THE SOVIET ECONOMY

THE SOVIET ECONOMY

A Collection of Western and Soviet Views

Edited by

HARRY G. SHAFFER
University of Kansas

 New York

APPLETON-CENTURY-CROFTS
Division of Meredith Publishing Company

Foreword

WESTERN experts on the Soviet economy have scattered some of their most valuable studies among a large number of journals, reviews, and quarterlies. Until recently, the would-be student was handicapped by having to look for these studies in a variety of not always accessible publications, which caused him frustration and wasted time. In the past year or two, his problems have been eased by the appearance of several collections of readings. This being the case, the potential reader of the present volume must ask himself whether there is any need for yet another collection of articles. Indeed, this volume would only be justified if it were different in coverage and conception to those which preceded it.

Fortunately, there are important differences. Not only have very few of the extracts from the work of Western scholars appeared in other collections of readings, but the editor has endeavored to present on each topic a selection of translated Soviet articles, so that one has a species of East-West confrontation. Since the student who knows no Russian often finds Soviet materials relatively inaccessible, the present volume tends to give the Soviet view a rather generous amount of space, which is justified in the present instance. It is true that translations are available, and indeed all the Soviet contributions in the present volume are reprints of translations made and published in the West. However, many students are unable to obtain them without a great deal of effort, and find it particularly difficult to identify in the mass of translated material the item of special interest to them in the context of their studies. This collection of Soviet views side by side with Western analyses of the Soviet economy is therefore a novel and useful contribution to the teaching aids available in this field.

It may be asked: How far do Soviet views represent what the authors themselves think or know? Are they not largely propagandist? The question is a legitimate one. At some periods and on some issues Soviet scholars had to serve up official myths regardless of their personal opinions, if they wished to be published at all. Even today, when pressures on scholars have greatly diminished, there are certain statements made of a declaratory character which may have little in common with reality, past, present, or future. For example, into this category must fall the quite common assertion made in Soviet articles that excessive consumption of Vodka is part of "the survival of capitalism in the minds of man." Part of the contribution of Bezuglov, in his article on the Moral Code of the Builders of Communism, suffers from this kind of tendency towards the unreal, official picture. It is also true that certain statements cannot be made, whatever the views of the authors concerned, or can be made only obliquely, or by implication. For example, no open attack can be made on the planning reform of 1957. However, even on such a topic, detailed criticisms are permitted, and it is in fact possible to build up a formidable critique of the existing planning arrangements using only published Soviet sources. Consequently, we are certainly not dealing with mere propaganda, but with economics, though argument is some-times presented in a partisan manner and with a certain limitation on the facts and figures that can be published. For example, Soviet authors are unable to quote systematic data on wage rates, and only very limited amounts of material appear in print on peasant incomes. Yet no one can deny that the flow of statistics and the amount of realistic and critical information about the Soviet economy have greatly increased in recent years. If some articles are phrased in combative and argumentative terms, the fact remains that Soviet economists are able to say a great deal that is of interest to Western students, that they argue among themselves, that they often present their own views in terms of scholarly discussions, and that a wide range of facts and statistics can be and are used in the process of the argument. Even where, for instance, Kudrov attacks West-ern statistical work on the USSR, he does not simply abuse his opponents, he cites data, discusses definitions, cites counter-arguments. While he does tend to select facts which suit his case, this tendency is not unknown among economists in many countries far to the west of the Soviet Union.

Consequently, the Soviet material used here represents a mixture: of official declarations and sincere argument, of economic and statistical analysis and a kind of superior advertising copy. Soviet economists have two tasks when they write for publication: to serve the purposes of the Soviet regime by highlighting its successes, and also to help discover better and more effective ways of running the Soviet economy. This sec-ond task has come increasingly to dominate their minds and their writ-ings. The Soviet economy has become increasingly mature and is more and more outgrowing the theory and organization devised under Stalin to speed the industrialization of a relatively backward country. The immense complexities of planning have given rise to many questions of the greatest interest to economists: these concern such matters as the role of prices, of the law of value, of exchange relationships between central planning and decentralized decision making, and of profits and incen-tives. Several of the articles chosen by Dr. Shaffer relate to these closely interconnected themes, and quite rightly too.

The readers should find much food for thought in this volume. If they are stimulated into thoughtful disagreement, or into taking the Soviet economy more seriously, this would certainly do no harm.

Alec Nove, *University of London*

Preface

Ever since the Bolshevik Revolution of 1917, social scientists in the English speaking world have shown some interest in observing, studying, analyzing, and interpreting the planned economy that has been taking shape in the Soviet Union, a country which occupies one-sixth of the entire land surface of the earth. But the widely-held view that a centrally planned, socialist economy could not function at all (and later the somewhat modified view that it could perhaps function, but at best very inadequately) deterred many social scientists from devoting their time and effort to the study of the USSR. Handicapped, furthermore, by lack of available information, travel restrictions within the Soviet Union, and language difficulties, only a relatively small number of Western scholars had become Soviet area specialists by the middle of the twentieth century.

When the first *sputnik* began to orbit a sleepy globe, people all over the world awakened to the realization that an economic and military power had arisen in the East which presented a formidable challenge to the supremacy of the economic and political institutions of Western capitalist or semi-capitalist democracies. By then Stalin had died, the publication of statistical information in the USSR had increased greatly, and the "Iron Curtain" was being lifted, permitting thousands of Westerners a personal glimpse at the country whose productive output and military strength were second only to those of the United States.

During the past few years, an ever increasing number of social scientists in the Western world have been devoting their efforts to the study of the various aspects—economic, political, social, historical, psychological, etc.,—of Soviet society. A veritable flood of scholarly books, monographs, and articles has been published; Soviet area courses have been added to the curricula of many liberal arts colleges and universities; instructors of introductory courses in the various social sciences have begun to pay increasing attention to a "comparative systems" approach; and the enrollment in Russian language courses on the college level has been expanding rapidly.

Until recently, the student who wanted to learn about the Soviet economy and who was not familiar with Russian had to depend almost exclusively upon the interpretations of Western scholars. This is no longer the case. Any university student interested in understanding the Soviet economy would be well advised to learn Russian, particularly if

he envisages extensive research in that area. However, he need not post-
pone his reading of original publications by Soviet scholars until he
knows the language, since English translations of large numbers of
Soviet articles and books are available.

As early as 1949, the Joint Committee of Slavic Studies began its
weekly publication of *The Current Digest of the Soviet Press* which translates, without comments, articles from Soviet newspapers and magazines.
The International Arts and Sciences Press began its unedited translations
of scholarly Soviet articles in the field of economics with the publication
of the first monthly issue of *Problems of Economics* in May 1958, and
since then has expanded its service by publishing similar journals in
such areas as sociology, education, history, and psychology. The United
States Joint Publications Research Service (JPRS) was established in
1957 to furnish the various units of the Federal government with translations of unclassified foreign documents, scholarly works, research reports, and other selected source material. During its first five years of
existence JPRS translated over 300,000 pages, more than 176,000 of which
were in the social sciences. While JPRS publications include translations
from non-Russian originals (such as Chinese, Hungarian, etc.), translations from Soviet sources alone for the fiscal year 1960-61 accounted
for 23,000 pages. (Organizations or individuals can subscribe to any JPRS
social science report series, to all reports published on any subject category, country, or area, or to any combination of these.) Other occasional
translations can be found in the publications of Radio Free Europe/
Munich, in the *International Economic Papers,* and in the *World Marxist
Review,* to name but a few. Furthermore, some English language journals
such as *New Times* and *International Affairs* (not to be confused with
the British journal by the same name) come straight from Moscow, and
so do translations of many Soviet books.

When Western Soviet area specialists study one or another aspect of
the Soviet economy, they utilize Soviet sources as well as Western interpretations. The purpose of this book of readings on the Soviet economy
is to introduce the student to this method. To this end, each of the
eleven main topics covered has been subdivided into *Western Views* and
Soviet Views.

Without further explanation, the subdivision into "Western" and
"Soviet" could easily be challenged. Marxian ideology itself, after all,
is "Western" in origin and so is most of the technological foundation
upon which rests the economic development of the Soviet Union. On
the other hand, several of the writers whose views are presented as
"Western" were born east of what today is generally referred to as "The
West." The division, then, is ideological rather than geographic. All
the writings presented in this book under *Western Views,* although they
may differ in many aspects of their approach and interpretation, have

one common denominator: they are anti-Marxist or at least non-Marxist. To maintain this ideological consistency, a separate category entitled *A Western Marxist's View* was reserved for the two contributions by Maurice Dobb, one of the most prominent Western Marxist economists. An alternate possibility would have been to subdivide the book's eleven main topics into "Anti-Marxist and Non-Marxist Views" on the one hand, and "Marxist Views" on the other. Such a subdivision, however, would have been misleading, as the selections included under *Soviet Views* represent only the current Soviet interpretation of Marxism-Leninism.

To enable the student to gain even a basic understanding of the Soviet economy more than mere sets of tables and graphs depicting output, consumption, and growth are necessary. To this end the eleven main topics in this book of readings encompass Western and Soviet interpretations of some of the theoretical and social, as well as the institutional economic framework of the Soviet economy. Apart from selections dealing with the problems, the past achievements and shortcomings, and the anticipated future progress of Soviet industry and agriculture, the reader will become familiar with Western and Soviet views on such topics as the reliability of Soviet statistics, the meaning of the transition to communism, and the position of the Soviet citizen as a consumer and as a worker. To make the study of the Soviet economy more meaningful to Western students, selections on some topics (such as national income) have been chosen that draw comparisons between the United States and the Soviet Union, and one section is devoted to a discussion of the problems and the methodology of comparing the economies of the two countries.

In choosing selections, articles that would be beyond the comprehension of all but well-advanced economics majors and graduate students were not included or were cut so as to exclude difficult mathematical or highly technical theoretical material. To further facilitate understanding for students unfamiliar with some of the terms used, a "Glossary of Important Economic Terms, Marxian and Soviet Economic Terminology, Russian Words, Abbreviations, Etc.," has been included at the end of this volume. Wherever considered necessary, somewhat detailed explanations, rather than mere brief definitions or translations, have been given. Furthermore, a list and description of periodic publications from which selections for this book have been taken has been appended at the end of the volume.

The identification of Soviet economists presented problems, since the same individual is frequently affiliated with several research organizations and on the faculty of various institutions of higher learning. V. V. Novozhilov, for instance, is on the economics faculty of Leningrad State University and of Leningrad Polytechnic Institute, and V. S. Nemchimov has been referred to as Academician of the Academy of Sciences, USSR; former head of its Department of Economics, Philosophy, and Law; Chairman of its Council for the Study of Productive Forces; Head of its Laboratory for the Application of Mathematical Methods in Economics; Head of its Study Group in Charge of Finding Ways to Improve Economic Planning; Academician of the All Union Academy of Agricultural Sciences; Economist associated with its Scientific Research Institute of Agricultural Economics; Specialist in Labor Economics and Statistics; etc. For purposes of this book, what appeared the most important or the most recent affiliation has been used in each case. Most identifications have been taken from *Survey of Soviet Economists and Economic Research Organizations,* Central Intelligence Agency, September, 1960. The assistance of Professor Robert W. Campbell of Indiana University and of Mr. Myron Sharpe of the International Arts and Sciences Press in ascertaining recent affiliations of several of the Soviet economists is gratefully acknowledged.

The cooperation of the authors, editors, and publishers who gave permission to reprint the selections contained in the volume is greatly appreciated and permissions are individually acknowledged on the first page of each of the respective selections.

I am indebted to my wife, Dr. Juliet Shaffer, for her editorial assistance which helped to make this preface, the introduction to the various sections, and the glossary less unwieldly and more readily understandable. I also want to thank Dr. Charles Staley for checking the economic terms contained in the glossary and for making helpful suggestions for improvements. Last, but by no means least, I wish to express my sincere gratitude to Professor Alec Nove, whose valuable critical suggestions have contributed greatly in improving the introductions, the selection of articles, and the glossary. It goes without saying that none of those who gave so generously of their time bear any responsibility for any errors of omission or commission.

Harry G. Shaffer

Contents

III. COMPARISONS OF UNITED STATES AND SOVIET NA-
TIONAL INCOME AND GROSS NATIONAL PRODUCT   57

IV. THE TRANSITION TO COMMUNISM: WHAT DOES IT
MEAN?   76

SOVIET VIEWS

SOVIET VIEWS

WESTERN VIEWS

A WESTERN MARXIST'S VIEW

SOVIET VIEWS

THE SOVIET ECONOMY

I

SOVIET STATISTICS: THEIR AVAILABILITY, ACCURACY AND RELIABILITY

FROM the late 1930's to Stalin's death, statistical information concerning the Soviet economy was hard to come by. Since then, and especially since 1956, a veritable flood of statistics concerning all aspects of Soviet economic life has been published and has been readily available to Western scholars. The USSR statistical yearbook of 1960 alone contains almost one thousand pages of statistical tables and has been translated into English *in toto*.[1] But how reliable are these statistics? To what extent can the Western student of the Soviet economy depend upon the information published under the auspices of the government of the USSR?

Literally dozens of articles and monographs on the reliability of Soviet statistics have been published in the United States and in Great Britain during the past quarter of a century, representing a variety of views.[2] For instance, Naum Jasny, author of many articles and several books on the Soviet economy, took to task such well-known Soviet area specialists as Alexander Gerschenkron, Abram Bergson, and Harry Schwartz for their views that the Soviet Union may withhold, but does not consciously falsify statistics.[3] Gerschenkron replied that Jasny's own extensive use of Soviet statistics is evidence that they must represent more than sheer invention and that Soviet data, while they need to be investigated critically, are definitely usable.[4] More recently, Nicolas Spulber has maintained that the Soviet Union not only withholds statistical information or presents it in a very ambiguous way, whenever it suits propagandistic purposes, but that its policy makers actually falsify it if it appears to be politically expedient.[5] Robert W. Campbell, on the other hand, considers

1 Translated by the US Joint Publications Research Service.

2 For a partial list of such articles and monographs, published during the 1940's and 50's, see, for instance, G. Warren Nutter, *Growth of Industrial Production in the Soviet Union* (1962), footnote p. 26.

3 Naum Jasny, "Soviet Statistics," *The Review of Economics and Statistics*, February, 1950, pp. 92-99.

4 Alexander Gerschenkron, "Comments on Naum Jasny's 'Soviet Statistics!'" *The Review of Economics and Statistics*. August, 1950, pp. 250-51.

5 Nicolas Spulber, *The Soviet Economy: Structure, Principles, Problems* (1962), pp. 143-44.

1

outright falsification quite unlikely, as cross-checks for internal consistency would reveal such manipulation. "By and large," he concludes, "our experience has been that the mass of Soviet statistics are more or less internally consistent, and this reinforces the doubt that the Russians are engaged in a process of double bookkeeping or outright statistical falsification." [6]

Whatever their views on falsification at the governmental level may be, Western economists are in essential agreement that Soviet statistics must not be taken at face value because of the possibility of error and of cheating on the local (plant and collective farm) level. In the section on *Western Views,* Alec Nove summarizes the most prevalent Western position on the availability and reliability of Soviet statistics, and Gregory Grossman reviews the Soviet government's own concern with the reliability of statistical information submitted to them by the lower echelons of the Soviet reporting hierarchy. Tampering with figures at the plant and collective farm level (to gain personal advantage or to cover up shortcomings) appears to be the main problem.

Under *Soviet Views,* the authors, while firm in their belief in the superiority of Soviet over Western statistical methodology and reliability, show awareness of shortcomings. Starovskii, Dean of Soviet statisticians, dwelling on the role of statistics in a socialist society, discusses past accomplishments, points to deficiencies, and proposes improvements. Kolpakov looks towards the future, outlining the road that is to lead towards the perfection of the statistical system of the USSR.

[6] Robert W. Campbell, *Soviet Economic Power* (1960), p. 35.

WESTERN VIEWS

1

A Note on the Availability and Reliability of Soviet Statistics *

ALEC NOVE
University of London

Availability

A few years ago, it would have been easiest to make a quite short list of the few figures which were available. The fact that the contrary procedure is now the most convenient one is a measure of the 'liberalization' achieved since the death of Stalin, or rather since 1956, when the systematic publication of economic statistics gradually began again after a long interval. However, there are still some conspicuous gaps, of which the following are the most important.

(*a*) Output figures for some *industrial products* are missing, among them non-ferrous metals, ships, aircraft, many chemicals, some machines, as well as military weapons.

(*b*) While more is now appearing about the breakdown of the *labour force,* including agriculture and the military services,[1] numbers in particular industries are not given in any detail.

(*c*) Very little has been published on earnings, either of wage-earners or of peasants. Such information as we have still has to be reconstructed from scattered and ill-defined statements. By contrast, Poland, Hungary and Czechoslovakia publish detailed wage statistics.

(*d*) Neither *national income* nor *gross industrial output* statistics are available except in the form of aggregate indices or of totals which are not broken down into their constituent parts, save occasionally into rough percentages.

---

* Reprinted from Alec Nove, *The Soviet Economy* (1961), pp. 307-314. By permission of the author and of George Allen & Unwin, Ltd. Published in the United States by Frederick A. Praeger, Inc., New York. (Footnotes renumbered.)

1 Until it was decided to publish the numbers in the armed forces (1960), the number of peasants and the age and sex distribution of the population were unpublished, no doubt to prevent calculation by residual.

However, let us give credit where credit is due. Gone indeed is the day when one had to search for statistics in leaders' speeches and make do with percentages of an unknown base. The statistical compendia on the economy as a whole, on agriculture, on various republics and localities, on transport, and so forth, together with the reports on the 1959 census, do give us a sizeable stock of statistics to work on, despite the remaining gaps. One difficulty is that many of the figures given are ill-defined; there is an unfortunate lack of explanatory notes; though minor attempts are being made to remedy this, we badly need longer explanations, and a new edition of a handbook on economic statistics is much overdue.[2] The lack of clarity about definitions, and especially changes in definitions, is a constant danger; it affects budget data, and also a number of the output figures and indices.

Credibility: Physical Output Figures

(a) *Industry*. Whatever the vagueness of definitions, the first question to ask is: are the figures true, or are they invented? Very few persons now believe that they are invented. The evidence against such a view is very strong. Despite captured documents,[3] despite the presence in the West of various Soviet officials who had defected, no evidence exists that the central Soviet statisticians invent figures to order, to produce propaganda effect. By this is meant that no one issues orders to print a figure of 400 knowing that the correct one is 350. Further support for this view comes from the fact that, when certain figures were discreditable, they were on occasion simply suppressed; many years later, they were published and showed that there was a fall in production in the 'suppressed' year. If it were possible simply to invent, then such behaviour would be pointless. Of course, we must note that selective suppression is a means of distorting a statistical table, but it is not invention. Not to tell the whole truth is not the same as telling a lie. Therefore we can legitimately conclude that when, for example, the Soviet authorities announce that 60 million tons of steel or 300 million pairs of shoes have been produced in a given year, this accords with the records of the Central statistical office in Moscow.[4] However, there are several qualifications to be made. One of these relates, not for the last time, to ambiguities of definition. Footwear sometimes includes only leather footwear, sometimes all footwear, the definition of leather footwear can and does alter, handicraft production can be omitted from the base-year without this being stated. Further-

2 There used to be such an explanatory handbook, entitled *Slovar-spravochnik po sotsia'lno-ekonomicheskoi statistike,* but this was last published in 1948.

3 Especially the *1941 Plan,* published in America by the American Council of Learned Societies, after it had been taken from the Germans.

4 This is also the broad conclusion of G. Grossman in his searching examination of *Soviet Statistics of Physical Output of Industrial Commodities* (Princeton, 1960).

more, most commodities for which statistics are published are not homogeneous, are in reality many different kinds of goods aggregated under a single head for statistical convenience. The methodology of aggregation is often unspecified. Of course, this is often true of similar statistics in all countries. But the point is that rewards for growth are so important in Soviet industry that the definitional changes, and the adjustment to definitions at local level, can aim deliberately at whatever result looks best from the standpoint of statistical publicity. This point is also relevant to the reliability of aggregate indices, and we shall return to it.

The figures may correctly reflect the data available in Moscow, yet this data could be wrong by reason of statistical 'padding' by the reporting agencies, especially the enterprises. They are interested in claiming plan fulfilment, and this could lead them to exaggerate. Scattered reports of measures against directors who indulge in such practices confirm that such dangers exist, but measures are taken to minimise them. The close link between production and disposals (*sbyt*) puts a limit on the amount of likely cheating: to report non-existent production which one would be called upon to deliver is asking for trouble. There are also some temptations to conceal output, in order to keep extra stocks in hand or to cover up pilfering or some semi-legal deal. Defective goods, on the other hand, seem frequently to be foisted on customers in the guise of standard products, the quality inspectors being overruled. On balance, one should expect some exaggeration in reporting, and no doubt the possibilities of getting away with it vary in different sectors and at different periods. Unless it can be shown that the *extent* of exaggeration changes, the rate of growth remains unaffected, for obvious reasons; this is the 'law of equal cheating', which the author of these lines 'invented' in 1956.[5] There seems no evidence one way or the other, in industry at least, to suggest that the rate of growth since (say) 1937 or 1950 has been affected by falsification from below.[6] However, it is manœuvring within the system of success indicators—without actually cheating—which seems much the most serious source of distortion. Reference back to the large number of plan-fulfilment 'dodges' listed in chapter 6 will provide a host of examples of how the wily director can distort the truth without actually breaking the regulations.

Clearly then, care is needed in interpreting the various figures, exaggeration is possible. But an excess of scepticism can lead to unfortunate results. Thus a certain American commentator noticed that cotton and wool cloth output figures were below the previous year in physical terms while the official statistical report claimed an increase, and jumped to the conclusion that this was evidence of cheating. It was not; there had been a shift of statistical reporting from linear metres to square metres, the

[5] In *Lloyds Bank Review*, April, 1956, p. 3.
[6] This is also the conclusion of Grossman, *op. cit.*, p. 133.

object of which was in fact to stop cheating by those who sought to fulfil plans by making cloth narrower. This illustrates the danger of using the 'cheating' hypothesis. Far better is it to assume that the figures represent some aspect of reality, and proceed, on that assumption, to examine with care the coverage and definition of the figures cited.

(b) *Agriculture.* For many years, until 1953, crop data were published in terms of 'biological yield', for reasons which cannot be gone into here.[7] It is very much to the credit of N. Jasny to have been the first to have documented and calculated with great ingenuity and surprising accuracy the extent of the consequent exaggeration.[8] This was due partly to the nature of the 'biological' statistics, which purported to represent the on-the-root crop, and were therefore gross of the considerable harvest losses, and partly to the tendency of the inspectors to exaggerate the on-the-root crop estimates, since certain delivery obligations of *kolkhozy* (payments to the MTS) were dependent upon them. In 1952, the grain harvest was said to have been 130 million tons. This has been officially revised downwards to 92 million tons, an exaggeration greater than many of the fiercest western critics thought possible.

Biological yield figures were dropped in 1953, and for several years no physical output data were published at all. Then they reappeared, and are now available in abundance, for every major farm product, down even to non-cow milk and non-sheep wool. However, there are several reasons for supposing that the 'law of equal cheating' may fail to operate in agriculture. Firstly, the large volume of unsold products makes it harder to keep track of reality. Secondly, a series of agricultural campaigns (grain, maize, meat, milk, and so on) have placed great pressures upon local officialdom, and we have Khrushchev's own word for it, at the January, 1961, plenum of the central committee, that it drove them into various kinds of simulation and exaggerated reporting (including the purchase of butter in the shops and its re-delivery to the state as new produce). Thirdly, the much better prices now paid for produce probably led to a discouragement of various forms of evasion by which production remained unreported.[9] Finally, the very large proportion of meat and milk originating in the private sector is very inadequately counted, through a sample survey, and seems to be unreliable and possibly overstated. For all these reasons, there are grounds for supposing that both the absolute level of and the rate of increase in the output of some farm products are overstated, though we cannot tell by how much.

[7] See A. Nove, 'Some Problems in Agricultural Statistics', *Soviet Studies*, January, 1956.

[8] See his *Socialized Agriculture in the USSR*, and other works.

[9] An interesting parallel may be found in Great Britain, where an increase in the official buying price for eggs shortly after the war led to a spectacular rise in the *reported* number of eggs laid.

It is also noteworthy that the definition of meat includes offal, lard, rabbits, poultry, and so is wider than that usually adopted in the West. Maize figures include the grain equivalent of ensilaged cobs since 1955. American analysts have claimed that milk sucked by calves is included in the Soviet milk statistics, but this has been denied.[10]

Indices: Are They Credible?

According to the official statistics, gross industrial output rose almost twenty-one times between 1928 and 1955. The highest western estimate, by F. Seton, allows for a twelve-fold rise. The lowest, by W. Nutter, supports a much lower figure, a five-and-a-half-fold increase. There are some others in between.[11] There is not the space here to comment in detail on the many western attempts to reconstruct an index of industrial production, based on Soviet physical output series. The point is that all are unanimous in completely rejecting the official index, even while at odds with each other about the 'correct' figure. My own view tends to favour the Seton index, because the much lower figures of Nutter and some other analysts seem to me inconsistent with what is known and accepted about Soviet fuel utilization and freight transportation. However, this still leaves the official index way up above the realms of possibility.

It is not that this index is deliberately 'cooked'. But all indices are conventional aggregations, necessarily lacking in accuracy. So much depends on price weights and on the treatment of new products, especially where, as in the machinery sector, these are extremely numerous. Anyone who wishes to make any such calculations should take an awful warning from A. Gerschenkron's calculations, in which he showed that, from 1899 to 1939, American production of machinery increased more than fifteen-fold with 1899 price weights, but less than doubled with 1939 price weights, and he emphasized the enormous difficulties due to changes in type and design. What is 'truth' when such divergences are possible? [12] This is why the care and refinements of some attempts to aggregate all available physical output data for the USRR seem to me to lead to such uncertain results, which would remain uncertain even if there were none of the sizeable statistical gaps in the output series.

The official series suffers from the following defects:

(a) Until 1950, the weights used were those of 1926–27. Apart from giving 'preindustrialization' weights to the fastest growing sectors of industry, the introduction of new products gave an opportunity (for directors) to manœuvre so as to adopt for them high '1926–27' prices.

10 See *Comparisons of the United States and Soviet Economies* (Washington, 1959), p. 236, and V. Starovski, *Vop. Ekon.*, No. 4/1960, p. 105.

11 See bibliography for references.

12 *A Dollar index of Soviet machinery output* (Rand Corporation, Santa Monica, 1951).

Despite occasional efforts to check this practice, the big rise in costs in the 'thirties meant that the prices at which new products were introduced into the index were higher than they would have cost in 1926–27. There was then a tendency to concentrate on the production of items bearing high '1926–27' prices, even at the cost of underfulfilling plans for the less highly valued items, because plan fulfilment was measured in 1926–27 prices. All this led to a creeping inflation of the index, made easier by the fact that it was genuinely difficult to determine what is a new product and what it would have cost to produce in 1926–27.[13]

(b) It is a 'gross' index, in the sense described in chapter 10. Therefore, it is affected by vertical disintegration.

(c) While since 1950 the index is no longer based on 1926–27 prices (it was calculated first in 1952 and then in 1955 prices), the growth rates prior to 1950 were simply chained on to the new index, and were not recalculated; or, if they were, the results have not been published. Much remains unclear about how the index is compiled. For instance, suppose that machinery output is expressed in 1955 prices, the problem of valuing new models remains, and, since in all countries such valuations are somewhat artificial, this makes possible the systematic selection of the highest of a range of possible figures, which can lead to distortion. It is only right to add that all analysts agree that the post 1950 indices are markedly less unreliable than those for earlier years. However, whatever the price base and whatever the regulations, the directors and local officials tend so to choose between possible alternatives as to be able to report a large increase in output. Because of the unavoidable imprecision of the regulations and of the definitions, the index can be affected by such choices in ways which are unlikely to arise in the West (where there is also a degree of imprecision and of arbitrary comparison), because increases in production as such are not vital 'success indicators' in a western firm.

With so much room for more or less legitimate manœuvre, Soviet statisticians can select the base and the weights which help them to show very large increases, and omit to publish calculations which reflect less credit on the system. For instance, base-year weights give a larger increase in output than end-year weights, so, in discussing industrial production indices, one Soviet statistician went so far as to proclaim that end-year weights were contrary to science, a remarkable doctrine indeed.[14] Yet, when Soviet statisticians calculate a cost of living index, they are careful to use end year weights,[15] which minimize the increase in prices and so represent real wages in a more favourable light.

[13] See A. Nove, '1926/7 and all that', *Soviet Studies,* October, 1957, pp. 117-30. Soviet journals have denied these exaggerations, but contemporary evidence, cited in the above-named article, is against them.

[14] D. Savinski, *Vest. Stat.,* No. 10/1958, p. 39.

[15] A. Gozulov, *Ekonomicheskaya statistika* (Moscow, 1953), p. 359.

National Income

The official index is at all times to be treated with a degree of suspicion. The official claim to a seventeen-fold increase in the period 1913–55, for instance, is utterly incredible. Thus it seems very widely agreed, by Soviet economists among others,[16] that the national income of the Russian empire in 1913 was approximately a fifth of that of the United States. If the official claim were even remotely correct, the Soviet national income would now be well ahead of that of the United States, which, even allowing for the familiar vagaries of index numbers, just is not acceptable. Then it is decidedly odd that the national income can increase by seventeen-fold when one of its principal components, agriculture, showed a rise (in gross output) of only 70 per cent. The computational methods are not properly explained. There seems to have been a substantial overstatement of the growth of the net product of trade and construction, at least during the period of '1926–27' prices.[17] But even in more recent years strange things happen to national income data. Thus the increase in 1958 was originally reported as 9 per cent (over the previous year), but then was revised to 11 per cent with not a word of explanation.[18] One can but show reserve in using officials claims, and seek explanations where possible to clear up doubtful points.

Some Other Items

Housing data (in square metres) may be given in *living* space (excluding kitchens, corridors, etc.) or in *total* space *(obshchaya ploshchyad')*. The former is roughly two-thirds of the latter, and the unwary are sometimes confused between them.

Real wage and other such figures are sometimes given by reference to the year 1940, or to some early post-war year. It should be noted that these were not good years for the consumer, and that a fairer picture of progress achieved requires a calculation based on some better year, say 1937 or 1928. This is never done by the official statisticians. It is important to distinguish data on real wages, which, allowing for the chosen base year, check well against other figures, from vague and barely credible claims about 'real income per head'; these include estimates of the value of social services and such indirect 'income' as the length of vacations with pay, and the methods used are never explained.

[16] Y. Kronrod in *Sovetskaya sotsialisticheskaya ekonomika, 1917–57* (Moscow, 1957), p. 168.
[17] See A. Nove, '1926/7 and all that', already cited.
[18] See *Pravda*, January 16, 1959, and *N. Kh. 1959*, p. 308.

Conclusion

Despite some justifiable scepticism about certain Soviet data, it should be clearly stated that the published physical output series and many other figures must be taken seriously, that they generally represent an expression (though sometimes an ambiguous or distorted expression) of reality. Much greater doubt attaches to some of the index number series, which are in some instances just not credible. Yet these comments are by no means intended to deny that the Soviet system has achieved rapid growth. Undoubtedly it has, though not at the tremendous pace which the official indices allege. Its achievements have, indeed, been such that it is surely about time that some of the wilder claims were quietly buried.

2

Soviet Concern With Reliability *

GREGORY GROSSMAN
University of California

Even a cursory reading of the Soviet literature reveals that the central statistical authorities have been well aware of the imperfect reliability of the data submitted to them. A closer study leaves no doubt that they have been gravely concerned over the problem, and that the question of accuracy of physical output data occupies the very center of this concern. It is also clear that the main source of inaccuracy is believed to be distortion of reported data by interested parties, aided by the negligence, if not abetted by the connivance, of the lower statistical agencies.

It is quite understandable that concern with data reliability should have been greatly intensified, as it was, in the early thirties, in view of the changes in the internal political atmosphere, the reorganization of industrial structure and management, especially the transition to a full-blown command economy, the turbulent economic conditions in general, and the mounting pressure for plan fulfillment, that characterized those years. It is also noteworthy that within two months of the completion of the First Five-Year Plan the USSR Supreme Court issued a resolution,

* Reprinted from Gregory Grossman, *Soviet Statistics of Physical Output of Industrial Commodities. Their Compilation and Quality* (1960), pp. 49-54, by permission of the National Bureau of Economic Research.

dated February 27, 1933, which read (in part): ". . . The special attention of courts must be directed to the following criminal acts in record-keeping and reporting . . . 6. Premeditated submission of incorrect data with the purpose of indicating fulfillment or overfulfillment of a plan." [1] This was followed in the same year by a resolution of the Central Executive Committee (*Tsentral'nyi ispolnitel'nyi komitet,* abbreviated as *TsIK*) and *SNK SSSR,* entitled "On the Liability for the Submission of Incorrect Statistical Information and Reports, and for the Violation of Forms and Dates of Submission of Statistical Materials and Reports," dated November 27, 1933. It extended certain sections of the criminal code of the union republics to apply to "intentional," "systematic," and "malicious" acts of the sort indicated in its title.[2]

Although the specialized literature of the middle thirties was on the whole more preoccupied with statistical organization, methodology, and coverage than with data reliability, it did occasionally reveal the seriousness of the authorities' concern on this score. For instance, the administrator of *TsUNKhU,* A. I. Kraval', is reported to have told the all-union conference on industrial statistics in December 1935 that: "The struggle against distortions in record-keeping and deception in reporting . . . must become an integral and important part of the work of statistical agencies." [3] Only a little over a year later, such distortions and deceptions were among the charges thrown at the alleged "wreckers" within the statistical apparatus, among them Kraval' himself.[4]

Since the middle of 1948, concern with the reliability of statistical information has been openly and frequently expressed in the specialized literature. It will be recalled that this was one of the reasons cited for the separation of the statistical apparatus from the *Gosplan* in August 1948, and attainment of a high level of data reliability was one of the principal assignments given to the new *TsSU* at the time. Shortly thereafter, on September 22, 1948, *TsSU* issued an order demanding that the personnel of the statistical apparatus "ensure the collection of truthful, scientifically justified, rigorously checked, and reliable statistical data, and fight against any outcropping of 'localistic' [*mestnicheskie*] tendencies in statistical work." [5] Similar orders are said to have been issued on subsequent occasions after inspection of the work of various local statistical

---

1 *Sbornik postanovlenii Verkhovnogo Suda SSSR* [Collection of Resolutions of the USSR Supreme Court], Moscow, 1946, pp. 18f., as cited in Kh. E. Bakhchisaraitsev, *Spravochnik po zakonodatel'stvu dlia rabotnikov gosudarstvennoi promyshlennosti SSSR* [Legal Manual for Personnel in State Industry of the USSR], Moscow, 1951, p. 499.

2 *Sobranie zakonov i rasporiazhenii Raboche-krest'ianskogo pravitel' stva SSSR* [Collection of Laws and Decrees of the Workers' and Peasants' Government of the USSR], Moscow, 1933, No. 70, p. 417, as cited in Bakhchisaraitsev, *op. cit.,* p. 499.

3 *Plan,* 1936, No. 3, p. 27.

4 Cf. *Plan,* 1937, No. 8, pp. 22-26.

5 I Dugin, "O nekotorykh nedostatkakh v rabote s kadrami" [On certain Shortcomings in Personnel Work], V. S., 1951, No. 5, p. 55.

offices. The question of data reliability has been—at least until the mid-fifties—one of the dominant themes of the editorials and articles in *Vestnik statistiki,* the organ of the new *TsSU,* and of the various other publications emanating from the statistical authorities in recent years.[6] Virtually every address by the administrator of *TsSU,* Starovskii, by one of his chief lieutenants (Volodarskii, Ezhov), or by one of the regional heads of the statistical apparatus before the frequent periodic conferences of statisticians from 1951 through 1953 dwelt at length on the theme of reliability.[7] It seems that in those years Starovskii hardly addressed his subordinates on any other subject, at least judging by the summaries printed in *Vestnik statistiki.*

The campaign to ensure the reliability of data submitted to the statistical offices reached its high mark approximately in 1952. After early 1953 —that is, after Stalin's death—the campaign, as such, virtually disappeared from the pages of the specialized literature, although occasional references to the problem of data reliability have continued to appear. On the other hand, no outright claim of substantial improvement in this respect has been made by the statistical authorities. It is difficult for the outside observer to decide whether there has in fact been any such improvement in recent years, or whether the apparent subsidence of the campaign was largely due to the internal political shifts following Stalin's death, coupled with the usual spasmodic occurrence of such events in the Soviet Union.

The existence of the problem of data reliability has been attributed to the presence of "individual persons in enterprises and ministries" who try to "embellish the true state of affairs, to conceal or minimize mistakes and defects by inserting false data in their reports." [8] These individuals, it is said, are a small, irresponsible, dishonest, and unconscientious minority; but few as they are, their work is insidious and must be thwarted. How can these dishonest few get away with their shady acts? They can, it is admitted, because not all functionaries of the statistical apparatus are sufficiently alert or conscientious.

Hence there is the insistence that the record-keeping and reporting of enterprises and departments be subjected to constant and thorough supervision and checking. But checking cannot reveal irregularities where there is strong intention to conceal and little motivation to uncover. This explains the exhortations to honesty and uprightness on the part of those

6 E.g. L. M. Volodarskii, *Promyshlennaia statistika* [Industrial Statistics], Moscow, 1954, pp. 11-13; *idem,* "Gosudarstvennaia statistika i narodnokhoziaistvennoe planirovanie" [State Statistics and Economic Planning], V. E., No. 8, 1955, p. 21; *idem, Statistika promyshlennosti* [Statistics of Industry], Moscow, 1956, p. 14; V. S., 1952, No. 4, p. 13; 1953, No. 1, p. 23; 1958, No. 6, p. 20; and especially the editorial entitled "Reliability— the Most Important Law of Soviet Statistics," 1952, No. 2, pp. 8-20.

7 E.g. V. S., 1951, No. 2, pp. 91-95, and No. 6, pp. 92-95, No. 2, pp. 92-95, and No. 5, p. 88.

8 *Ibid.,* 1952, No. 5, p. 88.

who submit the data and those who receive them. Thus we read in an article over the signature of the deputy chief of the personnel division of *TsSU SSSR*: [9]

The chiefs of the statistical administrations of the union republics must pay close attention to the personnel of the local agencies of *TsSU;* they must proceed painstakingly with the selection and deployment of [statistical] workers; they must educate them in the spirit of honesty, truthfulness, and responsibility for assigned tasks; they must analyze the personnel, replacing the unsuitable workers and promoting to responsible positions the able and promising ones. . . .

The chiefs of the statistical administrations must insist that, in resolving any question, all statistical workers bear only the interests of the state in mind, that they defend these interests in matters small as well as large, that they counter all expression of activity against the state, of localistic and narrowly departmental interests, and all forms of writing-up, misrepresentation, deception of the state, etc. . . .

A year later, an editorial entitled "Raising the Standards of Performance of the *Raion* and City Inspectorates of *TsSU SSSR*" asserted: [10]

Truthfulness and adherence to principle are the distinguishing characteristics of the Soviet statistician. [This statement, of course, really means that there is some question of that.—G.G.] Everything that *raion* and city inspectors, as all other Soviet statisticians, do must be suffused with a zeal to depict the actual state of affairs correctly, objectively, and honestly. In all their work *raion* and city inspectors, as all Soviet statisticians, must adhere to [high] principles, and must place the interests of the state above everything else. [Such interests] . . . require that Soviet statisticians produce absolutely reliable data, which permit the drawing of accurate inferences on the condition of the economy and the resolution of questions of its further development.

Raion and city inspectors are called upon to lead a decisive struggle against anti-state tendencies, against the attempts of some workers to place narrowly departmental and particularistic interests above those of the state, against attempts to distort reported data—to conceal unused equipment, raw materials, and supplies from the state, or to include in the reports of plan fulfillment output that has not been actually produced.

It is worth noting that the exhortations to honesty and appeals to high principles in these and other passages are aimed chiefly at the lowest levels of the statistical apparatus, that is, at those levels which come into immediate contact with the suppliers of data, and where, therefore, control is most crucial and corruption most likely.

The suppliers of data—especially the accountants of the enterprises and departments—must also remember their principles. A well-known

[9] Dugin, *op. cit.*, pp. 53 and 55.
[10] V. S., 1952, No. 4, p. 13. Cf. the editorial in V. S., 1955, No. 6, where the references to honesty are implicit however.

text on accounting in the industrial enterprise prefaces its section on the keeping of records of finished output with the following remarks: [11]

The quantity of output can be ascertained from the primary documents on the transfer of finished products [to the warehouse]. However, it is not a matter of the simple arithmetic addition of the data on output recorded [in the documents]. It must be remembered that such an economically and politically important indicator as the fulfillment of the output plan is determined from these computations. Therefore, the absolute accuracy and truthfulness of this indicator must be assured. Any deviation from absolute accuracy and truthfulness on the part of the figure for output represents, in our country, a deception of the state and constitutes a crime. In distinction to capitalist records, Soviet records in general, and the accountant's record of output in particular, give a completely objective picture of actuality.

Textbooks for students and manuals for inspectors and auditors also provide abundant evidence of widespread distortion at the enterprise and departmental level, and of the concern among the various controlling authorities with this fact.[12]

The leaders of the Party are not only aware of the imperfect reliability of the statistical data on which their day-to-day decisions must be based, but even see fit at times to speak out on the subject. From their point of view, the situation is doubly serious, in that individual Party members, far from being invariably the alert guardians of legality and morality, themselves commit acts of distortion and deceit.[13] At one time the Party Central Committee issued a demand to all subordinate units to uncover instances of writing up and to turn the culprits over for criminal prosecution; yet, the Party's "house organ" complained, the order was ignored "in some places." [14]

In sum, one can infer from the specialized literature on statistics that deception in reporting has been widespread, and that the authorities have been well aware of this fact and have been seriously concerned about

[11] M. Kh. Zhebrak, *Kurs promyshlennogo ucheta* [Course in Industrial Accounting], Moscow, 1950, p. 242. The last sentence of the quotation is, of course, to be understood in the hortatory rather than the positive sense. The source proceeds to list ways in which finished output may be recorded inaccurately, e.g. by the inclusion of items before their acceptance by the technical inspectors.

[12] I. Ia. German, *Finansovyi kontrol' i dokumental'naia reviziia v mestnoi promyshlennosti RSFSR* [Financial Control and Documents Audit in Local Industry of the RSFSR], Moscow, 1948; A. Kh. Ermolaev and G. R. Nak, *Dokumental'naia reviziia na zheleznodorozhnom transporte* [Documents Audit on Railroads], 2nd ed., Moscow, 1950; D. I. Alenchikov, *Organizatsiia i tekhnika dokumental'noi revizii* [Organization and Methods of Documents Audit], 4th ed., Moscow, 1954; N. A. Sokolov, *Kompleksnye dokumental'nye revizii na zheleznodorozhnom transporte* [Comprehensive Documents Audits on Railroads], Moscow, 1955; and W. Kalkutin and W. Mitrofanow, *Revision und Kontrolle der wirtschaftlichen Tätigkeit der Industriebetriebe* (translated from the Russian), Berlin, 1955.

[13] See P. Zh., 1955, No. 11, pp. 28-30. Cf. *New York Times,* June 26, 1955.

[14] P. Zh., 1955, No. 11, p. 29.

it; although of course we are not told the over-all magnitude, or even the preponderant direction, of distortion. The plaintive and sometimes near-alarmist tone of the Soviet literature on the subject of data reliability need not, however, mean that the degree of inaccuracy in Soviet output statistics is very high from the standpoint of the student of the Soviet economy. We must remember that the tolerances of inaccuracy acceptable for planning and administering the Soviet command economy, which is the chief end of Soviet statistics, may be considerably more exacting than those with which outside observers are typically satisfied, and moreover that the Soviets are wont to overdraw any evil that they may be mounting a domestic "campaign" against.

SOVIET VIEWS

3

The Tasks of Soviet Statistics *

V. N. STAROVSKII
Director, Central Statistical Administration, USSR

The historic decisions of the Twenty-Second Congress of the Communist Party of the Soviet Union and the new Program adopted by the Congress have defined tasks, paths, and methods for communist construction and have given the Soviet people a scientifically based, concrete plan for building communism. . . .

In the decision on tasks for communist construction set by the Party Program, accounting and statistics are called upon to play an important role. . . .

At the present stage of communist construction, when the building of communism in the USSR has acquired direct, practical significance, the Communist Party, in its new Program adopted by the XXII Congress of the CPSU, indicates that "the role of accounting and control over the conservation and proper use of national wealth will grow." The Program also indicates that one of the most important functions of centralized, planned direction is the realization of a uniform system of accounting

* From *Vestnik Statistiki*, 1962, No. 1. Translated in and excerpts reprinted from *The Soviet Economic System: Structure and Policy*, U. S. Joint Publications Research Service, April, 1962, Vol. II, pp. 207-241.

and statistics, and that "the increasing scale of the national economy and the rapid development of science and technology require a raising of the scientific level of planning, projecting, accounting, and statistics." Directly following these indications in the Program is a clause on the broad application which will be made during the next 20 years of cybernetics and electronic computers and control apparatus in production processes, in scientific research, in planning and project-design calculations, and in the sphere of accounting and management.

In essence, these clauses define the general line of development in accounting and statistics under conditions of advanced communist construction—the further strengthening of accounting and statistics as a uniform system, the raising of their scientific level, and their transition to a modern electronic technological basis. . . .

Let us remember that the Central Committee of our Party unmasked the vicious practice of accounting the biological harvest.[1] On orders from the Central Committee, the statistics of agricultural productivity, which were turned up in the course of a special inspection, were returned to organizations of the TsSU (*Tsentral'noye Statisticheskoye Upravleniye—* Central Statistical Administration), statistical organizations went over to accounting the barn harvest, data on the gross harvest of grain over a number of years were recalculated, and the true picture of the status of grain production was restored. In this connection, we must also emphasize another very important measure carried out on the initiative of the Central Committee of our Party—resumption of the publication of statistical data. Under conditions of the cult of the personality of Stalin, the opportunities to publish statistical data and to use them for scientific economic work were extremely limited.

The destruction of cadres during the period of the cult of the personality affected a number of statisticians—in particular, a number of workers who took part in the 1937 population census. Although methodological errors were committed in that census (carrying it out for a single day, inaccuracies, and contradictions in the instructions for carrying it out and for processing the materials), there was still no basis for accusing comrades of consciously falsifying the census data and denouncing them as "wreckers."

The condemnation of the cult of the personality and the restoration and tireless development by our Party of a Leninist style and Leninist principles has opened unlimited possibilities for creative solutions to problems in statistical theory and practice and for raising the level of

---

[1] This refers to the distortion of agricultural statistics by including among figures for crops harvested that part of agricultural produce that never reached the barn or the warehouse. Grain blown away by the wind or stolen during the harvest would be an example. Khrushchev estimated the "barn yield" for 1952 as 30 per cent less than the "biological yield." (Editor's note.)

statistical work in accordance with the demands of advanced communist construction.

In the new Program of our Party, in the resolutions of the Congress on the accounting of the CPSU Central Committee, and in the reports of N. S. Khrushchev, there is in essence no section from which conclusions applicable to accounting and statistics cannot be drawn, above all in relation to analysis of the economic development of the country and creation of the material and technological basis for communism, the rise in the material well-being of the people, the development of culture, and the study of the course of economic competition between the world socialist system and capitalism.

Of central importance for all of our work in the area of accounting and statistics is the clause in the Program stating that major attention in all spheres of planning and direction of the economy should be concentrated upon the most rational and effective use of material, labor, and natural resources and the elimination of excessive outlays. An immutable law of economic construction is the principle of achieving, in the interests of society, the greatest results with the smallest expenditures.

"Life itself," said Comrade N. S. Khrushchev at the XXII Congress, "demands a new, much higher class of scientific principles and economic calculations for planning and for economic leadership. Profound scientific work on problems of economic and technical development must precede the drawing up of plans and the approval of economic measures. Economic and technical research must facilitate the proper fulfillment of economic tasks. We are concerned here with establishment of the most favorable proportions in the national economy, with the most effective use of natural resources, productive capacity, and new technology, with the correct distribution of national income and capital investment, with the mobilization of additional means for accelerating rates of economic development, etc."

Upon which questions in the area of accounting and statistics is it necessary to concentrate our attention in the near future, in order to ensure fulfillment of the tasks set by the Party? Let us look at several questions which require particular attention.

First of all, among these, is the question of improving the indexes in the state plan.

The July (1960) Plenum of the CPSU Central Committee charged the State Economic Council of the USSR, the State Planning Committee of the USSR, the Academy of Sciences of the USSR, and the TsSU of the USSR, together with the Councils of Ministers of the union republics and the ministries, to work out and present to the Council of Ministers of the USSR proposals on the further improvement of indexes in the state plan, with a view toward increasing the interest of enterprises and *sovnarkhozy* in the most effective use of basic and working funds, in the output of products in the required assortment and of high quality, in the raising of labor productivity and the reduction of costs of production, and in improving the planning of the complex development of economic regions.

The enormous growth in the scale of socialist production and the acceleration of rates of technological progress during the period of advanced communist construction in the USSR demand continuity in the planning of the Soviet economy. The well-grounded, scientific working out of current (annual) plans for the development of the national economy is impossible without a thorough calculation of the perspectives for its development. In addition, perspective plans must be corrected by calculating the progress toward their fulfillment through annual plans. This requires a corresponding revision of statistical work and an increase in attention directed toward the more complete exposure of new reserves of production.

It is of course obvious that improvement in the indexes of planning does not seek to complicate the tasks of planning and accounting. The indexes in the plan must be only those which are actually necessary. In addition, much attention must be given to improving the use of existing accounts in management and planning. These offer great possibilities for a thorough analysis of the results of the work of individual enterprises and branches, and of the national economy as a whole. We must actively continue the struggle against collection of superfluous and illegal accounts. . . .

"In the past," states the accounting report of the CPSU Central Committee to the XXII Congress of the CPSU, "during the period of the cult of the personality, such shameful characteristics of Party, State, and economic leadership as faulty administration, the covering over of defects, working with caution, and fear of the new were widespread. Under such conditions, toadies, flatterers, and eye-washers often emerged. The Party is carrying on and will continue to carry on a decisive struggle against violators of Party and State discipline, against people who attempt to deceive the Party and the State. This struggle is boldly employing basic criticism and self-criticism as its sharpest and most effective weapons."

The state statistical organizations are required to take steps and have every opportunity to eradicate completely disgraceful cases of falsification in accounting. They are required to make those persons guilty of illegal additions answer to the law.

An important condition for ensuring the trustworthiness of statistical data is the availability of well thought-out, precise, and clear instructions which eliminate the possibility of incorrect interpretation. Instructions are the key to the correct accounting of plan fulfillment, the key which ensures the receipt of scientifically well-grounded, trustworthy data. The attention of theoretical and practical statisticians should be directed toward questions of drawing up and improving instructions—in particular, through discussing and throwing light upon these questions in the pages of *Vestnik Statistiki.*

Another condition for ensuring the trustworthiness of data is the intensification of control, through comparison of indexes from different sources. For instance, data from the accounting of areas under grain crops should be compared with data from the land balance. Data on fulfillment of the cost plan should be compared with data on fulfillment of the plan for profits. We are thus speaking of a higher type of control than that which is usually called logical control in statistics. It is very important that such control be introduced into statistical work.

In recent years, our Party and government have consistently followed the line of eliminating parallelism in accounting and of the further centralization of accounting work in statistical organizations. As we know, in the reorganization of the management of industry and construction, the accounting of enterprises and construction projects was concentrated in the statistical organizations. Later, agricultural accounting was transferred from agricultural organizations to organizations of the TsSU.

It is necessary to continue the work of ensuring uniformity in indexes and in periods for the presentation of statistical and bookkeeping data. It is time to consider the creation of centralized bookkeeping organizations, equipped with modern machines, which could carry out bookkeeping for individual enterprises on a contract basis. . . .

The volume of statistical and economic information needed for the planned management of the national economy will obviously increase as we move toward communism. In addition, greater demands will be made upon its usefulness. Of decisive importance in connection with this is the mechanization of all processes for obtaining accounting and statistical data—from the initial accounting to the receipt of over-all statistical totals.

The statistics of the communist society will be constructed through the efforts of those concerned with mechanization, who must place new machines at the service of statistics and utilize them correctly, and through the efforts of scientists—statisticians and economists—who must analyze statistical material.

The development of our whole system of state statistics is moving in this direction. The functions of obtaining and processing accounting and statistical data are being increasingly concentrated in machine calculation stations, permitting an intensification of the economic analysis and methodological direction of accounting and statistics in statistical organizations.

The task set by the government is that of raising the level of mechanization and automation in computational work connected with accounting and with economic-planning and engineering-technical calculations (in terms of numbers of workers employed) 40 percent by 1965. The mechanization of accounting work must, by 1965, release a significant number of accountants and bookkeepers for more rational utilization in the national economy. . . .

In addition, we may expect that the equipping of statistical organizations with electronic calculating machines—which has already begun—will mean a radical break in the whole organization of the collection and processing of statistical materials. Electronic calculating machines are machines of a communist society, and we must now, today, prepare more energetically and purposefully than ever before to master them. . . .

Very closely connected with the problem of placing accounting and statistical work on a base of electronic technology is the task of making broader application of mathematical methods in statistical work. Our age is the age of the intensive introduction of mathematics into all areas of knowledge. This very highly progressive process will undoubtedly have a most positive effect in the area of statistics. . . .

These great tasks for statistics which arise from the new Program of the CPSU demand deep theoretical knowledge, utter devotion to communism, and high work qualifications from all workers in Soviet statistics. It is important as never before that Soviet statisticians combine a high level of theoretical preparation in the area of Marxist-Leninist economic theory and statistics with practical experience in economic and statistical work. . . .

Now, as never before, the increasing importance of accounting and statistics for the planned direction of the national economy has become clear. The experience of using accounting and statistics in communist construction again and again shows how far-fetched and scholastic were the ideas about the future "dying-out" of statistics popular in the 1930's.

An important trait which we must instill in our young statisticians and in all statistical workers is a deep understanding that statistics, by their very nature, are sharp weapons in the ideological struggle.

Our statistics truly and scientifically indicate the great achievements of socialism and expose the falsifications made by bourgeois apologists, reformers, and revisionists in order to hide the unsightly picture of modern capitalism and, at any price, to understate the success of the socialist world.

The defenders of capitalism try with all their might to avoid an objective evaluation of the relationship between capitalism and socialism and to distort the actual state of things. But the facts are obstinate. . . .

The tasks for Soviet statistics arising from the historical decisions of the XXII Congress of the CPSU and from the new Program of our Party demand the full exertion of our powers and high creative incandescence in all of our work. Many unresolved problems have arisen. It is more than ever necessary to develop the initiative of accounting and statistical workers in every possible way in all areas, listening attentively to critical remarks and to proposals brought forward, and to study and generalize all new and valuable ideas in the field of statistical theory and practice. In this connection, our magazine, *Vestnik Statistiki,* must do a great deal, and much can be provided by conferences of accounting and statistical workers and by creative discussions of questions in dispute.

4

The Tomorrow of Our Statistics *

B. KOLPAKOV
Chief, Central Statistical Administration, RSFSR

. . . A centralized system of accounting and statistics is the most important lever of state control and direction of the economy, providing strict control over fulfillment of the economic plans and over the maintenance of overall state interests.

At all the stages of socialist construction, the Party and the Government have devoted great attention to state statistics. . . .

The realization of a single system of accounting and statistics, and the elevation of their scientific level, are among the tasks set by the new Program of the CPSU.

The new Program creatively generalizes the practice of the building of socialism and, expressing the collective mind of the Party, determines the principal tasks and the basic stages of communist construction. In the light of the program directives of the Party, it is important to trace the basic directions in which accounting and statistics are to develop in the period of large-scale communist construction in our country. . . .

1. What Do Balanced Accounts Give?

Over 750,000 persons in the RSFSR are engaged in computing work. But only an insignificant portion of them use special machines. Here is an untouched field of operations for mechanizers.

Before our eyes, office work is transformed into a form of highly quali-

* From *Ekonomicheskaya Gazeta,* 1962, No. 1. Translated in and excerpts reprinted from *The Soviet Economic System: Structure and Policy,* U. S. Joint Publications Research Service, March, 1962, Vol. I, pp. 312-331.

fied industrial work. The statistician, the accountant, and the bookkeeper become operators controlling the most complex mathematical machines. The now customary compilation and transcription "by hand" of bulky accounts, their breakdown and summarization, will soon recede into the past.

As the gradual transition to communism progresses, accounting will take on the functions of the regulation of social production, labor time, and products among the members of society.

Today, on the basis of accounting and statistical data, the planning organs compile current and prospective plans, correct them, and supplement them. Sometimes a considerable amount of time passes between the receipt of statistics' "signal" and the "answering command" to production via the planning organs. As a result of the mechanization and automation of accounting and statistical data, the "command" of the expedient volume of output and marketing of products will be passed by the statistical organs directly to the producer, in a manner similar to that in which instruments now maintain an assigned technological process in an automatic shop, or select optimum operating conditions. . . .

2. Electronic Equipment Transforms Accounting

In order to keep track of the fulfillment of state plans and to adjust to current developments, precise and objective data are required. In this connection arises the pressing necessity of the extensive employment of electronic computers in the field of accounting. The ability of high-speed electronic machines to analyze, to make generalizations on the basis of this analysis, and to prepare conclusions and recommendations signifies that man has acquired a powerful helper in the field of logical activity.

From the theoretical and technical points of view, the mechanization and automation of accounting work constitutes no problem. Automatic units to compute the work done by a metal-cutting machine tool are a conventional feature of contemporary machines. Automatic transmission of the data received by them to the computer installation at the plant also causes no difficulties. The problem lies in integration of the various types of data arriving at the plant installation. Mathematicians and engineers will, however, undoubtedly solve this problem too, if it is precisely formulated. The process of automatic transmission of information further along the chain of electronic computer installations, all the way to the TsSU (Central Statistical Administration), although it will grow in complexity, is fully realizable. Together with the passing of accounting data "upwards" along the chain, the issuance of necessary tables of such accounting data to the regional or oblast link must be organized. Thus, an account can be compiled without the intervention of human hand.

The time is not far in the future when having on the first of the month completed the calculation of all the plan indicators, the machine-computer station of one or several establishments, construction projects, or collective farms will by means of facsimile transmit the perforated cards or magnetic tapes to the machine-computer station of the oblast statistical administration. From there, as the perforated cards are processed, they will be passed on to the TsSU of the RSFSR, where a teletype, automatically linked to the perforators, will total up the data for any desired portion of the national economic plan. Thus, in many branches of the economy complex computers will not be required. It is sufficient to provide an establishment with a perforator, and this establishment will transmit its report not in the form of a table, but in the form of perforated cards.

Unfortunately, the scale of employment of electronic computers in our statistical activities is as yet insufficient. This is due not so much to lack of techniques, as to the extremely feeble development of the means of making use of these techniques. This is above all the fault of the TsSU's of the USSR and of the constituent republics. A group of statistician-scientists and practical specialists, together with mathematician-programmers, must be assigned the task of working out the problems of the mechanization and automation of calculation and accounting. The presently existing organizations are not solving these problems.

The electronic industry of our country is capable of developing and producing any machine desired, but it is not receiving any orders from the state statistical organs. And here the principal question is not, what kind of machines to produce—specialized or general-purpose ones. In our view, the general-purpose ones are more suitable, and they should be given preference. . . .

The introduction of electronic machines in statistics is also hindered by the insufficient preparation of economists and statisticians in the field of mathematics. It seems to us that it is now time to review educational programs with the object of devoting more time to the study of mathematical disciplines and the use of computers. We cannot afford to be restricted to but one department of mechanization at the Institute of Economic Statistics in Moscow. . . .

The extensive employment of electronics will become feasible when the country becomes covered by a network of electronic computers, tied together in a single system. In order for this to occur, however, it will be necessary to effect a radical change in the organization of the flows of accounting data (information), standardize its forms, radically improve the quality of lower-echelon accounting, and, possibly, alter the organization of work in some organs of state and economic control.

3. Centralized Summarization

The centralization of accounting data in the state organs of statistics, started in 1957, has been accompanied by the organization of an extensive network of machine-computing stations at each local statistical administration and at the central station in Moscow. The stations were equipped with digital computers (elementary mechanization) and punched-card computers (intermediate mechanization, if electronic computers are to be considered as advanced mechanization). Only in September 1961 did the TsSU of the Russian Federation receive two "Ural" electronic computers.

Here summarization remains decentralized as before. Each collective farm sends its report to the rayon. Here the state statistics inspector makes a summary. The oblast makes a summary on the basis of rayon summaries, and the center on the basis of the oblast summaries. In all cases there is no mass material, no "food" for the high-capacity, high-speed machines. And there is no point in processing 73 oblast summaries on the tabulator in the TsSU RSFSR. Of course, in practice we fully load the tabulator. For each oblast account, several dozen perforated cards are punched, and "food" is created for the machine. From the point of view of processing precision and speed, the results are of a positive nature. True enough, the cost of the operations is as yet high, but this is, after all, a break-in period.

Another procedure for centralized summarization can be presented. The industrial establishments send their accounts directly to the TsSU. The TsSU processes these accounts on high-speed electronic machines, extracts the oblast summaries, and passes them on "down," into the oblast. In this case the machines are loaded to the maximum, their speed is utilized, and the reliability and recentness of the information reaching the center concerning the processes occurring locally is assured.

The presence of mass material at the center makes it possible to carry out various kinds of processing in depth: groupings, comparisons, searches for optimum variants; mathematical procedures and generalizations can be employed. An extensive opportunity is opened up for scientific research and for plan calculations, which are the basis of our economic activity. It stands to reason that the organization of communications is first in order of importance. All the links in the statistical chain must function precisely and without interruption. Then the oblast will receive summary data through the center more rapidly than is the case today. Such is the principle of obtaining centralized summarization until such time when the complete mechanization and automation . . . can be realized.

As has already been said, a number of other labor-consuming processes connected with statistics should also be mechanized. In a number of cases at present we come up against obsolete methods of duplicating materials. Forty or fifty years ago, the typewriter and mimeograph were, of course, advanced equipment. To this day they can be efficiently employed in a small establishment with a restricted volume of materials, which are duplicated to the extent of 3-4 copies. However, in the state statistical organs, where in the course of several hours several hundred copies must be made of numerous tables with tens of thousands of indicators, the typewriter pool constitutes the principal bottleneck. Highly productive electrical and photographic duplication equipment exists, by means of which the process of duplicating statistical material can be accelerated several times over. But such facilities are as yet being produced in very small quantities.

4. Social Control Is a Mighty Force

Vladimir Il'ich has said: "In capitalist society, statistics used to be conducted exclusively by bureaucrats or by narrow specialists; we must take it to the masses, popularize it, so that the working people would themselves gradually learn to understand and to see how, and how long, it is necessary to work, how, and how long, it is permissible to rest—so that comparison of summaries of the economic activities of individual communes would become the object of general interest and study . . ."

Without participation of the masses there is no socialist accounting. If the "mystery" of accounts is in the possession of the plant director, the collective farm chairman, the director of the state farm and the bookkeeper . . . (while) the workers and collective farm members remain in ignorance, then this is not socialist accounting.

We need not only the official publications of the TsSU. Every worker must be informed of the financial and economic condition of his plant, collective farm, or state farm. That is why the Party has as its aim the further development of extensive management democratization, and constant leadership accountability. The accounts of the leaders must invariably be accompanied by financial and economic illustrative breakdowns, so that the workers and collective farm members will know what the result of their work is, what they have accomplished, and what remains for them to accomplish. Under such conditions it will be difficult, if not entirely impossible, for the chairman of a collective farm, for instance, to buy butter in the rural cooperative store and to deliver it as part of the farm's planned milk delivery. Control from below acquires constantly more active social forms. . . .

In the historic resolutions of the XXIInd Congress of the CPSU, majestic tasks have been placed before the Soviet people. The Party Program adopted by the XXII Congress has aroused the millions-strong masses to battle for building of the communist society and its material and technical basis. In this people-wide movement, no small part is to be played by statistics.

Statistics has been and always shall be at the service of our great state. To show the economic achievements of the people, to disclose the available reserves, to provide the cue for the most advantageous solution to economic problems—such are its aims.

The multithousand-strong regiment of Soviet statisticians is fulfilled with the desire successfully to solve the problems standing before it.

II

COMPARING UNITED STATES
AND SOVIET ECONOMIES:
PROBLEMS AND METHODOLOGY

A COMPARISON of two different economies that is to lay any claim to scientific validity presents problems of considerable magnitude, even to the well-trained statistician. An Arabian nomad lives in a tent on the edge of the Sahara desert, has two wives, and keeps a two-year-old camel for transportation. A shoe salesman in Lincoln, Nebraska lives with his family in a rented two-bedroom apartment, and owns a two-year-old Nash Rambler station wagon, almost paid for, that needs a major clutch repair. How does one weigh these items in an attempt to compare the standard of living of the Arab with that of the American? A capitalist country greatly increases its production of food while another country (where procurement and selling prices, wage rates, and the allocation of raw materials are all determined by government decree) sacrifices food production for increased industrial capacity. How does one make any meaningful comparisons as to their respective rates of growth? One nation lists the workers who transport crops from the farm to the city as "employed in agriculture," another as "engaged in marketing operations." One nation includes among its "unemployed" all those willing and able to work who are engaged in productive labor for less than twenty-four hours per week; another does not count as "unemployed" anyone engaged in productive labor, irrespective of the number of hours per week he works. These and countless other problems provide grounds for disagreement and make a valid comparison of two economies no easy task.

The two selections below are meant merely as an introduction to what economists in each of the two countries consider some of the major problems connected with comparisons between the United States and the Soviet economies. Many of the arguments presented here by Robert W. Campbell and N. V. Starovskii, respectively, we shall encounter again in much more elaborate form, as we proceed to read the views of Western and of Soviet economists on national income, agriculture, labor, living standards, and other aspects of economic life in the USSR.

WESTERN VIEWS

5

Problems of United States— Soviet Economic Comparisons *

ROBERT W. CAMPBELL
Indiana University

Introduction—Statement of Findings

The purpose of the present paper is to explain in a general way and illustrate with examples some of the most important difficulties involved in making comparisons of the economies of the United States and the Soviet Union. The past decade and a half of research has greatly increased the amount of solid evidence we possess concerning the comparative performance of these two economies. At the same time, however, it has also added greatly to the sophistication of economists concerning the pitfalls that await those who seek to appraise the relative performance of two economies so different as these. . . .

The current world situation has led to widespread recognition by the American people of the need to know more about the relative status of these two economies. Intelligent action on our part in many areas of public policy requires that we know how big Soviet output is in comparison with our own, how effectively the Soviet Union uses its resources by our standards, how fast their output and productivity are increasing, and what allocations the Soviet leaders make of their output. . . .

The obstacles to United States-Soviet economic comparisons may be said to comprise several distinct orders. It will be helpful to discuss them under three main headings as follows:

(1) The availability and interpretation of statistical data;
(2) The index number problems;
(3) The danger of comparing isolated indicators out of context.

* Excerpts reprinted from *Comparisons of the United States and Soviet Economies.* Papers submitted by Panelists Appearing Before the Subcommittee on Economic Statistics, Joint Economic Committee, Congress of the United States, 1959. Part I, pp. 13-30.

The availability and interpretation of statistical data. One of the most frustrating problems facing anyone who tries to make United States-Soviet comparisons is in securing the raw materials for his effort, namely the statistical data. This difficulty is most often presented by the Soviet side of the comparison rather than the American, although there are also instances where U.S. data make comparisons difficult. . . .

A second aspect of the information problem has to do with the interpretation of the data which the Soviet Government does vouchsafe us. . . .

The importance of clarity in statistical definitions warrants additional explanation. The difficulty is that it is possible for a notion which appears on the surface to be perfectly straightforward to be defined in a number of different ways and hence ambiguous in meaning unless the scope is clearly stated. Many of these apparently simple concepts actually have a number of dimensions that make alternative definitions conceivable. When one sets out to embody even such a notion as the output of electric power in numbers drawn from the actual workings of an economy, decisions must be made as to what producers will be included, at what point output will be measured, and so forth. This point can be illustrated with examples drawn from an actual exercise in comparison. Suppose that it is desired to compare the total industrial output of the United States with that of the Soviet Union, and it is decided to approach this problem by determining the relative outputs for as exhaustive a list of commodities as we can manage. The final step would be to weight these separate comparisons of output by some notion of the relative importance of each commodity (such as value added or employment) to obtain a single index expressing the overall relative output. In table I a few of the commodities that would be included in such a comparison have been listed and columns (1) and (2) show the outputs of these commodities in each country as given in the Soviet industrial handbook, and the Statistical Abstract of the United States. Column (3) shows the ratio of Soviet output to U.S. output.

TABLE I. *Comparison of selected commodity outputs in the United States and Soviet Union*

	Year	Unit of measure	United States	U.S.S.R.	U.S.S.R. as percent of United States
Electric power	1957	Billion kilowatt-hours	716.0	209.5	29.3
Coal	1956	Million short tons	529.8	472.1	89.1
Cotton cloth	1957	Million linear yards	9,563.0	6,119.0	64.0
Oil	1956	Million metric tons	364.0	83.8	23.0
Natural gas	1956	Billion cubic feet	10,082.0	483.0	4.8
Lumber	1957	Million board-feet	37,698.0	32,204.0	85.4

The specialist on the Soviet economy will immediately suggest many corrections that will have to be made in these numbers before they can be used as the raw material for a comparison of industrial output. For example, the first item on the list—electric power—is defined in the Soviet Union as the total output of power produced by the generators, gross of the amounts used or lost within the generating plant itself, whereas the U.S. figure is net of this amount. Fortunately the Russians tell us how much of the power generated goes for the needs of the stations themselves, so that it is possible to correct the Soviet figure to U.S. terms in this dimension. When the correction is made, it changes the comparison markedly, reducing Soviet output from 29.3 percent of U.S. output to 27.5 percent. There are uncertainties in some other dimensions as well, however. In both countries electric power is produced both by specialized utility plants, and by industrial plants for their own use. The output of most of these nonutility plants is included in the total for both countries, but the cutoff point is apparently not the same in both cases. For the United States the output of industrial plants covers only those with a capacity of 100 kilowatts and over, but it is clear from the statistics in Promyshlennost' SSSR, page 176, that the Soviet figure includes the production of plants much smaller than this. This difference again involves an appreciable fraction of output—namely, about 2.1 percent of total Soviet output in 1955.

For coal, the next item in the list, even cursory examination of the sources raises a suspicion that there may be an important difference in coverage. The U.S. figure is defined as mine shipments, mine sales, or marketable production, including consumption by producers. This seems to imply that it is measured after preparatory processes such as cleaning and sorting, and one breakdown in the Statistical Abstract of the United States gives a figure of 58.7 percent as the percentage of total production mechanically cleaned. The Soviet figure, on the other hand, may well involve measurement before these processes. Some 26 percent of Soviet coal output was sent to beneficiation plants in 1955, and in the process underwent a reduction in volume of 11.9 percent. So total output after processing was 3.08 percent less than the figure shown in table I. A second difference is that the U.S. figure for bituminous coal output covers mines with an annual output of 1,000 tons or more. It seems probable that the Soviet total would not make such an exclusion, though there are no data to indicate how important this difference in scope would be.

This possible divergence in the meaning of the coal figure also serves as a reminder that even though the output of many commodities is measured in physical units, comparison in these terms may be deceptive, since the commodity may not be at all homogeneous with respect to quality or some other dimension. This problem becomes most important when one is dealing with highly fabricated products, but is also serious even with commodities which seem to have easily identifiable physical measures, such as those in table I. For instance, the figures on output of cotton cloth, given in table I in linear yards as commonly measured in the statistics of both countries, are not at all comparable, since the average width of cotton goods produced in the United States is slightly over 40 inches, whereas it is slightly under 30 inches in the Soviet Union.

In the case of coal and electric power, the explanations in Soviet statistical sources are clear enough to make one aware of the differences in concept, though for neither country are the data detailed enough to permit bringing both figures to a common concept. For many commodities, however, the degree of comparability cannot be so easily ascertained. Output figures for the next two items on the list, i.e., oil and natural gas, are easily found in Soviet sources, but when U.S. sources are consulted for comparable data, it turns out that the petroleum extraction industry has another important output, namely, natural gasoline and natural gas liquids, equal in volume to about 10 percent of the crude oil output. These products are undoubtedly much less important in Soviet operations but must surely exist. Since they are not mentioned in the statistical source, one wonders whether they are perhaps included somehow in the oil output figure.

The notion of lumber output appears superficially to be a fairly simple idea, and the fact that the figures for both the United States and the Soviet Union are expressed in terms of physical volume is comforting. But even the briefest survey of U.S. statistical sources will disclose a number of alternative figures for lumber output differing slightly from each other in concept and accordingly in amount. To which of these concepts does the Soviet figure correspond? Moreover, if the breakdowns given in the census of manufactures are examined a number of possible differences in concept immediately suggest themselves. The U.S. output figures cover sawmills and planing mills, and include both rough and finished lumber. Since the U.S. figures are collected on an establishment basis, there is probably some double counting of lumber sawed in one plant and finished in another. To what extent is this true of the Soviet total? Furthermore, suppose a Soviet enterprise both rough-saws and finishes lumber; is its output measured in terms of the volume of the finished or unfinished wood? Careful study may succeed in unearthing answers to these questions, but the answers are not at all obvious from the statistical sources themselves, from handbooks on industrial statistical procedure or from the more generally available books dealing with the economics, planning, and administration of the lumber industry.

It should be admitted that definitions are not always presented along with statistics in the more general U.S. statistical publications. Nevertheless it is almost always possible to find in easily accessible sources detailed explanations of what a given statistic covers and how it has been derived. The difficulty of doing this for the U.S.S.R. often introduces an air of uncertainty into comparisons such as those in table I.

The existence of differences between the concepts underlying Soviet and U.S. economic data should not be surprising. Comparison of the statistics of any two countries will always reveal similar inconsistencies. They flow out of differences in the organization of the economy, different statistical traditions, divergent preoccupations among those who collect statistics. Statistics are often a byproduct of some concern other than economic analysis and their definition is controlled in part by competing objectives and expediencies. What is peculiar to Soviet statistical practice, however, is the great premium which the Russians place on the propaganda use of economic indicators, and in the service of this end concepts are sometimes deliberately defined in a misleading way. This propaganda objective is one of the explanations for their secretiveness concerning the actual definitions of the statistical material they publish. The propaganda uses of Soviet economic statistics also mean that definitions are sometimes changed to mask failure or exaggerate gains. The most infamous example of such a change is the shift from the "barn yield" concept to the "biological yield" concept of grain output in the thirties, adopted to make grain output appear larger than it actually was. Even though it was possible to find out from Soviet sources that this change in definition had been made, the appropriate correction to achieve comparability with a barn-yield concept remained unknown. Not until Khrushchev's speech to the plenary session of the Central Committee in December 1958, was it revealed precisely how great the difference was. The figures he cited for 1952, i.e., barn yield as 30 percent less than the biological yield, involved a bigger difference than had commonly been estimated. A more recent example of the subversion of intertemporal and international comparability to propaganda objectives is the change in the definitions of meat and milk output. Khrushchev has made catching up with the United States in meat and milk production one of the important goals of his agricultural program, and to make the fulfillment of this goal easier, the scope of the definitions of meat and milk output has been broadened beyond past definitions and beyond the American concepts.

The examples discussed so far all involve a very simple class of economic magnitudes, namely, physical outputs. The possible differences in concept that can confound comparison in such cases are multiplied many fold when one turns to more complex statistical indicators. Any attempt at qualification of such complicated concepts as gross national product accounts, labor force and employment statistics, or output indexes, offers so many conceivable alternatives in conceptualization, and involves so many expediencies in implementing the concept with data, that it may be impossible to make any reasonably accurate reconciliation of the actual numbers that the statistical systems of the two countries actually generate. The Soviet concept of national income is far different from that accepted in most capitalist countries, for instance. . . .

Deficiencies in the statistical raw materials on which comparisons are based are not confined to the Soviet Union. There are also cases where the U.S. side of a comparison may be obscure. Inventory statistics may be cited as a single illustration. Recent data on Soviet inventories have included a number of breakdowns that make it possible to ascertain fairly well the range of items that are included in the Soviet inventory concept, and our knowledge of Soviet accounting practices makes it possible to state more or less precisely how inventory values are calculated. In many ways the U.S. inventory figures [1] are more detailed than the Soviet ones, but variations in the accounting practices of individual firms makes it impossible to state with certainty just how comprehensive these figures are in terms of the items included and the basis of valuation. It may well be that there is a difference in the scope of the inventory concept and as a result comparisons using these data may be misleading.

Finally, it frequently happens that the concepts relevant to some comparison in which we are vitally interested are not well enough defined to be embodied very satisfactorily in actual statistical data in either country. The vagueness of what is being measured means that the definitions used in generating the data are chosen somewhat arbitrarily. For example, speculation about the relative efforts of the United States and the Soviet Union in science and in research has recently become a popular enterprise in economic comparison. As one of the main ingredients of technical progress both in military and civilian applications, the amount of research is supposed to be a powerful influence on our respective power and growth possibilities. The Russians, incidentally, are also interested in this comparison. In the United States, this aspect of national economic activity has been labeled research and development, and some statistics purporting to show how many dollars worth of research and development are being carried out have been published in recent years. These statistics have been strongly criticized, however, as arbitrary in definition and vague in meaning. After all, this is a very new concept and effort, and those who report such expenditures at the local level face many unsettled questions in deciding how much research and development their firm does.

The Russians call this activity science, and in the past few years Soviet leaders have quoted a figure showing a global total for this magnitude. This Soviet figure, however, represents more a reflection of certain budg-

---

[1] For an explanation of the uncertainties involved in the meaning of U. S. inventory statistics, see George M. Cobren, "The Nonfarm Business Inventory Component," in National Bureau of Economic Research, *Studies in Income and Wealth*, vol. XII, pp. 381-400.

etary and administrative conventions than any well-defined concept of effort devoted to the expansion of knowledge and improvement of technology. The uncertainty in any comparison of the Soviet and American research efforts, therefore, is not so much due to the fact that the specific content of the respective ruble and dollar amounts differs, as to the fact that neither of these amounts measures very exactly just what we would like to measure.

The discussion above has concentrated on the obstacles to obtaining comparable statistical raw materials as a basis for comparative studies of the United States and Soviet economies. To restore a balanced perspective, it should be added in concluding this section that most of these problems can be dealt with tolerably well. Finding data and establishing their meaning is the expected task of any economist who sets out to make comparisons of the two economies. Given experience and enough time he can usually settle such issues as those described with an acceptable margin of error. These are obstacles that will succumb to knowledge, and the recent increase in Soviet statistical output is beginning to clarify some former mysteries. So far, however, the problem has only been ameliorated, not eliminated. When a researcher is unable to deal with some data problem satisfactorily, he has a duty to present his figures with an appropriate statement of reservations. Similarly, those who make use of the comparative studies that are made must know that such problems exist, that they cannot always be settled completely satisfactorily, and that comparisons made in this situation are always subject to some qualifications. Hence, they should always ask for the qualifications and alternative interpretations along with the answers.

The index number problem. The second order of obstacles to international economic comparisons comprises a number of variants of what is known as the index number problem. These obstacles differ from those discussed earlier by the fact that they do not result simply from ignorance but rather from a number of unanswered, and perhaps unanswerable questions of theory and conceptualization. They are therefore more intractable than those discussed in the previous section. The index number problem arises whenever one tries to compare relatively large aggregates either between countries or over time. Most of the questions which international economic comparisons are designed to answer involve the comparative measurement of such large aggregates. The question of relative American and Soviet economic strength, for example, is usually posed as the size of Soviet output relative to our own, as measured by some indicator such as gross national product. Or people may ask for comparisons of smaller but still very heterogeneous components of this aggregate. It is common, for example to ask how well off the average Soviet consumer or industrial worker is relative to his opposite number in the United States. Those who are responsible for making U.S. defense policy would like to know how the Soviet military effort compares with our own in terms of its overall size. Making comparisons in these aggregative terms is the only way to escape getting lost in a host of contradictory details.

Economic aggregates such as those listed above can be measured only in value terms. The diverse physical goods and services encompassed in American or Soviet gross national product can be expressed in a single figure only through using the common denominator of monetary value. Hence, if it is desired to compare Soviet and American gross national product it is necessary to find some conversion factor, some exchange rate, that permits one to translate the rubles of one into the dollars of the other, or vice versa. Unfortunately, however, it so happens that the value of a ruble, expressed in how many dollars worth of output can be bought with it, varies markedly depending on the kind of product or service that is being considered. The structure of relative prices in the two countries is very different, so that the value of a ruble compared to a dollar is far greater in the purchase of some items than of others. This difference between the Soviet and American price structure is the result of many separate factors, including differences in the scarcities of the resources going into different commodities, the differential degree to which the Russians have caught up with American technology in different sectors of the economy, and the peculiarities of Soviet accounting, pricing, and fiscal practices. Hence any even moderately aggregative magnitude contains components for which the appropriate dollar-ruble conversion ratios diverge widely. The problem is to find an average ratio appropriate to the conversion of the aggregate we are interested in. The approach that springs immediately to mind is to average the individual conversion ratios, weighted by the relative importance of the various components of the aggregate.

The problem, however, is that the relative importance of the components is different in the two countries. As a result, there is a choice of weighting patterns and a choice of conversion ratios. The problem can be illustrated by the simple numerical example shown in the following table, in which the gross national product of two countries is compared. This example outrages reality in assuming that all gross national product is directed either to consumption or to military purposes, but this oversimplification makes the nature of the problem easier to see. We have called the two countries the United States and the Soviet Union, although the magnitudes shown for the gross national product and its components in each case are completely arbitrary. The proportions between consumption and military uses, however, and the implied difference in the price structures of the two countries are plausible reflections of reality. Columns (1) and (2) show the composition of the gross national product in each

country measured in its own prices. Column (3) shows the value of a
ruble in dollars in the purchase of the goods included in the respective
components of the gross national product. Using these figures as conversion ratios, it is possible to calculate the size of each country's gross
national product in the currency of the other. The results are shown
in columns (4) and (5). There are now enough totals so that the gross
national product can be compared either in dollars or in rubles, but a
glance at the figures shows that the result will not be the same for both
comparisons. When the output of both countries is measured in United
States prices, Soviet output appears to be one-third as large as that of
the United States, but if a comparison is made in Soviet prices, Soviet
output turns out to be only 28.5 percent of American.

TABLE II.   *Schematic illustration of the index number problem*

	U.S.S.R. (in billion rubles)	United States (in billion dollars)	Conversion rate (dollars per ruble)	U.S.S.R. (in billion dollars)	United States (in billion rubles)
	(1)	(2)	(3)	(4)	(5)
Consumption	100	40	.10	10	400
Military expenditure	20	5	.25	5	20
Total	120	45		15	420

NOTE. Soviet output as a percentage of United States output:
   In rubles: 120÷420=28.6 percent.
   In dollars: 15÷45=33.3 percent.

What is the reason for this difference in the two answers? A rigorous
explanation would involve going into the complexities of index number
construction, but the essence of the mechanism at work can be explained
as follows. Pricing in rubles is equivalent to converting total gross national product at an exchange rate of 10.71 cents per ruble, 10.71 being
the average of the separate ruble-dollar price ratios, weighted in proportion to the relative magnitudes of the components of U.S. gross national
product as they would look to a Russian. Valuation in dollars, on the
other hand, amounts to the use of a conversion ratio of 12.5 cents per
ruble, 12.5 being the average of 10 and 25, weighted by the relative importance of consumption and military expenditures as they would look
to one accustomed to American prices.

The same mechanism can also be explained in somewhat different
terms though with equivalent meaning. In the U.S. price system, consumer goods are priced cheaper relative to military goods than in the
Soviet price system. We have indicated this difference in price structure
in table II in an approximate illustrative way by the exchange rates

shown in column (3). These conversion rates imply that a dollar's worth of consumer goods would be worth 10 rubles in the Soviet Union, but a dollar's worth of military goods would be worth only 4 rubles. Ruble valuation of the output of either country will therefore magnify the significance of the consumption component of its gross national product and diminish the significance of the military component, compared with valuation in dollars. Since the composition of Soviet gross national product differs from the U.S. pattern by its relatively higher emphasis on military expenditure, it will look bigger relative to the U.S. total when both are seen in the light of a price system which prices military goods relatively high and consumption goods relatively low (i.e., the dollar price system) than in the light of one that has high prices for consumer goods and low prices for military goods (the ruble price system).

This ambiguity of answers in international comparisons is not uncommon. Whenever the price structures and the composition of aggregates vary between countries, different answers about the relative size of the aggregates will be obtained, depending on which country's prices are used. The greater the differences in price relationships and in composition, the greater will be the difference between the alternative answers. There are appreciable differences between the alternative measures of relative size of gross national product even when the U.S. is compared with countries with relatively high productivity and modern technologies such as Great Britain or Germany.[2] When comparisons are attempted between the United States and countries where allocation and price structures are more radically different, such as Italy or the Soviet Union, the degree of indeterminacy is even greater.

What guidance can be offered the person who finds that the answer to his simple question about the relative size of the United States and Soviet economies is given in the form of an indeterminate range? In terms of the example in table II, is the figure of 33.3 percent or 28.6 percent the "correct" figure for the size of the Soviet gross national product relative to our own? The answer to this puzzle turns on the fact that the two numbers represent answers to two different questions. The comparison made in rubles (i.e., the one showing the Soviet gross national product as 28.6 percent of American) answers the question "How big is Soviet output?" if it is assumed that it was as hard for them to produce a given collection of consumer goods relative to, say, a missile, as in the United States. The figure of 33.3 percent answers the question "How big was it?" if we assume that in the United States a given basket of consumer goods was priced as high relative to a missile as in the Soviet Union. One might argue that neither of these questions is "realistic." The relative

2 See Milton Gilbert & Associates, *Comparative National Products and Price Levels*, Paris, 1958, OEEC, for illustrations of the differences that alternative pricing makes in comparing U. S. output with some countries of Western Europe.

prices of consumer goods and military goods are not the same in both countries. The questioner did not intend it should be pretended they were when he asked how big Soviet output was relative to ours. This is perhaps true enough, but the researcher is forced to such expediencies in trying to make the comparison at all. The problem is that what appeared on the face of it to be a straightforward question; namely, "How big is Soviet output relative to our own?" really begs important issues, issues which the statistician must settle explicitly when he gets down to the mechanics of formulating a numerical answer. And though one may object that the way the statisticians have traditionally settled these issues (i.e., by seeing Soviet output in the light of U.S. value relationships or U.S. output in terms of Soviet scarcity relationships), he will find it difficult to suggest any more satisfactory approach. In a fundamental sense the two aggregates are not directly comparable, and the traditional approach has at least the virtue of marking out the limits that one might reasonably wish to set conceptually.

The above example is only one variant of the index number problem; even when comparisons involve much smaller aggregates than gross national product the same difficulty arises. In the numerical example of table II, for instance, it was assumed that a ruble is worth 10 cents in the purchase of consumption goods and 25 cents in buying the inputs of a military program. But how can a conversion ratio for such a component of gross national product be arrived at in the first place? Each of these aggregates (i.e., consumption and military expenditures) is itself a heterogeneous collection of goods and services, the composition of which varies between the two countries. Furthermore, the purchasing power of a ruble in terms of dollars is very different as between, say shelter and bread or between the maintenance of a soldier and the building of a missile. This means that one would have to choose among alternative weighting systems in order to compute conversion ratios for the separate components of gross national product before the problem of gross national product comparison could even be formulated as in table II. The existence of a range of possible values for the conversion ratio applicable to consumption or to military goods means that the range between the extremes of relative gross national product magnitudes would be even greater.

Another well-known variant of the index number problem arises in the calculation of rates of growth of various economic magnitudes such as industrial output, consumption levels, labor productivity, or others. In such problems it is necessary to determine the relative size of a given aggregate (e.g., consumption or industrial output) at two different points in time. Characteristically, the composition and the price structures for such aggregates change over time. (In the Soviet Union the changes in composition and price relationships have been exceptionally great.) The problem is formally identical with that of international comparisons of aggregates, and the same indeterminacy arises. In this case, however, there are good grounds for arguing that extremes at the ends of the range of possible answers flowing from different weighting systems can be ignored and something like the geometric mean of the extremes taken as an acceptable measure of the rate of growth. The sharp difference in weighting patterns chosen from points far distant in time is a function of how far apart the terminal dates of the comparison are. By looking at shorter periods, the changes in structure and price relationships are found to be less important, and the range of estimates of growth is greatly reduced. . . .

Another common exercise in these comparisons is to ask how soon the Russians will catch up with us in GNP or in some element of it such as industrial output. By estimating the relative size of the chosen economic indicator at the present time, and then projecting each of them forward at some rate of growth a date for the Russian catching up emerges. Because of the wide range of relative sizes that one can start with, and the wide choice of growth rates (reflecting in both cases the index number problem) it is possible to determine a period for the catching up process varying from a decade and a half to four or five decades. What is the purpose of a question that cannot be answered more definitely than that? Part of the indeterminacy comes from the fact that it is not clear what the comparison is aimed to show. If the question one ultimately wants to answer is something like "how soon will Soviet machinery output be great enough to cover a program of investment, trade, and military expenditure such as ours," then it might be more nearly answerable with an acceptable degree of exactness.

Dangers in comparing isolated indicators out of context. The third order of obstacles to meaningful comparisons of the American and Soviet economies involves the possibility of misinterpreting fairly specific indicators through ignoring important features of the context. If the index number problem makes the comparison of large aggregates difficult, at the other extreme differences in organization, in technology, and in resource availabilities often make comparisons of very narrowly defined magnitudes or overly specific indicators misleading. The Soviet and American economies differ from each other markedly in administrative structure, in the resource endowment within which each must operate, and in technology. Consequently the significance of a given economic indicator often varies between them.

In their zeal to make some comparison appear better than it really is, the Russians are frequently guilty of overlooking such differences. For instance Khrushchev has worked hard to make expansion of Soviet per capita butter production to the U.S. level a symbol of catching up with the United States in general. Apart from the question of differing at-

titudes of the two populations toward fats in their diets, this comparison overlooks the fact that butter production in the United States is supplemented by an output of margarine 3 percent greater than the production of butter itself, whereas in the Soviet Union the output of margarine is only 70 percent of butter output.[3]
cow, 1958, pp. 169-170.

Another such prestige output which they have elevated to the status of a symbol is the output of sugar. Soviet propagandists are fond of comparing sugar output in the two countries. For instance, in one of the standard statistical handbooks for agitators,[4] the production of sugar in the two countries is shown as 17 kilograms in the Soviet Union and 12 kilograms in the United States. This figure appears to be accurate enough as far as it goes, but what it fails to mention is that while Soviet sugar output is augmented by imports only to the extent of about 2 percent, U.S. domestic output is far overshadowed by imports so that per capita consumption is more nearly 45 kilograms than 12.[5]

Another common example is the preoccupation with individual commodity outputs, such as steel or electric power output, as general indicators of "industrial base," which in turn is thought of as being some indicator of relative Soviet military potential, or ability to implement other strategic objectives such as foreign aid capital accumulation or growth. What this comparison overlooks is the radically different pattern of consumption of these two products in the two countries. Consumer goods, such as automobiles and home appliances take a vastly higher proportion of United States, than of Soviet steel output. Similarly with electric power output; the Soviet output of 231 billion kilowatt-hours in 1957 compared to the American output of 716 billion kilowatt-hours seems to suggest that the productive capacity of the Soviet economy must be strongly restricted by the lack of this vital ingredient of productivity. Again, however, the pattern of utilization is very different. Only a tiny fraction of Soviet power output goes for such uses as household consumption, and municipal and commercial lighting, whereas a very large share of U.S. power output is devoted to these purposes. Hence it is erroneous to consider the relative outputs as a reliable indicator of industrial power.

One of the common areas of concern for people who are making these comparisons is the productivity of the Soviet economy, that is the amount of output they get per unit of the resources at their disposal. The rationale

---

[3] These figures are taken from *Statistical Abstract of the United States*, 1958 edition, pp. 674 and 681, and V. P. Zotov, *Pishchevaia promyshlennost' Sovetskogo Soiuza*, Mos-
[4] I. A. Ioffe, *Strany sotsializma i kapitalizma v.tsifrakh*, (*The Countries of Socialism and Capitalism in Figures*) Moscow, 1957.
[5] These figures are from *Statistical Abstract of the United States*, p. 671, V. P. Zotov, *Pishchevaia promyshlennost' SSSR*, p. 170, and *Ministerstvo Vneshnei torgovli SSSR, Vneshniaia torgovlia Soiuza SSR za 1957 god*, Moscow, 1958, pp. 21 and 33.

of such comparisons is a belief that productivity has something to do with the relative efficiency of the two economies. Here, however, a different context of technology and of resource endowments greatly beclouds the meaning of specific productivity comparisons. One of the most commonly studied indicators is labor productivity. Such studies always show that output per Soviet worker in any area of the economy is considerably below output per worker in the United States. The Russians themselves claim that output per worker in industry is about half the U.S. level, although this is the kind of comparison that is suspect because of the index number problem discussed earlier. The calculation presupposes some estimate of the relative size of United States and Soviet industrial output, and the great variety of possible weighting schemes means that such comparisons have to be examined very skeptically. In a number of individual branches of the economy, where it is possible to find more or less homogeneous physical measures of output, output per worker can be easily enough compared, however. The result of such comparisons is to show a great range of comparative labor productivity, but despite the variation from case to case, such comparisons show clearly that output per worker is far lower in the Soviet Union than in the United States.

It is but a short step from comparisons such as these to the conclusions that the Soviet economy is extremely wasteful and inefficient. This is a conclusion that is often drawn, but one that is by no means warranted on the evidence of comparative labor productivity. In general this low labor productivity is far less a reflection of inefficiency or waste than of the different resource situation confronting the Russian planners, a resource situation fundamentally different from ours. Soviet industrialization has taken place against the background of an abundance of manpower. The planners have faced a situation where it was never any problem to secure additional labor. The real difficulty was in finding the capital to create new capacity, new factories in which the labor could be employed. It was therefore economically sensible for them to use labor lavishly, substituting it whenever possible for capital goods, and bringing in more workers whenever it was possible by doing so to squeeze a bit more output out of existing enterprises. The result of such a policy was to make output per worker low, but it was still the correct thing to do in the light of the abundance of labor.

The low productivity of the Soviet industrial labor force can be explained alternatively as the low level of mechanical assistance which the Soviet worker has at his disposal. A good summary indicator of the amount of mechanical power which the worker has to assist him in doing his job is the amount of electrical power consumed per worker. Consumption of electric power per industrial worker in the Soviet Union is less than half the American level, and this factor alone goes a long way toward explaining why Soviet industrial labor productivity is so much below ours. It should be emphasized, again, however, that the failure of the Soviet planners to supply their workers with as much mechanical assistance as American workers enjoy does not necessarily imply a mistake in planning. Given the population situation and the amount of capital that could be accumulated, the Soviet planners have found that they could expand the industrial labor force much more easily than they could build more generating plants and other power facilities to increase the mechanical assistance provided for the worker.

The difference in resource endowments distorts other indicators in the opposite direction. Because of the intensive utilization of capacity the output per machine or per other unit of capital is much higher than in the United States. One of the best known examples is the high productivity of capital in Soviet railroad transportation. The Russians have a much higher output of freight turnover per mile of track and per freight car than we do in the United States—something over three times as much freight turnover per mile of track and almost three times as much freight turnover per ton of freight car capacity. Another industry in which Soviet equipment productivity is much higher is in blast furnace operation. Measuring the blast furnace capacity by the total internal volume of the blast furnace and output in tons, it turns out that the Russians get on the average 1.25 tons of pig iron per cubic meter of blast furnace capacity, whereas American producers get only 0.92 ton. It should be added that the productivity of blast furnaces is a function of their size, with larger furnaces being appreciably more productive per cubic meter of space than small furnaces are. Since American furnaces are rather larger on the average than Soviet furnaces, the higher productivity of Soviet furnaces is all the more notable.

Soviet economists are very fond of making such comparisons of capital productivity and concluding that they prove the greater efficiency of their economic system and the chaotic wastefulness of capitalism. This conclusion is as dubious as the reverse one that we sometimes make on the basis of labor productivity comparisons. The high rate of utilization of capital equipment makes sense for the Soviet Union but not for the United States. The relative abundance and cheapness of capital in this country makes it rational for a firm to provide itself generously with capacity.

The argument above should not be understood as implying that the American and Soviet systems are equally efficient in making use of the different resource endowments which each enjoy. The point is rather that the difference in relative scarcities of the basic factors of production makes productivity comparisons a very ambiguous kind of evidence on this score, though superficially they seem so suggestive of relative efficiencies. To what extent the difference in some productivity indicator is evidence of inefficiency and to what extent a reflection of different resource availabilities is a question that can be answered with certainty, if at all, only by a detailed scrutiny of many other aspects of the context.

Even when the influence of such radically different scarcity relationships is absent, more subtle differences in the parameters which confront decision makers and in technology may mean that technological indicators must be interpreted carefully. For instance in a comparative study of the electric power industry of the two countries, one question that would immediately draw attention to itself would be the expenditure of fuel per kilowatt-hour of electric power produced. The electric power industry is engaged essentially in the transformation of the heat energy of fuel into electric energy, and so this ratio is an important indicator of its technological perfection. There is no particular statistical problem to such a comparison—this is an important operating indicator used in the planning and administration of the electric power industry and it is a statistic the Russians collect and publish. Data of the same form can easily be calculated for the U.S. power industry. But as the comparison of the two industries went further, it would soon be found that one of the important differences between the United States and Soviet power industries is that Soviet generating equipment includes an appreciable proportion of installations in which some of the waste heat is captured and used for heating purposes. The generation of electric power inevitably involves the loss of some heat—it is impossible to convert all the energy in the fuel into electrical energy. The Russians use a considerable amount of this heat. Americans use it very little. In computing the fuel consumption per kilowatt-hour of electric power, the Russians assign a significant amount of the fuel burned in power stations (i.e., about 16 percent) to the heating operations.[6]

When it comes to choosing a fuel expenditure ratio for comparison with the American should one use the one cited by the Russians or one corrected to include all fuel burned in electric power stations? There are objections to either alternative. There would be little justification for basing the comparison on the total fuel burned since the Russians are correct in implying that this fuel is not one of the costs of power. It is true that most of this heat could not be converted to electric power even if they did not have the alternative use for it. Nevertheless they do have a use for it, and have made a choice of equipment which will permit them to capture it and avoid burning fuel in conventional installations for heating purposes. In the light of the alternatives open to them, then they are correct in saying that part of the fuel is really chargeable to heating rather than power generation. On the other hand we hesitate to use the Soviet fuel expenditure ratio as they present it because of doubts about the correctness of the amount of the fuel they assign to heating. The allocation between the two purposes is made on the basis of an engineer-

[6] This percentage can be calculated from data given in *Promyshlennost' S.S.S.R.*

ing convention rather than on the basis of what a sophisticated economist would consider correct. What it comes down to is that the power industry in the two countries employs two slightly different technologies, and as a result fuel expenditure per kilowatt-hour of power is an indicator with a slightly different meaning in the two countries. Even apart from this difficulty, other qualifications would have to be considered before this indicator could be taken as a measure of the relative efficiency of the Soviet Union and American power industries. Fuel expenditure per kilowatt-hour is a function of various design parameters of the equipment, such as the temperature and pressure of the steam. Rational decisions on these parameters are very sensitive to the costs of fuel relative to costs of the other inputs that go into the original construction and the operation of generating stations. Hence relatively small differences in price structure might mean that rational or "efficient" decisions would result in a different fuel expenditure ratio in the two countries.

A final illustration of the treacheries of comparing economic indicators torn from different contexts is provided by investment in the two countries. It has been a commonplace to explain the rapid rate of growth of the Soviet economy as flowing in part from the high rate of investment in the Soviet Union. The Soviet planners have been able to keep down consumption levels and in consequence devote a larger share of current output to building new production capacity than the United States does. To embody this argument in statistics, one commonly resorts to a comparison of the share of GNP devoted to investment purposes. Once attention is focused on this mode of analysis, actual statistical comparisons of investment in absolute terms or as a share of GNP are productive of considerable confusion. Investment as a percentage of GNP turns out to be not so radically different in the two countries, and this bolsters the suspicion that maybe the Soviet economy is not growing as fast as we have been led to believe. It also prompts the comforting thought that if small reallocations of Soviet GNP away from investment should take place the Russians will lose whatever advantage relative to the U.S. economy they may have had in the past. This confusion comes from focusing attention on gross investment as an explanation of growth rather than net investment which is the concept that covers the net additions to productive capacity. We have traditionally emphasized gross rather than net investment in our national income accounting and analysis because of the difficulty of measuring net investment meaningfully, and indeed for some international comparisons gross investment might serve well enough. Because the Soviet and American economies are so different with respect to the size and age of their capital stock and the rate of growth, however, the share of gross investment that represents real net additions to productive capacity is much greater for the Soviet Union than for the United States.

Conclusion. The task of this paper has been to discuss the problems involved in United States-Soviet economic comparisons. It would be a source of great chagrin to the author if this listing of obstacles should be taken as a justification for a belief that it is hopeless or pointless to undertake such comparisons. With respect to the first problem, data availability, the limitations of what can be accomplished has certainly not yet been reached. Indeed the rate of flow of data has increased recently much faster than our efforts to make use of it. Also the possible approaches for clearing up obscurities in the meaning of Soviet statistics are greater than may have been implied. The index number problem is not peculiar to United States-Soviet comparisons alone, but actually affects many measurement problems within our own economy. It is only that the attention of economists has been directed toward these difficulties in comparison and measurement most strongly in the comparative study of the United States and Soviet economies because intertemporal and international differences in economic structure are more striking when we try to evaluate their performance relative to ours than in many other kinds of problems that economists deal with. Likewise our preoccupation with the interpretation of data comes from the fact that the Russians are particularly persistent in choosing concepts that complicate comparability of economic indicators.

In this connection a final important implication of the discussion should be pointed out. The Russians are truly compulsive in making comparisons of their economy with ours, and in the process they turn all the ambiguities discussed above to good account in exaggerating their achievements relative to ours. They ignore important differences in the concepts underlying comparisons, choose weighting systems that present their achievements in the best possible light, and emphasize indicators the comparability of which is violated by differences in the context. All these misinterpretations can, of course, also be employed by those who would underemphasize Soviet economic performance. With a greater respect for truth than the Russians we should take pains to point out the errors involved in the Soviet comparisons, and with perhaps greater sophistication about the pitfalls of international economic comparisons we should be able to avoid the dangers of accepting misleading evaluations of Soviet economic performance from either end of the spectrum.

6

On the Methodology of Comparing Economic Indices of the USSR and the USA *

V. N. STAROVSKII
Director, Central Statistical Administration, USSR

In conditions of peaceful economic competition between the Soviet Union and the United States the proper scientific comparison of our indices with the indices of American statistics is of great importance.

Comparisons between the economic indices of the USSR and the USA are contained in recent highly important political documents of the Communist Party and the Soviet Government, particularly in the decisions of the 20th and 21st CPSU Congresses, plenary meetings of the CPSU Central Committee, the Seven-Year Plan target figures, and reports and statements by N. S. Khrushchev, First Secretary of the CPSU Central Committee and Chairman of the USSR Council of Ministers. These estimates, based on irrefutable facts, characterize the most important indices of our economy as compared with the economy of the United States.

For many years Soviet statisticians and economists have conducted important research on working out a system of indices to be used in comparing the Soviet and capitalist economies and in solving numerous and often highly complicated methodological problems arising in the process of comparison. This research has been especially fruitful in recent years, for it has been based on the highly important theoretical work of our Party on the question of economic competition between the two systems.

The USSR Central Statistical Administration is making comparisons of the major indices of the economy and culture of the Soviet Union with those of the capitalist countries. Its respective divisions are working out correct methods of comparison and are preparing comparable statistics for publication. Much work in this area has been done by the Institute of Economics of the USSR Academy of Sciences, the Institute of World Economics and International Relations of the USSR Academy of Sciences,

* From *Voprosy Ekonomiki*, 1960, No. 4. Translated in and excerpts reprinted from *Problems of Economics*, July, 1960, pp. 14-24, by permission of the publisher.

and the Economic Research Institute of the USSR State Planning Committee. Important work in comparing the economic indices of the USSR and the capitalist countries is also being conducted in the Business Studies Institute of the Ministry of Foreign Trade, the Labor Institute of the State Committee of the USSR Council of Ministers on Labor and Wages, the Moscow Institute of Economics and Statistics, the Chair of Statistics of the Economics Department of Moscow State University and the Moscow Financial and Economic Institute. Many Soviet economists have worked on the same subjects. Mention should be made of the studies of Academician S. G. Strumilin and a number of other scientists.

Much attention is also being given to the problems of comparing economic indices in the capitalist countries, particularly by American research organizations and some American economists. We must note with regret, however, that until recently the overwhelming majority of these economists (except for some progressive scholars) were engaged in the wholesale discrediting and groundless underestimation of the indices of Soviet economic growth. Only recently has there emerged a tendency to admit the achievements of the Soviet economy and give a somewhat more sober appraisal of them.

Our press has more than once rightly noted the obvious tendentiousness of American economists in assessing the indices of the Soviet Union's economic growth. Even some American scholars have begun to admit this lately. Thus, a US congressional committee recently published, among other reports, a paper by Lynn Turgeon about the standard of living in the Soviet Union. He was compelled to admit that Western economists "not only tend to give an inflated picture of the height of Russian prices but also, to some extent, magnify the size of the gap between the levels of living in the United States and the USSR." Lynn Turgeon regards a simple comparison of the wage and price levels in the two countries as incorrect and says that "these procedures, which have ordinarily been employed extensively in the past, will probably to an increasing degree tend to exaggerate the relative height of Russian prices as well as the gap between the two levels of living to an even greater extent in the future . . ."

As regards a number of indices, there is a difference in the method of calculation employed by Soviet and American statistics. Thus, a correct comparison of the respective indices requires that they be made comparable. For example, in the USA the production of electric power is figured on the basis of off-busbar output (that is, without the auxiliary power used by power stations for their own needs), while Soviet statistics give gross production of electric power. To make these indices comparable the Central Statistical Administration calculates either the generation of electricity in the USSR according to off-busbar output or the gross production of electricity in the United States. Raw cotton is used to compute cotton output in the USSR, whereas the United States and all other capitalist countries use cotton fiber, the weight of which constitutes approximately a third of that of raw cotton. Therefore, in comparing the indices of the production and yield of cotton in the USSR and the United States, it is necessary to convert US data into raw cotton (i.e., to treble the figures pertaining to fiber), or convert Soviet data into cotton fiber (i.e., take one third of the figures pertaining to raw cotton). Meat production statistics in the USSR include heads, feet and fat, whereas American statisticians sometimes exclude heads, feet and fat and often exclude poultry meat in the estimates of meat production. Therefore, in comparing data on meat output in the USSR and the United States the Central Statistical Administration of the USSR estimates meat output in the United States taking into account heads, feet, fat and poultry meat (according to US data, of course).

Official American statistics list among students of higher educational establishments people who attend junior colleges, as well as first- and second-year students of other colleges which, in the level of instruction, are equivalent to the senior grades of secondary school. Many American and British educators admit that this group is incorrectly listed among students of higher educational establishments. In 1958, Americans held that there were 3,226,000 college students in the United States. If the incorrectly listed students are excluded, the number of college students in the United States in 1958 was 1,738,000. According to official calculations the United States has more students than the Soviet Union, but according to correct calculations it has less.

In these and all other similar cases, Soviet statisticians strictly observe the principle of comparability of data and make the necessary recalculations to ensure their comparability.[1] But in addition to actual differences in calculations in the USSR and the United States (all of which can be overcome), there are many instances when there are no real differences but they are merely invented by dishonest critics. For example, the rather well-known Harry Schwartz, in an article published in *The New York Times* on January 16, 1959, cast doubt on Soviet milk production statistics on the pretext that these data include both milk consumed by the population and milk fed to calves. The impression created in the reader's mind by Schwartz was that American statistics calculate milk production in a different way. Yet, it is a fact that American statistics and American statistical manuals,[2] just as Soviet statistics, include in milk production

[1] The principle of comparability is strictly observed in the official statements of Party and Government leaders. For instance, in his report to the May (1958) Plenary Session of the CPSU Central Committee, N. S. Khrushchev directly pointed out, when he compared the rate of overall increase in production in the USSR and the United States, that the data on the output of electricity "did not include power expenditure by electric power stations for their own needs."

[2] See, for example, *Agricultural Statistics 1957*, issued by the US Department of Agriculture in 1958, p. 456.

both the milk consumed by farmers and the milk used for feeding calves. It is only the milk sucked by the calves that is not counted by American statistics, just as is the case with Soviet statistics. Harry Schwartz evidently needed this invented difference to gloss over the unpleasant fact that the Soviet Union has already outstripped the United States and has advanced to first place in the world in the total production of milk and the total and per capita production of butter.

There are essential differences between American and Soviet statistics in the system of calculating industrial production indices. In calculating these indices, Soviet statisticians draw on a complete accounting of the physical volume of production of all goods without exception evaluated in comparable prices. American statisticians do not have at their disposal a sufficient quantity of direct and reliable data and use less perfect methods in calculating these indices. For most branches of industry, instead of using the physical output of goods indirect indices are taken: number of man-hours worked (usually adjusted for changes in labor productivity), consumption or delivery of raw materials, consumption of electric power, indices of the value of output in current prices adjusted by the price index, etc. As weights for some branches of industry American statisticians use the so-called net product (to be more exact, the assumed net product, because depreciation is not excluded).

American statisticians criticize Soviet indices because they are based on an accounting of gross output. Without going into the details of why we are interested in calculating gross production (the most important reason is the need for dovetailing the output of enterprises and the output of industries), we shall merely mention that quantitatively the difference between average indices constructed on the basis of gross and net production is negligible; it is particularly negligible in comparisons covering a small number of years.

The differences are more serious in comparing such indices as the national income and the standard of living. Here it is a matter of different economic definition of the content of these indices.

Comrade N. S. Khrushchev, in his conversation in 1958 with E. Ridder, owner and publisher of the American *Journal of Commerce* and H. Luedicke, the editor of this newspaper, pointed out that "the economic concepts which underlie Soviet statistics, for example, clearly distinguish between the sphere of material production and that of non-productive branches, and correspondingly between the concepts 'production' and 'services.' In the USSR the volume of the aggregate social product does not include the value of 'services' in non-productive branches of the national economy, whereas in US statistics the 'gross national product' embraces all services irrespective of whether they are connected with production or not. Similarly, in defining the size and structure of the national income, Soviet statistics treat the national income not as a mere sum of all kinds of incomes, as is the practice in bourgeois statistics, but as the sum of primary incomes received in the sphere of material production."

American statistics, which include in the production of the national income not only the results of material production, but also services, artificially exaggerate the total size of the national income. American statistics also make serious mistakes in determining the indices of distribution of the national income, particularly the share of the working people.

Comparison of the Volume of Industrial Production

The first, and perhaps most important, methodological question in comparing economic indices is that of comparing the volume of industrial output.

A comparison of the levels of industrial production can be made by comparing both the data on the physical volume of production and also the value of the output in comparable prices. The most indisputable method is that of comparing the actual physical output of major industrial items, since this above all determines the industrial potential of one or another country. . . .

To characterize the relationship between the levels of total industrial output in the USSR and the United States it would be necessary first of all to compare the volume of gross industrial production. But in the United States it is now customary to publish an index not of gross industrial production, but of so-called net production, that is, the value of output less expenses for raw material, supplies and fuel. In other words, the assumed net production includes wages, profits and depreciation.

Several variants of calculations were made in order to compare the output of industry in the United States and the USSR in 1959. First, the magnitude of the assumed net production of Soviet industry was calculated and compared with the assumed net production of American industry. Second, the gross production of American industry was calculated and compared with the gross production of Soviet industry. Then, two variants of indices for converting rubles into dollars and dollars into rubles were derived. The conversion into dollars of the output of Soviet industry was done with due consideration for the industrial structure of the USSR, while the conversion into rubles was made by taking into account the industrial structure of the United States. As a result four variants were obtained. If we compare the assumed net production in rubles, we find that in 1959 Soviet output was 61% of the US output. If we compare it in dollars we find that it is somewhat smaller than 60%. As for gross production, in both variants the gross production of the USSR was equivalent to 60% of that of the United States.

Our official documents usually point out that in 1958 the industrial output of the USSR was not less than half of that in the United States. This is an absolutely indisputable appraisal both for 1958 and 1959. The above calculations show that in 1959 the volume of Soviet industrial production was about 60% of the output of American industry. The comparison of the physical volume of output given earlier also confirms that industrial production in the USSR is more than half of that in the United States.

Until quite recently the American press denied that industrial production in the Soviet Union was already not less than half of the US output. Some American economists asserted that Soviet industrial production was about one-quarter or one-third of the American. For example, in June 1959 William Byner, Vice-President of the Chase Manhattan Bank, stated that the latest statistics showed that the volume of production in the Soviet Union was probably not more than 20 to 25% of the American level.

Last November comparisons of the Soviet and American economies were made at meetings of the Subcommittee on Economic Statistics of the Joint Economic Committee of Congress. A number of American economists tried to repeat the absurd allegations that Soviet industrial output was only one-quarter or one-third of the American level. Allen Dulles, head of the US Central Intelligence Agency, who spoke at a meeting of the committee, had to dissociate himself from these overzealous attempts to discredit Soviet economic achievements. He stated that industrial production in the Soviet Union was not one-quarter and not one-third, but about 40% of the American level. Dulles said that "we should frankly face up to the very sobering implications of the Soviet economic program and the striking progress they have made over the last decade." This forced admission of Dulles speaks of a more sober approach to the appraisal of our successes, although even Dulles does his utmost to minimize our achievements.

A detailed reply to Allen Dulles was given in the editorial published in *Vestnik Statistiki* (No. 11, 1959) and in *Pravda* of November 28, 1959.

Progressive American economists also refuted Dulles. The well known American economist Victor Perlo, having studied available data, holds that the statement of Allen Dulles that in 1958 Soviet industrial output did not exceed 40% of the American level was absolutely groundless. In Perlo's opinion the calculations of Soviet economists which show that Soviet industrial output equalled 55% of the American level were much closer to the actual state of affairs. In a special study of the Soviet and American economies, Perlo arrives at the conclusion that in 1967 the USSR will overtake the United States in total industrial output, while in 1970 it will surpass it in per capita production.

The American Economic and Industrial Development Corporation has arrived at similar conclusions. A report of this corporation, published by the Senate Foreign Relations Committee, notes that if the present trend continues, by 1970 the gross national product of the USSR will rise by 130% as compared with an increase of less than 70% in the United States. By 1970, the report continues, the USSR will probably have a huge industry, relatively much stronger than at present and in some respects larger than the industry of the United States. . . .

A Comparison of Labor Productivity in Industry

To compare the levels of labor productivity in Soviet and American industry it is necessary to determine not only the relationship between the volumes of output, of which we have just spoken, but also the relationship between the number of workers.

According to American statistics, in 1959 the United States had 13 million industrial workers. For a comparison of this figure with that of the USSR it is necessary to take a comparable range of branches of industry, excluding branches which are not included in the industrial category in the United States. In that case the number of industrial workers, including those in cooperative industry, will be 18 million in the USSR. Another adjustment should be made for the difference in the methods of compiling the lists of employed personnel. American statistics practically exclude workers who are absent on account of sickness or other reasons. If, for the sake of comparison with American data, we exclude from the Soviet category of employed workers those who are absent on account of sickness or for other reasons, we find that in the USSR the number of workers engaged in industry, calculated on an average annual basis, was less than 17 million. Thus, the number of industrial workers in the USSR was about 130% of the American figure. Proceeding from these data (industrial output in the Soviet Union was more than half of that in the United States and the number of workers was 30% greater), we find that labor productivity of Soviet industrial workers in 1959 was 40 to 50% of labor productivity in American industry. This means that in 1959 labor productivity in American industry was approximately 2 to 2.5 times as high as in the Soviet Union. . . .

It is particularly important to study the factors making for a growth of labor productivity, and specifically, the different composition of workers and the considerable proportion of auxiliary workers in our industry.

Comparison of the Volume of Agricultural Production

A comparison of the volume of agricultural production is a relatively easier task because the number of separate items of agricultural output is much smaller than in industry. . . .

In total milk production the USSR overtook the United States in 1958. In 1958 the USSR produced 62 million tons of milk and the United

States, according to an official estimate, about 57 million tons. In 1959 the USSR produced 845,000 tons of butter, or 4 kilograms per capita, while in the United States, according to an estimate of the Department of Agriculture, per capita production, including the farmers' output, amounted to 3.7 kilograms. Thus, in per capita butter production the Soviet Union surpassed the United States in 1959. The Soviet Union exceeds the United States in the production of wheat, potatoes, wool and also in sugar beets and sugar cane combined (taking into account their sugar content). The USSR produces large quantities of flax fiber, sunflowers and some other crops which are not cultivated at all in the United States or are grown in small quantities. So far the Soviet Union lags behind the United States in the production of corn, raw cotton, vegetables, fruit, meat and eggs.

If we compare the value of the gross production of Soviet and American agriculture in 1959 in comparable prices, we find that in rubles Soviet output is 77% and in dollars it is 80% of the American output.

These calculations, just as a comparison of the production of separate items, show that total agricultural production in the Soviet Union in 1959 was only 20 to 25% less than in the United States, although last year the weather conditions were unfavorable in our country.

As for the rates of growth of agricultural production, they are several times higher in the Soviet Union than in the United States. In the last 15 years (1945–1959) the average annual rate of growth of agricultural production amounted to 6.7% in the Soviet Union and 1.7% in the United States. In the last six years (1954–1959) the average annual rate of growth of agricultural output was 7% in the USSR and only 2.3% in the United States.

Comparison of Labor Productivity in Agriculture

In comparing labor productivity in agriculture the main problem, after determining the relationship between the volume of output, is to establish the comparable number of people engaged in agriculture.

According to American statistics, the number of people employed on US farms amounted to 7.4 million in 1959 on the average. But American statistics, in large measure, do not take into account the number of hired workers and members of farmers' families who work only part time.[3] Moreover, American statistics do not include in agricultural work many jobs which in the USSR are performed by the collective farms and state farms themselves. Among these are the cleaning and drying of grain, the transportation of farm produce to the cities, delivery of the means of

---

[3] Members of farmers' families and domestic workers who do unpaid work on farms are included among those gainfully employed if they spend 15 hours or more in the course of the investigated week (*The Handbook of Basic Economic Statistics*, November 1959, p. 62).

production to the livestock sections, partial preparation of livestock fodder, repair of machinery and equipment, repair of buildings, etc.

To make the labor inputs comparable it is necessary to introduce the respective adjustments in the American statistical data. Taking into account the adjustments made by the Central Statistical Administration, we find that in 1959 approximately 12 million people, and not 7.4 million, were engaged in American agriculture. In 1959, 33 million people were engaged, on an average annual basis, in Soviet agriculture as a whole, including collective farmers, workers and employees engaged in their personal subsidiary husbandry (not counting, of course, the time spent in the household economy not connected with agricultural production). Thus, the average number of people engaged in Soviet agriculture was 180% greater than in the United States, while total agricultural production was 20 to 25% less than in the United States. Consequently, labor productivity in Soviet agriculture was approximately one-third of the American level. . . .

Comparison of the Magnitude of National Income

The methods of calculating the national income in the USSR and the United States differ considerably. The calculation of the national income in the Soviet Union is based on the principle that the national income is created in branches of material production, among which are industry, construction, agriculture, freight transportation, communications and trade, including the supply of materials and machinery and the procurement of goods. Incomes in the non-production branches, namely, education, public health services and the state apparatus are formed through the redistribution of the national income created in the branches of material production; consequently they have already been taken into account in the national income created in the sphere of material production.

In the United States, however, the national income is calculated as the sum of incomes formed not only in the branches of material production, but also in the non-productive branches. Thus, incomes of state institutions, the police and the army, which are formed out of incomes removed from the branches of material production, are listed in the national income. In other words, in the United States, some incomes are counted twice—in the branches of material production where these incomes are created and in the non-productive branches where these incomes are utilized. The non-comparability of the methods of computing the national income in the United States and the USSR is recognized by the Americans themselves. Therefore to make them comparable it is necessary to recalculate the national income of the United States according to the methodology accepted in the USSR, that is, without the double counting of the incomes in the non-productive branches, and to evaluate the national incomes of the two countries in the same prices. The appropriate calculations show that when properly compared the national income of the USSR in 1959 amounted to approximately 60% of the national income of the United States, while the per capita income in the Soviet Union was approximately half of what it was in the United States.

The rates of growth of the national income in the USSR are several times higher than in the United States. Hence, there is every ground for expecting that the USSR in the near future will surpass the United States not only in total national income but also in per capita national income.

A Comparison of Living Standards

The methods of comparing the living standards of Soviet workers and collective farmers with those of American workers and farmers present the most involved problems of all.

A comparison of the living standards of the working people of the USSR and the United States can be made on the basis of comparing a number of indices which indicate the level of satisfaction of the material and cultural requirements of different classes of the population.

In comparing the real incomes of the workers in the two countries one must not only compare money wages. It is a fact that in the USSR workers and employees, in addition to their money wages, receive considerable sums in the form of pensions, allowances, stipends, free education, free medical service and other payments and benefits at the expense of the state. Unemployment was fully abolished in the Soviet Union long ago. As a result of the higher living standard and the improved health services, the life span has been greatly lengthened in our country. In recent years the Soviet Union has had the lowest mortality rate in the world, while the increase in the population is higher than in most other countries. Account should also be taken of the fact that while in the United States a considerable part of the wages (approximately one-third) is spent on rent, in the Soviet Union only 4 to 5% of the budgets of workers' families go for rent and public utility services. The task set by the Party and the Government to eliminate the housing shortage in the next 10 to 12 years is being carried out successfully. All these factors affect the living standards of the population to a considerable extent and must be taken into account in comparing the real incomes of the working people in the USSR and the USA.

The living standards of the Soviet people so far are lower than those in the United States, a country which has not suffered a foreign invasion and has not fought wars on its own territory during the last 100 years. But although the individual wages of Soviet workers, when recalculated in comparable prices, are thus far lower than the wages of American workers, the working people of the USSR enjoy a number of advantages as compared with American working people. These include the absence of unemployment and security in the future, which scores of millions of American workers and members of their families lack. Other advantages include the lowest rent in the world, free education, including higher education. There are also the free medical services and a number of other benefits and services paid for by the state, of which the American worker cannot even dream. In the USSR there is no situation such as that in the capitalist countries, where the lion's share of the national income created by the working people is appropriated by the monopolists and other non-working groups of the population. In the Soviet Union the entire national income belongs to the working people and is used in their interests. Moreover, in the USSR the national income is growing several times faster than in the United States. Comrade N. S. Khrushchev, speaking on television in the United States on September 27, 1959, rightly said, in addressing the American people, that "though we are not yet as rich as you are, we are on the right path that leads to the achievement of the highest standard of living." . . .

The above-mentioned problems of the methodology of comparing various indices have been examined on the basis of Soviet and American indices, but they are also of more general significance in comparing the economic indices of the socialist and capitalist countries.

A great deal of work on elaborating unified methodological principles of determining the most important economic indices and scientific methods of comparing the indices of economic development of socialist countries has been carried on in recent years by organs of the Council of Mutual Economic Assistance.

It is necessary to pool the efforts of the economists of the USSR and the other socialist countries and direct them toward working out hitherto unsolved methodological problems connected with the peaceful economic competition of the two systems. These problems should be discussed collectively. We must also expose more actively the falsifying methods and misinterpretations of our indices on the part of bourgeois economists.

III

COMPARISONS OF UNITED STATES AND SOVIET NATIONAL INCOME AND GROSS NATIONAL PRODUCT

THAT THE gross national product and the national income of the United States exceed those of the Soviet Union, no economist in either country would deny. The *extent* of the excess, on the other hand, is a major point of controversy. Moreover, it does not help matters any that national income is computed quite differently in the two countries.[1] In the United States, national income is defined as the total of all incomes earned (equivalent to all expenditures incurred) in the process of the production of goods *and* direct services, in other words the aggregate of all wages, rent, interest, and profits. In the Soviet Union, on the other hand, only incomes earned (or expenditures incurred) in the production of material, tangible goods are counted, but not expenses for direct services. Hence, the cost of operating a freight train would become part of the national income as computed in the USSR, but the cost of operating a passenger train would not.

Below, Morris Bornstein compares the gross national product and the national incomes of the United States with that of the Soviet Union. In his comparisons, Bornstein inevitably obtains quite different results depending upon whether he converts the United States figures into rubles or the Soviet Union's into dollars—a point already touched upon by Campbell in Part I. This discrepancy, so puzzling to all who are not familiar with this type of problem, constitutes another major obstacle to any comparison of the national incomes of two different economies, or even of the same economy at two different stages of its historical development. And, unfortunately, the problem defies a definite scientific solution. Neither the conversion of the national income of the USSR into dollars, nor the conversion of the national income of the USA into rubles, nor any mathematical average of the two is inherently THE correct answer.

On the Soviet side, V. Kudrov, criticizing Bornstein among others, ex-

---

[1] In Soviet national income analysis, there is no "gross national product."

plains why he considers erroneous and unscientific the methods used by
American economists in computing the national income of the United
States and comparing it with that of the USSR.

WESTERN VIEWS

7

A Comparison of Soviet and United States National Product [1] *

MORRIS BORNSTEIN
University of Michigan

Introduction

The purpose of this paper is to make selected comparisons of the
structure, size, and growth of the national products of the U.S.S.R. and
the United States.

Of all the respects in which the economies of these two countries may
be compared, national product comparisons probably provide the
broadest, most comprehensive view, because they embrace, for each country, the net output of all goods and services produced during the specified
period.

However, because national product comparisons involve the aggregation of quite different items by value weights, the results obtained are
very sensitive to the weighting systems employed. The usual weighting
problems of intertemporal and interspatial comparisons are intensified
in a Soviet-United States comparison because of uncertainties about the
meaning of Soviet prices. Hence, it is desirable to consider national
product comparisons in conjuncture with other comparisons which are
less susceptible to weighting problems, such as selected physical output
comparisons and labor force comparisons.

At the same time, it should be recognized that while national product
provides a convenient measure of overall economic capability, this measure is not the most significant one for various economic, military, scien-

* Excerpts reprinted from *Comparisons of the United States and Soviet Economies.*
Papers submitted by Panelists Appearing Before the Subcommittee on Economic Statistics, Joint Economic Committee, Congress of the United States, 1959, Part II, pp.
377-395.

[1] The author wishes to thank Janet Riddle, Florence Roof, and Harold Demsetz for
their suggestions about various aspects of this paper.

tific, and political questions. For example, although Soviet national product may be only half the size of U.S. national product (by one measurement), the U.S.S.R. may, as a result of the particular composition and application of this smaller product, match or surpass the United States in military strength or in selected scientific programs. Thus, the usefulness of national product comparisons depends on the question at issue. For some questions, other measures are undoubtedly superior.

The national product comparisons in this paper concentrate on the period since 1950 because this period appears to be more representative of the conditions of economic competition between the two countries which may be anticipated in the future than would a longer historical period, such as that from 1913 or 1928 to the present. These longer periods span conditions of world war, the first rapid spurt of the Soviet industrialization drive, and a severe depression in the United States. In contrast, the period since 1950 has been more characteristic of likely future conditions in both countries. By 1950, the U.S.S.R. had largely recovered from the effects of World War II, while the United States had completed its reconversion from the war. In the conditions of international tension prevailing since 1950, both countries have endeavored to maintain a strong, up-to-date military posture while continuing to develop their civilian economies. So long as the international situation continues to be one of "cold war" and "competitive coexistence," analysis of the period since 1950 will be more useful for an appraisal of probable future trends and relationships than would reference to a longer period of significantly different political and economic conditions. . . .

Structure of National Product

In this section the structures of Soviet and United States national product are compared, first by analyzing the shares in the total product of each country of the principal end-use components, and second by analyzing the shares in the total national income of each country of the major sectors of origin in which income is generated. In both instances, reference is to each country's national product or income expressed in its own currency—rubles for the U.S.S.R. and dollars for the United States—with the resulting comparisons being only comparisons of the percentage shares of the specified uses or sectors in each country's total product or income. No comparison is made, at this point, of the relative size of the two economies. Rather only their resource allocation patterns are compared, without reference to the quantity of output produced in the two countries.

Before turning to these calculations, however, a few words are necessary regarding the serious conceptual and statistical problems encountered in such comparisons. Although these difficulties are not, in my judgment, so severe as to invalidate the basic conclusions to be drawn from such comparisons, they do qualify the precision which may be attributed to these figures, particularly the estimates for the U.S.S.R.

Two major conceptual problems are involved in such comparisons. First, output or productive activity in the two countries must be classified in comparable categories, which in some cases proves difficult because of the differences between the two countries in economic and political organization and objectives. Second, because of the different roles in the two countries of indirect taxes and subsidies, it is desirable to compare their economic structures not only in terms of established prices [2] but also in terms of adjusted prices, which allow for this difference and which, therefore, permit a somewhat more accurate comparison of real resource allocation.

The ability to make fairly precise comparisons of the structures of Soviet and United States national product is further hampered by a lack of necessary statistical data, chiefly for the U.S.S.R. The necessary basic national accounts are not published by the Soviet Government but must instead be compiled by a laborious and ingenious assembly of scattered Soviet data, supplemented by many estimates of varying precision. Likewise, Soviet data are lacking for many of the adjustments of basic accounts information which are needed to secure comparability with the figures for the United States. In contrast, most of the data needed for the U.S. side of such comparisons is readily available, primarily from the publications of the Department of Commerce. As a result, it ordinarily proves necessary to rearrange and adjust U.S. figures to match the categories used for the U.S.S.R., the opposite usually being impossible.

National product by end use. Table 1 shows the distribution of gross national product in the U.S.S.R. and United States in 1955 in terms of four end-use or purpose categories: Consumption, investment, defense, and government administration.[3]

[2] The term "established prices" is used in this paper in preference to "market prices" in recognition of the fact that Soviet prices, with the exception of collective farm market prices, are determined by administrative decree rather than by market forces.

[3] Figures for the United States are derived from data of the Department of Commerce and other U.S. Government agencies. . . . Figures for the U.S.S.R. are from an unpublished manuscript of the author, "Soviet National Accounts for 1955." This study follows the general approach of the pioneering studies of national accounts for the U.S.S.R. by Bergson, Heymann, and Hoeffding (Abram Bergson, *Soviet National Income and Product in 1937*, New York, Columbia University Press, 1953, Abram Bergson and Hans Heymann, Jr., *Soviet National Income and Product, 1940-48*, New York, Columbia University Press, 1954; and Oleg Hoeffding, *Soviet National Income and Product in 1928*, New York, Columbia University Press, 1954). The results of the author's study correspond closely to those in two other recent studies of Soviet national accounts for 1955, one by the Economic Commission for Europe (ECE) ("An Estimate of the National Accounts of the Soviet Union for 1955," *Economic Bulletin for Europe*, vol. 9, No. 1, May 1957, pp. 89-107), and one by Hoeffding and Nimitz (O. Hoeffding and N. Nimitz, "Soviet National Income and Product, 1949-55," RM-2101, Santa Monica, Calif., the Rand Corp., 1959). . . .

The consumption category in Table 1 includes both household expenditures on goods and services (including income-in-kind) and government current (i.e., noncapital) expenditures on health and education. This coverage is necessary to provide comparability, because in the U.S.S.R. virtually all outlays on health and education are made by the government, whereas in the United States a significant share of expenditures for these purposes is made by households. . . .

TABLE 1. *Gross national product by end use in the U.S.S.R. and the United States, at established prices and at adjusted prices, 1955*

| End use | U.S.S.R. | | | | United States | | | |
| | At established prices | | At adjusted prices | | At established prices | | At adjusted prices | |
	Billion rubles	Per-cent of total	Billion rubles	Per-cent of total	Billion dollars	Per-cent of total	Billion dollars	Per-cent of total
Consumption	840.8	65.4	566.4	58.9	269.7	67.8	240.1	66.3
Investment	263.5	20.5	241.8	25.2	77.2	19.4	73.5	20.3
Defense	144.6	11.2	125.2	13.0	38.4	9.7	36.9	10.2
Government admin-istration	36.9	2.9	27.6	2.9	12.1	3.1	11.7	3.2
Gross national product	1,285.8	100.0	961.0	100.0	397.5	100.0	362.2	100.0

Because the figures for the U.S.S.R. are derived from a national accounts study which (like all such studies for the U.S.S.R.) involves many estimates of varying reliability, they should be regarded as estimates intended to provide a fairly reliable, but by no means fully precise, indication of the pattern of resource allocation in the U.S.S.R. The consumption and investment figures may be considered to have a relatively high degree of reliability, because a substantial amount of data is available on these activities. On the other hand, the defense figure is necessarily more tenuous because of the need to make estimates for many items regarding which the Soviet Government discloses little or no information. The Government administration figure, being a residual of uncertain coverage, also is less reliable than the figures for consumption and investment, but its small size makes its deficiencies much less serious than in the case of the defense category.

In table 1, the distribution of Soviet and United States national product in 1955 among these four end-use categories is shown both at established prices and at adjusted prices. A comparison at established prices, however, does not adequately indicate the difference between Soviet and United States resource allocation patterns. A somewhat more accurate contrast is shown at adjusted prices, which attempt to exclude indirect taxes (which, although part of established prices, are not payments to factors of production) and to include subsidies (which are payments to factors of production not included in established prices). The resulting adjusted prices, intended to approach more closely a factor cost basis of valuation, depict more faithfully the distribution of resources among these end uses in the two countries.[4]

The effect of the adjustment is slight for the United States, where both indirect taxes and subsidies are of minor importance in the gross national product at established prices. For the U.S.S.R., however, the effect of the adjustment is striking, because indirect taxes account for over one-fourth of the gross national product at established prices and because they fall principally on the consumption end use, as a result of the heavy reliance of the Soviet budget on the turnover tax, an excise constituting about half of the value of state and cooperative retail sales. Subsidies, which were modest in 1955, also fell more heavily on consumption than on the other end uses in 1955, although this was not true in some earlier years, for example, 1948.[5] As a result of the importance and differential impact of indirect taxes, the share of consumption is much higher and the shares of investment and defense are significantly lower at estabilshed prices than at adjusted prices.

A comparison of resource allocation patterns at adjusted prices (cols. 4 and 8 of table 1) shows that in 1955 the U.S.S.R., in comparison with the United States, devoted a significantly greater share of its productive resources to investment (25 versus 20 percent) and defense (13 versus 10 percent) and a significantly smaller share to consumption (59 versus 66 percent). About the same share of resources went for general government administration in both countries.

National income by sector of origin. An alternative view of the difference in resource allocation patterns in the U.S.S.R. and the United States in 1955 is given in table 2. This table shows the distribution by sector of origin of factor incomes generated in the production of total national output in each country. The figures for the U.S.S.R., and the United States are, however, not strictly comparable, because of a difference in the national income concepts used for the two countries, which arises from

[4] These adjustments follow the method developed in Bergson's "adjusted factor cost" approach: see Bergson, *op. cit.* ch. 4, and app. E. and Bergson and Heyman, *op. cit.*, ch. III and app. D. Although these adjustments constitute only an approximation to a depletion of factor allocation in the U.S.S.R. because of many problems connected with the valuation of the services of land, capital, and enterprise in the Soviet setting, I believe they represent an improvement over the unadjusted established prices. For discussion of these problems, see the references just cited and also Peter Wiles, "Are Adjusted Rubles Rational?" *Soviet Studies,* vol. VII, No. 2, October 1955, pp. 143-160: Franklyn D. Holzman, "The Adjusted Factor Cost Method of Valuing National Income: Comment," *Soviet Studies,* vol. VIII, No. 1, July 1956, pp. 32-36; and ECE, *op. cit.,* p. 94.

[5] See Bergson and Heymann, *loc. cit.*

the difficulties of valuing the return to property factors in the U.S.S.R.[6] A serious shortcoming of the calculation for the U.S.S.R. is the inadequate allowance for land rent and the consequent substantial understatement of the contribution of agriculture to Soviet national income. As a result, the percentage figures for the U.S.S.R. in table 2 understate the share of agriculture, and overstate the shares of the other sectors, in total Soviet national income.

With this caution in mind, one can nevertheless draw certain conclusions from table 2 regarding differences in the use of resources in the two countries in 1955. The most striking conclusion is the much greater share of total resources engaged in agriculture in the U.S.S.R. This conclusion is confirmed by the much greater share of the agricultural labor force in the total labor force in the U.S.S.R., as compared with the United States, and reflects the inefficiency of Soviet agriculture relative to U.S. agriculture. Another prominent difference between the two countries concerns the share in national income of services and trade. The much larger share in the United States reflects the orientation of the U.S. economy toward the satisfaction of household demand for goods and services. In the U.S.S.R., on the other hand, consumer services and retail trade facilities have been sacrificed in favor of investment and defense production. Finally, in 1955, the U.S.S.R. devoted a somewhat smaller share of its resources to industry and construction and to transportation and communications than did the United States.

TABLE 2. *National income by sector of origin in the U.S.S.R. and the United States, 1955*

Sector	U.S.S.R.		United States	
	Billion rubles	Percent of total	Billion dollars	Percent of total
Industry and construction	332.0	36.6	134.5	40.7
Agriculture	245.7	27.1	15.2	4.6
Transportation and communications	45.5	5.0	21.2	6.5
Services and trade	283.3	31.3	159.2	48.2
National income	906.5	100.0	330.2	100.0

Comparative Size of National Product

In order to compare the size of Soviet and U.S. national product, the national product figures calculated in native currencies must be

[6] The calculation for the U.S.S.R. essentially follows the approach of Bergson, *op. cit.,* app. C. Although the profits component in the present national income calculation for the U.S.S.R. contains some elements of rent and interest on capital, it clearly does not represent them adequately, either in total magnitude or in distribution by sector.

expressed in a common currency, either dollars or rubles. In essence, the task is to price Soviet output at U.S. dollar prices and/or to price U.S. output at Soviet ruble prices. In practice, this is done by using international price deflators to convert the Soviet national product figures in rubles to dollars, and/or to convert the U.S. national product figures in dollars to rubles.

Foreign exchange rates are unsuitable as price deflators for such comparisons because they fail, for a number of well-known reasons, to measure the internal purchasing power of currencies, even in the case of market economies whose structure and pricing practices are broadly similar.[7] Because the official Soviet exchange rate is arbitrary and not intended to measure the relationship between foreign and domestic prices, it is particularly inappropriate for international comparisons of national product.

For a comparison of the size of Soviet and United States national products, it is necessary instead to use international price deflators which measure the internal purchasing power equivalents of the ruble and the dollar in purchasing the goods and services composing national product. The first step in obtaining these deflators is to derive ruble-dollar (or dollar-ruble) price ratios for individual products by comparing their internal prices in the U.S.S.R. and the United States. Then the ruble-dollar price ratios for individual items are aggregated into ruble-dollar ratios for categories of national product, such as consumption and investment. For this aggregation, it is possible to use as a basis for weighting individual items either their relative importance in Soviet national product or their relative importance in U.S. national product. In the former case, the aggregate ratios are said to be Soviet weighted; in the latter, United States weighted.

Table 3 presents the results of an effort to compare the size of Soviet and U.S. national product in 1955 by this method. It compares the national products both in rubles and in dollars. The ruble figures for the U.S.S.R. were taken from table 1, while the ruble figures for the United States were obtained by converting the dollar figures for the United States in table 1 to rubles by appropriate ruble-dollar ratios. Similarly, the dollar figures for the United States are from table 1, while the dollar figures for the U.S.S.R. were obtained by converting the ruble figures for the U.S.S.R in table 1 into dollars by appropriate dollar-ruble ratios. In both cases, the comparisons involve the established price figures, rather than the adjusted price figures, in table 1 because

---

[7] See Milton Gilbert and Irving B. Kravis, *An International Comparison of National Products and the Purchasing Power of Currencies,* Paris, Organization for European Economic Cooperation (OEEC), 1954, pp. 14-17; and Milton Gilbert and Associates, *Comparative National Products and Price Levels,* Paris, OEEC, 1958, pp. 29-33.

their purpose is to compare the output of goods and services entering national product in the two countries, rather than the quantities of factor inputs devoted to the production of national product in the two countries. In the figures taken directly from table 1, output is valued at established prices in each country. Where ruble-dollar (or dollar-ruble) ratios have been applied to figures in table 1 to obtain those in table 3, these ratios were constructed by comparing established ruble and dollar prices for individual items and aggregating the results by using established price weights.[8]

TABLE 3. *Comparison of gross national product of the U.S.S.R. and the United States, at established prices, in rubles and dollars, 1955*

End use	Ruble comparison			Dollar comparison			Geometric average of ruble and dollar comparisons
	U.S.S.R. (billion rubles)	United States (billion rubles)	U.S.S.R. as percent of United States	U.S.S.R. (billion dollars)	United States (billion dollars)	U.S.S.R. as percent of United States	U.S.S.R. as percent of United States
Consumption	840.8	4,045.5	20.8	105.1	269.7	39.0	28.5
Investment	263.5	540.4	48.8	52.7	77.2	68.3	57.7
Defense	144.6	192.0	75.3	36.2	38.4	94.3	84.3
Government administration	36.9	24.2	152.5	18.4	12.1	152.1	152.3
Gross national product	1,285.8	4,802.1	26.8	212.4	397.5	53.4	37.8

In examining the results shown in table 3, it should be remembered that they are offered only as approximate indications of the relative size of the two national products and their major end-use components. All of the problems and qualifications mentioned in connection with the derivation of the established price figures in table 1 of course apply

8 Thus, in this comparison no adjustment was made for indirect taxes and subsidies in either the national product figure or the ruble-dollar ratios. For a comparison of inputs, factor costs should be used both for value of produce and for the construction of ruble-dollar ratios. To obtain such factor cost, ruble-dollar ratios, individual established ruble and dollar prices should be adjusted to exclude indirect taxes and include subsidies. Cf. Gilbert and Kravis, *op. cit.,* pp. 91-92. Although rough adjustments of this type can be made for the U.S.S.R. for broad categories of national product, as was done in connection with table 1, data are lacking for similar adjustments of individual ruble prices.

also to table 3. In addition, the precision of the results in table 3 is limited by the rough character of the ruble-dollar ratio conversions, stemming from the problems encountered in obtaining price data, in matching Soviet and U.S. goods and services, and in deriving satisfactory weights.[9]

In the comparison of gross national product and its chief end-use components in table 3, the size of the U.S.S.R. relative to the United States differs considerably depending on whether the comparison is made in rubles (i.e., at Soviet prices) or in dollars (i.e., at U.S. prices). This difference is simply a manifestation of the fundamental index number problem encountered in both intertemporal and international comparisons and arising from the existence of alternative but equally appropriate weighting systems, corresponding to the Paasche and Laspeyres formulae.[10] Even the extent of the disparity in results, attributable to differences in the two price structures, is not unexpected. A substantial, although not so great, spread was also found, as a result of differences in price structures, in a comparison of the national products of various Western European countries with that of the United States at their own prices and at U.S. prices.[11]

Likewise, it is not surprising that, for national product as a whole and for its components (except for Government administration),[12] the U.S.S.R. is smaller relative to the United States in the ruble comparison than in the dollar comparison. The explanation lies basically in a negative correlation between the relative prices and relative quantities; that is, goods which have lower relative prices tend to be produced in greater relative quantities in a country. Thus, goods and services with lower relative prices in the United States are, on the average, those which are relatively more abundant in the United States, as compared with the U.S.S.R.; an analogous situation prevails in the U.S.S.R. Consequently, when the two national products are valued at U.S. prices, a greater price weight is given to goods which are relatively more heavily produced in

[9] The methodology and problems involved in ruble-dollar ratio calculations are discussed in Norman M. Kaplan and William L. White, "A Comparison of 1950 Wholesale Prices in Soviet and American Industry," RM-1443, Santa Monica, Calif., the Rand Corp., 1955; Norman M. Kaplan and Eleanor S. Wainstein, "A Comparison of Soviet and American Retail Prices in 1950," RM-1692-1, Santa Monica, Calif., the Rand Corp., 1956; and Abraham S. Becker, "Prices of Producers' Durables in the United States and the U.S.S.R. in 1955," Santa Monica, Calif., the Rand Corp., 1959, RM-2432. For an extensive discussion of the construction of similar price deflators for Western Europe and the United States, see Gilbert and Kravis, *op. cit.*, and Gilbert & Associates, *op. cit.*

[10] Likewise, there are two sets of answers for the relative purchasing power of the ruble and the dollar in regard to national product, depending on whether the price relationships between the two countries are weighted by the relative quantities of goods and services in Soviet or in U.S. national product.

[11] Gilbert & Associates, *op. cit.*, pp. 97-106.

[12] Where separate U.S.-weighted and Soviet-weighted ratios were not used; see notes to table 3.

the U.S.S.R. than if Soviet prices are used. Similarly, when the two national products are valued at Soviet prices, a greater weight is given to items which are relatively more heavily produced in the United States, than if U.S. prices are used.[13] When one country's output structure is priced at the other country's price structure, the effect is to apply relatively high prices to relatively large quantities and relatively low prices to relatively small quantities. Thus, the comparison is more favorable to a country when the other country's prices are used for both.

The existence of such a substantial disparity between the results of the ruble and dollar comparisons makes it inadvisable to use either one alone to depict the relative size of the two national products. Preferably, both comparisons should be used. However, because it is sometimes considered cumbersome to deal with two sets of comparisons, resort is sometimes made to an average of the results produced by the two sets of weights, such as the geometric averages in table 3. Such averages are convenient for various practical purposes, but it should be recognized that they have no unambiguous economic meaning. Where averages alone are presented, they may conceal a significant difference in results, corresponding to substantially different price structures, as in the case of Soviet-United States comparisons. Although the use of averages is often convenient for the sake of simplicity or brevity, a more precise discussion involves reference to both of the original comparisons.

The results in table 3 indicate that in 1955 Soviet gross national product was about one-fourth the U.S. level at Soviet ruble prices and about one-half the U.S. level at U.S. dollar prices. The geometric average of the ruble and dollar comparisons is about two-fifths. The relative size of the two economies (whether compared at Soviet or U.S. prices) differs, however, in regard to the several end-use components of national product.

Aggregate Soviet consumption was about one-fifth of the U.S. level at Soviet prices and about two-fifths at U.S. prices. If allowance is made for the 20 percent difference in population—about 200 million in the U.S.S.R. and 165 million in the United States in 1955—the respective per capita figures are even lower, approximately one-sixth and one-third. Such comparisons for consumption as a whole, however, conceal different relationships between the two countries regarding the various components of consumption, such as food, clothing, durable consumers' goods, etc. For example, Soviet per capita consumption levels are significantly closer to those of the United States in regard to food and basic types of clothing than they are in regard to durable consumers' goods, housing, and personal services.

---

13 See in this connection the results of Kaplan and Wainstein, *op. cit.*, pp. 30-31, for the U.S.S.R. relative to the United States; and Gilbert and Kravis, *op. cit.*, pp. 51-59, and Gilbert & Associates, *op. cit.*, pp. 23-24, for several Western European countries relative to the United States.

In the case of investment, Soviet product was substantially larger relative to U.S. product than in the case of consumption; it was about half of the U.S. level at Soviet prices and about two-thirds at U.S. prices. The spread between the ruble and dollar results is not so great as for consumption, indicating less difference in the Soviet and U.S. price structures for investment goods than for consumption goods. As in the case of consumption, however, the aggregate nature of the investment comparison obscures important differences in the relationship between the two countries in regard to different types of investment. Because of the emphasis of the Soviet regime on economic growth, a much larger share of investment is devoted to industry, and a much smaller share to housing and consumer services, in the U.S.S.R. than in the United States. As a result, in 1955 Soviet investment in manufacturing, mining, and public utilities was larger, and Soviet investment in housing was smaller, relative to the U.S. level than the relationship for aggregate investment shown in table 3.

According to table 3, Soviet defense outlays in 1955 were about three-fourths of the U.S. level at Soviet prices and almost equal at U.S. prices. However, because of the especially crude nature of both the initial national accounts estimate for Soviet defense expenditures and the ruble-dollar ratios for this end use, it seems prudent to allow for some understatement of the Soviet level both in rubles and in dollars and to consider Soviet defense outlays as approximately equal to those of the United States. Even if aggregate Soviet and U.S. outlays for defense are considered equal, however, it does not follow that the size, equipment, or effectiveness of the two military establishments is equal, for a number of reasons.

As in the case of the consumption and investment comparisons, the composition of the defense aggregate must be considered. Although total defense outlays may be equal in the two countries, the same relationship of equality obviously does not apply to all components of defense. The relationship of the two countries certainly differs in regard to troop strength and the various types of missiles, aircraft, ships, and other weapons. In a military contest, Soviet or U.S. superiority in one or more of these component categories of defense could be decisive, despite an accompanying inferiority in other categories. Other cautions must also be kept in mind in appraising national product comparisons of defense. For example, although Soviet and U.S. soldiers are, in this type of comparison, priced at the same pay rates, their productivity (i.e., combat effectiveness) may in fact not be the same. Also, because Soviet soldiers live more modestly than U.S. soldiers, Soviet subsistence outlays per man are less than U.S. outlays. Yet it should not be concluded from such a comparison that the effectiveness of Soviet soldiers is correspondingly below that of their U.S. counterparts. Instead, the U.S.S.R. may in fact support an equally effective soldier at less real cost in terms of resources devoted to his subsistence.

Comparisons of the relative size of the defense components of national product thus do not provide a sufficiently reliable index of the military strength of the two countries. For such an appraisal, other comparisons—of manpower, training, equipment, weapons technology, etcetera—are indispensable. The national product comparison does, however, furnish some corroborative evidence of the relative magnitude of the military programs of the two countries. The conclusion indicated by table 3, of an approximately equivalent military program in the two countries, seems consistent with other information on this question.

Little need be said about Government administration, the residual category in table 3. Outlays for the administrative apparatus concerned with planning, administration, and control in the U.S.S.R. far exceeded Government administration outlays in the United States, where some of the planning and control functions of the U.S.S.R. have no counterpart.

The general conclusions suggested by table 3 may now be summarized briefly in terms of the geometric average results. Although in 1955 the U.S.S.R. had a national product less than half that of the United States, the U.S.S.R. had an approximately equal defense effort and a level of investment about three-fifths that of the United States. In contrast, per capita consumption in the U.S.S.R. was only about one-fourth that in the United States. This performance reflects the desire of the Soviet regime for a strong and advanced military posture and a rapid rate of growth, and its willingness to pursue these objectives at the expense of the consumption level of the population.

8

Anti-Scientific Methods Employed by Bourgeois Economists to Compare the National Incomes of the USSR and the US [*]

V. KUDROV
Economics Research Institute, State Economic Council of the USSR

The question of comparing the national incomes of the USSR and the US assumes great significance in the period when the USSR has entered the decisive stage of economic competition with capitalism. The national income is the most important synthetic index of a country's economic power, standard of living, and economic structure, as well as the progressiveness of the social system from the point of view of utilization of resources and rates of economic growth. But in order to compare the national incomes of the USSR and the US the same methodology must be employed for measurement. The problems of calculating the US national income by the method used in the USSR have been frequently raised in our press.

Bourgeois economic literature devotes much attention to the comparative analysis of the national incomes of the USSR and the US. The questionable works of Bergson, C. Clark, Hoeffding, Wyler, Seton, Wiles, etc. have achieved a certain renown in the west. As the British economist Kaiser correctly observed, "most doubtful are the calculations (of bourgeois economists—V. K.), that try to present data on the USSR national income for international comparisons." [1]

The problem of comparing the national incomes of the USSR and the US was also taken up by the Joint Economic Committee of the US Congress, which arranged a series of special sessions to this subject at the end of 1959. The American economists Bornstein and Boddy spoke on the matter of the national incomes and products of the USSR and the US.

[*] From *Voprosy Ekonomiki,* 1961, No. 2. Translated in and excerpts reprinted from *Problems of Economics,* August, 1961, pp. 37-42, by permission of the publisher. All quotations from English sources have been re-translated from the Russian.—Ed.
[1] *Economic Journal,* March 1957.

"The purpose of this paper," Bornstein writes, "is to make selected comparisons of the structure, size, and growth of the national products of the USSR and the United States." [2] This problem is very important, indeed, and is of serious scientific interest. Let us see, however, the way in which it is being solved by American economists.

Whereas Marxist political economy defines the national income as new value created in the sphere of material production, the component part of the aggregate social product that remains after deduction of the compensation fund, bourgeois economic science regards national income as a simple sum of the incomes of individuals and enterprises. The American economist S. Kuznets writes that the national income constitutes "the net income from the economic activity of individuals, firms, social and political institutions, which in their entirety form the nation." [3] Bourgeois economic science includes any form of activity in the sphere of production as long as it satisfies someone's needs and yields income. . . .

In making comparisons with the USSR, American economists use not only the index of national income, but also the national product index. Bourgeois economists conceive of the national product as the aggregate of finished goods and services. Actually this is national income by end use plus indirect taxes, which are automatically reckoned together with the price. The national product is called "gross" or "net" depending on whether or not it includes the sum of depreciation of fixed capital (amortization). The national product breaks down into the consumption fund and the accumulation fund (in the gross product—the capital investment fund) and is tied in with the national income index.

When comparing the economies of the USSR and the US, bourgeois economists usually employ the gross national product index, inasmuch as it enables them to determine fairly exactly, by definite kinds, the entire mass of goods comprising the national product. The relation between national products of the two countries is roughly the same as that between their national incomes. However, the country with greater fixed capital will always have some advantage if the gross product, which includes amortization, is used.

In their comparative analysis of the Soviet and US national incomes and products, American economists have measured the Soviet national income and product according to the method accepted in the United States. However, they have not familiarized the reader with the primary sources of their statistical calculations. Therefore, we do not know, in effect, how they obtained their calculations, and it is very difficult to trust them. But it is clear that these calculations are based on the anti-scientific bourgeois theory that the national income is a simple arithmetic total of

[2] *Comparisons of the United States and Soviet Economies.* Part II, Washington, 1959, p. 377.

[3] S. Kuznets, *National Income. A Summary of Findings.* New York, 1946, p. 1.

almost all the incomes received by the population, and that the national product is the sum total of expenditures on goods and all kinds of services. Such an interpretation of national income and national product distorts their true magnitudes, structure and dynamics, since in the calculation of these indices there are included not only the basic incomes generated in the sphere of material production and expenditures for goods and material services, but also derivative incomes and expenditures for personal services, as a result of which there is repeated double counting. Thereby, the total size of the national income and national product is significantly over-stated, and their structure and dynamics are presented in a distorted light. . . .

Characterizing ironically the bourgeois interpretation of national income and national product, a contemporary American economist, Stanley Lebergott, writes: "how will people comparing gross national products be able to understand why one country has a greater 'economic power' than another, if their calculations include a greater complex of the financial system (a larger degree of control, a greater number of services rendered by financial intermediaries), high interest rates (a bigger total of paid interest), a greater scale of litigation (a higher quantity of legal services) and a larger number of people concerned with the future (large expenditures on life insurance)?" [4]

Therefore, inclusion of redistributed incomes or expenditures on personal services in the index of national income and product, as calculated by the bourgeois method, results in an exaggeration, when comparing the two countries, of the economic strength of the one that has a large government staff, a large financial banking apparatus, a huge army, an advertising business, "services," etc. This is why the bourgeois method of measuring the Soviet national income for the purpose of comparing it with that of the US cannot be regarded as scientifically correct. In this case the Soviet national income will inevitably be greatly understated relative to that of the US because the proportion of the nonproductive sphere in the USSR is much smaller than in the US. This is acknowledged also by the American economist Bornstein. He writes that the share of services and trade in the national income of the USSR, calculated by the American method, amounts to 31.3%, as against 48.2% in the US national income.[5] But this is not the only reason, though it is the basic one, for the relative exaggeration of the US national income and the understatement of Soviet national income.

It is common knowledge that the index for US national income includes part of the national income of other countries. This appropriation of the product of other countries occurs as a result of nonequivalent trade exchange and the export of capital. This international redistribution of

[4] *American Economic Review*, June 1955, p. 440.
[5] *Comparisons of the United States and Soviet Economies.* Part II, p. 383.

incomes finds partial reflection in the balance of income from foreign operations (rest of the world) and in the US balance of payments. The national income of the USSR actually reflects only the output of domestic production. However, American economists for some reason, have not scaled down the national income of the United States so as to make it comparable with the Soviet national income. But even if they were to rid their index of double counting and of redistributed incomes from other countries, it would not, strictly speaking, make the two national incomes completely comparable, since differences in the social systems of the two countries are not taken into account. The volumes of production in the USSR and the United States cannot be compared mechanically, because the products of labor are used differently in the two countries and have a dissimilar effect. The socialist system permits a more effective use of the national income, and, therefore, the Soviet Union can, indeed, catch up with the United States as regards economic strength even with a somewhat smaller national income. For example, the Soviet Union will not have to overtake the United States in the output of luxury items or advertising facilities.

Since it is not the production but the end uses of the national income that are usually compared, the question of the effectiveness of this use assumes great significance. There are non-productive expenditures of the national income in the USSR as there are in the United States. To make the indices for the two countries comparable, it is therefore necessary to reduce somewhat the American figure. It is known, for example, that some 31 billion dollars are spent on luxuries in the United States and more than 10 billion dollars on advertising. Furthermore, other smaller non-productive outlays are made annually from the American national income. . . .

Bornstein's calculation of Soviet national income in dollars and US national income in rubles is of great interest. . . .

The question arises, in what currency should the calculations be made —in rubles or dollars? Regardless of the differences in structure of the end use of the national incomes of the USSR and the US, evaluation of the comparable indices in rubles is especially affected by the structure of prices in the USSR and the evaluation in dollars is especially affected by the structure of prices in the United States. Under capitalism there is a definite inverse relationship between the structure of the physical volume of production and the price structure of the produced commodities. With insignificant exceptions, the most popular and representative goods on the market are usually relatively low priced. In other words, the higher the productivity of labor and the output of a given commodity, the lower its price. . . .

When we convert the Soviet national income, let us say, into dollars, the inverse relation between price and volume of production, characteristic of one country, often becomes a direct ratio. For instance, the USSR produces considerably fewer cars than the United States, but the price of an automobile in the US is relatively lower than in the USSR. So, if we value all the cars produced in the USSR during one year in dollars, the resulting figure will be very small. But if we attempt to express American car output in rubles, the figure will be unwarrantedly large. In general, when the Soviet and US national incomes are calculated in rubles, US national income will be overestimated, because its structure includes a high proportion of durable goods, which are expensive in our country, and a comparatively low proportion of food products, which are cheap in the USSR. This makes clear why the American economists love to calculate comparatively Soviet and US indices in rubles. It turns out, according to their data, that the ratio of the Soviet and US national products, calculated in dollars, was 53.4:100 in 1955, and if calculated in rubles, only 26.8:100. If the first figure is to some extent, close to reality, the second is nowhere near it.

We hold that a comparison of the national incomes of the USSR and the US should, from a methodological standpoint, be done in dollars, and if Soviet prices in rubles are used a number of important corrections must be made.

The Soviet Union has a specific system of price formation differing from that of the United States, and the law of value is not at all a regulator of production. As rightly pointed out by Ia. Kronrod, "the true rate of accumulation in the USSR is higher than what follows from the adduced index (one fourth of the national income). The current prices of means of production deviate, and substantially, below value, while those of consumers' goods are above it. Since the accumulation fund is largely formed from the means of production, and the consumers' fund is formed completely from consumption goods, the accumulation fund, if measured according to the mass of value in relation to the value of the national income, would be of a considerably bigger magnitude." [6]

A ruble evaluation of the US national income, on the other hand, would greatly distort its structure. Since the accumulation fund in the national income of the United States is comparatively small, it would become still smaller if expressed in rubles, because means of production in the USSR are priced below value. And, on the contrary, the share of the consumers' fund in the national income of the United States, if expressed in rubles, would be greatly inflated, since prices for consumers' goods in the USSR are above value.

Thus the calculated ratio between the US and Soviet national products, made by American economists in rubles (100:26.8), is absolutely incorrect. The ratio they have calculated in dollars—100:53.4—is nearer to the truth.

[6] Ia. A. Kronrod, *Obshchestvennyi Product i ego struktura pri Sotsializme.* Gospolitizdat, 1958G, str. 471.

However American economists use neither of these figures; they take an average of 37.8%. That is, they allege that in 1955 Soviet national income was 2.6 times smaller than that of the United States. This is also wrong, because in 1955 the relation of the national incomes of the two countries was close to 100:50.

Calculations show that in 1959 the ratio of the national incomes of the USSR and US was approximately 100:60. Consequently, if the Soviet national income equalled 1,350 billion rubles, the national income of the United States amounted to 2,254 billion rubles (according to the old price scale). According to our estimations, the 1959 US national income, free of double counting, amounted to 305 billion dollars (including indirect taxes for the sake of comparison). The Soviet national income, expressed in dollars, then equalled 183 billion dollars. . . .

It is an old story that American economists try to "prove" that the official figures on the dynamics of the Soviet national income are overstated. . . .

Obviously, the monopolistic bourgeoisie of the US is afraid of losing the economic competition between the USSR and the US. Therefore, the bourgeoisie and its spokesmen—the American economists and statisticians —take measures to bar the truth about the Soviet Union's economic successes from broad sections of the American people.

IV

THE TRANSITION TO COMMUNISM: WHAT DOES IT MEAN?

A RECENTLY published article which compared Communism and Fascism stated:

In marked distinction to Fascist ideology, no Communist ever proclaimed that a dictatorship would be the *final* goal of mankind. From Marx and Engels to present day Communist writers, the dictatorship is to be but preparatory for the time when, in Lenin's words, "mankind will inscribe on its banners: From each according to his ability, to each according to his needs." A pure Communist society, then, is mankind's promised land; a society without any government, police force, army, or jails; a society in which perfect freedom reigns; a society in which production will have been developed "to the n'th degree"; a society in which man will have been transformed into a "social being" who voluntarily and without special personal reward contributes to the best of his ability and takes from the common stores whatever he needs. It is this hope of an ideal order in which, quoting Lenin, "the *necessity* of observing the simple, fundamental rules of everyday social life in common will have become a *habit*"—it is this promise of a perfect world which Communism holds out to the hundreds of millions of its followers . . .[1]

The quotation above portrays the *fundamental, basic* notion of the perfect society which Marxists expect will somehow develop out of the "dictatorship of the proletariat." However, prior to 1961, the "final stage" of Communism has always been but a nebulous, vague concept in Communist literature, for neither Marx, Lenin, nor any of the theoreticians of "scientific socialism" had ever drawn a detailed blueprint of a Communist society, nor of the way in which the "withering away of the state" and the final goal were to be achieved. This was allegedly changed when the new draft program of the Communist Party of the Soviet Union was published in the summer of 1961 and adopted by the 22nd Party Congress before the end of the year. In this party program, the road at least was mapped out, the blueprint drawn, and the actions prescribed which, within twenty years, were to transform the Soviet Union into what the program refers to as an essentially (though not yet completely) communist society. Space limitations prevent the inclusion

[1] Harry G. Shaffer, "Communism and Fascism: Two Peas in a Pod?" *Queens Quarterly,* LXIX, No. 1 (Spring, 1962), pp. 146-156.

here of the entire Party Program, but excerpts are presented as the first selection below.

Naum Jasny, next, evaluates the 1961 Party Program and reaches the conclusion that the entire 20-year plan adopted by the 22nd Party Congress is utterly irrational, inherently self-contradictory, and impossible of fulfillment. Instead of a valid blueprint for surpassing the United States and reaching anything like a perfect society, the targets set in the "super-plan" are to Jasny but a "part in the pageant called the XXII Congress of the CPSU."

Concluding the section on *Western Views,* Alexander S. Balinky arrives at the conclusion that the Soviet Union will indeed reach "communism," but only by *redefining* the main features of communist society.

In the fourth selection Maurice Dobb, probably the foremost Marxist economist in the Western world, presents the Marxist case for what he refers to as "the first tentative blueprint for making the transition to Marx's 'higher phase of communist society.' "

Next, representing the Soviet point of view, I. Anchishkin attempts to clarify the meaning of "Communist abundance," stressing that a concentration of efforts on the production of unnecessary luxuries has no place in Communist society and would not be desired anyhow by the "new man" of the future. During the *transition* from socialism to communism, Anchishkin explains, the fulfillment of wants must be brought about not haphazardly, but gradually, step by step, according to a system of priorities based on the relative urgencies of the manifold needs of society. Inviting other Soviet economists to express their agreement or disagreement with the views expressed, the original article (and the translation in *Problems of Economics*) carried the footnote: "A posing of the question."

In communist ideology, an increase in productive capacity adequate to enable society to satisfy the needs of all its members is certainly an absolute prerequisite for the "final stage,"—but it is not the only one. As explained in the quotation at the beginning of this section, man would have to be "transformed into a 'social being' " before the state, in Marx's words, could "wither away" and a purely communist society be established. What, exactly, is this "social being," this "new Soviet man" as he is often referred to? What are his moral principles, what guides his actions, what makes him behave the way he does or is supposed to? The final, brief selection has been included to give the Western student a glimpse of the moral code of communism, as officially proclaimed in the Soviet Union today and by Marxists throughout the world for more than a century.

9

Excerpts From the Draft Program of the Communist Party Adopted by the 22nd Party Congress, Oct. 31, 1961 *

"The epoch making turn of mankind from capitalism to socialism, initiated by the October Revolution, is a natural result of the development of society."

"Capitalism, by concentrating millions of workers in its factories, socializing the process of labor, imparts a social character to production; nevertheless it is the capitalist who appropriates the fruits of labor. This fundamental contradiction of capitalism . . . manifests itself in production anarchy and in the fact that the purchasing power of society falls short of the expansion of production and leads periodically to destructive economic crises. (This leads to) . . . a relative and sometimes an absolute deterioration of the condition of the working class."

"V. I. Lenin developed the theory of the Socialist revolution in new historical conditions, elaborated the theory of the possibility of socialism triumphing first in one capitalist country taken singly. Russia was the weakest link in the imperialist system and the focal point of all its contradictions. On the other hand she had all the conditions necessary for the victory for socialism. Her working class was the most revolutionary and best organized in the world and had considerable experience of class struggle. It was led by a Marxist-Leninist party armed with an advanced, revolutionary theory and steeled in class battles."

"The enemies of Leninism maintained that Russia was not mature enough for a Socialist revolution, that it was impossible to build socialism in one country. But the enemies of Leninism were put to shame."

*. The complete text of the program can be found in the *New York Times,* August 1, 1961; in *Marxism,* edited by Arthur P. Mendel (Bantam Pocket Books, 1961), pp. 371-486; in *Program of the Communist Party of the Soviet Union, Adopted by the 22nd Congress of the C. P. S. U., Oct. 31, 1961,* Crosscurrent Press, 1961; and in many other places.

"Socialism, which Marx and Engels scientifically predicted as inevitable and the plan for the construction of which was mapped out by Lenin, has become a reality in the Soviet Union."

"The socialist principle 'From each according to his abilities, to each according to his work' has been put into effect in the Soviet Union."

"Monopoly capital has, in the final analysis, doomed bourgeois society to low rates of production growth that in some countries barely keep ahead of the growth of population. A considerable part of the production plant stands idle, while millions of unemployed wait at the factory gates. Farm production is artificially restricted, although millions are underfed in the world. People suffer want in material goods, but imperialism is squandering material resources and social labor on war preparations."

"The monopoly bourgeoisie is a useless growth on the social organism, one unneeded in production. The industries are run by hired managers, engineers, and technicians. The monopolists lead a parasitical life and with their menials consume a substantial portion of the national income created by the toil of proletarians and peasants."

"Fear of revolution, the successes of the socialist countries, and the pressure of the working class movement compel the bourgeoisie to make partial concessions with respect to wages, labour conditions, and social security . . . Even the relatively high standard of living in the small group of capitalistically developed countries rests upon the plunder of the Asian, African and Latin American peoples, upon non-equivalent exchange, discrimination of female labor, brutal oppression of Negroes . . . The bourgeois myth of 'full employment' has proved to be sheer mockery, for the working class is suffering continuously from mass unemployment and insecurity . . ."

"Taking cover behind spurious professions of freedom and democracy, U.S. militarism is in effect performing the function of world gendarme, supporting reactionary dictatorial regimes and decayed monarchies . . . The U.S. monopoly bourgeoisie is the mainstay of international reaction. It has assumed the role of 'saviour' of capitalism. The U.S. financial tycoons are engineering a 'holy alliance' of imperialists and founding aggressive military blocs. American troops and war bases are stationed at the most important points of the capitalist world."

"The American monopolies and their British and French allies are openly assisting the West-German imperialists who are cynically advocating aggressive aims of revenge and preparing a war against the socialist countries and other European states. A dangerous centre of aggression, imperilling the peace and security of all peoples, is being revived in the heart of Europe."

"The bourgeoisie gives extensive publicity to the allegedly democratic nature of its elections laws, singing special praise to its multi-party system and the possibility of nominating many candidates. In reality, however, the monopolists deprive the masses of the opportunity to express their will and elect genuine champions of their interests. Being in control of such potent means as capital, the press, radio, cinema, television, and using their henchmen in the trade unions and other mass organizations, they mislead the masses and impose their own candidates upon the electorate. The different bourgeoisie parties are usually no more than different factions of the ruling bourgeoisie."

"The dictatorship of the proletariat is a dictatorship of the overwhelming majority over the minority; it . . . is aimed at abolishing all exploitation of man by man."

"The world is experiencing a period of stormy national-liberation revolutions. Imperialism suppressed the national independence and freedom of the majority of the peoples and put the fetters of brutal colonial slavery on them, but the rise of socialism marks the advent of the era of emancipation of the oppressed peoples . . . The young sovereign states do not belong either to the system of imperialist states or to the system of socialist states. But the overwhelming majority of them have not yet broken free from world capitalist economy even though they occupy a special place in it. They constitute that part of the world which is still being exploited by the capitalist monopolies."

"Marxists-Leninists draw a distinction between the nationalism of the oppressed nations and that of the oppressor nations. The nationalism of an oppressed nation contains a general democratic element directed against oppression, and Communists support it because they consider it historically justified at a given stage."

"One of the basic questions confronting these peoples is which road of development the countries that have freed themselves from colonial tyranny are to take, whether the capitalist road or the non-capitalist . . . What can socialism bring these peoples?
Socialism is the road to freedom and happiness for the peoples. It ensures rapid economic and cultural progress. It transforms a backward country into an industrial country within the lifetime of one generation

and not in the course of centuries. Planned socialist economy is an economy of progress and prosperity by its very nature. Abolition of the exploitation of man by man does away with social inequality. Unemployment disappears completely . . .

It is for the people themselves to decide which road they will choose."

"A grim struggle is going on between two ideologies—communist and bourgeois—in the world today . . .

Imperialist reaction mobilizes every possible means to exert ideological influence on the masses as it attempts to discredit communism and its noble ideas and to defend capitalism. The chief ideological and political weapon of imperialism is anti-communism, which consists mainly in slandering the socialist system and distorting the policy and objectives of the Communist parties and Marxist-Leninist theory. Under the false slogans of anti-communism, imperialist reaction persecutes and hounds all that is progressive and revolutionary . . . Rallied to this black banner today are all the enemies of social progress: the finance oligarchy and the military, the fascists and reactionary clericals, the colonialists and landlords and all the ideological and political supporters of imperialist reaction."

"The contemporary Right-wing Social-Democrats are the most important ideological and political prop of the bourgeoisie within the working-class movement. They eclectically combine old opportunist ideas with the 'latest' bourgeoisie theories."

"To abolish war and establish everlasting peace on earth is a historical mission of communism. General and complete disarmament under strict international control is a radical way of guaranteeing a durable peace . . . Socialism has offered mankind the only reasonable principle of maintaining relations between states at a time when the world is divided into two systems—the principle of peaceful coexistence of states with different social systems, put forward by Lenin . . . Peaceful coexistence or disastrous war—such is the alternative offered by history. Peaceful coexistence implies renunciation of war as a means of settling international disputes, and their solution by negotiation; equality, mutual understanding and trust between countries; consideration for each other's interests; non-interference in internal affairs; recognition of the right of every people to solve all the problems of their country by themselves; strict respect for the sovereignty and territorial integrity of all countries; promotion of economic and cultural co-operation on the basis of complete equality and mutual benefit.

Peaceful coexistence serves as a basis for the peaceful competition between socialism and capitalism on an international scale."

"The building of a communist society has become an immediate practical task for the Soviet people. The gradual development of socialism into communism is an objective law; it has been prepared by the development of Soviet socialist society throughout the preceding period. What is communism?

Communism is a classless social system with one form of public ownership of the means of production and full social equality of all members of society . . . 'From each according to his ability, to each according to his needs' will be implemented. Communism is . . . a society in which labour for the good of society will become the prime vital requirement of everyone, a necessity recognized by one and all, and the ability of each person will be employed to the greatest benefit of the people . . . labour will no longer be a mere source of livelihood—it will be a genuinely creative process and a source of joy . . .

Family relations will be freed once and for all from material considerations and will be based solely on mutual love and friendship."

"In the current decade (1961–70) the Soviet Union, in creating the material and technical basis of communism, will surpass the strongest and richest capitalist country, the U.S.A., in production per head of population . . .

The material and technical basis of communism will be built up by the end of the second decade (1971–1980) ensuring an abundance of material and cultural values for the whole population; Soviet society will come close to a stage where it can introduce the principle of distribution according to needs, and there will be a gradual transition to one form of ownership—national ownership. Thus, a communist society will in the main be built in the U.S.S.R. The construction of communist society will be fully completed in the subsequent period."

". . . the C.P.S.U. (Communist Party Soviet Union) plans the following increases in total industrial output:

within the current 10 years, by approximately 150 per cent, exceeding the level of U.S. industrial output;

within 20 years, by not less than 500 per cent, leaving the present overall volume of U.S. industrial output far behind.

To achieve this, it is necessary to raise productivity of labour in industry by more than 100 per cent within 10 years, and by 300-350 per cent within 20 years . . .

The plan for the electrification of the country provides for an almost threefold increase in the power capacity per industrial worker within the present decade . . . The annual output of electricity must be brought up to about 900,000-1,000,000 million kwh by the end of the first decade, and to 2,700,000-3,000,000 million kwh by the end of the second decade . . .

As atomic energy becomes cheaper, the construction of atomic power stations will be expanded, especially in areas poor in other power sources and the use of atomic energy for peaceful purposes in the national economy, in medicine and science will increase . . .

Within 20 years metallurgy will develop sufficiently to produce about 250 million tons of steel a year . . .

In the 20 years comprehensive automation will be effected on a mass scale, with increasing emphasis on fully automated shops and factories, making for high technical and economic efficiency . . .

The C.P.S.U. will concentrate its efforts on ensuring a rapid increase in the output of consumer goods . . .

The growth of the national economy will call for the accelerated development of all transportation facilities . . .

The maximum acceleration of scientific and engineering progress is a major national task . . .

The Party will do everything to enhance the role of science in the building of communist society . . ."

"Along with a powerful industry, a flourishing, versatile and highly productive agriculture is an imperative condition for the building of communism . . .

. . . the task is to increase the aggregate volume of agricultural production in 10 years by about 150 per cent, and in 20 years by 250 per cent. In the first decade, the Soviet Union will outstrip the United States in output of the key agricultural products per head of population . . .

Productivity of labour in agriculture will rise no less than 150 per cent in ten years, and five- to sixfold in twenty years . . .

The further mechanization of agriculture, introduction of comprehensive mechanization, and use of automatic devices and highly efficient and economical machinery adapted to the conditions of each zone will be the basis for the growth of productivity of farm labour . . ."

"Increasingly equal economic conditions must be provided to improve the incomes of kolkhozes existing under unequal natural-economic conditions, in different zones, and also within the zones, in order to put into effect more consistently the principle of equal pay for equal work on a scale embracing the entire kolkhoz system. Farming on all collective farms must be based on the principle of profitability . . .

The economic advancement of the kolkhozes will make it possible to . . . effect a transition to a guaranteed monthly income; to develop community services more broadly (public catering, kindergartens and nurseries, and other services, etc.) . . . When collective production at the kolkhozes is able to replace in full production on the supplementary individual plots of the kolkhoz members, when collective farmers see for themselves that their supplementary individual farming is unprofitable, they will give it up of their own accord.

As the productive forces increase, interkolkhoz production ties will develop and the socialization of production will transcend the limits of individual kolkhozes. The building, jointly by several kolkhozes, of enterprises and cultural and welfare institutions, of state-kolkhoz power stations and enterprises for the primary processing, storage and transportation of farm products, for various types of building, the manufacture of building materials and elements, etc. should be encouraged. As the commonly-owned assets increase . . . these developments, which must proceed on a voluntary basis and when the necessary economic conditions are available, will gradually impart to kolkhoz-co-operative property the nature of public property."

"Elimination of socio-economic and cultural distinctions between town and country and of differences in their living conditions will be one of the greatest gains of communist construction."

"The building of the material and technical basis of communism calls for a continuous improvement in economic management . . . The immutable law of economic development is to achieve in the interests of society the highest results at the lowest cost. . . .

Communist construction presupposes the maximum development of democratic principles of management coupled with a strengthening and improvement of centralized economic management by the state. . . .

There must be a further expansion of the role of local bodies in economic management. . . ."

"In the process of communist construction economic management will make use of material and moral incentives for high production figures . . . In the course of the advance to communism the importance of moral labour incentives, public recognition of achieved results and the sense of responsibility of each for the common cause will become continuously greater. . . .

It is necessary in communist construction to make full use of commodity-money relations. . . . With the transition of the single communist form of people's property and the communist system of distribution, commodity-money relations will become economically outdated and will wither away."

"The C.P.S.U. sets the historically important task of achieving in the Soviet Union a living standard higher than that of any of the capitalist countries. This task will be effected by: a) raising individual payment according to the quantity and quality of work done, coupled with reduction of retail prices and abolition of taxes paid by the population; b) increase of the public consumption fund intended for the satisfaction of the requirements of members of society irrespective of the quantity and quality of their labour, that is free of charge (education, medical treatment, pensions, maintenance of children at children's institutions, transition to cost free use of public amenities, etc.). . . .

In the coming twenty years payment according to one's work will remain the principal source for satisfying the material and cultural needs of the working people. The disparity between high and comparatively low incomes must be steadily reduced. . . .

. . . as the country advances towards communism, personal needs will be increasingly met out of public consumption funds, whose rate of growth will exceed the rate of growth of payments for labour. The transition to communist distribution will be completed after the principle of distribution according to one's work will outlive itself, that is, when there will be an abundance of material and cultural wealth, and labour will become a prime necessity of life for all members of society."

"The national income of the U.S.S.R. in the next ten years will increase nearly 150 per cent, and about 400 per cent in twenty years. This real income per head of population will increase by more than 250 per cent in twenty years."

"Output of consumer goods must meet the growing consumer demand in full, and must conform to its changes. Timely output of goods in accordance with the varied demand of the population, with consideration for local, national, and climatic conditions, is an imperative requirement for all the consumer industries."

"Public transport facilities (tramways, buses, trolley buses, and subways) will become free in the course of the second decade, and at the end of it such public amenities as water, gas, and heating will also be free."

"In the coming ten years the country will go over to a six-hour working day with one day off a week, or a 35-hour working week with two days off, and on underground jobs and enterprises with harmful working conditions to a five-hour day or a 30-hour five-day working week.

By virtue of a corresponding rise in labour productivity, transition to a still shorter working week will be begun in the second decade.

The length of the annual paid holidays of working people will be increased together with the reduction of the working day. Gradually the minimum length of leave for all industrial, professional and office workers will increase to three weeks and subsequently to one month. . . .
All-round measures to make working conditions healthier and lighter constitute an important task in improving the well-being of the people."

"In addition to the existing free medical service, accommodations of sick persons at sanatoria and the dispensing of medicines will become gratuitous.
In order to afford the population an opportunity to rest in an out-of-town environment, holiday homes, boarding-houses, country hotels, and tourist camps will be built, where working people will be accommodated at a reasonable charge or by way of bonus, as well as at a discount or gratis."

"The transition to free public catering (midday meals) at enterprises and institutions will make it possible for more and more families, and in the second decade for every family, to keep children and adolescents free of charge at children's establishments if they so desire. The party considers it essential that everything should be done to fully meet in the next few years the demand in children's pre-school institutions.
In town and country there will be full and cost-free satisfaction of the population's need in nurseries, kindergartens, playgrounds, day-care schools and young pioneer camps. . . ."

"The set programme can be fulfilled with success under conditions of peace. . . ."

"The working class is the only class in history that does not aim to perpetuate its power. . . .
The Party holds that the dictatorship of the working class will cease to be necessary before the state withers away. The state as an organization of the entire people will survive until the complete victory of communism. . . .
As socialist democracy develops, the organs of state power will gradually be transformed into organs of public self-government. . . ."

"To improve the work of the Soviets and bring fresh forces into them, it is advisable that at least one-third of the total number of deputies to a Soviet should be elected anew each time so that fresh millions of working people may learn to govern the state. . . .
The Party regards the perfection of the principles of socialist democracy and their rigid observance as a most important task. . . ."

"Discussion by the people of draft laws and other decisions of both national and local significance must become the rule. The most important draft laws should be put to a nation-wide referendum."

"An effort should be made to ensure that the salaried government staffs are reduced, that ever larger sections of the people learn to take part in administration and that work on government staffs eventually ceases to constitute a profession."

"The transition to communism means the fullest extension of personal freedom and the rights of Soviet citizens. . . .
The whole system of government and social organization educates the people in a spirit of voluntary and conscientious fulfillment of their duties and leads to a natural fusion of rights and duties to form single standards of communist behaviour."

"The role of social organizations increases in the period of the full-scale construction of communism. The trade unions acquire particular importance as schools of administration and economic management.
The trade unions shall:
    work constantly to increase the communist consciousness of the masses . . . ;
    encourage the activity of factory and office workers . . . for higher productivity of labour . . . ;
    . . . protect the material interests and rights of the working people;
    . . . improve cultural services and recreation facilities for the working people; encourage physical training and sports."

"As socialist statehood develops, it will gradually become communist self-government of the people. . . . The bodies in charge of planning, accounting, economic management, and cultural advancement, now government bodies, will lose their political character and will become organs of public self-government . . . Universally recognized rules of the communist way of life will be established whose observance will become an organic need and habit with everyone.
Historical development inevitably leads to the withering away of the state. To ensure that the state withers away completely, it is necessary to provide both internal conditions—the building of a developed communist society—and external conditions—the victory and consolidation of socialism in the world arena."

"The Leninist principle of peaceful coexistence of states with differing social systems always has been, and remains, the general principle of the foreign policy of the Soviet state.

The Soviet Union perseveringly seeks to bring about the realization of its proposals for general and complete disarmament under strict international control. But the imperialist countries . . . openly proclaim their insane plans for the liquidation of the Soviet Union and the other socialist states through war. . . . The Soviet Union sees it as its international duty to guarantee, together with the other socialist countries, the reliable defence and security of the entire socialist camp."

"The Party sees the development of a communist attitude to labour in all members of society as its chief educational task. Labour for the benefit of society is the sacred duty of all. Any labour for society, whether physical or mental, is honourable and commands respect. . . .
Anyone who received any benefits from society without doing his share of work, would be a parasite living at the expense of others.
It is impossible for a man in communist society not to work, for neither his social consciousness, nor public opinion would permit it. Working according to one's ability will become a habit, a prime necessity of life, for every member of society."

"The peaceful coexistence of states with different social systems does not imply an easing of the ideological struggle. . . .
The Party will steadfastly propagate the great advantages of socialism and communism over the declining capitalist system."

"Cultural development during the full-scale construction of communist society will constitute the closing of a great cultural revolution. . . .
Absorbing all the best that has been created by world culture, communist culture will be a new, higher stage in the cultural progress of mankind. It will embody the versatility and richness of the spiritual life of society, and the lofty ideals and humanism of the new world. It will be the culture of a classless society, a culture of the entire people, of all mankind. . . .
The Party considers it necessary to expand the Soviet Union's cultural relations with the countries of the socialist system and with all other countries for the purpose of pooling scientific and cultural achievements and of bringing about mutual understanding and friendship among the peoples."

"The C.P.S.U. regards communist construction in the Soviet Union as a component of the building of communist society by the peoples of the entire world socialist system. . . .
The first country to advance to communism facilitates and accelerates the advantage of the entire world socialist system to communism. In building communism, the peoples of the Soviet Union are breaking

new roads for mankind, testing their correctness by their own experiences, bringing out difficulties, finding ways and means of overcoming them, and selecting the best forms and methods of communist construction. . . .

As Lenin foresaw, tendencies develop toward the future creation of a world communist economy regulated by the victorious working people according to one single plan.

The C.P.S.U. and the Soviet People will do everything in their power to support all the peoples of the socialist community in the construction of socialism and communism."

"The achievements of communism in the U.S.S.R. will be the greatest victory mankind has ever won throughout its long history. . . .

When the Soviet people enjoy the blessings of communism, new hundreds of millions of people on earth will say: 'We are for communism.'"

It is not through war with other countries, but by the example of a more perfect organization of society, by rapid progress in developing the productive forces, the creation of all conditions, for the happiness and well-being of man, that the ideas of communism win the minds and hearts of the masses."

"Under the tried and tested leadership of the Communist Party, under the banner of Marxism-Leninism, the Soviet People have built socialism. Under the leadership of the party, under the banner of Marxism-Leninism, the Soviet people will build communist society.

The Party solemnly proclaims: The present generation of Soviet people shall live in communism!"

10

Plan and Superplan *

NAUM JASNY
Author of many books and articles on the Soviet economy

After forty years of planning, the Soviets have announced their first general plan of twenty years' duration.[1] No less a task than the completion of laying the foundation of communism is assigned to it.

A single economic plan (single in the sense of covering the whole economy) presupposes the complete tie-in of all its parts. This would not guarantee that the plan is good. Some parts, although well tied-in with the others, may be too high, too low, or otherwise defective. But a plan-like document, in which the individual parts are programmed separately and not tied-in with the others, is not a single plan, even though some parts may be perfectly sensible.

In addition to planning for a time of which nobody can know anything definite, to putting in obviously absurd targets for vital items, and so on and so on, the provisions of the new plan display a flagrant disproportion between such crucial items as the targets for national income and those for labour productivity. This disproportion is so enormous, it so strikes the eye, that the suspicion arises that the real planners may not have seen the document at all. Incidentally, the agency which is supposed to have been working out the twenty-year plan, the Gosekonomsovet, does not appear to be mentioned in it.

The twenty-year plan is part of the programme of the Soviet Communist Party, the draft of which was released on 30 July 1961. The text actually does not use the phrase 'twenty-year plan' or, for that matter, the standard expression for the long-range plan, the general plan. It

---

* Reprinted from Walter Laqueur and Leopold Labedz, (editors), *The Future of Communist Society* (1962), pp. 29-43 by permission of Frederick A. Praeger, Inc., Publisher. (First published in Great Britain in October, 1961, as a special issue of *Survey*).

[1] The Soviets count the Plan GOELRO (State Committee on Electrification of Russia) of 1920 as the first general plan. But it did not embrace the whole economy even as drafted. The only part of it approved was the construction of thirty electric power plants. The rest was propaganda.

speaks simply of two decades, of 10 and 20 years. Features of the new 'plan,' which strike the eye and may possibly be interpreted as showing that, although very, very slowly, the Soviets are learning, are (a) that only few figures are given, and (b) that even those few are given in round numbers.[2] But these are relatively minor matters, included for the convenience of the planners in juggling with those figures that are given, and words of course flow easily. The basic requirement of a good plan is that it must be realistic. This was recognised at the party central committee meeting in December 1956, and was clearly in evidence in the annual plans of the subsequent years and in the targets of the general plan (a 15-year plan) for 11 industrial commodities announced in November 1957. This policy has now been abandoned. The targets of the new 'plan' are on the strongly optimistic side in almost all cases, and some important targets are clearly absurdly high.

On the technical side, it should be added that the new plan does not contain even a trace of a breakdown into 5-year periods, as seems to have been expected by writers in the Soviet press. The usual breakdown in the plan is by decades, but such important targets as those for grain and steel capacity have only one figure, that for 1980. At least in one case (real incomes of low-paid hired labour) there is a target only for the first decade.

While only a few figures are given, they enable us to form a rough idea about the expected development, although one would want to have in addition numerical data at least for the output of industrial consumer goods and for investment. For the first of these items one has to speculate from the data on the expected growth in personal incomes; for the second conclusions have to be drawn from the high rates of growth expected for the whole economy and from some verbal statements (the 20-year plan states that investment will have to be huge). Nobody expects from such a document as the new plan specific information about expenditure on the armed forces, but it goes out of its way to emphasise that 'defence' is fully taken care of.

Calculations as to the size and disposition of labour are one of the most important components of a plan. Not only are these items missing from the new 'plan,' but such immense errors have been made in respect to this question that it is impossible to accept the economic provisions of the programme as a plan.

Production

The few figures which can be extracted from the published document are set out in the table below:

2 The figures are frequently qualified with such phrases as "not less than" or "more than."

	Attained 1950–60 official	Attained 1950–60 corrected	Percentage growth as given in the 20-year Plan 1960–1970	Planned 1970–1980a	1960–1980
National income	159	97–113	almost 150	not less than 100	400
Industrial output	204	140	almost 150	not less than 140	not less than 500
of which:					
electric power	220	—	208–242	200	825–921
steel	139	—	—	—	284b
Farm output	60b	—	about 150	40	250
of which:					
grain	62	—	—	—	more than 100
meat	82c	—	about 200	nearly 33.3	nearly 300
milk	80	—	more than 100	—	nearly 200
Labour productivity:					
industry	104	—	more than 100	—	300–350
agriculture	—	—	not less than 150	100–140	400–500
Real income per employed person:					
Workers and employees	62c	—	almost 100	—	approx. 200–250
of which:					
low-paid	—	—	approx. 200	—	—
kolkhoz peasants	85c	—	more than 100	100	more than 300

a Implied.
b Capacity.
c 1950–59.

As far as can be seen from the data in this table, there is a violent contradiction between the targets for national income and those for labour productivity. The first implies a marked slowdown in the rate of growth in the second decade (1970–80) as compared with the first (1960–70), while this development is scarcely reflected in the targets for labour productivity. If the targets for national income are regarded as basic, as they should be, the question arises as to the reason for the slowdown. Since the Soviet planners are of course unable to visualise what will happen in the 1970s, the reason for the big discrepancy may be that the Soviets were mainly interested in having high rates of growth in the first decade and therefore set the target for this decade much higher than that for the second decade.

Because, clearly, the target for the growth of the national income in the 1960s, providing as it does a 2.5-fold rise and implying an annual growth of about 10 per cent, is very much on the optimistic side. The official estimates indicate a growth in national income in 1950–60 of almost 11 per cent per year, but there is no doubt at all that this figure is excessive. Most Western analysts agree on a figure of about 7–8 per cent.

Some analysts believe that the new plan is a projection of the development in the preceding years, but this is true only for output of electric power, as will be shown. The target for national income, the index which summarises the whole economy, clearly reflects expectations of a substantial speeding up in the first plan decade as compared with the preceding decade. A rate of growth approximately equal to that in the past is provided only for the second decade. In 1959 and 1960, the last two years, even the *official* indices showed a growth of 8 per cent per year, i.e. considerably less than scheduled for the 1960s. The first half of 1961, i.e. the initial portion of the 20-year plan period, was not better than 1959 or 1960.

The 20-year plan foresees a growth of 150 per cent in industrial output in 1960–70, or 10 per cent per year, i.e. the same as for the national income, and, incidentally, for the growth of agriculture.

The official estimate for the growth of industrial output in 1950–60 (about 11 per cent per year) is probably exaggerated, but much less than that for national income. (It is a mystery to this writer how this discrepancy comes to exist.) A growth of 9 per cent per year is assumed by this writer for this period. Thus here, too, the new plan goes beyond the previous attainments. The target of the new plan for industrial output also exceeds the targets of the 7-year plan for 1959–65, adopted little more than two years ago, which set a growth in industrial output of 8.6 per cent per year. The Soviet authorities may feel justified in raising this percentage because, according to their calculations, the rate of growth scheduled by the 7-year plan was exceeded in the first two years of its operation. According to these official calculations, industrial output grew by about 10.5 per cent in both 1959 and 1960. But, like most other recent indices, the indices for industrial production in 1959 and 1960 are likely to be at least moderately exaggerated. The real growth in industrial output in these two years is unlikely to have been as high as 10 per cent, the rate implied in the 20-year plan for 1960–70. And even if it were, can a 20-year plan be based on a 2-year development?

The growth of agricultural output of 150 per cent, or of 10 per cent per annum, foreseen for 1960–70, reflects nothing but Mr. Khrushchev's exuberance. There can be no doubt on this score. He takes the failure of his past predictions about the growth of farm production with amazing equanimity; his urge to get estimates down from the sky does not abate. Farm output grew at no more than 5–6 per cent per year from Stalin's death to 1960, with the growth in 1959 and 1960 definitely bogged down (even with the effect of unfavourable weather eliminated, this might still be true). The new target for the growth of agricultural output of 150 per cent in 1960–70 is also substantially above the target of the 7-year plan for 1959–65 of 70 per cent in seven years, which was in any case wholly unrealistic.

It has already been mentioned that the new plan shows a great decline in the rate of growth of national income from 150 per cent in

10 years, or about 10 per cent per year in 1960–70, to 100 per cent in 10 years or about 7 per cent per year in the 1970s. Whether even this rate can be realised, nobody of course can say. The growth in farm output is to go down substantially in the second decade (40 per cent instead of the 150 per cent for the first decade). Industrial output, however, is to continue its growth at almost the high rate of the first decade (about 9.5 per cent for the second decade as against about 10 per cent for the first). If the target of the 20-year plan for national income were to be fulfilled, this would mean that the national income of the USSR would in 1970 be slightly greater than the 1960 national income of the United States, and would be not much less than 2.5 times the latter after twenty years. The United States has of course 10 and 20 years respectively in which to counter these pleasant prospects.

Official Soviet indices (exaggerated) show that the output of heavy industry was increasing at a rate of almost 13 per cent in 1950–60, while the output of consumer goods was growing at a rate of not quite 10 per cent. The difference in the rate of growth between producer and consumer goods was actually not as large as indicated by these figures, but it should be noted that the share of consumer goods in total industrial production fell from 60.5 per cent in 1928 to 31.2 per cent in 1950,[3] and to less than 28 per cent in 1960.

At a reception in Moscow on 20 May 1961, Khrushchev is supposed to have said: "Now we consider our heavy industry as built. So we are not going to give it priority. Light industry and heavy industry will develop at the same pace." [4] There was every reason to assume that this important statement had been taken from the 20-year plan, then (according to Khrushchev) in preparation, that indeed it was one of the foundations of the whole plan and especially of its industrial component. Yet no such statement is to be found in the 20-year plan. Neither is there any statement on the priority of heavy industry, which has been present in every plan for over 30 years. The 7-year plan for 1959–65, approved little more than two years ago, still gave predominance to growth of heavy industry. Instead of this, the importance of heavy industry is stressed in the programme without reference (even by implication) to the growth in output of consumer goods. Heavy industry "insures the development of the economy" and therefore "deserves unflagging attention." Of consumer goods it is said: "The CPSU will concentrate its efforts on insuring a rapid increase in the output of consumer goods."

It has been suggested in the Western press that the omission of Khrushchev's statement about an equal rate of growth in output of consumer and producer goods was due to a conflict at the top level, in which Khrushchev was defeated. It is, however, not very likely that one

[3] _Soviet Statistical Handbook for 1959_, p. 149.
[4] _New York Times_, 31 July 1961.

of the foundations of the plan was really changed at what should have been a very advanced stage of its preparation. The targets of the new plan, giving the same rate of growth for consumer and producer goods, may have been retained [5] (there may have been some manipulation to make it easier to reach statistical equality) and only the words altered to omit the precise text of Khrushchev's statement; the specific rates of growth for the two groups of industrial goods, and possibly the targets for one or two individual consumer goods, were presumably present from the start. This assumption is reinforced by the very high target for output of farm products in the first decade, as well as the figures for real incomes, although the few round figures that are given in the new plan might well have been totally revised in the two months which elapsed between Khrushchev's declaration and the publication of the programme. Nevertheless it is still significant that, with the share of consumer goods in total industrial production as low as 28 per cent, the programme does not go so far as to ensure expressly that this percentage will be maintained in the future. There is not the smallest reason to treat Mr. Khrushchev as an entrenched advocate of consumer goods output and of adequate personal incomes in general. When he got the better of Malenkov, his victory signified *inter alia* the abandonment of Malenkov's efforts to speed up the expansion of the output of consumer goods and a return to Stalin's priority of heavy industry. Still, consumer goods are treated in the 20-year plan better than they were by Khrushchev in 1954–55, and in the 7-year plan for 1959–65. Indeed, no previous plan in the USSR has given anywhere near as much space to the well-being of the population as does the new plan. There is reason to believe that the change is due to the pressure of the population, which can make itself felt in spite of the dictatorship.

The new plan has only two individual industrial targets, namely, electric power and steel. Both are producer goods. The target for electric power provides about a trebling in each decade. This is equivalent to a rise of not quite 12 per cent per year, and represents an almost exact projection of the development in the decade 1950–60. In fact, this scheduled rate of growth seems somewhat too small relative to the target for total industrial growth, especially in view of the considerable reduction in the costs of constructing electric power plants. As for steel, the new plan speaks only of the technical production possibilities, i.e. of capacity to produce, which is not necessarily to be fully used. A capacity of 250 million tons of steel—the 1980 target—seems huge when compared with the present output of the United States. It is almost double the capacity of the United States plants; but it does not seem particularly

---

[5] But there may have been difficulties in setting this level of output of consumer goods for the second plan decade, when the rate of growth in output of farm products is scheduled to decline sharply.

large in the context of the other targets, specifically that for total indus-
rial production. The implied annual rate of growth, almost 7 per cent,
even appears small compared with the rate of increase attained by steel
production in the preceding decade. Of course it is hoped to economise
on steel by making machinery lighter, and more attention will certainly
be paid to the substitution of plastics for steel.

Three specific targets for farm products are given. Like the target for
total farm output, these must be judged as being more or less on the
fantastic side, considering the limited possibilities for the expansion of
farm production at anything like the rates implied.

When referring to overtaking the United States in total output, the
planners concentrate on the prospects 20 years hence, but with reference
to agriculture they say: "In the first decade the Soviet Union will outstrip the United States in output of the key agricultural products per
head of population." It is not difficult to overtake somebody who is
not running. There is no reason for the United States to expand its
farm output which already exceeds the demand.

The scheduled increase of more than 100 per cent in the grain output
in 20 years implies a rise of approximately 4 per cent per year—a great
rate for a crop like grain and for a country like the USSR. Most of the
grain areas are located in regions with inadequate moisture supply, and
where, therefore, commercial fertilisers have only a limited usefulness,
which in turn limits the possibilities for raising per-acre yields. A threefold increase in meat output in 10 years would mean a per capita output
of real meat of not much less than 100 kilograms in 1970. The further
increase in the second decade is then scheduled to be relatively moderate
(equal to about 15 per cent on a per capita basis). At anything like present
prices, this meat output might well outrun demand. But Mr. Khrushchev
does not really need to worry about this right now, when people are
standing in long queues for meat. The nearly trebled milk output
scheduled for 1980 implies a per capita output of over 700 kilograms.
Butter consumption is apparently believed to be capable of rising almost
indefinitely.

Labour Productivity and Labour Force

The crucial point in the development of the Soviet economy in the
coming two decades or so, in any serious plan, is the speed with which
labour productivity will grow. The provisions of the 20-year plan are
extremely optimistic on this score, especially of course in words but also
in figures.

Labour productivity in industry is to rise by fully 7 per cent per year
on the average in each of the 20 years. For some reason, its growth is
scheduled to be larger for the second than for the first decade. The

official statistics show, it is true, exactly the same rise in 1950–60, but the index of labour productivity in industry is exaggerated about as much as the index of industrial output. The target of the new plan for labour productivity in industry is definitely, and moreover substantially, higher than the past performance.[6] The new targets for labour productivity in agriculture far surpass even those in industry, and are wholly unrealistic. In the first decade labour productivity in agriculture is to grow by about 10 per cent each year. This would certainly be a great achievement, but the target for the second decade makes it a pygmy. It provides that labour productivity in agriculture, after having risen to 2.5 times its present performance, will go on growing at a not much slower rate for a further 10 years. By 1980 it would have reached a 5–6-fold as compared with 1960. The official estimates indicate a rise in labour productivity in agriculture in 1953–59 of not quite 7 per cent per year. This was, however, an overestimate and, moreover, the 6 years covered by the index are the most favourable ever, and the start was from a very low level.

The improbability of the labour productivity targets is enhanced by the comparisons with the United States made in the programme, where it appears that the USA is pretty backward compared with the level easily attainable on paper in the USSR.

It seems reasonable to assume that the rates of growth in labour productivity should decline as time passes. It has been increasing at a good rate in recent years, and it is obvious that the greater the growth of labour productivity in the past, the less remains for the future. Such gains as this are not repeatable.

There is however one thing which may prevent such a decline, possibly even permit an increase (but of course not over twenty years; this writer refuses to put down on paper his speculations on what will happen after 20 years). This is the great amount of irrationality and inefficiency in the Soviet economy. The partial removal of these features, now certainly in progress, may for a time prevent the decline in the rate of growth in labour productivity which is otherwise probably inevitable.

The immense amount of irrationality, inefficiency, and downright waste in the Soviet economy is apparently not generally realised.[7] Part of it is inherent in the Soviet system and cannot be eliminated. (This is not to say that this part is necessarily greater than that inherent in the capitalist system.) But a large part is unnecessary, and the Soviets are

[6] N. Kaplan and R. Moorsteen, "An Index of Soviet Industrial Output," *The American Economic Review,* June 1960, p. 316, calculated for industry other than machinery (including armaments) an average growth of 5 per cent in 1950–58. The addition of machinery would raise this percentage to say 6.

[7] The beginning of an analysis of this very important phenomenon may be found in my "Note on Rationality and Efficiency of the Soviet Economy," *Soviet Studies,* April and July 1961.

doing something to remove a good bit of it. Here only two items, electric power and fuel, will be briefly discussed. There is an immense waste of labour in Soviet agriculture, but the complications here are so vast that merely an attempt to touch on the topic would burst the permitted bounds of this article.

Of the electric power plants put into operation in 1950–59, 21.4 per cent were hydro-electric. One competent Soviet author has said: "As is known, hydro-electric plants cost four times as much as thermal plants per kilowatt to construct." [8] Moreover, the reported construction costs of hydro-electric plants are minimised in various ways in the USSR. It seems reasonable to assume that the relatively small proportion of hydro-electric plants among the 1950–59 constructions nearly doubled the total construction costs of all power plants.

On 10 August 1958, Mr. Khrushchev announced that the preferred treatment of hydro-electric power was to be discontinued; henceforth preference was to be given to thermal electric-power plants. The idea was incorporated in the 7-year plan for 1959–65, and in spite of Mr. Khrushchev's assurances that the change in policy would only be relatively short-lived, it may be regarded as accepted for good. If the share of hydro-electric power plants will be only 10 per cent of the total new capacity in the next 20 years, this alone may involve a saving on construction costs of about a quarter of what they would otherwise be. In addition, the majority of whatever hydro-electric plants will be constructed in the next 20 years, will be located behind the Urals, where the topographical conditions are much more favourable than in European Russia and construction costs are said to be only about half as large per kilowatt. Finally, if large thermal power stations are built, construction costs per unit of power will be substantially reduced.

After a delay much longer than the twenty years now envisaged, the Soviet rulers awoke to the idea (they did not need to develop it themselves; they could have borrowed it from the United States) that petroleum, and natural gas in particular, are very much cheaper to produce and, for that matter, to transport than coal, especially since this is particularly expensive in European Russia. The investment, including exploration costs, required for petroleum and gas is somewhat greater than for coal, but this hardly matters because the additional investment can be repaid from savings in less than two years, and for gas in less than one year. By the end of the 1970s the share of coal in total fuel is unlikely to be much higher than 25 per cent (it was 66.1 per cent in 1950), with the shares of petroleum and gas correspondingly higher. It has been calculated on the basis of the provisions of the "general plan," announced in November 1957 (this scheduled a decline in the share of

[8] *Economic Effectiveness of Fixed Investment and New Techniques,* ed. T. S. Khachaturov, Moscow, 1959, p. 466.

coal to about 30 per cent) that 36 milliard rubles would have been saved on this score by 1972,[9] a sum equivalent to roughly 3 per cent of the total 1959 national income. The savings (in rubles, not in per cent of national income) would of course be even greater by 1980, what with the total amount of fuel steadily rising and the share of coal in total fuel steadily declining.

All such savings are likely to affect favourably the growth of labour productivity in industry and construction. What can be expected is no more than holding on for some time to the relatively high rates of growth of labour productivity in the past few years, not its growth beyond this level and not for as long as 20 years.

So far as agriculture is concerned, the Soviet leaders presumably expect great savings of labour from the conversion of collective into state farms, accompanied by the elimination of the private plots and livestock of the collective peasants. These sources indeed may permit a temporary growth in labour productivity in agriculture greater than in the past several years, but nothing even remotely resembling a 2.5-fold rise in 10 years and 5–6-fold rise in 20 years is likely.

To turn now to the vital problem of the relation between the rate of growth of labour productivity and that of national income.

Assuming that the access of persons of working age will be about the same in percentage terms in both the 1960s and the 1970s, there should be a marked parallelism between the rate of growth of labour productivity and that of national income. This is, however, not the case. In the programme a somewhat greater rise in labour productivity in industry is set for the 1970s than for the 1960s. The target for the rise in labour productivity in agriculture is slightly less for the 1970s than the 1960s. Yet the rate of growth of national income is to decline from 150 per cent in the first plan decade to only 100 per cent in the second.

This glaring inconsistency can also be seen from the following data: In the first plan decade labour productivity in industry is to rise by "more than 100 per cent," that in agriculture by "not less than 150 per cent." If the access of new labour during the decade is taken into account, the growth in national income of "nearly 150 per cent" seems to have at least an outward appearance of a tie-in with that in labour productivity in industry and agriculture combined. But in the second plan decade we have a rise in labour productivity of 100–125 per cent in industry and of 100 to 140 per cent in agriculture. Taking into account the continued access of new labour to the extent of roughly 20 per cent, these rates of growth in labour productivity correspond to an increase in national income of not very much less than 150 per cent. Yet the new plan has only a 100 per cent rise. The reason for this immense discrepancy

[9] *Economic Effectiveness,* op. cit., p. 82.

can only be guessed at. It may possibly be due to failure to consider the changes in the labour force.

An indispensable part of a 20-year plan should be concerned with accessions to and utilisation of labour. Not a word can be found on these vital items in the document. The point is not only not discussed, it was obviously not given any thought. If it had been, the new plan would be a different document. The planners possibly thought that with the immensely optimistic prospects for the rise in labour productivity there was no need to worry about a possible shortage of labour. It seems to have escaped their notice that the combination of the provisions for output with those for labour productivity in the plan implies a tremendous amount of unused labour. After having boasted about the absence of unemployment for some 30 years, they suddenly programme unemployment on a fantastic scale. The relevant provisions of the new plan are shown in the table below:

Labour Force as Implied in the Programme

First decade (as % of 1960)

	Industry	Agriculture	Total
Output	250	about 250	——
Labour productivity[a]	more than 200	not less than 250	——
Labour force[b]:			
Millions in 1960	21	33	54
Percentage increase	25	less than in 1960	——
Millions in 1970	26	32	58
Second decade (as % of 1970)			
Output	not less than 240	133⅓	——
Labour productivity[b]	almost 200–225[c]	200–240	——
Labour force:			
Millions in 1970	26	32	58
Percentage increase +	+ about 15	− 30–40	——
decrease −			
Millions in 1980	30	19–22	49–52

[a] The calculations of the changes in the labour force are only rough owing to the nature of the data.

[b] Implied in the targets for output and labour productivity.

[c] A formula 'almost 100–125' does not make much sense but this is implied in the targets of a 'more than 100 per cent' rise for 1960–70 and an 'approximately 300–350 per cent' rise in 1960–80, and one naturally does not wish to meddle with official data more than absolutely necessary.

With the great rise in labour productivity in industry, the situation turns out very favourably for the industrial labour force. The targets for output and productivity in industry imply a rise in the industrial labour force in 20 years of only one-third to one-half. This compares with an increase of around 50 per cent in the 10 years from 1950 to 1960.

The corresponding data for agriculture imply a really fantastic development, if they were anything more than words on paper. For the

1960s the data of the 20-year plan imply an almost unchanged labour force in agriculture (for output we have a rise of "about 150 per cent" and for labour productivity one of "at least 150 per cent"), while in the next decade the labour force in agriculture, and consequently the whole farm population in about the same proportion, is to be cut by not less than 30–40 per cent. (This is expected to occur at a time when the real incomes of the peasants are rising fastest.) Ten to thirteen million workers (actually more because the figures for labour cited in the tabulation are not in physical terms but in units, and one unit is larger than one physical person) would be released from agriculture. What will happen about housing them? Is housing to be provided outside the village for this mass of people? And, most important, what will this mass of people be doing in the way of work and earning a living?

In two decades industrial and farm employment would go down from about 58 per cent of the total to little more than one-third. As the table shows, in the first decade industrial and agricultural labour together will increase by less than 10 per cent. The total access of labour may amount to say 20 per cent, and the economy, other than farming and industry, would have to expand its labour force by more than 30 per cent to make use of all available labour. Possibly it will be able to do so. We will not start guessing.

But the second decade shows an impossible situation. Industrial and farm labour together is scheduled to go down by 6–9 million. Employment other than industry and agriculture would have to double to take them in. The "planners" certainly did not realise it, but their beautiful plan implies unemployment on a vast scale.

Distribution

Of the roughly 10,000 words devoted to economics in the programme, a large part deals with the well-being of the population. "The CPSU puts before itself the task of world-historical importance—to insure in the Soviet Union the highest living standards as compared with any country of capitalism." It might easily escape the reader that the prospects are not quite so rosy, when one turns from words to examine the few figures given in the programme.

It must be remembered that the industrialisation drive was based on the severe exploitation and deprivation of the population, and that the share of personal incomes in national income was reduced by the time of Stalin's death to an incredibly low level and then held at approximately that level until today.

With all the great benefits, free lunches, etc., provided for the population in the programme, the extremely low share of personal income in national income is apparently going to remain almost stationary (an exact calculation is impossible because of inadequate data). The huge funds allocated for investment and the armed forces will grow (this seems to be implied in the data of the plan) only insignificantly less than personal incomes. Moreover, part of these incomes will reach the population in a form which will not be counted at full value (see below).

National income is scheduled to rise 5-fold in 20 years. (It is not stated, but is definitely implied in the combination of the rise in national income and the rise in personal incomes, that the funds in the hands of the State for investment and armed forces, huge even now, are to rise almost as much as national income, i.e., almost five-fold, during the same period.) This implies a per capita rise of 245 per cent during this period. Total per capita incomes of the population, which include all free public services, are to rise "more than 3.5-fold." The balance in favour of the population with reference to the distribution of the national income thus shifts only negligibly. The share of personal incomes, including free services, remains virtually at the low level at which it stood in 1960.

Real wages (targets for real wages include public gratuitous services throughout) are scheduled to rise by 200–250 per cent. The real incomes of the kolkhoz peasants (only few will be left by 1980 at the present rate of conversion of kolkhozy into sovkhozy), are to increase by more than 300 per cent.

Even a trebling of real wages in 20 years, the minimum "ensured" to hired labour in the plan, not to speak of the more than quadrupling provided for the kolkhoz peasants, would by no means be bad. But the fulfilment of the targets for real incomes obviously depends on attainment of the much too optimistic goals for output, especially for farm output. This dependence is even emphasised in the programme in reference to peasant incomes.

The policy of reducing the stratification of real wages is continued; it is indeed stated that by 1970 there will be no low-paid hired workers. The 7-year plan provided for the following increases in real wages:

>All hired labour, 40 per cent.
>Minimum wage, about 80 per cent.

The provisions of the new plan until 1970 are as follows:

>All hired workers, almost 100 per cent.
>Minimum wage, about 200 per cent.

The relationship in pay between minimum and average is more favourable in the new than in the 7-year plan. It must be remembered, however, that the 7-year plan is realistic and the new plan is not. The rate of increase in the minimum real wage is scheduled to reach by 1970 the level foreseen for increase in pay of all labour in 1980, but there is nothing about the course of the minimum wage in the 1970s. There are, however, provisions in the new plan which, if carried out, must further substantially improve the relative position of low-pay hired labour.

One feature of the new plan, potentially of importance, is the great increase in free services. Before discussing this point, it must be recalled that the rise in real wages is calculated *inclusive* of the "social funds." This phrase, however, is omitted from the statements on real incomes of the peasants. "Social funds" are the funds for providing gratuitous state services to the population. These are bestowed on the whole population, rather than on hired labour only. The reason for the use of different concepts in planning growth in real wages and the real incomes of the kolkhoz peasants is not made clear. Perhaps the peasants are not expected to get all gratuitous services.

The programme promises a vast expansion of these services. "In the movement towards communism, personal needs will be ever more satisfied at the expense of social funds of consumption; the rates of their growth will exceed the rates of growth of the individual payment according to labour." Some of the existing services are to be enlarged and a number of new ones added. Among the latter are the maintenance of children in children's homes and boarding schools (if the parents desire this), support of the disabled, free housing and some free communal services, lunches at the place of employment, etc.

Lack of space prevents a detailed examination. These services as a whole are to account by the end of the 20 years for "about half the total real incomes of the population." This phrase in the programme is given greater precision in an unsigned and consequently official commentary on the programme of great length in *Pravda,* 2 August 1961. According to this, social funds are to rise in 1960–80 "about eight-fold" on a per capita basis—a huge increase, if reached. A combination of these figures relating to gratuitous services yields the implication that the paid-out real wages are to be in 1980 about double those in 1960. The increase in cash payments is to be less, possibly much less, for those in the higher wage-brackets. It may be fairly assumed that the population would, in regard to at least many of these services, prefer cash, and that the relatively small increase in cash payments actually implies smaller rises of total wages than those stated in the programme. Since so much depends on the rise in the labour productivity of the better-paid labourer, the attempt to carry out the provisions for free services may become a handicap to growth in labour productivity, on the high targets for which the whole programme depends.

The fact that half of the real pay is to consist of gratuitous services, bestowed upon the population without regard to the amount of their labour, implies of course a great reduction in both stratification of real wages, and the differentiation in incomes between hired labour and kolkhoz peasants, especially since the wording of the programme seems to aim at reduced stratification in individual payments as well. If the minimum real wage paid out individually equals 50 per cent of the average wage payment, the total minimum real wage will have to be equal to about 75 per cent of the average total real wage. A full share in the gratuitous services on top of their incomes from the kolkhozy and their own farming enterprises would also mean higher incomes for the kolkhoz peasants. There is no indication how this difficulty is to be resolved, but it is impossible for peasants' incomes to differ substantially from the incomes of low-paid hired labour.

Expansion of gratuitous services is to go on after the expiration of the twenty years, and when all pay consists of gratuitous services, then, according to Mr. Khrushchev, there will be communism, the realisation of the principle "to each according to his needs." As compared with the ideas held for the last few hundred years, there is however this difference, that previously it was thought that the individual would himself decide what he needs. Now it turns out that the rulers will decree what the free Soviet population needs. A minor difference, to be sure.

Conclusions

Soviet planning is rich in bad plans. But to find an equivalent of the new "20-year plan" one has to turn back to Stalin's initial drive with its bacchanalian planning, the period called by this writer the All-Out Drive,[10] when in February 1932 an output of electric power of 100 billion Kwh was planned for 1937 (actual attainment, 36 billion Kwh), and this was by no means the only, or even the worst, target set in this period, which extended from Stalin's pernicious article in *Pravda* of 6 November 1929 to early in 1933. The deterioration in planning techniques in the new plan is especially marked as compared with the seven-year plan for 1959–65.

The question arises, how did all this get into the programme? It is impossible for real planners to have produced it. An explanation which seems least damaging is this: the Gosekonomsovet, with or without the participation of Gosplan, produced, on directions from above, a draft of the plan. Because these directions came from on high, the targets were made very optimistic, but probably the provisions were, if only crudely, tied in one with the other. The immense increases in productivity of farm labour may have been absent, and so, consequently, the precipitous decline in farm labour in the second planning decade, and so on. This crude draft was then, possibly very belatedly, taken to the central committee Presidium, where the planning "experts" drastically revised the draft. Mr. Khrushchev no doubt contributed his ideas on how agriculture

10 See *Soviet Industrialization*, 1928-52, Chapters 4 and 5.

had to develop. Tie-ins? Who at that level cares for them or understands the need for them? The real planners may not even have been given a chance to see this "plan" when the printers got to work, but they knew the moment they read the programme in the papers that the "plan" was absurd. Will they report their findings to Mr. Khrushchev? And will their advice be heeded?

In November 1957 Mr. Khrushchev announced the so-called general plan, in actual fact targets for the output of eleven industrial commodities, to be reached in about fifteen years. Even at that time the targets seemed not the product of serious prolonged work, co-ordinated with the probable development of the rest of the economy, but a hasty *ad hoc* affair, and they were dropped by March 1959 at the latest. The 20-year plan now announced seems no more serious. The targets for the eleven commodities constituted part of a pageant, the celebration of the 40th anniversary of the Revolution, and this function they fulfilled more or less successfully.

It looks very much as though the targets of the 20-year plan were designed to play the same part in the pageant called the XXII Congress of the CPSU. If the economic provisions were not incorporated in the programme, they might die at an even earlier age than the eleven targets of the 1957 general plan. Their incorporation in a more lasting document will make it more difficult to bury them, even if they become a corpse.

11

The Proclaimed Emergence of Communism in the USSR *

ALEXANDER S. BALINKY
Rutgers University

At the peak of the typhus epidemic that raged throughout western Russia during the winter of 1919, Lenin urged the Soviet people to action: "Comrades, either the lice triumph over socialism, or socialism will triumph over the lice!" [1] By inference he was thinking of the

* Reprinted from *Social Research,* Vol. 28, No. 3 (Autumn, 1961), pp. 261-282, by permission of the publisher.
[1] V. I. Lenin, "Report to 7th Congress of Soviets" (December 5, 1919), in *Selected Works,* vol. 8 (New York 1943) p. 72.

primitiveness, illiteracy, superstition, and economic backwardness that would have to be surmounted in order to build socialism out of a semi-feudal Russia. Four decades later, on January 27, 1959, Khrushchev informed the Twenty-First Party Congress that the "lice," so to speak, had been conquered. Proclaiming the period of socialist construction at an end, he declared that the Soviet Union was now ready to take its "first step into communism."

The emergence of communism had been periodically announced since the 1930s, and even earlier, but until now had been given little official attention beyond lip service. Khrushchev's 1959 speech, however, set the issue squarely in the limelight, and the Twenty-Second Party Congress, scheduled for October 1961, was assigned the task of formulating a new constitution that would reflect the emergence of a communist society. Communism, as contrasted with socialism, is envisaged in Marxist theory as having the following main characteristics: the "state" has "withered away"; there is economic abundance, with all the "reasonable and cultured" needs and desires of man met in full; everyone contributes to the best of his ability and receives according to his needs; the nature of man himself has changed (the "New Soviet Man"); physical and mental labor command equal respect; industry and agriculture are organized identically and run on the same principles; there is freedom from war, because there are no longer any capitalist imperialists.[2]

The fact that the USSR, in our eyes, has by no means met all, or any, of these requirements for the emergence of communism need not be belabored here, for this is one point on which there is unanimity of opinion among Western specialists on Soviet affairs. The intent of this paper is rather to answer three questions raised by this most recent Soviet development. First, how seriously does the Soviet leadership really take the broad issue of transition to communism? Second, why has Khrushchev chosen this particular moment in Soviet history to declare that the USSR is ready to enter a new era, the era of communism? And third, what is the likelihood of the USSR actually attaining full communism in the foreseeable future?

I

In the face of the realities of forty-odd years of Soviet rule, it is highly tempting to dismiss the secular eschatology of Marx and Engels as ritualistic nonsense. R. W. Campbell, for instance, says that "The vague Marxist goal of achieving communism is something they can make ritual obeisance to but their motivations and preoccupations are con-

[2] This is only a convenient summary of Section I of my article, "Has the Soviet Union Taken a Step toward Communism?" in *Social Research,* vol. 28, no. 1 (Spring 1961) pp. 1-14.

nected with more immediate problems." [3] Herbert Ritvo puts it even more bluntly: "Given the present nature of the party dictatorship, the vision of a future society where persuasion and sweet reason reign supreme must be dismissed as utopian nonsense at best, political cynicism at worst." [4] But to brush aside this ideological pillar of Soviet society, as so many do, is to obscure the importance of the psychological role it has played and continues to play in the lives not only of the Russian masses but, and especially, of the genuine Bolsheviks.

I do not wish to exaggerate the force that the promised land has had in luring the post-revolutionary masses to voluntary sacrifice. The absence of alternatives has been a far greater factor. But the dream has had and continues to have some effect. It is said that much of the power of the mediaeval church over the minds of men was based on its bipolar concept of heaven and hell, reward and punishment in the hereafter. Correspondingly in the communist world the spirit of the masses is anchored in anticipation of a terrestrial ideal—an anticipation that is strengthened by the utopian streak that has always been present in Russian thought. And the inevitable emergence of communism—as salvation not only from capitalist exploitation but from the admitted sacrifices pursuant to socialist construction—has been one of the few gratifications the Kremlin oligarchy has had to offer the Russian masses in any abundance.

But the hopes of the masses, according to Leninist doctrine, are not what really matters. During the period of the "dictatorship of the proletariat" it is the small, hard-cored, disciplined, and dedicated elite which provides the leadership for the march into communism. The rest follow. The true Bolshevik is propelled by the rainbow at the end of the road. It is to keep him on the right path—overcoming obstacles, warding off external and internal enemies of socialism, elevating the masses—that the communist utopia is essential. To dismiss the utopia as visionary propaganda is to forget that since the middle of the nineteenth century communist leaders have justified most of their actions by the Marxian apocalypse of an earthly paradise, one far richer, far more just, brotherly, and aesthetic than any that appeared in the blueprints of the Utopian Socialists. And for the true Bolshevik, belief in this utopia is not a simple matter of rendering lip service, of a mechanical recital of Marxist dogma. It is the force that drives him not only to personal sacrifice but to the imposition of sacrifice on others. Much in the manner of the early Christian missionary, it compels him to save souls, by kindness and persuasion if possible, by fire if necessary.

Thus if the opiate of utopia has done less than is assumed for the Russian masses, it has done more than is generally recognized for those

[3] R. W. Campbell, *Soviet Economic Power* (Cambridge, Mass, 1960), p. 8.
[4] Herbert Ritvo, "Totalitarianism without Coercion?" in *Problems of Communism*, vol. 9, no. 6 (November-December 1960).

who rule them. It has provided the Bolshevik with the simplicity of a single and known goal, and has immunized him from any scruples in attaining it by any or all means. By the splendor of its artificial illumination this vision of a radiant future has enabled the believer to soothe his conscience, resolve his doubts, and reconcile humane objectives with inhuman practices. In short, as so eloquently expressed by the Polish poet Czeslaw Milosz, it has enabled the Bolshevik to rationalize everything by the historic necessity of attaining the ultimate good.[5]

These, then, are some of the reasons why the "specter of communism" has never been permitted to fade out in the Soviet Union,[6] even during the darkest days of the civil war. As Schumpeter insisted, it is the assurance of inevitable salvation and not the cold economic logic of scientific socialism that has given Marxism its survival value and whatever universal appeal it may have.[7]

The point is sometimes made that while rank-and-file Bolsheviks may be motivated by a communist utopia, the sophisticates in the Kremlin are not. But the notion that Soviet leaders merely use the instrumentality of utopia, while cynically disbelieving it themselves, is not a tenable or at least a provable one. There is little basis on which to presume that men like Khrushchev are ordinary, if high-powered, pragmatists, out after personal gain in whatever form. Nor is there any solid ground for the view that Khrushchev has been able to escape from the hypnotic effect of dialectical materialism, or that he believes Marxism is meant only for lesser men.

Another view often expressed is that no *apparatchik* would believe in or work toward a goal that would render him powerless and place the entire governing apparatus in a museum alongside other antiquities. But to view the matter in this light is to ignore one of the characteristic

[5] Czeslaw Milosz, *The Captive Mind* (New York 1959), p. 225.

[6] On the eve of the Bolshevik revolution, Lenin reminded everyone that "Mankind can pass directly from capitalism only into socialism . . . but . . . our Party looks farther ahead than that: socialism is bound sooner or later to ripen into communism": V. I. Lenin, *The Tasks of the Proletariat in our Revolution,* published in 1917 (English ed. London 1932). The prospect of achieving communism surrounded the launching of the First Five-Year Plan in the spring of 1929, *Agitprop* succeeding to some extent in convincing the people that soon after the successful completion of the plan a "bright future" in the form of communism would begin to appear: see Wiktor Sukiennicki, "The Vision of Communism—Marx to Khrushchev," in *Problems of Communism,* vol. 9, no. 6 (November-December 1960) p. 8. In November 1936 Stalin announced "the complete victory of the socialist system in all spheres of the national economy," and concluded that "in the main we have already achieved the first phase of communism—socialism": J. Stalin, *Problems of Leninism* (Moscow 1947) p. 548. Again in March 1949, at the Eighteenth Party Congress, and in October 1952, at the Nineteenth Party Congress, it was officially proclaimed that the building of socialism had been completed, and that the Soviet Union was about to embark on communist construction: *KPSS v rezoliutsiiakh i resheniiakh sezdov konferentsii i plenumov TsK,* 7th ed. (Moscow 1954) Part 3, pp. 340 and 579.

[7] Joseph Schumpeter, *Capitalism, Socialism and Democracy,* 2nd ed. (New York 1947) pp. 3-8.

differences between Marxism-Leninism and other ideologies leading to a different brand of totalitarianism. Marxism-Leninism teaches its disciples that the emergence of communism is not something to be linked with any one man or group of leaders. Each individual, living in a particular historical moment and subject to immutable historical laws, has a specific role to play toward the attainment of the ultimate objective. As long as full communism remains in the future, as long as the Bolshevik can remain on his historical path in pursuit of the goal, his claim to total power is not threatened—especially since Leninist doctrine holds that communism is not achieved "by the subsiding of the class struggle, but by its intensification. The State will die out not as a result of the relaxation of the state power, but as a result of its utmost consolidation." [8] Thus Khrushchev, as a Marxist, can believe in the inevitability of communism and work for its realization free of the anxiety that the "dictatorship of the proletariat" may no longer be needed in his lifetime. And, as will be brought out later, Khrushchev has hedged even more by taking the position that while the state will wither away, the party will remain.

II

The crucial question, however, is less whether Khrushchev believes in the inevitability of communism than why he sees the Soviet Union of today as historically ripe for its emergence. According to available evidence, the current Soviet leadership has calculated that the attainment of its ultimate goal, world communism, can be facilitated by pushing up the time table for achieving communism in the USSR—and this, too, is consistent with the Marxian concept that while man cannot change the direction of history, he can shorten or lengthen the birth pangs involved in the arrival of a new social order. But why is the effort being made at this particular time?

The underlying factor in Khrushchev's decision to take the "first step into communism" now is directly related to the carefully measured (but non-linear) economic and political "liberalization" that has characterized post-Stalinist Russia. It is my contention that Khrushchev sees in a policy of imminent transition to communism at least a partial solution to the series of complex problems posed for the Soviet regime by the shift from coercion to persuasion. For purposes of clarity it is necessary, therefore, to consider the implications of this post-Stalinist "liberalization." In using the term I am referring to such events as the abolition of Stalinist-type slave-labor camps and the freeing of political prisoners; the relaxation of labor discipline; the downgrading of the secret police;

---

[8] J. Stalin, "The Results of the First Five-Year Plan" (January 7, 1933), in *Problems of Leninism* (Moscow 1940) p. 457. Stalin took this from Lenin, and Khrushchev has not repudiated this particular Stalinist view.

the program of two-way tourism, student exchange, and trade; the literary and artistic thaw (especially in 1956–57).[9]

A frequent and dominant explanation of such tendencies is that the Soviet Union, having passed the period of "primitive accumulation," has now reached a stage of economic development in which the earlier Stalinist instrumentalities of compulsion and negative incentives are no longer workable or effective.[10] Advocates of this position hold that a highly industrialized society cannot operate efficiently with the kind of submissively frightened labor force that the political circumstances of the preceding era tended to generate. To emerge victorious in all spheres of competition with the capitalist world, the Soviet Union, it is held, must have a permissive atmosphere in which initiative, imagination, and creativity can flourish.

A broader and more realistic interpretation, in my view, rests on the fact that by the early 1950s the Soviet regime had sharply reduced its fear of capitalist encirclement, and had succeeded in significantly narrowing the gap between the pre-revolutionary values of the Russian masses and the post-revolutionary socialist institutions. In other words, the USSR had passed from Lenin's fearful admission that "we are but a hair's breadth from some invasion" to Khrushchev's confident "Who is encircling whom now?"; [11] and the Bolshevik revolution had succeeded, as such revolutions can, in overturning in very short order almost all the existing social, economic, legal, and political institutions. What no such revolution can do, however, is to reshape the values, prejudices, and behavior patterns of the vast majority of the people in the same short span of time. Thus what Lenin and Stalin faced was the unavoidable post-revolutionary necessity of forcing the new socialist institutions on a people not ready for them—unavoidable, that is, if the revolution was to succeed. Marxist theory is entirely consistent on this point. It makes no assumption about the readiness of the masses for socialism, especially in a semi-feudal country where the centralizing and "civilizing" forces of a mature capitalism cannot even do part of the task Marx and Engels had in mind. Lenin and Stalin knew perfectly well that the Russian masses,

[9] An account of the specific nature of this "liberalization," or of the changing ratio of force to public control in economic, political, social, and legal spheres, is beyond the scope of this paper. The best summary of the earliest of these changes (1953–56) may be found in "Russia Since Stalin: Old Trends and New Problems," in American Academy of Political and Social Science, *Annals* (January 1956). For more recent evidence see A. Ulam, "The New Face of Soviet Totalitarianism," in *World Politics* (April 1960); Herbert Ritvo (cited above, note 4) pp. 19-29; L. Schapiro, "Has Russia Changed?" in *Foreign Affairs* (April 1960); and there are many others.

[10] See Solomon Schwarz, "Why the Changes," in *Problems of Communism*, vol. 9, no. 1 (January–February 1960) pp. 10-12.

[11] Lenin, *Collected Works*, vol. 27, p. 117, as quoted by Stalin in 1926; see the latter's *Problems of Leninism* (1940) p. 156. N. Khrushchev, *For Victory in Peaceful Competition with Capitalism* (New York, 1960) pp. 206-07; he asked the question in an interview given to a correspondent of *Le Figaro*, March 19, 1958.

90 percent of whom were peasants, had little comprehension of what the Bolshevik revolution was all about. The majority, ground into the dust by an oppressive and decadent czarist regime, wanted change. What the Bolsheviks had in mind was change on a scale undreamed of by the peasants.

The point is that once revolution occurs, it must bear the bitter fruit of a period of coercion, during which either the new takes firm root or is destroyed. This is what the Bolshevik means when he says that "you can't make an omelet without breaking eggs."

But even totalitarianism seeks legitimacy. Stalin's willingness to use terror does not, in itself, prove that he preferred tyranny as an end in itself. Ultimately every ruler or governing clique wishes to govern by the consent of the subjects rather than by permanent and exclusive reliance on brute force, and this preference is especially characteristic of Marxism and Bolshevism, because of their messianic nature. That the Bolshevik triumvirate has forced supreme sacrifices on the Soviet people for four decades is due principally to its intention to safeguard the socialist start on Russian soil as a base from which to launch a worldwide communist offensive. For the same period it has been engaged in the most massive program of "reeducation" yet witnessed by history. Under conditions of iron-curtain isolation, Soviet rulers have purged the incorrigible, intimidated the weak, cajoled the doubtful, rewarded the willing, and "educated" the newly born—all for the purpose of reducing the pre-revolutionary "vestiges" and instilling the values of communist morality.

The reduction of the gap between the socialist institutions and the pre-revolutionary values of the people has been a gradual, almost imperceptible process, one that Stalin was too old and rigid to take into account during the last years of his life. To borrow a term from Hegel, Stalin's death was the "node"—the point at which what is continually changing becomes suddenly and dramatically visible. On coming to power, Khrushchev undoubtedly had a mixture of motives for initiating a degree of "liberalization." His ability and willingness to do so stemmed, however, from a reassessment of the risk involved. He recognized that there now existed a significant acceptance of the Soviet way of life on the part of the majority of the people.

Though it would be illusory to deny that the Soviet regime has reduced the gap between the new and the old, this does not mean that the gap is entirely closed, that deviation or dissidence has entirely disappeared. Even official Soviet pronouncements do not go that far. There is an integral relationship between the Kremlin's estimate of the extent to which the people accept the current Soviet institutions and the degree of "liberalization" it is willing to permit. I cannot, therefore, agree with those who see in the thaw a tendency toward greater real freedom or a move in the direction of democracy as we understand it. Ideally, Khrushchev seeks to loosen the reins only to the extent that there is no danger that the Soviet people will use such relaxation to question or act contrary to the Kremlin's intent.

But this is precisely the point at which a delicate problem confronts the Soviet rulers. It is difficult, if not impossible, to know exactly the the ratio of acceptance to dissidence at a given moment in time. As the events of the past eight years have shown, there have been numerous occasions on which the Soviet leadership has been forced to tighten controls, because of miscalculation. Therefore, in order to reduce the risks involved in progressive liberalization, Khrushchev has seen the need for some noncoercive instrumentality as an aid to continued control. Proclaiming the emergence of communism appears to serve just such a purpose.

III

One aspect of "liberalization" has been the steady rise in the Soviet living standard. This has been occurring since 1953 despite the fact that one of the reasons given for Malenkov's demotion was his expressed desire to place more emphasis on the consumer-goods sector of the economy, as against Khrushchev who insisted on continuing the policy of concentration on the capital-goods industries. In a recent statement Khrushchev seems to have swung completely around to Malenkov's position, promising still greater emphasis on consumer-goods production.[12] This stress on material improvement has done more than meet some of the long neglected needs of the Russian people. It has excited their expectations. During a recent visit there I heard the expression *zaftra budit* (tomorrow it will be) with surprising frequency. In the many discussions I had with Russians in all walks of life, their interest in the United States centered around our material circumstances rather than our political philosophy. Some say that this was so only because the Soviet people are afraid to discuss the latter but not the former. I did not find that to be the case. It seemed to me that they were avidly interested in the material aspects of American life, and were genuinely far less concerned about our ideology.

In an atmosphere of "catching up with and surpassing America," expressions of desire, even impatience, for still greater material wellbeing have official sanction. Khrushchev, speaking to the workers of the Baltic Works in Leningrad, recently (1958) promised them an end to the housing shortage within ten or twelve years. A voice from the audience boomed out "Let's make it shorter," to which Khrushchev replied that it

[12] See Harry Schwartz in *The New York Times*, May 21, 1961, p. 26.

all depended on the workers themselves.[13] An incident of this sort would have been unthinkable, on several counts, during the Stalinist period. The present Soviet leadership is not only taking this craving for material improvement into account; it is encouraging it and, to some extent, catering to it. To be sure, it has given the party serious concern lest it take the form of "crass Western materialism," of which the leaders have always been so critical. Conveniently, however, Marx and Engels made economic abundance a key requisite for the realization of communism, and thus the increasing Soviet concentration on worldly goods can be seen as different from bourgeois materialism.

From the Soviet standpoint a high rate of economic growth and a continuing improvement in the living standard have, of course, a purpose quite beyond the mere satisfaction of consumer demand. Khrushchev points repeatedly to the economic progress taking place in the USSR as proof of the superiority of socialism over capitalism. He has been saying to the working class in every non-communist country what he said in July 1958 in East Germany: "There is an abundance of wealth for everyone in the world—it must simply be rationally and economically used. Marxism-Leninism teaches us that only under socialism can this wealth be most rationally used for the good of all the people. That is why we advise people who are living without a compass or with a faulty one: Throw your bad compass into the sea, equip yourself with our communist compass and take the road of building a new social system—the socialist system. You may be confident that the Marxist-Leninist compass will unerringly lead mankind to a radiant future." But, as he told two groups of Hungarian workers in April of the same year: "It is only by raising the productivity of labour that we shall beat capitalist production, demonstrate the superiority of the socialist system, and thereby create the conditions for building a communist society . . . [if only] the imperialists do not stick their pigs' snouts into our socialist garden." [14]

Thus an economic problem facing Khrushchev is how to increase the productivity of Soviet labor in the existing circumstances. For reasons already cited, he prefers not to rely so heavily as in the past on the negative force of coercive labor discipline. Recent evidence also indicates that, for a different set of reasons, he does not currently favor a further widening of income differentials or an extension of special non-monetary privileges as incentives to productivity. In fact, recent Soviet legislation has been directed toward: raising the national minimum-wage and social-security benefits; reducing the income differential between industry and agriculture; holding back any further rise in the income of the "elite" class; de-emphasizing piece-rate work that leads to sharp differences in wages in the same occupation; and even cutting back, some say, the high

---

13 Khrushchev in *For Victory* . . . (cited above, note 11) pp. 709-10.
14 *Ibid.*, pp. 538-39, 325, 297.

monetary and non-monetary earnings of those at the peak of the managerial and party hierarchy.[15]

The official Soviet view is of course that all this is a logical consequence of the process of transition to communism. Western analysts see it in quite a different light. Robert Feldmesser, for instance, explains these trends as part of Khrushchev's offensive to revitalize the force and insure the dominance of the party over all the other groupings in the USSR.[16] Specifically, Feldmesser believes that he has become fearful of *administrirovanie,* that is, of all the "little Stalins" whom the "big Stalin" created: Khrushchev now wishes to weaken or destroy those who, in a "highhanded, arrogant" way, exercise "petty tutelage over subordinates . . . gloss over shortcomings, suppress criticism and persecute critics," all with the aim of entrenching a hereditary caste that would be safe even from the party. Recently exposed cases of petty bureaucracy, embezzlement, cheating, falsification of statistics, stealing of state property, and "familyness" (as well as the newly legislated severity of punishment for such crimes) make Feldmesser's thesis appear credible indeed.

In addition, however, it seems likely that Khrushchev, having reason to avoid both negative and positive incentives in their traditional forms, has selected to rely (at least in part) on what some psychologists call the principle of the "goal gradient." In non-technical terms, this principle holds that as a person comes near the realization of a goal, his incentive to reach it grows stronger. There are known cases, for example, of prisoners who, after serving almost twenty years of a sentence, join a jail break a month before their legal release. Thus Khrushchev hopes that by bringing the long-promised but distant communist utopia almost, but not quite, within grasping distance, he will stimulate the Soviet people to greater productivity in order to make it all come true.

That "transition to communism" may serve as a non-specific incentive to productivity is given increased plausibility by the prevailing mood of optimism that exists in the USSR today. The Soviet people, in the main, do not judge their present or future economic circumstances by what exists in the Western world. Rather, they measure progress by what they have had, what they have now, and what they are told they are going to receive. And by their norms there has been welcomed improvement. (In discussions with Soviet citizens I was struck by the extent to which their knowledge about the American standard of living is distorted. It seems

[15] See Decree of July 12, 1954, in *Sbornik Zakonov SSSR i Ukazov Presidiuma Verkhovnovo Soveta SSSR* (Moscow 1959) pp. 411-13, 505-06; *Pravda,* September 9, 1956, June 21 and November 14 and 25, 1958; *Izvestia,* April 4 and June 6, 1959; *Komsomolskaia Pravda,* March 20 and April 6, 1956; Lazar Volin, "Reform in Agriculture," in *Problems of Communism,* vol. 8, no. 1 (January–February 1959); *Voprosy Ekonomiki,* no. 2 (February 1959) pp. 80-88, 113-22, 143-49.

[16] Robert A. Feldmesser, "Equality and Inequality under Khrushchev," in *Problems of Communism,* vol. 9, no. 2 (March–April 1960) pp. 31-39.

to go to extremes, and is often inconsistent. I have been asked such questions as "Is it true that every American has two automobiles?" and "Do Americans have enough to eat?" In one case I was asked both of these questions by the same individual. The degree of distortion increases as one goes deeper into the provinces.) Further, the Soviet regime is reenforcing the prevailing optimism by creating experimental islands of communism at the present time. The Red Proletariat Foundry in Baku, of which I have already written in this journal(note 2, above), is one important case in point. Beyond that, several communities called "agro-towns" have been erected and populated; their residents live in specially designed buildings suitable for the type of communal living envisaged under full communism.[17] The noted Soviet economist S. Strumilin has written an important piece outlining what life will be like when communism is achieved, and in fact, Soviet literature is replete these days with details about the society of the very near future.[18]

IV

Economic considerations are not the only ones behind the decision to move up the arrival of communism. Isolation and expansionism are mutually exclusive. During most of the Stalinist period, when the emphasis was on building and securing socialism within the USSR, contact between the Soviet masses and the rest of the world was not only unnecessary but risky from the Bolshevik point of view. Today, with the focus on Soviet imperialism, the Kremlin is forced to lift the Iron Curtain for those on both of its sides. Soviet leaders cannot expect to spread communism throughout the world without sending large numbers of their own people into the target areas. Nor can they hope to sell their socialist system by example without allowing visitors from the noncommunist world. It will be recalled that it was the USSR, and not the Western nations, that initiated the idea of tourism and cultural exchange.

Given the USSR's current international objectives (especially in the context of peaceful coexistence), the Stalinist variety of iron-clad control over the Soviet people no longer appears possible or desirable. This does not mean that no control is needed, but it does mean that the cir-

17 See B. Svetlichny, "Designing Beautiful Cities," in *Nauka i Zhizn* (Knowledge and Life), no. 9 (1960); A. Zhuravlyev and M. Fyodorov, "The Micro-District and New Living Conditions," *ibid.*; A. Obraztsov, "What Will our Future Cities Look Like?" in Nedelya (Weekly), December 25, 1960.

18 S. Strumilin, "Communism and the Workers' Daily Life," in *Novy Mir* (New World), no. 7 (1960). Three important works on transition to communism written by Soviet scholars are: A. Loginov, "Chitaia knigu o kommunizm," in *Kommunist*, no. 12 (1960) pp. 111-18; D. I. Chesnokov, *Ot gosudarstvennosti k obshchestvennomu samoupravleniiu* (Moscow 1960); S. Strumilin, *Rabochi den i kommunizm* (Moscow 1959).

cumstances of the present phase of Soviet development require a greater
emphasis on self-control and self-discipline on the part of the population,
both those at home and those sent abroad. There is no doubt that some
measure of broadening is produced by the relative freedom with which,
say, American tourists, students, and delegates speak with Soviet citizens
(and vice versa) or bring pro-Western literature and ideas into the Soviet
Union. The Soviet leaders would much prefer that the Soviet citizen remain immune from such contamination as a matter of conviction and
acceptance of his own system to his doing so through continued fear of
the secret police. It is in this context that Khrushchev speaks of the
imminent "withering away" of the various organs of the state. What he
wants is a greater reliance on the people, as distinct from the external
control of the state, in the matter of enforcement of communist morality.
This is why there has been so much talk, and some action, about the
establishment of such para-police and para-judicial public organizations
as the Brigades of Communist Toil, the People's Militia, the Comradely
Courts,[19] and why there has been renewed interest in the role of the
aktivist, the citizen who not only obeys the rules of communist morality
but takes it on himself to see that others do the same thing.

The official explanation for the vigor with which the party is currently
urging the people to "work and live like true communists" appears in
the following quotation from an eminent Soviet scholar: "Despite the
connection and mutual relationship between the material and moral
foundations of communism, the former develops more quickly than the
latter. . . . We will in the near future attain the abundance and surplus
of consumer goods which are necessary. . . . A much more difficult
matter, which will take much more time, will be to form in every member of society the inner necessity to work and live in a communist
manner." [20] In other words, the stage is all set for the appearance of
communism, if only the people will begin to behave accordingly. This
official position is derived from the Marxist materialist interpretation of

[19] There is by now a good deal of Soviet literature dealing with these public organizations, which are expected to replace the existing state organs. On Brigades of Communist Toil see *Pravda,* June 1, 1960; *Voprosy filosofi,* no. 10 (1959). On the People's
Militia see *Pravda,* March 10, 1959; *Izvestia,* June 24, 1959; *Kommunist,* No. 10 (1960);
Komsomolskaia pravda, August 30, 1960. On the Comradely Courts see *Izvestia,* September 10 and October 24, 1959; *Pravda,* January 28, 1959. For Khrushchev's position
on the significance of these public organizations see his speech to the Twenty-First
Party Congress, as reported the following day in *Pravda,* January 28, 1959. For a non-
communist interpretation of the meaning of these organizations (with which I do not
entirely agree) see R. Schlesinger, "The Discussion of Criminal Law and Procedure," in
Soviet Studies (January 1959).

[20] Ts. Stephanyan, "Stages and Periods," in *Oktyabr,* no. 7 (1960). The same point
is made by S. Strumilin in *Novy Mir* (cited above, note 18). The best analysis of the
whole role and concept of the New Soviet Man may be found in an excellent little book
by Hadley Cantril, *Soviet Leaders and Mastery over Man* (New Brunswick, N. J., 1960).

history, which holds that change occurs first in the economic substructure, then, after a lag, in the superstructure of human behavior.

Soviet leaders recognize, however, that obstacles remain. One such obstacle to the fuller development of a society of New Soviet Men is the progressive disappearance of whatever revolutionary élan the Soviet masses may have had in the past. I believe that Professor Cantril puts the matter too strongly when he writes (note 20, above) that "The danger facing Soviet leadership is . . . a passive and apathetic attitude of its citizens toward it. The revolutionary élan has largely disappeared and may almost completely evaporate before long" (pp. 85-86). It is a fact, however, that the mood of the Soviet people today is one of wanting to reap the fruits of their earlier sacrifices. The forces that once provided a common goal (real or fancied danger, World War II) are greatly reduced. In a far broader sense than simply increasing labor productivity, the Soviet regime has been forced to find some new approach to revitalizing the waning revolutionary spirit. It appears to have found it in a policy of more rapid moving into communism.

Political liberalization and a rising living standard have posed a very special ideological problem as well. As noted earlier, "the inevitability of communism" and the concepts associated with it (such as "worker control," "withering away of the state," "the leap from necessity to freedom") have never been allowed to die out as ideological slogans. In recent years, however, national communism in Yugoslavia, revisionism in Poland, revolt in Hungary, and the beginning of a faint intellectual thaw in the USSR itself have awakened the Soviet leaders to the fact that their own ritualistic phrases contain two-edged swords. Dissident Marxist elements outside the Soviet Union have been turning such promises as the withering away of the state and a classless society into weapons with which to fight Soviet totalitarianism and imperialism. That the party leaders have been annoyed, if not concerned, over this issue may be seen from the following quotation: "The problem of the withering away of the . . . socialist state is the main thesis, indeed a veritable *idée fixe,* of contemporary revisionism. No sooner does the question of the state arise than they steer it to the issue of the withering away." [21]

In turn, the Soviet people too, experiencing material improvement, have been asking pointed questions about the specific nature of the promised land. Thus *Kommunist,* the theoretical organ of the party, declares (no. 12, August 1960) that communism must not be oversimplified or turned into "harebrained plans," that "The days of utopia, or arbitrary flights of fancy, have passed, giving way to higher responsibility in analyzing reality and in foresight" (p. 113). In that same issue *Kommunist*

---

[21] *Voprosy filosofii,* no. 4 (1960) p. 14.

described (p. 117) what communism will not be like: it will *not* be that "you rise in the morning and you begin to reflect: where shall I go to work today—to the factory as the chief engineer, or shall I gather and lead the fishing brigade? Or perhaps fly to Moscow to conduct an urgent session of the Academy of Sciences?"

Apprehensive of what such flights into fancy might lead to, the party has found it wiser and safer to take this ideological bull by its utopian horns and give it a specific and desirable content. And when Khrushchev announced the arrival of the first stage of communism to the Twenty-First Party Congress he also took pains to stress that it was not to be a "vulgar, . . . formless, unorganized, and anarchic mass of people. No, it will be a highly organized and arranged cooperation of workers . . . [with everyone] fulfilling his functions as a laborer and his social duties at a determined time and in an established order" (*Pravda*, January 28, 1959). Transition to communism has thus come to serve the purpose of keeping the expectations of the Soviet people in check and purging the heretical elements outside the party.

Deviation from the Moscow interpretation of Marxism-Leninism is far from the only problem confronting the Communist Party of the Soviet Union in its relations with other communist-bloc nations. A very practical problem is that many of the East European satellites have not been progressing along the path of socialist construction at a rate fast enough to satisfy the Kremlin. Khrushchev has found the policy of transition to communism useful in this connection as well—although I doubt that it was designed expressly for this purpose. In a concerted effort to spur socialist construction and reduce existing resentment and disaffection, Khrushchev has been saying to each of the satellites he has visited that the path the USSR has followed is the historically correct one, as proved by the fact that it is now ready to enter communism, and if the other socialist countries wish to arrive at the same destination they must pattern themselves after the Soviet model. He has been telling them:

Comrades, the victory of world communism is beyond all doubt. The task that now faces all of us is to advance toward the cherished goal under the Marxist-Leninist banner. And since we march along a single path—face one and the same task—there is and can be no antagonism, no competition between us. We must work in unity and intimacy, hand in hand, in order to build communism. Our socialist countries are, however, at different stages in their advance toward communism. Up to now the building of socialism has been completed only in the Soviet Union. But I can assure you that we have no intention of entering communism alone—of eating ham every day while the rest of you look on and lick your chops. That would be immoral and wrong. The more developed country must help those who are less developed. The more we help each other the quicker communism will triumph everywhere. But you must do your share. You must develop your socialist economy and increase labor productivity in order to equalize and eliminate differences. Then, and only then, shall we all be able to enter communism together along a united front.[22]

Khrushchev has been trying to make a somewhat similar point with the Chinese communists. After the Russian Revolution the Bolsheviks tried and discarded the commune as the basis for organizing economic life. Early experience indicated that the masses were not ready for the commune system, which requires of its participants (among other things) a degree of socialist mentality and behavior presumably possible only after living in a socialist environment for many years. Thus the conclusion was reached that to begin with communes before completing the period of socialist construction would be to begin backward. But communist China, until very recently, insisted on using the communes in agriculture, despite Moscow's persistent urging to the contrary. By claiming the successful end of socialist construction in the USSR and the beginning of the "first stage of communism," Khrushchev has, in effect, been saying to the Chinese communists: "As you can see by the fact that we have already arrived, there is only one correct way to attain true communism—our way."

These, then, are some of the practical, pragmatic reasons underlying Khrushchev's decision to move up the time table. It is reasonable to presume that after the October 1961 meeting of the Twenty-Second Party Congress, and the ratification of the first communist constitution, further advantages (as well as some disadvantages) of this policy will come to light. Thus far, on net balance, transition to communism, resting comfortably on ideological belief in its historic inevitability and desirability, seems to be serving some highly useful purposes for the Soviet leadership.

v

What is the likelihood of the USSR actually attaining full communism in the foreseeable future? Any attempt to provide even a reasonably full answer to that question would require an analysis and evaluation of every aspect of Soviet society, a task that is entirely beyond the scope of this paper. There is one sense, however, in which the question can be answered more easily. I venture the guess that full communism will indeed be attained in the USSR in the near future—*by definition.* The four key features of communism are: the withering away of the state; economic abundance; from each according to his ability, to each according to his needs; and the New Soviet Man. As briefly as possible I shall indicate below how each of these features is being currently interpreted

---

[22] This quotation is entirely in Khrushchev's words, but since he often repeated himself, even in identical words, I have drawn passages from various of his speeches; see his *For Victory* . . . (cited above, note 11) pp. 323-24, 327, 350-51, 506, 511, 537, 545-46, 574-75, 697, and 731.

or reinterpreted to enable the Soviets to declare full communism a reality within the general time limit (1970–80) that has recently been set.

One of the principal reasons why so many non-Marxists have scoffed at the Marx-Engels vision of a communist utopia has been the common-sense notion that no modern society can possibly exist without a state or some form of government and law enforcement. From the Soviet point of view, Khrushchev has resolved the problem. While advocating the gradual extinction of the state organs, he has also stated (in *Pravda,* February 16, 1958) that "The party has stronger foundations than the state organs. It arose and exists not as a result of obligations of a legal order. Its development was called for by circumstances derived from political concepts, and mankind will always be in need of moral factors." Thus the state will indeed wither away, quite as Marx, Engels, and Lenin predicted. But the party, about which Marx and Engels had nothing to say in this connection, will remain forever, being rooted, as Khrushchev now finds it, in communist morality.

The requirement of economic abundance has also been given a specific meaning that makes communism appear more likely. Taking the slight cue provided by Engels, Khrushchev has enlarged on the idea that economic abundance does not mean an economy of "free goods" in the technical sense in which bourgeois economists use the term. His position, as stated in his speech to the Twenty-First Party Congress (*Pravda,* January 28, 1959), is that "When we speak of satisfying the needs of people, we have in mind not the whims and desires for luxury but the healthy requirements of a culturally developed man." The party, which never disappears, remains of course the arbiter of what is to be regarded as a whim and what constitutes the real needs of a cultured man.

The communist dogma "from each according to his ability, to each according to his needs"—which entails a break in the functional relation-ship between productivity and reward—is a somewhat more complicated proposition to reinterpret. By way of an official effort the current tendency is to point to the growing share of welfare expenditures in the total governmental budget.[23] Such items as medical care, education, old-age pensions, holidays are, by their very nature, more closely tied to need than to contribution. An expansion of such services, coupled with a few dramatic gestures such as free bread and free public transportation, could easily be cited by Soviet authorities as evidence of one or another stage of a communist system of distribution. (I have heard talk, in the Soviet Union, that bread may soon be placed on the free list and, after that, public transportation. This is not surprising in light of the fact that rent has been virtually free almost from the inception of the Soviet regime; the rental charge for workers has been negligible and, according

[23] See Alec Nove, "Toward a 'Communist Welfare State?'" in *Problems of Com-munism,* vol. 9, no. 1 (January–February 1960) pp. 1-10.

to some reports, is soon to be abolished entirely.) In the meantime, however, Khrushchev is saying that the traditional system of incentives is still necessary in order to reach fully an economy of abundance.

Finally, there is the thorniest problem of all—attainment of the New Soviet Man. Anyone who is even casually acquainted with recent Soviet developments is aware of the drive to force behavior into the mold of communist morality, and the severity of the penalties for failure to comply. The Soviet view is that the publicity given to acts contrary to communist morality in no way indicates a rise in vestigial behavior. And official statistics on the secular decline in crime and juvenile delinquency are cited as proof. The current campaign is explained as the final grand effort to get rid of the remnants of bourgeois mentality and behavior in order that full communism may emerge on schedule.

Should this offensive fail or fall short of expectation, there is still, however, a possibility of maintaining the myth—a possibility coming from the Soviet people themselves. Perhaps it was best stated in a fascinating book by Joseph Novak, a recent defector from the communist world. Telling of the fact that the party regards divorce among its members as a violation of communist morality, Novak says: "But our married couples anxious to part aren't so stupid. They try to give reasons for their desire to divorce which won't harm them, which may even improve their reputations in some places. They use political, ideological, social, and labor excuses, and lie like old veterans. For instance, a case will come up . . . where . . . a husband applies for a divorce. His reason? His wife . . . refuses to 'improve her intellectual and political standards by attending an ideological course organized by the union.' The husband continues to give examples of the 'political backwardness' of his wife, quoting views allegedly uttered by her." [24]

Over the years of Bolshevik rule, the Russian people have found many ways of adjusting and adapting their thinking and behavior to new and often sudden conditions and requirements. It may yet be that, in order to survive, they can find even more subtle means by which to make the fiction of a communist utopia appear real—at least real enough to satisfy their party leaders.

[24] Joseph Novak, *The Future is Ours, Comrade* (New York 1960) p. 63.

12

Transition from Socialism to Communism: Economic Aspects *

MAURICE DOBB
Trinity College, Cambridge, England

From time to time in the past the criticism has been levelled against Marxism that it had no clear blueprint of what a socialist economy would be like. Marx was himself careful, it is true, to avoid the errors of the "utopian socialists", and of what he sometimes called the "sectarian socialists", and emphasised that the precise shape of the new society, since it was an historical product, could not be defined until one was confronted by the actual situation from which it would directly emerge. In this he was being realistic. Concrete circumstances, as we know, modify cases (we may recall Lenin's well-known saying: "Whoever expects a 'pure' social revolution will *never* live to see it."). In his famous *Critique of the Gotha Programme* in 1875 (criticising some of the "Lassallean" formulations in the draft programme of the new unified German Workers' Party) Marx indicated some of the broader features of that new society, but no more.

Today we have before our eyes socialist societies (in being or in the building) over more than one-third of the world; and we now have also the first tentative blueprint for making the transition to Marx's "higher phase of communist society" a century after he wrote the *Critique of the Gotha Programme*. Critics can no longer complain of lack of definiteness; instead, some of them perform a *volte-face* to utter cries about "unrealistic utopian promises", "propaganda wishful thinking in service of the cold war", etc. But some people like to have it both ways.

Socialist Society

We may remember that in the *Critique* Marx emphasised that in the first stage after the social revolution "we have to deal with . . . a society,

* Reprinted from *Marxism Today,* November, 1961, pp. 340-345, by permission of the author and the publisher.

not as it has *developed* on its own foundations, but, on the contrary, as it *emerges* from capitalist society; which is thus in every respect, economically, morally and intellectually, still stamped with the birthmarks of the old society from whose womb it emerges". Economically, a leading consequence of this is that the share of each individual in consumption will depend on the amount of labour he gives to society (wages according to amount and quality of work). The total consumption fund of society available for distribution among its members can never equal the total social product; since from the latter has to be deducted the product needed for the expansion as well as replacement of means of production (also for a "reserve or insurance fund against misadventures", for maintaining "non-productive services" such as health and education, and for pensions). These deductions were described by Marx as "an economic necessity", and their amount as "determined by available means and forces, and partly by calculation of probabilities, but in no way calculable by equity". The individual worker or producer accordingly "receives back from society, after the deductions have been made, exactly what he gives to it . . . his individual amount of labour". In *this* sense (by contrast with capitalist society) there is "equal right" as between all workers; but it is equal *only* in relation to labour as a standard of judgement, and men are unequal physically and mentally, and, hence, in the labour they can supply. This "limitation on equal right", "inevitable in the first phase of communist society [i.e. socialism] as it is when it has just emerged from capitalist society after prolonged birth pangs", can only disappear

"after labour, from a mere means of life, has itself become the prime necessity of life; after the productive forces have also increased with the all-round development of the individual, and all the springs of co-operative wealth flow more abundantly" (Marx, *Critique of the Gotha Programme*).

In 1917 Lenin was to enlarge on this in his *State and Revolution*, but he did not add materially to it as regards the conditions that would make a transition to communism possible. In connection with the simultaneous "withering away of the state", he speaks of

"such a high stage of development of communism that the antithesis between mental and physical labour disappears, that is to say, when one of the principal sources of modern *social* inequality disappears—a source, moreover, which cannot be removed immediately by the mere conversion of the means of production into public property, by the mere expropriation of the capitalists.

"This expropriation will *facilitate* the enormous development of the productive forces. And seeing how capitalism is already *retarding* this development to an incredible degree, seeing how much progress could be achieved even on the basis of the present level of modern technique, we are entitled to say with the fullest confidence that the expropriation of the capitalists will inevitably result in an enormous development of the productive forces of human society.

But how rapidly this development will proceed, how soon it will reach the point of . . . removing the antithesis between mental and physical labour, of transforming labour into 'the prime necessity of life'—we do not and *cannot* know."

He added: "The question of length of time, or the concrete forms" of the further transition to communism must for the present be left open "because there is *no* material for an answer to these questions". (Further on he says: "The political difference between the first, or lower, and the higher phase of communism will in time, probably, be tremendous; but it would be ridiculous to take cognisance of this difference now, under capitalism; and only isolated anarchists, perhaps, could invest it with primary importance.")

Soviet Experience

Today there *is* material, at least for part of an answer of these questions. In the first place, the growth of the productive forces of the Soviet Union has by now laid the basis for a sharp increase in the consumption fund of socialist society, and, hence, in the standard of life and of individual culture—this despite the devastation of two world wars and invasion, and the continuing diversion of huge resources to guard against a third. This is the basic historical fact which has enabled the new programme of the C.P.S.U. to forecast a sufficient state of economic affluence by 1980 to permit such important elements in the standard of life as canteen meals, public transport and houseroom to be supplied free according to the principle of "to each according to his needs", as well as a great extension of medical services and health facilities and the maintenance of the old and the young and the disabled.

Meanwhile, the experience of building socialism has yielded, in addition to much-enhanced productive power, certain lessons about the path and methods of socialist development, which were not (nor scarcely could be) available before.

Firstly, there was the lesson of the prime importance of continually raising the productivity of labour and to this end improving and modernising technique. From this followed the importance of maintaining the rate of expansion of the sector of industry producing capital goods (Marx's Department I): if its rate of growth were to be seriously reduced, then (except in so far as new techniques have so-called "capital-saving" effects) the expansion of the economy as a whole must be reduced. We know that today in the Soviet economy (and in most other socialist countries) the disparity in growth-rates between the two main sectors or departments of industry is much smaller than it was formerly, especially in the pre-war and immediate post-war years; but so-called heavy industry continues to take the lead.

At the same time, on the basis of past achievements in expanding the output capacity of fuel and power and steel and engineering, it is now possible to maintain also a high rate of expansion of consumer goods industries and of housing. The previous serious lag in agricultural production, especially livestock, has meanwhile been overcome. Thus, the scarcities and austerities of the pre-war period (and the immediate post-war years) have come to be things of the past; and attention has been directed towards a reduction of income differentials for different grades of work by raising the lower grades and basic rates relatively to the more highly paid. It is also clear that during the past decade the difference between rural and urban incomes has been considerably narrowed by an increase of the former at a proportionately higher rate.

Secondly, there has been the lesson that commodity production and market exchange (and, hence, value-categories and the "law of value") continue under socialism. This is not only because of the existence of the "two forms of socialist property" (collective farm property in agriculture and state property in the means of production in industry), but because of the sale of consumer goods on the retail market, where wage and salary earners (as well as collective farmers) who receive their incomes in cash "realise" these incomes and exercise free consumers' choice. (Clearly, wage differentials would lose much, if not most, of their force as economic incentives if this were not so.)

In the discussions of the last few years it has been emphasised that the importance of commodity production and of market categories, and with this the use of economic incentives in production, will continue and even increase during the transition from socialism to communism. An illustration of this is the revision a few years ago of tax scales and prices for collective farmers which had previously been exerting a negative effect on agricultural production (and the draft programme refers to the continuing need to keep "the level of state purchase prices" high enough to ensure "greater incomes for *kolkhoze*" and sufficient encouragement to them to raise labour productivity). Similarly in industry there have been changes designed to associate the interests of workers more closely with the productive results of their own factory, especially as regards increased efficiency and improved quality. With greater decentralisation of economic administration and planning since 1957 this question has acquired added significance.

Says the draft programme:

"It is necessary in the course of constructing communism to make full use of commodity-money relations in keeping with their meaning in the period of socialism. In this, such instruments of economic development as cost accounting, money price, production-cost, profit, trade, credit and finance play a big part. . . . There will be a further strengthening of the monetary and credit system. . . . The price system should be continuously improved. . . . Prices must, to a growing extent, reflect the socially necessary outlays of labour, ensure return of productive and distributive expenditures and a certain profit for each enterprise that is operating normally. Systematic price-reductions based on growth of labour productivity and reduced costs of production are the main trend of price-policy in the period of constructing communism."

Planning

Thirdly, socialist economy has acquired experience of planning methods which enable the general statements of Lenin nearly half a century ago about "social accounting and control" to be transformed into much more detailed precepts and rules. This greatly enriched experience of three decades of planning both gives a firmer knowledge of the internal structure and relations of the productive system than a capitalist state can ever have, and provides also the instruments whereby balanced and proportional development can occur, harnessing the full potential of productive capacity and steering its growth in such a way that excess capacity and oscillations do not occur. (This is not to say that planning is always perfect and makes no mistakes: it is to say that it has a *potentiality* altogether different in kind from a capitalist system.)

This is the basis for the kind of forecast of the next twenty years contained in the new Soviet programme, and forming, indeed, its keystone; and this is why these are not just "forecasts" and "guesses" such as we know in the capitalist world with its "anarchy of production", but are sober, even conservative, estimates, based on projecting into the future the possibilities that planning experience has already revealed as actual and realistic. In connection with planning, the programme emphasises the need for further improving "the scientific level of planning, accounting, statistics and industrial designing", with particular reference to increasing the effectiveness of investment (a matter on which there has been much recent discussion) by "the choice of the most profitable and economical trends in capital construction, achieving everywhere the maximum growth of output per invested rouble, and reducing the time-lag between investment and the return on it". ("Cybernetics, computers and control systems must be introduced on a large scale in industry, research, designing, planning, accounting, statistics and management.")

Reference is also made to the need to combine centralised planning, which concentrates on the setting of "key targets" and on "co-ordinating and dovetailing plans drawn up locally" with "economic independence and rights of local organs and enterprises", with an increasing role for "plans and recommendations made at lower levels" and with "timely correction and amendment of plans in course of their fulfilment". Not only "extension of operative independence and *initiative of* [industrial] *enterprises* on the basis of state plan-targets", but "direct and most active participation of *trade unions* in elaborating and realising economic plans" and in "management of enterprises" at both top level and lower levels is emphasised.

The "Two Forms of Socialist Property"

It should be explained, perhaps, that a few years ago there was a good deal of discussion about the question of the "two forms of socialist property" in agriculture and of their future in the course of the transition to communism. Stalin in his *Economic Problems of Socialism in the U.S.S.R.* of 1952, while repudiating proposals that collective farm property should be nationalised, spoke of the need "to raise collective farm property to the level of public property", on the ground that the existence of collective farm property, with the commodity relations connected with it, was already "beginning to hamper the development of our productive forces . . . since they [i.e. the commodity relations] create obstacles to the full extension of government planning to the whole of the national economy including agriculture". Linked with this contention went the proposal to substitute for market relations between industry and agriculture some form of direct "products exchange".

In the discussions of the following years the view gained ground that, instead of the perspective of collective farms being converted at some stage into state farms, *both* forms of property should undergo development and evolve into a new and common socialist form.

Thus, at the time of the transfer of Machine and Tractor Station property (machinery) to the collective farms, Ostrovitianov wrote as follows:

"It is becoming clear that co-operative collective farm property can grow into the common form of property belonging to the whole people without being turned into state property. . . . The idea has gained currency in recent years that commodity exchange is incompatible with the prospect of going over from socialism to communism. Such a formulation of the question is wrong."

The new programme says of the collective farm system:

"The *kolkhoz* blends the personal interests of the peasants with common, nation-wide interests, individual with collective interests in the results of production. . . . It is essential to make the most of the possibilities and advantages of the *kolkhoz* system. . . . The *kolkhoz* is a school of communism for the peasantry. Economic advancement of the *kolkhoz* system creates conditions for the gradual *rapprochement* and, in the long run, also for the merging of *kolkhoz* property and the property of the whole people into one common property."

Some Misconceptions

Some possible misconceptions about the nature of communism are removed by the draft programme. Some might suppose that communism would be an anarchic, entirely go-as-you please, *Cannery Row*-kind-of-existence, in which only the conscientious or the "squares" worked and the remainder did as they pleased—a sort of *beatnik* paradise. In fact, it is stated that

"Communist society, which is based on highly organised production and advanced technology, alters the character of work, but it does not release the members of society from work. It will by no means be a society of anarchy, idleness and inactivity. . . . Communist production demands high standards of organisation, precision and discipline, which are ensured, not by compulsion, but through an understanding of public duty, and are determined by the whole pattern of life in communist society. . . . Labour will no longer be a mere source of livelihood—it will be a genuinely creative process and a source of joy."

Some might suppose that individual property in means of consumption would disappear as well as property in means of production. On the contrary, we are told that while "people's requirements will be satisfied from public sources . . . articles of personal use will come into the full ownership of each member of society and will be at his disposal".

Some might (indeed do) suppose that all individual differences will be ironed out, and everyone be made to conform to a uniform pattern in his mode of life and in what he consumes. On the contrary, "the purpose of communist production is . . . to provide all its members with material and cultural benefits according to their growing needs, their individual requirements and tastes". The difference will be, not that individual variations disappear or are ignored, but that increasingly "people's requirements will be satisfied from public sources".

In case old *canards* about communism and the family should be revived, it is worth noting the statement that, since "communism is the system under which . . . (man's) best moral qualities blossom forth and reveal themselves in full . . . family relations will be freed from material considerations and will be based solely on mutual love and friendship".

In case, again, some should argue that in talking of such changes Communists are ignoring human nature (an old gibe), it should be stressed that there is no proposal to abolish economic incentives at one stroke. The programme realistically states that:

"Proper combination of *material and moral* incentives is a great creative factor in the struggle for communism. In the course of the advance to communism the importance of moral labour incentives, public recognition of achieved results and the sense of responsibility of each for the common cause will become continuously greater."

Be it noted that they will "become greater", but their increase will be a gradual process, and they will replace the former only to the extent that they have sufficiently developed and matured.

The Economic Basis of Transition

What, then, can be said to be the material basis on which the notion of a forthcoming transition from the socialist stage of development to a yet higher stage is based? Is this transition conceived as coming suddenly, in a single dramatic "leap", or coming gradually step by step? And what are to be the outward and visible signs of the change?

It is to be noted that the programme is careful to state that "the C.P.S.U., being a party of scientific communism, proposes and fulfils the tasks of communist construction in step with the preparation and maturing of the material and spiritual prerequisites, considering that it would be wrong to jump over necessary stages of development, and that it would be equally wrong to halt at an achieved level and thus check progress. The building of communism must be carried out by successive stages".

Quite clearly, the material basis for the transition can be nothing else than the growing abundance of consumer goods (and of other elements in the standard of life) as a result of expanded productive power and heightened productivity of labour. This will make possible shorter hours of work, greater leisure, new attitudes to work as well as new cultural and moral standards. A leading feature of the transition will be a rise in the specific weight of socially-provided services and facilities as elements in the standard of life, compared with commodities and services provided through the market (i.e. sold in shops or realised at a price in exchange for the money incomes of citizens). At the same time, the "two forms of socialist property" of which we have spoken will tend to come closer together as a result of changes *both* in the organisation of collective farms (and of other forms of co-operative production) *and* in state-owned agriculture and industry in the direction of greater decentralisation and democratisation. The effect of greater mechanisation will simultaneously be to diminish greatly the number of laborious unskilled manual jobs. With such changes it is the intention to narrow existing differences in monetary rewards by raising the lower categories towards the level of the highest, and to assimilate both conditions of work and the consumption level of the rural population to urban conditions and standards.

Says the programme:

"The disparity between high and relatively low incomes must gradually shrink. Increasingly large numbers of unskilled personnel will become skilled, and the dwindling difference in proficiency and labour productivity will be accompanied by a steady reduction of disparities in the level of pay. As the living standard of the whole population rises, low income levels will approach the higher, and the disparity between the incomes of peasants and workers, low-paid and high-paid personnel and the populations of different parts of the country will gradually shrink."

At the same time

"personal needs will be increasingly met out of public consumption funds, whose rate of growth will exceed the rate of growth of payments for labour. . . . The transition to communist distribution will be completed after the principle of distribution according to one's work has outlived itself, that is when there is abundance of material and cultural wealth and labour has become a prime necessity of life for all members of society."

This material basis for the transition is no wishful thinking, but represents the level of production *per capita* of the population which can be reasonably expected two decades from now (given that peace is maintained) as a result of extrapolating into the future the production-increases of recent years. A few figures and some simple arithmetical calculation will show this to be so. Gross industrial output in recent years has been increasing in the U.S.S.R. by 10 per cent or slightly more per annum (with production of capital goods by 11 or 12 per cent and of consumer goods by about 8 per cent)[1]. The national income has been increasing (on the average of the last five years) by 8 per cent.

This growth-rate is somewhat higher than was envisaged by the seven-year plan for 1959–65, which provided for an annual increase in gross industrial output of 8.6 per cent; amounting to a rise of 80 per cent over the seven-year period as a whole. (The increase in the whole national income over the seven-year period was to be between 62 and 65 per cent, and in "consumption expenditure" between 60 and 63 per cent.)

Forecast of the Next Two Decades

To come to what is said about future economic growth in the draft programme: this provides for a rise in industrial output of 150 per cent over the next ten years (i.e. by the end of 1970). This level would be attained with an annual (compound) rate of growth over the coming decade that was somewhat *less* than that of the past five years (say, just over 9 per cent instead of 10 per cent). In *this* sense it is a cautious target, and by no means fanciful and optimistic as some Western commentators (including some on the B.B.C.) have maintained. This level of industrial output would substantially exceed the *present* level of U.S. industrial output; and unless U.S. production grows during the coming decade appreciably faster than its growth-rate during the past decade, the Soviet level would by then surpass the U.S. level *of that year* (1970).

[1] *Planovoe Khoziaistvo*, the Gosplan journal, in its issue for September (1961, No. 9, p. 9) states that 10.6 per cent has been the mean yearly growth of industrial production for the last sixteen years; that Soviet industrial production in 1960 was 60 per cent of the American; and that the Soviet Union will reach 106 per cent of the present American level by 1966 and 156 per cent of that level by 1970 if Soviet industrial production continues to grow at 10 per cent per annum.

The same can be said of what is forecast for the *second decade*. A continued annual (compound) rate of growth of 10 per cent per annum would raise production by the twentieth year to a level of rather *more* than six times the present level: i.e. raise it by more than 500 per cent. In the draft programme 500 per cent is given as the increase in industrial production by the year 1980 (and 400 per cent as the increase in total national income). This will involve raising labour-productivity in industry over the two decades (mainly through improved technique) by three times, or rather more, to a level that will be about double the present U.S.A. level; and labour productivity in agriculture by more than five times (probably the most difficult to forecast of all).

At the same time efforts will be concentrated

"on ensuring a rapid increase in the output of consumer goods. The growing resources of industry must be used more and more to meet fully all the requirements of Soviet people and to build and equip enterprises and establishments catering for the household and cultural needs of the population. Along with an accelerated development of all branches of light and food industries, the share of consumer goods in the output of heavy industry will also increase.[2] More electricity and gas will be supplied to the population. . . . Output of consumer goods must meet the growing consumer demand in full, and must conform to its changes."

On this basis it is estimated that the real income *per head* of the population will increase by more than two-and-a-half times by 1980.

Thus, it is hoped and anticipated that by 1970 the Soviet Union "will surpass the strongest and richest capitalist country, the U.S.A., in production *per head* of the population", that the housing problem will be solved, and "the U.S.S.R. will have the shortest working day", thereby "creating the material and technical basis for communism".

In the *following* decade (1971–80) "the material and technical basis of communism will be created and there will be an abundance of material and cultural benefits for the whole population". In consequence "Soviet society will come close to a stage where it can introduce the principle of distribution according to needs, and there will be a gradual transition to one form of ownership—public ownership". The threshold of the communist stage of society will have been reached. In the period subsequent to this "the construction of communist society will be fully completed".

This is not a romantic picture of a leap from one stage of development into the next; but a carefully graduated phasing of development in which consequences are made to follow upon pre-conditions, and future achievement is related to present and past achievement to form a rational and realistically-grounded pattern of advance.

2 Presumably this is a reference to so-called "consumers' durables" from refrigerators and washing machines to motor-cars.

Human Wants and Use-Values: Capitalism and Socialism

A general question arises here, of some interest to economists at least. As the productive power of a country grows and the supply of consumer goods becomes more abundant, there is a sense in which the use-value aspect of these goods becomes more important as compared with their aspect as exchange-values. Some economists of the marginal utility school have even been apprehensive about a possible conflict between these two aspects. A leading member of the Austrian school, Friedrich von Wieser, towards the end of last century, spoke about the "antinomy" between use-value and exchange-value; pointing out that as the supply of goods in relation to wants became sufficiently abundant (i.e. as the *satisfaction* of wants grew) they would tend to lose their exchange-value. This is, of course, a prospect to be feared by bourgeois economy.

One may remember that Marx in a different context spoke about capitalism halting the increase in productive power "at a point determined by the production and realisation of profit, not by the satisfaction of social needs". For obvious reasons too great an increase of production creates a problem for capitalism—a problem which it meets either by concerted measures to restrict production or by measures to boost effective demand (often in a quite artificial manner). Thus, in recent years there has been a great deal of anxious discussion about ways in which capitalism can be kept going (surplus value continue to be "realised", in Marxist language) by pressurising consumers to buy what salesmen want to dispose of and by creating various forms of social waste.

Hence, the important role in modern capitalist society of the "admen" and the "hidden persuaders", the attempts to cultivate a social atmosphere of competitive emulation among consumers in buying new gadgets and maintaining standards of expenditure which are valued for the social prestige or status they yield, rather than for the real human wants they satisfy. Hence, the popularity not only of armament expenditures by the state but of what one may call "premature obsolescence" of durable goods (scrapped before they are worn out because meantime a new style or model has been introduced and everyone is under pressure to have the latest thing). Hence, also the kind of wasteful expenditure that the American writer Thorstein Veblen called, with intentional pomposity, "conspicuous consumption" and "honorific waste". All this, liberally bolstered up by the hire-purchase system and a growing structure of hire-purchase credit, has become an organised system under modern capitalism, whereby the conflict between growing productive power and consumer demand is staved off for a while. With it go a whole tribe of moral distortions in the social life of modern society which it is not in place to describe at the moment, but which are only too patently before our eyes.

It is, perhaps, a commonplace to say that the problem of abundance is no problem for a socialist society (provided that the necessary changes in the structure of production can be planned sufficiently far ahead). On the contrary to being a problem, it confronts socialist society with a unique historical opportunity—the opportunity of beginning a transition to a yet higher phase of socialist society. And if there should remain any doubt in anyone's mind as to whether this statement is true, the issue will be tested by the facts of development in the Soviet Union over the present decade and the next.

Can it be this that the champions of the so-called "free world" of unplanned private enterprise, on both sides of the Atlantic, at present so reluctant to contemplate an international *détente* and disarmament, are really afraid of?

SOVIET VIEWS

13

The Problem of Abundance and the Transition to Communist Distribution *

I. ANCHISHKIN
Institute of Economics, USSR Academy of Sciences

"The highest goal of the Party," states the Program of the CPSU, "is to build a communist society which will have as its banner: 'From each according to his abilities, to each according to his needs.'" In this basic thesis of our Party, one finds the end of the entire struggle of the working class for a revolutionary transformation of society, and this thesis expresses the highest and ultimate goal in fulfilling its historical mission. From this thesis also follows that one of the most important tasks in building communism is the growth of socialist distribution into communist distribution. . . .

* From *Voprosy Ekonomiki*, 1962, No. 1. Translated in and excerpts reprinted from *The Soviet Economic System: Structure and Policy*, U.S. Joint Publications Research Service. May, 1962, Vol. IV, pp. 127-146.

The Universal Abundance of Products and
Communist Distribution

The basic condition for a transition to communist distribution is the creation of the material and technical basis of communism. In order to solve this fundamental question of communist construction, one must erect a first rate production system based upon the extensive utilization of the most recent achievements of science and technology, and the complete application of up-to-date production equipment. As a result of solving this task, the society will possess a highly mechanized extensive production system which will provide a high level of labor productivity, a short working day and a universal abundance of products. . . .

Abundance serves as a basis for the complete and general satisfaction of needs for consumer goods on the part of a highly aware and cultured man in a new society. It presupposes an abundant, high calorie and richly assorted food which corresponds to the demands of science and which contains all the necessary food elements in the required amount and combination. It should be tasty, varied and healthy, and have nothing in common with the primitive gluttony of curs or the perverted gourmandism of today's plutocrats who do not know how to fill their belly —either with nightingale tongues and oysters or the trout delivered thousands of kilometers by airplane.

Universal abundance presupposes that each member of society will obtain a sufficient amount of high-quality, comfortable, practical and handsome clothing, undergarments, footwear, etc. But here abundance in no way presupposes superfluousness or extravagance. For satisfying the needs of a cultured person, he need not have scores of suits, shirts or dozens of pairs of shoes. In the aim of providing the fullest mechanization of labor in housework, we are extensively developing the production of home equipment and machines, the need for which will also be determined within reasonable limits. No one need have several electric ranges, washing machines, vacuum cleaners, refrigerators, etc. The possibility of free access at any time to the needed item from the public store room makes the accumulation and hoarding of these things superfluous and unthinkable. This equally relates to clothing and footwear.

Abundance also means the full satisfaction of the needs of the members of society for ordinary cultural goods such as radio receivers, television sets, pianos, musical instruments, bicycles, motorcycles, etc. The need for the amount of these goods designed for a definite purpose and requiring expenditure is limited by the possibilities of each family for their placement and practical utilization. And, finally, abundance presupposes the satisfaction of people's needs for housing and home comfort.

This is the most complex of the tasks linked with achieving full and complete abundance, but it as well undoubtedly will be solved, regardless of all the difficulties.

In reviewing the problems of abundance, there arises the question of how one should understand the complete and thorough satisfaction of the needs for the members of society? We can look into this through a few examples. Due to the development in technology there is appearing a new and improved type of television set. But as long as they are producing only experimental models, it is impossible to satisfy the given need for many of them right away. The same thing can take place in regard to many other articles, the demand for which cannot be fully satisfied until mass production has begun. Here such instances will be more probable and frequent the more rapidly technology develops. And the problem of satisfying the demand for rare items is even more complex. Admirers of old valuable things, collectors and people who value unique antiquities will probably exist under communism. We will also find "collectors" who would like to surround themselves with pictures by Leonardo da Vinci, Michelangelo, Raphael, Rembrandt, Rubens, Repin, Surikov, Levitan and others. It goes without saying that such "demand" cannot be satisfied.

There will possibly be other instances when society cannot satisfy such "needs" for individual persons. But this in no way means a violation or a negation of the communist principle of distribution according to need. The communist principle of distribution cannot be considered the caprices of individual persons, and it consists of completely and generally satisfying the needs of conscientious and cultured members of society for mass produced consumer goods. Its realization should be possible under two conditions: in the first place, with the universal abundance of consumer goods, and, in the second place, with a high conscientiousness of people. Therefore, the transition to communism, the communist education of the members of the society assumes particular significance. . . .

The Gradual Character of Creating an Abundance and the Transition to Communist Distribution

An abundance of consumer goods cannot arise all at once for all products and for all citizens in a socialist society. It is created gradually in a dual relationship: in the first place, with the development of the productive forces, abundance encompasses over a definite sequence a greater and greater number of goods; in the second place, it is spread throughout a greater and greater circle of workers on the basis of realizing the socialist principle of distribution according to labor. Approaching the question concretely, it is essential to determine in what sequence any good will be created in abundance for all members of society. There is every reason to suppose that at the beginning there will be an abundance of material goods, and then cultural goods.

As production grows, the socialist society will gradually move from an abundance of some goods to an abundance of others. Here, an abundance of any product is achieved more rapidly the less the expenditures of labor required for its production and the smaller the amounts of it needed for satisfying the demands of a person. . . . Thus, the production of meat and milk products generally requires greater labor expeditures than the production of bread or certainly potatoes. Therefore, the complete satisfaction of demand on the part of the entire population for meat and milk products becomes possible significantly later than the satisfaction of demand for bread and potatoes. On the other hand, the cost of tea, coffee and different specialties is higher than the cost of meat and milk products, and nevertheless the demand for the former products can be completely satisfied much earlier, since they are consumed in small doses.

It can be fully assumed that abundance will be achieved first for such food items as potatoes and vegetables, bread, and then meat and milk products, and confectionary goods. As for clothing and the materials necessary for manufacturing it, abundance will first of all be achieved for cotton articles and later for natural silk and wool. An enormous role in the rapid and complete satisfaction of these needs will be played by articles from synthetic fibers, due to the great savings in labor from replacing the natural raw product with them.

The satisfaction of the need of members of society for well-equipped housing is an even more complex problem, since it requires great expenditures. The total solution to this task will therefore be achieved after the complete satisfaction of the other needs of people.

In the Soviet Union, consumer goods are distributed according to a differentiated system, related to the quantity and quality of labor expended by each citizen capable of working. As a consequence of this, the products are distributed unequally. Some people can buy the most essential, the less varied and cheapest consumer goods, while others can acquire more varied and sufficient food products, by limiting themselves to a good degree in clothing and footwear. Finally, a small group of skilled specialists and individual highly qualified workers can purchase many consumer goods in abundance according to their need. In a word, in carrying out the socialist principle of distribution there is a complex differentiation in the degree of satisfaction of demands for the members in socialist society. Now, for example, livestock products are not produced in an amount sufficient for the complete satisfaction of demand for all members of society. When this will be achieved, then once again through distribution according to labor, each person will also obtain these products corresponding to his need. Thus, gradually on the basis of achieving an abundance in any consumer good it is possible to carry out even with the distribution according to labor the complete satisfaction of demand for all Soviet citizens for these products. Consequently, not all at once for all products, but gradually and in a definite sequence we will achieve an abundance of consumer goods for all.

The creation of abundance means not simply increasing the mass of consumer goods, but above all presupposes greater and greater variety and an improvement in the quality of the products. The complete and thorough satisfaction of the needs of members in a socialist society basically changes the structure of personal consumption. The demand for high-quality products is increased, new consumer goods appear, and one reduces the proportional amount of goods which are extensively consumed when there is a characteristic low level of prosperity for the masses. . . .

At present in our nation prosperity is becoming the achievement of many; in time, when the wages for the lowly paid workers will be raised, it will become possible for all Soviet workers. The question of the day is to create abundance and to accomplish this it will require the solution to many complex questions. . . .

The growth in the productive force of social labor is a basic condition for creating an abundance of products. The less the labor expenditures require for producing each product, the more rapidly it will be achieved. From here it follows that a systematic reduction in production costs is the decisive precondition for spreading abundance over the entire large circle of workers in a socialist society. For achieving general abundance, one must pay particular attention to rapidly reducing the cost of livestock products (meat, milk items, wool, leather, etc.), and also clothing and footwear on the basis of development of the industries producing these consumer goods. Therefore, a rise in agriculture, and in particular an important branch like animal husbandry, and the rapid development of industry producing consumer goods at present comprise the basic task in the struggle for changing the socialist principle of distribution into the communist one.

Under contemporary conditions, the cost of the type abundance still significantly exceeds the income of the workers with average skills in the Soviet Union. The average budget for a working family in our nation is still below the budget of abundance, that is, a family income which would make it possible to acquire the material and cultural goods according to need.

In the area of distribution, the most important feature of changing socialism into communism is the gradual liquidation of actual material inequality. . . .

Overcoming the Actual Material Inequality and Leveling the Income Level for Workers

At present in our socialist society there still exists a significant difrentiation between workers according to qualifications and wages. In the transition to communism, this wage differentiation will gradually be liquidated. But the differences in the skills of the workers and their general and special training cannot be completely eliminated. . . . However, under communism, the inequality linked with differences in qualifications will disappear in the distribution of products.

At the definite stage of the gradual transition from socialism to communism, the distribution of products will cease to correspond to the quality and quantity of expended labor. . . . Society will still not be in a situation to move as a whole to the distribution of consumer goods according to need, but it will already distribute them not in strict accordance to the quality and quantity of expended labor. . . .

In a socialist society, since the production of consumer goods is still insufficient for completely meeting the needs of all citizens, the very distribution according to labor is a consumption measure, and most likely, also a measure for limiting it. Communism, however, on the contrary, removes the limitation in consumption and here consumption itself becomes its own measure. It is also a measure of need. . . .

The process of establishing actual material equality for the members of a socialist society is long and complex, and it reflects deep social and economic changes which are occurring in the transition from socialism to communism. This process will be complete only with the construction of a communist society, when on the basis of a rapid increase in the productive forces and the abundance of products, we will establish a communist principle distribution according to need. This task will be solved completely when a communist society can provide complete and full automation of production and liquidate the existing differences between mental and physical labor.

"In the second decade," states the Program of the CPSU, "we will achieve an abundance of material and cultural goods for the entire population, and we will create the material preconditions for a transition in the subsequent period to the communist principle of distribution according to need." . . .

14

The Moral Code of the Builders of Communism *

ANATOLIY BEZUGLOV
Soviet Journalist

We are on the threshold of communism. Communism! For centuries this, for the best sons of mankind, was a dream, a bright and attractive dream but only a dream, and only likely to come true in the very remote future. Philosophers, writers and ardent revolutionaries persistently and courageously sought the path which would lead to a social system in which all working people could lead a free and joyful life, and where material and spiritual assets would abound. This system has been found —it has been outlined by Marx and Engels. Along the unexplored path to this goal Lenin and the Party of Communists have led the working people. Today the dream and the reality have approached each other . . . The new program of the CPSU—this profoundly scientific and profoundly practical plan for building communism—proposes to achieve this in the main over a period of 20 years. This means that it will be not some beautiful strangers but, we and our children who will have the honor of being the first citizens of a communist society.

What sort of people must we be to enter this bright future? We agree, every day and everywhere one can come across people for whom the moral code of the builders of communism has become the law of their lives. Some go to sea in bad weather to save victims from a shipwreck, others argue with the doctors that it is precisely their skin that is suitable for grafting on to a patient, others go to a team at a factory that is lagging behind to help their comrades become first-class workers, or leave a comfortable flat in Moscow to go to Siberia to work on a building project, or rush to rescue people from a burning house, or risk their lives to stop a train, or dive into icy water to save someone's life. All this is done for the sake of a human being, for the sake of someone who more likely than not is just a stranger, yet is regarded as if he were a next-of-kin. All this

* From a radio broadcast delivered over Radio Moscow on May 11, 1962, as part of the series "The Moral Code of the Builders of Communism." Abridged and translated under the title "What We Shall Not Take with Us into Communism," in *Radio Free Europe/Munich, Research and Evaluation Department, Background Information USSR,* May 30, 1962, pp. 2-6. Excerpts reprinted from the translation by permission of Radio Free Europe.

is done for the common weal. For these people the road to communism is open, they are worthy of communism and they constitute the overwhelming majority of our people.

But . . . there are among us others who have goals different from this. It is easy to recognize them by their words, life and actions. With them everything is subordinated to their own selfish interests. Such concepts as faithfulness, justice and honesty are but empty sounds to them. Although they are few in number, and with every day they are becoming fewer, such people do still exist. I remember that when the "Komsomolskaya Pravda" public opinion poll asked readers the question "Have you any aim?" the editorial office received thousands of letters, fine, warm letters testifying to the richness of the soul of the young Soviet citizen. Yet what a discordant note was sounded in a letter from a building engineer in Askhabad. He wrote: "My aim is to lead a life of pleasure, to build a career . . . I get R.210 in new currency; soon I shall be arranging to marry the daughter of a senior official: this promises me a 'Volga' and a further advance in my work." Career, a "Volga," advance in his profession—for these things this man is prepared to stoop to anything. He is prepared to arrange a marriage, precisely "to arrange" . . . The main thing to him is that the girl of his choice is the daughter of a senior official. That is how cynics and careerists argue. . . .

But whatever path they choose, each of them is equally loathsome and incompatible with the standards of the communist attitude to work, to life and to people . . . They are on the look-out for every chance to defraud: they are not above cooking the wage accounts, entering the names of non-existent people and obtaining money for them; they are not above using timber earmarked for the building of a factory, to build their own country house. They are capable of stealing expensive components in short supply, . . . collective farm grain, and their conscience will not stir, or, to be more precise, they simply have no conscience.

People of this kind are not condemned in a world where dog eats dog because bourgeois morality puts up with the fraud, deceit and hypocrisy. But in our country where men are friends, comrades and brothers, there is no room for such behavior. With us respect and mutual trust are the basis of relations between people. Today at many Soviet enterprises the services of a cashier are no longer used to pay wages. In cinemas in hundreds of towns and villages, ticket checkers have been done away with. In almost every industrial center there are enterprises where workers have been put on their honor to hand over the completed product without technical checking. These and other similar facts in our life show the visible features of the communist future.

But there are also those who abuse this trust, who act dishonestly, unscrupulously. Yes, unfortunately, there are. As a rule, passengers pay their fares without any reminder, but there are those who try to get a free ride . . . It seems to me that a "free rider" does not always understand that acting dishonorably, he is deceiving both himself and the society as a whole. Surely, the money from passengers' fares does not go into the pocket of some private employer but the State, and the Soviet State uses the money in the interests of the whole people . . .

Will it thus be the frontrankers, the fully aware people, who will march forward into communism, leaving the others lagging somewhere behind? No, this will not happen. The Communist Party has solemnly proclaimed: The present generation of Soviet people will live under communism. So it will not be just the chosen ones, but all—the whole generation—which will live under communism. Our Party has set us this historic task . . . The point at issue is to educate everybody and not just some in the spirit of communism. This is why the moral code of the builders of communism provides that the norms of behavior of Soviet man must include an uncompromising attitude to injustice, sponging, dishonesty, careerism. . . .

V

SOVIET AGRICULTURE: PROBLEMS AND PROSPECTS

FROM THE days of the first attempts to collectivize Soviet farms to the present, agriculture has been the millstone around the neck of Soviet economic progress. Even from 1953 through 1958—the years of the greatest advances in Soviet agriculture—the rate of growth of the agricultural sector lagged far behind that of the industrial sector and was barely adequate to take care of the increasing population and the increased demand resulting from enhanced purchasing power. The bumper crop of 1958 made the Soviet planners unduly optimistic. In spite of increased efforts on their part, agriculture lost ground during the following four years and actual performance fell substantially behind plans.

Why has the nation that has astonished the world with its economic successes in the field of heavy industry been unable to match its accomplishments in the vital area of food production? Will agriculture remain an impediment, blocking the road towards the promised era of abundance for all? Or will the Soviet Union eventually be able to achieve its hoped-for abundance of agricultural output?

In the first two selections, Roy Laird and Alec Nove discuss what to each of them appear to be the major difficulties encountered by the USSR in its operation of the agricultural sector. Each of them evaluates some of the recently introduced measures aimed at improving agricultural performance. And each of them, while granting the likelihood of increased agricultural output and the *theoretical* possibility of great strides forward, is rather pessimistic that anything close to the plans envisaged by the 22nd Party Congress will be accomplished in the foreseeable future. In the third, briefer, selection, Radio Free Europe addresses itself specifically to the decree of June 1, 1962, that raised the retail price of meat and butter, a decree that was taken throughout the Western world as clear evidence of the failure of the agricultural system of the USSR.

Although Soviet authors, in general, never fail to point out how far Soviet agriculture has progressed since the days of the Czars, they admit that progress in that economic sector has left much to be desired and that rapid advance has now become a matter of great urgency if their other goals are to be accomplished. They also acknowledge the present superiority of United States agriculture but they disagree with Western economists on the extent of the superiority, some of the major reasons for it, and the outlook for the future. They proclaim their confidence that the Soviet Union can achieve its plans for agriculture—although some concede that it may take somewhat longer than originally envisaged.

In the section on *Soviet Views* below, Braginskii and Dumnov challenge some Western claims that labor productivity in American farming is eight to twelve times that of the Soviet level, but even by their own computations arrive at a three to one ratio. There is little doubt in their minds, however, that the discrepancy is but temporary. Once the advantage of the United States in the areas of agricultural mechanization and electrification has been overcome, socialist agriculture, they are convinced, will prove its superiority over capitalist farming methods.

In the final selection on Soviet agriculture, the Central Committee of the CPSU and the USSR Council of Ministers defend the necessity of raising the price of meat and butter. They explain that the shortage of these consumer items was brought on by a combination of factors: a rapid growth in population, a considerable rise in the purchasing power of the masses that resulted in a substantial increase in the per capita demand for meat and butter, and a procurement price paid by the government to the collectives so low that the raising of livestock was unprofitable. Confident that higher procurement prices would induce farmers to devote more time to livestock raising and that increases in farm productivity would soon cut costs of production, the Party Central Committee and the USSR Council of Ministers proceeded to decree for that purpose increases in the price of meat and butter. (Note that simultaneously a decree was issued lowering the prices of sugar and of rayon textiles.)

15

Soviet Goals for 1965 and the
Problems of Agriculture *

ROY D. LAIRD
University of Kansas

In view of the impressive rate of Soviet economic growth during the past three decades, it seems likely that the Soviet leaders may make good their promise "to catch up with and surpass" the United States' level of production. Although estimates vary, most analysts agree that in recent decades the rate of Soviet industrial growth has been two to three times as rapid as that of the United States. The present Seven-Year Plan, to be concluded in 1965, aims at approaching American economic output in all sectors. Even in the troubled area of agriculture, the achievements of recent years appear to have been considerable.

Table 1, prepared by the Soviet analyst Artemii Shlikhter, gives Soviet agricultural advances over 1953, Soviet projections for 1965, and a comparison with United States levels of output.[1]

In the development of the Soviet economy thus far, nearly all growth has been in industry, achieved at the expense of the agricultural sector of the economy. As the Soviet writer A. Koriagin reports, in the "pre-war years (1930–1940)" and the "post-war years 1947–57, the volume of industrial production increased by an average of 16.2 per cent per year, and that of agriculture by a little more than 4 per cent." [2] These figures

* Reprinted from *Slavic Review*, October, 1961, pp. 454-464, by permission of the author and the publisher. References to Russian authors, articles, and books (in letters of the Russian alphabet in the original article) transliterated especially for this reproduction by Professor Laird.

[1] Artemy Shlikhter, "Nekotory voprosy sorevnovaniya mezhdu SSSR i S Sh A v selskom khozyaistve," *Mirovaya ekonomika, i mezhdunatodniye otnoshenia*, No. 9 (Sentyabrya, 1959) pp. 33-51. A condensed version of this article appeared in *The Current Digest of The Soviet Press*, Vol. XI, No. 36 (October 7, 1959) pp. 3-8 & 13. According to Khrushchev the plan for 1965 involves a 70% rise in agricultural output by 1965. *Pravda* (January 28, 1959) pp. 2-10.

[2] A Koryagin. "O sootnosheny tempov razvitiya promishlennosti i selskovo khozyaistva SSSR," *Voprosi ekonomiki* No. 3, 1959, p. 43.

TABLE 1

| | U.S.S.R. | | | U.S.A. |
	1953	1958	1965	1958
Gross Grain harvest (mil. tons)	82.5	139.5	164.0-180.3	179.8*
Including:				
Wheat (mil. tons)	—	75.4	—	39.8
Raw cotton (mil. tons)	3.5	4.4	5.7-6.1	Approx. 7.0
Meat and lard (slaughter				
weight; mil. tons)	5.8	7.9	16.0	16.4
Milk (mil. tons)	36.5	57.8	100.0-105.0	56.8
Butter (thous. tons)	497.0	770.0	1150.0	687.0
Wool (thous. tons)	235.0	321.0	548.0	134.0
Eggs (bil. units)	16.1	23.5	37.0	64.0

* Harvests of wheat, corn, barley and sorghum for 1958. The 1958 grain harvest far exceeded the usual harvest. In 1957 the harvest came to 158,200,000 tons, including 25,900,000 tons of wheat.

do not reveal that most of the 4 per cent "average" increase in agriculture has come about since 1954—"largely," as Shlikhter recognizes, because some 100,000,000 acres were newly plowed in the virgin lands campaign.[3]

Shortly before his death Stalin admitted that, unless corrected, the backwardness of agriculture "will hamper the continued growth of the productive forces of our country more and more as time goes on." [4] Acutely conscious of this problem, Khrushchev has devoted more attention to improvements in agriculture than to any other economic objective. However, impressive though his list of innovations is, Khrushchev has refused to adopt any scheme that would fundamentally alter the Stalinist collective system or abandon the priority given to industrial growth.

In spite of the recent gains in total agricultural output, the needs of a population of some 210,000,000, increasing by nearly 4,000,000 a year, are not yet satisfied. The widening gap between industrial and agricultural growth has made ever sharper demands on agriculture. As Khrushchev acknowledged late in 1958, "A definite lack of correspondence developed between the development of industry and agriculture, and between the actual needs for grain and other products by the government and their real levels of production. This divergence carried the possibility of serious consequences. It could have inhibited further rise in socialist industry, improvement in the living standards of working people, and the advance of our country to communism, and this in the long run would have weakened the economic power of the Soviet Union and the entire socialist camp." Suggesting that the problem belonged to

3 Shlikhter, *op. cit.* Both the 1959 and 1960 harvest in the new lands were disappointing.

4 J. Stalin, *Economic Problems of Socialism in the U.S.S.R.* (Moscow: Foreign Languages Publishing House) 1952, p. 76.

the past, Khrushchev nevertheless went on to say that "overcoming the lag in agriculture, and the need for a sharp upsurge therein was not only of internal but of international significance." [5]

According to the Seven-Year Plan, agriculture will virtually close the gap with industry by 1965. Soviet plans are regarded as law; moreover, it is a myth of the system to look upon plans, once made, as virtually carried out. There is no such restriction upon the analyst outside the Soviet Union, and to this writer there seem to be some serious weaknesses in the plan.

Many Western economists assert that the problems of Soviet agriculture arise chiefly from the lack of economic incentives for the kolkhozniki (the peasant members of the collective farms). It is true that much of the recent increase in agricultural investment has gone to the kolkhozniki. It is asserted that their real incomes advanced 60 per cent between 1952 and 1958; [6] but the 1952 level was so low that the increase still does not provide adequate incentives.[7] By 1965 a further rise of 40 per cent is anticipated. However, the economic burden of purchasing the machinery of the MTS, in the absence of further rise in agricultural prices, makes such a further increase in incomes unlikely.

In 1952 Stalin argued that the indirect subsidy of the collectives through state investments in the MTS was so large that if, as two of his economists suggested, the machinery were to be sold to the farms, the effect "would be to involve the collective farms in heavy loss and ruin them, to undermine the mechanization of agriculture, and to slow up the development of collective farm production." [8]

Only six years later, encouraged by Khrushchev, Soviet economists were prepared to assert not only that the kolkhozy could afford the purchases but that "on the whole we may conclude that the collective farms of the USSR will be able to buy the needed machines from the MTS for cash

[5] *Pravda* (December 16, 1958) pp. 1-7.

[6] T. Zaslavskaya, "Garantynaya denezhnaya oplata truda v kolkhozakh," *Voprosi ekonomiki*, No. 2, 1959, p. 115.

[7] According to Lazar Volin the greatly increased amount of cash distributed to the peasants in 1956 as compared to 1952 (the period in which the greatest increase occurred) only amounted to a total average income per peasant family of "a little more than $200 at a realistic rate of exchange." "Reform in Agriculture," *Problems of Communism*. Vol. VIII, No. 1, (January–February), 1959, p. 39.

[8] *Stalin, op. cit.,* p. 100. The fact that the MTS have been operated at a loss should not be taken as an indication that, on balance, agriculture has been subsidized by the industrial side of the Soviet economy. Indeed, the contrary is true. To speak of the state subsidizing agriculture through operating the MTS at a loss is only a reflection of the fact that agricultural prices have been kept at such a depressed level (in order that the collectives can contribute to the continued expansion of industry) that, at least in the past, forcing them to pay for the actual costs of the MTS work would have forced peasant standards of living even lower than they have been. In short, the subsidy implied by Stalin in this instance was merely a reflection of the Soviet system of bookkeeping and not economic relationships.

in the next two or at most three years." [9] The basis of their estimate was as follows:

The majority of our collective farms have the necessary means for the purchase of agricultural machines needed by them, as may be seen from the following figures. The income of all collective farms from state deliveries and sale of products to the state amounted in 1956 to 81.3 billion rubles (in 1955 it amounted to 60.7 billion rubles) and, with the inclusion of receipts from the sale of products at kolkhoz markets, to 94.6 billion rubles. [All ruble values are in the old (pre-1961) ruble.]

Money contributions of the collective farms to the indivisible funds amounted in 1956 to 16.7 billion rubles, while in 1958, according to preliminary calculations, they would rise to about 25 billion rubles. The balance value of the basic production means of all MTS in the country on January 1, 1957, was 53.5 billion rubles, of which tractors made up 13.5 million rubles, combines 8.9 billion rubles, other agricultural machinery, implements and inventory—15 billion rubles. The balance value of that part of the machine-technical means which collective farms can buy from the MTS was 40.6 billion rubles. This is only 40 per cent of the money income which collective farms obtained in one year—1956. We have, however, to keep in mind that the basic production means of the MTS in their balances are valued at their original cost. Actual expenditures of the collective farms for acquiring the necessary MTS machines (considering their wear and tear) may be approximately estimated at 18 to 20 billion rubles. A comparison of this figure with the above-mentioned figure of 40.6 billion rubles shows that the MTS have many obsolete and worn-out machines.[10]

Conspicuously absent from these calculations is any consideration of the substantial additional expense of fuel and spare parts, and of purchasing the large quantities of new machinery whose production by 1965 is projected. Also ignored is the cost of remunerating the relatively highly paid workers who have been transferred from the MTS to the kolkhozy with a guarantee of income at least equal to their old wage.[11] On the MTS there were well over 1,500,000 machine operators alone, so at least that many persons must be added to kolkhoz payrolls.[12]

However, the estimated expenditure by the kolkhozy of 18-20 billion rubles (cited above) to finance the purchase of the MTS machines is far from the total cost of the transaction. Entirely absent from the Soviet calculations of the cost to the kolkhozy of the MTS transaction is any consideration of the additional burden that they now must bear for

[9] P. Karotamm, "Neobkhodimy i svoevremenny shag," *Voprosi ekonomiki*, No. 3, 1958, p. 30.

[10] *Ibid.* p. 30.

[11] Counting agricultural specialists, machine operators, administrative personnel, clerks, and all other categories of workers, there were some 3,000,000 MTS employees. Some, of course, have been retained by the newly created Repair-Technical Stations. Khrushchev, *Pravda*, March 1, 1958, pp. 1-3.

[12] K. Ostrovityanov, "Concerning Two Forms of Socialist Property," *Komsomolskaya pravda*, March 18, 1958, p. 2. Translated in *The Current Digest of the Soviet Press*, Vol. X, No. 12, 1958, p. 11.

fuel, repairs, machine replacements, and other running costs that were previously carried by the MTS. Prices that the state pays for agricultural produce were advanced somewhat in 1958 along with the MTS sales.[13] Nevertheless, when the burden of the salaries of the highly paid specialists (transferred to the kolkhozy from the MTS) are added to the new and heavy burden of running costs, the asserted annual assets of the farms of from 16.7 to 25 billion rubles (only part of which can be expended on machinery) seems hardly adequate. The above citation implies that the burden upon the farms of the demise of the MTS would be only some 20 per cent of one year's income, and only for the first year. In reality, however, the first year's cost was probably closer to double this figure, plus a continuing additional annual burden that might well equal 20 per cent of the average collective farm's income. On balance, therefore, the total costs of the average kolkhoz have probably increased.

Lazar Volin estimated that the average cash income of each peasant from its kolkhoz labor (excluding income in kind) was only 2,100 rubles in 1956.[14] This probably was still valid in 1960. Because of the burden of MTS sales, the average peasant family's income may even have fallen since 1956.

The post-1953 reforms have noticeably improved the situation in agriculture. No doubt Khrushchev sincerely desires better living standards for the Soviet workers and peasants, and further advances may well be achieved. However, such goals must remain secondary and can be realized only very slowly. Even in consumer-oriented economies, substantial improvement in the welfare of the population as a whole requires decades and the best possible circumstances. The observation has been accurately made that the impressive industrial base created in modern Russia provides the means for a rapid advance of consumers' welfare, *if* the Soviet leaders ever decide to reorient the economy. In the words of the Soviet economist S. Kheinman, however: "The cardinal proposition of Marxist-Leninist economic theory to the effect that heavy industry must be given priority in development has again been embodied in the Seven-Year Plan for the development of the national economy of the USSR for 1959–1965." [15] Even in the "glorious socialist motherland" one cannot have his cake and eat it too.

Soviet officials will undoubtedly continue to point to the "millionaire" farms, arguing that the plight of the less fortunate kolkhozy is due to inefficiencies for which the kolkhoz administrations are largely responsible.

13 Indeed, although I was unable to verify it in my visit to rural Russia in June, 1960, there is a persistent rumor among colleagues abroad that at least some agricultural prices have been reduced during recent months.

14 Volin, *op. cit.*, p. 39.

15 S. Kheynman, "Razvitie promyshlennosti v semiletnem plane," *Voprosi ekonomiki*, No. 2, 1959, p. 41.

In the past, the MTS monopoly of the agricultural machinery was considered an essential "lever" for maintaining economic control over the farms and political control over the peasants. Now that the party is fully entrenched on the farms, the financial drain of the MTS on the state treasury is no longer thought justified. Administrative reorganization, improved controls, and increased efficiency, rather than raised incentives, remain as before the chief means for expanding Soviet agricultural output under the Seven-Year Plan,[16] and the priority given to industry continues in force.

Shlikhter has made very clear the probable effect of the retention of the priority for investment in industry. The achievement of the USSR's "main economic task . . . [overtaking] the USA in per capita output of both industrial and agricultural products," Shlikhter declares, must "ultimately" rest upon very great increases in Soviet agricultural output per man-hour.[17] Such increases would free the millions of additional workers that Soviet industry needs, along with ever-rising capital investment, if it is to continue its rapid growth. Shlikhter points out that although the total area under cultivation in the USSR is not much greater than in the United States, "43 per cent of the population," or some ninety million, in the Soviet Union are engaged in agriculture as compared with 10 per cent, or less than twenty million, in the United States.[18] If the efficiency of Soviet agricultural labor could be doubled, as the 1965 goal envisages, some twenty million workers could be transferred to industry

TABLE 2

	Labor (hours) per centner of output			Percentage by which U.S.S.R. exceeds U.S.A.	
	U.S. farms	State farms	Collective farms	State farms	Collective farms
Grain	1.0	1.8	7.3	80%	630%
Potatoes	1.0	4.2	5.1	320%	410%
Sugar beets	0.5	2.1	3.1	320%	520%
Raw cotton	18.8	29.8	42.8	60%	130%
Milk	4.7	9.9	14.7	110%	210%
Added weight, cattle	7.9	52.0	112.0	560%	1320%
Added weight, pigs	6.3	43.0	103.0	580%	1530%

16 A comprehensive study of the political role of the MTS is presented in a work by the present author and two colleagues. Roy D. Laird, Darwin E. Sharp, and Ruth E. Sturtevant, *The Rise and Fall of the MTS as an Instrument of Soviet Rule* (Lawrence, Kansas: Governmental Research Center), 1960.

17 Shlikhter *op. cit.*

18 *Ibid.*

—assuming that about one-half of the farm population are in the category of "able-bodied kolkhozniki." How serious labor inefficiency in Soviet agriculture is was indicated by figures for 1956–57 that Khrushchev cited in his December, 1958, address (Table 2): [19]

The claim is repeatedly made that Soviet agriculture has become the most mechanized in the world; no wonder Soviet agricultural economists are convinced that it is about time for such mechanization to bring about the release of large numbers of workers. They can cite the Soviet experience in labor output on the sovkhozy (state-owned and operated farms) in support of this view; the above table indicates that in the all-important area of grain production the sovkhozy are much more efficient than the kolkhozy.

However, Khrushchev's comparisons need serious qualification, since they are based on Soviet production for 1956–57. In 1956 the virgin lands, almost entirely farmed by sovkhozy, enjoyed the heaviest rainfall in some fifty years, and produced a bumper crop. Selection of another year would have yielded a comparison much less favorable to the sovkhozy. In any case the sovkhozy have always had the advantage, which the kolkhozy lacked, of substantial state subsidies. Solid evidence for this observation was provided by the Minister of State Farms, Benediktov, who bragged —for the first and last time—that in 1956 the sovkhozy paid their own way.[20] Furthermore, the sovkhozy do not have the incentive problems that hamper the kolkhozy, since workers in the former enjoy a guaranteed wage. Thus the sovkhozy (especially their 1956 performance) furnish no reliable evidence of what the kolkhozy, under the present system, can be expected to do.

However serious is the desire of Soviet leaders to overtake the United States in agricultural production, they continue to appear unwilling to make the sacrifices in other sectors of the economy necessary to achieve that goal. As Shlikhter indicates, increased livestock production—regarded as the key to rivaling American standards—is a direct function of expanded fodder production.[21] However, the measures he recommends seem in fact to be less relevant to producing more fodder than to saving labor generally. Shlikhter lists: (1) "socialist competition," (2) corn-growing, (3) increased production of "protein-rich fodders such as alfalfa, clover, and lupine," (4) increased mechanization, (5) expanded electrification of the farms, with concentration on labor-saving devices, and (6) increased production of fertilizers.[22]

[19] *Ibid. Pravda*, December 16, 1958, pp. 1-7.
[20] I. Benediktov, "Za dal'neishy razvitie sovkhoznovo proizvodstva," *Kommunist*, No. 18, December, 1956, p. 73.
[21] Shlikhter, *op. cit.*
[22] *Ibid.*
[23] *Ibid.*

Though its achievement is doubtful, the planned increase in the production of commercial fertilizers by 1965 (31,000,000 tons) would rival United States levels and could have a significant effect on yields.[23] However, increased yields depend not only on fertile soil but also on labor and abundant moisture, whereas the plans reveal an attempt to reduce labor drastically, ignoring the costly business of expanding the area under irrigation. Indeed, without sufficient moisture the addition of fertilizer often can do more harm than good. Although the Soviets have attempted to learn the lessons of American farming experience, in failing to stress the expansion of irrigation they have missed one of the most important of such lessons. In recent years large additional areas of the United States have been put under irrigation. For example, irrigation has transformed much of central Nebraska, where natural conditions are roughly comparable to large sections of agricultural Russia, into an important corn-growing area; and Khrushchev, whose favorite subject in agriculture is America's corn and corn-hog production, could afford to take note. However, it may be that the Soviets are slighting irrigation for what are to them sufficient reasons: the high cost of installing irrigation systems and the fact that irrigation is one of the most labor-expensive of all agricultural practices.

As for increases in output of "protein-rich fodders" (which require more moisture than most grains), they will be helpful in achieving the livestock goals, but expansion of these crops will require land now devoted to other crops that are slated for increased production.

Now that possibilities for expanding the cultivated area are largely exhausted, the Soviet analysts recognize that future advances must depend chiefly on increase in yields and mechanization. However, evidently they do not realize that mechanization does not itself guarantee increased yields except in a few cases—for example, when machines are used in additional applications of fertilizer or the expansion of irrigation. As the experience of the American truck farmer or the Russian peasant working his private plot shows, higher yields depend more on labor intensification than on mechanization. As Shlikhter correctly points out, although the United States leads the world in the efficiency of agricultural labor in yields, it lags far behind other areas where more intensive cultivation is employed—for example, Japan and Denmark, where grain yields per acre are nearly double those in America.[24] Extensive agricultural mechanization, coupled with specialization in single crops, has produced greater total output in areas where tillable land is abundant and labor scarce, but not in areas where all available land is already under cultivation. The American farmer has found greater profits in investing in machinery,

24 *Ibid.* Of sixteen countries listed by Shlikhter only Argentina, Mexico, and Canada lag behind the U.S.A. in grain yields per acre.

specialized crops, and large farms, rather than in diversified farming that requires expensive manpower; but, as shown by the example of other nations, this has been at the cost of maximized yields.[25]

Machine cultivation of corn is excellent, but no machine has been invented that will keep a field as clean of weeds as can a man with a hoe. Mechanical sowing saves labor, but no machine is as efficient as a Japanese farmer who goes over every inch of his land, planting each gap by hand. The Soviet leaders desire increases both in yields, which would feed the people better, and in labor efficiency, which would enable workers to be transferred into industry, but since either could only be maximized at the expense of the other, they have had to choose, and have chosen the latter, as before.

Some increases in yields will probably be realized during the next few years, but in the light of the means to be employed, the achievement of the 1965 goals would seem most unlikely. If surpassing the American economy in over-all output is, as the Soviets have plausibly concluded, "ultimately" dependent on a major improvement in the efficiency of agricultural labor, the most crucial question concerning the future of the Soviet economy lies here.

It does not seem likely that the enormous amount of fat on the carcass of kolkhoz labor can be trimmed to anything like Western proportions. However, the reasons are not primarily economic—a point missed by Soviet analysts and by many Western economists as well. The bloated labor requirements of the kolkhoz are chiefly a result of the administrative system and only secondarily of inadequate incentives. This point was vividly illustrated several years ago in a comparative study of the employment of labor in combining and threshing crews in Nebraska and the USSR. The study demonstrated that, using comparable machines, a combining crew regarded as exemplary by the Soviets required ten workers for every one employed in an average Nebraskan crew. A similar comparison of threshing crews yielded a ratio of 14:1.[26] Khrushchev's 1958 comparisons indicate that in spite of organizational changes partially intended to save labor, little or no improvement in labor efficiency has been achieved. According to Khrushchev's statistics, the total labor requirements for growing grain in the kolkhozy in 1958 (plowing, sowing, cultivating, and harvesting) was 7.3 times greater than American require-

[25] This point was emphasized in a British evaluation of American agriculture when the author noted: "The American authorities fully realize that the economic advantages of specialization and of the resultant high output per man may be outweighed by lower yields per acre and by long-term adverse effects of poor husbandry." A. N. Duckham, *American Agriculture: Its Background and Its Lessons* (London: Her Majesty's Stationary Office, 1952), p. 55.

[26] A. Nove and R. D. Laird, "A Note on Labour Utilization in the Kolkhoz" *Soviet Studies*, Vol. IV, No. 4, April, 1944, pp. 434-442.

ments.[27] Since harvesting always requires the peak utilization of labor, ten to fourteen times as many workers must still be required for this operation in the Soviet Union as in Nebraska.

Arguing that electrification (i.e., mechanization) of agriculture was the proper basis for socializing agricultural Russia, Lenin laid the foundation for a collectivized system that would fulfill both the theoretical and practical demands of the Soviet state. Stalin found that a planned totalitarian system required an additional element, the bureaucratization of farming. Today Soviet economists regard the administrative organization of the country's agriculture as its key feature.

Thus when Shlikhter argues that Soviet agriculture requires fewer machines than are needed in the United States, Great Britain, and France, he concludes that the "socio-economic" system of the USSR is less wasteful of machinery than the capitalist countries.[28] However, he, like other Soviet writers, wisely avoids opening Pandora's box through a discussion of the problem of labor efficiency.

When early experiments in equalized peasant income removed all work incentive, the effects were disastrous. Soviet leaders felt compelled to adopt a new device: an extreme piece-work scheme. A peasant's income came to depend upon the number of "labor-days" (units actually based on work done and not on time at all) earned. Today each collective has classified literally thousands of tasks, assigning them to one of nine "labor-day" categories. A peasant's work must be measured daily by one of an army of checkers employed by the farm. Everything must be recorded by a staff of bookkeepers in the peasant's work book and in the kolkhoz accounts. In addition, the collective has an administrative and technical staff charged with the task of guiding and supervising the actual work.

As a result of Khrushchev's reforms, each collective now contains also a party unit that is entrusted with the political welfare of the farm and its members—which according to Soviet definition includes the whole spectrum of human activity. District party and state officials are charged with keeping continual "day-to-day" checks upon the work of the farms

[27] Pravda (December 16, 1958) pp. 1-7. According to figures supplied in a discussion with Mr. Seivek, chairman of the multimillionaire Red Star Kolkhoz near Krasnodar (where labor efficiency is surely better than the national average) the collective has one able-bodied kolkhoznik for every 14 acres of land, calculated on the basis of those who are engaged solely in field work (each field brigade has 200-250 hands and is responsible for 7,500 acres). The collective has one field hand for every 33 acres. The average Kansas or Nebraska farmer probably cultivates ten times this area of land; other crops will, of course, require more intensive labor employment. On the Red Star the major crops were small grains (8,300 acres), corn (7,300 acres), sugar beets (7,780 acres), sunflowers (1,900 acres), vegetables (600 acres), annual and perennial grasses (8,400 acres), and gardens and vineyards (1,500 acres).

[28] Shlikhter, *op. cit.*

in order to ensure proper fulfillment of the state plan. Each collective has so-called "inspection commissions," consisting of peasants not on the administrative staffs who are charged with keeping a check on the kolkhoz administration. These and numerous other nonproductive tasks, such as guarding the kolkhoz produce against peasant stealing, occupy a multitude of able-bodied workers and hamper the efficiency of those directly engaged in production.

Although Khrushchev's post-1953 reforms have included several attempts to improve the system of remuneration, such as allowing the peasants to collect monthly advances on their earnings rather than waiting until the end of the year, crucial problems remain. The ultimate value of a kolkhoznik's "labor-day" depends not only upon the whims of nature, but also upon the efficiency of several hundred fellow workers. The Soviet press continually reports situations in which the value of one farm's "labor-day" is three or four times greater than that of a neighboring farm. Under these circumstances a kolkhoznik can ill afford to leave his assigned field task to take care of a strayed or injured animal or to take extra pains or precautions of any kind. Bureaucratic farming has yet to find a way to challenge him to make such efforts.

Even though the Soviets claim to have taken advantage of the West's industrial experience, they have ignored the human lessons of the industrial revolution. Through his labor union the Western worker can and often does influence the policies of his employers and in turn his own working conditions. Although the Russian peasant is supposed to have similar rights in the allegedly democratic kolkhoz general meeting, in practice its infrequent sessions only rubber-stamp orders relayed from above. The Soviet kolkhoznik is completely denied the stimulus and satisfaction that an individual receives from personally deciding when, how, and what work should be done. David Mitrany's observation that there is as yet no proof of any advantage in adapting large-scale industrial techniques, accompanied by the inevitable bureaucratic organization, to agriculture is clearly borne out by the Soviet experience,[29] in which the disadvantages of bureaucracy are reinforced by the inflexible demands of a totalitarian dictatorship.[30] Shlikhter and his colleagues want the advantages of the American agricultural system but fail to realize that an

[29] The often noted penchant for "gigantomania" in agriculture is expressed in the large working brigades and huge machines, but most dramatically in the changing size of the farms themselves. Before the 1950 amalgamations there were more than 250,000 collective farms in the USSR. Amalgamation reduced the total number of farms to some 70,000 by 1959; and *Pravda*, April 1, 1960, reveals that further unifications have cut the total number of kolkhozy to only 54,000. The average collective was about 1,600 acres in 1950; the 1960 collectives must average nearly 8,000 acres.

[30] David Mitrany, *Marx Against the Peasant*, (London: George Weidenfeld and Nicholson, Ltd.), 1951, pp. 228-229.

inseparable part of this system is the very "socio-economic" organization of an "open society" which Marxism-Leninism so completely rejects.

By 1965 "socialist competition," increased electrification, and more machinery are supposed to induce a 100 per cent increase in the efficiency of agricultural labor.[31] The past two decades, in which "socialist competition" has been tried, the number of tractors has doubled, and the kilowatts of power consumed on the farms have increased tenfold [32]—while the agricultural population has not grown appreciably—have brought no corresponding increase in efficiency, and there is no reason to expect the same methods suddenly to produce a different result. Unless and until the Stalinist agricultural system is recognized as the major flaw in the Soviet system, the lag in agriculture will increasingly retard the growth of the economy, and the possibility of achieving United States' levels of production will elude the Soviet leaders.

16

Soviet Agriculture Marks Time [*]

ALEC NOVE
University of London

Nine years ago, Khrushchev addressed the first "agricultural" plenum of the Central Committee since Stalin's death. His frank exposure of the poor state of Soviet agriculture was followed by action along a wide front. Prices paid by the state for farm produce were substantially raised, investments in agriculture increased, peasant incomes showed a much needed and rapid rise from very low levels. Tax and other burdens on the private activities of peasants were eased, to the benefit of all concerned; for example, in five years the number of privately owned cows increased 25 percent. In 1958 a major organizational weakness was corrected: Tractors and other machinery formerly owned and operated by the Machine Tractor Stations (M.T.S.) were sold to the collective farms

31 Shlikhter, *op. cit.*
32 *Ibid.*
  * Reprinted from *Foreign Affairs,* July, 1962, pp. 576-594, by permission of the author and the publisher. (Articles in *Foreign Affairs* are copyrighted by the Council on Foreign Relations, Inc., New York.)

which the M.T.S. had previously "serviced" (and also supervised). In 1958, too, the government dropped its complex multiple-price system, under which farms received a low price for a quota of produce and a higher one for deliveries in excess of their quota; this was replaced by a single price for each product, with zonal variations.

The period 1953–58, then, was one of reform, of higher incomes, of large investments, of new methods. It was also one of higher production. The 1958 grain harvest set an all-time record. Sugar beets and cotton also did very well. Milk yields benefited from the improved diet of the cows. According to the official statistics, the *annual* rate of growth of gross agricultural output in the five years 1953–58 was 8.6 percent. This would be a remarkable achievement, if the statistics were reliable, but there are ample grounds for suspecting some degree of exaggeration. Even so, no serious observer doubts that a substantial advance was recorded in these years.

No doubt inspired by the figures with which they were supplied, Khrushchev and his colleagues projected an even more rapid growth of agricultural output in the Seven Year Plan (1959–65), and onward through 1970. Extremely ambitious plans were envisaged for meat production, in particular, and for other scarce items such as fruit and vegetables. Yet for three consecutive years since 1958 the figures have shown no appreciable change, merely some fluctuations reflecting better or worse weather. Indeed, grain harvests have been below the 1958 record (see table on next page). How far performance lags behind plan can be seen from the following table (totals are in millions of tons):

	1961 plan	1961 performance
Grain	155.2	137.2
Meat	11.8	8.8
Milk	78.4	62.5

Source: Khrushchev, *Pravda,* March 6, 1962.

Allowance for statistical inflation of output would make the shortfall even greater. There is no doubt that Khrushchev is alarmed, because he has admitted as much at great length, and has proposed a number of remedies.

It is the purpose of this article to examine the reasons for the difficulties in which Soviet agriculture finds itself, and to assess the likely efficacy of the measures proposed to set matters right. But before doing so it is important to repeat that there has been a sizable advance since the death of Stalin, and that the crisis in Soviet agriculture is essentially to be seen as a failure to expand, a failure to measure up to very ambitious plans, rather than as a collapse. Various foods are in short supply in many cities at different times of the year, but there is some truth in Khrushchev's assertion that the shortage has been exacerbated by an increase in personal incomes (with retail prices broadly unchanged).

In considering the problems of Soviet agriculture, it is necessary to distinguish several types of difficulty, and, correspondingly, different kinds of policies or remedial measures. There is, first, the complex of problems related to soil utilization, agricultural techniques, equipment and the like, which may be called problems of production. Secondly, there are questions connected with the peasants, with their private interests, incomes, incentives. Finally, there are the many problems of agricultural planning, administration and control. These are all to some extent interconnected, as when, for instance, an administrative measure designed to improve technique affects the peasants' private activities. None the less, it remains true that these various matters are to some extent distinct and can be separately analyzed.

Problems of Production

One of the principal objects—though not the only object—of Soviet farm policy is to increase production. Under any political system, this would involve overcoming serious obstacles, for a large part of Soviet territory is unsuitable for agriculture. Where the soil is fertile there is usually a high risk of drought, and where rainfall is adequate the soil is generally poor. Two of Khrushchev's principal remedies—designed to provide more crops and especially more grain for human and animal consumption—were the virgin-lands and the corn campaigns. The first involved enlarging the area of extensive farming, the second was an attempt to intensify farming. Both have now been running for six years or more, and so some assessment of their effectiveness is possible.

The virgin-lands campaign was a truly formidable undertaking. It added to the farmland of the Soviet Union an area equal to the cultivated land of Canada. Between 1953 and 1956, the total sown area rose from 157 to 194.7 million hectares. So great an expansion in so short a period has no parallel in agricultural history. It was achieved through a major diversion of machinery and with a minimum number of permanent settlers, reinforced at harvest time by migrant labor (volunteers or "volunteers," probably both). The areas brought under cultivation were in the northern half of Kazakhstan, in parts of west and central Siberia and in the territories east of the lower Volga and the southern Urals. The principal crop was grain, largely spring wheat. The following table gives the official production figures (in millions of metric tons) for the total grain harvest in the years 1953–1961, with a breakdown showing that part of the total harvested in the virgin lands, of which Kazakhstan (shown as a further subtotal) is one region.

	1953	1954	1955	1956	1957	1958	1959	1960	1961
Total Grain									
Harvest	82.5	85.6	106.8	127.6	105.0	141.2	125.9	134.3	137.3
Harvested in									
virgin lands	27.1	37.6	28.0	63.6	38.5	58.8	55.3	59.1	n.a.
Harvested in									
Kazakhstan	5.4	7.7	4.8	23.8	10.5	22.0	19.1	18.8	14.8

Sources: for 1953–60, *Narodnoe khozyaistvo* S.S.S.R. v. *1960 godu,* p. 440–1; for 1961, *Pravda,* March 6, 1962.

Clearly, grain production did increase greatly through 1958. In 1954, the first year of the campaign, yields were good but little had yet been ploughed. In 1955, on the other hand, drought ruined the crop; in Kazakhstan, for instance, yields in that year averaged a mere 3.8 quintals per hectare, against a nation-wide average of 8.5 quintals in a not very favorable year. In 1956 the harvest was very good—the best to date in the areas with which we are concerned. The 1957 crop was a poor one. Since 1958, a good year, no further progress has been made, and the figures for Kazakhstan, the territory with the highest drought risk, have shown an alarming downward trend.

The difficulties encountered have been of the following kinds:

1. The nature of the campaign itself caused the ploughing up of some land with unsuitable soil, or with excessively sparse rainfall. The causes of such errors will be discussed when we come to analyze administration.

2. A surprisingly high proportion of the machinery is not kept in good repair and cannot be used, owing to lack of spare parts, skilled mechanics and workshops. The situation has been getting steadily worse; thus there were 32,000 combine-harvesters inactive in Kazakhstan in 1959, but 60,000 were in disrepair at the start of the 1961 harvest.[1]

3. The right kind of rapidly ripening seed is seldom available. This, in combination with the shortage of working machinery, delays the harvest, and, in this area of early frosts, heavy losses result.

4. Lack of amenities has driven away some of the permanent labor force, despite repeated criticisms of this state of affairs by Khrushchev and by many lesser officials.

5. The land has been misused. Spring wheat has been sown year after year, although there was no lack of warnings as to the consequences. Weed infestation, soil erosion, reduced natural fertility are all named as causes of falling yields. No acceptable system of cultivation and crop rotation has yet been agreed upon.

Despite these difficulties, the campaign to date has paid good dividends.

[1] These figures are taken from the remarkable speech by the premier of Kazakhstan, Sharipov, in *Kazakhstanskaya Pravda,* Dec. 24, 1961.

It was clear from the start that there would be some bad years, and, whatever discount is made for statistical exaggeration, it is surely true that a substantial contribution has been made to Soviet grain supplies, which could not otherwise have been obtained so quickly. Moreover, poor weather conditions in the Ukraine have often coincided with good ones in Kazakhstan, so that one effect of the campaign has been to spread the risks somewhat.

The future, on the other hand, looks much less satisfactory. It is known that some of the newly opened lands are of good quality, while others appear to have been ploughed up on orders from above and against the better judgment of local experts, but we do not know how much land may be in each category. Nor have we the means of assessing the extent of damage done by prolonged monoculture, or wind erosion, though these factors have certainly contributed to the steady drop in output and yields in Kazakhstan, where the bulk of the least suitable lands happens to be situated. Probably some of the ploughed-up land will have to be abandoned. Remedial measures at present being discussed may well run into administrative difficulties, because of Khrushchev's strong distaste for fallow and grasses, which presumably should be extended in some areas if the land is to be saved. Increased application of fertilizer is unlikely to provide a solution because of lack of moisture. (Very little is used on the somewhat similar Canadian prairies, though rainfall there is slightly higher.) In all the circumstances, it would be sensible to assume that a bigger contribution will be needed from traditional agricultural areas, and that the Soviet Union will be fortunate if means are found to maintain average yields in these marginal lands at the modest levels of the last few years.

Khrushchev was conscious from the first of the need to increase substantially the output of fodder, particularly fodder grains, in the "old" cultivated areas. This was the primary object of his corn campaign, which was facilitated by the growing of so much wheat in the virgin lands. Corn had been neglected, and its acreage in 1953 was actually somewhat lower than in 1940 and 1950. To enforce a rapid change, Khrushchev had recourse to continuous propaganda and administrative pressures. As a result, the area under corn rose rapidly from 3.5 million hectares in 1953 to 19.7 in 1958 and 28.2 in 1961. With strong pressure to sow corn on good land and to give it a large share of the available fertilizer,[2] yields rose also, as the following table shows:

	1953	1958	1959	1961
Total corn harvest (millions of metric tons)	3.7	16.7	12.0	24.0
Yield (quintals per hectare)	10.6	20.6	13.8	18.2

2 Perhaps this is why potatoes, which "compete" for scarce fertilizer with the more fashionable corn, have been doing badly of late.

However, these official averages conceal vast regional variations. Thus in some areas in which corn was sown "by order," yields were exceedingly low; these include the Volga area and the Urals, where average yields for the period 1957–59 were respectively 5.1 and 4.5 quintals per hectare. This represents utter failure.

None the less, as in the case of the virgin-lands campaign, the underlying idea behind Khrushchev's corn plan was sound, and the substantial increase in silage supplies (from 32 million tons in 1953 to 186 million tons in 1960, largely due to corn) certainly helped in raising milk yields and providing a better diet for an expanded livestock population. The trouble, as in the case of the virgin-lands campaign, has been the "campaigning" methods themselves, which caused rapid expansion under conditions which were often unsuitable. (Khrushchev has repeatedly claimed that corn can grow even as far north as Archangel.) Orders from the center demanded that all corn be sown in "square clusters," although, as several local agronomists sought vainly to point out, it is often more convenient to sow in rows.

Khrushchev has also set unrealistic goals. Thus whole provinces in the Ukraine were expected to achieve a yield of 50 quintals of corn per hectare in 1961, whereas American yields, with more suitable soils and warmer climate, averaged around 32 quintals. Even though the 1961 harvest in the Ukraine was an all-time record, with excellent weather conditions, no province came within 15 quintals of this target. Instead of learning his lesson, Khrushchev has repeated his demand for 50 quintals per hectare in 1962. One is left wondering which would do more harm: failure (with or without simulation of success), or success bought at the cost of neglecting all other farming needs of the Ukraine; presumably the former. It is this chronic tendency to overdo a good idea, to impose it by decree, which ruins its application and does so much harm to Soviet agriculture. More will be said below about the causes of such practices.

Meanwhile we must turn to consider the latest of Khrushchev's campaigns—to plough up meadows and reduce the area of sown grasses. Its motive, like that of the corn campaign, was the need for fodder, more in quantity and more diversified in type. This called for a further intensification of agriculture, which, as Khrushchev rightly saw, was inconsistent with the previously fashionable *travopolye* (rotational grass) crop system, associated with the name of Vilyams (Williams) and imposed under Stalin on all parts of the Soviet Union, regardless of local conditions. While grass could be a valuable source of fodder in the Baltic States or the northwest, in central and south Russia it grows poorly and provides little hay. Consequently there was much to criticize in these cropping practices. Khrushchev attacked the indiscriminate enforcement of *travopolye* in 1954, but agronomists had been trained in this way of thinking, officials were used to it, and those experts who had opposed it in Stalin's day had been punished or demoted. Consequently, little change actually occurred.

Khrushchev launched an all-out assault on *travopolye* in 1961—in speeches in many parts of the country and at the Twenty-second Party Congress. He pointed to the vast areas of sown grasses, of meadows, of low-yield crops such as oats. He ridiculed those provinces, including Leningrad and Moscow, where 50 percent or more of all arable land consisted of grasses and fallow. He demanded that such crops as corn, peas, beans and sugar beets be sown instead, in virtually all parts of the country. Only by intensification of agriculture of this kind, he asserted, would it be possible to produce sufficient fodder. Agricultural experts or officials who did not see this would have to be reëducated or removed. Crop rotation, too, must be drastically altered forthwith.

Again, as in the case of the virgin-lands and corn campaigns, Khrushchev appears right in general principle, but the method of enforcing his ideas almost ensures that very serious errors will be made in some parts of the country. The new system will not be understood. New crops will be grown by order in areas where soil conditions or labor shortage or the lack of necessary machinery or fertilizer will make it impossible to apply the directive effectively. For example, in parts of the Baltic States or in the Leningrad province it may well be rational to grow grass, because, although it would certainly be possible to produce more fodder per hectare by planting, say, beans, it would not be worth the extra labor involved. Incredibly enough, Khrushchev hardly mentioned that additional inputs would be necessary; all he declared himself concerned about was the amount of fodder produced. Of course, Khrushchev was careful to warn against excesses; grass was not to be universally banished, fallow might be necessary here and there, and so on. But the general sense of his instructions was such that they are bound to be followed by orders to plough up grass, to ban fallow and sow beans, corn, etc., regardless of circumstances. Thus the premier of Latvia mentioned that some of his colleagues in the Baltic States were already treating clover as a "forbidden crop." [3] Khrushchev must know all this. Yet presumably he can see no other way of breaking up existing irrational farm practices, since his only available weapon is the party machine, and this is the sort of way it works. In his impatience with low yields and general inefficiency, these crude administrative methods must appear to him as irreplaceable.

One cannot envisage a rapid advance of Soviet agriculture by such methods—the more so as the agricultural machinery industry has been undergoing a painful period of readjustment. Production of some vital items has fallen drastically. Khrushchev himself cited with dismay the

[3] Y. Peive, *Ekonomicheskaya gazeta,* March 5, 1962, p. 5.

fact that output of corn silage combines, urgently needed as a result of the expansion of the corn acreage, actually fell from 55,000 in 1957 to 13,000 in 1960.[4] Other sources confirm that the new system of industrial planning has caused much confusion in farm machinery factories.[5] The chronic shortage of spare parts continues, and decrees about expanding their output and making them available to farms on free purchase (as distinct from administrative allocation) have remained on paper.[6] Finally, fertilizer production and output of other important agricultural chemicals (sprays, weed-killers, etc.) are far behind schedule. Khrushchev contrasted the Seven Year Plan target for mineral fertilizer—an increase from 12 to 35 million tons—with the "achievement" of an increase of a mere 2.9 million tons in three years. New capacity is being delayed, and the completion plan for the three years is only 44 percent fulfilled.[7] No wonder the Ukrainian party leader, Podgornyi, complained that fertilizer supplies were inadequate: "For instance, deliveries to the Ukraine of fertilizer for sugar beet growing, per unit of land, has actually diminished in the past few years." He also deplored serious difficulties in supplies of timber, vehicles, tires and metal.[8] These are products of obvious importance to agriculture. The addition of even the best techniques cannot bring results if the required machines are not available, or if they break down and cannot be repaired, or if, as in some areas, farms do not even have carts or trailers to move into the fields the fertilizer which they do have available.

One purpose of the Party's recent declarations may be to restore a high priority to the industrial sectors which serve agriculture, and surely some improvements are both possible and likely. However, these shortages, which hamper agriculture even with existing cropping arrangements, must greatly hinder the application of the anti-*travopolye* policies, which call for much increased utilization of both machinery and fertilizer. If this call cannot be met, the result is likely to be a large additional expenditure of peasant labor without sufficient return.[9] It should be added that, as a consequence of the ploughing up of grasses, private livestock may be deprived of pasturage, to the further detriment of production and peasant morale. (When the corn campaign was launched, the peasants were promised part of the corn for their animals; but no such promises are being made at present.)

[4] *Pravda,* March 6, 1962. Khrushchev there cites other examples.

[5] See in particular the article by the director of the Tula farm machinery factory, *Ekonomicheskaya gazeta,* Jan. 15, 1962, p. 8.

[6] A 1961 decree provides for severe punishment for allowing farm machinery to deteriorate, but often enough the cause of the trouble is lack of spare parts, or of materials with which to build shelter and storage space.

[7] *Pravda,* March 8, 1962.

[8] *Pravda,* March 7, 1962.

[9] The burdens on the labor force which present policies impose were stressed at the Central Committee plenum by P. Abrosimov (*Pravda,* March 8, 1962).

The Peasants

By the end of 1957, many collectivized peasants must have felt considerable grounds for satisfaction. Cash distributions from the farms had risen almost fourfold in five years. They were about to be freed from all delivery obligations to the state from their private holdings, and their private livestock was expanding at a fairly impressive rate. It is true that work discipline was being tightened. But clearly things were improving.

In the past four years, the peasants have been in a much less satisfactory situation. Space precludes anything like a full analysis of the many factors involved. The following is a summary of unfavorable developments:

1. Attempts, sometimes encouraged by the authorities, to pay collective farmers a guaranteed minimum "wage," instead of in "workday units" of uncertain value, have broken down in many areas [10] because there is still no financial basis for any regular payment for work done, except on the richer farms. For seven years the press has been publishing articles and letters insisting on the necessity of earmarking a fixed share of farm revenue to pay the peasant members. Yet nothing effective has been done.

2. The 1958 reforms had the unintended consequence of increasing disparities in income between rich and poor farms. This was because, until that year, the more fertile areas were charged a kind of disguised differential rent by having to pay more for work done by the M.T.S. and by being compelled to deliver a bigger quota of produce at low prices. The abolition of the M.T.S. and the unification of delivery prices eliminated these methods. It is true that the unified delivery prices are lower in fertile areas, but the difference is quite small.

3. Peasant income from collective farms appears to have declined since 1957. The evidence for this lies, first, in the fact that there has been statistical silence since 1957, which usually indicates that the figures look bad. Second, two Soviet scholars have used regional and/or sample data to show a fall in distributions to peasants since that date; one of the writers, citing a 15 percent reduction between 1957 and 1960 in the province of Rostov, lists a number of other areas in which "the situation is broadly similar." [11] This happened despite a rise in gross revenues, and appears to have been due to pressure to spend large sums on investment, to exorbitant charges for repairs in state-run workshops, and the need to pay black-market prices to obtain desperately scarce tires, building materials and spare parts.[12]

4. Restrictions have been imposed on private activities of peasants,

[10] See evidence in A. Kraeva, *Voprosy ekonomiki*, No. 8/1961, p. 74.

[11] *Ibid.*, p. 77, and E. Kapustin, *Ekonomicheskaya gazeta*, April 9, 1962, p. 8.

[12] E.g. see articles in *Ekonomicheskaya gazeta* by M. Semko and A. Severov, respectively March 5 and March 19, 1962.

and the number of privately owned cows has declined sharply since the end of 1957. In consequence, and also because of a decline in free-market sales, peasant incomes in cash and produce from their private plots have fallen too. Thus there is evidence of a significant decline in peasant living standards, which must affect incentives.

Several measures have been taken to ease the financial burdens of the collective farms: prices of some items which farms must purchase were reduced in 1961, credit terms were eased, and payments for produce were made in advance. Also, nearly two million collective-farm peasants have been converted to state-farm status since 1957, making them regular wage earners (though the wages are low). However, possibly because of financial stringency, the government has done little indeed to improve peasant incomes, and must have caused much irritation by its measures against private livestock.

Perhaps the renewed restrictions on private activities of peasants are designed to persuade them to work harder for the collectives. Certainly, it could be shown that millions of man-hours are dissipated on private landholdings and millions more on taking produce to market. The Soviet leaders could well argue that these are not efficient ways of using labor. Yet, in existing circumstances, the private plot and the free market are indispensable, both for the peasants and for urban consumers of foodstuffs. In the first place, the private holdings, though primitively cultivated, are often much more productive, per unit of land, than collective or state farms, due partly to hard work and partly to the concentration of manure on a small area. To take a particularly striking example, in 1959 a hectare of potatoes on private holdings yielded 11.6 tons, as against 6.6 on state and collective farms.[13] Second, particularly in small towns and in rural districts, the state distribution network is utterly incapable of coping with food supplies, except for a narrow range of staple items. In this situation a cut in the number of private cows may create serious shortages.

Why, since milk production on state and collective farms has fully offset the decline in private output, does this situation occur? Some would point to exaggerations in the reporting of milk production, asserting that output has in fact fallen. This may well be so. But there is another and simpler reason. To distribute milk in a "modern" manner is a complex affair. It requires storage, refrigeration, specialized transport, bottles or cartons, and so on. All these are lacking, outside of a few big cities. In these circumstances, even if milk does exist on some farm 30 miles away, it is impracticable to distribute it, and so the local woman and her one private cow are irreplaceable. In villages, except in a very few showplaces, the private plot is almost the sole source of milk

[13] Calculated from detailed figures given in the statistical compendium, *Selskoe khozyaistvo S.S.S.R.* (Moscow, 1960).

and vegetables for peasant families. Given the present structure of Soviet farming and food distribution, measures against the private sector must have unfortunate results, and the quickest way of ensuring an increase in production of many much-needed items is to permit some enlargement of private farming activities. It is extraordinary that Khrushchev, who so strongly criticized the measures taken under Stalin against private plots, should be adopting his present policies—or permitting them, since it is not impossible for the party machine in the villages to take some initiative in these matters. Surely he must know better than anyone that such interference damages not only the supply of food from the private sector but also the morale of the peasants and their work for the collective and state farms. Yet only recently it was proposed that private plots on state farms be done away with and that communal vegetable-growing be substituted.[14] One can imagine the unpopularity of such imposed measures. Here ideology and administrative habit seem to stand directly in the way of increasing production.

Administration and Planning

The Soviet leaders must surely be fully aware that agriculture does not take kindly to centralized planning, that local initiative is vital. Yet ever since collectivization they have interfered with farming operations. This is to some extent explained by the fact that collectivization itself was imposed by the Party, and it has required constant vigilance to maintain collective farms and to "protect" them from their peasant members. Party watchdogs must also supervise the party-nominated "elected" chairmen who were often peasants themselves and therefore liable to give priority to the farm's needs rather than the state's. Low prices, which helped to finance industrialization but offered no financial incentive, made it necessary that the coercive apparatus of Party and state be mobilized annually to enforce deliveries to the state. For many years the principal task of the local party officials in rural areas, and of the political officers within the M.T.S., was to squeeze out produce for the state from reluctant and potentially backsliding peasants, who had to be restrained from spending their time on their private holdings. Farms could not be allowed to pursue the principle of maximizing revenues, since the price system was (and still is) geared to other objectives. The existence of a free market exercised a particularly distracting influence. Thus collective farms have been accused of marketing vegetables in distant cities at high prices, or growing sunflowers instead of sugar beets because they could sell sunflower seed in the free market at a profit,[15] or

---

[14] V. Grishin, the "trade union" chief, *Pravda*, March 10, 1962.

[15] I. Bodyul, *Ekonomicheskaya gazeta*, March 5, 1962, p. 6. Many similar examples could be cited.

even—in the case of a state farm in 1961—growing grass instead of grain because, as a surprisingly honest director told Khrushchev to his face, grass does not need to be delivered to the state and grain does.

Consequently, the habit developed of controlling agriculture from above, and of so organizing farms and planning as to facilitate this control. To some extent the amalgamation of collective farms, which has more than quadrupled their average size since 1950 (and which is still going on), is explained by the greater convenience in exerting control from above, rather than the convenience of management. From the latter standpoint, most state and collective farms are much too big. This tendency to very large size is also explained in part by the traditional Marxist belief that there are substantial economies of scale in agriculture.

When, in 1953, the appalling state of Soviet farming called for drastic remedial measures, Khrushchev showed himself very conscious of the harm done by inefficient central planning. The Soviet press printed a long series of articles criticizing the stupidity of inflexible production plans passed down the administrative hierarchy to farms for which they were quite unsuitable. Khrushchev and others declared that this must cease. In 1955, a decree was adopted freeing the collective farms from having production plans determined for them; they were to be given delivery quotas, and were to be free to decide their crop and livestock plans, so long as these were consistent with the quotas. It was repeatedly asserted that farm management and agronomists should be free to decide their own methods in the light of the very varied circumstances which always exist in agriculture.

In practice, since prices of neither output nor inputs reflected either needs or scarcities, direction from above had to continue. The period 1955–61 was one of experiment and frequent change in administrative arrangements. The Ministry of Agriculture was gradually shorn of its powers, part of which were transferred to *Gosplan* (the central planning agency) and part to a new body responsible for supply and utilization of farm machinery and fertilizer (*Sel'khoztekhnika*). A number of changes in purchasing arrangements culminated in the setting up, in 1961, of a Procurements Committee with local organs in close touch with farms, whose production programs they were supposed to influence. But production planning was also supposed to be the responsibility of the provincial agricultural department, while state farms came under a provincial trust which took its orders from organs of the individual republics.

The result was confusion. Everyone was to some extent responsible, therefore no one was. In practice, the local party organs at provincial (*oblast*) and district (*rayon*) levels exercised the most effective control over collective farms (and to a lesser extent over state farms). They issued orders on a variety of topics, they could and did dismiss the "elected" chairmen of farms and "recommend" others. But the responsibilities of the local parties, and the pressures to which they were subjected, gave rise to an administrative disease which is worth analyzing more closely.

A rural party secretary has always spent the bulk of his time dealing with agricultural problems. His promotion, or dismissal, depends on his success in coping with them. But how is his success or failure to be determined? The answer in practice has been: by his ability to report the fulfillment of plans to his superiors, if possible ahead of time. These plans tend to be very ambitious, and Khrushchev has systematically encouraged party secretaries to "compete" with one another by offering to overfulfill them. The plans in question are of many different kinds: they might concern grain procurement, meat deliveries, milk production, the completion of sowing by a certain date, the quadrupling of the corn acreage, the use of some fashionable method of harvesting, and so on. Almost invariably, the plans are either impossible of fulfillment, or (and this is the cause of much trouble) can be fulfilled only if other agricultural activities, which may be important but not at the moment the subject of a campaign, are neglected. Party secretaries are therefore repeatedly placed in an impossible situation. They are, of course, told to administer their areas efficiently, to take into account all the multifarious needs of agriculture. But they simply cannot do this while they are being cajoled to fulfill plans which, in the circumstances, are inconsistent with a healthy agriculture.

By long training, party officials have tended to adapt their behavior to the need to report success in the current campaign. Therefore cases like these recur repeatedly (all the examples are genuine and could be multiplied): seed grain is delivered to the state to fulfill delivery plans, and later other grain, unsorted and unsuitable, has to be returned for seed; farms are ordered to sow before the ground is fit for it, and/or to harvest by a fashionable but, in the given circumstances, unsuitable method; meat quotas are met at the cost of slaughtering livestock needed in the following year; to fulfill the procurement plan the local party boss orders the state elevators to receive what Khrushchev (in his speech at Novosibirsk) described as "mud, ice, snow and unthreshed stalks," which damaged the elevator's equipment. Party officials have repeatedly broken up established crop rotations to compel the adoption of whatever was the subject of the current campaign; if they understood the long-term damage which this might do to the soil, they would, in any case, probably be in charge of some other area by then. Other party secretaries inspired or condoned large-scale falsification of plan fulfillment, by such methods as instructing farms to buy butter in retail stores for delivery as their own produce (note that the cost of this operation falls on the peasants), or more simply by "writing in" non-existent figures (*pripiski*). They did not do these things because they enjoyed cheating or damaging the farms of their area, but as a response to pressures to achieve the impossible.

It is interesting to speculate why agricultural plans are so much less realistic than industrial ones. The uncertainties of the weather constitute one reason, but another is surely the habit of "campaigning," which is of such long standing, has done so much damage to sound farming and which still continues. A campaign must have clearly defined objectives, priorities and dates on which achievements are to be measured; it must involve strain and effort to achieve success, and must lead, therefore, to neglect of other considerations. But in agriculture this does great harm.

Given these administrative habits, it followed logically that the planning autonomy granted to collective farms in 1955 could never be a reality. It is also easy to understand why all decentralization measures were doomed to failure. Devolution of authority in the existing setting meant in practice devolution to party secretaries, who alone were in a position to enforce decisions, and this led to the systematic neglect of anything for which there was no pressure from the center. In a genuine effort to encourage local initiative, Khrushchev announced in 1958 that only grain-surplus regions were to be given grain delivery quotas. The idea was to encourage other regions to meet their own needs from their own resources, and in particular to concentrate on fodder grains for their livestock. What happened was that both grain acreage and production fell sharply in the areas freed from delivery quotas. In returning to centralized procurement planning in 1961, Khrushchev himself explained the reason: party secretaries, finding themselves no longer under pressure to deliver grain, instructed "their" farms to pursue other objectives in which the center seemed more interested; consequently, the fodder shortage was accentuated.

It is in the light of all this that one must assess Khrushchev's latest administrative reforms. There were two possible ways out: either to grant much more autonomy to farm management, or, on the contrary, to attempt to organize a more streamlined and flexible machine of central control. He chose the latter. Given his own background and the traditions of the Party, he could hardly have done otherwise.

A completely new hierarchical pyramid of control has been created in 1962. A new All-Union Committee on Agriculture is to be headed by a deputy premier, and is to include the head of the agricultural department of the Central Committee of the Party, and the heads of other relevant organizations, which retain their identity within, or alongside, the new structure: the Procurements Committee, *Setl'khoztekhnika,* the Ministry of Agriculture (reduced to purely research and advisory functions), plus representatives of the planning agencies. This new committee will apparently not be a policy-making body (Khrushchev would have headed it if it were); it is merely to ensure that party and state directives for agriculture are carried out. But below the all-union level the situation is different in one all-important respect: the heads of the agricultural committees in republics and provinces are to be the first secretaries of the republican and provincial parties. At provincial level and below, the tasks of procurement as well as production planning, for collective farms and state farms, will be unified under the new committee within a provincial agricultural department. The basic unit of agricultural planning, operating on the instructions of the provincial committee, will now be a new "territorial state and collective farm administration," which, as a rule, will group together several districts (*rayony*). In each of these territorial administrations there will be a "party organizer" deputed by the republican or provincial party organization.

This new hierarchy is to have authority to plan production, to issue directives as to methods, crop rotations, procurements, and in general to be in charge of both state farms and collective farm operations. "Inspector-organizers" employed by the territorial administrations will work within the farms and "will decide on the spot questions of production and procurement." The large number of workshops and other minor enterprises carried on jointly by two or more collective farms will be placed directly under the territorial administrations. An end is finally made of the doctrine, so often disregarded in practice, that collective farms are autonomous coöperatives governed by their members.

The reorganization marks a drastic alteration in, and a tightening of, the entire system of administration. Within it, the role of territorial party officials has undergone an important change. Hitherto, however frequently these officials interfered with plans and operations, they were not directly in charge of them. Their job was supposed to be to ensure that the relevant state organs did their job, to act as political commissars and not as army commanders, so to speak. It is true that they did in fact frequently issue commands, but—and this point was made several times—they could and often did dodge responsibility by putting the blame on one or more of the state officials whose formal duty it was to plan this or that aspect of agriculture. Now, the most senior party secretaries at the republic and provincial level have been put in direct command over farming in their areas, have been given full powers to issue orders to ensure that the agricultural plans are fulfilled. The state organs at their level, and beneath them, are at their command. The most powerful man in the new basic territorial controlling organs will be the "party organizer" whom they will appoint, and even the nominal chiefs of these organs will clearly be party officials for the most part, certainly not professional agricultural managers; both Khrushchev and Voronov warned against appointing farm managers to these posts.[16] One category of party official loses—the district (*rayon*) secretaries—and protests from them were mentioned by Khrushchev. (They will sit on a council which will be attached to the territorial administrations, but so will farm managers and other lesser lights.) Apparently their behavior vis-à-vis the farms is regarded as having contributed to past distortion, which is true enough. Khrushchev appears to believe that the past failures of party control were due to the fact that it was unsystematic, spasmodic, with many overlaps with various state organs which in turn confused one another and, as he put it, left the farms "undirected." Presumably he imagines that, if a party secretary knows he is personally responsible for all agriculture in "his" province, he will no longer concentrate only on the immediately current campaign, and the many defects of party activities in rural areas will thereby be corrected.

But will they? If our analysis is correct, then the essential weakness arises not from irregularity of their interference but from the overambitious nature of the plans which, willy-nilly, they have to force down the throats of their subordinates, and from the contradiction between these plans and the self-interest of farms and peasants. Party officials will surely continue to try to please their superiors and to organize matters so as to be able to report what these superiors wish to hear. While it is true that a more logical administrative structure has been achieved, it lessens the effective powers of farm managements and farm agronomists. It is on the farms that crops are grown, and it cannot be right to diminish the range of choice open to those who can actually see the crops growing, who bear formal responsibility for farm operations and, in the case of collective farms, for the incomes of the labor force.

Conclusion

Soviet agriculture is indeed marking time. The liberal post-Stalin policies did produce quick results, but since 1958 the growth rate has been negligible, for a number of interconnected reasons which I have endeavored to analyze here. It clearly does not follow that growth cannot be resumed. If more investment funds can be made available for the fertilizer and farm-machinery industries, for instance, then the very low crop yields in the naturally unfertile lands of the center, north and west of European Russia can be increased. Success in agriculture tends to reinforce itself (higher yields of fodder grains, more livestock, more manure, higher yields, higher productivity, increased incomes, more incentives, therefore still higher productivity, etc., etc.). None of this is

[16] Voronov in *Pravda*, March 28, 1962. The big role played by Voronov in carrying out this reform is surely a significant pointer to his rapidly increasing position of power in the U.S.S.R.

impossible, despite the adverse natural conditions under which Soviet agriculture operates. The trouble is that policies toward the peasant and the organizational arrangements of the régime seem inconsistent with the great advance in food production which Khrushchev desires with evident sincerity. And paradoxically, his impatient urgings, and their organizational and "campaigning" consequences, are among the principal obstacles to soundly based progress. Although we should expect to see some increases in production, there can be no question of fulfilling—or anything like it—the plans for 1965 and 1970, to which so much publicity has been given in the Soviet Union.

Finally, it is only right and fair to emphasize that there is no easy solution to the problems with which the Soviet leadership is wrestling. It is easy to criticize the price system, but it ill behooves us to lecture Khrushchev about the virtues of a free price mechanism when not a single major Western country permits it to operate in the agricultural sector. Difficulties arise in ensuring even modest efficiency in traditional peasant farming in many non-Communist countries, and agricultural plans have a regrettable habit of going awry in places well to the west of the Soviet border. Thus at the moment of writing there is an acute potato shortage in England, due largely to the fact that the Potato Board restricted plantings in the incorrect expectation of favorable growing weather; if there were a 1962 sheep plan in Scotland it would be a failure, since so many sheep have been killed by the severe winter. It is also not to be forgotten that, seen historically, Soviet agriculture has served as a means of financing and sustaining industrialization and has suffered in consequence. This is a disadvantage unknown to farmers in developed Western countries.

Yet it remains true that the huge farms of the Soviet Union have been inefficient in the use of resources and have shown a deplorable lack of flexibility and a failure to mobilize necessary human ingenuity. It is also significant that the only country in the Communist bloc which fulfills its agricultural plans is Poland, where most farms are privately owned and privately run. One reason for this is that Polish plans are reasonable: had Gomulka been so foolish as to promise to treble meat production in five years, he too would have "failed." Polish farming has its own weaknesses, and it is surely impossible on practical as well as ideological grounds to apply the "Polish model" to the Soviet Union. Yet, Polish experience underlines a fact too often overlooked: that with all the familiar inadequacies of small-peasant agriculture, it possesses advantages which Marxist theory has failed to recognize and Soviet practice has yet to find a way of emulating. Khrushchev is making an all-out effort to seek efficiency within the basic institutional and political framework of the Soviet system, and has mobilized the Communist Party machine for this purpose. The next few years will show whether a breakthrough can be achieved under these conditions. Much depends on the outcome—perhaps Khrushchev's political standing, probably also the influence of the Soviet Union on other peasant countries, within and outside the Communist bloc.

17

Prices . . . and Pork *

RADIO FREE EUROPE
Munich Research and Evaluation Department
Background Information USSR

On June 1 (1962) an "appeal" and a decree were published (by the Central Committee of the CPSU and the USSR Council of Ministers) which raised the delivery prices for meat from cattle, pigs, sheep, and poultry by an average of 35 percent and for butter and cream delivered to the state by 10 percent respectively. At the same time retail prices at state shops were raised by an average of 30 percent for meat and meat products and 25 percent for butter. . . .

The price increases reflect the failure of Soviet agriculture to meet both consumer demand and the unrealistically high goals planned in livestock products. The Seven-Year Plan called for a doubling of meat output by 1965, or 16 million tons, compared to an actual output of 8.75 million tons during 1961. In fact, the performance of the livestock industry during the last two years has been on the order of a near debacle. The actual performance in production is meaningful.

PLAN VS. PERFORMANCE
(million tons)

	Meat	Milk
1961	8.75	62.5
1960	8.7	61.7
1959	8.9	61.7
1965 Planned Goal:	16.0	100—105

1961 CSA report, *Pravda*, 23 January 1962
Narodnoye Khozyaistvo SSSR v 1960 godu, 1961, p. 378.

* Excerpts reprinted from *Radio Free Europe/Munich, Research and Evaluation Department, Background Information USSR*, June 23, 1962, pp. i-v, by permission of Radio Free Europe.

Thus instead of a 33 percent rise in output of meat there was actually a regression! In milk output, where the number of cows rose by 15 percent during the first three years of the Seven-Year Plan, instead of an annual growth of 10.8%, in actuality, less than one-half of one percent increase was achieved! The table scarcely needs further comment; it stands as a devastating commentary on the irrationality of some of Khrushchev's inspired agricultural planning. It also contains some seeds for the policy of raising prices for livestock products.

The disparity between prices paid Soviet farms and their costs of production has been the main constraint on the development of agricultural output. Apart from the subsidized technical crops (cotton, flax), the Stalin era of socialized farming (1928–1952) saw no basic changes in the price structures. After 1953 this disparity began to be recognized and two major price changes were instituted (in 1953 and 1958) for livestock products. Cost accounting studies did not appear until 1956, which then acknowledged the principle that prices received by farms were well below costs of production. This recognition, at least was a positive and rational step toward some semblance of price-market economy. The distorted price relationship acted as a disincentive in livestock production as it was more profitable for farms to sell grains and potatoes than feed it to their livestock.[1] The introduction of the single price system in 1958, which abolished the multiple price schedule of "procurement" and "purchase" and MTS payments in kind was based on the principle that prices would cover average costs of production and provide for accumulation. However, Khrushchev put a constraint upon the increase by fixing the total cost to the state of all deliveries from the collective farms not higher than the former outlays for paid deliveries plus MTS operating costs and investment.[2] It is now admitted, after a three-year lapse, that the 1958 prices did not cover the costs of production: thus collective farms have suffered losses instead of making profits—or more directly, the collective farmers have been "subsidizing" urban consumers in their meat and dairy food purchases.[3]

The new prices set in the June 1, 1962 decree bring average production costs and selling prices more into line. However, for many farms, as the appeal warned, the margin is still too narrow for profits unless the farms institute sharp labor and feed economies in their operations. The decision to raise prices must have been a difficult one for Khrushchev and

[1] For example, to produce 1 kilogram of pork liveweight (worth 7 rubles) required 16 kgs. of potatoes valued at 8.48 rubles. As feed costs are generally 60% of the cost of production, the net loss on such operations was prohibitive. *Voprosy Ekonomiki*, No. 3, 1958, p. 65.

[2] *Pravda*, 25 January 1958.

[3] *Ibid.*, 1 June 1962.

For example, Cost of producing 1 quintal beef 1960— 91.6 rubles
              1960 price for beef (aver. khol.-sovkh) 59.1 "
              1962 " " " " " " 84.0 "

certainly tarnished his reputation as an agrarian authority. In February, 1961, a plenary session of the Ukrainian CC at Kiev, he had warned that the state could not further subsidize livestock-product prices and that the only way out was for farms to improve labor productivity and establish cheap fodder sources to achieve doubling in meat output by 1965.[4] Or, again, at the December agricultural plenum of the CC, following the record harvest of 1958, when he predicted that the state would shortly purchase farm products from collectives in regions where the lower cost of production would be reflected in lower prices. Those farms, he added, unable to cut costs would be forced to sell on the market for whatever prices prevailed.[5] These warnings were uttered at a time when a spectacular breakthrough in agricultural productivity was, in the First Secretary's belief, just around the corner. To borrow one of his descriptive phrases, this breakthrough now belongs in "the dustbin of history."

The decisions of the March, 1962 agricultural plenum scarcely brought joyful demonstrations in the villages, either among the rank-and-file collective farmers, who were then denied any increase in the distribution of farm income, or among party and farm officials, who were saddled with more hemming controls. Perhaps in a recognition of this discontent in the countryside, so in contrast to the favorable public response following the MTS take-over in 1958, prompted the Kremlin to boost prices as a concession to the peasantry. At best the marginal income accruing the farms will be approximately 9 percent, less taxes and indivisible fund deductions. With the stress on accumulation for capital allocations it is not likely that a substantial share of the added income will appear in the labor-day payments to collective farmers.

The effect of the price rises on the operations of the private herds of collective farmers and employees is as yet uncertain. A 30 percent increase in the retail price of meat at state shops will act as an automatic brake on the consumption of meat products and may well depress demand. It is in effect a form of rationing by the price mechanism. With meat prices already 25 percent higher on the kolkhoz city markets over the state retail outlets, a further rise in the price differential may be more than the traffic would bear. Although 45 percent of the gross meat production (49 percent of the milk with 51% of the cow population) came from the private herds in 1960, the substantial share of this product is privately consumed or exchanged on the provincial markets. This private output has increased significantly in recent years; thus a considerable section of the Soviet population is furnishing its own protein-mineral-vitamin foodstuffs without benefit of Soviet planning. So when Khrushchev speaks of the insatiable demand for livestock products and of the inadequacy in their supply, he could admit that this applies to

[4] *Pravda*, 1 February 1961.
[5] *Pravda*, 16 December 1958.

only one-half the Soviet population. The price decree will place no constraint on the further development of the private plots and herds; in fact, any substantial upward price shift on the kolkhoz markets would attract the available meat and milk supplies from the private sector. For as long as the shortages exist there is no likelihood that punitive measures against the private plots will be undertaken by the Kremlin.

The appeal stipulates that the price increases are of a temporary nature and will ultimately be repealed. About one billion rubles additional income is to accrue to the collective farms, but as many will still operate at a loss in producing livestock (the appeal is explicit on this loss), added inducement may be minimal to collective farmers. Spread out among 31 million collective farm workers the extra pay would be less than one ruble a month.[6]

On balance, the temporary price boosts for livestock products will scarcely create the spectacular breakthrough in agricultural production that the Kremlin plans call for. Investment in agriculture remains crucially inadequate—agricultural output does not correspond even to that insufficient outlay. Only massive allocations of capital injected at a constant flow will solve some of Khrushchev's agricultural production problems. Or a more effective policy would be the doubling of the private plots. This would not place a drain on spare resources; it would admit, however, to the failure of collectivization to solve Russia's chronic food underproduction.

---

6 Even this modest indicated rise does not apply to sovkhoz workers: the decree states that prices paid state farms are to be 10% less for the same products as those paid to the kolkhozy.

18

Labor Productivity in Agriculture in the USSR and the USA *

B. I. BRAGINSKII
Chief, Section on Statistics,
Scientific Research Economic Institute of Gosplan, USSR
D. DUMNOV
Department of Agricultural Statistics, USSR Central Statistical Board

In analyzing the present position and the prospects of economic competition between the USSR and the USA in agriculture, we must not forget that although in scale, multiplicity of crops, and diversity of soil and climatic conditions, agriculture in the USA is most closely comparable to our own, nonetheless climatic conditions in the USA are immeasurably more favorable to agriculture than in the USSR. This must be remembered in comparing labor productivity in Soviet and American agriculture. First of all, however, we must briefly analyze the social and economic conditions under which the productive forces in American agriculture have developed.

As a result of specific historical circumstances, labor productivity in American agriculture far exceeded that of all European countries for many decades, let alone that of economically backward pre-revolutionary Russia. Agriculture in the USA developed in newly settled regions, without feudal survivals, and under conditions of a relative abundance of land, low prices and a shortage of labor. All this stimulated the use of machinery and economical methods of farming, particularly livestock farming.

Thanks to favorable climatic conditions and an abundance of highly fertile land, the American farmer used relatively little fertilizer and received a much greater return per unit of labor than the peasant of France, Germany, Italy or Britain, where the survivals of feudalism and serfdom made themselves felt. In Russia these survivals greatly hampered

* From *Vestnik Statistiki*, 1961, No. 2. Translated in and excerpts reprinted from *Problems of Economics*, May, 1961, pp. 3-9, by permission of the publisher.

the development of productive forces in agriculture. Labor productivity in farming was particularly low. Before the Revolution (in 1913) 75% of the gainfully employed population of Russia worked in agriculture; in the USA in 1910 only a little over 30% of the gainfully employed population worked in agriculture and produced a much higher level of output.

As we know, the growth of labor productivity in capitalist agriculture is a deeply antagonistic process. Higher labor productivity on the big farms brings ruin to the mass of small farmers. Between 1910 and 1959 average labor productivity in American farming almost tripled. This increase led to the impoverishment and pauperization of many hundreds of thousands of farm families. Between 1945 and 1958 alone the number of farms in the USA dropped from 6 million to 4.7 million and the farm population from 25.3 million to 21.4 million.[1] The increase in labor productivity on American farms is being effected more and more through backbreaking intensification of labor. The working day on American farms is very long and the output quotas exceedingly high, and farm owners use only physically strong and experienced persons as farm laborers, dooming the less capable and older workers to chronic unemployment.

Constant fear of unemployment and ruin forces the hired laborers and small farmers to work beyond their strength. But the increase in labor productivity benefits only the monopolies and capitalist farmers.

An entirely different situation exists in the USSR. The growth of labor productivity in Soviet agriculture leads to substantial increases in living standards both in the city and the countryside. Between 1940 and 1959 labor productivity in the socialized economy of the collective farms registered a 77% increase. During the same period the average real incomes of the peasants increased 2.2 times (calculated per working person). In 1965 labor productivity on the collective farms should be about twice the 1958 level, with at least a 40% rise in collective farmers' real incomes.

The advantages of the planned socialist economy make for a steady and rapid growth of labor productivity in all branches, including agriculture. But at present the USSR is still considerably behind the United States in agricultural labor productivity. However the lag is less pronounced than the enemies of socialism would have us believe. Bourgeois statisticians and economists, in comparing labor productivity in the USSR and in the capitalist countries, resort to falsification and often use obviously absurd figures. Thus, the report of the Joint Economic Committee of the United States Congress, *A Comparison of the Economic Growth of the Soviet Union and the United States,* makes the claim that labor productivity in American farming is between 8 and 12 times the Soviet level.

---

[1] *Statistical Abstract of USA,* 1960, p. 615.

The same figure is repeated by *Fortune* magazine and other journals. An analysis of statistical data on agriculture in the USSR and the USA shows that these figures have nothing in common with the facts.

For the real dimension of the lag to be determined, the indexes of labor productivity in the USSR and USA must be placed on a fully comparable basis. This requires comparable data on output, employment and labor time expenditure. We have already referred to the level of output in agriculture. As for the number of persons employed in American farming and the number of man-hours worked, the US statistical data are understated and not quite comparable with similar data in Soviet statistics. American farmers keep records of their personal labor and paid labor only, but do not record much of the work performed by their families. A sizeable part of the work done by other workers in agriculture is also not recorded.

Let us first consider the data on agricultural employment. The figures for the USSR and USA cannot be mechanically compared. The fundamental differences in the social and economic structure of agriculture in the USSR and USA lead to substantial differences in employment. American farmers operate on a capitalist basis, under conditions of competition and the ruthless exploitation of labor. In the USSR, on the other hand, agriculture is run along socialist lines. All the collective farmers are equal participants in the artel. But they do not all work the same number of hours, of course: the elderly folk, the youngsters, and women having large families work limited hours, to the extent of their possibilities. Apart from farming operations, the collective and state farms do a great deal of building work and have subsidiary establishments as well as welfare and children's institutions. For these reasons, Soviet agriculture will inevitably employ more people than in the USA, even when the labor expenditure per unit of output in the USSR drops below the American standard.

Because of the seasonal nature of agriculture, farm employment varies with the seasons. It is highest when the major crops are being harvested, and it is at this time that the employment figures are most fully recorded. Let us compare the agricultural employment figures in the USSR and USA during the height of the farming season (September in the USA, July and August in the USSR) and in terms of average annual figures. According to current American statistics, the average number of people working on American farms in September 1958 and 1959 was 9.3 million.[2] On an average annual basis employment in US agriculture in 1958 was 7.5 million.[3]

The data of various US official sources on farm employment differ

[2] *Handbook of Basic Economic Statistics*, 1960, No. 4, p. 65.
[3] *Ibid.*

considerably.[4] Without going into the causes of these discrepancies, we shall merely note that all sources admit the possibility of an appreciable understatement of the number of people employed on farms, both at any given time and on an average yearly basis (including the period of highest employment in agriculture). This applies in the first place to the unpaid members of farmers' families. But it also applies to the number of hired workers.

American statisticians exclude from the farm employment figures those able-bodied and juvenile members of farmers' families who worked less than 15 hours during the week recorded. Hence, if the unpaid members of farmers' families worked even 50 to 60 hours a month or 7-8 normal working days they do not appear in the agricultural employment statistics.

According to the *Statistical Abstract* for 1959 (p. 24) there were five million able-bodied women living on American farms in 1956. But according to the *Monthly Labor Review* only 1.9 million women worked on farms in September 1956.[5] We are thus led to believe that 3.1 million able-bodied women did not do any work at all. This is a distortion of the facts. In reality, during the height of the season on farms which do not employ hired labor (and they are in the majority), women work in the garden, look after the cattle and poultry, etc.[6] The statistics also ignore the work of children below 14 who are employed less than 15 hours a week, while the Census Bureau keeps no record of the work of children of this age employed even more than 15 hours a week.

This means that the number of persons—members of farmers' families —who are employed in farm work but are not included in the American statistics is at least 2 or 3 million, according to our estimates. They are for the most part women and children working less than 15 hours a week. In the Soviet Union the collective farms' annual reports on employment by months cover both the able-bodied men and women and all those children and old people who in any way participate in farm work. Hence, for the purpose of comparability the American farm employment figures should be increased by some 2 or 2.5 million in terms of the yearly average, and by 3 million during the period of highest employment.

The current US statistics which are used as a basis for calculating employment figures also considerably underestimate the number of hired

---

[4] A detailed analysis of US farm employment statistics is given in *Statistika sel'skogo khoziaistva v kapitalisticheskikh stranakh,* a collection of articles translated from English and edited by L. M. Tsyrlin. Gosstatizdat, 1960, pp. 4-5, 136-144.

[5] *Monthly Labor Review,* No. 1, 1957.

[6] The former US Secretary of Labor, Mitchell, in his *Farm Labor Fact Book* (1959), writes that women and children work on the farms in winter, spending "a little time" feeding the cattle and poultry and collecting eggs. As the seasonal demand for labor grows, adds Mitchell, they may spend as much as 40 hours a week and more on farm work.

farm laborers. This is particularly true of seasonal workers, especially of the migratory, juvenile and imported workers (Mexicans, Puerto Ricans, and others). About 500,000 workers in the USA keep wandering with their families in search of work.[7] The seasonal workers have only part-time employment and are really semi-employed workers. During the harvest season more than 4 million hired laborers work on the farms, according to Department of Labor figures.

That the statistics on hired workers are incomplete may be seen from the figures for 1950. Current statistics set the number of hired workers and office employees in American agriculture at 2.3 million, while the Department of Agriculture figure was 5.5 million, a difference of more than 3 million. More recent figures on hired workers also vary widely depending on the source. Thus, according to the *Handbook of Basic Economic Statistics,* in July-September 1958, i.e., at the height of the farming season, there were 3 million hired workers employed on American farms,[8] but *Agricultural Statistics* placed the number of hired workers in 1958 at 4.2 million, with 2 million as the yearly average.[9]

It should also be noted that the number of persons who worked on American farms in any single month is recorded in accordance with the figures for the last week of the month, so that those who worked during the previous weeks but not the last one may not be accounted for. In the Soviet collective and state farms the records are complete, and anyone who has worked even a single day during the month is accounted for.

Finally, for the Soviet and American data to be comparable, those persons on American farms who provide them with services and help to dispose of their produce should be registered as employed. The point is that in the USSR these operations are for the most part performed on the collective and state farms directly and the persons performing them are classed as agricultural workers (according to the summary annual report of the state farms for 1958, the sale and procurement of products and materials accounted for 7% of total labor expenditures), while in the USA these functions are performed by special enterprises and agencies whose employees are not classed as agricultural workers. The services rendered to farms include such operations as repair of tractors and farm machinery, production and marketing of fodder, processing, drying and cleaning of grain at the elevators, processing of mineral fertilizers, transportation of grain, milk and other farm produce, etc. Most of these operations are performed by commercial and transport companies. In 1958 some 800,000 persons were employed in these operations in the USA.

[7] These data were taken from an article in the *American Federationist* republished by the Soviet magazine *Za Rubezhom,* 1960, No. 18.

[8] *The Handbook of Basic Economic Statistics,* 1960, p. 65.

[9] *Agricultural Statistics,* 1959, p. 452.

If we take all these adjustments into account and bring the number of persons employed in farming in the USA into a pattern comparable with that used in the USSR, we will find that in 1958 and 1959 some 12 million persons worked on American farms, the number rising to 14-14.5 million during the height of the season.

What are the respective figures for the USSR? In terms of average yearly employment throughout Soviet agriculture, including the collective farms, the RTS, MTS, state farms, state subsidiary agricultural enterprises, as well as the personal subsidiary farm plots of the collective farmers, factory and office workers, a total of 33 million people were employed in 1959, including not only the able-bodied but children and elderly people.

As for the peak season, if we add the RTS workers and take into account the work done by the collective farmers and state farm workers on their personal subsidiary farm plots, the total number of persons employed in Soviet agriculture at the height of the season will be approximately 38 million.

On the basis of these data, agricultural employment in the USSR and the USA will appear as follows (the figures apply to 1958 for the USA and 1959 for the USSR):

	USSR	USA	Excess of USSR over USA
During the peak season, in millions	38	14	2.71 times
On an average annual basis, in millions	33	12	2.75 times

Thus, during the period of maximum employment, and on an average yearly basis, 2.7 times as many persons worked in farming in the USSR as in the USA. The total agricultural output of the USSR in 1959 was some 20% below that of the USA in 1958. Hence, labor productivity in Soviet agriculture is about one third of the American level.

Let us also compare labor productivity in Soviet and American agriculture on the basis of output per man-hour.

The data on labor inputs in man-hours contained in the American statistics are not actual inputs but norms, i.e., they reflect as a rule the labor requirements of big farms. According to these figures, American agricultural operations in 1958 required 13.7 billion man-hours. A footnote to the table in the *Statistical Abstract* from which this figure has been taken says that this is the standard number of hours required by male workers of average skill to perform various jobs. Hence, the actual number of man-hours spent by all workers, without their being recalculated in terms of hours of skilled male workers, is much greater than would appear from the American sources.

According to Hecht and Barton,[10] the average length of the American farmers' working day in 1946–1947 was 12 hours in summer and 10 hours in winter. The authors point out that nothing had substantially changed in this respect in 30 years. Nor has there been any substantial change in succeeding years.[11]

If we consider that the bulk of farmers work all the year round, we find that farmers themselves, without hired workers and those members of the family who help them, actually worked some 14-15 billion man-hours in 1958, i.e., more than the standard number of hours cited above. To this should be added the labor of hired workers amounting to some 5 billion man-hours,[12] as well as the work of those members of farmers' families who work less than 15 hours a week and who are not taken into account by American statistics at all. Their work adds up to at least a billion hours even if they work only one or one and a half hours a day on the average.

According to our calculations the actual labor inputs on all American farms, including the small ones, are about one and a half times as large as the standard expenditures of skilled male labor, as calculated by American statistics for big specialized farms.

If we calculate the total yearly inputs of labor in man-hours in Soviet farming (including the subsidiary personal plots) for the range of operations comparable to those performed on American farms, we will again find a difference of some 2.8 times in favor of the USA. Hence, labor productivity in Soviet agriculture on a man-hour basis in 1958 was about one third of the American level, i.e., we arrive at the same figure as before.

Natural and climatic conditions have an enormous influence on labor productivity in agriculture. As already noted, the Soviet Union as a

[10] *Voprosy proizvoditel'nosti truda v sel'skom khoziaistve S Sh A*, Selkhozgiz, 1957, p. 141.

[11] Mitchell, the former US Secretary of Labor, in his *Farm Labor Fact Book* mentioned above (1959), cites data on the number of working hours per week spent by people whose basic occupation is farming. In 1952–1957 the average was 48 hours a week (p. 179) or 2,500 hours per year. This figure applies to farming as a whole, but on the big farms the working week exceeds 60 hours. Mitchell cites numerous instances of a 60 to 70 hour working week on livestock farms.

[12] This figure has been calculated as follows: according to the *Statistical Abstract* (1958, p. 442), hired workers were paid 2.9 billion dollars in 1957; if we divide this sum into the daily wages of a hired laborer and multiply the result by the number of working hours per day—8.8—(see *Statistical Abstract*, 1958, p. 215), we get about 5 billion, which is the number of man-hours worked by hired laborers in 1957.

It is also necessary to bear in mind that the farmers have to pay for the hire and repair of machinery. In 1955, for instance, these expenditures amounted to 2 billion dollars (*ibid.*, p. 637). In paying for machine repairs (about 1.5 billion dollars) the farmer pays for the labor spent on repairs. Let us recall that in Soviet agriculture the cost of machine repairs is included in agricultural expenditures.

whole has much less favorable conditions than the USA,[13] and it takes a much greater expenditure of effort on the average to produce a unit of output in the USSR than in the USA. It would therefore be more to the point to compare labor inputs not between the USSR as a whole and the USA as a whole, but by separate regions with more or less identical natural and climatic conditions. Thus, in grain crops the regions most closely resembling the USA are the Ukrainian SSR (the steppe areas), the North Caucasus, Kazakhstan and Western Siberia. In these regions the labor inputs per centner of grain on collective farms in 1956–1958 were lower than the average for the USSR as a whole: in the North Caucasus—2.1 times, in Western Siberia—2.4 times, in Kazakhstan—3.2 times.

The differences in agricultural labor productivity between the USSR and USA is decisively influenced by the differing levels of mechanization and electrification of agriculture in the two countries. Livestock breeding and some branches of crop production in the USSR are less mechanized than in the USA. In 1958 the USA had 5,180,000 tractors (including orchard and garden tractors) and the USSR only 1,001,000, or 1,750,000 in terms of 15 h.p. units; the number of grain harvesting combines in the two countries was 1.1 million and 0.5 million, and of trucks —2.9 million and 0.7 million respectively.[14] True, on Soviet farms the machinery is used more intensively than on the capitalist farms of America, and the average output per tractor h.p., foot of combine width and truck tonnage is higher.

The advantages of large-scale socialist agriculture enable the Soviet Union to complete the all-round and integrated mechanization of all farm operations with a smaller number of tractors, combines and other machines per 100 hectares than are used in the USA.

In recent years many of the more efficient state and collective farms have substantially reduced labor inputs per unit of output. The measures taken to secure a sharp expansion in agriculture on the basis of Party and government decisions, have created opportunities for a rapid growth of agricultural labor productivity. Thus, while the big American farms require one man-hour to produce a centner of grain (exclusive of processing time), some of the state farms in 1956–1959 required less than one man-hour to produce a centner of grain. In 1956–1958 it took only 0.5 man-hours (including processing time) to produce a centner of grain at the Kirov State Grain Farm, Akmelinsk Region, 0.54 man-hours at the Gigant State Farm, Rostov Region, 0.8 man-hours at the Stavropolskii State Farm, Stravropol Territory, and at the Kropotkinski State Farm,

13 See the article by A. Pavlov and V. Sobakinskigh "A Comparison of Soviet and US Levels of Agricultural Output," *Vestnik Statistiki*, 1961, No. 1. [See *Problems of Economics*, April 1961—editor.]

14 See the Statistical Yearbook *Narodnoe khoziaistvo SSSR v 1959 godu*, p. 416; the magazine *Mirovaia Ekonomika i Mezhdunarodnye Otnosheniia*, 1959, No. 9, pp. 41-45.

Krasnodar Territory, and so on. There are quite a few state farms in Kazakhstan and Western Siberia where production per man has in recent years exceeded 1,000 centners which is considerably more than on the big grain farms of the Central North-West in the USA.

A mass movement for the organization of all-round mechanization brigades on row crops (corn, cotton, sunflower seeds, sugar beets) developed on the collective and state farms in 1957–1960. These groups require much less labor than the average for the collective farms as a whole to produce a centner of produce, and less than is required in the USA.

In livestock breeding we must apply the economical methods used by the big American farms to maintain productive stock if production costs per centner of output are to be reduced further. We are referring to the loose housing system for dairy cattle and pigs, the use of automatic feeders, etc. The Peremoga State Farm, Zaporozhye Region, the Piatigorskii State Farm, Stavropol Territory, the Provalskii State Farm, Lugansk Region, all of which have adopted the loose housing system for cows, required 3.5 man-hours in 1958 to produce a centner of milk, 20% less than on the big American farms. On the mechanized dairy farms, where one milkmaid tends 35 to 50 cows, it does not take more than two hours to produce a centner of milk. On a number of pig-fattening state farms employing modern methods of tending pigs, less labor is required to gain a centner of increased weight than in the USA. Pig-tenders Ragulina and Strigunovskaia of the Kommunar State Farm, Stavropol Territory, required only two man-hours to gain a centner of increased weight in 1959; the same applies to other pig-tenders who fattened between 1,000 and 2,000 pigs a year. In 1960 there were more than 1,000 pig-tenders in the RSFSR fattening 1,500 and more pigs a year each.

Our collective and state farms have great opportunities for rapidly increasing labor productivity in the near future. This is especially true of livestock breeding, where we are considerably behind the USA in labor productivity.

Addressing the Des Moines Chamber of Commerce in September 1959, N. S. Khrushchev said: "Our agriculture's lag in mechanization and labor productivity compared with yours is temporary, of course. The socialist system of agriculture makes it possible to overcome this lag quickly and to secure a higher labor productivity than exists on your farms."

19

Meat Prices Raised to Cover Costs, Spur Output *

Appeal of the Party Central Committee and the U.S.S.R. Council of Ministers to All Men and Women, Workers, Collective Farmers, and State Farm Workers and the Soviet Intelligentsia, to all Soviet People

The Soviet People know with what persistence our party has been striving to increase the output of agricultural products.

If we look back and carefully survey the path our agriculture has traveled since the September, 1953, plenary session of the Party Central Committee, we can say with good reason that the rural working people have accomplished much in bringing about an advance in agricultural production. The gross output of agriculture rose 60% between 1953 and 1961. In this period grain production increased from 5,036,000,000 poods to 8,422,000,000 poods, which represents a great victory. The country's food-grain needs are now being met in full. The production of meat in this same period rose from 5,800,000 tons to 8,800,000 tons (slaughter weight), of milk from 36,500,000 tons to 62,500,000 tons and of eggs from 16,000,000,000 to 29,000,000,000; the manufacture of sugar from sugar beets increased from 3,434,000 tons to 6,085,000 tons, etc.

While paying tribute to the efforts of the working people on the collective and state farms, we can by no means be satisfied with the results achieved in agricultural production. Its level is still insufficient to meet the public's greater demand for certain foods, above all animal products.

What is the matter?

It is easy for any open-minded person to see that the difficulties in question are difficulties of our tempestuous growth.

The Soviet economy is developing swiftly. The population of our country, especially the urban population, is growing very rapidly. Between 1953 and 1961 it rose by 29,000,000, of whom 28,000,000 are city dwellers. The money income of the working people has been rising year by year. In 1961 it was 42,000,000,000 rubles, or 87%, higher than in 1953.

Socialism gives every Soviet family confidence in the future. The un-

* From *Pravda*, June 1, 1962, p. 1; *Izvestia*, pp. 1-2. Translated in and excerpts reprinted from *The Current Digest of the Soviet Press*, June 27, 1962, pp. 3-6 by permission of the publisher.

employment problem has long since been done away with in our country, and the state provides for people in old age and in the event of their disability. It assumes the enormous costs of housing construction, free medical care and free tuition in schools and higher educational institutions.

Whereas under capitalist conditions every worker's family is forced to spend a great part of its income on rent, medical care and children's education and to lay aside savings for a rainy day, our Soviet family uses a great part of its income to improve its diet and dress. This naturally heightens the demand for such foods as meat, sausage products and butter. Look, comrades, at how much more of the highly valued foods people have been buying in our country in the past few years! For example, in 1953 the amount of meat and meat products sold through the state trade system was 1,757,000 tons, while in 1961 it was 4,033,000 tons; the corresponding figures for milk and dairy products are 1,980,000 tons and 9,393,000 tons, for butter 330,000 and 632,000 tons, for sugar 2,410,000 tons and 4,550,000 tons, and for eggs, 2,045,000,000 and 5,860,000,000.

There can be no doubt that as time goes on the requirements of the Soviet people, including their requirements for food products, will rise even faster. The constant growth of the people's well-being is a law of socialist society and a matter of primary concern for the Communist Party and the Soviet government. . . .

Every adult knows that before meat, milk and butter show up on the table a great deal of labor must be expended, particularly under our rigorous climatic conditions, with the autumn and winter seasons lasting seven or eight months in most parts of the country, which makes the keeping of livestock and production of feed more difficult. The building of livestock premises and the mechanization and electrification of livestock sections require huge outlays of funds and labor.

With the present level of mechanization in animal husbandry and of labor productivity on the collective and state farms, the cost of meat and milk production is very high, substantially exceeding the prices at which the state purchases these products. . . .

Consequently the collective farm takes a loss on every kilogram of meat and milk it produces. This being the case, the collective farm obviously has no material incentive to increase its output of these products. What is the solution? The purchase prices of meat and milk must be raised so that the production of these products becomes economically profitable for the collective farms, so that they yield the necessary accumulations and provide the farms with a material interest in rapidly increasing the output of livestock products. . . .

Some people may ask: Would it not be possible to raise the purchase prices of meat and still maintain the current retail prices of meat and meat products? Even if we suppose that the state could find the additional funds for this by increasing the prices of, say, vodka, tobacco and certain other items, it would still be impossible to keep retail prices at their former level. . . . With meat in short supply, this would provide the soil for speculation and would make it even more difficult to accomplish the task of ensuring the cities a steady supply of livestock products. . . .

Taking all this into consideration, the Party Central Committee and the U.S.S.R. Council of Ministers have decided to raise the purchase prices of beef, pork, mutton, goats' meat and poultry an average of 35%. It has been decided that the retail prices of meat and meat products should simultaneously be raised an average of 30% and of butter an average of 25%. . . .

In taking the step of raising the purchase and retail prices of meat, meat products and butter, the Party Central Committee and the Soviet government have been concerned to keep the cost to the public of the rise in retail prices as small as possible. With this end in view, the retail prices of sugar and of staple fabrics and articles made from these fabrics have been reduced. . . .

Dear comrades, Raising prices somewhat for meat and meat products, as well as for butter, is a temporary measure. The Party is confident that the Soviet people will successfully carry out the measures outlined by the March plenary session of the Party Central Committee in the field of agriculture. The level of mechanization will rise, labor productivity will increase and production costs will come down, which will make it possible in the not too distant future to lower the prices of farm products.

The Party Central Committee and the Soviet government are confident that the Soviet people will understand correctly the questions raised in this appeal and will make every effort to translate the great plans for communist construction into reality as quickly as possible.

PARTY CENTRAL COMMITTEE
U.S.S.R. COUNCIL OF MINISTERS

In the U.S.S.R. Council of Ministers

. . . With the object of heightening the material interest of the collective and state farms in sharply increasing the production and delivery to the state of livestock and poultry, the U.S.S.R. Council of Ministers has decreed:

that purchase prices for livestock and poultry sold to the state by collective farms shall be raised as of June 1, 1962, an average of 35% for the country . . .

For the purpose of reducing the losses incurred by the state in the sale to the public of meat, meat products and butter and of establishing a sounder correlation between the purchase and retail prices of livestock products, effective June 1, 1962, the retail prices of meat and meat products shall be raised an average of 30%, itemized as follows: beef, an average of 31%; mutton, 34%; pork, 19%; and sausage products, 31%; the price of butter shall be raised an average of 25%.

The U.S.S.R. Council of Ministers believes that the rise in the purchase and delivery prices for livestock products will be of great financial help to the collective and state farms. Turning this aid to good account, the Union- and autonomous-republic Councils of Ministers, territory and province executive committees, territorial collective farm-state farm (state farm-collective farm) production administrations and collective and state farms should this very year achieve a sharp increase in the production of meat and other livestock products, a rise in the productivity of labor and a reduction of production costs, so that livestock products are produced at a profit on every collective and state farm.

* * *

On the Reduction of State Retail Prices for Sugar, Fabrics of Staple Rayon Yarn and Articles Made From These Fabrics. The U.S.S.R. Council of Ministers resolves:

that effective June, 1962, the state retail prices of the following consumer goods shall be reduced:

—sugar, an average of 5%;

—fabrics of staple rayon yarn, an average of 20%.

The Union-republic Councils of Ministers are instructed to reduce retail prices effective June 1, 1962, of sewn articles, haberdashery and other items made from staple rayon fabrics proportionately to the reduction of the retail prices for these fabrics.

VI

SOVIET INDUSTRY [1]

A. The Reorganization of Soviet Industry: Results and Expectations

THE RAPID post-World War II industrial development of the USSR made it increasingly difficult, inefficient, and wasteful to continue the old system wherein control and supervision of all Soviet industries was centralized in some forty economic ministries in Moscow, each in charge of a branch of industry. On July 1, 1957, Soviet industry was reorganized along territorial lines, with most supervisory powers over enterprises transferred to more than one hundred newly established regional economic councils, called *sovnarkhozy*.[2] To Western thought this reorganization may amount merely to a change, for better or for worse, from centralized branch-of-industry to somewhat less centralized territorial control, perhaps even in part brought on by a political struggle for power.[3] Soviet writers, however, refer to it as the embodiment of "the Leninist principle of democratic centralism," of utmost importance for the completion of the tasks connected with the anticipated "transition to communism."

The Central Intelligence Agency, in the first selection below, describes and evaluates, somewhat sceptically, the sovnarkhoz system during its first four years of operation and discusses Soviet proposals for further changes. A. Vedishchev, in the first selection under *Soviet Views,* appraises the system, after three years, from the Soviet perspective and raises questions in regard to the need for further improvements.

[1] No selection on Soviet industrial *growth* has been included here, as Part X deals with "Soviet Economic Growth and the Prospects for Catching Up with and Outstripping the United States."

[2] Under the reorganization of November, 1962, the number of *sovnarkhozy* was decreased to about forty and their respective areas enlarged accordingly.

[3] See, for instance, Alec Nove, "The Soviet Industrial Reorganization," *Problems of Communism,* November–December, 1957, pp. 19-25.

20

The Territorial System of Economic Organization and Planning: Summary and Conclusions *

CENTRAL INTELLIGENCE AGENCY
Office of Research and Reports

The organization of Soviet industry along territorial lines—a radical departure in mid-1957 from the traditional branch-of-industry patterns of ministries—remains basically unchanged after nearly 4 years of operation. Small changes introduced since 1957 suggest a regime restlessly seeking still more effective organizational forms but reasonably satisfied that the territorial system is a workable basic administrative arrangement as was the ministerial system before it. Each system has exhibited obvious shortcomings which have evoked continuing innovation and refinement, and each has presented some problems which have defied easy solution.

Either system, in practice, has owed part of its success to the incorporation within it of basic elements of the other. Under the ministerial system, the branch-of-industry principle was supplemented by territorial divisions both in the ministries and the gosplans. Under the system of territorial councils of national economy (sovnarkhozes), the gosplans have expanded their branch-of-industry divisions by assuming many of the functions and acquiring many of the personnel of the former ministries.

Either system, in practice, has owed part of its inadequacy to its inability to encompass simultaneously and with equal effectiveness both departmental and regional considerations. The departmental barriers of the ministerial system often led adjacent enterprises of different ministries on circuitous routes through official channels to Moscow to effect the simplest transactions and obscured the requirements for unified planning of national and regional economic development. The regional barriers of the sovnarkhoz system have led to local distortions of the

---

* Excerpts reprinted from *Developments in the Organization and Planning of Soviet Industry,* Office of Research and Reports, Central Intelligence Agency, August, 1961, pp. 1-4, by permission of the Central Intelligence Agency.

national interest, and campaigns to curb these localist tendencies probably have inhibited the local initiative that the reorganization sought to promote.

The industrial reorganization of 1957 and subsequent changes in industrial planning and organization have contained elements of both centralization and decentralization. A considerable amount of administrative detail has been decentralized. Control over basic economic decisions has been tightened at the all-union level, and many decisions regarding investment, production, and allocation of materials—controls formerly exercised by the ministries—were centralized in the Gosplan [1] during the first year under the new system. Some of these decisions, particularly those bearing on allocation of materials, were passed down to the republic gosplans and to the sovnarkhozes in 1958 and 1959, but decisions bearing on interrepublic supply and other major planning decisions were retained by the Gosplan. In an attempt to strengthen central planning, long-term planning was taken from the Gosplan in 1960 and placed in a relatively new agency at the national level, the State Scientific-Economic Council (Gosekonomsovet).[2]

A similar move was made in 1960 to strengthen planning at the republic level by relieving the republic gosplans of the heavy administrative burden of handling intersovnarkhoz production relationships as well as problems of supply and sales in those republics containing a number of sovnarkhozes.[3] These administrative responsibilities were shifted to newly created republic-level sovnarkhozes that were superimposed over the existing regional sovnarkhoz structure in the first three of these republics, and the five regional sovnarkhozes in Uzbek SSR were replaced with a single sovnarkhoz.

In May 1961 a long-discussed scheme to further an old objective—the integrated development of natural economic regions broader in area than the regional sovnarkhozes—was put into operation with the division of the country into 17 large economic regions. Each region, except Kazakh SSR, was to have a council for coordinating and planning the work of the sovnarkhozes. These councils are to study basic problems of complex regional economic development and work out recommendations for presentation to the republic gosplans, the national Gosplan, and the Gosekonomsovet.

Most of these changes, both in organization and in planning, have involved lateral transfers of functions with little shifting of authority from one level to another. Those which have involved vertical transfers of functions have been directed toward either relieving central agencies

---

1 Unless local organizations are specified, the terms *Gosplan* and *Council of Ministers* refer to organizations at the national (USSR) level.

2 Abolished in November, 1962. (Editor's note.)

3 Earlier in 1960 the RSFSR contained 67 sovnarkhozes; the Ukrainian SSR, 14; Kazakh SSR, 9; and Uzbek SSR, 5.

of administrative details or supplying central agencies with a better basis for planning and control. If Soviet hopes are realized, the sovnarkhozes will have progressively less freedom to express undesirable localist tendencies, and opportunities to exercise local initiative along approved lines, which was one objective of the 1957 reorganization, will increase very little. In this sense, the changes since 1957 may be viewed as attempts to refine the operation of the new system rather than as a return to the old, and the system itself may be viewed simply as centralization along territorial lines compared with the previous centralization along branch-of-industry lines.

A long list of economic achievements of the last 4 years has been attributed by Soviet writers to the sovnarkhoz system, including gains in output, increases in profits, reductions in costs, better utilization of materials and equipment, reductions in the number of unfinished construction projects, better training and utilization of manpower, reductions in the average length of haul of rail freight, improved relationships between industry and agriculture, more efficient combinations of technically related enterprises, and reduction in the size of the managerial apparatus. For the most part, these claims have not been demonstrated conclusively to be products of the sovnarkhoz system, and some of the claims, themselves, have not been adequately substantiated.

In any event, Soviet writers also have admitted important areas where the sovnarkhoz system is in need of further improvement. Serious shortcomings have been cited in sovnarkhoz arrangements for introducing new technology, solving problems of industrial specialization and cooperation, meeting intersovnarkhoz delivery plans, and planning and coordinating the total economic requirements within the sovnarkhoz. The sovnarkhozes, lacking well-defined legal rights even after 4 years of operation, perhaps have operated too cautiously to realize their full potential in coping with these problems.

In addition to these admitted shortcomings which are susceptible of treatment within the general framework of the existing organizational system, is the problem of improving economic efficiency at the enterprise level. The enterprise manager now operates in an environment substantially different from that preceding the 1957 reorganization, and he generally has described the new system as an improvement over the old. His opportunities, however, to select optimum levels and mixtures of output, the most economical combinations of inputs, schedules for introducing new production techniques, and rates of capital investment are little greater than under the old system. As long as higher echelons retain authority over these basic decisions, which are important determinants of economic efficiency, the response of the enterprise manager to recently instituted incentive measures must necessarily be limited, and the problem of improving the planning and control activities of higher echelons will remain a basic part of the leadership's efficiency drive.

Recommendations for improving central planning and control were presented in March 1961 to the Council of Ministers, as requested by the plenum of the Communist Party of the USSR (CPSU) in July 1960. These recommendations were directed toward overcoming the defects of physical and value indicators now used in the planning and reporting of industrial activity, providing greater continuity in economic plans over longer periods, and improving the quality of regional planning. Some of the recommendations have been discussed for years, but none seems to promise a spectacular solution to the problems considered. Nevertheless, greater precision in industrial indicators might improve the communication between planner and manager that is essential for realistic planning, and greater use of regional planning balances might provide some of the integrated development of local resources originally sought in the reorganization. The attempt to obtain greater continuity in plans, whether it succeeds or not, will force planners to look ahead in greater detail and may lead to a more accurate anticipation of the requirements of future planning periods.

SOVIET VIEWS

21

The Territorial System of Economic Organization and Planning: Advantages, Accomplishments, and Suggested Further Improvements *

A. VEDISHCHEV
Council on Studying Productive Forces

It is three years since the implementation of the truly revolutionary decision on the reorganization of management in industry and construction. Historically, this is a brief span, but even these three short years have given convincing proof of the vast advantages of the new system. . . .

* From *Planovoe Khoziaistvo,* 1960, No. 7. Translated under the title "Three Years of Work under New Conditions—An Economic Survey," in *Problems of Economics,* January, 1961, pp. 52-61. Excerpts reprinted from the translation by permission of the publisher.

The reorganization of management in industry and construction has extended the rights of the Union Republics in the management of economic construction. This has contributed to the further enhancement of the Soviet people's material and spiritual forces, strengthening their friendship and promoting mutual aid in their triumphant advance to communism. . . .

On the eve of reorganization, Soviet industrial enterprises and construction sites were under the jurisdiction of 438 ministries and departments. Today, instead of this cumbersome system there are only 102 economic councils managing these enterprises and construction sites. . . .

The advantages of the new forms of management in industry and construction are manifested most vividly in the further expansion of the socialist economy, the better utilization of internal production potentialities and natural riches, the pre-schedule construction and commissioning of industrial enterprises, the growing labor productivity and greater profitability. The territorial principle of management has eliminated departmental barriers which weakened and often even led to violation of normal relations of production. It has also created conditions for greater specialization and cooperation, elimination of irrational shipments, better employment of engineers and technicians, and reduction of managerial staffs. The organization of industrial and construction management on the territorial principle has made it possible to run enterprises and superintend construction in a more concrete manner and has given rise to an extensive socialist emulation movement.

Much experience and factual material have been accumulated in the course of the three years and they allow us to thoroughly assess the merits of the new system of management, draw the necessary conclusions and make proposals for its improvement. . . .

The maintenance of high annual rates of industrial growth makes it possible to rapidly increase the absolute volume of growth of industrial output. In the economic councils' first year of operation the increase in gross industrial output exceeded the preceding year's increase by 17 billion rubles, in the second year—by 32 billion rubles, in the third year—by approximately 52 billion rubles. In the three years from July 1957 to July 1960 the increase in gross industrial output was about one-third above the increase in the preceding three years. . . .

The establishment of economic councils accelerated the fulfillment of the construction program. The volume of construction and assembly work in 1957–1959 was 46% above that of the preceding three-year period. Some 2,600 large industrial enterprises were commissioned in three years. Large-scale housing construction was started throughout the country and in most areas the plans are being overfulfilled. . . .

Much has been done in the sphere of invention and rationalization in the years since the reorganization of management in industry and construction. The number of inventors and rationalizers increased from 1 million in 1956 to 2 million in 1959. The savings obtained from the introduction of rationalization proposals in industry came to more than 11 billion rubles in 1959 as against 7 billion rubles in 1957.

The training of skilled workers has improved with the establishment of economic councils. Instead of departmental educational institutions the economic councils are building up a centralized educational network in accordance with the peculiarities of the economy of each given area.

The territorial system of management brings research, building and designing organizations closer to production and involves local research institutes in the solution of vital problems of technological progress. A new geography of the country's research institutes is in the making. Large research institutes have been set up in Gorkiy, Cheliabinsk, Stalingrad, Novosibirsk and other cities. Economic councils are establishing experimental and research workshops at enterprises, enlarging and strengthening designing bureaus. Many economic councils have set up economic laboratories. Workers are taking part in industrial management through the technical and economic committees of the economic councils, a new form of worker participation in management.

Development of Progressive Forms of Organization of Productive Forces

General indices of the development of industry and construction do not suffice to assess the economic effectiveness of the territorial system of management. To do so it is necessary to analyze the sum total of economic indices which reveal the specific nature of the influence which the territorial system exerts on the development of the country's economy.

The new system of management has created conditions for accelerating the social division of labor in all its forms. It has furthered the concentration of production and widened the scope for the development of such progressive forms as specialization, cooperation and combined production.

In three years the economic councils have consolidated more than 2,000 industrial enterprises. The process of increasing the concentration of output on the basis of district economic organization has spread to all branches of industry. The implementation of these measures has led to an increase in the volume of output and made it possible to achieve a considerable economy of manpower and funds. As a result of the amalgamation of technically related enterprises the economic councils of the Russian Federation have reduced the managerial apparatus by 17,000 people with an aggregate annual payroll of 180 million rubles.

A big job is being done in all areas in concentrating widely scattered auxiliary, transport and repair enterprises employing over 7,000,000 workers. The economic councils are reorganizing these enterprises on a district basis, centralizing the output of equipment, establishing district repair bases, etc. According to sample statistical data the concentration of service and auxiliary enterprises has made it possible to release 10 to 18% of the workers and transfer them to basic production work. . . .

The problem of specialization in the economic areas is being solved on a new basis. Proceeding from the concrete economic and natural conditions, the economic councils are intensifying economic specialization in the areas, giving priority to the development of those branches of social production for which the most favorable natural and economic conditions exist, ensuring production with the least expenditure of labor and funds. . . .

An important aspect of integrated economic development in the economic areas is the coordinated development of industry and agriculture. The territorial system of management produces new relationships between industry and agriculture. The economic councils organize production of agricultural tools on the spot, set up repair shops and produce fertilizers. At the same time the volume of output of agricultural raw materials is increasing rapidly and they are being processed more and more in the areas of their origin.

The territorial system of management in industry and construction makes it possible to better utilize the various natural resources and to thoroughly study them and the productive forces of each economic area. . . .

Certain Questions of Further Improving the Organization and Planning of the National Economy

The three years' experience accumulated by the economic councils has shown that the territorial system of management in industry and construction is effective. At the same time it shows that the great possibilities available in the national economy under the new conditions are not being fully used by far.

There are serious shortcomings in the assimilation and introduction of new technology, in mechanization and automation of production methods. Some economic councils procrastinate in reconstructing enterprises and modernizing equipment and are very slow in mastering new technological processes. All this retards the rise of labor productivity and the reduction of production costs. . . .

There are many problems still unsolved in the sphere of specialization and coordination in industry. . . .

The new system of managing the economy has created possibilities for developing a new system of interregional ties which will increase the economic efficiency of the territorial organization of the national economy. In improving industrial coordination the economic councils have performed a big job in the past three years. But some of the shortcomings born in the days of departmental management persist to this day. There are still irrational shipments.

Serious shortcomings exist in the system of material-technical supply. There are still cases of certain economic councils and enterprises failing to fulfill cooperative delivery plans.

Elimination of these shortcomings is the chief task confronting the economic councils and planning organizations. At the same time attention should be paid to the further improvement of the organizational forms of management in industry and construction. This is required by the rapidly developing productive forces. . . .

On the whole, the new system of economic administrative areas constitutes a firm base for managing and planning the Soviet Union's national economy. This, however, does not preclude its further improvement.

The elaboration of the industrial development plans by the economic councils in different economic administrative areas is a big step forward in perfecting national economic planning. Prior to the establishment of the economic councils, the job of drawing up plans at the enterprises and construction sites was done by dozens of departments. Now these plans are worked out at the enterprises with the participation and assistance of the economic councils.

The organization of the economic councils does not, however, solve the problem of elaborating a unified plan embracing all the branches of production and all types of economic activity on the territory of each economic administrative area.

The economies of the economic administrative areas, distributed among many departments and organizations, are not yet sufficiently coordinated economically. . . .

Integrated plans should ensure the economic development of the areas as component economic parts of the national economy based on a carefully selected combination of economic branches within the area, and resting on solid economic ties. Unified plans may be worked out jointly by regional planning committees and the planning bodies of the economic councils. To prepare a unified plan it is necessary to thoroughly study all the branches of the area's economy and to enlist the broad, creative assistance of workers, engineers, technicians and scientists. . . .

It should also be noted that as the result of the further territorial division of labor there will be, in addition to the economic administrative areas, large economic areas tackling economic problems of nation-wide import and developing specialization and cooperation in production.

The economic administrative areas are the component parts of the large economic areas. Life itself has made it necessary to coordinate the activities of the economic councils in large areas. . . .

The large economic areas are the territorial basis for the elaboration of long-range plans for the development of the country's productive forces embracing whole groups of economic administrative areas. On this basis, the central planning bodies will be able to select the most effective and economical variants for developing the country's productive forces.

The extremely rapid development of the productive forces thus confronts the system of planned economy with ever new problems. A creative approach to these problems and the perfection of the methods of planned economy are necessary to create the material and technical base of communism, to solve our basic economic task and to steadily raise the material and cultural level of the working people.

B. Heavy Versus Light Industry:
More Machines, or More Consumer
Goods Now?

No AUTHOR who describes Soviet industrialization can fail to point to the great emphasis that has been placed on heavy industry at the expense of light industry and agriculture. This emphasis, the sacrifice of present consumption for greater future output, has been evidenced not only by the relative quantities but also by the quality of goods produced by the various branches of Soviet industry. G. Warren Nutter, dealing mainly with the pre-1957 period, discusses these "favored" and "neglected" sectors in selection 22 below. Radio Free Europe, in selection 23, points to the quite considerable change in emphasis (in favor of consumers' goods) that had taken place by 1961.

On the Soviet side, the question of what should be the relative emphasis on heavy as compared with light industry does not find Soviet economists (nor Soviet party and government leaders) in complete agreement. While all Soviet economists and leaders are fully aware of the importance of "Subdivision I" (producers' goods sector of the economy), A. I. Notkin in selection 24, for instance, advises against making a fetish out of the over-emphasis on the rate of growth of producer as compared with consumer goods. A. Koryagin in the final selection, however, cites Marx, Lenin, and past Soviet experience to prove that technical progress depends upon continued emphasis on producer goods and he claims that the equalization of growth rates of heavy and light industry is favored by the "Antiparty group." This strong stand is particularly interesting in light of the fact that Khrushchev, a year earlier, had apparently declared that there was no longer any reason to give priority to heavy industry and that from then on "Light industry and heavy industry will develop at the same pace." [1] This statement, how-

[1] See *New York Times*, July 31, 1961. Restated in Naum Jasny's article, selection 10. See also Leopold Labedz, "Ideology and Utopia, The New CPSU Program," *Survey*, October, 1961, p. 20.

ever, never found its way into the Party Program of the 22nd Party
Congress. The Program, as a matter of fact, does not go explicitly into
the heavy-versus-light industry controversy. It should be pointed out,
however, that at the Plenary Session of the Central Committee of the
CPSU in November, 1962, Khrushchev returned to his previous position.
"We shall continue unswervingly," he proclaimed, "to follow the Leninist
policy of preponderant development of means of production." [2]

WESTERN VIEWS

22

The Product Mix: Composition, Quality, and Variety *

G. WARREN NUTTER
University of Virginia

As we shall measure it, economic growth means expansion in the
capacity to produce things, and this cannot be fully revealed in figures.
If produced things did not change in nature, there would be only the
technical problem of measuring quantities; but growth and change go
hand in hand, and the gray area of "qualitative change" cannot be captured in quantitative form.

We are interested in the qualitative changes resulting from greater or
lesser productive activity with a given technology. For our purposes, the
quality of an item may be taken as improved when more resources
are used to produce it, and worsened when fewer are used.[1] The term is,
therefore, being used in a very restricted sense, since in ordinary usage it
also refers to such things as change in the efficiency with which something
is produced, or in its value in use.

Soviet attitudes on production differ from those in the West, and for

[2] *Pravda* and *Izvestia,* Nov. 20, 1962, p. 1. Translated in *The Current Digest of the
Soviet Press,* Dec. 12, 1962, p. 46.

* Excerpts reprinted from G. Warren Nutter, *Growth of Industrial Production in the
Soviet Union* (1961), pp. 52-54, 57-58, 60-63, 64, 82-83, by permission of the National
Bureau of Economic Research.

[1] Improved quality does not, of course, always result from additional expenditure of
resources. With inefficiency not difficult to imagine, a leaky fountain pen could be more
costly than a leakproof one. We must suppose that the optimum available technology
is, or would be, used in every case being compared.

this reason the pattern of qualitative change has been different. In the background lie two basic factors. First, Soviet industry has been split in two, one sector—heavy and military industry—being systematically favored over the rest. Second, the economic system has an inherent quantitative bias, traceable in part to the working of the system itself and in part to the crusading nature of communism.

These forces work both for and against each other, and the result is mixed as far as the qualitative aspects of growth are concerned. Alec Nove is justified in warning us against sweeping conclusions based on the volume and sharpness of internal complaints about the quality of goods: [2]

It is generally assumed that poor quality is a characteristic of Soviet production. This assertion has some truth in it, but needs to be carefully qualified. There is evidence that Soviet industry is capable of first-class precision workmanship, and also plenty of evidence to the contrary: of bathroom taps which do not run and textile dyes that do. One should beware of concluding that poor quality is an inherently "Soviet" characteristic. It would be wiser to bear in mind that these things are, at least in part, consequences of the sheer pace of Russia's industrial revolution. An industry staffed by half-trained ex-peasants is apt to produce a high proportion of spoiled work, under communism, fascism, feudalism or any other system known to man. With the passage of time, Russia has acquired a fairly large skilled-labour force, but there has not been enough of it to go around, and priority has been given to heavy industry. This, and the inevitable effect of a constant seller's market, has certainly tended to depress the quality of consumers' goods and the standard (as well as the rate) of house building. Even so, this state of affairs cannot be assumed to last indefinitely, and the visitor who finds (as the author of these lines did) that door handles come off in hotels should not conclude that Soviet industry produces defective railway locomotives or machine tools. Door handles have no priority.

It is important not to be misled by the large number of criticisms of defects which appear often enough in the Soviet press. It is easy to catalogue these criticisms and derive from them a picture comforting for the complacent but fundamentally inaccurate. The system as a whole is not chaotic, even though examples of chaos can be properly cited; it does work. The essential fact is that the U.S.S.R. is a vast country of contrasts, which has developed very unevenly, with the good and the bad existing still side by side. One should also remember that inefficiencies in Western countries would be better known if the private affairs of firms were liable to be released to the press. In the U.S.S.R., the authorities use publicity in a carefully selective way. Hence an outburst of criticism directed at some sector is not necessarily proof that it is peculiarly defective, or that its efficiency has declined; the reason may be a decision to launch a campaign to improve it, or possibly even a desire to discredit the minister in charge.

Most of what Nove says should be heeded, but his warning is in a sense too strong. Whatever might be true for the future, Soviet industry in the

[2] A. Nove, "The Pace of Soviet Economic Development," *Lloyds Bank Review,* April 1956, pp. 11 ff.

past has been the model of austerity, and this is relevant in studying its growth. In the emphasis on quantitative growth, the simple has been generally favored over the complex and amount over quality. The result has been an economy with products less varied than in the West, with a product mix more heavily weighted in favor of producer and military goods, and with a quality of goods generally lower.

Many Soviet products in areas like heavy industry and the military sector now equal or excel Western products, demonstrating rapid progress in these fields. But there has not been the across-the-board improvement that has characterized Western industrial growth. The most marked improvements have been in metallurgy, machinery, and munitions; otherwise, growth has been primarily quantitative, consisting in expanded output of standardized commodities.

An anecdote of the second world war [3] portrays this contrast. During an air raid a Western ambassador and his military attaché watched a Soviet anti-aircraft battery manned by young women who maintained a rapid rate of fire on attacking aircraft. The attaché, an artillery officer, was fascinated by the Soviet guns and the efficient way they were being handled. After the raid was over, he took out his pipe for a smoke and broke a dozen matches before getting one to light. Pointing to the matches and the guns, he burst out: "How can people who make and work guns like that make matches like this?"

This contrast needs to be understood, especially in relation to other Soviet developments. . . .

Like most economic details, the problem of quality was not commented on widely in the Soviet press during the decade following World War II, but it received increasing attention toward the end of the Fifth Five Year Plan, particularly after Premier Bulganin's report of July 1955 on problems of industrial development.[4] In setting the tone for succeeding discussion, he stated: "It is necessary that those who neglect the quality of production, and thus crudely trample underfoot the interests of the state and the population, be severely punished. Party organizations are called upon to play a great role in the struggle for the quality of production." His references to poor quality included consumer goods, fuels, metallurgy, and machine building.[5]

Bulganin singled out the difficulties in meeting "assortment plans": [6]

A serious defect in the work of industry is the mistaken practice, which

---

[3] Related to me by Professor John H. Young.

[4] N. A. Bulganin, "Concerning Tasks in the Further Advance of Industry, Technical Progress and Improvement of Production Organization" (a speech at the Plenary Session of Communist Party Central Committee, July 4, 1955), *Current Digest of the Soviet Press*, VII, 28, pp. 3-20 and 24 (original text in *Pravda* and *Izvestia*, July 17, 1955). Henceforward this will be cited as: Bulganin, "Tasks."

[5] Bulganin, "Tasks," p. 16.

[6] *Ibid.*

is most harmful to the national economy and which we have not outlived, of the nonfulfillment of the production plan in terms of category quotas.

. . . For example, although the Ministry of Ferrous Metallurgy over-fulfilled the 1954 plan for rolled metal production as a whole by 173,000 tons, it failed to produce 155,000 tons of special large and small rolled steel sections, which are in short supply, 85,000 tons of rolled wire and 25,000 tons of rolled wheels.

Several branches of machine building also do not fulfill the plan for the established categories of goods.

The Ministry of Heavy Machine Building, which overfulfilled the over-all production plan for 1954, failed to fulfill the plan for the production of metallurgical equipment, forging and pressing machines, various types of lifting and transport equipment, diesel engines, and gas generator motors. The Ministry of Machine Tools overfulfilled the plan for 1954 for the total quantity of metal-cutting lathes and forging and pressing machines. However, it has not fulfilled the plan for production of the more important types of heavy machine tools and forging and pressing equipment.

The Ministry of Electrical Equipment overfulfilled last year's over-all production plan. However, the tasks of production of such important types of goods, essential for the national economy, as electric motors exceeding 100 kilowatts, power transformers and generators for steam and hydraulic turbines have been considerably underfulfilled by the ministry.

One can find many similar examples in other fields of industry.

The volume of criticism grew around the end of 1956 and early in 1957, following a year in which difficulties had been encountered in meeting the goals of the new Sixth Five Year Plan, leading finally to abandonment of the plan in the fall of 1957. . . .

Against this volume of complaints about quality in very recent years, we must place the accumulating evidence of a trend toward improvement in the quality of consumer goods since the death of Stalin. We see this reflected in eyewitness accounts of qualified observers who have visited the Soviet Union at different times separated by passage of years, in the postwar as well as the interwar period.[7] We may infer the same thing from the increasing diversion of resources to consumer goods: from 1950 through 1955, output of consumer goods apparently grew more rapidly than total industrial output.

In drawing a moral from the instances of quality deterioration described in the Soviet press, we must therefore bear in mind the warnings of Nove and not conclude too much. The focusing of criticism on particular industries—as agricultural machinery, textiles, footwear, furniture —may represent special campaigns to bring about improvements. At the

[7] See, e.g., the articles by Elizabeth Swayne in *Printer's Ink,* August 14 and 21, 1959 and *Profit Parade,* July and August, 1959.

same time this does not explain the bunching of complaints, spread over a wide area of products, that seems to occur when industry is having difficulty fulfilling the quantitative tasks set for it. In times of stress, quality tends, in response to the pressures described in the preceding chapter, to depreciate as the growth rate slows down, making the quantitative record look better than it is. These temporary deteriorations in quality get concentrated in areas of lower priority—particularly consumer goods—but they may spill over into more favored areas if the stress is great enough, as it apparently was in the early Soviet period and during the short-lived Sixth Five Year Plan. Whether such "cyclical" worsening of quality persists over the long run is another story, to which we now turn.

Qualitative Changes in the Long Run [8]

Trends in quality also reflect the basic contrast in priorities. In the favored sectors of industry— primarily within the three "M's": metallurgy, machinery, and munitions—rapid growth in output has been accompanied by substantial improvement in quality; in the neglected sectors—primarily within the three "C's": consumer goods, construction materials, and chemicals—quality has improved slowly and, in some cases, even depreciated. . . .

By its very nature, analysis of qualitative change must be descriptive; the results cannot be put in figures, though much of the pertinent evidence may be presented that way. In any case, most of the evidence comes from Soviet sources, and this poses certain problems. As we noted in the preceding chapter, performance in some sectors of industry is shielded from view, and this applies to changes in quality as well as in output. On the one hand, these sectors include declining or very slow-growing industries, where quality is also probably improving very slowly or not at all—possibly even worsening. On the other hand, they also include industries closely related to military production, where, by all visible signs, quality has improved in pace with output.

[8] The discussion in this section and the following one is based largely on data in the tables and notes of *Statistical Abstract of Industrial Output in the Soviet Union, 1913–1955*, New York, NBER, 1956. Citations will be made only when other sources are used.

Our knowledge of technical conditions has been greatly improved as a result of recent visits to the Soviet Union by U.S. industrial delegations under the cultural exchange programs. Some of the reports that have been issued are: "Russian Metallurgy," *Journal of Metals,* March 1958; *Report on Visit of U.S.A. Plastics Industry Exchange Delegation to USSR, June 2 to June 28, 1958* (Society of the Plastics Industry), New York, n.d.; William E. Vannah, "A Team Reports on Control Inside Russia," *Control Engineering,* November 1958; *Steel in the Soviet Union* (American Iron and Steel Institute), New York, 1959; *A Report on the Visit of an American Delegation to Observe Concrete and Prestressed Concrete Engineering in the USSR* (Portland Cement Association), Chicago, 1959; *A Report on USSR Electric Power Development, 1958/59* (Edison Electric Institute), New York, 1960; and "Soviet Computing Technology—1959," *Transactions* (Institute of Radio Engineers), March 1960, and *Communications* (Association for Computing Machinery), March 1960.

Again as we have already noted, criticisms of specific industries appearing in the Soviet press may at times be more directly related to campaigns for reform than to worsening conditions. One must be careful to go beyond these sporadic outbursts before drawing conclusions about long-run developments. But this is made difficult by the fact that the qualitative aspects of growth have not been systematically discussed in the Soviet technical literature. The picture of historical changes in quality within a particular industry must be pieced together from widely scattered fragments of information.

Any discussion of qualitative changes, no matter how extensive it may appear to be, is bound to be annoyingly incomplete. Moreover, too much remains unseen to know how representative the fragmentary description actually is. With this repeated warning, we proceed to say what can be said.

Examples of improving quality. The world has witnessed the rapid Soviet progress in the three "M's" and little more need or can be said here. Metals such as steel, aluminum, and tin have been entering increasingly into world trade and have competed successfully with the products of other countries. According to first-hand reports of qualified Western observers, the postwar Soviet iron and steel industry—except possibly for rolling mills—is technically on a comparable footing with the British and American industries,[9] though the products are of somewhat lower quality.[10]

Soviet machinery and equipment, though often copied from Western prototypes and produced on a more standardized basis, have apparently kept pace with technological developments in special areas. This is certainly true of military weapons and equipment, in novel as well as conventional lines, as we know from the fact that fission and fusion bombs have been exploded, powerful rockets launched, satellites orbited, and so on. In warfare itself, the world has observed the high quality of tanks, aircraft, artillery pieces, and rockets. Unfortunately, these "eyewitness" observations cannot be fortified by systematic evidence from open source materials, but there would seem to be no reason to question the Soviet advances in these fields, as far as quality of production is concerned.

Industrial products connected with other favored activities, like education and science, have also probably shown marked improvement over the Soviet period, though extensive documentation is again lacking. Even within the more neglected sector of consumer goods, there has been improvement in durable goods, at least in the sense that new products have been introduced: television, long-playing records, aluminum pots and

9 *Steel in the Soviet Union; Economist,* December 3, 1955, pp. 863 ff; *The Russian Iron and Steel Industry,* Special Report No. 57, London, Iron and Steel Institute, 1956; and "The Russian Steel Industry," *Steel Review,* April 1956, pp. 24-48.
10 *Steel in the Soviet Union,* pp. 191 and 247.

pans, cameras, watches, and so on. As an example regarding consumer perishables, higher-grade tobaccos have displaced the traditional low-grade *makhorka* absolutely as well as relatively.

In another relatively neglected area, construction materials, there has been a notable improvement in the quality of portland cement—though incidents such as the powdery floors at the recent U.S. exposition in Moscow suggest that there is room for further advance. . . .

These random notes cover only a portion of the cases that might be cited. The imprecise and incomplete nature of the discussion illustrates the handicap an outsider labors under in trying to assess a region of activity shrouded in secrecy. This handicap is further highlighted by the importance attached to travelers' tales—Marco Polo economics—as a source of information on these qualitative matters. We do not yet know enough about the products of Soviet industry to make anything approaching a definitive appraisal of trends in quality.

Examples of unchanging or worsening quality. There are a number of industries in which quality of product has failed to improve or has worsened. In part, this has been the kind of development always observed in the early stages of industrialization, as machines replace handicrafts and standardized production begins to serve mass markets. The very word "brummagem," from Birmingham, has been adopted into the English language to stand for shoddy, standardized merchandise. Beyond this, it is characteristic of a centrally directed economic order for the product mix to be simplified and for variety to be de-emphasized in favor of standardized goods. Centralized planning becomes less and less efficient as the number of products multiplies. . . .

Concluding Remarks

This less than adequate look at the qualitative aspects of Soviet industrial production, hampered by the selective nature of Soviet statistics, can be summarized only in broad terms. In general, industrial products are less complex and varied in the Soviet Union than in the West, and they have improved in quality more slowly. The picture is, however, one of contrasts between the favored sector of the three "M's"—metallurgy, machinery, and munitions—and the neglected sector of the three "C's"—consumer goods, construction materials, and chemicals. In between these extremes lies a number of industries that have experienced mixed qualitative developments. Finally, Soviet industry has been subject to "cyclical swings" in the quality of production, coinciding with swings in the rate of growth of industrial output. When the growth rate slows down, quality begins to deteriorate; when it speeds up, quality also tends to improve. The mounting attention being paid in recent years to formerly neglected sectors suggests that this characteristic pattern of qualitative changes, both short- and long-run, may be undergoing transformation. But that is for the future to say.

23

Relative Decrease in the Emphasis on Heavy Industry *

RADIO FREE EUROPE
Munich, Research and Evaluation Department
Background Information, USSR

. . . In accordance with the Program of the CPSU, there was a narrowing gap between the growth rates of heavy and light industry:

Growth Rates in %

	Group A	Group B
1960	"almost 11%	more than 7%" [1]
1961	"more than 10%."	6.6% *

[1] For 1960 figures see *Pravda,* 26 January, 1961.
* The plan for 1961 had aimed at 6.9%.

The long-term planning on which this convergence is based is shown by a table in the latest issue of *Planned Economy* (No. 12, 1961):

Average Growth Rates (in %)

	Total	Group A	Group B
1954–1960	11.1	12.0	8.9
1961–1970	10.1	10.5	9.2

Thus the average priority margin in favor of heavy industry is to be narrowed from 3.1% in the past seven years to 1.3% in the present decade.

In 1961 the fastest growth rates were shown by some of the specialized agricultural machinery (e.g. maize combine output at 245% more than the 1960 level, in response to Khrushchev's favorite campaign), washing machines at 44%, and electric locomotives at 41% more than 1960 output. Refrigerator production (30% up) and granulated sugar (32% up in response to Castro) were also notably good performers. . . .

* Excerpts reprinted from an article entitled "Soviet Industrial Performance in 1961," in *Radio Free Europe/Munich, Research and Evaluation Department, Background Information USSR,* January 24, 1962, pp. 1-5, by permission of Radio Free Europe.

Capital Investments

The shortage of investment resources is illustrated by the fact that the capital investment plan was underfulfilled by 5%. The first four growth industries as regards *rate of increase* of investments in 1961 were:

	Increase on 1960 investments
1. Agriculture (3rd last year)	+22%
2. Light Industry (not placed last year)	+18%
3. Engineering (second last year)	+14%
4. Chemicals (top last year)	+13%

(The metallurgical industry came sixth with +8%.)

Hence two consumer industries have now emerged in the leading positions for the first time since the seven-year plan was launched. The fundamentalists may well be disturbed, but the pattern of the 1962 plan with its 33.5% increase in light industrial investment shows that their objections are not being heeded by *Gosplan* any more than by *Gosekonsovet*. . . .

Conclusion

The USSR's industrial output grew faster in 1961 than that of any other major power with the exception of Japan and Italy. The most serious failure was in productivity, and the most novel feature was the emergence of agriculture and light industry at the head of the table of investment growth rates. A long-delayed but still welcome development.

24

Closer Approximation of Rates of Producer and Consumer Goods *

A. I. NOTKIN

Institute of Economics, Academy of Sciences, USSR

. . . During the period of full-scale construction of Communism we will achieve proportions, auspicious for the quickest building of Communism, between production and non-production accumulations, between the accumulation of basic and of working production funds, between accumulation and current consumption. Systematic increase in national income and in the effectiveness of material and labor resources, and above all of the fund of production accumulation, will be the basis for achieving the corresponding optimum during this period. . . .

A leveling of the rates of development of subdivisions I and II, with the faster growth of Subdivision I, will be characteristic of the period of full-scale construction of Communism in the USSR . . .

Why has a leveling of the rates of growth of subdivisions I and II become possible in 1951–60, as well as during 1961–80? In the prewar period, to overcome technical and economic backwardness and strengthen the country's defense in short periods, it was necessary to form, in essence, a large number of branches of heavy industry and to use the comparatively small fund of production accumulation first of all in these branches. A very high level of development of the production of producer goods was achieved as a result of Soviet industrialization and the postwar upsurge of the Soviet economy. Its share in industrial production comprised 39.5 per cent in 1928, 61.2 per cent in 1940, 68.8 per cent in 1950, and 72.5 per cent in 1960. The establishment and development of new and the expansion of old productions in Subdivision I no longer calls for a swift growth of the entire Subdivision I as a whole, as was the case in the prewar period when its volume was small. In addition, the high level of development of

* From *Ekonomicheskaya Gazeta,* November 13, 1961. Translated in part in *Radio Free Europe/Munich, Research and Evaluation Department, Background Information USSR,* March 20, 1962, pp. 1-3. Excerpts reprinted from the translation by permission of Radio Free Europe.

the production of producer goods signifies that in each given year this production can, besides covering the needs of compensation of expanded means of production, secure incomparably larger absolute increases in the basic and working funds of the national economy than in the prewar period, even with a leveling of its development and the rates of growth of Subdivision II.

But the leveling of the rates of development of the production of producer goods and consumer goods does not mean their leveling to the rates of the capitalist world. In the general perspective, higher rates of growth of both the first and the second subdivision are planned than have been planned for the Seven-Year Plan (1959–1965). As is well known, the control figures of the Seven-Year Plan provide for a 9.3 percent average annual increase in products of Industrial Group A and 7.3 per cent in products of Group B. In 1961–70, the average annual rates should comprise 10.6 per cent for Group A and 9.2 per cent for Group B; in 1971–80 they should comprise 9.8 per cent and 7.8 per cent respectively, and for the entire 20-year period they should comprise 10.2 and 8.5 per cent, respectively.

The leveling and maintenance of high rates of expanded reproduction in both subdivisions promotes an increase in the quality of manufactured equipment and of the economic effectiveness of capital investments. Therefore, the achievement of optimum proportions in the development of the production of producer and consumer goods, as well as of accumulation and consumption, is inseparably tied to the struggle of the Soviet people and the party for technical progress and effective use of the material and labor resources of our society.

In the light of Soviet reality and the planned calculations for the general perspective, it would be incorrect to make a fetish of great differences in rates of growth of the production of producer goods and consumer goods being a kind of natural law of socialist expanded reproduction in all its stages. But from the leveling of these rates we must not draw the conclusion that a gradual diminution of the effect of the law of the greater growth of the production of producer goods will inevitably occur with a high level of economic development and a general harmonic upsurge in the entire national economy. Of course, in certain years a quicker upsurge of Subdivision II of public production is possible in the aim of immediately overcoming lagging in the production of items and funds of consumption. However, over somewhat prolonged periods, the relation of the growth of subdivisions I and II is always influenced by such basic factors of expanded reproduction as intensive technical progress and the growth of labor productivity, which necessitate the quicker development of the production of consumer goods, primarily instruments of labor and energy . . .

The swift development of all branches of heavy industry secures the development of a new scientific and technical revolution and the achievement of a higher labor productivity than with capitalism. Nevertheless, the leveling of the rates of growth of subdivisions I and II makes demands on the development of the production of producer goods. It necessitates the intensification of output of producer goods for production consumer goods, which at present is insufficiently developed. In the period 1961–80, industrial production of producer goods will increase 600 per cent, while the industrial production of means for producing consumer goods will increase 1,300 per cent. A tremendous upsurge in the production of consumer goods will be realized on the basis of this, with an improvement in their assortment and quality in accordance with the growing demands of the Soviet people.

There is no doubt that Soviet industry can manufacture consumer goods not only in ever growing amounts, but also on a level corresponding, to use an expression of the Financial Times, to the complex character of consumer demand. The country which has achieved unheard-of successes in mastering the cosmos is capable of developing the production of cars, television sets, radios, and cameras, of building housing and social and cultural institutions, and of sewing footwear and clothes on a level which answers the demands of technical and social progress and the tastes of consumers. There is no free business competition in socialist society, but we have our own methods of influencing production, and they must be developed in every possible way.

25

Why the Equalization of Growth Rates of Heavy and Light Industry Must be Opposed *

A. KORYAGIN
Candidate of Economic Sciences

. . . The conclusions of K. Marx concerning the organic and technical structure of capital in the process of expanded reproduction show that an increase in the production of consumer goods occurs with the out-

* From *Ekonomicheskaya Gazeta*, May 7, 1962. Translated under the title "Excerpts from Article Claiming 'Antiparty Group Representatives Favored Equalization of Growth Rates of Heavy and Light Industry,'" in *Radio Free Europe/Munich, Non Target and Russian Department, Background Information USSR*, July 2, 1962, pp. 1-3. Excerpts reprinted from the translation by permission of Radio Free Europe.

stripping growth of the production of producer goods. This thesis of K. Marx was further developed in the works of V. I. Lenin. "The whole meaning and significance . . . of the law concerning the increase of producer goods," he wrote, "consists only in the fact that the replacement of manual labor by machine labor—the progress of technology in the machine industry in general—demands the intensified development of production in the mining of coal and iron, these genuine 'means of production for producer goods'." . . .

Lenin showed that the very character of technical progress dictates the need for the fastest output rates of machine equipment and materials which are used for expanding the production of producer goods as a whole. And this in turn determines the rates and scales of the output of equipment and material for the production of consumer goods.

The economic law of the preferential growth of the production of producer goods acts also under the conditions of socialism . . .

The party line on the preferential development of heavy industry was subjected to fierce attacks by antiparty elements who proposed a course toward the primary development of light industry, or as they said, "the cotton-print industry." This would have meant the preservation of the technological and economic backwardness of the country, an increase in its dependence on the capitalist world, the undermining of defense capability, and in the final analysis, the loss of the socialist victories of the people. The party destroyed the right-wing capitulators and rejected their opportunistic theories.

However, even in recent years certain relapses into similar views have been discovered. Representatives of the antiparty group tried to assert that during the transition from socialism to Communism, a line should be taken toward establishing the same growth rates for heavy and light industry. This correlation of rates would undermine the material and technical basis of the increase of production of consumer goods. The party showed the complete groundlessness of the views of the antiparty group.

The experience of socialist construction in our country has supported the Leninist thesis that the outstripping growth of the production of producer goods as compared with the production of consumer goods is an absolute condition of expanded socialist reproduction.

The correlation of growth rates between the two subdivisions of public production at each historical stage is determined by specific conditions of the economy's development and depends on a number of factors, namely, the achieved level of production and its structure, the rates and directions of technical progress, the maturing of great advances in the development of science and technology, the level of industrial development in socialist countries, the need to help poorly developed states, the international situation and tasks of strengthening the country's defense capabilities, and others. . . .

The experience accumulated shows how, as we move from one stage to another, the correlation of rates of development of the heavy and light industry changed. This is seen from the correlation of the growth rates of the two subdivisions of public production in industry in the USSR . . .

In 1960, the industrial product was 45 times as great as in 1913; production of producer goods (Group A) was 103 times as great, while production of consumer goods (Group B) was 16 times as great. Consequently, the product of heavy industry grew approximately 6.5 times as fast as the product of the light and food industry. This shows that for a number of years, our country has directed means primarily to heavy industry and has limited capital investments in the light and food industry to overcome its technological and economic backwardness.

The considerable outstripping in the development of heavy industry changed fundamentally the structure of industrial production. This is testified to by data concerning the proportion of the "A" and "B" groups in the industry of the USSR . . .

The proportion of the product of heavy industry has risen steadily. This created an ever more powerful basis for the further expansion of production and for high rates of socialist accumulation for the resolution of the grand tasks of Communist construction.

The 22nd Party Congress posed the task of creating the material and technical base of Communism within two decades; this requires complete electrification of the country, the improvement on this basis of the techniques and technology of production, the introduction of comprehensive mechanization and ever broader automation of production processes, the development of the chemical industry, etc. This can be achieved only on the condition of the preferential development of heavy industry . . .

For the period of the general long-range plan, an outstripping development of the production of equipment and materials for the development of the production of consumer goods has been planned. Thus, the product of enterprises which manufacture producer goods for the production of the same producer goods will increase to approximately six times the present level, while the production of producer goods for enterprises of the light and food industry, agriculture, housing construction, and cultural and everyday services will increase to 13 times the present level.

As N. S. Khrushchev showed, this correlation is conditioned by the fact that a considerable reserve of the preferential growth of heavy industry, which was necessary for its own development, was already accumulated in preceding years. However, this "reserve" was never an end in itself; it was formed in accord with the demands of the basic economic law of socialism, in the interests of the rise of all branches directly connected with satisfying the vital demands of the workers. Now all conditions have been prepared for a sharp increase of the production of equipment and materials for an intensified production of consumer goods which will secure an abundance of material goods and the transition to the Communist principle of distribution . . .

Heavy industry is called on to secure the comprehensive mechanization of all production processes in farming and animal husbandry and to greatly increase the delivery of mineral fertilizers, poisons and chemicals, and construction and other materials to kolkhozes and sovkhozes.

At present, there is a certain disproportion between the tasks of the upsurge of agriculture and the level of the material and technical supply of kolkhoz and sovkhoz production. The party considers it necessary to expand existing plants which manufacture tractors, agricultural machines, and equipment for the mechanization of animal husbandry and to build a number of large new ones . . .

VII

THE SOVIET CITIZEN
AS A WORKER

To ANY student of the Soviet economy, the study of labor in the USSR must be of special interest, for in Marxist-Leninist philosophy the working class was to be the ruling class during the period of the "Dictatorship of the Proletariat"—that "intermediary stage" which "inevitably" was to lead from the era of capitalism to the pinnacle in the economic, political, and social development of mankind: pure communism.

Two main topics will be covered in this part: the economic conditions of the Soviet working class and the functions of labor unions in the USSR.

A. The Soviet Worker Under Changing Conditions

That the condition of the Soviet citizen as a worker has improved decidedly during the past twenty or twenty-five years is undeniable. The Soviet worker certainly has progressed since the days when, in 1940, the working day was lengthened from 7 to 8 hours, there were six working days per week, changing jobs without permission was prohibited, and criminal penalties were imposed for tardiness and absenteeism. These decrees, not much enforced since Stalin's death, were officially repealed in 1957; a gradual decrease of the working day was legally provided for in 1956 (and has apparently been carried out according to schedule); and increased wages combined with an almost continuous decline in all retail prices during most of the 1950's have greatly enhanced the Soviet worker's real income. Yet, retail prices are still above and average wages well below those of the United States, and the approximately 30 per cent increase in the price of meat and butter in the spring of 1962 obviously had a detrimental effect on purchasing power. "Not Good—But Better," one of America's experts on Soviet labor problems entitled an article on the current status of the Soviet worker.[1]

[1] Emily Clark Brown, "Not Good—But Better," *Problems of Communism*, November–December, 1960, pp. 38-41.

In the first selection below, Margaret Dewar presents a rather critical evaluation and analysis of recent labor reforms in the USSR. Kazanskii and Ul'ianova, on the other hand, give the official Soviet interpretation which views the reforms with pride as a great social achievement on the road to communism.

WESTERN VIEWS

26

Labour and Wage Reforms in the USSR *

MARGARET DEWAR
British specialist on Soviet labor and author of several books on the Soviet economy

No industrially-developed country other than the USSR has employed so great a degree of compulsion to discipline its workers or such refined methods of material and psychological incentives to induce higher productivity. This is not a moral judgement, but a statement of facts, for which there are objective reasons. The first labour laws of the young Bolshevik Government reflected socialist aims, but in the existing economic and cultural context these laws were utopian. During the Civil War and the period of the New Economic Policy (NEP), Soviet labour policy was imposed by the grim struggle to survive. Finally, it was shaped by the primarily political decision of the new rulers to enter, "at all cost," upon a productivity race with the most industrialised countries of the West. As pointed out by Werner Hofmann in his comprehensive study "Die Arbeiterverfassung in der Sowjetunion," [1] the USSR was not a virgin country like the USA, Canada, Australia, or South Africa where industrialisation proceeded simultaneously with political development. In order to achieve her industrial revolution, she had, like some of the West European countries, to overcome an established order and to combat deeply ingrained social habits of thought. The advantages of highly developed twentieth-century techniques were offset by a lack of capital and a skilled labour force. Profound changes and radical measures were re-

* Excerpts reprinted from *Studies on the Soviet Union*, New Series, Vol. II, No. 3, 1962, pp. 80-91, by permission of the Institute for the Study of the USSR, Munich, Germany.
1 *Volkswirtschaftliche Schriften*, Heft 22, Dunker and Hunblot, Berlin, 1956, 542 pp.

quired to overcome the obstacles and to accelerate the high pace of industrialisation, which was dictated on the one hand by the modern techniques, and on the other by the fear of "foreign intervention."

Hence the forcible collectivisation in the early thirties and the subjection of the industrial workers to rigorous discipline by depriving them of any escape routes and of means of expressing their needs or discontent in an organised way.

The various methods of compulsion, which included imprisonment for leaving one's job and various types of material, moral and psychological pressure brought to bear on the Soviet worker throughout the thirties and the war period, are sufficiently well known to need no reiteration. Suffice it to say that force of one kind or another became the dominant feature of Soviet labour policy. It must be recognised, however, that it did create —with terrible hardship and appalling suffering—a large industrial labour force in a relatively short time. It also brought into existence a hierarchical apparatus of functionaries who are exempt from the worst sacrifices demanded of the rest of the population. This group has had the power to enforce the Government's policy and a tendency—only lately checked—to increase in disproportion to the growth of industry.

Between 1926 and 1959, the number of people employed rose from 11,300,000 to 62,961,100.[2] In 1959, the active working population, including kolkhoz workers and armed forces, was stated to be 99,130,000, i.e. 47.5 per cent of the total population (52 per cent of workers were men and 48 per cent women). Of this 99-odd million, 78,635,000 were manual workers (i.e. 79.3 per cent) and 20,495,000 (or 20.7 per cent) white collar workers. The latter category included 392,000 executives of state administrative bodies and social organisations (88 per cent of 1939); 955,200 executives in industry, building, agriculture, transport and telecommunications; 4,205,900 engineers and technicians; and 3,501,900 planners, book-keepers, cashiers and inspectors. Compared with the 1939 census, the last three groups showed an increase of 26 per cent, 154 per cent and 13 per cent respectively.

The organisational structure of the Soviet labour force up to the time of Stalin's death displayed no essentially novel or advanced methods of disciplining labour and increasing productivity which had not been employed in the West. By and large, the industrialisation of the USSR showed features also inherent in the periods of industrialisation of other countries, modified, of course, by contemporary methods of production and labour incentives. All that was novel was also retrogressive; that is, the arbitrariness, the totalitarian manner, and the total disregard for the individual, with which the policy was put into practice.

Also the Soviet worker under Stalin did not occupy a higher position

---

[2] *International Labour Review*, No. 3, 1961, "The Active Population of the USSR," pp. 198-203 quoting *Vestnik Statistiki*, No. 12, 1960.

in the social structure, nor had he more to say in distribution of the social product than have workers elsewhere. In many respects he was, in fact, in a worse position than his counterpart in the West, since he had no independent trade unions to stand up for his interests and—if need be— to call him out on strike. He had, in spite of the claims of the Soviet rulers, no possibility whatsoever of exerting a direct and organised influence on the shaping of industrial policy.

Since the death of Stalin, particularly since 1956, there have been considerable changes in Soviet labour legislation and more are foreshadowed for the period of "creating the material and technical basis of Communism." Therefore, the question arises: Are the present changes and the discernible trends in the future of a fundamental nature, affecting the entire relationship of social forces in the USSR, or are they merely a long overdue liberalisation, a softening of the harsh laws governing labour conditions, which will be carried out strictly within the limits of existing social relations?

From the point of view of the worker, the most important decree of the post-Stalin period was, no doubt, that of April 25, 1956, revoking the June 1940 decree which tied him to his job under threat of imprisonment or corrective labour. In practice it has apparently been possible to leave one's job without express managerial permission since 1953, but the official, generally valid decree was not promulgated until 1956.[3] The labour force had by then become more stable and the danger of the spontaneous and anarchic fluidity of the earlier years had passed. The only large-scale movement of workers was that organised by the authorities themselves: the mass transfer of workers to the East, especially to the virgin land areas, the transplanting of agricultural and other experts from large towns to farms and production sites and the dispersal of administrative personnel into the provinces in connection with the decentralisation of industry in 1957. Although these transfers may not always have been entirely voluntary, there was nothing of the compulsion and brutal force of the thirties.

Next in importance was the re-introduction of the seven-hour day, made possible, as Khrushchev said, by higher productivity and an in-

---

[3] *Vedomosti Verkhovnogo Sovieta SSSR,* August 5, 1956, No. 10/203. The decree states that workers will no longer be liable to court proceedings if they leave their job on their own accord. But the stipulation that continuity of work would be considered interrupted, and that social insurance would not become operative until after six months at the new job, was maintained. It was later amended so as not to be applicable to workers who left their jobs because of industrial injuries or disease (*Vedomosti,* February 8, 1957, No. 3/55). This stipulation was finally repealed a year ago (*Vedomosti,* January 28, 1960, No. 4/36). Sickness benefits will now be paid irrespective of the length of employment at the worker's new place of work. Continuity of work will not be considered as having been interrupted if work is started within a month of leaving the old job. This is important, as the sum total of years at work affects old age and disability pensions.

creased social product. It was hailed as the shortest working day in the world. It is a matter of speculation how much this measure may also absorb latent unemployment due to the mechanisation and automation drive, the rapid expansion of industry in general, and also to a certain flight from the land.

The seven-hour day was first promised in 1927, on the occasion of the tenth anniversary of the October Revolution, in the Manifesto of the USSR Central Executive Committee. In 1928 it was operative in the textile industry. Its introduction by stages throughout industry was made obligatory in January 1929 and envisaged as being fully operative by October 1933. In 1931, 58.2 per cent of all industrial workers were already said to be on a seven-hour day. After 1932 no more information was published on this. Under the impact of the all-out industrialisation drive the decision is hardly likely to have been strictly adhered to, though it was not officially repealed until June 1940, when the eight-hour day and the seven-day week with Sunday as the general day off (as against the former so-called six-day week) was once more introduced. In June 1941 overtime of up to three hours a day was made mandatory.

Thus, in fact, the present introduction of the seven-hour day is no more than a return to a previously existing condition, though admittedly the reduction of working hours has now been carried out on a much sounder economic basis than before. The decision concerning its introduction (seven hours in general, six hours for underground workers in the iron ore and coal mining industries), without loss of pay, was announced by Khrushchev at the Twentieth Party Congress in February 1956. In March of that year, the working hours on the eve of days off and holidays were cut from eight to six,[4] thus making a 46-hour week. Juvenile work was reduced to six hours in May,[5] and in December the government imposed a ban on work by juveniles under the age of 16. Apprentices aged 15—16 were to work only four hours a day.[6]

The first switch-over to the seven- (or six-) hour day was made towards the end of 1956 in the Donbas coal region. Other coal regions and industries, such as iron ore mining, ferrous and non-ferrous metallurgy, and the coke-chemical industry followed between 1957 and 1959.

The Twenty-first Party Congress (January–February 1959) decided on a completion of the switch-over in 1960, and foreshadowed the introduction of a general 40-hour week in 1962 and a 35-hour week in 1964 (30 hours for workers engaged in hazardous occupations or in work detrimental to health).

The time limits for the introduction of the seven-hour day in various geographical regions and the remaining branches of the national econ-

4 *Pravda,* March 9, 1956.
5 *Pravda,* May 29, 1956.
6 *Pravda,* December 14, 1956.

omy, including cultural and scientific organisations and sovkhozes
were published in *Pravda,* as a resolution of the Central Committee, the
Council of Ministers and the All-Union Central Council of Trade Unions
on September 20, 1959. The whole question of the switch-over was approached cautiously, by stages, to avoid chaos in the national economy.
Even so, the impact must have been considerable.

One condition of the successful transfer to the shorter working day
without loss in pay and the introduction of new wage scales, was the
establishment of the most rational form of pay, instead of the wholesale
use of piece-work rates hitherto existing even where most unsuitable. It
was suggested that the ministries, economic regions, enterprises, etc.,
adopt the system of individual bonuses based on qualitative indices, together with collective bonuses for quantity of output. Careful preparatory
work was to precede the switch-over, to avoid time lags, fall in productivity and consequent need to hire additional personnel, thereby exceeding the fixed wages fund. The reduction from the 48-hour to the 42-hour
week,[7] was carried out over a period of five years, and has meant a reduction of the available labour force by 12.5 per cent.[8] The switch-over from
the 48-hour week to an eventual 40-hour week, with a reduction of the
labour force by 16.6 per cent, will take seven years to complete. . . .

Apart from a further revision of minimum wages, the decision to
simplify the wage and salary scales, and to "put in order" the entire system
of pay was a positive step of the first order. This reform is to be carried
out simultaneously with the reduction of the working day. It is to be
completed throughout the national economy, including sovkhozes and
auxiliary agricultural enterprises in 1962. . . .

A revision of wage and salary scales had long been overdue. In the
course of thirty years they had become so numerous, complicated and
unwieldy, so overlaid with supplementary payments, such as bonuses,
progressive piece rates, etc., that they had lost a great deal of their practical value. . . .

Before the reform there were, Sukharevsky * reveals, about two thousand different rates for Grade 1 (the lowest, basic grade). After the
reform there will be a total of six wages scales with about forty different
rates for Grade 1. These will cover all branches of the national economy
and all types of work. For some trades and professions the same scale will
be in force in all industries throughout the country. As before, the new

[7] It is not quite clear whether work on Saturdays and on the eve of holidays has been
extended to 7 hours, or whether it is still 6 hours, which would mean a 41-hour week.
An article in *Sovietskoe gosudarstvo i pravo,* No. 8, 1961, pp. 3-16, states that at the end
of 1950 the average working day, taking into consideration the shorter day of the
miners, was 6.67 hours, or 39.4 hours per week.

[8] N. Klimov, "Shortening of the Working Day and Problems of Labour Productivity,"
Voprosy ekonomiki, No. 9, September 1959, pp. 49-57.

* Reference is made to B. Sukharevsky's article "Working Day and Wages in the
USSR" published in *Kommunist* No. 3, Feb., 1960, pp. 22-37. [Editor's Note].

wage scales will lay down the statutory minimum rate for the job. This will be supplemented by bonuses, piece rates for exceeding the norm, and zonal allowances (the so-called coefficients), as the case may be. These supplementary payments may constitute 15 to 20 per cent of the basic wage, which will thus at last really become "basic." Grade 1 will be based on the statutory national minimum wage in force at any particular time.

In 1956 minimum wages (and students' stipends) were raised to between 270 and 350 roubles a month, but the existing Grade 1 rates were not altered. In 1962 the minimum is to be increased to 400–450 roubles. According to Sukharevsky, the wage for Grade 1 in light industry and the food industry will be roughly 400–500 roubles a month; in the manufacturing branches of heavy industry 500–600 roubles, and in mining 500–700 roubles. In some branches of industry the basic Grade 1 wage will thus be some 50 per cent above the statutory minimum and, taking into consideration the supplements, actual earnings of workers in Grade 1 can be as much as 100 per cent above the minimum. As announced by Khrushchev at the Twenty-first Party Congress, in 1965 the statutory minimum will rise to 500–600 roubles.[9] The wage rates for Grade 1 will, no doubt, rise correspondingly. Certain differences in the wage rates for the same grade and within the same branch of industry will, however, remain, due to differences in actual working conditions. A Grade 1 piece worker in the engineering industry will earn 530–560 roubles a month if he is on "cold" work, but 610–640 roubles if on "hot" work.** . . .

As to engineers and technicians, their salaries are, as before, laid down in special scales. The minimum salary of a Grade 1 foreman of a production section is to be "higher" (Sukharevsky does not specify by how much) than the basic wage of the most highly skilled worker. The foreman's salary will then serve as the lowest basic unit for the salaries of other engineers and technicians. A director's salary is, "as a rule," limited to two or three times that of a foreman (as against three to five times before the reform). This again is a step in the direction of closing the gap between minimum and maximum earnings. It should be noted, however, that a considerable gap remains. The national minimum in 1962 is to be 400–450 roubles a month. The minimum Grade 1 wage in heavy industry was stated to be 500–600 roubles (see p. 85); the highest wage, at a ratio of 1:2, would then be 1,000 to 1,200 roubles. A foreman whose basic salary is to be "higher," would then presumably get at least 1,100 to 1,300 roubles, and a director two to three times more, i.e. anything between 2,200 and 3,900 roubles, which would be nine times more than statutory minimum. If we add to this the maximum supplements of 20 per cent for

9 *Pravda,* January 28, 1959.
** All figures are expressed in old roubles. To obtain equivalent figures in new roubles, divide by ten. [Editor's Note].

a worker and 60 per cent for a director, we arrive at extremes of roughly 480 and 6,240 roubles a month (in the old currency). This means that if our calculation is correct we still have a differential of about 1:15.

The salaries of leading administrative and technical personnel will be worked out by groups of industries and laid down in two scales (instead of the former 700-odd): a higher one for the more important branches, including heavy industry and the other for the rest. Sukharevsky antici-pates, however, a single salary and a single wage scale to be operative throughout the country. Maximum bonuses for salaried workers will now be limited to from 40–60 per cent of the monthly salary. For the first time in the history of state enterprises and agricultural organisations there will also be a "unified wage and salary scale" for all.[10]

The new system of bonuses introduced in the majority of enterprises since October 1959 lays far more stress on quality and on lowering the cost of production to or below that required by the plan. This will be measured in "cost per rouble of production." In key enterprises of heavy industry, however, overfulfilment of the production plan will still count. It is, no doubt, hoped that this will eliminate excesses in bonus payment which in the case of salaried workers can, as we have seen, still be con-siderable.

Summing up the aims of the wage reform, the Department of Labour Legislation of the Institute of Government and Law explains that for the time being the system of pay is still based on "material interest" and that certain "privileges for workers in key industries or leading profes-sions" will be maintained or introduced. It considers, however, that future legislation must strictly define the competence of the trade union organi-sations at all levels in matters of wage policy.[11] The rights and functions of the trade unions and dispute-settling bodies have already been ex-tended and modified during the last few years.

Right from the beginning, i.e. when the shorter day on the eve of free days and holidays was introduced, stress was laid on the absolute necessity of maintaining the level of production, since only this would make it economically possible to maintain the level of wages. . . .

How far the revision of output norms has been successful is difficult to assess.

Reports by the Central Statistical Administration on the fulfilment of the annual plan goals give the following figures as compared with the preceding year: increase of labour productivity in 1959 was 2 per cent in the coal industry, which is working on the reduced day, and between 5–12 per cent in other branches of industry, most of which had ap-parently not yet switched over at that time. The increases in labour

[10] A. Volkov, "Shorter Working Day and Wage Reform," *Kommunist*, No. 13, Sep-tember 1960, pp. 28-37.
[11] *Ibid.*

productivity in 1960 and 1961 were "over 5 per cent" and "over 4 per cent" respectively in industries with the reduced day and "taking into account the reduction in working time," labour productivity increased by over 10 per cent in 1960 and 11 per cent in 1961 (in the building industry it was 3.5 per cent and 12 per cent).[12] . . .

The present effort to improve the workers' living standards and their working conditions has also been reflected in the field of labour protection, especially for women and juveniles. Examples are the re-introduction of the ban on underground work, longer leave for expectant and nursing mothers, and social services, such as sickness benefits, maternity benefits, pensions, provision of work for old-age pensioners, and the like. The rates for old-age and disability pensions have gone up. The minimum is now 300 roubles a month, plus certain supplements. For workers disabled while at work, the minimum basic rate is 360 roubles. For both categories the ceiling is 1,200 roubles. For workers retired on grounds of general ill health, the minimum basic pension is 300 roubles and the maximum 900 roubles.[13] But Article 60 of the 1960 Labour Law still speaks of "personal" pensions for citizens and their families for "special services to the state." Instituted originally in 1920 towards the end of the Civil War, when they were not to exceed "four times the average local wage," these "personal" pensions, together with gratuities, reached fabulous heights under Stalin. Even before his death, however, publication of information about them had ceased, so that there is now no indication as to their amount. They obviously still exist, however, since the 1956 law stipulates that these pensions, as well as those given to scientists and their families, are to be dealt with separately by the USSR Council of Ministers.

Further increases in minimum pensions will probably accompany the rise in minimum wages in 1962 and 1965. . . .

There is now also an awareness of the need to give security to the old and the sick on the collective farms, who have hitherto not been and are still not covered by the state social insurance scheme.

The institute of Government and Law advocates handing over the entire social insurance system to the trade unions as a step on the road towards the gradual transition to Communist self-government.

Finally, there are the cuts in, and the proposed eventual abolition of income tax. In 1956 the limit for tax exemption of low wages, salaries, and stipends was raised to 370 roubles a month and in 1960 to 500 roubles.[14] At the Supreme Soviet session in May 1960 Khrushchev outlined the plan for the total abolition of income tax in stages by the end of

---

12 *Pravda*, 22 January, 1960; January 26, 1961; January 23, 1962.
13 Law passed by the Supreme Soviet of the USSR on July 14, 1956, *Zbornik Zakobodatelnykh aktov a trude*, Moscow, 1956, p. 420 ff.
14 *Pravda*, July 23, 1960.

1965 and a simultaneous automatic raising of incomes.[15] . . . The Soviet government can afford to make a gesture in regard to income tax, which constitutes an insignificant part of its revenue: 5,800 million roubles in 1962, out of a total estimated revenue of 74,400 million roubles. One of the chief sources of revenue being the turnover or sales tax on most consumer goods (estimated at 32,400 million roubles in 1962, i.e. roughly 43.5 per cent of total revenue as against less than 8 per cent in the case of income tax). . . .

We can only guess at future trends from the pronouncements of the Soviet leaders at Party Congresses and Supreme Soviet Sessions, and from press reports. A theoretical explanation and forecast of future wages policy is given by Sukharevsky in the customary tortuous and abstract way. The socialist system, he says, knows two methods of distributing the total consumer fund: first, payment of wages for work performed, and second, supplementary payments or allocations from public funds, not connected with any work performed. The latter are sickness benefits, pensions, hospitals, schools, stipends and so on, i.e. what used to be called "the socialised part of wages." Under the socialist system, during the period of the transition to Communism and the eventual distribution "according to individual needs," the socialist system will continue to pay "wages," i.e. use the form evolved under capitalism, but will give it a "new content." In a socialist society, Sukharevsky explains, wages play a different role in the system of distribution insofar as they are used as a material incentive for the individual in order to raise the standard of living of the entire working class in strict accordance with their productivity. While allocations from public funds (i.e. indirect payments) under capitalism are—here Sukharevsky quotes Lenin—either "huckstering" or "acrobatics of bourgeois charity," in the USSR they will eventually lead to Communism, and will apparently gradually replace monetary wages, at which point the differences between manual and brain work and between work in industry and work in agriculture will have disappeared.

Soviet theoreticians have been writing in this vein for a great many years and it is quite possible that many of them have finally become convinced by their own propaganda that a fundamentally new and vastly superior social system is being evolved in their country. What, however, does the entire present trend of Soviet labour policy reveal? Simply that the political process of "de-Stalinisation" has been carried into the economic field and into the field of labour relations.

Now the world and the Soviet people have been told by Khrushchev that freedom and democracy did not exist under Stalin. The recent economic and social reforms are an admission that the happy and prosperous condition of the Soviet working class was also a delusion. However, de-Stalinisation does not go so far as to upset the basic system established

---

[15] *Pravda,* May 6, 1960.

during the Stalin era and therefore the economic and labour policy reforms leave the situation of the mass of the population fundamentally unchanged.

The paternalistic measures that have been and are being taken to ease the lot of the Soviet workers are undoubtedly progressive, but there is nothing to support the claim of a new form of society, superior to capitalist society. None of the measures recently taken have so far touched upon the social status of the Soviet worker. They have not given him that essential means of expressing and achieving his aspirations, which workers in the capitalist democracies possess—free trade unions.

SOVIET VIEWS

27

Higher Wages, Shorter Hours, Smaller Wage Differentials, and Increased Output: A Great Social Achievement *

A. KAZANSKII
Retired. Formerly with Labor Statistics Department,
USSR Central Statistical Board

A. F. UL'IANOVA
Chief, Section of Labor and Wage Statistics,
Central Statistical Administration, USSR

The program for the comprehensive building of communism in our country provided for the complete transfer by 1960 of factory workers and office employees to a seven-hour working day and workers of the leading professions engaged in work underground to a six-hour working day. This program, proclaimed in the historic decisions of the 21st Congress of the CPSU, contained many other exceptionally important measures providing for the further development of the Soviet economy and an improvement in the material well-being of the working people.

Guided by the decisions of the Congress, the CPSU Central Committee, the Council of Ministers of the USSR, and the All-Union Central Council

* From *Vestnik Statistiki*, 1961, No. 5. Translated under the title "A Great Social Achievement (On the Results of the Transfer of Factory Workers and Office Employees of the USSR to a Shorter Working Day)", in *Problems of Economics*, August, 1961, pp. 28-36. Excerpts reprinted from the translation by permission of the publisher.

of Trade Unions passed a decision in September 1959 which established specific dates for completing the transfer in 1960 of all factory workers and office employees to a reduced seven or six-hour working day.

This decision has been carried out. By January 1st, 1961, factory workers and office employees of all enterprises, institutions and organization of the USSR had a seven-hour working day, and those who were engaged in work underground had a six-hour working day. Furthermore, in accordance with earlier decisions of the government, those engaged in work under harmful conditions had a four to five-hour working day, young people aged 16 to 18 six hours a day, and those 15 years of age—4 hours a day. It should be borne in mind that the work of these youths is paid for as a full working day of workers of the respective categories. There are several other categories of employees (school teachers, professors and instructors, doctors, medium level medical personnel, etc.) who also enjoy a shorter working day in accordance with laws passed previously. . . .

As a result of the shifting of all workers and employees to a shorter seven or six-hour working day, the average length of the work week established for all workers and employees of the Soviet Union (bearing in mind that part of the workers and employees work seven hours a day and that some have a shorter working day) is 39.4 hours.[1]

The already achieved transfer of Soviet factory workers and office employees to a shorter working day is an important step towards the establishment in our country of the *shortest working day in the world*. The free time of the worker "for rest, for his development, and for the enjoyment of his rights as a human being, a family man, and a citizen" (V. I. Lenin, *Collected Works,* Vol. II, p. 276) was increased by one hour, and for some categories of workers, by two hours. In other words, the workers and employees transferred to a shorter seven or six-hour working day, received an additional 41-45 free days per year. . . .

Reduction of the working day has always been and remains one of the fundamental policy questions of the Communist Party. Among the first decrees of the Soviet Government signed by V. I. Lenin was the decree of November 11 (October 29) 1917, on the introduction of an eight-hour working day as the maximum working norm for adults, and a six-hour working day for juveniles. . . .

The restoration of the national economy after the imperialist and civil wars, the rise in labor productivity and the strengthening of economic leadership enabled the Party and the Government to further lighten the labor of the working people. In October 1927, on the occasion

---

[1] The figures quoted are determined on the basis of the annual amount of working time, i.e., taking into account the shorter working day on days preceding the day off and holidays, and also the holidays themselves which are in addition to the regular day off.

of the Tenth Anniversary of Soviet power, the Central Executive Committee of the USSR published a manifesto proclaiming the transfer, within the first five-year plan period, of workers of industry, railway transport, the public utilities and communications to a seven-hour working day, and workers engaged in work underground—to a six-hour working day without any decrease in wages.

The measures provided for by the Manifesto were successfully carried out. In the years following the transfer of the workers to a shorter working day all branches of industries showed a considerable increase in gross output, labor productivity, and the wages of the workers.

On the eve of the Great Patriotic War, in view of the serious international situation, the Soviet Government was compelled, in June of 1940, to increase somewhat the length of the working day for factory workers and office employees. In particular, the working day was increased from seven to eight hours at enterprises with a seven-hour working day, and from six to seven hours at enterprises with a six-hour working day (with the exception of trades with harmful working conditions), and from six to eight hours for office employees.

In the post-war years the Soviet Government passed a number of new laws reducing the length of the working day (the working day was shortened on days before the day off and before holidays, a shorter working day was introduced for juveniles, and a number of privileges were established for working people who study in correspondence and evening higher and specialized secondary schools, etc.).

After overcoming the terrible losses which our country suffered from the bandit attack of the fascists, losses which were unprecedented in the history of warfare, the Soviet State succeeded in considerably advancing all branches of the national economy. This achievement was due to the great labor enthusiasm of the Soviet people and the wise domestic and foreign policy of the Communist Party. Economic development provided the real basis which made it possible to raise the question of introducing a shorter seven and six-hour working day. It is quite natural that this measure was first introduced in heavy industry, the coal industry, ferrous and non-ferrous metallurgy, the chemical, cement, reinforced concrete and other industries.

The average length of the working day established for adult factory workers at the end of 1960 was 6.94 hours. If we consider the average annual working time, i.e., if we take into account the shorter working day before days off and holidays and also the holidays in addition to the usual days off, the average length of the working day for adult workers in industry amounts to 6.67 hours. The average length of the work week for industrial workers is now 40 hours.

There are two essential features that distinguish the transfer of Soviet workers and employees to a shorter working day.

The first is that the shorter working day was introduced under conditions not only of absolute maintenance of the achieved volume of output and the level of labor productivity, but even of a further increase in production and a rise of labor productivity. . . .

A number of economic and technical measures taken prior to the transfer of workers and employees to a shorter working day assured the fulfillment and over-fulfillment of the plan for output and labor productivity, and also helped lighten labor as much as possible. Among the chief measures taken were the wide introduction of new techniques, the modernization of lathes and other machines, the use of progressive, improved technology, and better repair of equipment. Furthermore, the mechanization of the production processes at a large number of enterprises was effected not only in the main operations, but also in the auxiliary ones which call for a great amount of manual labor. . . .

As a result of these measures labor productivity in industry per worker increased more than twofold in 1960 as compared with 1950, and by 13% since 1958. . . .

The second most important feature of the transfer of workers and office employees to a shorter working day is that when this measure was taken the wages of workers and employees not only did not drop, but were even raised in branches where new higher rates and salaries were introduced. This is possible only in a socialist society.

The decisions of the 21st Congress of the CPSU provided that when wages were regulated, the wages of the lower and middle-paid workers and employees be raised in order to reduce the gap between the lower and higher paid categories of workers. During the seven-year period the wages of the lower paid workers and employees are to be raised from 27-35 rubles to 50-60 rubles a month.[2] These measures will be carried out gradually, in two stages.

In the years 1959–1962 (the first stage) it is planned to complete the regulation of wages of workers and office employees, which has already been begun, and simultaneously to increase the minimum wage to 40 to 45 rubles per month in all branches of the economy.

In the years 1963–1965 (the second stage) the minimum wage of workers and employees in all branches of the national economy is to be raised to 50-60 rubles a month, and the wages and salaries of middle-paid workers and employees will also be somewhat raised.

As a result of measures already taken to regulate the wages of factory workers and office employees, the number of people in industry who receive less than 60 rubles a month has become considerably less.

In all branches of the national economy the transfer of factory workers and office employees to a shorter working day was effected without any drop in wages. In industry and in a number of enterprises of other

2 Here, as elsewhere, the wages are given in terms of new currency.

branches of the national economy, where the transfer of workers and employees to a shorter working day was effected simultaneously with the regulation of the wage system, the earnings of the workers and employees not only remained at the former level, but as a result of the introduction of new, higher rates and salaries, they were raised, especially those of the lower-paid categories of workers. The average money wage of workers in industry increased by 17% [3] in 1960 as compared with 1955, and by 27% in the construction industry. . . .

Uniform wage scales were established for enterprises of one and the same branch. While the new wage scales retained considerable differences between the rate categories, they put an end to excessive differences between the pay of the higher and lower categories. For example, at the machine-building and metal-working enterprises the previously existing eight-category wage scale, in which the relation between the extreme categories was 1:2.4, 1:3.0, and 1:3.6, was replaced by a uniform six-category wage scale with a relation between the extreme categories of 1:2.0. . . .

As a result of the regulation of the wage system, such forms and systems of payment for work were introduced as best stimulated a rise in labor productivity and afforded a material incentive to the workers. The piece-work progressive system of pay was wiped out almost completely, and was replaced by the direct piece-work or piece-work-bonus system. In a number of branches of industry in various production sections where the piece-work system of pay was not justified, payment on a time basis was introduced (mainly a time-bonus system). . . .

As a result of the transfer of factory workers and office employees to the new system of pay, the material interest of the workers in the results of their labor greatly increased. In all branches where the wage system was regulated simultaneously with a cut in the length of the working day output considerably increased, as did labor productivity and the workers' wages. . . .

After the shift to a shorter working day more favorable conditions existed for the workers to increase their knowledge and raise their qualifications, to study while continuing to work by attending the general education schools for young city and agricultural workers, evening and correspondence higher and specialized secondary schools, evening schools, schools for professional and technical education, and other educational institutions.

In 1960 the number of people who, while continuing to work, studied in the higher and specialized secondary schools, in the general education schools for young city and agricultural workers, and also in schools for adults, amounted to almost five million. Furthermore, in 1960 about

---

[3] This does not include enterprises of producers' cooperatives transferred to the system of state enterprises in 1960.

ten million workers and employees were taught new specialties and raised their qualifications directly on the job.

In the period when the workers and employees were transferred to a shorter working day there arose new ways for the workers to raise their technical and general cultural level: instruction in people's universities, acquaintance with the concrete economics of various branches of industry, and the extension of lecture and group work at workers' clubs.

The shift of the workers and employees to a shorter seven and six-hour working day, which was completed by January 1, 1961, is not the final stage in reducing the length of working time. The 21st Congress of the CPSU decided to complete the transfer of workers and employees to a 40-hour work week in 1962 and in 1964 to begin the gradual transfer to a 35 and 30 hour work week with two days off a week. When these measures are effected, the USSR will have the shortest working day and the shortest work week in the world.

In his speech at a meeting of the builders of the Bratsk hydro-electric power station in October 1959, N. S. Khrushchev defined the prospects for the further reduction of the working day in the period of the building of a communist society. "The time is not far off when, on the basis of the further development of production, science and techniques and on the basis of technical progress and the automation of production the people of our country will work 3 and 4 hours a day," he said. "Man will control intricate machines and mechanisms, and in this brief period he will produce considerably more products than he now does; this will ensure the greater satisfaction of the needs of the country and all the needs of every citizen of communist society."

The apologists for capitalism, in trying somewhat to support their fabrications about a change that is taking place in the nature of capitalism, its transformation into a sort of "people's capitalism," demagogically speculate on certain social achievements which the working class won through many years of stubborn struggle, exaggerate their significance in every possible way, and at the same time distort the general picture of the position of the working people in capitalist countries. In particular, a slight decrease in the absolute length of the working day in various countries during the past decades, despite what the bourgeois economists write about it, is by no means evidence of a lightening of labor inasmuch as the reduction in the length of the working day is accompanied by an increased intensification of labor.

According to the latest published data, the actual average length of the work week in England is 46.7 hours and in France—46.1 hours.

In the USA there is a law about a 40-hour week. But the law does not restrict the use of overtime work, and if an employer finds it profitable to do so, he can compel a worker to work beyond the established time merely by paying him additionally for the work done above 40 hours a week. It must also be pointed out that in the USA, where there is chronic unemployment of millions of workers, it is a widespread practice to employ people for a lesser number of hours per week with correspondingly lower wages. For instance, according to a selective poll by the Census Bureau, in June 1959, 49.8% of the workers and employees in non-agricultural branches in the USA in 1959 had a 40-hour work week, 21.9% worked less than 40 hours a week, that is, actually they were partially unemployed, 28.3% worked more than 40 hours a week, and 12.5% worked more than 48 hours a week.[4]

As regards the position of the working people in the colonial and semi-colonial countries, it is much worse than that of the workers and employees in the so-called "civilized" capitalist countries.

In the USSR, in contrast to the capitalist countries, a cut in the length of the working day is not accompanied by an increased intensification of labor. The rise in labor productivity is achieved in the main by mechanization and automation of production, by production training of the working people, and a rise in their cultural and technical level. There is no unemployment in the USSR. On the contrary, the number of workers and employees engaged in the national economy increases every year. . . .

The real incomes of Soviet workers and employees are constantly increasing. In 1960 they had increased 2.1 times as compared with 1940. The real incomes of industrial and construction workers in 1960 had increased 5.8 times since 1913, the liquidation of unemployment and the reduction in the length of the working day being taken into consideration.

The cut in the length of the working day is a most important social achievement of the working people of the USSR. Once again the Soviet Union has demonstrated to the entire world the great advantages of socialism over capitalism.

4 Compiled from *Current Population Reports,* Series, p. 57, No. 204.

B. The Soviet Worker and His Labor Union

SOME LABOR unions in the Western World have pursued political goals which, to a greater or lesser extent, have been in direct opposition to a capitalist free enterprise system. Britain's major labor unions, for instance, are the backbone of Britain's Socialist Labor Party; France's CGT has at times been under the influence of France's Communist Party; and Argentina's labor unions provided the foundation upon which rested Peron's dictatorial powers. In the United States, however, most labor unions are opposed to any *fundamental* changes in American society and consider it their task to improve the lot of American workers within the framework of a basically capitalist democracy. Higher wages, shorter hours, better working conditions, and recently a gamut of fringe benefits—these are the issues for which American labor leaders bargain collectively with the representatives of their employers.

But what is the role of a labor union in a society in which there is but one industrial employer, the state? How can a labor union bargain collectively with this one employer if, in the very theory of the system, all industries are owned by society at large? To what extent do labor unions in such a society have the power to influence managerial decisions? How much of a voice does the individual worker have—in other words, how democratic are labor unions—in a society in which the one single political party has a preponderant influence over the direction of most aspects of national life?

Emily Clark Brown, whose extensive studies of Soviet trade unions include prolonged personal observation of industrial relations in the USSR, finds that the reorganization of Soviet industry in 1957 brought in its wake considerable and beneficial changes for Soviet trade unions, in terms of enhanced rights, responsibilities, and power. She concludes, however, that the required adherence to the overall plan and the position of power of party members necessarily prevents any real independence.

On the Soviet side, A. Piatakov presents the official Soviet position in regard to the purposes and functions of trade unions in the USSR, their relationship to the state, their role in the drafting of laws and in local, state, and central planning, their participation in management, and their duties and responsibilities towards their members.

28

The Local Union in Soviet Industry: Its Relations with Members, Party and Management *

EMILY CLARK BROWN
Vassar College

Soviet trade unions, as "mass nonparty organizations," are now said to be playing an increasingly important role in Soviet life, under the leadership of the Communist party. Their central task, according to the most authoritative statement, is: "the mobilization of the masses for the struggle for further mighty progress of all branches of the economy . . . for the maximum utilization of all reserves and possibilities for rapid growth of . . . production, for the further development of the material security and culture of the working people." At the same time: "Improving the conditions of work and life of workers and employees is a most important task of the trade unions." [1] Khrushchev said of the trade

* Excerpts reprinted from *Industrial and Labor Relations Review*, January, 1960, pp. 192-215, by permission of the author and the publisher.

During the past year, Professor Brown spent almost three months in the Soviet Union, pursuing her interest in the industrial relations system of that country. This article reports her findings on the nature of unionism at the plant and shop levels, based on observations made in a variety of industries. These findings contrast markedly with earlier appraisals of the role of the trade union in Soviet industry. Although unions must conform to the broad objectives of the state, the author finds that the function of protecting workers' rights and interests is becoming increasingly important, that the powers as well as the responsibilities of the local unions (or factory committees) have been enlarged, and that union leadership at the "grass-roots" level has become more representative of, and possibly more acceptable to, the workers which it represents. Much of this change in the role of unions resulted from important changes in 1957–1958 in Soviet policy on the organization of industry, including labor organization. For additional background on this development and a discussion of its implications for labor relations in the Soviet Union, the reader is referred to the author's earlier article, "Labor Relations in Soviet Factories," in the January 1958 issue of this *Review*, pp. 183–202. EDITOR (of the *Industrial and Labor Relations Review*).

[1] Resolution of Central Committee of the Communist Party of the Soviet Union on the work of trade unions, Dec. 17, 1957. *Pravda*, Dec. 19, 1957, translated in *Current Digest of the Soviet Press*, Vol. 9, No. 50 (Jan. 22, 1958), pp. 11-15. See also *Statutes of the Trade Unions of the USSR*, adopted March 27, 1959. *Trud*, April 2, 1959.

unions in 1957, "Not a single event of any importance in the life of our country takes place without their active participation." [2] Under the terms of a highly significant decree of July 1958, on the rights of factory and other local trade union committees, "Factory, plant and local committees of the trade unions, elected on the basis of the statutes of the appropriate trade unions, effectuate representation in the name of the workers and employees of enterprises, institutions, organizations, on all questions of labor, life, culture." [3]

The claim of these organizations to be voluntary associations, representing and working for the interests of their members, is widely disputed in the West. Our understanding of the Soviet economy would be furthered if we could have conclusive answers to the questions about their role in the still highly centralized planned economy, their relationship to party and government and to their members. Are they "real" trade unions, according to the classic definition, "a continuous association of wage earners for the purpose of maintaining or improving the conditions of their working lives?" [4] Do they perform a function useful to workers in the particular system of industrial relations that exists in the Soviet Union? What is the real nature of industrial relations in the Soviet system?

This article contributes some tentative answers to these questions by presenting an analysis of available evidence on Soviet unions especially at the local level, in the plant, where their relationship with their members is most direct. Useful evidence comes from the Soviet press, Soviet professional journals dealing with labor, and numerous pamphlets reporting in detail on local experience. In addition, the writer spent a month in the Soviet Union in 1955, and again in 1959 was allowed to stay in the country for ten-and-a-half weeks as a tourist, engaged in field study of labor relations. Visits to a total of twenty-one plants, usually involving long talks with the director or other management officials and, whenever possible, with the chairman of the trade union factory committee, were supplemented by interviews with regional trade union council officers, regional economic council personnel, economists, and experts on labor law.[5]

[2] N. S. Khrushchev, "On further improving organization of the management of industry and construction," *Pravda*, May 8, 1957 in *Current Digest of the Soviet Press*, Vol. 9, No. 18 (June 12, 1957), p. 16.

[3] Pravda, July 16, 1958, *Current Digest of the Soviet Press*, Vol. 10, No. 28 (August 20, 1958), pp. 3-4. The decree was given final approval as law (*zakon*) by the Supreme Soviet in December 1958.

[4] Sidney and Beatrice Webb, *The History of Trade Unionism*, 1920, p. 1.

[5] I am grateful to Vassar College for the faculty fellowship which made possible the trip in November–December 1955, and for releasing me for a half year in 1959; and to the Social Science Research Council for a grant, which, supplemented by a grant from the Inter-University Study of Labor Problems in Economic Development, made possible the extensive stay from February to May 1959. The friendly cooperation of many Soviet citizens is gratefully acknowledged: managers and trade union officers who gave their time freely, many economists and legal experts who were helpful, several hard-working

New evidence was obtained on the people who operate this industrial relations system, their attitudes and beliefs, and their organization and methods of work. The evidence is limited in value by its largely subjective character. Little objective evidence could be obtained in the field, especially since, in spite of some cooperation and a number of promises, it never proved possible to attend a union meeting, production conference, disputes committee session, or other examples of trade unions actually at work. It was only rarely possible to talk directly with workers in any fruitful way. The representativeness of the plants visited is a serious question also, since they were primarily in light industry, especially textiles, and among larger plants and plants which are shown to tourists.[6] Experts with whom this question was raised, however, were sure that these were typical, no better and no worse than many others. In any case it is useful to know what the industrial relations system is supposed to be, what official policies are seeking to promote, and what people involved intend and say about how it works. Soviet publications gave confirmation and added detail to the impressions obtained in the plants.

The analysis starts, after briefly noting the special conditions of the Soviet environment, and the structure of the trade unions, with a discussion of the factory committee and its officers, in relation to the members, to party policy and local party organization, and to higher levels in the union structure. It then turns to the plant directors, who they are, their attitudes and relations with the union and workers, and the climate of labor relations in the plants. Finally, the new rights and functions of the factory committee are discussed, and the job of the chairman is described.

Intourist managers and guides who went beyond the call of duty to help an odd tourist who w∠nted contacts not usually made by Intourist (though it must be said that some others did not meet the unusual situation with the ingenuity and initiative that their system is said to call for), and Voks, the Union of Societies for Friendship and Cultural Relations with Foreign Countries, who were most helpful in arranging contacts in four cities. Interviews were conducted through interpreters, except in the rare cases where an economist spoke English. The writer's knowledge of spoken Russian was enough to help in interviews and to give some opportunity for other contacts.

Cities visited were Moscow, Leningrad, Kharkov, Kiev, Ivanova, Rostov, Tbilisi, Alma-Ata, Tashkent, and Samarkand. Plants visited included machine-tool production, 3; tractors, 1; textiles, 9; tea-packing, 2; champagne, 2; and one each in shoe, tobacco, food, and printing plants.

Reports on the earlier stage of the study appeared in "The Soviet Labor Market," this *Review*, Vol. 10, No. 2 (January 1957), pp. 179-200, and "Labor Relations in Soviet Factories," Vol. 11, No. 2 (January 1958), pp. 183-202.

6 While it was denied that there are lists of plants to which tourists may be taken, it was clear that Intourist knew what plants were available. A request to see a printing plant, because of the author's acquaintance with that industry in the United States, was without result in two cities, and succeeded in a third only when Voks made arrangements through the Minister of Culture of the Republic.

The Soviet Industrial Environment

To understand Soviet trade unions the first essential is to see them in their economic and political context. First, since all basic policies in the Soviet system are centrally decided by the Communist party and the authoritarian, Communist-controlled government,[7] the role of trade unions is the role decided by the party. A second major point is the extremely rapid pace of industrial growth, with large-scale production [8] and increasing mechanization and even automation. Productivity of labor is increasing rapidly under the great drive to "overtake and surpass" the United States in major fields, although it is still relatively low and surprising amounts of manual labor are still to be seen.

Third, central planning of the economy still rules, under the State Planning Commission and the Council of Ministers of the USSR. The decentralization of industry put through by Khrushchev in 1957, however, placed detailed planning and the administration of most of industry under regional economic councils, thus considerably increasing the scope for local initiative.[9] Along with this change in management, a need was evidently felt for more scope for union influence and activity at the local level, probably both to promote local initiative and to provide a further check on local management.

Fourth, although the labor force is now largely the product of the Soviet period and much of it of peasant origin, the educational level is rising rapidly. One-third of the workers in industry are now said to have secondary education, at least in part.[10]

Fifth, labor relations and the rights of citizens at work are controlled in detail by laws and regulations covering hiring and firing, training and recruitment, mobility, safety and health, hours, regulation of the work of women and children, vacations, holidays, social security, and the powers of trade unions, among other points. Wages and salaries are de-

[7] In spite of real indications of liberalization since the Twentieth Congress of the party in 1956, with greater individual security and more freedom for local initiative, the authoritarian environment is still reflected in the inability of officials, local trade union people, and professional men to act except within the limits of their clear authorization. "It is not within our competence," or "We do not make such contacts," was heard from Intourist and from others whose aid was asked in making contacts.

[8] Of the plants visited in 1959, only the champagne and tea-packing plants had 500 or less employees, while others ranged from 1,000 employees up to 10,000 in a shoe plant and 5,000, 10,000, and 17,000 in textile plants.

[9] Khrushchev, *op. cit.,* pp. 3-17. For a good analysis of the change see A. Nove, "The Soviet industrial reorganization," *Problems of Communism,* Vol. 6, Nov.–Dec. 1957, pp. 19-25.

[10] E. Manevich, *Sotsialisticheski Trud, 1959,* No. 5, p. 30. The number graduating from secondary schools increased from 220,000 in 1950 to 1,340,000 in 1958. Nicholas DeWitt, "Upheaval in education," *Problems of Communism,* Vol. 8, Jan.–Feb. 1959, p. 30. For comparison, in the United States in 1950 one-half of the workers in industry had more than eight years' education, and the median has risen since then. United States Census, 1950, *Occupational Characteristics,* Special Report P E No. 1 B, Table 10.

termined centrally by the government, in consultation with the trade unions, on the basis of incentive pay, to ensure "individual self-interest in the results of one's work."

Sixth, it is assumed in the Soviet Union that there is harmony of interests in industry, that workers know that they are "the owners of industry," and that "working for themselves they also are working for society." The daily papers, booklets bought in large quantities, and the public speeches of leaders, all stress this harmony, the common effort, the glorious future for which all are supposed to be working. Whatever scepticism workers may have about all this, it seems inevitable that they are now conditioned by it and that it does affect their attitudes and behavior. Moreover, having seen notable progress in recent years in real earnings and in the availability of consumption goods and better housing, workers are optimistic about further progress, in line with the promises made in the current Seven-Year Plan.

Finally, it is to be noted that the trade unions operate within a union structure similar to that of many Western countries, with a hierarchy of interunion councils and functional organizations from the local to the national level. At the top is the All-Union Central Council of Trade Unions, which exercises authoritative control over the trade unions, under the guidance of the Communist party, and has important roles in considering and deciding basic questions related to labor legislation, wages, and labor conditions, jointly with the State Committee on Labor and Wages.[11]

Industrial unions (only twenty-two since 1957) are headed by their central committees, with functions relating to the wage system, safety, and other matters special to the industry in question. At the Republic and regional levels, interunion councils of trade unions operate, with much greater powers than formerly, and working closely with the new regional economic councils. Also at the regional level are branch or industrial union committees, under their central committees. At the bottom are the "primary organizations," the factory and other local union committees with their members.[12]

[11] A decree of the Council of Ministers of the Russian Federated Republic of April 22, 1958 is reported to provide that all proposals before regional economic councils, councils of ministers of autonomous republics, executive committees of local Soviets, ministries and departments, on economic plans, plans for cultural and living construction and for introduction of new techniques, and all current questions of labor and life are to be examined with participation of the appropriate trade union organizations and to be decided with consideration of their opinion. G. N. Pemelin, *Sovetskoe Gosurdarstvo i Pravo*, 1958, No. 10, pp. 28-29. For a discussion of the role of the national organizations see Brown, "The Soviet Labor Market," p. 181, n. 14.

[12] The functions and powers of all these groups were considerably altered in 1927–1958. See above ns. 2-3. Immediately after the reorganization of industry the Central Council of Trade Unions issued on August 17, 1957 a regulation on Republic, area, and regional councils of trade unions. *Spravochnik Profsoyuznovo Rabotnika* (Handbook of Trade Union Workers), 1958, pp. 433-437.

Soviet trade unions work on the basis of "democratic centralism," with elections democratic in form. Unions at each level of the hierarchy are responsible to the membership or subordinate unions which elect them; at the same time, each union operates under the authoritative direction of its superior body. . . .

Concluding Observations

The evidence presented above, in spite of all its limitations, gives the basis for certain conclusions, although they must be tentative and subject to check when it becomes possible for some social scientist to make more intensive field studies of labor relations in the Soviet Union.

1. Soviet trade unions differ from those of the United States and other Western nations because they operate within a different economic, political, and social system, and they should be appraised in that context—one-party dominance, central planning, Communist ideology of harmony of interests and common interest in production in a so-called "workers' state," strict discipline, and broad emphasis on democratic participation in control, "control from below as well as control from above." To the extent that the attitudes implied are now broadly accepted, and we have no conclusive evidence that they are not, they change workers' attitudes toward management and their expectations of the unions.

2. Soviet trade unions are not and cannot be independent in any real sense in such a society. The influence of party members active in the union keeps them in line with party and government policies. Higher union officers quote party dogma and never express independent trade union sentiments. Lower union organs and leaders are independent only to the extent that they exert their initiative in performing tasks set for them by the party and higher union agencies. It would be wrong, nevertheless, to assume that this usually means conflict between the aims and desires of the party and of the workers—though this has been true to some extent in the past and could be true again.[13]

3. At local levels there appears now to be an increasing degree of responsibility ("answerability") of union officers to their membership. Elections are now democratic in form and probably as a rule in practice, although the influence of party members is disproportionately strong. The extent of participation of members in the work of the local union in some plants, perhaps many, would put to shame most American local unions. Increasingly, attention is paid to "the demands of the workers" for improvement of conditions and protection of rights. The functions of "Communist-upbringing" and discipline of the workers are still present, as well as an important role in promoting production. But sometimes

[13] It may be that the same person may combine the attitudes of "good party member" and "good local trade union officer concerned for the interests of the members" without feeling any conflict between these positions.

in the minds of factory committee chairmen the protection functions are in the foreground, especially when they think of the increased rights of the union committee. These functions all seem to them closely intertwined and to the interests of the workers. The talk of many of these people in the plants has a familiar "trade union" flavor.

4. Relations between workers, union officers, and management in many plants are self-respecting, friendly, and cooperative, promoting increases of efficiency in production and jointly solving problems, and assuring individual workers of protection of their interests against arbitrary action and illegal conditions. Relationships are not likely to be universally as good as those in many of the plants visited, but the channels of appeal, while sometimes clogged, can be opened, and often are. It is not surprising if, as some evidence suggests, workers are now showing increased confidence in the trade unions.

5. The powers of the unions, especially at the local level, have significantly increased, and barring a drastic reversal of the trends of Soviet policy, they are likely to increase further. In some respects these powers are greater than those of American trade unions. They involve the sharing of decision-making nationally and in the regions on broad economic policies, as well as in the plants on matters directly affecting the interests of workers. The encroachment on "management prerogatives" goes surprisingly far and would shock most American managers and many trade unionists. This is true even though the unions have no power to bargain on wage levels. The increasing educational level of workers and their resulting awareness of developments and discontent with failure of the promises of Communist theory to be made reality may have had some influence on the development. Even more, the trend may have been dictated by the need to obtain the cooperation of workers in making a highly developed industry operate efficiently on its present basis of planning with decentralization of management.[14] Both grounds point to a continuing need for a vital place within the Soviet system for organized and, to some degree, spontaneous activity of workers. Increased protection of the interests of workers, which seems to be intended and to some extent becoming effective, can be expected, nevertheless, to remain within whatever limits are decided upon by party policy.

6. Developments within the unions may be affected by the growth in numbers of responsible, educated leaders in the plants, up from the rank and file. This could lead to more regional union leaders who were advanced from the plants rather than coming from management or party posts. Such a development would seem desirable if the intent is to increase initiative and some degree of independence on the part of the unions. Most higher officials will continue to be party members as well

[14] See Solomon Schwarz on this point, in "Beginnings of Economic Democracy," *Sotsialisticheski Vestnik,* September 1958, pp. 163-164.

as trade union officers, with their highest loyalty inevitably to the party. However devoted to their union jobs these party member, trade union leaders may be, the confidence of outsiders, and perhaps of union members, too, would be increased if more of them came up through the ranks of trade union organizations and gave more indication of being representatives of workers.

7. The self-confidence and vitality observed in some areas among factory committee and regional union officers indicate a grass-roots quality in the local union organizations currently, which is healthy and could lead to more initiative from below. The needs of the Soviet system of planned economy will prevent any movement out of line with the main purposes of the régime. Still, it seems that earlier appraisals of the Soviet trade unions need reconsideration in the light of recent changes. At least in the better instances, Soviet local unions appear now to be doing a job for their members which goes farther toward democratic representation and protection of workers' interests, within their particular system, than has been generally supposed.

SOVIET VIEWS

29

The Purposes and Functions of Trade Unions in the U.S.S.R.*

A. PIATAKOV

Assistant Chief, Legal Department of the State Committee on Labor and Wages, U.S.S.R. Council of Ministers

The socialist economic system with national ownership has provided possibilities in the Soviet Union for the people to develop new ways of organising the work of society, on the basis of fellowship and mutual assistance between workers. The State, representing the whole people through the councils of deputies which embrace the whole urban and rural population, is responsible for ensuring that the rights and liberties laid down in the Constitution are equally available for all citizens, regardless of sex, religion, race and nationality, including the right to

* Excerpts reprinted from an article entitled "Labour Administration by the State and Trade Unions in the U.S.S.R." in the *International Labour Review*, June, 1962, pp. 558-572, by permission of the International Labour Office, Geneva, Switzerland.

work, the right to be paid for work according to its quantity and quality, the right to rest, and the right to security in old age, sickness and disablement.

The state authorities regulate labour relationships in socialist society with the aim of improving working conditions, increasing labour productivity and ensuring a constant rise in the material well-being and cultural level of the working people. In addition to enforcing the law and maintaining the basic rights of citizens, they plan the economy so that material and manpower resources can be used efficiently to satisfy the growing needs and development of the members of society. This direction of the economy follows the principle of "democratic centralism," combining centralised control with freedom of initiative for regional and local authorities.

The trade unions (as well as other social organisations) play a major part in implementing measures to improve working conditions and, as mass organisations with extensive rights, collaborate with the state authorities on the most important questions relating to labour and remuneration. They encourage workers' initiative in developing new forms of work—socialist emulation, the shock-worker movement, the Communist labour brigades and enterprises—and help workers to acquire experience in dealing with production, state and community matters. As society has developed and its material level has risen, the unions have taken over functions previously performed by the State. They at present participate directly in public administration in fields closely related to workers' needs such as social insurance, the running of sanatoria and rest homes, physical culture and sports.

Legislative Powers

Under the U.S.S.R. Constitution (article 14) and the constitutions of the constituent republics, the basic principles of labour legislation are a matter for the supreme organs of the Union, while labour legislation itself is a matter for each republic. Laws are enacted by separate votes in the two chambers of the Supreme Soviet (the Council of the Union and the Council of Nationalities) after close consideration by the deputies at sessions of these bodies.

In virtue of the legislation the Praesidium of the Supreme Soviet issues decrees for the purpose of improving conditions of work and raising living standards, such as the decree of 26 March 1956 to extend the period of maternity leave and the decree of 10 February 1960 to regulate the special allowances of persons employed in the far northern areas and in places assimilated thereto. The Acts of the Supreme Soviet and decrees by its Praesidium are published in the "Gazette of the Supreme Soviet of the U.S.S.R."

On the basis of the existing legislation, the Council of Ministers of the U.S.S.R. issues regulations and instructions regarding the method and concrete details of implementation of the measures in the field of labour and wages prescribed in the legislation.

Decisions of the Union Council of Ministers which have a generally binding (normative) character are published for general information in the "Ordinances of the U.S.S.R. Government."

Taking this Union legislation as a starting-point, the supreme soviets of the federated republics regulate under their constitutions the various aspects of labour relations in the light of regional conditions. . . .

Drafting of Laws and Regulations

The trade unions play an active part in the drafting of laws and regulations on labour questions, as well as on questions of production, material living conditions and culture:

(1) The Central Council of Trade Unions and the central or republic committees of particular unions submit draft laws and regulations to the Praesidium of the Supreme Soviet or Council of Ministers—in either case at the federal or republic level. Specific regulations of major importance are adopted jointly by the Union Government and the Central Council of Trade Unions (C.C.T.U.); for instance the decree of 19 September 1959 to reduce hours of work was jointly issued by the Central Committee of the Communist Party of the Soviet Union, the Union Council of Ministers and the C.C.T.U.

(2) The C.C.T.U. issues instructions, rules and explanations on the application of labour legislation, except on matters within the jurisdiction of the State Committee of the U.S.S.R. Council of Ministers for Wages and Labour.

(3) The C.C.T.U., the central committees of particular trade unions, and the republic, regional and provincial trade union councils take part, through their representatives, in the preparation of draft laws and regulations by the Supreme Soviet, the Council of Ministers and other governmental bodies.

(4) The central committees of trade unions, in conjunction with the appropriate ministries and government departments, issue rules and standards on occupational safety and health. . . .

Labour Questions in Relation to Planning

Side by side with the regulation of labour relations, the state authorities devote a large part of their time to labour aspects of planning. . . .

The public plays an active role in this planning. A decree of the Praesidium of the Supreme Soviet of the Soviet Union, dated 15 July

1958, gave factory and local trade union committees the right to participate in working out the preliminary plans for production and capital investment and to hear reports by managements of undertakings and offices on the execution of the production plans. Before confirmation, production plans of undertakings are discussed at general meetings of employees.

The trade unions play an active part at all stages in the preparation of state plans (in undertakings, on the regional economic councils, provincial executive committees of the local soviets of workers' deputies, the councils of ministers of the autonomous republics and the state planning authorities of the federated republics).

The Central Council of Trade Unions is entitled to tender advice to the Soviet Government on the draft economic plans in so far as labour questions are concerned (decree of the Union Council of People's Commissars and Central Council of Trade Unions dated 10 September 1933).

Entry into Employment

In the Soviet Union employment relationships arise between citizens on the one hand and undertakings, institutions or organisations on the other. The substance of the relationship and the rights and obligations of the parties are determined in a manner laid down in labour legislation.

The basis for the existence of an employment relationship is the individual contract. In the exercise of their right to work, citizens choose their employment according to their particular trade and skill. The right to enter into a contract of employment starts at the age of 16 years; in exceptional cases, with the consent of the factory or local trade union committee, a young person may start work at the age of 15.

When unemployment was liquidated in 1929–30 there ceased to be any practical need for employment exchanges, and these were disbanded. Undertakings and establishments inform the public of vacancies on their workforce for technical and manual workers in the various trades by means of advertisements in newspapers or notices in special display windows. Engagements for work in a different town are arranged on a voluntary basis by the recruitment departments of the regional and provincial executive committees of the soviets of workers' deputies, and their district representatives; in such cases contracts of employment are concluded for specific periods and provide for an allowance to meet the cost of removal and of settlement at the new workplace. State undertakings and institutions are entitled to engage employees within the limits of their planned or estimated personnel establishment and total wage bill. When concluding a contract of employment, the individual negotiates the terms and conditions which would be acceptable to him, including the date for starting work, the post and trade category, the duties, the rate or scale of pay and the housing to be provided.

Labour in the Individual Enterprise

Management in the Soviet Union is based on a combination of two principles—centralised command and initiative by the rank and file. The managing director bears full responsibility for implementing the production and financial plan, directing the work procedures and processes, and administering the undertaking. Engagements and transfers of all personnel (with their consent) are a matter for the managing director, though he must take the views of the trade union into account.

Managements of undertakings have a great deal of freedom of decision in labour questions, guided by current legislation and the targets set in the plan. The managing director organises recruitment, the distribution and assignment of skilled workers within the undertaking, and arrangements for training at the various levels. He ensures that the pay system is correctly applied and that wages are paid at the proper times. He determines and may modify the structure and size of the staffs of the workshops and administrative departments of the undertaking within the limits of its labour plan, as well as the numbers of salaried employees, engineers and technicians, guided by the appropriate salary scale. He decides and may modify the rates of pay of individual administrative and production workers within the limits of approved salary scales and of the total funds available for wages and salaries, and approves advances of pay to wage-earning and salaried employees, etc.

The wage-earning and salaried personnel is associated with the conduct of the undertaking as regards internal questions, usually through the trade union organisation (factory committee). In particular, extensive rights were given to the factory and local committees of the trade unions by a decree of the Praesidium of the Supreme Soviet of the U.S.S.R., dated 15 July 1958. No labour problem can be decided by the management of an undertaking without the participation of the trade union committee.

It will be sufficient to indicate briefly some of the rights vested in the factory and local committees: representation of the wage-earning and salaried personnel in all questions concerning work, living conditions and culture; participation in the drafting of the production and capital investment plans and of the plans for construction of housing and welfare premises; conclusion of collective agreements; receiving of reports by the management on the execution of the production plan, commitments undertaken under collective agreement and other matters affecting the personnel; submission of proposals to higher authority for improving the operation of the undertaking or institution as well as for improving conditions of work and life and the material and welfare services provided; expressing an opinion on the candidates proposed for managerial posts and raising with the responsible bodies any questions of the removal or punishment of managerial personnel who fail to perform their obligations under collective agreements, behave bureaucratically or infringe labour legislation; participation in decisions on job evaluation and remuneration (application of pay scales to particular jobs, allocation of wage rates to workers, determination of standard rates of output, introduction of incentive pay systems, fixing of amounts of bonus, etc.); operation of the state social insurance system for employed persons; examination of labour disputes; ensuring observance by managements of labour legislation and rules and standards of occupational safety and health; organising the standing "production conferences," etc.

These standing conferences, which provide one of the main means of employee participation, comprise manual workers and salaried employees, representatives of the trade union committees and of scientific and technical societies, etc., and also the management. The conference discusses questions relating to the fulfilment of the planned quotas, maximum utilisation of internal production reserves, creation of working conditions conducive to high productivity, and improvement of material and welfare facilities for the workers and their families.

Work in each undertaking is governed by rules of employment issued by the management after consulting the trade union committee: these are based on—and may add to—model rules issued by the State Committee on Labour and Wages of the Union Council of Ministers in agreement with the Central Council of Trade Unions on 12 January 1957. . . .

An important factor in the determination of conditions of work in undertakings is the collective agreement, concluded by the factory or local committee of the trade union acting on behalf of all wage-earning and salaried employees, and by the management of the undertaking. At present collective agreements are being used more and more as a means of providing for employee participation in management.[1]

The agreement lays down the respective obligations of management and personnel as regards improved organisation of production and work, due application of remuneration systems, execution of production plans, increases in productivity of labour, improvement of skills, improvement of safety and health arrangements, and also provision of housing and of material and welfare facilities for employees. Many clauses of collective agreements have legal force. . . .

A decree of the Praesidium of the Supreme Soviet of the U.S.S.R. dated 25 April 1956 laid down that a wage-earning or salaried employee is

[1] See also G. K. Moskalenko: "Collective Agreements in the U.S.S.R., in *International Labour Review,* Vol. LXXXV, No. 1, Jan. 1962, pp. 18-29.

entitled to terminate his employment and dissolve his agreement (where it was for an indefinite period) on giving the management two weeks' notice. On the other hand, Soviet legislation strongly guarantees the individual's right to work: if the management wishes to terminate an employment relationship, it may do so only on grounds explicitly stated in labour legislation and only provided the factory or local trade union committee gives its consent.

Supervision of Undertakings

Regulations for the regional economic councils, approved by the Council of Ministers of the U.S.S.R. on 26 September 1957, provide that the economic councils shall direct industry and construction in their areas, with extensive participation by the workers. With this object, technical and economic commissions have been attached to the economic councils, consisting of scientists, professional men and women, high-output workers, innovators, inventors and rationalisers, and leaders of government, economic, trade union and other organisations. The councils also regularly convene meetings of managerial and technical personnel and industrial innovators who have been active in popularising progressive methods of work to study together the means of introducing such methods on a wider basis. The orders and instructions of the economic councils on basic questions of work and wages, safety and health questions and material and cultural facilities for employed persons are issued with due regard to the proposals of the trades union councils.

Special Rules for Safety and Health

Much importance is attached in the Soviet Union to occupational safety and health. Increased output of commodities, widespread introduction of new techniques, the progress of mechanisation and automation are being accompanied by improved safety and health conditions at work. In addition, there is special state action to protect the health of employed persons while at work, enormous sums being spent on such action every year.

Federal legislation deals mainly with occupational safety and health questions requiring uniform action throughout the Union: these include elaboration of schedules of safety and health measures, drafting of safety and health standards to apply in projected industrial undertakings, general rules on safety and health and rules for particular industries, lists of occupations involving unhealthy processes and therefore requiring specially advantageous conditions of work (shorter working day, longer holidays), lists of occupations with unhealthy or arduous conditions of work in which women and young persons are not to be employed, rules regarding pre-employment and periodical medical examinations, instructions on the issue of special working clothes, etc. . . . .

In accordance with section 7 of an order by the Union Council of People's Commissars and the Central Council of Trade Unions dated 10 September 1933, many orders on occupational safety and health in particular industries have been issued by the central committees of the trade unions in agreement with the ministries, departments and economic councils concerned. Special safety rules of inter-occupational scope have been issued by the Central Council of Trade Unions (on the provision of workshop personnel with aerated or salt water, etc.).

The legislation of the republics has supplemented federal standards by laying down a whole network of measures on occupational safety and health. . . .

Inspection and Enforcement

Inspection to ensure compliance with safety and health rules is primarily the responsibility of the appropriate organs of government.

A public prosecutor is entitled to order an undertaking or institution, and also officials, to desist from any illegal action taken. He can challenge the legality of any order or instruction, make investigations, suggest disciplinary action or initiate criminal proceedings for infringement of labour laws, and prosecute offenders in the courts, etc. . . .

Current legislation places on managing directors of undertakings and worksites the responsibility for safety and health arrangements and for conformity with the labour laws. In undertakings there are special officials whose responsibilities include enforcement of safety rules—the deputy director for safety, the safety engineers, safety technicians, etc. Managing directors of undertakings conclude special agreements with the factory trade union committee embodying obligations as regards safety and health.

The activity of the state inspecting bodies is combined with a great deal of labour protection work by the trade unions. These supervise observance of safety and health rules, acting through their "technical inspectors of labour." The work of the inspectors is directly administered by the republic, provincial and regional trade union councils.

These technical inspectors have wide powers, including the right to check safety and health conditions and arrangements in undertakings and institutions and the right to take proceedings against persons infringing labour laws.

A great deal of work is also done by the "social inspectors for labour protection" and the safety and health commissions attached to the provincial and the factory or local committees of the trade unions. A social inspector for labour protection is elected at the level of each trade union group.

These social inspectors, who act under the direction of the technical inspector, are agents of the factory trade union committee: they have special powers to supervise observance of labour legislation, including power to require the management to produce or give necessary documents or explanations, to issue orders binding the management in agreement with the technical inspector, etc. The safety and health commissions comprise social inspectors and industrial innovators (workers) under the chairmanship of a member of the trade union committee. The commissions participate in the planning of safety and health measures, supervise the expenditure of money for these purposes, check the medical equipment of undertakings, and investigate the causes of employment injuries and occupational diseases.

More than 2 million members of trade unions take part in this way in the supervision of safety and health on the workers' behalf.

Disputes

The Soviet state authorities and trade unions also enforce the law on employment relationships through their handling of disputes between employees and managements. Labour disputes are very rare in the Soviet Union, mainly arising through inadequate knowledge of labour legislation on the part of individual management representatives or workers, or through its faulty application.

Under the regulations for the examination of labour disputes approved by decree of the Praesidium of the Supreme Soviet on 31 January 1957, such disputes are handled by (a) labour disputes boards, (b) the factory or local trade union committees and (c) the people's courts.

The labour disputes boards are set up in undertakings, institutions and organisations and are composed of equal numbers of permanent representatives of the factory or local trade union committee and of the management. They are thus joint union-management bodies. The two sides are on an equal footing at meetings of the board: the functions of chairman and secretary are performed at alternate sessions by representatives of the trade union committee and of the management respectively. Decisions are reached by agreement between the two groups of members.

The disputes board acts as court of the first instance for all labour disputes arising between employees on the one hand and the management on the other, excluding those in which the employee can apply directly to a court (in case of dismissal by the management).

In large undertakings with separate workshops there are workshop disputes boards as well as one for the whole undertaking.

Cases are examined by the labour disputes board only where the employee has failed to overcome the disagreement through direct discussion with the management. The factory, workshop or local trade union committee receives complaints for consideration by the board.

Disputes are considered in the presence of the employee. If necessary, the board may summon witnesses to its sittings, delegate technical or financial investigations to individuals, and require submission of documents or accounts by the management.

The decisions of the board come into force as soon as they are issued. Each decision must give reasons and be based on the labour legislation, the collective agreement, the contract of employment, the rules of the undertaking, or relevant regulations or instructions. If agreement cannot be reached between the representatives of the management and the trade union on the disputes board, or if the employee concerned appeals against the decision of the disputes board for the whole establishment, then the case goes to the factory or local trade union committee. After considering an appeal against a decision by a disputes board, the committee may uphold the decision or issue a new one.

Decisions by the disputes board and orders by the factory or local committee must be put into effect by the management within ten days. If a decision is not put into effect, the committee gives the employee an attestation which has the force of a writ of execution.

Workers enjoy extensive possibilities as regards defence of their employment rights before the courts. Any labour dispute which has been examined by a factory or local committee (and, in first instance, by a disputes board) can be referred for decision to a people's court if the employee is not satisfied with the committee's order or if the management considers this contrary to law.

Under an order issued by the Praesidium of the Supreme Soviet on 27 January 1959, the people's courts also have primary jurisdiction for disputes regarding the reinstatement of employees dismissed by the management with the consent of the trade union committee.

In a labour case the employee may make his complaint orally or in writing, oral statements being recorded by the people's court and signed by the judge and the complainant. Employees are exempted in such proceedings from state charges and from payment of costs. To ensure proper examination of the case, the judge is required to order production of the necessary documents and other exhibits, to summon witnesses and (where the management alleges that the committee's order in the employee's favour was contrary to the law) to allow a representative of the trade union committee to defend the employee.

If the court orders payment of a sum of money to the employee, settlement of any amount not exceeding one month's earnings must be immediate.

An appeal against the court's decision may be brought by either party or by the public prosecutor within ten days of its announcement. The appeal goes to the next higher court, which is entitled in a labour case either to annul the decision of the people's court and order a re-examination or to issue its own decision on the merits (if the facts are sufficiently clear or if only the explanatory part of the decision requires to be modified).

The tendency of the Soviet State is in the direction of stronger links between governmental agencies and the mass of the people, better services for the workers, more extensive self-administration by the public and a greater role for the trade unions in Communist construction, particularly as regards the settlement of labour and wages questions.

VIII

THE SOVIET CITIZEN AS A CONSUMER

"Not Good—But Better," the term mentioned in the introduction to THE SOVIET CITIZEN AS A WORKER (part VII) certainly applies also to THE SOVIET CITIZEN AS A CONSUMER. While in standard of living the Soviet Union is still far behind the United States, or even almost all the Western European countries, it is well ahead of much of the rest of the world.

As has become apparent from many of the readings above, significant international comparisons in general are not easy to make—and this, certainly, holds true for international comparisons of standards of living. While we know that the standard of living in the United States is substantially higher than that in the Soviet Union, only a detailed, thorough study can provide us with even an approximation of *how much* better off the U. S. citizen is. There are more doctors per thousand people in the Soviet Union than in the United States and their services are offered free of charge, but medicines and sickbed supplies are much more readily obtainable in the United States. The Soviet worker hardly ever pays more than 5 per cent of his income for rent (as compared with around 20 per cent for the American worker) but he is definitely limited in the number of square feet per person that is legally permissible—and the prevailing housing shortage makes even this maximum space unobtainable for most workers' families. Few Russian workers pay any income tax, which so greatly reduces the take-home pay of the American wage earner, but as much as one-half of a Soviet citizen's weekly expenditure on consumer goods may go for the payment of the "turnover tax," an excise tax varying in rate depending upon the type of consumer goods.

When comparing living standards, Soviet writers always stress communal consumption, i.e., that type of consumption (such as free education), the costs of which are borne by society at large rather than by the individual consumer. No doubt communal consumption plays an important role in the economic well-being of the Soviet citizen and leaves the Soviet worker a larger percentage of his income for expenditure on such things as food or clothing, but to measure precisely the per capita value of communal consumption in the USSR is no easy task.

In the first selection under *Western Views* below, Jan S. Prybyla discusses the overall standard of living of the Soviet citizen, giving due recognition to communal consumption. Imogene Erro, next, takes some important, selected consumer goods and compares the quantity and quality of these goods available to citizens in the respective countries. Her article endeavors to prove on the basis of these chosen examples that the Soviet consumer has (and is likely to continue to have) fewer consumer goods of much lower quality and within a much more limited range of choice than the consumer in the United States.

Under *Soviet Views* A. Aganbegian, while not denying that the USSR still lags behind the United States in many (though not all) of the indices which he uses to compare levels of living, paints a much rosier picture of the Soviet consumer's present—and still more of his future—living standard. P. Oldak, finally, outlines the steps which, in the opinion of Soviet economists, need to be undertaken to increase further the well-being of the Soviet citizen as a consumer.

WESTERN VIEWS

30

The Soviet Consumer in Khrushchev's Russia *

JAN S. PRYBYLA
Pennsylvania State University

The present study attempts to analyze relatively recent trends in the Soviet citizen's living standards. In other words, how has the Soviet consumer been faring under Khrushchev? There is substantial agreement amongst non-Soviet economists that from 1928 to 1953 the Soviet consumer shared only to a limited extent in the overall growth of the economy. Although Professor Maurice Dobb (*Soviet Economic Development Since 1917*) regards the contention that the rapid pace of Soviet industrialization in the inter-war years was promoted at the expense of the standard of life of the people as "loose and ill-informed chatter in the West," the available (Soviet) figures are against him. Not only have realizations in the consumer sector run consistently behind cheap promises, but even by minimal standards the Soviet citizen in 1953 was still

* Reprinted from the *Russian Review,* July, 1961, pp. 194-205, by permission of the publisher.

shoddily clad, deplorably housed, poorly equipped in household goods, fed primarily on bread and cereals, and working forty-eight hours a week. In recent years, however, important developments have taken place which it is imperative to analyze in some detail.

Two sets of preliminary remarks must be made in this connection. First, there seems to be no necessary connection or correlation between trends in material prosperity and political freedom. The oft-repeated forecasts that a substantial rise in Soviet living standards will automatically bring with it a liberalization of the totalitarian political structure are unwarranted and smack of wishful thinking. This is not to say that a relaxation of the political excesses of the Stalinist era has not taken place, or that further easing of the political dictatorship may not make itself felt in the future. However, the motive forces behind such development in the political sphere are very largely autonomous and not necessarily connected with either higher wages or a more abundant supply of washing machines. The growing satisfaction of consumer needs is a two-edged sword, and it would certainly be erroneous to adopt without serious reservations the thesis of the gradual *embourgeoisement* of the Soviet political set-up.

The second set of remarks concerns more purely methodological problems involved in the evaluation of living standards in a planned economy of the Soviet type. The usual tools of analysis are clearly insufficient in that context. In measuring changes in the standard of living it is usual to watch changes in real wages, a procedure which implies evaluations of movements in the general price level (as indicated by the consumer price index), and movements in money wages. In studying Soviet living standards, however, these measures tend to give insufficient, incomplete, and biased results, the bias being a downward one. The Soviet standard of living is characterized not only by money wage and general price level shifts but by the significant impact of items of communal consumption, the extent of leisure time, and the chronic problem of the nonavailability of many lines of consumer goods which theoretically figure on the retail price list. In addition, any international comparisons of living standards come up against the incommensurable problems of the quality of consumer goods: a Russian pair of "middle quality" shoes is not the same as an American pair of shoes of "middle quality."

With these warnings in mind, it seems that since 1955 there has occurred a definite improvement in the situation of the Soviet consumer. On this point there appears to be fairly general agreement. There continues to be, however, substantial disagreement on the extent of this improvement. Again, it is generally conceded that the upward trend will continue, but the rate of improvement over the next six years is subject to debate.

The upward trend in Soviet living standards is shown by the more generous provision of communal consumption items, selective money wage adjustments (accompanied by a virtually stable price level), and increased leisure. Each of these is examined in turn.

Communal consumption. The term "communal consumption" includes the provision of health services, educational services, subsidized housing, and social security items such as social insurance and maternity assistance. A portion of the annual gains in the economy is passed to the consumer in this form. It is the ideologically favorite form in a system in which the individual matters principally as the component part of the group. In the Soviet system communal consumption items are in a number of cases attached to restrictive provisions relating to labor discipline and the government's desire to keep labor turnover in check. They are also used as a variety of productivity incentive. The interesting feature in recent developments has been the relaxation of some of the more blatant restrictions attached to social security benefits, especially *sick pay.* In the past, job changes involved loss of sick-pay rights for a period of six months. A decree of the Presidium of the Supreme Soviet approved by the Supreme Soviet in May of last year, practically removed this restriction. Most social benefits (including sick-pay) continue, however, to be scaled according to the length of uninterrupted employment in the same enterprise. Although rates of sick-pay have in recent years remained substantially unchanged, the payments are generous. The same applies to *maternity benefit rates.* Maternity leave is now back to the 1938 period of 112 days.

Old age pensions have doubled between 1955 and 1958 and scales of payments have been revised so as to benefit workers with previous lower earnings. Official Soviet sources claim that the reforms and increases in old age pensions have added some 5 billion rubles annually to consumer income. It is thought that one of the effects of the reform has been to lower the wage-earners' propensity to save, a fact reflected in the under-fulfillment of recent annual personal savings plans. Lower old-age payment rates for partially employed retirees may also have the effect of cutting into the labor force. There is, however, little doubt that the changes in this sector have tended in the direction of greater income equality. Free secondary and university *education* has been restored since 1956, but with the exception of an accelerated school building program, overall budgetary expenditure on education has been maintained at approximately the pre-1953 rate.

Expenditures on *health services* continue at the pre-1953 rates, and are steep. Free medical and dental services are provided for all workers and employees, and only nominal charges are made by nurseries. Outpatients are required to pay for the great majority of drugs. Professor Lynn Turgeon has summarized the trends in recent expenditures on transfers and communal consumption in a table prepared for the Joint

Economic Committee of the Congress, from which it can be seen that the average annual increase in budgetary allocations for these items between 1956 and 1959 was of the order of 11 per cent. The figure becomes more meaningful when it is compared with the annual average population increase in the same period which was about 1.4 per cent, and with the corresponding average annual increase in the industrial labor force of a little over 3 per cent. The percentage increase in expenditures on communal consumption and transfers for these years is somewhat distorted by the unusually heavy disbursements in 1956–57, and is likely to run in the future at an average annual increase rate nearer 8 per cent. The particularly heavy rise in expenditures on pensions must also be viewed in the perspective of the slow but steady increase in the percentage of those over 60 years of age who today comprise about 8.2 per cent of the population (as compared with 7 per cent in 1950).

The following table based on and calculated from data supplied by Professors Turgeon and Body (J. E. C. documents 48448 and 46283, Part II) throws further light on the increasing importance of communal consumption items in the life of the Soviet citizen in recent years.

TABLE 1.   *U.S.S.R. State Budget Expenditures, 1956–1959*

Year	Tot. Exp. Bil. of rubles	% over preced. year	Tot. exp. on commun. cons. and transfers. Bil. rubles	% over preced. year	Exp. on communal cons. & transfers as % of tot. exp. in each year
1956	561.0	4.3	169.0	10	30.1
1957	598.0	6.6	202.0	19	33.7
1958	626.7	4.8	215.0	6	34.3
1959	707.2	12.8	232.2	8	32.8

These figures and the preceding discussion show that the Soviet government has been and will probably continue to be able to provide the consumers with increasing amounts of communal consumption items without any deflection of resources from other uses. There remains, of course, the question of the quality of communal services. By Western standards they still appear very primitive. This is especially true of much hospital equipment and of clinical facilities. Medicines are often unavailable and rural health clinics tend to be staffed with insufficiently —by Western standards—trained personnel. The deductions to be made from the average monthly money income of a Soviet family of four for medical, dental and child care are relatively modest—something of the order of 5 per cent.

Residential housing seems to be in a category of its own. It continues to be the gaping sore on the Soviet body economic. Since it is the government who is the landlord in the majority of cases, and since rents being based on the income of the principal wage earner bear little relation to housing costs, it is correct to regard the provision of domestic housing as a variety of social service. In spite of a sharp increase in construction in the last three years, the available housing space is still appalling and apartments are poorly maintained and shoddily equipped. Although it is true that the rents charged are insufficient for maintenance and repairs, the run-down appearance of Soviet houses is also attributable to poor construction materials and bottlenecks in the supply of qualified repair and maintenance services. It is likely that there has been some improvement in per capita floor space since 1953 (at that time 4.5 sq. metres per urban dweller, this figure including kitchen, bathroom, hallway and stairway space) but even on the assumption that present plans are fully carried out, the improvement over the next six years is not likely to reach, much less exceed, 10 sq. metres per urban dweller. The situation in the countryside appears to be even worse. Given these negative factors, it remains true that the deductions for rent and household operations to be made from a wage earner's average money income are very modest, probably not exceeding 7 per cent.

Finally, the abolition in 1958 of the so-called "voluntary" *bond subscriptions* (which, in fact, took the form of compulsory deductions from the pay packet) has no doubt added several billions of rubles annually to the consumers' disposable income.

Money wages and the price level. The pre-1955 favorite method of passing to the consumer the annual gains in the productivity and the labor force of the food-processing and light industries was by means of periodic, indiscriminate price reductions. This method was part and parcel of the Stalinist policy of fostering income inequalities as a spur to productivity and as a means of tying a privileged stratum to the top directorate. The last massive price cut took place in 1954 when the consumer price index stood at 43 (fourth quarter of 1947 = 100). Money wages in the period 1947–54 increased at a moderate annual rate of about 15 per cent. Since that time massive price reductions have been relegated to the dust heap of history, and replaced by selective adjustments of money wages, the upward movement being particularly important in the lower income brackets. The 1956 minimum wage law— 350 rubles per month in urban and 270 rubles in rural areas—revealed the fact that at that time some 8-10 million Soviet wage earners were below these minimal, subsistence levels. Not only were money income inequalities rife, but there existed privilege gulfs which would hardly have been tolerated in a thorough-going capitalist economy. Although little information is available on recent trends in upper incomes, there is little doubt that Khrushchev's wage policy is tending in the direction of greater income equalization. The whole wage structure in the U.S.S.R.

had by 1954 reached an unprecedented point of chaos with phoney piece-work bonuses and artificial time-work upgrading spiraling under the stimulus of a developing labor shortage. The recent wage reforms have all tended both to eliminate such abuses and to reduce basic wage differentials. They have also attenuated some of the harsher aspects of Stalinist labor discipline (such as, for example, punitive restrictions on job changing and absenteeism). The average increase in money wages between 1956 and 1958 was 3.6 per cent, the increase being most important in the lower brackets. The trend is likely to continue, and is sustained by the abolition of direct taxes on subsistence income (300 rubles per earner in urban areas) and a lowering of tax rates on income below 450 rubles per month. It should be remembered, however, that the bulk of Soviet taxes is indirect. Collective farm workers' incomes continue to lag behind although some attempts are being made to pass to these workers some of the increases in the collective farms' money receipts following the rise of prices of agricultural goods decreed in 1958. The collective farmer, however, does not benefit from the social insurance and pension rights of the industrial wage-earner except insofar as the collective is able to provide relief for its sick and aged members from its own funds—which is still rarely the case.

Selective money wage increases since 1955 have been accompanied by modest selective price cuts on such items as children's clothing, radios, aluminum kitchenware, medicines, watches, and a number of foods (vegetables, fat, poultry, pork, fruits). Soviet official sources claim that these price reductions have added annually between 5 and 6 billion rubles to the consumers' disposable income. Inevitably any such increases were largely offset by the persistence of a strong sellers' market for most of the items subject to price cuts. The chorus of consumer complaints about the inadequate matching of supply to consumer demand continues unabated in the Soviet press. Thus, *Pravda* on October 16, 1959, in announcing a Party decree "on measures for increasing the production, expanding the assortment, and improving the quality of cultural, everyday, and household goods," deplores the severe shortages in stores of the very goods on which consumers were supposed to gain their 6 billion rubles of disposable income. The list is worth quoting, since it points up the real limitations of the 80 per cent balance of money income left in the hands of the average, urban wage-earner after deductions for direct taxes and communal consumption items: television sets, pianos, children's and teenagers' bicycles, washing and sewing machines, refrigerators, electric irons, meat grinders, china and earthenware, glass and enamel utensils, household and chemical goods, plastic and synthetic goods, metal beds, lampshades. On October 20, *Pravda* laconically informed its readers that "models of the most varied cultural, everyday and household goods can be seen these days in the departments of the Moscow City Economic Council." Complaints about the quality of such goods as did make their way to the shops were even more poignantly revealing.

After discounting excessive claims, and in view of the relative stability of the general price level since 1955, it probably remains true that the Soviet consumer has in recent years experienced some rise in his disposable income. This conclusion is confirmed by net additions to private savings (currently running at an annual rate of 7 billion rubles), although, as has been pointed out earlier, the increases have been less than anticipated by the planners. In this respect some of the current savings must be regarded as somewhat "forced." A poll of some 1,400 persons traveling from Moscow on 65 routes showed that the reasons assigned to increases in living standards included wage adjustments, discontinuation of forced loans, pension increases, lower taxes on income, and price cuts on a number of consumer items. *Komsomolskaya Pravda* (October 7, 1960) which sponsored the poll drew from this the conclusion that "first and foremost the comrades support the Party and government policy in reducing the gap in payment for work by raising the lower-paid categories to the level of other categories." For once *Komsomolskaya Pravda* may have been getting tolerably near to the truth. The poll also revealed the major areas of weakness: more than half of the people polled complained bitterly both about the quality and the allocation of housing—the most satisfied appeared to have been a senior engineer, father of two children, his wife fully employed who was the proud possessor of an apartment with a total floor space of 32 sq. meters. Other grievances centered around the inadequate provision of consumer services (shops, cafés, repair facilities), shortages of consumer goods, and of children's institutions indispensable in time.

In a series of important studies, Professor Turgeon has evaluated the meaningfulness of Soviet retail prices.[1] His findings give the American consumer some idea of the current situation of his Soviet counterpart. Taking the money income of an average-income urban family of four to be 1,120 rubles per month net (i.e., after deduction of sums for communal consumption, housing and household operations, transportation, and savings), and of an urban subsistence-level family to be net 520 rubles monthly, the families are likely to be faced with the following sample prices as in Table on p. 259.

Under these circumstances the average-income family will tend to spend about half of its net disposable income (as defined above) on food, beverages, and tobacco, a further 25-30 per cent on its low stock of

[1] Lynn Turgeon, *op. cit.*, pp. 319-40, and Turgeon & D. P. Lomberg, "The Meaningfulness of Soviet Retail Prices," *American Slavic and East European Review*, April, 1960, pp. 217-233.

TABLE 2. *Some representative Soviet retail prices for consumer goods and services in 1958*

(Food prices are in rubles * per kilogram unless otherwise indicated)

Chicken	16.50	Cheap cotton print (meter)	100.00 plus
Beef (stewing)	12.00	Cotton print dress	200.00
Pork	19.50	Wool dress	475.00
Average fish	11.00	Man's overcoat	720.00
Butter	28.00	Man's all wool suit	2,000.00
Margarine	14.00	Man's wool mixture suit	700.00
Eggs (10)	7.50	Poplin shirt	50.00
Sugar	10.00	Man's felt hat	69.00
Tea	70.00	Wool socks	11.00
Rye bread	1.24	Shoes (adequate)	200.00
White bread	2.35	Canvas shoes	27.00
Potatoes	1.00	Aluminum frying pan	7.50-8.50
Carrots	3.50	Fountain pen	17.50
Coffee	40.00	Bicycle	450.00-600.00
Cigarettes (25)	2.25	Radio receiver (good)	400.00
Noon meal at work	6.00	TV (14 inch)	2,400.00
Apples	20.00	Alarm clock	30.00-50.00

Toilet soap (bar)	2.20
Haircut	.90-1.50
Shoeshine	1.00
Gasoline (gallon)	3.00
Newspaper	0.20
Movie admission	3.00-5.00
Balalaika	40.00

* These are old rubles. To convert to today's rubles (for which American tourists in the USSR pay $1.10 each) divided each price by 10. [Editor's note.]

clothing, leaving little for the purchase of such durable goods and personal care items as are available in the stores.

Consumption of leisure. Sotsialisticheskaya Zakonnost of October 1959 published the provisions of a draft law on labor principles which among many significant changes proposed the reduction of the working day to 7 hours, and of the working week to 40 hours, the changeover to the first to have been completed in 1960, and to the second in 1962. This would imply a 5-hour day on the day preceding the day off, or in capitalist terms a "week-end." Generous provisions were also made for young workers and for workers in unhealthy or arduous jobs. These changes should not be shrugged off as mere propaganda, although in the past legal provisions have not always corresponded to reality. If the new working schedule is actually put in operation, and this does appear to be happening, the Soviet planners will have to rely heavily on mechanization and scientific management to achieve their productivity goals. This may prove rather difficult in the food-processing and light industries since these industries are not scheduled to receive in the coming seven years any significantly greater portion of total industrial investment (although, of course, the absolute amount of investment will rise sharply). On the other hand if the present inflow of labor into these sectors is maintained (as it is likely to be owing to a gradual relaxation of the war-time deficit in the recruits for the labor force), the present increase rates in productivity will tend to be sufficient to provide the consumer with an annual increase in consumer goods of about 5-6 per cent. A relaxation of international tension with a concurrent reduction in Soviet occupation forces abroad and of the "conventional" military establishment at home, may push that rate even higher on the assumption that some of the released manpower shall be made available to the consumer goods sector.

Conclusions. Since 1955 the living standards of the Soviet citizen have risen, although there exist wide deficiency areas, especially in housing and consumer services. The upward trend was sustained by increases in the labor force and in the productivity of the consumer goods industries, without any significant deflection of resources from other sectors. The major forms in which these gains in the economy have been passed on to the consumer are: wage increases, especially at lower levels, increased provision of communal consumption items and rises in social security payments (again the stress being put on the lower levels), some small decreases in selected consumer goods prices, and increased leisure. The future trend appears to be primarily in the direction of further increases in communal consumption items, lower-bracket wage adjustments and increased leisure. Both communal consumption and leisure are centrally controllable items. However, any conclusions as to future political liberalization prospects are risky and highly uncertain if they rest only on the hope that a higher standard of living implies less state control or coercion. All that can be said at present is that some of the more brutal economically coercive measures of the Stalinist period have been softened or eliminated. Russian history shows that such trends are reversible. More significantly, the solvent of greater prosperity may work either in the direction of a revolution of higher consumer expectations or in the direction of a softening-up of such social tensions as exist in the Soviet Union.

31

Textiles, Clothing, Footwear, and Selected Consumer Durables in the Soviet Union and the United States: a Comparison of Quantity and Quality *

IMOGENE ERRO
American Student of the Soviet Economy

That the Soviet consumer is better off today than he was in 1950 or even 1955 is open to little doubt. Although consumer prices are still high, the price trend has been downward, while production has registered annual increases. Nor is there any doubt that the gap between Soviet and American outputs of consumer goods has narrowed. There is little likelihood, however, that the gap will be closed by 1970 as Khrushchev has pledged—even for a minimum number of basic commodities. Indeed, neither past Soviet performance nor the production targets of the Seven-Year Plan support Khrushchev's optimism. Even if the increases called for by the plan are achieved, Soviet per capita outputs of consumer goods in 1965 will on the whole remain far below even the present US production levels for goods of comparable quality. Probably, in a few instances, the Soviet Union will be able to claim that it has surpassed the United States in total production, if not in production per capita. In wool fabrics, for example, the Soviet Union claims to have surpassed the United States already (though the Soviet production figure includes fabrics not classed as wool in the US). But in the vast majority of basic consumer goods the United States will continue to outproduce its Soviet competitor.

* Excerpt reprinted from an article entitled " 'Catching Up and Outstripping': An Appraisal," in *Problems of Communism,* July–August, 1961, pp. 24-30, by permission of the United States Information Agency.

Soviet production data used in this article are officially announced figures as published in the press and in handbooks. Production figures for 1960 appeared in *Pravda,* January 26, 1961. Definitional information is from *Tovarovedeniye promyshlennykh i prodovostvennykh tovarov* (Science of Staple Commodities as Applied to Industrial Goods and Foodstuffs), Moscow, 1955; and from *Promyshlennost SSSR* (Industry USSR), Moscow, 1957. Data for the United States are from publications of the US Department of Commerce: *Survey of Current Business,* January, 1961; *Statistical Abstract of the United States,* 1959; and *Facts for Industry,* M22T, 1958, 1959.

In setting up consumption standards for textiles, clothing, and footwear, Soviet planners have based their norms on "complete satisfaction of
need," taking into account regional differences of climate. But the list
of commodities considered "really necessary" is extremely limited by
comparison with the wide range of goods available, for example, in the
average American department store. Although the Soviet norms approach
US consumption levels for food items, they are generally lower for textiles
and clothing. The following data for 1958 (when the norms were announced) compare the norms for these latter items with actual Soviet
consumption and with US consumption of the same commodities, on
a per capita basis:

| | Consumption | | Soviet |
	USSR	US	Norms
Textiles (sq. meters)	28.3	66.5	58.1
Leather footwear (pairs)	1.8	3.4	3.5
Knit underwear (pieces)	1.9	8.3*	6.6
Knit outerwear (pieces)	0.5	2.9*	1.6

* 1959

Khrushchev has pointed out that "satisfaction of need" means meeting all "the healthy requirements of a culturally developed man" but
does not include catering to individual whims and desires for luxuries, a
definition which severely limits the Soviet consumption pattern. The
Soviet government thus visualizes the citizen as a culturally developed
person (or expects him to become one), clinically prescribes his requirements for consumption, and seeks to stimulate production in consumer
industries so as to supply these narrowly-defined needs by 1970, or sooner
if possible. But the norms require more goods than are planned for
1965, and to achieve the required levels even by 1970 would necessitate
a sharp step-up of present rates of growth in consumer industries.

Limited Consumer Satisfaction

In textiles, clothing, and footwear, the Soviets aim in general at emulating American consumption standards. In other commodities, however,
such as home furnishings, appliances, and automobiles, they are developing consumption patterns peculiarly their own. For example, the cramped
living space typical of Soviet housing (less than 400 square feet in the
average urban apartment) restricts both the number and types of furniture and household appliances which can be utilized within the family
unit. As for automobiles, Khrushchev has made it clear that the Soviet
Union does not intend to emulate the "excessively wasteful" American
pattern.

It is far more economical and ideologically correct, says Khrushchev, to provide public service facilities (such as taxi "pools") for transportation, rental centers for home appliances, and communal services for laundry, rather than attempt to supply each family with its own automobile, washing machine, and vacuum cleaner. In addition, the regime is encouraging the use of restaurants and public facilities providing carry-out food in order to restrict the need for kitchen appliances and equipment in the home. Thus, while Soviet officials speak on the one hand in terms of catching up with US production levels in basic consumer goods, they denounce American consumption practices on the other as grossly wasteful and extravagant.

Certain problems inherent in a planned economy directly affect consumer purchases. Without the stimulus of competition, Soviet consumer goods production lags behind not only in quantity but even more in design, quality, and range of commodities, all of which limits consumer selection. Retail outlets are ancient in methods and approach; sales personnel are uninterested in customers' desires, and only recently has installment buying been introduced even on a limited scale. Furthermore the system of production quotas gives rise to serious imbalances in consumer goods. For example, where the quotas are fixed in units, as for shoes, the number of models produced tends to narrow because the quotas are more easily met with fewer models; where they are fixed by value, as for overcoats, the tendency is to concentrate production in the more expensive styles; and where fixed by weight, as for cooking utensils, heavier items often are favored at the expense of the lighter.

Resort to such expedients by production managers often results in the accumulation on retailers' shelves of goods for which there are no buyers, either because they are in excess of demand or because they are luxury items too expensive for most consumers to afford. Some of the devices that have been adopted in order to resolve these retailing problems—such as price-cutting, advertising, and limited installment buying —appear remarkably close to capitalistic retailing methods but are nevertheless becoming accepted procedures in the Soviet distribution system.

So much for the broader aspects of the problem. The following sections will be devoted to a closer examination of relative Soviet and US performance in the basic areas of consumer goods production.

Textile Production

In both quantity and quality, the Soviet Union still has far to go to catch up with the United States in this category of consumer goods. Total Soviet production of textiles in square meters is only about half the American volume—a level that is far from adequate to supply, at anything approaching the consumption standards of most Western countries, the needs of a population about 20 percent larger than that of the United States. Where the two countries stand in relation to each other in total and per capita production of the major types of textiles is shown in Table 1.

TABLE 1. *Soviet and US Textile Production, 1960*

	Cotton	Wool	Silk*	Linen
Production per capita:	(in million sq. meters)			
Soviet Union	4,800	439	675	516
United States	9,335	417	2,782	(a)
Total production:	(in sq. meters)			
Soviet Union**	22.4	2.1	3.2	2.4
United States	51.7	2.3	15.4	(a)

* Also includes rayon and synthetic fabrics.
** In 1959 the Soviet Union changed from linear to sq. meters in reporting textile outputs; hence, comparison of pre-1959 with later figures requires conversion of the former into sq. meters by multiplying by the following width factors (derived from 1959 data): cotton, 0.75; wool, 1.27; silk, 0.82; linen, 0.91.
(a) Negligible.

Besides the volume of production, certain aspects of quality must also be considered since they affect both appearance and utility. Quality in textile products is related principally to the technical efficiency of the various processes of manufacture—spinning, weaving, dyeing, and finishing—and to the characteristics of the raw fiber used. Although comparisons of this nature between Soviet and American textiles are seldom possible, the shabby appearance of Soviet wearing apparel and household fabrics, as reported by foreign travellers to the USSR, is at least *prima facie* evidence of the relatively low technological efficiency of the Soviet textile industry.

As shown in Table 1, cotton fabric is the basic textile in both the Soviet Union and the United States. Soviet production per capita is less than half the US figure, and the ratio is approximately the same for the per capita supply available for domestic consumption since it is not appreciably altered by imports and exports. However, Soviet prospects of catching up with the United States in cotton fabrics are enhanced by the fact that US production has tended to level off during the last ten years —even declining in some years—in response to a moderation of consumer demand. In this period the American industry has concentrated on research and development aiming at special improvements in fabric characteristics, such as increased wrinkle-resistance, the "drip-dry" finish, and interesting new textures in yarns and weaves. The development of improved fabrics made from synthetic fibers or from blends of natural and synthetic fibers has contributed to the slackening of demand for cotton fabrics, and this in turn has been reflected in a marked shift from natural to synthetic fibers in mill consumption. As more new kinds of synthetic fiber with improved characteristics are developed, this gradual trend may be expected to continue. In spite of the leveling-off of US production and the planned expansion of Soviet output of cotton fabrics, however, the Soviet target for 1965 production, as shown in Table 2, is only 61 percent of US output in 1960.

Soviet interest meanwhile has centered largely on boosting total production of cotton fabrics to meet expanding consumer needs. Improvements in quality and surface characteristics have received relatively little attention, and cotton-like synthetic fibers are not yet available in appreciable quantities.

Several factors relating to measurement and quality are of basic importance in comparing US and Soviet production and consumption data. American-made cotton fabrics are both wider and heavier than their Soviet equivalents, having increased in average width by about 9 percent in the past 20 years, with the largest proportionate increase in fine-quality fabrics. In the Soviet Union, the average width and weight of cotton fabrics have tended to remain fairly constant, suggesting that Soviet mill managers dislike width increases which reduce linear output.

TABLE 2. *Soviet 1965 Production Targets for Consumer Goods Compared with 1960 US Production*

Commodity	USSR 1965		US 1960	
	Total	Per capita	Total	Per capita
Textile fabrics a				
Cotton	5,700	24.7	9,335	51.7
Wool *	635	2.7	417	2.3
Rayon, synthetic fiber, and silk	1,218	5.3	2,782	15.4
Linen	578	2.5	(negligible)	
Hosiery b	1,250	5.4	1,814	10.0
Leather footwear b	515	2.2	604	3.3
Refrigerators c	1,450	6	3,750 d	21
Washing machines c	2,570	11	4,210 d	23
Radios c	6,000	26	11,090 d	61
Television sets c	3,300	14	5,716	32

a Total production in million sq. meters; per capita, sq. m.

b Total production in million pairs; per capita, pairs.

c Total production in thousand units; per capita columns show units per 1,000 of population.

d 1959 figures.

* Soviet figures include wool-like fabrics of synthetic fiber; US figures do not.

IN THE PRODUCTION of wool fabrics, the Soviet Union boasts that it already surpassed the United States in 1957. This claim is true only if such important factors as fiber content, quality, and consumer preference are completely disregarded, and the propaganda implication that the Soviet consumer actually fares better in wool textiles than his American counterparts is definitely false. At present, the United States still leads in both production and consumption of wool fabrics per capita, even without taking into account quality factors and consumer preferences for wool substitutes. Moreover, although Table 2 suggests that the Soviet Union may outproduce the United States in wool fabrics by 1965, an important qualification is how the term "wool fabric" is defined.

Some fabrics statistically reported as "woolen" in the USSR are not so classified in the United States. Wool fabric by Soviet definition includes anything containing at least 30 percent wool as compared to a US minimum of 50 percent wool, although the most common blend in the Soviet industry appears to be about half wool and half cotton or rayon. Moreover, pure wool fabric accounts for less than 10 percent of the total Soviet production, suggesting one reason why good-quality suits and coats for both men and women are scarce and extremely expensive. The Soviet practice of blending in non-wool fibers is mainly designed to augment production, whereas US blending is more often directed toward achieving a specific type or quality of fabric.

The claimed Soviet gains in wool fabric production as compared to the United States have been significantly aided by the fact that US production of these fabrics has been continuously declining since 1947 as a result of the development of synthetic substitutes such as Orlon, Dacron, and Acrilan. Although the Soviet Union is now making plans for the large-scale production of these synthetics, it presently does not produce any wool-like synthetic yarns or fabrics in substantial quantities and remains dependent on wool-based fabrics for its warm clothing.

American-made wool fabrics are wider, but of lighter weight, than those made in the USSR. The heavier weight of the Soviet fabrics may be attributed in part to the use of coarser wool, which has a greater fleece weight than fine wool; to the use of heavier substitute fibers in wool blends than are used in the United States (*e.g.,* cotton is generally heavier than synthetic fibers); and to the fact that the colder Soviet climate requires heavier fabrics. The predominance of part-wool fabrics in Soviet production reflects inadequates domestic supplies of raw wool and a preference for making up the deficit by blending with non-wool materials rather than by raw wool imports.

IN SOVIET USAGE, "silk fabrics" include all fabrics that are silk-like in appearance, whether woven from natural silk or from rayon and other synthetic fibers. Heavy consumer demand for clothing and household furnishings made of rayon and other silk-like synthetics has stimulated the development of these industries in the USSR, but the Soviet rayon industry still remains far behind its American counterpart, while the production of most other synthetic fibers is not yet past the experimental stage. Total Soviet production of "silk fabrics" is at present about one-fourth the US output (Table 1) and is scheduled, by 1965, to reach a planned level equal to only 44 percent of 1960 US production (Table 2).

Nevertheless, if the presently planned expansion of these industries is continued, chances are that Soviet consumers will eventually enjoy an abundance of rayon and other silk-like synthetic fabrics. The raw materials (cellulose for rayon; coal, petroleum, and natural gas for synthetics) are cheap and plentiful in the Soviet Union, and the necessary machinery, processes, and technology are available from abroad, mainly the United States, Western Europe, and Japan. Although the Soviet Union has already begun producing *kapron* (nylon 6) and, on a smaller scale, two other types of nylon (*anid* and *enant*), *nitron* (Orlon), and *lavsan* (Dacron), much of this production is presently going into military and industrial items and very little into fabrics for consumer use.

Whereas in the United States linen is usually an expensive luxury fabric imported from abroad for use in the manufacture of quality dresses and table linens, in the Soviet Union it is a more commonplace fabric devoted to utilitarian rather than luxury uses. This is no doubt related to the fact that the Soviet Union has a centuries-old linen industry producing rather ordinary grades of cloth, while the United States has none. Seventy percent of Soviet linen production is for industrial purposes, mainly packaging material, the rest going into clothing and household fabrics for consumer use.

Clothing, Hosiery and Footwear

Soviet-made clothing, as a rule, is notoriously shoddy, ill-fitting, and unattractive, reflecting both the poor quality of the textile fabrics used and the inexperience and lack of fashion-consciousness of the so-called "fashion" designers. Its low quality, lack of durability, and poor appearance have evoked widespread complaints from the buying public, and defective merchandise reaching the retail market has resulted in a high rate of factory returns. Though not accustomed to fine quality in personal apparel, Soviet consumers have become keenly aware of the plainness of their attire as a result of the increasing flow of Western visitors to the USSR. They also are sensitive about the high prices they have to pay for clothing, and in return they expect at least a modest response to consumer taste and a reasonable measure of durability, if not fine quality and style. Since Khrushchev himself has recently criticized the backwardness of the clothing and related industries, Soviet consumers can probably look forward to some increase in the availability of wearing apparel and possibly some improvement in quality.

Soviet clothing factories are equipped with machinery which, though not of the most modern design, is adequate for the fairly uncomplicated methods in use by the sewing industry. Production, however, is geared to volume rather than quality, and certainly not to fashion, the same models being duplicated monotonously year after year. A large part of the Soviet clothing supply comes from producers' cooperatives, which are soon to be integrated into the state industrial system and from private tailors—one of the very few groups of private entrepreneurs still permitted to function.

Hosiery is mostly a cheap cotton product lacking in durability and unattractive in appearance, comparable to American-made hosiery of 30 or 40 years ago. Of the total Soviet output in 1955, 79 percent was of cotton, and the remainder of rayon, nylon, or wool. By contrast, 67 percent of US hosiery production in 1958 was of nylon, and elasticized yarns are widely used, whereas these are still in the experimental stage in the Soviet Union. If the target fixed by the Seven-Year Plan is met total Soviet output of hosiery by 1965 will still be only about two-thirds of US production in 1959.

Turning to leather footwear, not only is Soviet production still inadequate to meet consumption needs, but lack of durability and poor selection of styles and sizes are constant sources of consumer complaint. Shoes of quality materials and good construction are available but so excessively priced as to be inaccessible except to the upper income groups. Pig and goat leathers, relatively less durable than other kinds of real leather, are widely used, especially for children's shoes; and artificial suede and other simulated leathers, which are extensively used as substitute materials, are far less durable, although the composition soles in common use appear to be an acceptable substitute. Poor durability also results in part from fabrication methods that are often either outmoded or geared to achieving maximum output rather than quality. Many Soviet shoe factories are poorly equipped; some are consolidations of small handicraft enterprises using extensive hand labor.

Even disregarding quality factors, the per capita supply of footwear available to the Soviet consumer is not much over half that available to the American buyer. Production of leather footwear in the two countries in 1960 was as follows:

	Soviet Union	United States
Total production (in million pairs)	418	604
Production per capita (in pairs)	1.9	3.3

Planned Soviet production of leather footwear by 1965 is scheduled to reach 85 percent of US production in 1960 (Table 2). While this may narrow the quantitative gap, there is little question that catching up with the United States in per capita production of leather footwear of equal quality is still a distant goal for the Soviet Union.

Durable Consumer Goods

Soviet preoccupation with building the country's industrial base and expanding its scientific frontiers is reflected nowhere more strongly than in the scarcity of consumer durables such as refrigerators and household laundry equipment. The low priority of such items is evidenced by the fact that they have largely been produced as side-line products of automobile, aircraft, and other heavy industrial plants. Soviet officials recently admitted that there is not a single plant in the Soviet Union specializing in the manufacture of refrigerators, and this situation is typical of the production of most major appliances.

Although supplies of most consumer durables in the USSR have increased somewhat since 1950, these commodities are still scarce and expensive. Radios and television receivers, because of their value as means of propaganda dissemination, enjoy a relatively favored place in consumer goods production and can be bought fairly cheaply. On the other hand, such household appliances as refrigerators and washing machines remain in the luxury class, and many others that are common in the United States—*e.g.*, freezers, dishwashers, and clothes dryers—are still virtually unknown to the Soviet public. Shortages also exist in supplies of ordinary household furniture and have been accentuated by the increasing availability of apartment housing.

A comparison of 1960 Soviet production of major electrical appliances with the latest available US production (or sales) figures (1959) is given in the following table:

	USSR	US
	(in thousands of units)	
Refrigerators	529	3,750*
Washing machines	953	4,210*
Radios	4,200	11,090
Television sets	1,700	6,270

* Sales

The lead held by the United States is even greater when these figures are translated into ratios of output to population. Thus, for each 1,000 of population, the United States produced 11 times as many refrigerators,

7 times as many washing machines, 3 times as many radios, and 6 times as many television sets, as the Soviet Union. (It should be noted also that these large production differentials are only a partial indication of the over-all difference in the volume of appliances in actual consumer use as they ignore appliances already installed and operating.) As shown in Table 2, the planned Soviet output goals for these consumer items by 1965 are still far below the actual US production levels of 1959.

While admitting the shortages of durable household goods, Soviet officials have tried to twist them to propaganda advantage by claiming that the growing public *demand* for durable goods is itself evidence of a rapidly rising standard of living. As one such statement put it,

> . . . the desires of the working people today radically differ from those of yesterday. They [the workers] say . . . that it is still difficult to buy a television set, a household refrigerator, good furniture, an upright piano. Undoubtedly this . . . shortcoming serves at the same time as a striking illustration of the rising standards and higher requirements of the Soviet people.[1]

To outside observers this statement, on its face, is ridiculous and only serves to underline the sacrifices of personal comfort, well-being and freedom of choice that are still demanded of Soviet citizens.

In conclusion, although each year is bringing some improvement in the lot of Soviet consumers, the Soviet Union will not—in spite of Khrushchev's boasts—surpass the United States in *per capita production* of consumer goods by 1970. Even assuming successful fulfillment of the Seven-Year Plan targets, Soviet production of most major consumer goods in 1965 will still remain far below the US production levels.

While the Soviet leadership has committed itself to providing a more adequate supply of basic consumer items such as textiles, clothing, and footwear, it clearly does not intend to emulate Western consumption standards in the broader range of consumer goods. In a few commodities of the Soviet planners' choosing, the USSR may possibly surpass the United States in over-all production (for example, in wool fabrics), but such gains will not be impressive on a per capita basis because of the expected increase in population. Moreover, quality improvements are not likely to be commensurate with production increases, and most consumer items will probably remain well below the quality levels of these goods in the United States. As for the hitherto grossly-neglected area of consumer durables, there will undoubtedly be a substantial increase in the availability of some household appliances, but Soviet consumption standards will continue to be far below those of the United States even in this narrowly circumscribed sector.

[1] *Komsomolskaia pravda,* October 7, 1960.

32

Living Standards of the Working People in the USSR and the USA *

A. AGANBEGIAN
*Institute on Economics and Organization of Industrial Production,
Siberian branch of the USSR Academy of Sciences*

The transition to the comprehensive building of communism in the USSR marks the beginning of a new historic era for the whole of mankind. Under the leadership of the Marxist-Leninist Party, the Soviet people are mobilizing all their material and spiritual forces in order to be the first people in the world to create a society which realizes the principle "from each according to his ability, to each according to his needs." The ways and means of building communism are defined in detail in the draft of the new Program of the Communist Party of the Soviet Union.

A communist civilization is being built in the process of the economic competition with capitalism. The decisive question in this competition, in the final analysis, is which system will provide the working people with the greatest material well-being and spiritual wealth.

Capitalism, having developed its productive forces tremendously, became subsequently the greatest obstacle to social progress. "If the 20th Century—the Century of the colossal growth of the productive forces and the development of science—has still not put an end to the poverty of hundreds of millions of people, has not provided an abundance of material and spiritual riches for all men on earth," the Draft Party Program points out, "only capitalism is to blame."

Relying on the laws of social development, which afford irrefutable proof of the superiority of the socialist system, the Communist Party of the Soviet Union has posed the world-historic task of providing the population of the USSR with a living standard which is higher than that of any capitalist country. The Draft Party Program contains a com-

* From *Mirovaia Ekonomika i Mezhdunarodnye Otnosheniia*, 1961, No. 10. Translated in and excerpts reprinted from *Problems of Economics*, March, 1962, pp. 10-24, by permission of the publisher.

prehensive system of concrete indices for raising the living standard of the Soviet people in the coming decade and the next twenty years.

In the current stage of the competition Soviet society has already surpassed the capitalist world and its richest country, the USA, in some of the most important indices of a people's living standard. As it fulfills its magnificent plans for building communism, the Soviet Union will outstrip the USA in a growing number of indices of living standards. In the peaceful competition with capitalism, the socialist system will provide the people with a level of material well-being which the working people cannot even dream of in any capitalist country. . . .

A living standard covers a very wide range of indices. However, a fairly complete picture of a people's living standard can be obtained by analyzing the following basic socio-economic indices:

1) real incomes;
2) level and structure of consumption;
3) employment provided;
4) length of the working day and working conditions;
5) housing and living conditions;
6) public health services;
7) education and cultural services;
8) social security, child care.

A mere enumeration of the basic indices of the living standard reminds us that in many of them the Soviet Union is ahead of all the countries of the capitalist world. There is general knowledge of the USSR's unsurpassed achievements in public education and in cultural services for the population, in providing full employment and completely eliminating unemployment, in establishing healthy working conditions, in public health, in state social security, etc. However we still lag behind in several other indices. Surpassing the US living standard involves outstripping it in all the basic indices.

In order to gain a clear idea of the successes and immediate tasks of the USSR in the course of the competition, it is necessary to compare the indices of the two countries on the basis of a scientific methodology. . . .

Naturally, this comparison will bring out the most profound qualitative differences between the socialist and capitalist, American ways of life. To begin with, the Soviet Union has completely and finally done away with capitalist exploitation and its consequences: the deepening gulf between wealth at one social pole and poverty at the other, unemployment, inhuman intensification of labor, discrimination against women, young people and national minorities, moral degradation of working people, etc. The development of socialist production, which, unlike capitalist production, does not serve as a source of profit for the exploiters, is dedicated to raising the living standard of the working people. In the same way, the national income is distributed in the interests of the working people.

In contrast to the USA and all other capitalist countries, the socialist system provides every honest working man with access to all the good things of life, to education, public activities, scientific and technical work, the arts, etc. The Soviet citizen can freely apply and develop his abilities in any field of endeavor: he is not confronted with the property, political, national, racial and other barriers which capitalism puts in the way of the ordinary man. All Soviet statesmen, directors of enterprises, military leaders, scientists and artists have come from the ranks of the workers, peasants, or working intelligentsia. Soviet people go through life with heads proudly erect: they are the collective owners of all of their country's wealth, of all the fruits of their labor; they are the rulers of their state, the builders of the most perfect and just social system. It is difficult to measure all these unshakable and indisputable advantages of the socialist system in figures. However, their paramount significance is obvious without doing so. They inspire the simple people in the capitalist countries in the struggle for social progress, and the most sober leaders of the capitalist world must recognize them, directly or indirectly.

The achievements of the Soviet Union are especially striking if they are compared with the past, with the economic backwardness, poverty and lack of culture of the working people in pre-revolutionary Russia, with the devastation of World War I, the foreign intervention and World War II. These historic facts explain why the volume of production and labor productivity in the USSR are at present lower than in the USA, and why the USSR still lags behind the USA in the level of real incomes and wages, in the consumption of a number of goods, in housing conditions and in several other elements involved in material well-being. It can be said with confidence that if there had been no wars on the territory of the USSR, as there have been none on the territory of the USA, the population of our country would have a higher standard of living than the population of the USA.

It should immediately be emphasized, however, that, first, this lag seems significant only when a comparison is made of average indices, which in the USA, unlike the USSR, do not reflect the living conditions of considerable strata of the working people because of the very great differences in the material well-being of different classes and groups of the population; second, this lag is being overcome rapidly as a result of high rates of growth of social production, and, consequently, improvements in the life of the entire population of the USSR. The constant improvement of the living conditions of every Soviet family is in contrast with the precarious material position of many working people in the

USA, especially in connection with frequent economic crises, work stoppages in branches of the economy, capitalist automation of production, accomplished at the expense of the working people, etc.

The USSR Will Outstrip the USA in the Level of Real Incomes of the Population

We know that a country's national income is the source of the population's material well-being. The size of the national income is determined by two factors: the level of labor productivity and the number of workers employed in material production. . . .

The productivity of living labor in the national economy of the USSR in 1960 was lower than in the USA by approximately 2.5 times. Consumption of raw materials, fuel and electric power per unit of output is somewhat smaller in the USA than in the USSR. However, this is compensated for by the more effective use of fixed productive capital, something which is natural for a planned, socialist economy. Consequently, the superiority of the USA in the saving of past labor is so small that it may not be taken into account in a rough estimate. In both countries the production of net output by one worker in industry, construction and transport is approximately 2 to 2.5 times greater than by one worker in agriculture. Inasmuch as agriculture in the USA employs a much smaller percentage of all the workers of material production than in the USSR, this factor raises the volume of the national income produced by an American worker, as against that produced by a Soviet worker. . . .

In 1960 the national income used in the USSR came to, in round figures, almost 144 billion rubles. About 75% of the Soviet national income is used for satisfying the material and cultural requirements of the population; the remainder is directed towards expanding socialist production and for other social requirements.[1] This means that in 1960 about 104 billion rubles went into the consumption fund and 40 billion rubles went into the accumulation fund, the reserve fund and other expenditures. The national income of the USA in 1960, calculated on the basis of the non-scientific American method (as the sum of all incomes in the society), amounted to 418 billion dollars, but after discounting the double counting of incomes, it really came to approximately 320 billion dollars.[2] Of this, about 230 billion dollars goes into the consumption

[1] See also the statistical yearbook *Narodnoe Khoziaistvo SSSR v 1960 Godu,* Moscow, 1961, p. 154.

[2] The methodology for these re-estimates has been worked out by the Soviet economists A. Pal'tsev, M. Kolganov, A. Petrov and others. Their re-estimates for other years have also shown that calculations based on the American method exaggerate the real volume of the national income in the USA by 25 to 30%. Sources: *The Handbook of Basic Economic Statistics,* April 15, 1961, p. 231; *Survey of Current Business,* June, 1961.

fund of the population and 90 billion dollars goes for accumulations, for expenditures on military technique, reserves, material outlays on administration, science and other items.

In order to compare the level of real incomes of the Soviet and US populations, the consumption funds in the two countries should be compared in identical currency. The purchasing power of one dollar for food and manufactures sold in the retail trade may be accepted as approximately equivalent to one ruble. The volume of retail trade in the Soviet state, cooperative and collective farm trading network amounts to approximately 75% of the total consumption fund of our national income. The remaining 25% of the consumption fund is made up of consumer goods acquired by the population outside of the retail trade system (consumption in children's institutions, hospitals, payment in kind on the collective farms, goods obtained from the subsidiary farms, etc.), as well as material outlays in institutions and organizations providing services for the population, amortization of housing, schools, hospitals, etc. This portion of the consumption fund is calculated in prices which are far below retail prices, and therefore the purchasing power of one dollar here will be smaller than one ruble, in all probability about 0.5 to 0.7 of the ruble. As a result, with regard to the consumption fund as a whole in the national income, the purchasing power of one dollar will approximate 0.9 rubles ($1 \times 0.75 + 0.6 \times 0.25 = 0.9$), which corresponds to the official rate of the ruble in relation to the dollar.

Taking into account the indicated purchasing power of the dollar, the consumption fund in the USSR approximates 120 billion dollars as against 230 billion dollars in the USA. . . .

When speaking of comparative well-being in the USSR and the USA it should be remembered that there is a great gap in the USA between the average living standard of the population and the living standard of the working people: real per capita income for the population as a whole in the USA is 25% higher than in the families of the working people.[3] Therefore, if a comparison is drawn between the real incomes of the working people of the USSR and the USA, rather than between the real incomes of the population as a whole, the difference will be much smaller. . . .

The average per capita real income of the working population of the USSR today comes to about 55% of the American level. In the seven years from 1959 to 1965 the per capita consumption fund should increase by about 1.5 times in the USSR, or at the rate of 6% a year. In 1965 the

[3] About 30% of total income is concentrated in the hands of 10% of the richest families, the remaining 90% of the families receiving 70%. See the *Statistical Abstract of the United States,* 1959, p. 318.

average real per capita income of the working population in the USSR will amount to 70 to 75% of the American level.

The Draft Party Program indicates that the national income of the USSR will rise by almost 150% in the coming ten years, and by about 400% in twenty years. Real incomes per head of population will increase in twenty years by more than 250%. . . .

In the current decade the USSR will in the main attain the average level of real incomes of the working people in the USA, and by 1975 it will also surpass the average level of real incomes of the entire population of the USA. Twenty years later the real incomes per head of population in the USSR will be higher than in the USA by at least 30 to 40%, and per working person by at least 60 to 70%. . . .

In comparing the average real incomes of the Soviet and US populations, account should always be taken of the tremendous gaps between the incomes of different groups of the American population and the incomparably smaller differentiation of incomes in the USSR. In order to measure this differentiation, let us compare the incomes of the 10% of the families which are most prosperous and the 10% which are least prosperous. In 1957 the 10% of poorest families in the USA received 1% of the money incomes of the population (before taxes), while the 10% of richest families received 29%; thus the difference in income levels comes to 29 times.[4] In the USSR in 1958 the relationship between the incomes of the 10% most prosperous families of workers and employees and the 10% least prosperous was, according to rough estimates, 4.75 times, and in 1965 it will drop to about 3 times.[5]

The vast differences in the incomes of different groups of the US population is explained not only by the gulf between the bourgeoisie and the working people. There are also very great differences in the living standards of different strata of the working people. This is due, first, to discrimination in payment for the labor of women, Negroes and numerous categories of workers and employees (farm workers, workers in commerce and the services, etc.), and, second, to the losses resulting from full or partial unemployment. Approximately 1,300,000 families (2%) have incomes which are 10 or more times below the average—under 500 dollars; 3,250,000 families (6%)—from 500 to 1,000 dollars; 7,400,000 families (13%)—from 1,000 to 2,000 dollars; 6,258,000 families (11%)—from 2,000 to 3,000 dollars. Thus, with a relatively high average income level, millions of American working class families live in poverty, other millions simply are in want, wear cast-off clothes, live in slums, and cannot afford to pay for medical assistance, which is quite expensive.

[4] *Statistical Abstract of the United States,* 1959, p. 318.
[5] *Voprosy Truda,* IV, Moscow, 1959, p. 148. The differentiation will be somewhat higher for the population as a whole, including peasant families.

The Soviet Union Will Surpass the USA
in Consumption and Housing

The difference between the levels of nutrition of the Soviet and US populations has been reduced sharply in the last few years. Nevertheless, the USSR still lags behind the USA in average per capita nutrition norms, as is evident from the comparison made in Table 1.

TABLE 1 *

	USSR (1960)	USA (1958)	USSR in % of USA
Milk and dairy products in terms of milk (kg.)	283	317	89
Meat and meat products (kg.)	45	94	48
Fish and fish products (kg.)	11	11	100
Eggs (pieces)	123	348	35
Sugar (kg.)	28	39	72

* A. N. Kosygin, "Doklad o Plane Razvitiia Narodnogo Khoziaistva na 1960 G.," *Pravda,* Oct. 28, 1959; *Ekonomika Kapitalisticheskikh Stran Posle Vtoroi Mirovoi Voiny. Statisticheskii Sbornik,* Moscow, 1959, p. 886; *Statistical Abstract of the United States,* 1959, p. 85.

Appraised in rubles or dollars, the value of the average per capita food products consumed in the USSR is approximately 60% behind that of the USA. This is the average, but it is known that the nutrition of the working people in the USA is substantially below that of bourgeois families. Expenditures on food per person in families with annual incomes of more than 10,000 dollars are 2 to 2.5 times greater than in families with incomes of under 2,000 dollars. The average indices of nutrition for working people, who constitute about 90% of the population, are about 5 to 10% lower than even the average per capita consumption norms for the entire population of the USA. This means that in per capita nutrition of the working people the lag of the USSR behind the USA is actually smaller, about 1.5 times. Under the Seven-Year Plan, the food products supplied to the Soviet population will increase on an average by more than 1.5 times. Consequently the existing lag in this area will be eliminated by 1965.

Moreover the diet of the Soviet population will be the best in the world. Proteins of animal origin will comprise more than 50% of the total consumption of proteins. There will be a substantial increase during the next twenty years in the share of animal produce (meat, fats and dairy products). The assortment of food products will be much improved. Thus poultry and veal will make up a larger share of the meat products. Fruits, especially citrus fruits and grapes, and high-quality vegetables will constitute a large share of products of vegetable origin.

The USSR lags behind the USA in the consumption of manufactured goods to a somewhat greater extent than in food consumption. For example, in 1959 per capita sales of manufactures in the USSR (excluding automobiles) came to about 165 rubles (or, relatively speaking, 165 dollars), while in the USA they amounted to about 400 dollars, or about 2.5 times more.[6] The extent of the lag may be judged approximately also by the per capita production of certain consumer manufactured goods (see Table 2).

TABLE 2 *

	USSR		USA	Indices of USSR in % of 1959 indices of USA	
	1959	1965 (planned figures)	1959	1959	1965 (planned figures)
Cotton fabrics (square meters)	24	28-29	49	50	60
Woolen fabrics (running meters)	1.6	2.2	1.6	100	140
Silk fabrics (running meters)	3.8	6.5	12.5	30	50
Hosiery (pairs)	4.4	5.5	11	40	50
Leather shoes (pairs)	1.85	2.25	3.6	50	65
Radios, Radio-phonographs, and TV sets (per 1,000 people)	25	39	100	25	40
Refrigerators (per 1,000 people)	2	7	18	10	40

* See *SSR v Tsifrakh v 1959 Godu*, pp. 57-58, 80-81; *Kratkii Spravochnik o Semiletnem Plane SSSR*, Moscow, 1960, pp. 74, 76; *Voprosy Ekonomiki*, 1960, No. 4, p. 106.

Account must be taken, of course, of the fact that there is also a vast differentiation in the USA in the consumption of manufactured goods by different classes and sections of the population, a much greater differentiation than in food consumption. The consumption of manufactured goods by families of American working people is 25 to 30% below the average indices. Therefore, in comparison with the working people of the USA, consumption by the working people of the USSR in this sphere lags behind not by 2.5 times, but by approximately 2 times. The most substantial lag is in the consumption of durable domestic goods (refrigerators, etc.), the production of which got under way in our country only in recent years, but is developing quite rapidly. Here, too, consumption is evenly distributed among the population of the USSR, while in the USA distribution among the different groups of the population is extremely uneven. American family budgets show that rich families

[6] The calculations are based on data presented in the statistical yearbook *Narodnoe Khoziaistvo SSSR v 1959 Godu*, Moscow, 1960, p. 642. See also *SSR v Tsifrakh v 1960 Godu*, p. 342; *Statistical Abstract of the United States*, 1959, pp. 308, 833.

(with annual incomes above 10,000 dollars) spend 20 times as much on durable goods than the poor families (with incomes of up to 2,000 dollars a year).

At the end of the Seven-Year Plan the difference in per capita consumption norms of manufactured goods in the USSR and the USA will be substantially reduced. If in 1960 the consumption of manufactured goods per member of families of working people in the USSR was about 40% of the corresponding level in the USA, in 1965, as based on the Seven-Year Plan targets, it should increase to 60%. But the Government of the USSR and the Soviet people are exploring new possibilities for accelerating the output of manufactured mass consumer goods to the utmost. . . .

Realization of the rapid rise in the general level of public consumption provided for in the Draft Party Program will enable the USSR to surpass considerably the American indices on both the consumption of food and manufactured goods. Calculations of the population's requirements for textiles, shoes and other manufactured mass consumer goods are based on rational, scientific standards which take account of the habits and climatic conditions of our country.

What are the prospects in the competition in housing conditions? Taking average indices as a basis, the provision of housing to the US population is at present approximately twice that in the USSR. At the end of 1958 there were 8 square meters of general living area per person in the cities and workers' settlements of the USSR; 1.7 people on an average lived in one room.[7] In the USA in 1956 an average of 0.65 persons occupied one room in the cities.[8] True, the average size of a habitable room in the USA is somewhat less than in the USSR, but what matters most is that, just as for other indices on living standards, the provision of housing in the USA is very different for various groups of the population.

One can indirectly form a judgment on this from rent statistics: the wealthy families, with average annual incomes of about 10,000 dollars, spend five times more on rent than the poor families (with incomes of up to 2,000 dollars a year).[9] This means that the latter live in greatly inferior, more congested conditions. . . . It follows from these facts that the average housing provided for the working people in the USA is 10 to 15% below the average for the entire population. Many working people, primarily Negroes, Puerto Ricans and other national minorities, live in slums, barracks and ramshackle houses in congested and unsanitary conditions. New York alone has 50,000 barracks [*Baraki*] inhabited by about 1.5 million people.

In the USSR the overwhelming majority of workers and employees are

7 *Narodnoe Khoziaistvo SSSR v 1958 Godu,* pp. 9, 641; *Novoe Vremia,* 1960, No. 22, p. 10.
8 *Statistical Abstract of the United States,* 1959, p. 768.
9 *Ibid.,* p. 316.

given apartments in state-owned houses. Rent is low in the USSR (not more than 13.2 kopecks per square meter) and covers only a small portion of state expenditures on housing. Rent and communal services consume only 4 to 5% of the family incomes of Soviet workers and employees. In the USA these expenses amount on average to about 20% of incomes; in the low-income families of working people they go up to 30%.[10] The share of rent in the expenditures of American families is growing year by year, and, moreover, at a faster rate than the general index of the cost of living. American families now spend on housing (not counting communal services) an average of about 800 dollars a year, while in 1940 they paid 320 dollars.[11]

The gap between the USSR and the USA in providing housing is shrinking from year to year. The rates of housing construction in our country are higher than in the USA. About 15 million apartments will be built in cities and workers' settlements between 1959 and 1965; the available housing will increase by 60%, an increase of approximately 40% per inhabitant. If at present the working people in the USSR are provided with approximately 2 times less housing than the population of the USA, this difference will be reduced to 1.5 times by 1965. After another 7 to 10 years, evidently, the USSR will also surpass the American level for this index. As stipulated in the Draft Party Program, the achievements of the second decade (1971–1980) will result in every Soviet family enjoying, free of charge, a private, modern apartment. The Soviet Union will surpass the level of housing provided in the USA and in the other more developed capitalist countries. Moreover, thanks to the vast new housing construction, Soviet housing will consist in the main of modern houses with all the communal amenities.

Falsifying Methods Used by Bourgeois Economists in Comparing Incomes and Consumption

Comparisons of real incomes of the populations of different countries should be made on the basis of the net incomes used for the acquisition of consumer goods. Bourgeois economists often violate this requirement by comparing nominal rather than net incomes. They reason as follows: the weekly wage of the American worker amounts to about 90 dollars, which is equivalent to 90 rubles. This should come to more than 360 rubles a month and almost 4,700 rubles a year, i.e., much more than the workers earn in the USSR (precisely this method was used by R. Nixon in his speech at the opening of the American Exhibition in Moscow).

Soviet economists [12] have already exposed such falsifying manipula-

10 *Ibid.*

11 Calculated on the basis of *Statistical Abstract of the United States,* 1959, p. 770; *The Handbook of Basic Economic Statistics,* April 15, 1960, p. 104.

12 See, for example, the article by P. Mstislavskii in *Novoe Vremia,* 1960, Nos. 21 and 22.

tions with the so-called dollar equivalent in which one dollar was generally equated with one ruble. A deliberately distorted picture of real incomes is obtained when the 1:1 dollar rate, calculated for food and manufactured goods of mass consumption, is extended to the whole of the nominal wage of the American worker without considering what part of this wage is really used for purchasing manufactured goods and foodstuffs. Meanwhile, there is a fundamental difference between the composition of expenditures in the budgets of Soviet and US workers and employees, as is illustrated by Table 3.

TABLE 3

Indices	USSR		USA
	1960	1965 (estimates)	
All money expenditures, including (in %)	100	100	100
Direct taxes	7		12
Contributions to social insurance fund			4
Rent and communal services	4	5	19
Medical treatment and education	(approx.) 0.1	(approx.) 0.1	6
Transportation (including private automobiles)	3	3	13
Other everyday expenditures	11	12	9
Remainder for purchasing food and manufactured consumer goods	75	80	37

The people of the USA can spend on manufactured goods and food only 37% of their money incomes. Therefore, in the comparison of the incomes of American and Soviet families made in Table 3, net incomes of US workers from wages should be estimated not at 90, but at most at 33 dollars a week. Moreover, this part should be compared not with the nominal incomes of the workers in the USSR, but with their real income after tax payments, etc.

Certain other comparisons drawn by American economists are also incorrect. Thus, they make comparisons not on the basis of total real income, but only on wages. As regards the working people of the USA, their incomes are actually almost completely limited to their wages. In addition to their wages, the workers and employees receive only small additional incomes in pensions, benefits and additions to their base pay. All these additional incomes amount to no more than about 8% of wages.[13] Benefits provided free of charge by the state constitute a very

13 *The Handbook of Basic Economic Statistics,* April 15, 1960, p. 231.

negligible share of the real incomes of US workers and employees—elementary and secondary education for a part of the population, and certain others. These benefits amount to only about 5% of the real incomes of the population.

In the USSR the payments and benefits provided to the population through the state budget and the funds of enterprises amounted in 1960 to 24.5 billion rubles, or 22% of the consumption fund of the national income. The share of payments and benefits from public funds in the real incomes of Soviet workers and employees is still greater; on average they amount to 50% of their real incomes, and substantially more for lower-paid categories. As the Draft Party Program indicates, the share of the public consumption funds in the total real incomes of the Soviet population will increase up to 50% in twenty years. As Soviet society advances towards communism, the needs of the people will be satisfied to an increasing degree out of funds intended for collective use, for the "joint satisfaction of needs." As Karl Marx wrote: "This share will increase substantially at once as compared with what it is in contemporary society, and it will increase constantly with the development of the new society.[14]

US economists, in comparing the incomes of American and Soviet workers while operating only with the size of wages, do some flagrant juggling, embellishing the American way of life. Bourgeois economists commit a forgery even in comparing the wages of workers in the USSR and the USA. They operate with data on the earnings of the most highly-paid workers in the US manufacturing industry and compare it with averages for the USSR. But the wages of workers in other branches of the American economy lag substantially behind earnings in the manufacturing industry. For example, in 1958 farm workers received only 40 to 45% of the wage paid to workers in manufacturing, people in retail trade —75 to 80%, workers employed in the services—50 to 60%, etc.[15]

Lastly, there is a typical falsification in the fact that incomes of American workers are usually calculated on the basis of their hourly or weekly wages. While in the USSR annual or monthly wages correspond as a rule to the aggregate weekly earnings because the working people are employed throughout the year, the situation is quite different in the USA. In 1957, for example, only 55.1% of US workers and employees were employed 50 to 52 weeks during the year, 15.5% worked 27 to 49 weeks, 10.4%—less than 27 weeks, and 19.0% worked part-time.[16] As a result, annual earnings are actually far below the amount obtained by multiplying weekly earnings by the number of weeks in a year. In 1958 the weekly

[14] K. Marx, *Izbrannye Proizvedeniia*, Part II, p. 13.
[15] *Statistical Abstract of the United States*, 1959, pp. 228, 230, 233.
[16] *Ibid.*, p. 208.

wage of US workers and employees was about 75 dollars. That would seem to amount to 3,900 dollars a year, that is, 52 weeks. Actually, however, it was only 3,160 dollars for all US workers and employees.[17] Consequently, an honest approach to the question requires that actual annual incomes be compared, and not magnitudes obtained as a result of statistical gymnastics.

There is still another method of comparing consumption levels in different countries in wide use in American economics literature; it is also based on the substitution of nominal for real incomes. This method is often used at exhibitions arranged by bourgeois countries abroad; it was used, in particular, at the American Exhibition in Moscow. We refer to indices which characterize what a worker or employee can purchase with his hourly earnings. The following example is produced: a garment worker in the USA earns 2 dollars an hour, and the fabric used for making her dress costs 3 dollars. Thus the incorrect conclusion is suggested that in one and one-half hours the worker earns enough to pay for her dress. "Calculations" of this kind obscure the fact that before she can buy anything the worker must pay taxes, insurance fees, rent, charges for communal services, bills for medical treatment, tuition fees, transportation, etc. And only what remains, and this, as we have seen, amounts to about one-third of wages, can be used for purchasing food and manufactured goods. This calculation, just as all others made by the bourgeois economists, ignores the fact that there is not full employment and assumes that workers and employees are regularly employed during the year and on a full-time basis. This means that such comparisons grossly distort the real picture, greatly exaggerating the indices of real incomes of the working people in the USA.

As we have seen, the methods of comparing real incomes in the USSR and USA which are often employed in American economics literature are incorrect. It should be noted, however, that the outstanding economic achievements of the Soviet Union have recently forced some American economists to make more sober judgments about the relationship between the standards of life in the USA and the USSR. This was reflected in particular in the reports submitted to the Economic Committee of Congress on the comparison of Soviet and US economic indices. The American economist Lynn Turgeon, who prepared a report on the standard of living, does criticize, though timidly, the method of comparing nominal incomes in the USA and USSR. She [*sic*] notes the need for taking into account the different expenditure structures in the two countries and the supplementary incomes over and above wages.

17 *The Handbook of Basic Economic Statistics,* November 15, 1959, p. 208.

Superiority of the USSR in Employment and Working Conditions

The superiority of the Soviet Union with respect to the employment of the population has an effect on every aspect of the living standard. Our able-bodied population is being drawn into production with increasing completeness. The share of those employed in the social and cultural branches is increasing, while it is declining in the state apparatus, financial and credit institutions, etc. At the same time, the use of labor resources in the USA is deteriorating. The number of totally and partially unemployed workers is growing from one economic cycle to another; the share of those working among the able-bodied population is declining; the number of workers employed in material production is diminishing not only relatively, but also absolutely; at the same time, the number employed in trade, in financial and credit institutions and the state apparatus is growing rapidly. Employment in the USSR and in the USA can be characterized from the data given in Table 4.

TABLE 4 *

	USSR	USA	USSR in % of USA
Entire population at the beginning of 1960 (millions)	212	179	120
including those able to work by age	120	96	125
Number employed in the national economy (millions, in 1959)	100	70	140
including partially employed (from 1 to 34 hours a week)	none	14	
Number of totally unemployed (millions)	none	4**	
Percentage of all workers in the national economy employed in:			
a) branches of material production	79	50	160
b) non-productive branches and trade including:	21	50	40
social and cultural branches (education, science, public health and the arts)	10	9	110
trade, financial institutions, the state apparatus and other non-productive branches	11	41	25

* Compiled on the basis of data in the handbook *SSSR v Tsifrakh v 1959 Godu*, pp. 35, 281; *Narodnoe Khoziaistvo SSSR v 1958 Godu*, pp. 655, 654; *Voprosy Ekonomiki*, 1960, No. 4, p. 114; *Statistical Abstract of the United States*, 1959, sec. 1, 8; *The Handbook of Basic Economic Statistics*, April 15, 1960, p. 13.

** The official statistics on unemployment in the USA which we have used underestimate the actual number of totally unemployed.

How do matters stand in the USSR and the USA with respect to the length of the working day? American propaganda proclaims that the average working day in the USA is shorter than in the USSR. But by the end of 1960, when the transfer of all Soviet workers and employees to a 6- and 7-hour day was completed, the USSR had moved ahead on the length of the working day. This is clear from the data in Table 5.

TABLE 5 *

	Average work week (hours)	
	USSR (at the end of 1960)**	USA (at the end of 1959)
Workers and employees in the national economy as a whole	40.2	41 (approx.)
Workers in industry	40.5	40.6

* *Trud,* October 13, 1959; *The Handbook of Basic Economic Statistics,* April 15, 1960, p. 25. The average work week in the USSR was calculated with due account for measures taken in 1960 to transfer to a 6-hour day all workers employed in underground work.

** Counting holidays, the average work week of workers and employees in the national economy of the USSR was 39.4 hours; for workers in industry it was 39.7 hours.

The average length of the working day in the USSR reflects the actual situation. Overtime work does not occur in the Soviet economy on a mass scale; it is resorted to in special cases only with the special permission of the trade unions. In the USA, on the contrary, the average working day does not reflect the real state of affairs. The law on the 40-hour work week in the USA does not prohibit work over this norm; it provides only for higher pay for overtime work. In the last few years 7-8% of the American workers and employees have been working from 41 to 47 hours a week, 6 to 7%—48 hours, 4 to 5%—49 to 54 hours, about 5%—55 to 69 hours, and about 2%—70 and more hours a week. Consequently, more than 25% of all the US workers and employees are working more than 40 hours a week. At the same time, millions of working people are compelled to work only a few hours a week, that is, they are partially unemployed: 5 to 6% of the workers and employees work from 1 to 14 hours a week, 3 to 4%—15 to 21 hours a week, 3 to 5%—22 to 29 hours, and 3 to 4% from 30 to 34 hours a week.[18] If we calculate the average working day in the USA without the partially employed workers, it will come to about 45 hours a week. Unlike the USA, the USSR has neither fully nor partially unemployed workers.

In the next ten years the USSR will make the transition to a 34- to 36-hour work week (30 hours in harmful occupations and in underground work), and in the following decade—on the basis of a corresponding growth of labor productivity—the transition to a still shorter work week will begin.

The working day is being reduced in the Soviet Union without wage reductions, and in those branches of the national economy where adjustments in wages are being made simultaneously, the wages of workers and employees are being increased, lower paid-workers receiving the most substantial increases. In the USA, where payment is based on hours of

[18] *Current Population Reports,* 1956–1959.

work, a reduction in the working day entails a cut in wages. That is why the American workers, along with workers in the other capitalist countries, are fighting not only for a shorter working day, but also against wage cuts and for increases.

While reducing the working day, the Soviet Union will be increasing the duration of paid annual vacations. The minimum vacation for all workers and employees will gradually be extended from two to three weeks, and later to one month. There is no general provision in American legislation for paid annual vacations. True, as the result of a stubborn struggle against the employers, some American workers succeeded in getting provisions for paid vacations incorporated in collective agreements, but as a general rule they are for one week. Only workers with an uninterrupted service record of more than five years are given a two-week vacation. . . .

Superiority of the USSR in Social and Cultural
Services and in Social Security

The socialist state, acting in the name of society as a whole, is concerned with the satisfaction of the material and cultural requirements of every person. This concern greets man at the very threshold of his life. A long, fully-paid maternity leave has been established in the USSR; mothers are provided with free medical consultation and medical assistance during childbirth. Nurseries and kindergartens are provided for the children, with the parents paying, on average, only 20% of the cost of maintaining the children and the remaining 80% being covered by the state. Instruction is free in all general education schools. The state bears the bulk of the expenditures required for the maintenance of children in the boarding schools and in the prolonged-day groups. Furthermore, the students in specialized secondary schools and higher schools not only study without charge, they also receive stipends. Advanced training in production is provided at the expense of the respective enterprises.

Many workers are accommodated in sanitoriums or holiday homes during their vacations at reduced prices (the remaining costs are paid from social funds). Medical assistance is available to every Soviet citizen free of charge in the event of illness; the state also pays sick benefits during periods of illness. State pensions are paid to the aged and to incapacitated workers and employees.

The following data testifies to the tremendous scope of the social and cultural services provided from state and social funds in the USSR. There were 5.7 million children in kindergartens, nurseries and children's homes in 1959. More than 6 million children are sent each year to Young Pioneer camps, summer playgrounds and excursion centers. State allowances are paid to about 7 million mothers of large families and single mothers for the care of their children. Some 400,000 children were maintained and taught in boarding schools at the beginning of 1960. There were 33.3 million people studying in general education schools, the schools for young workers and young villagers and the schools for adults, and at no charge. The state provided stipends and dormitory accommodations for 3.4 million students of technical schools, universities and other schools. Some 8.7 million workers and employees either acquired skills or increased existing ones at enterprises and institutions in 1959 at no charge. More than 20 million pensioners receive their maintenance from the state, collective farms and public organizations. All Soviet citizens enjoy free medical assistance. Allocations from the state budget of the USSR and from the funds of enterprises for the indicated payments and benefits amounted to 24.5 billion rubles in 1960; they will come to 36 billion rubles in 1965, an average of 380 rubles a year per person employed in the national economy. This does not include state capital investments for the construction of houses, schools, institutions for cultural and everyday services and medical services, which in 1965 will amount to an additional 80 rubles per worker.

The capitalist system does not put concern for man as one of its tasks. Capitalists need the worker and they provide for him only to the extent that it increases profits. Expenditures on social and cultural services in the USA are borne in the main by the working people themselves. Expenses for medical care are especially burdensome. . . . Many types of treatment are inaccessible to a substantial portion of the American working people because they are so expensive. Education in the USA is to a significant extent provided from the people's own resources. This is particularly true of specialized and higher education. Approximately 50% of the pension fund in the USA comes from deductions from the wages of workers and employees.[19] It should also be emphasized that the social services in the USSR are superior to those in the USA. This becomes clear in comparing the indices in Table 6 (p. 288).

Soviet pension provisions and the amounts paid are much more favorable than in the USA. The age at which pensions are paid is lower in the USSR: 60 years for men and 55 for women (reduced by 5 and 10 years respectively in the case of preferential pensions); in the USA it is 65 years for men and 62 for women. The average old-age pension in the USSR amounts to 60% of a worker's earnings; it is only 20% in the USA. Pensions are paid to all workers and employees in the USSR, while only some of them receive pensions in the USA. The Soviet state spends very substantial amounts on pensions—more than 7 billion rubles in 1960.

The Draft Party Program provides for further development and improvement of the social and cultural services for the population of the

19 For greater details on social security in the capitalist countries see *Mirovaia Ekonomika i Mezhdunarodnye Otnosheniia,* 1960, No. 2.

TABLE 6 *

	1913		1958-1959	
	Russia	USA	USSR (1959)	USA (1958)
Number of doctors for every 10,000 inhabitants	1	11	17.9	12.0
Expenditures on treatment in % of money incomes of a family	No information available		0.1	5.2
Number of deaths per 1,000 inhabitants	30.2	13.2	7.6	9.5

* Compiled on the basis of statistics in the handbook *SSSR v. Tsifrakh v 1959 Godu,* pp. 241-248; *Statistical Abstract of the United States,* 1959, pp. 59, 62, 316.

USSR. Within the next two decades the Soviet Union wil have introduced free maintenance of children in children's institutions and boarding schools (at the request of parents), free use of apartments, communal services and urban transportation. There will be a gradual transition to free public meals (dinners) at enterprises and institutions, and for collective farmers at work.

A comparison of the basic data on the standards of life in the USSR and the USA shows that as regards providing jobs, the length of the working day, working conditions, public health, education, cultural services, social security and the care of children, the working people in our country have attained indices which are unattainable for the working people of the USA and other capitalist states today.

After the Great October Socialist Revolution, the Soviet Union made a colossal leap in its historic development. Under the leadership of the Communist Party, the peoples of the USSR have converted a once backward Russia into a great socialist power which is marching in the vanguard of mankind.

The standard of living in the USSR has grown immeasurably in comparison with the impoverished living conditions of the working people in Russia before 1917. The living standard of the Soviet people continues to rise at rapid rates in all its aspects. By the end of the Seven-Year Plan, the Soviet Union will be really close to the USA in the size of real incomes of the working people, the level of consumption and the provision of housing, and subsequently it will surpass the USA in these indices. The working people of the USSR will then have the highest living standard in the world.

This will not only be a great victory for the peoples of the USSR. The Draft Party Program notes: "Every new step made towards the shining peaks of communism inspires the working masses in all countries, serves as immense moral support in the struggle for the liberation of all peoples from social and national oppression, and brings closer the triumph of the ideas of Marxism-Leninism on a world-wide scale."

33

Ways to Increase National Well-Being *

P. OLDAK
*Institute on Economics and Organization of Industrial Production,
Siberian branch of the USSR Academy of Sciences*

In the period of the extensive building of communist society and in the conditions of a new era of economic competition between two systems, the growth of the well-being of peoples is becoming the most important criteria of evaluating a social structure.

In the last few years, in connection with the vast successes of the socialist structure in the USSR and in countries of peoples' democracies and with the rapid growth in the living standard of people in these countries, the problem of national well-being has become the object of a sharp ideological battle. What regularities and perspectives of the growth of the standard of living of the people in the condition of socialism and capitalism, by which ways the task set forth by the party in the Soviet Union will be decided in the nearest future—to attain the highest standard of living in the world—these questions inevitably acquire the significance of the most important aspects of modern analysis in the problem of national well-being.

In bourgeois economic literature a whole series of works has appeared which has as its purpose to discredit the successes in the socialist countries and to represent capitalism as a system which is growing in the direction of a "state of universal prosperity." [1] . . .

Under the guidance of the Communist Party, the people of the Soviet Union successfully built socialism and have entered into the new and most important period of its development—the period of the comprehensive building of the communist society. Communism grows immediately from socialism and is its direct extension. The degree of the approaching of socialist society to that of communism is determined by the level of the development of productive forces. The prerequisites for the solution promoted in the plan of the Program of the CPSU for the task of world-

* From *Voprosy Ekonomiki*, 1961, No. 9. Translated in and excerpts reprinted from the U.S. Joint Publications Research Service pamphlet number 11473, December 8, 1961, pp. 1-13.

[1] J. K. Galbraith, *The Affluent Society*, London, 1959; K. Colegrove, *Democracy versus Communism*, New York, 1957; A. Harris, *Economics and Social Reform*, New York, 1958.

wide historical significance—the attainment of the highest standard of living for people in the world, and for the guaranteeing of the complete satisfaction of the requirements of the population in principal products and services, will be created according to the measure of its increase. In the course of the solution of this problem, from the economic point of view, the Soviet Union must surpass the US, the richest capitalist country which possesses the largest material opportunities for securing the basic goods and services for the population. But the US, which has attained a high level of development in the productive forces, is a capitalist country and that is why she did not bring an authentic well-being to the people. The US is a country of chronic mass unemployment, where, notwithstanding the abundance of material wealth created by the labor of the masses, there are not enough housing, school buildings, hospitals, and qualified teachers and where medical aid is exceptionally expensive and there also exists an abusive discrimination of the negro population. In this way, the US cannot at all be looked at as the country with the highest standard of well-being in the world. According to the most important indices of the standard of well being for the people, the Soviet Union and other socialist countries have far surpassed all that which can be gained by the working masses of even the richest capitalist country.

The absence in the USSR of the exploiting classes, the liquidation of unemployment, and the presence of the widest opportunities in education and in the improvement of one's skills for the workers of the USSR, are the factors putting the workers of the USSR in immeasurably better conditions in comparison with the capitalist countries. The growth of public funds, at the expense of which free medical service, education, and an expansive pension plan for the workers is realized in the USSR, creates great advantages. Thanks to the rapid growth of public funds the consumption of the Soviet worker exceeds that level, which is provided for by wages, by approximately one-third.

At the same time according to the measure of the most important indices, the standard of living in the USSR for the time being continues to lag behind the living standard in the US. A significant number of American families are now better provided for by basic products, nourishment, living facilities and many goods of prolonged utilization. Here is the result, from one side, of the consequence of the economic backwardness of Tsarist Russia and that colossal loss which was suffered by the national economy of the USSR by the wars, especially by the Second World War, and from the other side, the exceptionally favorable historical and suitable condition in which the economic growth of the US took place, and also that massive profit, which the United States as an imperialist power in the course of many years extorted from the exploited people of the underdeveloped countries directing a significant part of it for the development of its own production.

"It is generally known,—said comrade N. S. Khrushchev in a speech at a luncheon given in his honor by Cyrus Eaton, in September 1960,— that the American people have accomplished much in the development of their country but we do not envy this. To the US we offer a peaceful competition in economic growth and in the increase of national well-being." . . .

Among the theoretical problems of the growth of national consumption in the conditions of the transfer from socialism to communism, the question on the correlation of the rates of the growth of the productivity of labor and the level of consumption occupies an important place. It is well known that the level of consumption, which socialist society in each given segment of time can provide to its members, is determined by two factors: the magnitude of created national income and the envisaged volume of accumulation. The national income is that source at the expense of which the fund of accumulation and the fund of consumption is formed. Therefore, within the limits of each given year, the absolute magnitude of these funds is found in an inverse dependence on each other. Within limits of a prolonged segment of time the dependence between consumption and accumulation is significantly complex. Without a doubt, accumulation presupposes a known abstraction on the part of material values which create the physical volume of national income from current consumption. However, these means are used on the expansion of productive and non-productive funds of the country: the construction of factories, plants, canals, and homes; cultivation of gardens and the organization of public services and amenities in the cities, etc. All this provides for an increase in the level of consumption in the near and distant future. In realizing accumulation, society makes a certain postponement of consumption in the present for the sake of a more significant increase of consumption in the future. It is completely evident, that the workers in socialist countries cannot be interested in a short term increase of the level of consumption at the expense of reducing accumulation, for this would call for a lowering of the rates of reproduction on an enlarged scale, which would very rapidly bring about a lowering in the rates of the growth of consumption. Socialist accumulation must be sufficiently high in order to provide for complete utilization in the process of attaining technical progress. Only in this case, can society achieve the highest rate of growth in the productivity of labor, so that, in its turn, it will appear as the necessary condition for the realization of optimal rates of growth in the national consumption for a prolonged perspective.

In the conditions, when the socialist revolution was victorious in a backward country, the only way for a radical increase of the living standard for the people was industrialization and the creation of its own technical personnel. With this in mind, the shorter this historical period, in the course of which it is necessary to achieve the foremost industrially developed country, the greater must be the degree in which the growth of the national income is directed for the increase of the fund of accumulation. The latter finds its expression in the significant outstripping of the rate of growth of the productivity of labor in comparison with the rate of growth of the fund of accumulation. . . .

The largest discrepancy between the rates of growth of the productivity of labor and the real incomes of workers occurred during the first Five-Year Plan. In the course of the second and third Five-Year Plans, this discrepancy was already significantly less. In the period from 1940 to about 1959, the productivity of labor in industry grew 180% and the real income of workers and servicemen—100%. The control figures of the Seven-Year Plan provide for a further approach of the rates of growth of these indices. . . .

Resting on powerful industry and its wide utilization in the process of attaining a modern scientific-technical revolution, socialist society in its further development can single out still more means for satisfying the constantly growing material and cultural needs of the population. Comrade N. S. Khrushchev said: ". . . We, apparently, at the moment, will not carry out a policy of developing the ferrous metal industry to the limits of its possibilities. Evidently, we are transferring part of the capital investment to agricultural economy and to light industry. Communism cannot be built by machines and ferrous and non-ferrous metal industry alone. This is necessary, in order that people could dress and eat well, having housing and other material and cultural needs. This is not a revision of the general line, but a reasonable utilization of our material resources. When we were surrounded by the enemy and our industry was weaker than that of the capitalist countries, we economized on everything and as Lenin said, even on schools. But now it is a different situation: we have a powerful industry and our armed forces have the most modern armaments. Then, why should we refuse that which man can receive without a loss for the further development of our socialist state?" [2] . . .

One of the important problems of the growth of national consumption in the period of comprehensive building of a communist society is the question on the perspectives of the development of two principal parts of the fund of consumption: the fund of personal consumption and the public fund of consumption. In previous years in the USSR, an extremely rapid growth of public funds of consumption was observed. Thus, if the real income of workers and servicemen in 1959 increased in comparison with 1940, 100%, and the real income of the peasant increased 120%,

[2] N. S. Khrushchev, *Za novye pobedy mirovogo kommunisticheskogo dvizhenija.* Gospolitizdat.—N. S. Khrushchev, For new victories of the peaceful communist movement. State Political Publications. 1961, p. 17.

then the public funds of consumption taking into account for one worker grew 300%. At the beginning of the First Five-Year Plan, the public funds of consumption composed a total of 24% of the fund of individual wages and in 1958 it was already 41.5%.

The outstripping rate of the growth of public funds in comparison with that part of the fund of consumption, which is distributed according to labor, was stipulated by the necessity of solving a series of the most important social tasks. The interests of socialist construction in the USSR demands from the Soviet people in the shortest historical time to not only create their own heavy industry, and provide a defense potential for the country and its economic independence, but, simultaneously with this to overcome a centuries' old illiteracy as soon as possible, to organize the necessary medical service for the population, to care for the invalids of society, to create a network of children's institutions, and to sharply increase the number of schools, technical institutes, higher institutes of education and scientific research institutes. In these historical conditions, the provision of the primary growth of the public funds of consumption permitted the socialist state to single out the necessary means for protecting the health of the population, to create a system of educating the rising generation and of social welfare, which is responsible to the demands of a new order and to prepare its own engineering-technical intelligentsia and personnel of learned men in all the principal fields of knowledge.

The first and most important tasks of satisfying the social and cultural requirements of population were successfully solved. According to the level of the growth of public education, health administration and social welfare, the Soviet Union has far surpassed the most progressive capitalist states. At the present time, free public education and medical service are being realized and children's institutions are being founded at the expense of the public funds of consumption. At the expense of these funds, the population of the socialist countries receives the opportunity to live in well built dwellings under a low rent plan, to freely attend and join clubs, readings rooms, palaces of culture and many sports establishments and receive free or with a discount passes into rest homes, sanitariums, tourist facilities, etc.

The growth of the indicated parts of the fund of consumption signifies at the same time a growth of two principal forms of the distribution of products in a socialist society and in corresponding forms of consumption. The free distribution of a part of the fund of consumption is one of the elements of communist aspects which are already maturing in the conditions of socialism. In this plan, the future belongs to the public funds of consumption and the growth of these funds is of great social significance. . . .

It is completely without doubt that socialist society must henceforth provide a steady growth of public funds of consumption, while paying special attention to the expansion of the network of children's institutions and to the system of medical service for the population. Namely, in these fields, a completely free satisfaction of requirements will be provided for first. The growth of public funds and the creation of more favorable conditions for the all-round education of the rising generation, for the care of public health and necessary welfare of the aged is the historical advantage of the socialist system. It is one of the brightest manifestations of the humanistic principles of communism.

At the same time, the party finds that in the Leninist position, the building of communism must rest on the principles of material incentive. Distribution according to labor in the forthcoming twenty years will remain the principal source of satisfying the material and cultural requirements of the workers. . . .

At a later stage, when the level of the monetary incomes of the population becomes higher, and the principle of material incentive will be used by us to the fullest degree, socialist society can start on the road to a rapid increase of a portion of the public funds of consumption. In the sum total of the twenty years, as indicated in the plan of the Program of CPSU, the public funds of consumption in proportion to the sum will reach, approximately, half of the sum of the real incomes of the population. In these conditions, in a higher degree of our growth, the primary growth of the public funds of consumption as authentically the communist path of increasing the well-being of the workers appears as an important prerequisite and continuous basis of transformation to the communist distribution according to the requirements and to the communist form of consumption. . . .

The nearest step of the achievement of the communist level of national well-being and our immediate goal is the creation of abundance and the complete satisfaction of the requirements of the population in the principal goods and services. It must be especially emphasized that the creation of abundance of products even during a high level in the growth of techniques demands significant expenses on the part of human labor and expenditures on the part of many natural resources and material values already created by man and which in the future cannot always be replaced rapidly. Therefore, the movement toward abundance and distribution according to the requirements does not in any case permit wastefulness of created material and spiritual values. For the complete satisfaction of the rapidly growing requirements of the members of society, a careful expenditure of the initial natural resources, the economy of human labor and the reasonable utilization of created consumer values will be absolutely and exceptionally necessary.

IX

SOVIET ECONOMIC GROWTH
AND THE PROSPECTS FOR
CATCHING UP WITH AND
SURPASSING THE UNITED STATES

DURING most of the years since the introduction of the first five-year plan in 1928, the Soviet Union has shown a remarkably high rate of economic growth. A mere generation ago, the USSR, though already more advanced economically than most of Asia and Africa, was still an "underdeveloped" agricultural country. By 1960, in spite of a devastating war that had destroyed one-tenth of her population and much of her industrial and agricultural capacity, the Soviet Union had become a world power, second only to that of the United States. Her per capita gross national product in 1961 was more than ten times that of many of the underdeveloped countries in Asia and Africa, and considerably higher than that of any Latin American nation. Yet, it still lagged far behind that of Canada, Australia, New Zealand, and most of Western Europe and—according to some Western estimates—amounted to less than one-third of the United States per capita GNP. The exact rate of economic growth of the USSR during the 1950's is a matter of dispute. However, it was certainly at least twice that of the United States and well above that of all the countries referred to above, with the possible exception only of West Germany.[1] Should the Soviet Union be able to maintain such a high rate of economic growth, without a material increase in the rate of growth of the United States, it would of course be a mathematical certainty that within a relatively few years she would overtake the United States, first in aggregate output, then in per capita output, and eventually in aggregate and per capita wealth. Is that what is going to happen? And, if so, what is its significance for the Western world? Western opinions on the matter vary considerably.

[1] For figures showing the per capita gross national product of almost 100 countries for 1961, see, for instance, Clair Wilcox, Willis D. Weatherford, Jr., and Holland Hunter, *Economies of the World Today* (1962), pp. 16-19, (Adapted from P. N. Rosenstein-Rodan, "International Aid for Underdeveloped Countries," *Review of Economics and Statistics*, Vol. XLIII, 1961, pp. 107-138). For a comparison of 32 countries as to their average annual rate of growth in GNP during the 1950's, see p. 20.

In the first selection below, Joseph A. Kershaw reflects on the economic growth of the USSR. He points to differences in growth rates among the various sectors of the soviet economy; he refers to some of the problems which may prevent it from maintaining its post-World War II rate of growth; but he concludes that the West will have to learn to accommodate itself to a USSR whose economy may continue to grow at a rapid rate.

Alvin Hansen, next, discusses some of the conditions which, in his opinion, may enable the Soviet Union to maintain a higher rate of economic growth than the United States. He shows great concern over this challenge and urges that effective steps be taken by the Federal government to raise the rate of growth of the United States.

Though in disagreement as to the fundamental reasons for higher growth rates in the USSR, K. Bieda, commenting on Hansen's article, grants the likelihood that the situation may continue to prevail. Bieda, however, considers it generally ill advised and totally unnecessary for affluent societies such as the United States or Australia to devote their efforts to a race for increased rates of growth.

The point of view that in the economic race with the USSR the United States has little to worry about in the foreseeable future has been taken by Naum Jasny. His "Plan and Superplan," contending that the entire twenty-year program adopted by the 22nd Party Congress is unrealistic and impossible to fulfill, has been reprinted as selection 10 above.

While Western scholars are in disagreement on the outcome of the economic race between the US and the USSR, Soviet sources seem united in their views. They express no doubt that the Soviet Union will surpass the United States and that this will prove once and for all the superiority of their system and ensure its eventual victory over capitalism. This point of view is vividly exemplified by an agency of the USSR Economic Council in an article entitled "Different Systems—Different Results,"— the selection chosen to represent *Soviet Views* on the topic.

34

Direction for Future Growth of the Soviet Economy *

JOSEPH A. KERSHAW
The RAND Corporation, Santa Monica, California

This subject is at once fascinating and frustrating. Part of the fascination lies in the fact that our lives are going to be dominated in good part by the economic struggle between the Soviet Union and the United States. It is fascinating to the professional economist because the USSR seems to provide a laboratory in which are exhibited many of the problems that economists are most concerned with. The nature of economic growth is laid bare in the Soviet Union in terms more graphic than in almost any other nation. It is no accident that those interested in the economics of the Soviet Union are almost without exception interested also in that new and fashionable branch of economics called "the economic growth of underdeveloped areas."

There are of course many other problems which fascinate the economist who studies the Soviet economy. What is the role of economic planning and how effective can it be? What is the impact on growth and welfare of an allocation of resources very different from our own? How is the rate of investment determined in a centralized economy? How was it possible for a primitive agricultural economy to compress the period of growth and leave behind completely some of the stages which some economic historians tell us must be gone through? How applicable are some of the newer techniques in economics, in particular what role can mathematical economics play in the planning process? These are but a few of the problems that the economist interested in the Soviet Union has to wrestle with before he can understand this strange beast. Small wonder then that the specialist in the area will insist that his speciality is as interesting and challenging as any.

But there are frustrations, too, and these are no less impressive. For one thing, many of the data that one needs to work with in understand-

* Reprinted from Nicholas Spulber (editor), *Study of the Soviet Economy* (1961), pp. 3-16, by permission of the author, the RAND Corporation, and the Indiana University Press. The author is now Professor of Economics at Williams College, Williamstown, Mass.

ing any economy are simply not available from the Soviet Union. There is the infuriating Soviet practice of releasing data in percentage terms without giving the base data, and leaving it to the foreign investigator to make his guesses about the base year. In the last few years this situation has become a good deal better. The Soviet statistical people have been releasing information in much greater quantity and apparently of adequate quality. This is not to indicate that everything we need has been made available. But the data drought of the war and immediate post-war period has certainly been alleviated.

This may be an appropriate place to refer to one of the most annoying occupational diseases that is endemic among Soviet specialists. We might refer to it as revisionitis, which is a technical term for the need for wholesale revisions of large empirical manuscripts which reach completion just as a new statistical handbook on the same subject is released by the Soviet Central Statistical Office. The Russians are maddeningly efficient at timing the release of these handbooks—at Rand we have sponsored a study of Soviet populations which has been wrapped for mailing to the publisher countless times; its author is threatening to change his field of specialization to welfare economics.

There is a more fundamental sense in which the economist finds the study of the Soviet economy frustrating. In dealing with the United States or almost any Western economy, one can safely assume that individuals and business units will behave in accordance with motives that are well enough understood. For example, suppliers will normally be able to sell when they are able to produce something more efficiently than their competitors. International trade takes place when the division of labor indicates that it's a good idea for it to take place. Investment is attracted to those areas that are the most profitable; and the areas that are most profitable are normally determined by the tastes, desires, and incomes of consumers.

I realize that I am painting an over-simplified picture of the Western or free type of economy. All of us are familiar with the exceptions to these easy generalizations, but in the case of the Soviet Union, factors which we have come to call non-economic are instrumental to a far greater extent in determining the flow of resources. The market place plays a role in the Soviet Union and it is an important one. Nonetheless, compared to the role it plays in the free economies of the West, the market place is a very secondary instrument. I need only mention the recent Soviet purchase of Egyptian cotton, or Soviet behavior with respect to gold, for that matter. Behavior in these instances is not dictated by any economic calculus but by some other criterion which Soviet planners hold to be more important than the economic considerations.

All of these things make it difficult for the economist to decide when he should be looking for economic explanation and when something else may be dominating a particular case. Let me cite an example. Those who have studied Soviet transportation are fond of pointing out that the Russians have obtained a highly intensive use of their rail freight system. With a country a good deal larger than the U.S., the rail mileage in the Soviet Union is not much more than half ours. Furthermore, the reliance on the rail network is much greater than it is here. It is an interesting question whether this indicates that the Russians have succeeded in being very economical with the use of their railroads, or whether they have made some bad decisions and the economy would be much better off if there were a more extensive rail network. Then one comes to notice Soviet practice in civil aviation. Every traveler has pointed out the tremendous number of jet aircraft sitting idly on almost every commercial airfield in the Soviet Union. Apparently what the Russians have done with respect to civil aviation is to substitute idle capacity in the form of these aircraft for maintenance facilities, repair crews and so on. You will notice that this is exactly opposite from their practice in rail transportation. Are there satisfactory economic explanations of this striking difference, or is the explanation to be found in some completely non-economic consideration, such as a desire to maintain a reserve of civil air transport capacity for possible military use?

Comparative Rates of Growth

Let us turn now to a brief description of the Soviet economy, and in doing so examine some of the fascination and some of the frustration involved in its study. I suppose the most outstanding characteristic of the Soviet economy since the planning period began in 1929 has been the consistent and high rate of growth that it has enjoyed. There have been short periods of small or negative growth—for example the years of World War II and, earlier, a part of the period of the peasant resistance to agricultural collectivization. But these have been exceptions to the general trend.

As anyone who reads the newspapers is aware, there has been some dispute as to just what the rate of growth of the Soviet economy has been. This is certainly not the place for us to try to decide whether that rate of growth has characteristically been five per cent a year or six per cent a year or seven per cent a year. It seems to me that the important fact is to recognize that it has been consistently high. In particular, it has been, and continues to be, substantially higher than our own. Furthermore, in my view this disparity in the rate of growth between the USSR and the USA will continue to exist, though it *may* narrow somewhat in the relevant future. For this there seem to me obvious reasons, and on some of these I will touch in a few moments.

But confining the comparison to growth rates of gross national product seems to me to be an exercise of very limited meaning. For one thing, to the extent that we are interested in the relative economic power of the economies, some sectors are more significant than others. For another, gross national product is an aggregate made up of very different sectors growing at very different rates. Like so many aggregates, this one covers up as much as it reveals. I'd like to disaggregate a little and discuss agriculture and industry separately.

Turning first to the agricultural sector, here there is no doubt that the United States is extremely efficient compared to the Russians. The agricultural problem in the U.S. is of course one of trying to persuade farmers not to produce so much food and raw materials that they will embarrass whatever administration happens to be in power. This is a problem that the Soviet officials would dearly love to face. The Soviet agricultural sector has been a consistent laggard and has created perhaps the most persistent overall problem that the Soviet planners have had to face. Indeed, for many years the sheer job of increasing total agricultural output by the one-and-a-half per cent by which the population was increasing seemed to be an impossible one. The missing of goals in agriculture has been chronic, and for many years the inability to correct the agricultural deficiencies in the Soviet Union seemed to threaten the progress of the entire economy.

In recent years, some significant changes have been made, particularly changes with respect to price and tax policy. These changes are having a very real impact on the incentives of agricultural workers, and for the first time since the planning period began some significant gains were realized in the middle and later 1950's. These institutional changes were coupled with the so-called "new lands" policy, and there appears to be at least a chance now of getting the agricultural situation in hand. The year 1959 and the year 1960 were both poor years weatherwise and the substantial increases that had been achieved up to 1959 have been interrupted. Whether the increases will be resumed in the future is not completely clear, but the steps that have been taken would certainly seem to have been in the right direction. No longer can one assert with confidence that the agricultural problem remains unsolved. At the same time one must note that, as of now, the 1965 agricultural output targets look as unrealistic as these targets have turned out to be under preceding plans. Headlines in recent weeks indicate that solutions are certainly not yet at hand.

In industry the story is different. Here are the favored sectors in the Soviet economy, as they have been since the beginning of the planning period. In consequence, this is where the rapid rates of increase really show up. This is where the statistics can really play tricks on unsuspecting investigators, too; and over the last decade a great deal of effort has been put into the matter of straightening out the Soviet statistics and even into creating new indexes of Soviet industrial output. I think we are now in a position to understand pretty accurately what is going on.

The picture of comparative rates of growth of industry in the U.S. and USSR is not an encouraging one. All of you know that one can prove almost anything by a careful selection of a beginning and a terminal year for industrial production statistics. This, of course, explains the disparate figures that were used during our recent political campaign. I think, however, that if one looks objectively at what has been happening in the United States and does not pick an unusual beginning or ending period, he has to come to the conclusion that industrial production here has been growing recently at a rate that is something less than four per cent per year. I think a careful scholar who looks at the situation in the Soviet Union cannot help coming to the conclusion that the rate of increase of industrial production has been in the neighborhood of nine per cent per year. I am referring to Soviet experience in the pre-War period and since 1950. During the war the rate was of course very low; between 1945 and 1950 it was much higher than nine per cent, but this was to be expected during reconstruction. Incidentally, munitions are excluded from the index I am using.

However one looks at it, it seems to me inescapable that the rate of increase in Soviet industry is at least double that in the United States. This disparity used to be explained by saying that the Soviet industry started from so much lower a base. If this explanation ever had any validity, and I for one doubt that it did, it certainly does no longer. The Soviet industrial base is today a large one, generally second only to our own. Indeed, in a number of not inconsequential cases, the Russians are now out-producing us. They produce more iron ore and machine tools than we do now, for example, and the outputs of steel in the two countries are now close enough so that before long the leader will be determined by the duration of the steel strike in the United States in any given year.

Growth and the Competition for Resources

Let us turn briefly to what seems to me to be the explanation for these high and persistent rates of growth, particularly in the industrial sector. I shall have to over-simplify, of course, but it seems to me that the explanation can largely be found in Soviet policy with respect to investment. Our studies of Soviet national product and its allocation indicate that, except for the war years, there has been a persistent practice of allocating to investment a very high proportion of total resources; high, that is, when compared to the experience in most Western countries. Year in and year out, always excepting the war period, the rate of investment in the Soviet Union (that is, the proportion of total investment to gross national product) has been well in excess of 20 per cent. But that's not all. In addition to a high rate of investment, the actual allocation within the investment sector has been to those industries that have a high payoff in rate of growth. I'm referring to the ferrous metallurgical industries, electric power, petroleum, chemicals, and so forth. If one looks at a pie chart showing investment allocations in the Soviet Union and in the U.S., one sees a significantly higher proportion of the Soviet total going to those industries that we might characterize as "growth industries." In particular, commercial and residential construction in the Soviet Union has taken a lot less relative to the total than has been the case in the United States, while machinery and metal working have taken a lot more.

The difference in investment policy, of course, rests in the nature of the economy itself. These decisions in the United States, with modifications associated with the name of John Maynard Keynes and others, are to a large extent made in the market place; they reflect time preferences of individuals and profit estimates of firms. In the Soviet Union, both the size of the investment and the direction of investment are essentially political decisions, made at the highest planning levels, and made with a view to keeping the rate of the growth of the economy as high as possible. And this leads us, I think, to a most significant distinction between the Soviet and American economies. I refer to the purpose for which the economy exists. I think it can be said that by and large the purpose of the American economy has been the satisfaction of consumer desires, and at this we have had no peer. The purpose of the Soviet economy appears to be to maximize the rate of growth over time, and at that they seem to have excelled.

It would be misleading to conclude from this that since we are winning the consumption battle and they the growth fight, we can relax because of a stalemate. For one thing growth seems a good deal more appealing to the uncommitted areas than high consumption (which indeed seems to be regarded as immoral in many quarters). But more important, there are strong interrelationships here. As I will stress later, the Soviet standard of living is rising, more or less in proportion to the growth of the total economy, and if this continues the gap in standards of living will close rapidly. This, it seems to me, is why we must look closely at the health of our own economy. Possibly a doubling of our growth rate is not compatible with the maintenance of our free institutions, but some increase surely is.

This brings us to what I suspect most people regard as the most interesting question of all. I refer to the possibility that the rate of economic growth in Soviet industry can remain high for the more or less indefinite future. I suspect that part of the answer to this lies in the recognition that the high rate of investment, and the particular direction of investment which we have described in preceding paragraphs, can to all intents and purposes continue so long as the aim of the Soviet economy is rapid growth. There is always the possibility that diminishing productivity of capital will set in, and indeed this appears to be taking place. But the planners have been able to offset this by raising the rate of investment. Basically, then, the answer to the question is that there is no obvious and inherent reason why substantial slowing down in the Soviet rate of growth should be expected to occur.

But there will be competition for resources; competition, that is, from other sectors of the Soviet economy which will make it at least questionable whether the growth sector will continue to receive as much favor as it has in the past. I'd like to discuss two or three of these competing areas.

One is foreign aid. Within the last few years, the Russians have entered the foreign aid business. They've not done it quite the same way as we have; in some respects their performance has been more impressive than ours and in others less. The current rate of Soviet foreign economic aid is running something like a half billion dollars a year, well below that of the U.S. total. But the Russians characteristically concentrate their aid in a few countries, and one consequence is that the impact on these selected countries is perhaps more substantial than the simple absolute members might indicate. Another thing they are prone to do is to concentrate their aid within a given country on those items of capital investment which have aspects of public monuments about them. They are rather likely to contribute to the construction of dams or other large ventures which the public can see and associate with Soviet foreign aid. They seem less interested in agricultural assistance programs and other things which are less visible, though frequently more important.

Given the modest size of Soviet foreign aid, there is little question but what the Russians could increase it substantially without undue impact on their domestic economy. One wonders whether they will do this, and one wonders what the U.S. response to either the existing level of Soviet foreign aid or a very much stepped-up level ought to be. If it be the case, as we seem to think, that foreign aid to underdeveloped countries will have the result of increasing the political stability of those countries, then presumably an inflow of capital, from whatever source, would contribute toward our own goals in these areas. Does it follow that we welcome the assistance of the Soviet Union? The case of Cuba indicates that it can't be that simple. About all that does seem clear is that in the area of foreign aid we may expect that cold war conflicts will remain fairly constant.

Another sector of the Soviet economy that is competing with the growth sectors is national defense. There is little I can say about this except that the Soviet defense budget seems to absorb, very roughly, the same proportion of GNP as does ours, and the proportion has not been increasing, as far as we can tell. You will realize, however, that the problem of relative efficiencies in different parts of the economy is most acute here, so that we have to attach a good deal of uncertainty to this sort of estimate. Moreover there is a real possibility that the Soviets may be booking what are in effect defense outlays under other budget headings. There has been in recent years, apparently, a fairly significant decrease in the number of men in uniform in the Soviet Union, and though the impact of this is probably minimal or non-existent on the over-all military strength of the nation, as Khrushchev has insisted, nonetheless there are interesting economic implications with respect to the need for a continually growing civilian labor force.

I come now to the third, and in many respects much the most interesting, of the sectors of the economy competing for resources with the growth sectors. I refer to what has been going on with respect to living standards in the last few years. As one would suspect, since there has been a great and continuing emphasis on the heavy industry sector and a continuing maintenance of a sizable military establishment, the standard of living in the Soviet Union has accordingly suffered. If we regard food and housing as the two most important consumer goods, I think it is not far from the truth to say that in 1950, by the time the consumption levels had regained their pre-war status, consumption per capita in the Soviet Union was not substantially above what it had been in 1913, before the Revolution.

Since 1950, however, Soviet consumption has continued to grow. As pointed out earlier, consumption's share of GNP has not increased in recent years, but consumption has shared fully in the high and sustained rate of over-all growth. The cumulative result has been a very substantial rise in the standard of living over the past decade. As you know, every American who visited the Soviet Union in 1956 or thereabouts and revisits it now is impressed by the very large visible evidences of real changes. Queues are no longer so much in evidence; the goods on the shelves in the stores are not only there, but are of much better quality than they were; people are dressing better; and above all, of course, the construction of housing is proceeding at a tremendous rate. Let me make clear that the Russians have a very long road to travel before they will have a standard of living that approaches that in the West. An American cannot visit the Soviet Union without coming away tremendously depressed at the lot of the ordinary civilian. The point is, however, that the situation is changing, and apparently it is changing fast.

For our story, perhaps the most important part of this change is what has taken place in housing. Housing had, for many decades, been completely, or almost completely, forgotten, and indeed even today the number of square meters available per person is pitifully small, probably not larger than it was 30 years ago. The important point, however, is that housing is built on a large scale, and ordinary Soviet citizens in general are not only aware of this, but all have friends who have recently moved into some of the new housing. The new housing is nothing substantial or fancy by our standards, but the major point about it is that it holds out promise for a family to have its own flat, with its own bathroom and its own kitchen, not shared with any other family. This must be something devoutly to be desired, and indeed one can sense the great feeling of expectation about real improvements in housing when one talks to any appreciable number of people in the USSR.

Improvements in the standard of living have come before, and then something has happened that has caused the leaders to change their policy once more and go back to austerity. The significant thing in terms of the housing splurge that is now going on, it seems to me, is the extent to which the state has committed itself to continue with the housing construction program until people are housed in decency all over the USSR. I should judge that it would be extremely difficult, though of course not impossible, for the regime to reverse itself on this count; and if this is a valid analysis it emphasizes the long-term nature of the commitment for the continued construction of housing. At the present time, incidentally, the volume of housing construction is running about double what it was a few short years ago, and the single most impressive thing that a visitor to the Soviet Union now sees is the tremendous volume of housing construction which stretches in all directions in most of the larger cities, and for all I know perhaps in the smaller cities as well.

The importance for our story is that resources put into housing—cement, steel, construction equipment services, etc.—are not available for what I have earlier identified as the growth sectors. In point of fact, as we all know, housing is an expensive way to spend resources. The payoff in human comfort and dignity is high, but the payoff in economic growth from housing construction is small.

What are we to say about the total impact of this competition for resources; competition, that is, with the growth sectors? My guess is that the future will see some decline in the rate of growth of Soviet industry, partly as a result of the factors that I have just been discussing, and partly as a result of other factors, some of which I will mention shortly. We have already begun to notice a peculiar phenomenon taking place. The capital output ratios in the Soviet Union, both average and marginal, have been rising in recent years. In part I am sure that this is a result of the greater emphasis on domestic housing construction, where capital output ratios, of course, are extremely high. But this is not enough of an explanation, and when one contrasts the situation in the Soviet Union with that in the United States, where capital output ratios have remained constant for decades, one is face to face with a very interesting question, a question, however, which we unfortunately do not have time to address today. If these ratios continue to rise, it is clear that it will take a greater and greater effort to achieve the same amount of growth.

Another phenomenon to notice, I think, is what is happening to the labor supply in Soviet industry. Two recent developments of interest may be noted. The first is that the wartime losses, in terms of a low birth rate, are proving to be tremendously high. Indeed, some of our research indicated that they were so high that we were loath to believe the results we were getting. The recent publication, however, of the census of 1959 has indicated that we were very much on the right track. In any case, the deficit in the population age groups coming onto the labor force is just now becoming important. Babies who should have been born in the early 1940's would be coming onto the labor market about now. What the demographers love to call "a relatively short cohort" is severely handicapping the labor recruiters in the Soviet cities. There has been some tendency to explain the demobilization of some of the armed forces as a means to offset the impact of this development. Similarly, the recent changes in education which have resulted in shunting youngsters of 15 and 16 into the labor market rather than into educational institutions is viewed as an answer to this demographic deficiency.

Another, and equally important, development is taking place with respect to the labor supply. For a good many years the number of laborers in agriculture has been declining year by year, so that the cities have been receiving not only the total growth in population of working age, but also an augmentation resulting from the decline in the labor force on Soviet farms. This movement of labor from the country to the city is of course characteristic of any economy that is developing. In recent years, however, the movement seems to have stopped, and the labor force in agriculture is as large now as it was five years ago. It is not clear whether this tendency can be reversed so that the movement could be resumed, but if it is not it means a further deficiency in the rate of growth of the labor supply in Soviet cities.

It is worth noting that these factors are apparently regarded as being less significant by Soviet policy-makers. A progressive shortening of the work week was promised in the seven-year plan and in fact is now taking place, the ultimate goal being a seven hour day and 35-hour week. The planners seem confident that the resulting loss of labor time will be more than offset by an increase in labor productivity.

One should be cautious, I think, and not attribute too much significance to these various developments. Every economy has its problems, and certainly one proceeding under forced draft has more than its share. The external evidence, however, indicates that at least up to now there is little or no tendency for any substantial slow-down in growth rates to take place. When we computed the growth rates implied by the seven-year goals, that is to say, the goals for the plan ending in 1965, we discovered that the rates were somewhat lower than they had been in earlier plan periods. Before taking this as evidence of a slow-down in the rate of growth, however, one needs to wait and see what is likely to happen with respect to the Seven-Year goals. Indeed, it already looks as though there is a strong possibility that major fulfillment of the important industry goals will take place in six rather than in seven years. If this should happen, the annual rate of growth will not be lower than it has been in the past.

Concluding Comments

I'd like to conclude this paper with a few observations on some problems that seem to be of rather broad philosophical interest to economists. It is paradoxical that some of the very real problems that the Russians are now facing have come as a result of their generally successful achievements. They have brought their economy, in a short space of time, from a primitive agricultural one to the second most powerful industrial nation in the world today. And if they cannot be called "The Affluent Society" as yet, nonetheless when the writer of that estimable best-seller visited the Soviet Union 18 months or so ago, there seemed some danger that he might produce another best-seller comparing the United States and the Soviet Union, and it was perhaps not completely inappropriate that a colleague of mine suggested that the title of this book might be "The Confluent Societies."

But affluence has brought some problems with it. Planning is rather simple when it's a matter of picking out a few lead commodities, emphasizing them, and pulling the rest of the economy along as you force the rapid growth of the selected few. Today the Russians have opportunities for more choices, and the size of the input-output table that they must have to consider each time they sit down for a planning session staggers the imagination. There has been great interest on the part of economists outside as to how the planning is actually done, how the balances are reconciled, and how consistencies are built into the system. It's interesting to note that Gosplan, which does this, has been the most difficult of all for foreigners to penetrate, and it's my belief that there's been no visit by an American economist or economists to the Gosplan itself. We have noted, of course, a very great interest in some of the newer techniques in economics, and when Wassily Leontief visited the Soviet Union summer before last, he was received as a hero for having pressed forward in the general field of input-output and linear programming, and he a Russian too. There is an intellectual ferment going on now among economists, a ferment to be sure that has not reached very far down into the profession as yet. But it is clear that linear programming, econometrics in general, and some others of the new fads in economics are being pursued with diligence by many of the leading economists in the Soviet Union. Indeed, one wag has said that the great hope for the West is that Soviet planners will embrace linear programming!

The word "rationality" has now become semi-applicable to the management of the Soviet economy. We watched with interest a couple of years ago when industry was apparently decentralized, and we began to wonder whether we might actually see the Lange-Lerner model put into action. We didn't, of course, and at least up to now there has been no real release of control, nor attempt to decentralize the control to a price system designed to minimize or to maximize, let alone to optimize. But these things are at least being talked about, and this is something new.

What should be said in conclusion? We have learned much about the Soviet economy since economists began serious study of it a decade or more ago. We have much more to learn. If our current understanding has general validity, we have in the Soviet Union an adversary whose economy is growing at a rapid rate and promises to continue to do so. It seems almost crystal clear that we have to accommodate somehow to this development. Just how is not so clear, but the world is going to look more and more at the economic performance of East and West, and the relative growth rates of the two will be perhaps the most significant indicator of all.

35

The Economics of the Soviet Challenge *

ALVIN H. HANSEN
Harvard University

This special issue of *The Economic Record,* in recognition of the distinguished work of Sir Douglas Copland, will reach a wide international circle and will be read in many lands. The topic which I have chosen to write about is obviously of the greatest international importance. I shall, however, consider the problem from the standpoint of the United States. What I shall have to say about American practices

* Reprinted from *The Economic Record,* March, 1960, pp. 5-12, by permission of the publisher.

and policies will, here and there, in part apply to other countries. But it is, nevertheless, the United States that I am writing about, not the so-called western bloc in general.

The *trend* rate of growth of real income—gross national product at constant prices—compounded per annum, has been around 3 per cent during the last three decades in the United States. As nearly as one can learn from the most competent researches on Soviet rates of growth, the Russian GNP growth rate in real terms has been around 7 per cent. The growth of industrial production, as distinct from the GNP, has apparently been considerably greater—around 10 per cent. In contrast, our industrial production, compounded annually, has grown at the rate of $3\frac{1}{4}$ per cent.

If we could assume that these rates of growth will continue over the next two decades, the Soviets would catch up with us by 1980 at a GNP of 900 billion dollars in terms of 1959 prices.

It could with a good deal of justification be argued that the Soviet rate of growth is in large part due to the fact that they started from a low base. Possessing potentially rich resources, still largely under-developed, together with a physically strong and energetic labour force, the possibilities of growth in the earlier stages of development were naturally very great. This is all the more true in view of the fact that it was possible to import the whole accumulated technology of the western world as rapidly as it could be installed without having to wait for the slow and tedious processes of invention and experimentation. It can therefore be argued that once the Soviet economy has measuredly caught up, its rate of growth will slow down to that of the United States and other western countries.

I believe that there is very much force in this argument. Nonetheless, it would be a mistake to become too easily convinced that the spread between their rate of growth and our own will completely disappear automatically in a sufficiently short time span to ensure the maintenance of American economic superiority.

There are certain factors favourable to growth which are not permitted to come into play in our system as we now operate it. Unless this is remedied, there is reason to believe that the Soviet rate of growth, while not as large as in recent decades, will continue to exceed that of the United States.

Basically, the matter simmers down to this. Under our system, as it is now operated under currently dominant political tenets, the federal government is not permitted to play the role which is requisite for adequate growth and for the fulfilment of the cultural needs of modern urban communities. The government is prevented from helping private enterprise to attain its full potential, and it is not assuming sufficient direction of production to ensure the optimum use of our productive resources. The current practices and conventions which limit our rate of growth [1] are detailed below.

I

Under currently accepted economic precepts, the development of power and other natural resources is stopped at the point where the investment is self-liquidating. This is true whether the development is undertaken by the government, as in the case of the TVA, or by private enterprise.

Consider the TVA. It is generally held that no such project should be undertaken unless it can reasonably be expected to yield a monetary return sufficient to amortize the initial capital investment and to cover the market rate of interest over and above all operating expenses. Indeed, the TVA has demonstrated thus far that it fully measures up to these rigid standards.

At the time of its inception the TVA involved, it is true, a tremendous risk. No one knew whether or not it could pay out. Opponents regarded the whole project as a piece of political folly. And supporters were quite aware that they were assuming a grave calculated risk. There was, however, general agreement that if the venture could not, within a reasonable period, cover full amortization and interest charges over and above all operating expenses, the project would have to be deemed a failure.

Now the solid economic facts are quite otherwise. But this is a lesson that the country has not even begun to learn. It is indeed one of those many economic truths which run counter to commonly held views, and which will never win wide acceptance except on the basis of actual experience. Congress and the electorate have never grasped the fact that even though power and other resource developments may not *directly* pay out, they may nonetheless be economically profitable to the country as a whole.

To appraise the economic justification of any development project, account must be taken not only of its direct and immediate earning possibilities but also its impact upon the agriculture and industry served by it. In short, account must be taken of the role of external economies. And while the theory of external economies has long since been fully developed, economists have done very little to educate the country generally on a matter which is of the utmost importance.

[1] It could be argued, as Professor Galbraith indeed has in his widely read *The Affluent Society*, that leisure may be as important, or even more important, than growth. This could well be true at some future date, but in the kind of world in which we still live I am unable to follow this line of thinking. We still desperately need growth, partly because we have a long way to go before income distribution has reached a tolerable degree of equality, partly because the backlog of unsatisfied community needs is overwhelming, and partly because a peaceful world is not yet in sight.

Yet the point can easily be made quite clear to the general electorate if one compares: (a) the profit outlook of a private corporation contemplating a power development in an area in which it owns no business whatever except the power project itself, and (b) the profit outlook which confronts a private corporation that already owns all the industries in the region. In the latter case, the increased profits accruing to these industries may far more than offset any losses sustained by the power company itself. Under the circumstances, the overall private corporation would certainly undertake the power development even though it itself may operate at a loss.

This simple illustration explains precisely *one* reason why the Russian system may be capable of a more rapid rate of growth than the American system as now operated. Not until we are able as a nation to grasp the overall vision of the impact of resource development *on the economy as a whole* will we be able to match, so far as this one factor is concerned, the Russian rate of growth. To compete on equal terms, public investment in resource development will have to be pushed far wider and deeper than we have thus far been prepared to go.

II

The Russian system may, moreover, continue to provide a rate of growth in excess of that achieved by the American system as now operated by reason of our conventional method of dealing with obsolescence.

Under a system of private enterprise, established businesses with heavy investment in plant and equipment are loath to scrap existing facilities, and will certainly not do so *merely* because the new technology is more efficient than the old. New machinery will not be introduced, the old will not be scrapped, until it becomes quite clear that the new lower costs more than offset the losses involved in writing-off the old equipment. There is, furthermore, the great risk that, in a rapidly changing world, investment made today in the most up-to-date equipment may by tomorrow be rendered obsolete by still newer techniques. It might well be the part of wisdom to wait until time will have sharply reduced the write-off losses.

In the days of ruthless competition when new firms were constantly entering almost every field of manufacture, established companies were compelled to write off obsolete equipment whether they liked it or not. The new competitors entered the market with the most recent techniques. Old concerns were forced into line or driven to the wall. Survival required a rapid rate of obsolescence. Nowadays, when only a few giant firms occupy the field, and when the capital required to compete runs into hundreds of millions and even billions, new entrants no longer threaten established firms. The firmly entrenched companies can calculate more coolly than formerly the cost of a write-off of old equipment against the economies of the new techniques. Pressure to introduce new processes is indeed strong, and vast sums are spent on technological research. But the pressure is less compelling in a monopolistic or quasi-monopolistic situation.

All studies, from Hoover's famous report on *Waste in Industry* in the early 'twenties to the present, disclose the fact that a large part of American industry falls far below the level of what could be achieved if full advantage were taken of known management and production techniques. Under the Russian system, however, decisions to introduce *all around* the most up-to-date equipment can be made purely on the basis of productivity, not on the basis of profit calculations of giant concerns relatively free from severe competition, or of smaller concerns in fields dominated by sluggish custom and practices. To be sure, Russian technology still falls far short of current technological knowledge. The available resources are limited. The GNP is still relatively small, and the amount of capital formation that can be squeezed out over and above the military output and the urgently necessary consumers' goods, while *relatively large,* is absolutely small. Yet as GNP grows the capacity to pump out capital formation will progressively increase. In the Russian system the speed with which obsolescent equipment is depreciated is not based on profit calculations but only on the rate of technical progress and the limits imposed by scarcity of resources.

An obvious solution for American industry is to stimulate investment in the newest techniques by the device of accelerated depreciation. This amounts to an interest-free loan from the government to private business. Accelerated depreciation was indeed incorporated into our tax legislation in 1954. It should be carried much farther than the present law permits. But it should be administered countercyclically. Long-term growth requires a rapid rate of depreciation and replacement. But stability requires a cyclical adjustment of the accelerated depreciation privilege. The burst of investment of 1955–57 was primarily responsible for the recession of 1958. Bursts of investment are inimical not only to stability, but also to sustained rates of growth. Tax provisions relating to accelerated depreciation should be very generous in order to permit maximum growth. But they should be cyclically adjusted in order to foster stability and *sustained* growth.

III

The Soviet system may be able to maintain a higher rate of growth than the American system as now operated because their system permits in the long run an overall investment in industry as a whole to the point of "full investment." This means that investment in plant and equipment can be carried to the full limit of capital productivity, namely the point at which any further investment (given the state of technology) would yield no additional net output. New techniques and a growth in the labour force would of course open up further outlets for investment. These new outlets could then again be exploited to the full.

It is, of course, highly probable that for a considerable time at least, investment cannot be carried to the point of *full* investment in the Soviet Union. Up to date it has certainly not been carried that far by a wide margin. This is due partly to the fact that in the earlier stages of development she has experienced a marked shortage of capital goods. Thus the marginal product of capital has in fact been high—indeed, much higher than in the more developed countries of Europe and the United States. Moreover, even though the condition of severe capital shortage were overcome, it would still be true that for a long time to come the military requirements and the sorely needed minimum of consumer goods would preclude a volume of capital formation large enough to reach the point of "full investment."

Thus the outlet for investment in the Soviet system for the foreseeable future appears to be practically limitless. The outlet is large because Russia has still considerable distance to go before her stock of capital has caught up with the advanced countries. And taking a larger view of the matter, the outlet for investment can remain very large even after her greatly enlarged capital stock has driven the marginal productivity of capital down to the level of the western countries. This is true because investment in Russia need not stop at the point where the net marginal yield will cover the interest cost. Investment can, if the party leaders so decide, be pushed on to the point of "full investment." [2]

Under the American system, operating under present procedures and practices, investment cannot be pushed to the point of "full investment." Investment cannot be pushed beyond the limits imposed by the prevailing interest rate.

Here again something could be done about it if we were prepared to throw overboard outmoded conventional ideas. What is needed is a drastic and sustained reduction in the rate of interest.

It will at once be said that such a policy would produce a terrible inflation. This indeed might be true under certain conditions if no means were taken to check it. But there are powerful and effective ways of controlling inflation by means other than monetary. This is not the place to elaborate, but I hope to be able to do so in a forthcoming book. The answer would, of course, involve some considerable departure from the

[2] Economists (Mises, Lange, F. M. Taylor, and others) seeking to apply the principles of marginalism, have sought to show that optimum use of resources requires that account be taken of the rate of interest not only in the allocation of capital to different industries, but also in the allocation of production resources to the output of capital goods in relation to the output of consumer goods.

concept of "business as usual." But we are not living in a "business as usual" world. Unless we wake up to that fact before long we may pay dearly.

IV

Finally, the Russians may succeed in maintaining a higher rate of growth because they are able to devote a *larger proportion* of GNP to growth than is feasible in the United States under existing mores and practices. The possibility that we may be unable to match their rate of growth of output capacity can in part be explained in terms of the manner in which American consumer wants and consumer values are influenced under the powerful sway of modern advertising. A not inconsiderable part of our production resources are wasted on "manufactured wants."

Social values in former times were inculcated into the social fabric primarily through education in the home, school and church. In the United States today, it is no exaggeration to say that the radio, television and movies are more important as educational media than the home, the school and the church combined. And the programmes as well as the commercials are largely controlled not by educators but by salesmen and advertisers. Under this tutelage, value standards inevitably fall to the lowest denominator. This is private enterprise at its worst. Private enterprise is wonderfully efficient in the production end, but it is not a good educator of social values.

Economists used to argue, and some still do, that the consumer in a free price system is entitled to what he wants, foolish though it may be. "Consumer sovereignty" was the phrase. This line of reasoning could indeed claim solid validity in the days of free and well-nigh perfect competition. But it is difficult to see how an economist who has been instructed in the theory of monopolistic competition can still adhere to the "consumer sovereignty" dogma. Nowadays consumers no longer act on their own free will. The demand curve is no longer the product of spontaneous wants. It is manufactured. The operating costs of modern corporations relate not merely to the *supplying* of wants but also to the *creation* of wants. The consumer is "brain-washed" into believing that this or that gadget is necessary if for no other reason than to keep up with the Joneses. Social values are created. One comes to feel that a longer, wider and lower car heavily weighted with chrome is more important than the education of one's children. Price comparisons are lost sight of when brand names become all-important. Controlled consumer tests, for example, indicate that one branded product which costs $182 is in fact superior to another which costs $232. Another at $89 is rated superior to one priced at $359. And so the reports go on and on with a long list of branded products. The process of consumer brain-washing has become a branch of psychoanalysis. Consumer wants are no longer a matter of individual choice. They are "mass produced."

"Consumer education" operates in two directions, each reinforcing the other. In one direction an immense effort is made to create social values which will build up a demand for gadgets and thus hold the line for established manufacturing capacity. We have reached a point at which American prosperity (so business journalists tell us) rests heavily on the continued output of 7 million cars per year. Citizens who are deeply interested in the crying needs that continue to go unsatisfied may perhaps be forgiven if they tend to view this situation as a kind of treadmill, a species of pyramid building.

In another direction, the various media of communication, including pronouncements by public officials (particularly in the Eisenhower Administration) are engaged in a powerful, and it appears successful, campaign to persuade the public that government expenditures should be reduced or at least not permitted to rise. Private expenditures are encouraged by all manner of alluring devices like consumer loans—trips to Europe with no down payment. But public expenditures are labelled as spendthrift and inflationary.

In the United States we have gigantic surpluses of some material goods. Farm surplus—partly political and partly technological in origin—we hear much about. But we also have other surpluses which advertising attempts to hide. Our stock of automobiles is so large that we could take the entire population—babies included—of the United States, the United Kingdom and West Germany out for a Sunday "buggy ride" with only five persons in each car. And even so we would not be using the idle stock of new and used cars piled up in dealers' inventories. The surplus reveals itself not merely in numbers but also in size, weight, and unused horsepower capacity. We could stop producing cars for five years and scarcely feel any pinch in automobile travel. The waste of resources that has gone into the leviathans produced in the period 1947–59 (in contrast with the more sensible 1947 models) could reasonably be set down at a figure of around 50 billion dollars.

At the same time, we have a great need for teachers, nurses and doctors, schools, hospitals, housing for middle and lower income groups, urban renewal, roads, resource conservation and development—all essential for vigorous and sustained growth. I do not wish to go into detail. The facts are well known. Yet funds for schools are voted down all over the country. We are confronted with a set of social values, artificially created, which block progress and growth.

The more pressure advertising succeeds, the more will we reach a point at which private spending plus necessary outlays for defence will together absorb so large a part of GNP that no room is left for public investment in schools, hospitals, housing, urban redevelopment, resource development, etc. We have already reached this point. The Administration at Washington drives this clinching argument home day after day. Having reached this point, public spending brings inflation. To prevent inflation it is imperative to hold public expenditures to a bare minimum.

Conclusion

How might we be able to lift our historical 3 to 3½ per cent rate of growth to perhaps 5 per cent? I suggest that any such rate of growth is not likely to be reached or even approximated without a greatly enlarged role of the federal government. In particular I have suggested four lines of attack: (a) greatly increased public investment in both natural and human resources; (b) accelerated depreciation to encourage private investment; (c) low long-term interest rates designed to push investment closer toward "full investment"; (d) turn our modern media of communication into powerful instruments of public education thereby raising the standard of social values.

All four suggestions involve, as already noted, an enlarged role of government. Yet the first three of these programmes (and to some extent also the fourth) would induce increased private investment. Public resource development opens up private investment outlets. So also do accelerated depreciation and low rates of interest. And saner values with respect to social priorities would enable us to devote a larger proportion of our productive energies to those investments, both public and private, which ensure a more rapid rate of growth. Once again, the fear that public investment will supplant private enterprise does not appear to be well grounded. We already have a mixed public-private economy.

36

Professor Hansen and the Economics of the Soviet Challenge [*]

K. BIEDA

The University of New England, Australia

In the March 1960 issue of *The Record,* Professor Alvin H. Hansen expresses his concern about his expectation of the Soviet Union reaching, by 1980, the same G.N.P. as that of the U.S.A. His forecast is based on the "most competent researches." [1] Hansen is inclined to explain the faster annual rate of Soviet progress up to the present solely by the advantages in development of the beginner who can imitate the more advanced and draw on their experience. This, of course, is a fairly conventional argument. Most of its adherents argue that owing to the very nature of its advantage the Soviet growth is likely to slow down in time. Hansen, however, argues that unless the West makes some adaptations to its system the Soviet rate of growth "while not as large as in recent decades will continue to exceed that of the United States."

Since some of the detailed arguments of Professor Hansen about this very important problem appear unconvincing and since he is an eminent and influential economist some discussion [2] of the issues and remedies seemed more than warranted.

More precisely the explanation for the past disparity of growth, given almost solely in terms of the Russians importing the accumulated western technology, appears inadequate. To be sure every country imports foreign

[*] Excerpts reprinted from *The Economic Record,* June, 1961, pp. 157-170, by permission of the publisher.

[1] These almost certainly are American. Several of them appeared in the past few years. It is interesting to note that the figures quoted by Hansen are virtually identical to the figures quoted in the *Soviet Handbook 1959–1965* (Soviet Booklet No. 57 London, November 1959). There on p. 19 the figures of "average annual rate of growth of industrial production between 1918–1957 are: U.S.S.R. 10.1 per cent, U.S.A. 3.2 per cent, Great Britain 1.9 per cent, and France 3.2 per cent." It appears somewhat puzzling that the independent American researchers with incomplete information and using in all probability different statistical techniques should get the same result as the Soviet officials.

[2] I am grateful to Dr. K. A. Blakey, Dr. J. W. Nevile, and Mr. P. H. Davies for comments, and especially to Professor J. P. Belshaw and Mr. J. A. Withers for lengthy discussions on and around the topic. They are, however, in no way responsible for errors of commission or omission.

technology and it is obvious that the Russians could do that more than some Western countries (e.g. U.S.A., or the U.K.). There are, however, many other Western and non-Western countries who were or are at the same level of technology as the Soviet Union was and yet they do not show the same rates of growth. The general picture given here would be a more balanced one if Hansen had at least hinted at some other factors, some of which would operate only in the early stages of growth (and would not be unique to the Soviet Union) and some which may be operative in the Soviet Union all the time. It seems necessary to mention here that a beginner in development has two powerful purely, or almost purely, *statistical* advantages. In the first instance it is usual in estimating National Income to calculate the value of the market-bound activities only. This means that a great deal of useful economic activity performed in Russia in the 'twenties or the 'thirties by the housewife, the product of which was consumed directly by the family, was excluded. Now this housewife works in a factory for wages and the bread she bakes as an employee is counted, whereas the bread she baked as a housewife was not. Thus some of the advantage is illusory, but not all, because presumably baking the bread in a factory is much more efficient.

Secondly, a country just starting has little capital stock. This means that in the earlier years of the last three decades a given sum of capital investment went in Russia almost entirely to *net* investment whereas in the U.S.A. it had to go in a large proportion merely to replace some worn-out equipment. Thus the beginner shows *in that period* a faster increase in production. It is interesting to mention in this context that the industrial growth of Federal Germany is only very slightly lower than that of the Soviet Union in the period 1950–1957.[3]

It is true, however, that Hansen skipped deliberately over the past and discussed the more important future. It is here that the gravest doubts arise as to the very validity of his arguments, not to speak of their adequacy.

I. "Full Investment"

Hansen argues that the Soviet Union may have a faster rate of progress in future because its system unlike the Western one

permits *in the long run* an overall investment in industry *as a whole* to the point of 'full investment.' This means that investment in plant and equipment can be carried to the full limit of capital productivity, namely to the point at which any further investment *(given the state of technology)* [4] would yield no additional output.

[3] Zbigniew Lewandowicz, "Problemi Economici dell' U.S.S.R.," *Economia Internazionale,* November 1959.

[4] Italics by the present writer.

It should be obvious that this statement could be valid only if the Russians had an abundance of capital compared with their needs. Yet this vital assumption is nowhere even mentioned. If capital is not abundant "full investment in industry as a whole" is impossible. Hansen admits that so far there is "a severe capital shortage" which prevents "full investment." Yet he argues that in the future "investment can, if the party leaders so decide, be pushed to the point of full investment." The present writer tried very hard to make Hansen's argument plausible and came to the conclusion that there is here a necessity for a miraculous air-lift to match Russia's needs for capital with an abundant stock of capital (in fact a series of air-lifts would be necessary as technology would grow).

The argument against the possibility of an abundance of capital can be empirical or a priori. In the first instance, in the very long history of mankind we have had all sorts of societies, ascetic and hedonistic, dynamic and stagnant, collectivistic or individualistic, yet capital has always been scarce. On a priori grounds there is no doubt that capital in future will grow, possibly very quickly, but unfortunately the needs for capital are likely to grow at least as fast. As soon as a gadget or a product appears we find many new uses for it (with or without modification). It seems hardly conceivable that capital stock would grow without a growth of technology and that technology would not open vistas of new products or services each of which would create fresh demand for capital.

The assumption then of an abundance of capital is extremely unrealistic. Anybody who postulates such an unrealistic assumption explicitly or implicitly ought to provide some reasons for it. Hansen does not provide a shadow of evidence in this respect, indeed appears unaware of making this assumption. Thus the argument must be faulty [5] in its very essence, or at least is entirely unproven. But even on his own assessment of the nature of the problem, Hansen's policy prescription for pushing investment in the U.S.A. further is dubious. He suggests that investment cannot be pushed far enough in the United States, because interest rates are not low enough. Apart altogether from the uncertain effects of interest rates on investment, interest rates (if one takes into account the steady increases in prices) are already, in real terms, low and may sometimes be negative. In conditions of full employment

---

[5] The reasons for falling into a trap like this might be as follows. It is usual to talk of full employment, which has some meaning. Some writers, e.g. Hutt, have spoken of full employment of resources (which is erroneous, because owing to our ignorance we never utilise our resources fully). Hansen's preoccupation with the Soviet stress on capital formation gave his idea of "investing more fully" some treacherous attraction. In addition Hansen's argument was constructed with one leg in the realm of "long run" analysis, which allows him to argue the growth of capital stock, and the other leg in the other world of "short run," which allows him to keep technology and needs constant.

there are a tremendous number of people who would pay the ruling rates of interest if only they could get hold of any loan capital.

II. Obsolescence Policy

(a) Hansen further argues that American growth is hindered by the usual method of dealing with obsolescence. He starts with the statement that under the capitalist system new technology will not be introduced *merely* because it is *technically* more efficient than the old one and argues that the switch-over to the new technology should be made irrespective of the total real costs of doing so. Hansen then proceeds to say (without supplying any proof) that the latter is the Soviet practice [6] and a source of their success. But surely whether it is a Western monopolist or a Soviet planner who is making the decision, when a new technology appears the rational thing to do is to calculate the cost of the adoption of the new technology. One has to estimate here the remaining working life of the old capital asset. Say this is ten years. Then one has to estimate how much dearer in respect of labour, power, or raw materials the old technique would be over that period of ten years than the new technique. This extra cost X of labour, power, or raw materials has to be compared with the extra cost of labour needed to produce the new machine, more precisely that part of the new machine which would have to be depreciated in ten years. Let us call that cost Y. A rational capitalist monopolist would be under the same logical compulsion as a rational Soviet planner to scrap the old equipment if the extra cost X of working the old machine were greater than Y, and conversely. The West and the Russians have electronic brains, which could do many jobs better than human beings do with the present equipment. Does this necessarily mean that bus drivers should be replaced by an electronic brain irrespective of cost in terms of labour and resources? Productivity (in any economic system whatever) requires that a planner should save labour, power, and materials in the *whole economy and not just in one sector*. In this case a small saving of the labour of bus drivers would involve incomparably much greater waste of labour and capital in the electronic goods industry.

(b) As a matter of fact, to the extent that some forms of competition still exist in the West, it can be argued that the replacement of obsolete capital takes place faster in the West than in the Soviet Union. Hansen appears to think in black and white terms here. The past is depicted as one of ruthless competition and the present completely without it. Though the competition of to-day is not that of perfect competition of the textbook, though there is not much price competition (there is a threat of it) there is the powerful threat of the new product, and the com-

[6] A. Erlich argues in *Soviet Economic Growth,* edited by Abram Bergson (Row, Peterson & Co., Evanston, Ill.), that in fact the opposite is the case. Erlich quotes as his authorities two Soviet economists, A. Notkin and A. Arakelian.

petition of the firm from another industry, or just the fear of what the rival oligopolist firms are doing. There are many industries, indeed all the industries supplying durable consumer goods, e.g. the car industry, where obsolescence is rapid and innovation of the process or the product excessively rapid. Here all firms spy on one another and as soon as one plans to introduce a new product or a new process the others try to beat him to it. Indeed, as Galbraith argues: "In industries where firms are few and comparatively large—oil, metallurgy, cars, chemicals, rubber, heavy engineering—the investment in technological advance is considerable." [7]

(c) Briefly, Hansen has not established that the Western obsolescence policy is wrong, nor that the Soviet obsolescence policy is different, and it would follow that his prescribed medicine would be irrelevant to the real situation. But even for the problem as seen by Hansen the advice is strange. What he recommends is accelerated depreciation allowances cyclically adjusted. Now this might or might not help the problem of stabilisation much. But how would it speed up replacement over the whole period of the downswing and the upswing? What one would gain on the swings one would lose on the roundabouts. While some producer would find benefits in installing new capital equipment during the phase of the accelerated depreciation allowances of the downswing, this would be offset by the postponement of replacements during the upswing when the privilege would be withdrawn (by Hansen). The producers would wait then until later when accelerated depreciation allowances are restored. But even on this very narrow issue of the effect of accelerated depreciation allowances Hansen takes too much for granted. The stimulating effect during the downswing is fully dependent on there being no income tax increase after the period of the accelerated depreciation ends. If the period of the accelerated depreciation is, say, 3 or 4 years, some time early in the subsequent 6 or 7 years the downswing phase might be replaced by the upswing (to the extent that this and other policies were successful) and the excessive growth of the upswing would presumably soon have to be checked both by removal of the accelerated depreciation allowance and by a very probably increase in income tax. (Hansen could not fight inflation by credit squeeze because he insists on lower rates of interest.) In effect then, the firm would have shifted a substantial part of its income from the low tax years into the high tax years, and the "interest-free loans from the government" would then prove to have high interest charges. Thus the stimulating effect would seem to be most uncertain.

It would be much simpler, if it were desired to speed up innovations, for the government to organise research for all the industries where the representative firm is too small to finance its own. This would speed up innovations where they are sluggish and leave unaffected the in-

[7] *The Affluent Society* (Hamish Hamilton, London), p. 99.

dustries where the stimulus is unwanted. Galbraith gives convincing arguments to prove that innovation is very unevenly [8] supported in various industries.

III. Should Investment Be Self-Liquidating?

Hansen is right when he argues that when approaching an investment decision the government should consider not only the direct returns, but also the more remote indirect ones. The argument used to justify investments even if they are not self-liquidating is based on the "social" external economies. This argument has been recognised since at least the time of Adam Smith.[9] The newer factor that Hansen introduces here is the conventional argument that the United States public authorities, by ignoring the external economies, have not carried public investment far enough. That may well be true. But if Hansen continues to argue that this explains the faster Soviet growth two points may be brought out. Firstly, other Western governments e.g. British, French or Australian, are probably not guilty of that mistake, and yet the performance of their economies is not better, in fact that of Great Britain is much worse. Secondly, the Russians themselves may be making the opposite error of not carrying investment far enough in the field of light industry, i.e. consumer goods industries. Surely external economies can arise in either field. Moreover it could be argued with considerable justification that the social external economies of any given project are much less in a highly developed economy like that of the U.S.A. than in a relatively underdeveloped one as the Soviet Union was in the early stages of her growth. After all, if one or two big public projects were not carried out in the U.S.A. the external economies lost would not be very great—some land would not be irrigated, but the U.S. has an excess of agricultural products. Perhaps some skilled labour (skilled in public works) has not been developed, but other skill has been gained (in private industry). Perhaps some knowledge or experience has not been gained, but other offsetting know-how must have been acquired. But the same could not be argued in an underdeveloped economy, where an excessive development of "natural resources" producing some asset does not add perhaps so much skill or useful experience as could have been gained in industry.

Perhaps Hansen could make out some argument here on the lines of external diseconomies of private enterprise, but he does not even hint at that. Moreover if he did, the question would come up whether there do not arise external diseconomies as a result of governmental actions, some institutions or even the very size of government machine under certain circumstances.

[8] *Ibid.*
[9] Cf. *The Wealth of Nations,* p. 681 (The Modern Library, New York, 1937).

There is also the additional point, that Hansen is somewhat vague on this paragraph. When he suggests that investment in "natural resources" need not be self-liquidating, what exactly does he mean? Does he mean that an investment in, for example, a coal-mine in an advanced country need not be self-liquidating? This ambiguity, together with the general suggestion of the whole article that capital is a free good, could easily lead an unwary reader to think that insisting on self-liquidating even in the wide sense does not matter.

IV. How Much Investment?

Hansen gives here a conventional argument that communist countries devote a much larger proportion of their national income to investment than capitalist countries do. Indeed throughout his whole article the volume of investment is taken as virtually the sole cause of economic growth and increasing investment is virtually the sole prescription. It is true, of course, that in this error he is not quite alone. Since the growth of the popularity of the so-called "production functions," some writers have come to believe that there is some rigid dependence of output and productivity on the capital stock. Those writers seem to be blind to the fact that whether one takes business in New York or Sydney, the most profitable firms and the firms growing fastest are often not highly capitalised. If this mechanical dependence of output on capital stock does not apply in the same cultural and social *milieu*, why should it apply in vastly differing environments? Even in the same country and the same industry a massive application of capital does not necessarily increase physical productivity of labour, as is clearly shown, for example, in the well known Reid Report on the British coal industry. Again on what grounds did Hansen reach the view that the Soviet Union puts a higher proportion of G.N.P. into capital formation than the U.S.A. or Australia? Further even if the Soviet Union did so, and if quantity or growth of capital were such an all-important factor, is it not the case that the average worker in the Soviet Union is still aided by a great deal less capital equipment than the worker in the U.S.A. and that the current *absolute* per capita addition to the equipment of the Soviet worker may well be much less than the addition enjoyed by the American worker?

It is true that statistics on capital formation as a percentage of G.N.P. leave much to be desired, but presumably if Hansen did look for any factual support he would have to consider such statistics as are available. Here are some estimates: (See table on p. 324).

Kaplan argues that the proportion of G.N.P. invested in the Soviet Union greatly resembles the U.S. investment rates for the last eighty years. Yet the U.S. did not show anywhere nearly so high rates of growth of G.N.P. as Hansen's Soviet figures. In the period 1949/50–1958/9, Aus-

Soviet Gross Investment as a Percentage of G.N.P.

	Estimate of Bergson * "established prices"	Estimate Bergson "adjusted prices"	Kaplan's Estimate **
1937	19.2	22.9	15.9
1940	13.7	16.6	13.3
1944	11.5	13.5	9.2
1948	18.5	25.6	17.2

* Abram Bergson and H. Heymann, *Soviet National Income and Product 1940–48* (Columbia University Press, New York 1954).

** *Soviet Economic Growth,* edited by A. Bergson (Evanston, Ill., 1953).

tralia's total Gross Capital Formation amounted to 28 per cent of G.N.P. or, if cars are excluded, 25 per cent. Yet Australia's G.N.P. grew by post-war standards at the quite moderate rate of about half that of Japan (sometimes much slower than that; the exact figure greatly depends on the period chosen). Among the countries that easily exceed the economic growth of Australia are Federal Germany, Austria, Communist China, Nationalist China, Philippines, Japan,[10] and probably there are quite a number of others.

It could be argued that it is the rate of investment and the rate of growth of population in conjunction with the abundance or paucity of natural resources that affect the rate of growth of G.N.P. If that were the case Australia should definitely have one of the fastest rates of growth in the world and Japan one of the slowest. Japan's recent rate of investment is similar to that of Australia (in earlier periods it was much lower) and while in the period 1953–58 the number of people in employment increased in Japan by 10 per cent, it increased in Australia by 13 per cent! Further, it cannot be argued that the natural resources of Japan are rich but in the words of U.N. *Economic Survey of Asia and the Far East* 1957 the growth of real income in Japan ". . . in recent years has been at the rate of 10 per cent per annum . . . by far the highest increases among industrial nations. In 1956 industrial production had risen by 23 per cent over the previous year." [11]

Nor can it be argued that the fast growth of Japan's G.N.P. can be explained by the advantages of the beginner as Japan, though poor, is now a highly developed country. In fact, contrary to such an argument, now that she has presumably exhausted the advantages of the beginner, she has shown a dramatic *acceleration* from the pre-war annual rate of growth which used to be approximately 4 per cent. Neither is this fast post-war growth a result of starting from a low base existing at the end

[10] U.N. *Economic Survey of Asia and the Far East* 1957 (Bangkok 1958).

[11] (Sic.) Nor was that year exceptional as, between 1954 and 1959, Japan's industrial production doubled. U.N. *Economic Survey of Asia and the Far East* 1959 (Bangkok 1960).

of the war, as Japan's recovery was completed by 1950 or 1951 [12] and the rates quoted apply to the subsequent period.

Briefly, if Hansen was searching for some simple secret of growth he should have given more consideration to the conditions of growth in the Soviet Union and at least some to the remarkable case of Japan.

V. The Pattern of Investment

It might, perhaps, be argued that the pattern of investment, i.e. its distribution between industrial investment and durable consumer goods, is significantly different in the countries discussed. There are some differences to be found, though for some countries the breakdown of capital formation is incomplete or not available. Figures available are:

Percentages of Gross Capital Investment in the U.S.S.R.[13] and Australia[14]
Made in Various Fields

	U.S.S.R. Seven Year Plan 1952-8	U.S.S.R. Seven Year Plan 1959-65	Australia 1958/9
Industry incl. agriculture	76.6	76.7	66.5
Motor cars	—	—	10.4
Housing and Public Facilities ..	19.4	19.3	20.0
Education and Public Health ..	4.0	4.0	3.0

A rough calculation made out for New Zealand also shows a lower proportion of total investment made in the industrial field.

There is of course a possibility that some of the Australian industrial investment is in the wrong sector (e.g. too much in manufacturing and not enough in mineral extraction). But it is impossible to make a statistical comparison of the extent of mal-investment in various countries.

In the case of Japan the U.N. statistics [15] single out from the total capital formation only the expenditure on dwellings. There only about 7 per cent of the total capital formation is spent on housing against Australia's 15 per cent. Nevertheless Australia's capital formation is so large that these differences should not invalidate the view that differences in the rate of growth do not depend on the rate of industrial investment in any simple and mechanical fashion. Further evidence in support of this view is supplied by the U.N. statistics [16] of Net National Income growth in the period of 1952–6 and the Gross Fixed Capital Formation

12 Cf. G. C. Allen, *Japan's Economic Recovery* (O.U.P., 1958), p. 21; also U.N. *Economic Survey of Asia and the Far East* 1957, p. 45 (Bangkok 1958).

13 Absolute figures taken from *Soviet Handbook 1959–65. Statistics and Data Relating to the Seven Year Plan.* (Soviet Booklet No. 57, London, November 1959), p. 52.

14 *National Income and Expenditure of Australia* 1959. Government Printer, Canberra.

15 *U.N. Economic Survey of Asia and the Far East* 1959 (Bangkok 1960).

16 *U.N. Economic Survey of Asia and the Far East* 1958 (Bangkok 1959).

for such countries as, for instance, Philippines, Communist China and Nationalist China. All of these have a much lower rate of investment and a faster rate of growth of national income than Australia.

VI. Excess Capacity, the Soviet Stress on Capital Goods Industries, and the Concept of National Income

(1) There are strong reasons for thinking that the Soviet Union uses at all times such capital equipment as it has to a fuller extent than the West does.

It is generally known that the Western type of economy has considerable excess capacity in depressions. What is much less well-known is that countries like the U.S.A., Australia, or New Zealand have considerable excess capacity in some sectors even in boom periods.[17] The fact that there is in boom periods a large number of unfilled *immediate* vacancies is itself suggestive that there must be some excess capacity in capital generally. In addition certain specific industries have been run in the best post-war years only at a fraction of their capacity.

Even in normal times excess capacity is likely to arise because of:

(a) Mistakes in the assessment of the market for goods and labour by individual producers in the West and by the planners in the Soviet Union.

(b) Sudden and dramatic changes in the Government policies in the matter of import controls, exchange controls, various qualitative credit controls, hire-purchase restrictions, indirect tax changes, etc. All of these policy changes aim at various objectives with a considerable disregard of their effects on the pattern of investment and the problem of capacity utilisation.

(c) Capricious behaviour of the "spoilt" consumer in the Western society, and his effective insistence on a high degree of choice, which can be purchased only at the expense of a more or less permanent excess capacity and the holding of very large stocks, all of which reduce our overall average return on capital invested.

(d) Fluctuations in the foreign sector. These affect all countries but not in an equal degree and not in the same fashion.

(e) Monopolistic organisations, especially of the cartel type common in Australia, have, as is well known, a strong tendency to create permanent excess capacity.

---

[17] In the U.S.A. in December 1956 capital was utilised at no more than 91 per cent and in August 1957 at no more than 88 per cent. Both estimates are claimed to have been made in the most conservative fashion and both in periods of prosperity. Calvin B. Hoover, "Employment Growth and Price Levels," *Quarterly Journal of Economics,* August, 1960.

(2) Of the above five factors only the first two are equally liable to occur in the Soviet Union. If they produce in the West a sectoral excess capacity this may prove either permanent or fairly long-lived. In the Soviet Union such errors can be more readily and more quickly eliminated and at a lesser cost in terms of the accepted statistical G.N.P. growth measurement. The Soviet Union can eliminate excess capacity very quickly because:

(a) If Russia tends to have a faster growth (for other reasons which will be argued later) then a faster growth of demand for goods generally will eliminate the excess capacity more quickly.

(b) The consumer goods industry is kept in the Soviet Union at such a capacity compared with the potential demand that an excess capacity is almost unthinkable.

(c) The Soviet Union is aided by the fact that it strongly favours investment in the capital goods industries compared with investment in consumer goods industries. It is still true, of course, that a particular capital goods industry could develop an excess capacity. But as the capital equipment in many capital goods industries is relatively unspecific (compared with that of the consumer goods industries) it can often be easily switched to other production. Although the capital equipment in *some* capital goods industries is highly specific (e.g. in a coal mine, electric power plant, water control installations, etc.) their *product* may be relatively unspecific and therefore excess production may be used up easily in practically any industry (provided that the economy is as the Soviet one always tight-stretched, with a repressed inflation). For the rest if the Soviet planner should still face an excess capacity, he could easily switch resources to some sort of sputnik (not that it is argued that this need has arisen).

In addition, to the extent that the Soviet economy develops something like an excess capacity in an industry producing capital goods the planners can easily eliminate that excess capacity by a small alteration in the plan and by putting a bigger supply of some product on the consumer market, which will gratefully take it up even if the price is not reduced (and the price if necessary may be reduced by a reduction of the turnover tax). Alternatively the product in excess supply can be sold to the Ministry of Foreign Trade. Lavishing resources on the base of the economy, that is on the capital goods industries, has at this level the advantage that the products are undifferentiated: they can equally well be used by the capital goods industries as by the consumer goods industries.

As a result of these features of the Soviet economy, if the planners make a mistake it is easily corrected. One is tempted to say that the

Soviet planner in a sense "cannot do wrong"! Such investment as he has determined will be fully utilised and the product sold at a price he determines. Then the estimator of the G.N.P. takes the total output at the planner's prices, or his own country's prices, and says that the G.N.P. of the Soviet Union rose so much. This situation may, however, co-exist with a severe shortage of, say, shaving blades where the planner did not provide sufficiently, and an excess of books where he may have over-provided.

(3) If free market consumer valuation of G.N.P. were available this sort of discrepancy would force the G.N.P. down, but if a free market does not exist whose prices should be used? Some writers have chosen the Soviet planners' prices either of the early period or some later period, or the prices ruling in a particular year in some other country. Each set of prices, whether that of a different year or a different country gave a *completely different* rate of growth.[18] None of them could reflect the true consumer's valuation otherwise than by an unlikely accident. National income and its growth are essentially welfare concepts. Since inter-personal comparisons of utility are impossible, since the consumer's valuations change all the time (which brings an insoluble index number problem) and since even such changing consumer valuations are distorted in the West by monopoly elements and are smothered by the planners' preferences in the Soviet Union, there arises the problem of what value, if any, we should put on national income statistics.[19]

VII. Some of the Possible Causes of the Faster Growth of G.N.P. in the Soviet Union

The present knowledge of the mechanism of economic growth is still so inadequate and the factors facilitating growth are so numerous, complex and often intangible, that not only would the monistic diagnosis of Hansen be insufficient, but the following list of probable factors may well be incomplete. The present writer thinks that the faster Soviet growth is at least in part explained by the following:

(1) Different attitudes of labour and management to effort in a country that has already "arrived" and in a country that is passionately trying to catch up.

(2) The present unsatisfactory patent arrangements in the West which lead to a vast multiplication of costly research effort and restrict the use of latest inventions, whereas in the Soviet Union any

18 See *Soviet Economic Growth,* edited by A. Bergson (Row, Peterson & Co., Evanston, Ill.).

19 This article was written sometime in May 1960, the final draft was written in October and sent to the Editor at the beginning of November 1960. Since the time of writing it K. Polanyi developed, independently of course, a somewhat similar idea in the Oct.–Dec. issue of the *Soviet Survey* quarterly.

invention is shared out with all the other enterprises. In addition the Soviet Union has a system of bilateral agreements with the other Communist countries providing for free mutual exchange of inventions, information, plans and specifications.

(3) The Soviet Union uses material incentives to a similar extent as the West and in addition makes incomparably greater use than the West of moral and social incentives, conferring recognition and distinction for effort on worker or manager.

(4) The Soviet Union uses piece work and shift work more than the the West.

(5) The U.S.A. while talking in general terms of increasing growth, is actually making no mean effort and this at very high cost, to discourage growth of output and indeed to reduce output in an important sector of its economy, namely agriculture—precisely the opposite to what Khrushchev is doing.

(6) The Soviet Union places greater emphasis on education, especially in technology. Various kinds of truth are not all equally worth knowing, and from the point of view of G.N.P. growth especially they are not equally useful. The Soviet Union in conformity with its materialistic outlook places great stress on education and research in the severely practical and useful.

(7) The U.S.A. has been for some time withdrawing its main effort, in terms of manpower, from production of goods to the production of services. In the post-war period about 80 per cent of the net addition to the labour force in the U.S.A. went into the tertiary sector.[20] Such a trend has not yet manifested itself in the Soviet Union. Since services invariably show much slower growth of productivity than secondary industry such a disparity would affect the growth of G.N.P.

(8) The Soviet Union makes much greater use of women's contribution to the market-bound national effort. Because of our prejudices, our values, and our way of living we produce our "national income" with only a small contribution from women. In fact in the intellectual field we have managed very successfully to prevent women from contributing.

VIII. Conclusions

Should we invest more? Hansen appears to have no doubt at all that we should. All he worries about is the method of bringing about higher investment. Quite apart from the fact that his methods of increasing investment are dubious, there arise three hurdles.

[20] *U.N. Economic Survey of Asia and the Far East* 1957 (Bangkok).

(a) There is serious doubt whether an increased investment would increase the growth of G.N.P. significantly.

(b) There is also the question whether, in the conditions of the U.S.A. or of Australia, an increase in output (if so badly desired) could not be obtained more economically by other sacrifices preferable to the community.

(c) Finally why should we make any very heavy sacrifices to-day so that we should be so very rich to-morrow? Is it not the case that the U.S.A. and Australia belong to the very rich countries? After all the U.S.A. is not trying to make up lee-way in her per capita income as is the U.S.S.R. Surely provided that there is *some* growth, provided, that is, that our children shall be somewhat richer than we are, there is no superior moral, economic or welfare virtue in high consumption to-morrow instead of consumption to-day.

It is true that the Soviet Union has been making great sacrifices in the past and is making them now because it wants to catch up on the U.S.A. But if we push up our sacrifices for the sake of faster and faster growth and keep on at it, when, if ever, are we going to stop, or to slow down? If we keep on making great sacrifices for the sake of future for ever, we would be in effect building pyramids. If at a distant time we slow down sacrifices to enjoy very high consumption, such a sudden switch would lower the utility of the total product over the whole period of the very lean and the very fat years, in a similar way as it is argued that gambling does.

Hansen's concern here must have arisen either because he fears that divergent rates of growth would produce an unfavourable change in the balance of military power, or an unfavourable psychological impact on the third countries. Galbraith [21] gives a brilliant argument that future war could not ". . . even remotely be called a G.N.P. war . . . ," which presumably means, that within a range of differences of G.N.P., the total productive power in itself is entirely irrelevant to military power nowadays. The dilemma facing the West arises then from the fact that the western opulence does not endear the West to the undeveloped (and uncommitted) nations, who rather may be presumed to be strongly attracted to him who shows faster rates of growth. Thus we may be forced into lower consumption and greater sacrifices merely to prove ourselves and our system to the uncommitted nations.

[21] J. K. Galbraith, *The Affluent Society* (Hamish Hamilton, London).

SOVIET VIEWS

37

Different Systems—Different Results *

Sector of Economic Competition, Economic Research Institute,
USSR State Economic Council

The Year Under Socialism and Capitalism

Another year of the economic competition between the two social
systems has passed. Its results show that in this competition socialism is
winning in the most important sense—it is winning an edge in time,
which we measure by the development of the productive forces. This is
graphically borne out by the report of the Central Statistical Administration of the USSR on the fulfillment of the Soviet national economic
plan on the one hand, and the economic results of the year in the United
States on the other.

The past year was a good one for Soviet economy, for the Soviet
people. Industrial output grew by almost 10%, considerably exceeding
the planned assignment for the second year of the Seven-Year Plan. There
was a rapid increase in the extraction of oil and gas, the most economical
fuels. Technical progress was marked by a particularly rapid growth in
the output of modern electrical, power and chemical equipment, automatic instruments and synthetic fibers. The foundations were laid for a
further improvement in the structure of production: with a total increase
of 11.5% in capital investment, investment in the chemical industry
grew by 33% and in the machine-building industry by 23%.

Despite unfavorable weather conditions, good results were scored in
agriculture. According to preliminary data, in 1960 the gross harvest of
grain was 445 million poods higher than in 1959. There was an increase
in the output of meat, milk and eggs. This resulted in greater sales of
consumer goods to the population.

Real incomes per working person went up by 5%. From the social
welfare funds (those for public education, medical services, social maintenance and various payments and benefits) the population received 24.5
billion rubles or 1.5 billion rubles more than in 1959.

* From *Trud*, February 10, 1961. Translated in and excerpts reprinted from *Problems of Economics*, February 1961, pp. 12-16, by permission of the publisher.

But in the United States of America, the main capitalist country, the development of productive forces declined sharply. After skidding for many months, its economy again began to slip down slowly toward the end of the year.

"The present state of the economy is disturbing," President Kennedy stressed in his recent State of the Union Message. "We take office in the wake of seven months of recession, three and a half years of slack, seven years of diminished economic growth, and nine years of falling farm income."

American economists call 1960 "a year of frustrated hopes and disappointments." It began with much pomp and fanfare, however. Former President Eisenhower claimed in his January message to Congress that it would be a year of "unprecedented prosperity" for the United States. The newspapers of the monopolies assured their readers that not a single cloud obscured the prospects of the US economic growth. But the end of the year heard wailing about "economic instability," "coming depression," and an increasing number of "distressed areas." "The clouds of recession are thickening," *Newsweek* wrote in December.

There are more than enough reasons for alarm.

By the end of the year industrial production in the United States dropped by 5% compared with the beginning of the year. Enterprises in some industries operated at 40 to 50% below capacity. The backlog of orders shrank to the level of the worst months of the 1958 crisis.

All this greatly affected the position of the United States in the economic competition with the Soviet Union—both materially and morally. "The Americans are stunned, not so much by the decay of the American system, as by some supernatural effectiveness of the Russian system," wrote US journalist Alexander Werth.

Victory in Economic Competition Is Approaching

The end of the Seven-Year Plan is still far in the future, but it is already clear that it will be fulfilled ahead of schedule. The time required for the Soviet Union to occupy first place in the world in the level of economic development is approaching faster than we expected two years ago at the 21st Congress of the CPSU.

Under the Seven-Year Plan, by 1965 the Soviet Union is to reach the 1958 level of industrial production in the United States—if the average annual rate of increase in industrial output is maintained at 8.6%. However, the actual rate in the first two years of the Seven-Year Plan was 10.5%. This makes it possible for Soviet industry to reach the US level of 1958 not in 1965 but in 1964. This is borne out by the following simple calculations.

In 1958 Soviet industrial output equalled about 60% of the US level at that time. With annual increases of 10%, in 1959 it reached 66% and in 1960, 73% (of the US level in 1958). If this pace is maintained, in 1964 Soviet industrial output will be 107% of the 1958 level in the United States.

For some of the most important industrial goods this level will be surpassed even earlier; for instance, in steel—in 1962–1963, and in cement—in 1961–1962. And if it is borne in mind that the Soviet Union is already ahead of the United States in the volume of production of a number of industrial and agricultural goods (iron ore, timber procurement, mainline electric and diesel locomotives, woolen cloth, butter, milk, fish catch, etc.), it becomes clear that the Soviet Union is already approaching the US level of 1958.

Recent years have also seen a marked change in the relationship between the current (i.e., simultaneous) levels of industrial output in the USSR and the USA. At the present time industrial output in the USSR is approximately two-thirds of gross industrial production in the United States.

The rapid and steady development of all branches of Soviet industry on the one hand, and recessions and crises in the development of American production on the other, inevitably diminish the gap between the levels of output in the USSR and the USA. This is vividly illustrated by the following figures in steel output:

Steel Output in the USSR and the USA
(in millions of tons)

Year	USSR	USA
1950	27.3	87.8
1951	31.4	95.4
1952	34.5	84.5
1953	38.1	101.2
1954	41.4	80.1
1955	45.3	106.2
1956	48.7	104.5
1957	51.2	102.3
1958	54.9	77.3
1959	59.95	84.8
1960	65.3	90.1
1961 (plan)	71.3	. . . .

And steel output is a most important indicator of the economic might of a country and the level of development of its productive forces.

It has already become a normal feature for the United States—and this is pointed out in the Statement of the Moscow Meeting of Representatives of the Communist and Workers' Parties—that the rate of growth of production barely exceeds the growth of population. In the Soviet Union, production is growing 5 to 6 times more rapidly than population.

Dynamics of Industrial Production and Population Growth in the USSR and the USA (in % of 1957)

Year	USSR		USA	
	Industrial production	Population growth	Industrial production	Population growth
1957	100	100	100	100
1958	110	101.8	93	101.7
1959	122	103.6	105	103.4
1960	134	105.6	107	105.4

Eighty years ago the United States emerged in first place in the volume of industrial production, and it has since maintained a considerable edge on the other capitalist countries. Only a socialist country could set itself and successfully tackle the task of reaching the American level of industrial production. The feasibility of this task is no longer called in question by many bourgeois economists, although they consider that this will take more time than we in the Soviet Union think necessary. But what they fail to understand is that to overfulfill their plans has become a rule with the Soviet people. That is why their victory in the economic competition is coming ever closer.

For an Abundance of Foodstuffs

In 1958, on the eve of the 21st Congress of the Party, the volume of agricultural production in the USSR amounted to approximately 75 to 80% of the US level. The total and per capita production of wheat, rye, barley, potatoes, flax, sunflower seed, sugar beet and wool in the USSR was then and is now higher than in the USA. The USSR, however, is still behind the USA in the total harvest of grain crops and cotton, and in the output of meat, eggs, fruits and vegetables.

In order to reach and exceed the American per capita level in the output of all agricultural products, their production in the USSR must exceed that of the USA by 18 to 20%. This task will be fully solved with the fulfillment of the Seven-Year Plan.

During the 1953 to 1960 period our country considerably increased the volume of agricultural production. We have never experienced such high rates of growth of agricultural production as during the past seven years. They considerably exceed the US rates of growth.

This superiority in rates of growth has made it possible for the Soviet Union to considerably alter the relationship between the USSR and the USA in the output of major foodstuffs.

Increase in Agricultural Production in the USSR and USA, 1953 to 1960
(1960 in % of 1953)

	USSR	USA
Grains	161	137
Sugar beet	246	136
Meat	150	115
Milk	169	105
Butter	171	89

Volume of Agricultural Production in the USSR
(in % of USA level taken as 100)

	1953	1960
Grain crops	58	68
Sugar beet	212	382
Meat	39	51
Milk	67	108
Butter	68	127

Grain production in the USSR is behind that of the USA first of all in the output of corn. The implementation of the resolution of the January Plenary Meeting of the CPSU Central Committee on expanding the area under corn in the Ukraine, the RSFSR, Moldavia and Georgia with the aim of producing not less than 50 centners per hectare, will make it possible to considerably narrow the gap between us and the USA in the production of grain crops and will greatly increase the country's fodder supply.

The USSR has exceeded the US level in the total and per capita production of butter. In 1960 the per capita production of butter in the USA was 3.7 kg.; in the USSR it was 4 kg.

As for total milk production, the USSR has exceeded the US level but is still behind in per capita production. This lag can and should be overcome within the next year or two.

The USSR lags behind the USA above all in the production of meat per capita. During the past seven years per capita meat production in the USSR has increased from 31 to 42 kg. It has outstripped by far such countries as Italy (24 kg. per capita), Finland (32 kg.) and Norway (34 kg.). However, it still lags behind the USA which produces 98 kg. per capita.

The January Plenary Meeting of the CPSU Central Committee posed the task of sharply stepping up the production of grain, industrial crops, potatoes and vegetables, meat, milk and other products during the current year. "The interests of building communism and achieving a steady rise in the people's living standards," the resolution of the Plenary

Meeting reads, "today calls for new and still higher rates of growth in agriculture. The task is to make agricultural output always outpace popular demand."

Although the USSR is still behind the USA in the volume of agricultural production, the paths of agricultural development in the USSR and the USA are profoundly and basically different.

In the Soviet Union the people, the state and the Party are concerned with one problem; what should be done to utilize the great advantages inherent in socialist agriculture, to *increase* production and to flood the country with foodstuffs. It is pointed out in the resolution of the Plenary Meeting of the CPSU Central Committee that "we shall not have a prospering socialist economy without a well developed agriculture, without an abundance of agricultural products. The effort to steadily advance agriculture is a prime condition for building a communist society. It is truly the concern of the entire people."

Today, when the results of the January Plenary Meeting of the CPSU Central Committee are being discussed throughout the country, collective farmers and state farm workers once more are checking their possibilities, finding new reserves for further development, and deciding the tasks to be tackled. This nation-wide movement is the best guarantee that the resolution of the Plenary Meeting will be fulfilled within a short period. The time is not far off when our socialist agriculture will leave the USA behind both in the total volume of production and in per capita output. . . . .

Growth of the People's Welfare Is Main Aim

The purpose of increasing production and labor productivity in the USSR is to raise the Soviet citizen's material and cultural standards. By the end of the sixties the Soviet Union should surpass the USA in per capita output. This will give the Soviet people a higher living standard than that in any other country, including the USA.

When one compares living standards one must not forget that in a capitalist society the "average level" is a rather relative concept. Bourgeois economists include in this "average" both the fabulous incomes of a handful of monopolists and the high salaries of their bootlickers on the one hand, and the earnings of the workers who now have, as President Kennedy put it, "less money to buy things which now cost them more" and "the incomes" of the millions of jobless on the brink of starvation on the other. All these marked contrasts in the material standards of the classes in capitalist society are glossed over by this "average." To realize its real meaning one could quote from old statisticians who used to say that the "cow drowned in a puddle, the average depth of which was 20 centimeters."

Today the population of the USSR is less well off in clothing, footwear and housing than the *employed* factory and office worker in the USA. The USSR is also behind the USA in the standard of consumption of meat, milk, eggs, and fruit.

Nevertheless the working people of the Soviet Union enjoy, as far as material standards are concerned, advantages over the working people of the USA and other capitalist countries which the latter can only dream of.

Every working man knows that material and cultural standards are steadily rising in the USSR, that today we are better off than yesterday, and that tomorrow we shall be still better off than today. This is a tremendous source of optimism, for every new day opens up new vistas and new bright prospects.

Look how much has been done for the Soviet people's benefit in the past two years of the Seven-Year Plan!

All factory and office workers have been transferred to a 6- and 7-hour day. The working week in the USSR averages 39.4 hours today. The wage adjustments which accompanied this process resulted in greater wages and salaries for a considerable number of employees, chiefly for those in the lower-paid categories. The gradual abolition of the income tax, begun last year, will result in the complete elimination of this tax by 1964. Mankind has never known anything like this in all its history!

The fact that there is no unemployment in the USSR and that all doors to science and production are open wide to young people is something we have long grown used to. But in the USA, according to the latest statistics, there are 5,500,000 unemployed and a still greater number of partially unemployed. Every year more than a million young people reaching working age hunt in vain for jobs. Taxes and prices are going up while earnings are going down. All that the American working man hopes for is that tomorrow will be no worse than today. It is not because today is good, but because the prospects are gloomy. The stormclouds of a new crisis constantly threaten to deluge the country with more suffering and privation for those who work, let alone the jobless. There is nothing sadder than the lot of a man who realizes that society does not need him and that he cannot feed himself and his family.

With obstinacy worthy of a better cause, the bourgeois press is repeating the allegation that in the capitalist countries everyone has "equal opportunities" and that all can become millionaires. Ruthless reality is showing, however, that it is only the millions of the disinherited that are multiplying.

What can the bourgeois newspapers, journals and books compare with the following facts about life in the USSR? Full employment. Social insurance for all factory and office workers without exception. No discrimination in pay for reasons of seniority, sex, or color of skin. A state-paid 16-week maternity leave. State aid for unwed mothers. More nurseries, kindergartens and boarding schools every year. Free compulsory education for all children of school age. Free university and college education and scholarship stipends for practically the entire student body. More university and college students per 1,000 of the population than anywhere else. More engineers graduated in 1960 than the USA graduated in the last three years taken together. Some 20 million pensioners with nothing to worry about.

In the last few decades, thanks to medical achievements and rising cultural standards, infant mortality rates in many countries have dropped considerably, while the average expectation of life has gone up, as a result of which the age pattern of the population has changed greatly. The proportion of children and aged people, in other words, those who need medical help and care most, has increased.

With an eye to all this, the Soviet state has taken a number of measures to train more doctors. Today the USSR has 18 doctors for every 1,000 of the population, compared to the US figure of 12. This is not the only thing. Since the proportion of children and aged people is increasing the number of doctors for every 1,000 of the population must grow every year. In the USSR the number of doctors has increased by 29% in the last 9 years, while in the USA there has been no increase for many years now. One must also take into consideration the fact that in the USSR medical assistance is free, whereas in the USA it is very costly, being out of reach for the low-paid brackets and a considerable burden on the American working man's budget.

Before the revolution our country had one of the highest death rates in the world. Quite an achievement. Today it has the lowest.

Or take the rate of housing construction. In the last three years we have built more than 8.7 million apartment units in the urban and rural areas. Meanwhile the USA has built only 4.1 million. Last year the USSR put up more than 14 apartments for every 1,000 of the population compared to the US figure of 7.6.

In the USSR the number of schoolteachers for every 1,000 of the population is growing while in the USA it is declining. In the USSR the number of newspapers, magazines and books published for every 100 of the population is growing, while in the USA it is either continuing at the same level or is going down.

The Soviet system has proved for all the world to see that it is incomparably better suited to satisfy all the increasingly complicated requirements of human society. The USSR is fashioning its own way of life, one that has no ostentatious tinsel and accords with human aspirations for genuine progress.

The rate of growth in national income is the best general indication of the degree to which the people's material living standards are rising.

Between 1957 and 1960 Soviet national income increased by 30%, the increase per capita being 24%. In the USA the respective percentages were 7 and 4. In the last three years the growth of the per capita national income in the USA has averaged only one per cent a year. A snail's pace!

These varying results reveal best of all the advantages of the socialist system which asserts the human being's right to a decent life, opens up unprecedented vistas for the blossoming of the country's material and spiritual culture, guarantees to the working people rising living standards and advances society to communism.

X

THE GREAT VALUE-PRICE CONTROVERSY IN THE USSR AND THE PROSPECTS FOR THE USE OF MATHEMATICS TO IMPROVE THE EFFICIENCY OF SOVIET PLANNING

Man's wants are limitless. The resources available to satisfy these wants are definitely limited. How to allocate these scarce resources among alternative ends —this is the subject matter of the science of economics.

IN HIS introductory economics course, a student in the Western world is introduced to a definition of economics similar to the one above. From that time on, he presumably comes to realize that to economists the world over, the efficient allocation of resources is a matter of utmost concern. The student learns how in a "perfectly competitive" free enterprise society, productive resources are allocated not by government decree, but by the "automatic" forces of the market, how price on the one hand is determined by the interaction of demand and supply, and how it, in turn, acts as a consumption-rationing and production-inducing device. He learns that, at least according to theory, the seller will sell wherever he can get the highest price, and the buyer will buy wherever he can buy most cheaply. He understands that the producer is expected to produce the number of commodities that will yield him the largest total profit and that he will attempt to produce this output with a combination of the factors of production that minimize his cost for the given output. (And the student may even remember afterwards that the best point of output is the point where marginal costs equal marginal revenues and that the optimum combination of the factors of production is such that the marginal product of any factor divided by the marginal cost of the factor is equal to the marginal product of any other factor divided by the cost of that other factor.)

But even the student who has forgotten some of the technical aspects of economic theory will, upon brief reflection, realize that a planned economy in its attempt to maximize output is faced with certain problems that do not confront the producer in a capitalist society. If a farmer in the United States decides to buy a tractor (instead of buying another piece of land or hiring another worker or two) his reason probably is that he expects to obtain the highest return on his monetary outlay from the purchase of the tractor. But how does a planner make such a "rational" decision in an economy in which land is not for sale, in which wages are determined by government decree and not by the interaction of demand and supply, in which raw materials are allocated by the government, in which interest on capital investment is not computed as part of the cost of production of any commodity, and in which, finally, retail prices are not necessarily cost-connected? If efficiency is in any way measured by the profitability of the producing unit, how can it be measured in a society in which some commodities are purposely priced far below cost of production to encourage their consumption, while the consumption of others is discouraged by relatively high prices?

These are but a few of the economic problems that confront the planner in a noncapitalist, planned economy. During the Stalin era any attempt to solve problems related to the rational allocation of resources by the application of mathematics was discouraged if not prohibited outright. Since Stalin's death, Soviet economists have shown great interest in improving the efficiency of planning by the utilization of such tools as input-output analysis and linear programming, and by the use of electronic computers. But as these economists are supposed to accomplish their goal without ever deviating from Marxian analysis, their task is not an easy one. In their "great value-price controversy" Soviet economists today debate these and related issues and openly disagree with one another, something one would have been hard pressed to find during the Stalin era.

The first selection of *Western Views* is taken from Vsevolod Holubnychy's thorough study of the development of Soviet economic theory. Holubnychy discusses the stifling influence of the Stalin dictatorship and the reawakening of Soviet economic discussion in the post-Stalin era. However, his conclusion that Soviet economists have ample opportunities to develop meaningful economic ideas on the basis of orthodox Marxian analysis would probably be challenged by the majority of Western scholars.

Robert W. Campbell, secondly, stresses the importance of economic theory to economic planning ("Economic theory bears the same relation to planning that physics does to engineering"), discusses the contributions made towards the reconstruction of Soviet economic science by Kantorovich and Novozhilov, and comments on the reaction of other Soviet economists to the new proposals for the improvement of efficiency in Soviet economic planning. As Campbell conceives it, Soviet economists are greatly hampered by the ideological necessity imposed upon them to fit the use of mathematics and of modern economic theory into the framework of Marxian analysis.

Next, Wassily Leontief traces in his frequently quoted article what he refers to as "The Decline and Rise of Soviet Economic Science." Leontief asserts that the reawakening of Soviet economic science amounts to a long overdue adoption of Western economics, Soviet claims to the contrary notwithstanding.

Though discussing the same basic topic as the three preceding selections, British Marxist Maurice Dobb presents quite a different view of a development which he sees as "a new maturity of Marxist thought" leading towards the goal of "building a Political Economy of Socialism."

In the first selection under *Soviet Views,* V. S. Nemchinov explains the vital role that mathematics can and should play in the improvement of economic research and planning in the USSR. Nemchinov warns, however, that unless the application of mathematical methods remains but a tool subordinate to the qualitative goals of a socialist society, it could become "a 'Trojan horse,' making for the penetration of an alien and inimical ideology." A considerable part of Nemchinov's article is devoted to an attempt to refute specifically most of the arguments in Leontief's *Foreign Affairs* article (reprinted as selection 40 below).

Next, short excerpts from the writings of seven of the participants in the great Soviet value-price controversy are presented. Among the participants selected is S. G. Strumilin, statistician since 1899, central figure in the formulation of the drafts for the first and second five-year plans, and recognized dean of Soviet economists. Excerpts are included from the writings of Kantorovich and Novozhilov, whose contributions to the recent developments in Soviet economic science have been discussed in several preceding selections. Also represented are such "orthodox" Soviet economists as Kats and Boiarskii, who are critical of at least some aspects of the new theories. [It is interesting to note, in this connection, that the editors of *Voprosy Ekonomiki,* the leading theoretical economic journal in the Soviet Union, as late as February, 1961, took an official stand, backing Boyarskii's basic criticisms of Kantorovich and Novozhilov. (See their comment in the first footnote to Boyarskii's and also to Kantorovich's article on pp. 410 and 406 respectively.)] The purpose of presenting these excerpts is merely to introduce the reader to the great controversy regarding economic theory that is going on in the Soviet Union at this time. The technical, mathematical details have been omitted.[1]

A rapidly industrializing and growing planned economy must necessarily encounter ever more complex problems. If mathematical methods are to be used to aid in their scientific solution, electronic computers are undoubtedly destined to play a prominent role in the expanding spheres of economic planning, economic analysis, economic management, and economic record keeping. In the last selection, N. Kovalev, chief of the

[1] Kantorovich's famous 1939 article has been translated in its entirety by Robert W. Campbell and W. H. Marlow in *Management Science,* July, 1960.

Computer Center of the State Economic Council of the USSR, discusses this role which he expects electronic computers to play in the future. He shows some of the uses to which mathematics in general and electronic computers in particular have already been put by his agency in conjunction with other governmental institutions; he points to existing shortcomings; and he offers concrete proposals for their rectification.

WESTERN VIEWS

38

Soviet Debates on Economic Theories: An Introduction *

VSEVOLOD HOLUBNYCHY
Researcher, Institute for the Study of the USSR, Munich, Germany

The Stifling Impact of Stalin's Dictatorship

The discussion began when Stalin announced that not only political power but also the economy and society in the Soviet Union had become socialist. At first he seems to have been aware, as every other informed person was, that he was saying something utterly incompatible with the letter and spirit of Marxism-Leninism. So, at the Sixteenth Party Congress in 1930, he said that the USSR was only entering the stage of socialism, and immediately qualified his declaration by saying that this did not imply abolition of the NEP because money, commerce, and commodity relations were not yet going to be liquidated.[1] But at the Seventeenth Party Congress in 1934, having silenced all opposition, he felt free to revise Marxism-Leninism without qualification, and completely forgetting his continuation-of-the-NEP formula, he declared that full-fledged socialism had been built in the USSR, while money, commerce, and commodity production were here to stay because they did not contradict socialism, in which centralized planning dominated everything.[2]

Soviet economists knew very well at the time how Marx, Engels, and

---

* Excerpts reprinted from an article originally entitled "Recent Soviet Theories of Value," in *Studies on the Soviet Union*, New Series, Vol. I, No. 1, 1961, pp. 47-72, by permission of the Institute for the Study of the USSR, Munich, Germany.

[1] J. V. Stalin, *Sochineniya* (Works), Vol. XII, Moscow, 1949, pp. 306-307.
[2] *Ibid.*, Vol. XIII, p. 342.

Lenin envisaged their socialism, but no one would dare to question Stalin's authority if he wished to avoid the sad fate of Ryazanov, Rubin, Kushin, Groman, Bazarov, and other Marxists silenced at that time by the GPU. Moreover, Stalin's emphasis on centralized planning as the dominating force in money-commodity relations looked like an innocent and plausible item of revisionism, especially since he also promised that money-commodity relations were only temporary. Everyone understood him correctly and sycophants started to sing his praises. In 1930 he was placed on the same footing as Marx, Engels and Lenin. A legion of minor writers began to popularize his economic theories, while those with authority started to elaborate on them. K. Ostrovityanov, who had successfully mutilated his outstanding "Bukharinite" past, unequivocally declared that Soviet economics "should know no objective economic laws whatsoever" because it had just "jumped into the Realm of Freedom" in which there was only one economic category left: "the plan of the dictatorship of the proletariat." [3] For the former "semi-Trotskyite" A. Leontiev this was nothing new; he had only to reprint his 1925 *Notes on Transitional Economics* in which he had predicted that centralized plans would take the place of economic laws in Soviet economy. While for S. Strumilin all this was nothing but a triumph of his ideas about planning; he proclaimed that from now on there remained only one law: "the will to rush towards Communism." [4]

Were it not for Stalin's arbitrariness and terror, Soviet economic thought would probably have developed normally along the promising paths opened up in the twenties by such thoughtful economists as I. Rubin and E. Slutsky, instead of straying off for more than a decade in the jungle of voluntarism.

The painful consequences of the lack of economic theory and methods, however, began to be felt soon enough. It is enough to mention such facts as the complete financial collapse of the entire Donbas mining industry in 1939, when even wages were not paid for months. Yet the change was very slow, for it was only in September 1940 that an editorial in *Planovoe khozyaistvo* called for the first time for "more attention to economics and economic theory."

It was around this time, in 1940 or 1941, that in an unpublished statement Stalin urged economic theorists to work out a text-book of Soviet economics; it is said that at this time "Stalin, as the first Marxist, put forward a thesis about the necessity of commodity production under socialism as well as the operation of the law of value in an altered form." [5] This was the consummation of Stalin's economic revisionism.

The war delayed the work on the new theory, but finally, in the last

3 *Vestnik Kommunisticheskoi Akademii*, No. 4, 1933, pp. 10 ff.
4 *Planovoe khozyaistvo*, No. 8-9, 1934, pp. 200 ff.
5 *Zycie Gospodarcze*, Warsaw, No. 12, 1959, p. 12.

issue of *Pod znamenem marksizma,* in 1943, an editorial was published that reverberated throughout the world.[6] The paper did not refer to Stalin but nonetheless authoritatively declared that "commodity production" and a "transformed law of value" were operative in the USSR. This editorial was probably written by L. Leontiev. Anyhow, it was put in imperative terms, which, however, displayed nothing but intellectual calisthenics. R. Meek agrees that the logic of the argument was dubious and the use of Marxian economic terms arbitrary and inconsistent.[7] Yet to some neophytes the paper was a revelation: an attempt was even made to prove that Engels in 1844 had known what Marx would say in his *Critique of the Gotha Programme* in 1875, and that both had presaged exactly what was said in the Soviet paper.[8]

Soviet economists, however, were not at all enthusiastic about the editorial of 1943: they ignored it almost unanimously until, in 1948, Leontiev in a signed article reminded them of its main theses.[9] Instead, in the meantime, they were interested in somewhat more meaningful and immediate issues: E. Varga's debacle over the thesis of "planned capitalism" in the West, S. Strumilin's discussion of the "time factor" in capital investments, A. Notkin's theory of a "technological factor" in economic growth, E. Sollertinskaya's courageous statement on the existence of differential rent on collective farms, etc. It was not until 1951 that a group of senior economists was finally directed to write the first draft of a textbook on Soviet economics. The completed draft was sent for comments to Stalin, and these comments were published in the autumn of 1952.[10] Of particular import was Stalin's declaration to the effect that the law of value, although having "no regulating function in socialist production . . . nevertheless influences production" and as such "cannot be ignored" in price-fixing as hitherto.[11] As the two major causes of the existence of the law of value under socialism Stalin stressed (1) the difference between state and collective farm property which necessitated a commodity exchange between industry and agriculture based on money, and (2) the existence of a retail market for consumer goods in which consumers had free choice in spending their incomes. He thus confined the operation of the law of value to only those economic relations which were not yet wholly controlled by the state; in particular, he remarked, the law did not operate within the capital goods industry where products were not really bought and sold but were simply transferred from one enterprise

6 An English translation of this editorial appeared under the title "Teaching of Economics in the Soviet Union," in the *American Economic Review,* Menasha, Wis., USA, September, 1944, pp. 501-530.

7 R. L. Meek, *Studies in the Labour Theory of Value,* London, 1956, pp. 272-273.

8 *Les Cahiers de l'économie soviétique,* Paris, January–March 1947, pp. 3-4.

9 *Vestnik Akademii Nauk SSSR,* No. 1, 1948, pp. 3 ff.

10 J. Stalin, *Economic Problems of Socialism in the USSR,* Moscow, 1952.

11 *Ibid.,* pp. 23 ff.

to another by order of the planners. However, apparently still conscience-stricken because of his revision of the views of Marx and Lenin on socialism, Stalin invented a non-existent leftist critic of his doctrine, named him "Comrade Yaroshenko," quoted his views on the institutions of a moneyless and marketless economy, very similar to Marx's, ridiculed them as obviously Utopian under the present conditions, but promised that they would come true in the future, under the "second stage" of Communist society.

Needless to say, Stalin's pronouncements were hailed by all as the ultimate in wisdom. Yet the work on the economics text-book proceeded rather slowly, so much so that it even outlived Stalin. The book appeared in the autumn of 1954, incorporating everything bequeathed to it by that greatest of all economists.[12] It was full of abstruse and unpalatable ideas in the tradition of Stalin's historical materialism as outlined in the notorious Chapter IV of his *History of the CPSU, Short Course,* but as far as economics was concerned it was insipid and inane.

Yet it cannot be gainsaid that Stalin at least reminded the majority of the Soviet economists of their professional duties by having swerved their thoughts from blissful voluntarism to something called "objective economic laws." Thenceforth Soviet economic discussions began to acquire more meaning and significance, their scope began to broaden, and their character became lively and spontaneous. Of great political import was the 1954 debate over the comparative rates of growth of heavy and light industries; then, in 1954–55, there developed a revealing discussion of the nature of the turnover tax; and in 1955 the question of capital depreciation and obsolescence was raised, the debate over which continued through 1958.

The next notable change occurred in 1956, when at the Twentieth Party Congress Mikoyan openly called for a revision of Stalin's *Economic Problems of Socialism.* This brought a breath of fresh air. Economic discussion acquired new freedom and vigour. A long series of great debates on the law of value and price policy, on the efficiency of capital investments, and on agricultural costs and prices started in 1956 and lasted through 1959. In 1957–60, ground and mining rents came under discussion, and in 1959–60 the question of the location of industries, the laws of monopoly capitalism, and finally, the basic law of socialism.[13] In the post-1956 discussions, for the first time in some thirty years, Soviet econ-

[12] *Politicheskaya ekonomiya: Uchebnik* (Political Economy: A Handbook), Moscow, 1954.

[13] For these discussions the reader must consult not only *Voprosy ekonomiki* and *Planovoe khozyaistvo,* but also such journals as *Nauchny doklady vysshei shkoly; Ekonomocheskie nauki; Vestnik statistiki, Ekonomika selskogo khozyaistva; Finansy SSSR; Gorny zhurnal; Ekonomicheskaya gazeta;* as well as the journals of the universities of Moscow, Leningrad, Kiev, and Tbilisi, and the republic economic journals such as *Ekonomika Radianskoi Ukrayny,* etc.

omists tackled problems of real theoretical importance and profound political implications.

It should not be construed, of course, that these debates provided the opportunity for an entirely free expression of thought. The most important of them were thoroughly organized in the form of conferences under the auspices of the Institute of Economics of the Academy of Sciences of the USSR; others were stimulated by the editors of journals, who solicited contributions on a pre-arranged topic; but, above all, the debates were, of course, carefully watched by the apparatus of the Central Committee of the Soviet Communist Party, and, as a result, most expressions were confined to a more or less strict Party orthodoxy.

These Soviet debates have already deservedly become a current issue with leading Western students of the Soviet economy.[14] . . .

The quintessence of all recent Soviet economic debates has been a search for some objective, material, scientific method of decision-making. Most participants have in one way or another admitted and recognized that, until now, major Soviet economic decisions have been for the most part subjective and arbitrary, and have led to direct and indirect losses. It has been suggested that the reasons why Soviet economists have only now turned to this problem are: (1) that the concern with scarcity deepens as an economy gets richer,[15] (2) that, in pursuit of the aim to overtake the West at the earliest possible date, Soviet economists have become acutely conscious of the need for maximum efficiency,[16] and (3) that they have succumbed to the Western criticism of their methods.[17] All these explanations are plausible, though as to (1) and (3) it must be added that it is only now that they have been freed from the stifling pressure of Stalin's authority,[18] and as to (2) it must be pointed out that, in addition, they have realized that, during the past decade, Soviet economic growth has been steadily slowing down.[19] . . .

14 R. Schlesinger, "Strumilin and Others on the Theory for a New Price Structure," *Soviet Studies*, Oxford, July 1957, pp. 92-98; M. Dobb, "A Comment on the Discussion About Price-Policy," *Soviet Studies*, Oxford, October 1957, pp. 131-41; A. Nove, "Recent Developments in Economic Ideas," *Survey*, Washington, D.C., November–December 1957, pp. 19-26; A. Nove, "The Problems of 'Success Indicators'," *Ekonomica*, London, February 1958, pp. 1-13; W. Leontief, "The Decline and Rise of Soviet Economic Science," *Foreign Affairs*, New York, January 1960, pp. 261-72; M. Dobb, "The Revival of Theoretical Discussion Among Soviet Economists," *Science & Society*, Washington, D.C., Fall 1960, pp. 289-311; B. Ward, "Kantorovich on Economic Calculation," *The Journal of Political Economy*, Chicago, December 1960, pp. 545-56; A. Zauberman, "The Soviet Debate on the Law of Value and Price Formation," in G. Grossmann (ed.): *Value and Plan*, Berkeley, 1960, pp. 17-46. (Includes comment by A. Bergson.)

15 Zauberman, *op. cit.*, p. 17.

16 Nove, in *Survey, op. cit.*, p. 21.

17 Leontief, *op. cit.*, p. 265.

18 Cf. Dobb in *Science and Society*, op. cit., pp. 289 ff.

19 Cf. V. Holubnychy, "Le ralentissement des rhythmes d'accroissement de l'économie soviétique," *Problèmes soviétiques*, Institute for the Study of the USSR, Munich, No. 2, 1959, pp. 52-85.

Doctrinal Limitations and Opportunities

It is not easy to appreciate fully the significance and trends of these debates without sufficient knowledge of Marxian economic theory. The statements to the effect that Marxism (it would be more accurate to say Stalinism) hampers the development of Soviet economic thought and prevents Soviet economists from understanding and embracing Western economic ideas and Western critiques of Soviet economics, though to a large extent true, nonetheless belong to those few hackneyed clichés which have become petrified through conventional repetition, yet have produced little, if any, positive effect on the study of the Soviet economy. While most writers thus blame Marxism and some even strangely deny its significance entirely,[20] only a few voices are heard calling for serious study of the role of Marxism in Soviet affairs, and even these come largely not from the economists but from political scientists and historians.[21] Paradoxically, in spite of all the ado about Marxism, not a single satisfactory empirical study of its relation to Soviet economics is as yet in existence. As a result, we have an appalling situation: while Soviet economists are truly hampered by Marxism in their appreciation and acceptance of Western views, but have no other way out, Western economists, in turn, do not realize or foresee the opportunities still open to Soviet economists within the framework of a Marxism freed from Stalin's stifling authority.

Recent debates and events in the field of publication in the USSR seem to call for a careful re-examination and differentiation regarding the persons and views in the West against which Soviet dogmatism is really directed. Recent translation and publication in the USSR of several American, British, and German books on the methodology of input/output analysis, linear programming, location theory, and mathematical statistics indicate that Soviet Marxists are not opposed to practical, methodological Western suggestions applicable to the Soviet economic system. They are, however, invariably opposed to Western psychological theories of value and their outgrowth, welfare economics. Yet, whether accidental or not, the fact is that the foremost students of Soviet economics in the West have come from the welfare and neo-liberal schools

---

[20] A. Gerschenkron's article in *Soviet Economic Growth,* ed. by A. Bergson, Evanston, Ill., 1953, p. 26.

[21] Cf. D. von Mohrenschild, "Russian Area Studies and Research Since World War II," *The Russian Review,* Washington, D.C., April 1953, p. 113; H. Koch, "Experience in Research on the USSR," in *Proceedings of the Sixth Conference of the Institute for the Study of the USSR: The Aims and Methods of Research in the USSR,* Munich, 1955, pp. 5-6. The only notable exception among the economists was a paper by H. Raupach, "Uber den Ausgangspunkt einer kritischen Wertung der Sowjetwirtschaft," *Schmollers Jahrbuch,* No. 5, 1951, pp. 57-68, though he suggested that more attention be paid to Lenin than to Marx.

of thought, and they have also been regularly in the forefront of the criticism of Soviet economics. As a result, there has developed a strikingly incongruous relationship between the economic ideologies of Soviet economists and Western students of Soviet economics.

Whereas Marxism is undoubtedly the thick lead wall which protects Soviet economists from the critical radiation of Western welfare ideas, it would be wrong to construe that, by itself, it is completely vapid and can no longer give birth to interesting and meaningful economic ideas. Such impressions usually arise from a smattering and rudimentary knowledge of Marx's writings. . . .

The reason why Marx is misinterpreted is rather simple: barring prejudiced twisting of his positions, it is merely insufficient reading and research. It is a fact that can be adduced merely by looking at sources cited in the footnotes of most writers. Most interpreters of Marx both in the Soviet Union and abroad have read at best only the three volumes of *Capital.* Yet these comprise, according to the number of pages, not more than some 45 per cent of all the mature economic papers of Marx! Disregarding various subjective reasons for not having read Marx fully or carefully, the objective reason for such an incomplete knowledge of Marxian economics is that Marx is not available complete in any single language. Having studied all major bibliographies of the published works of Marx and Engels,[22] the author of the present article has arrived at the conclusion, based on an approximate count of pages, that of all the economic papers of Marx there have appeared, up to 1956, in German—98%, in Russian—69%, in French—56% and in English—50%. In all other languages, less than one half of Marxian economics is available. . . .

The salient feature of the Soviet-type total state monopoly is its ability to control not only the supply and prices of commodities but also, to a significant extent, the demand for them. This happens because the monopoly is here almost the only employer of all factors of production (*i.e.,* it is a total monopsonist) and hence the only payer of all national income. . . .

After all, it was Lenin who said that "socialism is nothing else but a state-capitalist monopoly, turned over to the use of the people and, to that extent, one that has ceased to be a capitalist monopoly." [23] Whether or not the present Soviet state monopoly is for the use of the people, is, of course, the crux of the matter and a big question.

22 L. A. Levin, *Bibliografiya proizvedenii K. Marksa i F. Engelsa* (Bibliography of the Works of K. Marx and F. Engels), Moscow, 1948; M. Rubel, *Bibliographie des oeuvres de Karl Marx,* Paris, 1956 and 1960.

23 V. I. Lenin, *Izbrannye proizvedeniya* (Selected Works), Moscow, 1946, Vol. II, p. 100.

39

Marxian Analysis, Mathematical Methods, and Scientific Economic Planning: Can Soviet Economists Combine Them? *

ROBERT W. CAMPBELL
Indiana University

Like other aspects of Soviet life, economics has been revivified by Stalin's death. The most visible part of its reawakening has been an extensive discussion of, and experimentation with, institutional arrangements, though even questions of strategy and basic policy have also been exposed to an unwonted amount of free discussion. The real measure of this freedom, however, is that the search for theoretical clarification, which inevitably accompanies discussion of practical issues, has been allowed to develop in a way not permitted since the late twenties. One aspect of this dramatic change is the controversy which has developed around the use of mathematics in economics. After long aversion to any introduction of mathematical reasoning into analysis of economic relationships, the Russians are now thinking about the possible usefulness of input-output techniques in balancing supply and demand and in price planning and about the application of linear programming to enterprise planning, and have begun to resort to mathematical models to explore the abstract essence of practical problems.

The expectation was that mathematical economics could be borrowed from the capitalist world just as implements and techniques are. One of the common themes in the post-Stalin discovery of what economists in the capitalist world have been up to is the need to sort out the usable from the nonusable, and to purge mathematical methods of their bourgeois interpretations before they are applied in the Soviet economy. As one might expect, hopes for such an antiseptic transfusion are likely to be

* Reprinted from an article entitled "Marx, Kantorovich, and Novozhilov: *Stoimost'* versus Reality," in *Slavic Review*, October, 1961, pp. 402-418, by permission of the author and the publisher. English translation of references to Russian authors, articles, and books in footnotes (in letters of the Russian alphabet in the original) from the reprint in *Radio Free Europe/Munich, Research and Evaluation Department, Background Information USSR*, January 2, 1962, pp. 1-16, by permission of Radio Free Europe.

disappointed, and even the beginning of Soviet work on mathematical techniques has led to a search for clarification of the theory of value. Mathematics and computers in themselves are ideologically neutral; but the mathematization of any science implies measurement, and in economics the unit of measurement is value. Hence, as one of the participants in the controversy has said, understanding how to measure value is basic to all practical problems of calculation. But progress toward an improved explanation of value and an understanding of its connection with the problem of allocation will require Soviet economists to free themselves from the limitations of Marxist theory. In fact this emancipation has nearly been accomplished already in the writings of two of the participants in the discussion of the use of mathematical methods in economics, L. V. Kantorovich and V. V. Novozhilov. Thus apart from its manifest content, the term "mathematical methods in economics," which is bandied about so freely by Soviet economists, has also become a euphemism for a new theory of value. The present article describes this search for a new theory of value.

Deficiencies of the Labor Theory of Value

As an introduction we must review briefly the divergent histories of the mainstream of world economic theory and Marxism. The basic theory of economics has come of age only in about the last half century. In this period the bits and pieces, the partial insights of earlier years, have been integrated into a unified general theory. Marxist economics, on the other hand, has spent this period marking time in a blind alley, to use a favorite Soviet metaphor. Marxist value theory broke away from the tradition that prevailed in the time of Ricardo, and has missed out on the great scientific success of generalization and unification which has taken place in Western value theory since then.

The nature of this achievement can be explained as follows. One of the central preoccupations of economics has always been what determines price. Movements of foreign exchange rates, the distribution of income among social classes, changes in the general price level, and so on, all involve questions of relative prices, how much one thing is worth in terms of others. Hence the search for a general explanation (i.e., theory) of value has always occupied the center of the stage. The practical questions that economists have struggled to unravel have always led back to this as the basic theoretical problem to be solved. During most of the nineteenth century no consistent and satisfactory explanation was offered. There were cost theories and utility theories, to mention only one dichotomy, and any one theorist might well try to embrace several different theories and use them in different parts of his book for different problems. Ricardo, for instance, has two theories of value—one for the value of land, and another very different one for the value of everything else. The reconciliation of all these conflicting partial explanations into a unified general theory of value came only in the late nineteenth century with the concept of general equilibrium and the reduction of all explanations to the common denominator of utility by the writers of the utility school.

In the process, it also came to be understood that the explanation of value is only one aspect of the central problem of economics. The question of relative prices is inextricably intertwined with the explanation of relative quantities. Indeed the reconciliation and integration of all the conflicting parts of value theory as it had previously existed was made possible only by widening the perspective to take in the question of what determines the proportions among different kinds of output along with the question of what determines value. One reflection of this new insight into the problem of value was the formulation of a new definition of economics, the one commonly used today, as the theory of allocation of scarce resources among competing ends. This definition slights the value aspect of the problem, but its rapid adoption was a response to the profound insight that economic theory must explain not only value but also quantities and the interdependence of both these sets of magnitudes.

It was this achievement that the Marxists and their Soviet intellectual heirs missed out on. The Russians retain, through Marx, ideas about value extant at the time of Ricardo. Marx took the theory of value as it then existed, and compounded from some of its confusions a theory of the dynamics of the capitalist system. (It might be more accurate to describe the process the other way round: Marx had the conclusions and was trying to show how they flowed rigorously and inevitably from the theory of value then generally accepted. With the benefit of hindsight we may look back on his effort as a *reductio ad absurdum* technique for proving the deficiencies of Ricardian value theory.) Thus the bondage of a Marxist heritage in economic theory is not so much that the Marxist view is simply wrong in one particular (i.e., that it assumes that value is created only by labor) as that it does not comprehend the basic problem of economic theory; it has not achieved a full understanding of what a valid economic theory must illuminate. That achievement came in the mainstream of world economic theorizing only after Marxism had already taken the turning to enter the blind alley mentioned above.

This isolation of Marxist economic thinkers from the rest of the intellectual community has not been natural or easy to maintain. Marxist groups have had to wage a constant struggle to preserve the sanctified shortcomings of their economic doctrine against the encroachments of greater sophistication, but they have considered it important to do so because of the central place that the labor theory of value holds in the

Marxist theory of the transition from capitalism to socialism. The stagnation of economic theorizing within the Marxist tradition of economic thought has resulted in an irony often commented on. The Soviet planned economy, in which the efficient allocation of resources to achieve competing goals is a constant preoccupation, has muddled through with no body of theory to explain the implications of actual and potential choices. It must seek its guidance in a theory which not only misunderstands value but which does not even envisage the question of value as having any connection with rational allocation.

This is a supremely unsatisfactory situation, full of tension. As explained above, in the market economy the notion of describing an optimal allocation of all society's resources was essentially an abstract construct, imagined in the process of integrating all the bits and pieces of economics into a theory of choice and value. The social necessity for such an allocation among the competing ends is not self-evident to the individuals in Western society, where the allocation results from the impersonal operation of the price system. In the Soviet economy, on the other hand, the allocation of all society's resources among alternative uses is a highly visible and operational process, which calls out for some sort of theoretical conceptions to clarify and inform the manipulation of it. At the same time a strong motive to find a unified theory of economics grows out of preoccupation with questions of measuring cost and value. Despite central planning there is still a tremendous need in the Soviet system for decentralized calculation of benefits and gains among alternatives, and these calculations must always be cast in terms of some common denominator of value. At the micro-economic level the Russians are engaged in a quest for what they call "effectiveness," but their efforts to calculate effectiveness always founder on the inadequacy of their understanding of value and how it is related to the problem of choice in its allocation aspects. This is clearly an unstable situation; the practice of planning calls for theoretical guidance which Marxist value theory is incapable of providing. Economic theory bears the same relation to planning that physics does to engineering. It provides a model of concepts and interrelations that makes it possible to comprehend the dependence of consequences on other variables as a prelude to manipulation. When Soviet planners seek such insight in Marx, they are not likely to find anything relevant, or if they find something on the subject, it is likely to be misleading. What is needed is some way of seeing the process whole—a vision that makes clear the interdependence of the problem of allocation and the problem of value.

Failing to find such a vision in Marx, practical planners in the Soviet Union are continually trying to make one up for themselves. There are innumerable instances in which planners in some corner of the economy are rediscovering some of the basic ways of economic reasoning, figuring out for themselves some of the basic ideas of value and allocation. It was surely inevitable, for instance, that electrical engineers and mining engineers would come to realize that the condition for efficient allocation of a program among production units working in parallel is equality of marginal cost.[1] Those who are called on every day to decide how far to carry the substitution of capital for labor in designing production facilities quickly come to realize that there must be a limit, and common-sense considerations soon suggest what the nature of that limit is. The difficulty is that these creative responses by individual thinkers have never coalesced into a general theory of allocation and value on the scale of the entire national economy, and that is what is needed. The failure to achieve such unification has been due partly to the fact that the theorists to whom this responsibility is allotted in a modern specialized society were hobbled by Marxism, and such generalization would inevitably contradict some of the Marxist simplicities. Moreover, the task of generalization and integration is probably more difficult than the development of partial theories and explanations.

The seminal works on the problem of value and allocation by V. V. Novozhilov and L. V. Kantorovich originated in precisely the way we have described, as efforts to deal with partial problems of calculation. Novozhilov is an economist who at one point tried his hand at the problem of rational criteria for investment choice, with which Soviet economists have long struggled. In trying to set out conditions for maximizing the effectiveness of investment expenditures, he found that no answer could be given except as part of the answer to a larger question of criteria for the effective allocation of *all* resources. Kantorovich, who is really a mathematician rather than an economist, was drawn to the problem when he was asked to solve a highly specific, parochial, and actually insignificant problem of allocation. But in bringing to bear the broad vision of a mathematician upon this problem of allocation within a limited framework, he discovered concepts and operations for clarifying the whole problem of value and resource allocation on a national economic scale. In making these advances, both men inevitably came into conflict with the labor theory of value as developed by Marx, and this is the revolutionary and controversial feature of their work.

The Objectively Determined Valuations of Kantorovich

The development of Kantorovich's thought can be briefly summarized as follows. In the late thirties, the Plywood Trust in Leningrad asked

[1] Such propositions are developed, for instance in V. M. Goristein, *The Most Profitable Distribution of Loads Between Power Stations Working in Parallel* (Moscow–Leningrad, 1949) and N. V. Volodomonov, *Mining Rent and Principles of Assessing Ore Deposits.* (Moscow, 1959).

the help of the Institute of Mathematics and Mechanics of Leningrad State University for help in solving a production-scheduling problem. The Trust had several different kinds of machines for stripping logs for plywood, and the machines had different productivities, in terms of volume of logs handled, depending on what kind of logs were to be handled. The proportions among the different kinds of logs to be worked on the machines were given, and the problem was to assign the different kinds of logs among different machines so as to make possible the maximum throughput per unit of time, or in other words to maximize the productivity of the machines. Kantorovich was asked to help find the solution to this problem.

It is logical enough to appeal to a mathematician for help in such a problem. There is a whole branch of mathematics concerned with just the problem of finding *maxima* and *minima* of interrelated variables under specified conditions. But when the problem of the logs and machines was formulated as the maximization of a function subject to certain conditions, it was not the kind of problem that could be solved by the traditional methods of analysis. This did not mean that it was insoluble but that some practically usable technique for finding the solution had to be worked out, and this is what Kantorovich did.[2] His method involved a modification of the use of Lagrange multipliers of traditional analysis to the needs of the problem as he had formulated it. The multipliers could be found by an iterative process, and once found they could be used to find the solution of the problem. That he happened to stumble on this technique for solving the problem was purely an accident. The whole class of linear programming problems, as this kind of problem later came to be called, were rediscovered in the United States, but were solved here at first by a different approach called the "simplex method."[3] That Kantorovich happened on this particular technique, however, was of great significance, since the multipliers he employed turned out to have the same significance as prices in Western value theory, and his trial-and-error search for them an analogue of the process of price determination in a market economy. At the time, Kantorovich thought of these multipliers as simply an intermediate step in the process of finding the set of variables he was interested in, that is, the allocation of log types among machines to maximize throughput. He did note that the multipliers had some significance in relation to the problem: they represented certain trade-off possibilities that one

[2] His explanation of his approach is in *Mathematical Methods for Organizing and Planning Production.* (Leningrad, 1939). This has been translated and published as "Mathematical Methods of Organizing and Planning Production" in *Management Science,* July, 1960.

[3] For a history of linear programming and an explanation of its relationship to traditional value theory, see Robert Dorfman, Paul Samuelson, and Robert Solow, *Linear Programming and Economic Analysis* (New York: McGraw-Hill, 1958).

might wish to consider in making decisions about the allocation involved. However, it seems quite clear that he did not then realize the broad significance of these multipliers as indexes of value.

As is widely known, this discovery was almost completely neglected in the Soviet Union. Such a fate is somewhat difficult to understand. Besides solving the specific problem of the Plywood Trust, Kantorovich had remarked that a great variety of production planning problems could be cast in the same form and hence would be amenable to solution by the same means. Moreover, he made no little effort to pave the way for the widespread application of linear programming to practical problems. The original publication contains a classic defense of abstract theorizing in the form of a rebuttal to all the objections that he supposed "practical" people would make to the mystifications of a mere mathematician. He also took pains to describe a wide variety of situations faced every day by Soviet planners where his method could provide useful guidance; and the Institute sponsored several conferences to bring together mathematicians and planning personnel to explore the feasibility of such practical applications.

Nevertheless, Kantorovich never succeeded in arousing much interest, although he apparently continued to work on linear programming. There is a short list of articles on the subject,[4] which appeared during the forties, but it seems doubtful if more than a handful of Soviet economists had even heard of Kantorovich up to the early fifties.

In the meantime, linear programming was rediscovered independently in the United States a short while after Kantorovich's original paper. In sharp contrast to the Soviet history, it quickly found wide application in practical problems of production planning in the United States, and was also quickly reconciled with and assimilated by the body of traditional economic theory. Ironically, one can find in the extensive literature outside the Soviet Union practical applications illustrating all those potential uses which Kantorovich had pointed out in his pioneer article.

Despite the lack of interest in his discovery, Kantorovich apparently continued to think about its applications and about its general economic significance. When the Soviet infatuation with mathematical methods in economics after Stalin's death had finally made the climate right, Kantorovich was rediscovered as a Soviet pioneer, the original inventor of linear programming. The Academy of Sciences published a full length book by him entitled *Economic Calculation of the Opti-*

---

[4] These include L. V. Kantorovich "On the Transference of Mass," *Reports to the Academy of Science,* No. 7-8, 1942, L. V. Kantorovich, "Selection of Supplies Giving the Maximal Output of Sawn Timber with a Given Assortment," *Forestry Industry,* No. 7, 1949, and L. V. Kantorovich and M. K. Gavurin, "The Application of Mathematical Methods in the Principles of the Analysis of Loads," in the volume *Problems of Raising the Effectiveness of Transport* (Moscow, 1949).

mum Utilization of Resources,[5] in which the method and its implications for value theory and for allocation are explained.

This is a remarkable book. The title itself represents a significant advance, betraying as it does a focus on the problem of the allocation of resources. What distinguishes it from the earlier work is that in it Kantorovich has now fully recognized the significance of his multipliers as indexes of value, and that he has integrated the theory of value and the theory of allocation. This vision is boldly proclaimed by relabeling the multipliers of the earlier work as "objectively determined valuations" (*ob'ektivno obuslovlennye otsenki*). The term is an artful invention. It not only goes as far as one may with propriety in a Marxist society toward saying that these multipliers actually express value, but it also symbolizes the integration of the value problem and the allocation problem. He calls the values "objectively determined" because they are uniquely defined by the conditions of the problem. The allocation of resources which maximizes (or minimizes, depending on the nature of the problem) the variable of interest is consistent with only one set of values for the multipliers. Kantorovich does not use the word *stoimost'* to describe his indexes of value since that term has already been pre-empted by orthodox Marxist value theory. Nevertheless he is perfectly clear on the point that "value" in any meaningful sense is defined by his *otsenki* rather than by *stoimost'*.

The new book contains much else in addition to this basic discovery. Kantorovich has used his method to deal with problems of capital allocation, and he has long sections developing the proposition that the familiar deficiences of *khozraschet* (which we can define for our purposes here as the technique of administrative decentralization in a centrally planned economy) can be overcome if the objectively determined valuations are substituted for the kind of prices, based on bookkeeping costs, that the Russians now have. His *otsenki* reflect not only the cost aspects of value but also the demand aspects, and their use will therefore discourage those characteristic irrationalities of the Soviet system in which a producer is tempted to do something that looks cheap but is actually a waste of scarce and valuable resources, or to do something that seems very productive but really produces something not vitally needed. In short, Kantorovich has reconstructed most of the significant propositions of the body of production theory previously developed in the West, though in the modern linear programming form rather than in the traditional form which assumed continuous differentiable production functions. And in contrast to the neglect of his earlier work, his ideas are now being widely disseminated not only by

[5] *The Economic Calculation of the Best Utilization of Resources* (Moscow, Publishing House of the Academy of Sciences, USSR, 1959).

the book, but also through articles, papers at conferences, and educational programs for training young economists in the new mathematical methods.

Novozhilov's Theory of Value

The second contributor to the renaissance of economic science in the Soviet Union, Novozhilov, also arrived at general conceptions of value by way of a limited problem of resource allocation—the capital allocation problem. The history of that problem cannot be recapitulated in detail here, and the reader is referred to the paper by Grossman.[6] The basis of the controversy over capital allocation was that ideological difficulties were encountered in any attempt to formulate practical rules for deciding how far Soviet designers should go in substituting capital for labor in designing new products, new plants, and new processes. Any workable rules necessarily implied the productivity of capital, a proposition in conflict with the labor theory of value. Moreover, there was a danger of getting involved in the question of the proper division of investment between the consumer-goods and producer-goods industries. The subject was therefore politically as well as ideologically treacherous, and after a short flurry of discussion in the twenties, most economists carefully avoided it. Novozhilov published several papers in which he tried to find an approach that would avoid both these dangers.[7] Actually his basic proposition concerning the theory of value and allocation were developed in these early papers, and his more recent publications contain only restatement, extension to additional problems, and mathematical demonstrations. Nevertheless, we will take as the text for the following discussion one of these more recent papers, "The Measurement of Expenditure and Its Results in the Socialist Economy," published in 1959.[8]

This paper is a wonderful document. It has great appeal to a Western economist as a vicarious rebuttal of all the traditional nonsense of Soviet economists. Novozhilov goes unerringly to the point, with pithy comments on the sterility of the clichés with which Soviet economists treat problems of value and allocation. The following paraphrase of his introduction gives the tone of the whole paper:

[6] Gregory Grossman, "Scarce Capital and Soviet Doctrine," *Quarterly Journal of Economics*, August 1953.

[7] V. V. Novozhilov, "Methods of Measuring the Economic Effectiveness of Planning and Project Variants," *Works of the Leningrad Industrial Institute*, No. 4, 1939, and "Methods of Finding the Mimimal Expenditure in a Socialist Economy," *Works of the Leningrad Technical Institute*, No. 1, 1946. These two papers have been published in translation in *International Economic Papers*, No. 6, 1956.

[8] "Measurement of Expenditure and its Results in a Socialist Economy," in the volume *The Application of Mathematics in Economic Research*, ed. by V. S. Nemchinov (Moscow, 1959).

One of the most important problems of our economic science today is the problem of measuring the expenditure and results of socialist production. In fact, that is the main problem. It is natural that much attention is devoted to the methods of economic calculation. There are many books and articles on the subject and not a few conferences have been concerned with the discussion of this question. However, all this huge effort has not yet led to a solution of the problem. The confusion stems from the absence of a correct methodology of measuring expenditure [i.e., the absence of a correct theory of value]. In practice our planners have found it indispensable to make adjustments in the value magnitudes they manipulate in order to avoid absurd conclusions. My objective in this paper is to reconcile theory and practice and to improve the latter through clarification of the theory.

His answer to the problem of how to measure cost is a theory of value based on "opportunity cost." That is, it takes account not only of the labor used in the production of a commodity but also of other resources used, such as land and capital, on the grounds that these are limited in supply, and that their use in the production of one good means that they cannot be used to save on the labor required for the production of some other good.

He begins by formulating the general task of calculation in the socialist economy as one of maximizing the effectiveness of labor, by which he means producing the national output with as little labor expenditure as possible. However, this is not possible just by minimizing the labor cost of producing each component of the total output separately. The problem is that in addition to the direct, obvious labor input into each good there is a second kind of labor expenditure, which he describes as "inversely related expenditures of labor" (*zatraty obratnoi sviazi*). This concept is identical with the concept of opportunity costs. These originate in the circumstance that there are some kinds of input that are in short supply in any given planning period. If the labor input into a particular product is minimized by substituting these scarce inputs for direct labor, then the labor cost of outputs elsewhere in the economy will rise in consequence. To reconcile the local efforts to minimize the cost of each good separately with the objective of achieving the minimum labor input for all output taken together, these inversely related costs must be taken into account. To make this possible, it is necessary to have a measure indicating the effectiveness of each scarce input in saving labor. If these costs are known, then they should be taken as the appropriate price tags for such nonlabor inputs in economic calculation. Thus all partial decisions aimed at minimizing costs will take into account not only direct expenditures of labor but also the indirectly related expenditures of labor, and the totality of partial efforts at cost minimization will be consistent with the aim of minimizing the labor input for all output taken together. He later on develops a mathematical proof for these assertions, and before he is done he has shown how the allocation and value problems interact. Value is something that cannot be determined just by accounting; it emerges only from the problem of allocating resources optimally.

All this is perfectly familiar to economists outside the Soviet Union, except for the formulation of the problem as one of minimizing the labor input required to produce an assigned program of total output. The Western economist would formulate the problem as one of finding the values coincident with maximizing the output from given resources. The formal essence of the two problems is identical, but Novozhilov's approach permits him to avoid analyzing what determines the proper assortment of final output, and also expresses all his values (including the inversely related expenditures) in terms of labor inputs, thus preserving an appearance of Marxist orthodoxy.

Armed with a competent conception of value, Novozhilov vanquishes a good share of the problems that confuse the Soviet planner and economist. With a mere flick of this powerful weapon he parts those Gordian knots that Soviet economic theorists have worried fruitlessly for three decades. How can the comparative performance of enterprises in unlike circumstances be compared? Charge for the differential advantages that some enjoy! How stint the importunate demands of project designers for "deficit" good? Price goods not at *stoimost'*, but at their opportunity costs! How maximize the effectiveness of investment resources? Suffer them not to be used except where the returns justify their opportunity costs! How should a socialist society reckon with obsolescence? Novozhilov's answer is not the customary twenty pages of twaddle, but a few short paragraphs directed faultlessly at the essential issues.

Altogether it makes exhilarating reading for a non-Soviet economist, and one suspects that most Soviet students would have the same reaction. This is not to say that Novozhilov never stumbles. His theory of value has the fundamental deficiency of dealing with value only as it reflects production constraints, and when he approaches a problem such as the proper rate of accumulation or the proper choice of output mix, his concept of value is of little help. In these passages, in contrast with other sections of the paper, there are no mathematical formulas, and even his vocabulary—terms like welfare, wants, useful results—becomes fuzzy. It lacks analytical power since it is not infused with meaning drawn from his theory of value. It does not necessarily follow that he does not understand these issues. His vagueness may only reflect discretion.

With so much accomplished, what remains to be done? Have not the Russians overleaped a century of Western thought and made good at last their cultural lag in the science of economics? That would be too sweeping a judgment, as we shall see in a moment, but certainly these two works represent a great achievement. Kantorovich and Novozhilov have shown convincingly that other things besides labor are scarce, and that the problem of value and the problem of allocation are inseparable. They make it clear that value is not something metaphysical, as Marx made it, but that what something is worth is clearly defined as an index of its scarcity in relation to objectives. What are the prospects for the success of this revolution?

The Response of Soviet Economists

It is too early to predict with assurance whether these innovations in the theory of value will be able to make their way into Soviet economic thought and teaching. There are, however, very strong factors favoring their survival. Much damage has been done just in the opportunity allowed for their expression; once Soviet economists have had a chance to ponder them, they can scarcely be rejected except by arbitrary repression. If these innovations are as unorthodox as we have argued, then one might hold that such must be the outcome. But the counter-argument is that heretical though sophisticated value theory may be, it is wonderfully useful, like traditional logic and quantum mechanics. Hence there must be strong pressure on Soviet economists to gain an understanding of it, even though the novices in those secular seminaries, the economics and philosophic faculties of universities, may still be required to learn by rote the old catechism.

In the meantime Soviet economists are not willing to be converted without at least a protest. Kantorovich's book contains a foreword by Academician Nemchinov, expressing strong reservations about some of the implications Kantorovich draws. Similarly the reviews of both men's works in the authoritative economic journals have been unfavorable. However, the most interesting thing about this criticism is that the critics seem to understand very well what Kantorovich and Novozhilov are doing. The new theory has been given competent, if reluctant, sponsors for its debut. They have done their homework well and have thoroughly grasped the logic of the new approach. Their reactions reflect the difficulties of dealing with this threat to orthodoxy. Nemchinov agrees that the objectively determined evaluations and the inversely related expenditures are useful concepts, acceptable when kept in their proper place, as techniques for solving particular production problems. The main theme of his protest is that the temptation to find a more general significance in them must be resisted. The novel concepts have nothing to do with value, but are just a special kind of indicator used in a technical problem. Nemchinov is embarrassed by Kantorovich's intransigence in openly labeling his numbers as objectively determined valuations, though he sees perfectly well that this is precisely what they are. In fact he is sufficiently convinced that he equivocates in his denial of their general significance, and in the end does not really deny the possibility of their extension to an economy-wide framework but only says that such applications have not yet been worked out. In evaluating Novozhilov's work he is much comforted that labor remains the *numéraire* for all elements of Novozhilov's measure of value, but is upset by the problem that in Marxist theory rent-like elements (which is one way to describe the opportunity costs) have nothing to do with value but are only a distributive category.

Boiarskii, too, in the review in *Planovoe khoziaistvo* [9] seems to see the truth of Kantorovich's arguments, but also sees that they lead to the wrong conclusions. His review has a schizophrenic air. The first part is devoted to explaining the ideas and praising the practical usefulness of linear programming. But in the second part he says that the book demonstrates the danger of turning a mathematician loose to deal with issues that Marxist economic science has already settled. The real conclusion of his review seems to be that there is nothing wrong with these theories about the proper allocation of resources except that they lead to un-Marxist conclusions about the measurement of value. Boiarskii is never able to explain, however, where Kantorovich got off the track toward something useful and arrived at something harmful.

The review by Kats in *Voprosy ekonomiki* [10] also exudes intellectual distress. He begins with praise, but is then at such a loss to explain what is wrong with the mathematical approach that he is obliged to resort to all sorts of irrelevant and ridiculous criticisms. For instance he complains that it is a weakness to take the composition of output and the amount of resources as given, but as will be explained below, that is one of the ground rules imposed by the Soviet setting. The reasons for the distress are obvious. The only refutation would be to say that the assumptions are wrong or that the mathematics is wrong. For instance, it might be denied that factors other than labor are in short supply or that they can be substituted for labor. (This is indeed the implicit difference between the Marxist conception of value and better ones.) But such a criticism would outrage common sense. It is hard to see how the reviews could be otherwise, of course. Reviewmanship is an exacting art in the Soviet Union, and one of its first rules is to evaluate the conclusions rather than the logic of an argument.

What is really subversive about Kantorovich and Novozhilov is that they are right, and to allow them to propagate their views is to give

[9] A. Ya. Boiarskii, "On Mathematical Methods and the Demands of Economic Science," *Planned Economy*, No. 1, 1960.

[10] A. Kats, "Economic Theory and Application of Mathematics in Economics," *Voprosy Ekonomiki*, No. 11, 1960.

them the victory. They have formulated the problem, found the solution, derived the corollaries, and all one can do is challenge either
their formulations or their mathematics. It is disquieting to good
Marxists to see such concepts as rent, returns for capital, and opportunity costs emerge as implications of assumptions with which they
cannot quarrel, but this unpleasantness is no refutation. The only
protection is to bar mathematicians from the temple. Once they are
allowed intercourse with the rest of the intellectual community, they
have a tremendous advantage. The veneration of science in the Soviet
Union confers great prestige on mathematics, which is after all, the
"queen and servant of science." Kantorovich is by all accounts an un-
assuming, even diffident, man, but shielded by mathematics he has
shown no hesitation in pressing his attacks on existing Soviet value
theory. At the recent conference on the use of mathematics in economics he replied quite boldly to his critics. Nemchinov in his closing
remarks at the conference made a point of rebuking Kantorovich for
upsetting the "creative and comradely spirit" of the conference by
"underestimating and deprecating the work of Soviet economists." [11]
Just what Kantorovich had said to merit this rebuke is not revealed,
but it is well known that he considers Soviet economic theory mostly
claptrap. At the 1959 annual meeting of the Division of Economics,
Philosophy and Law of the Academy of Sciences he expressed the following unflattering opinion of the contribution made by economists
to the economic achievements of the USSR:

How great is the role of economists in these achievements? The accumulation
of practical experience in economics and planning has played a definite role
here, but this has not been at all generalized by economic science. . . . In the
forty-second year of the existence of the socialist state our economic science
does not know precisely what the law of value means in a socialist society or
how it should be applied. It does not know what socialist rent is, or whether
in general there ought to be some calculations of the effectiveness of capital
investment, and if so, just how. We are offered as the latest discovery in the
field of economics, for example, the proposition that "the law of value does
not govern but only influences," or that "the means of production are not simply commodities but commodities of a particular kind," and so on.[12]

The probable outcome of this co-operation with mathematicians is
foreshadowed in one of Nemchinov's remarks in summing up the results of the volume on *The Application of Mathematics in Economic
Research.* He warns:

[11] Summaries of some of the presentations at this conference, held in April 1960, in
Moscow, are given in *Voprosy Ekonomiki,* No. 8, 1960. The rebuke to Kantorovich is
on p. 122.

[12] *Vestnik Akademii Nauk SSSR,* No. 4, 1959, p. 60.

. . . the chief peril in applying mathematical methods to economics is that the qualitative nature of the economic phenomena being studied falls into oblivion. In the winged expression of V. I. Lenin, directed at idealistic theories in physics and mathematics, the perversion of the role of mathematics both in natural sciences and social sciences is that in these theories matter disappears and only equations remain.[13]

Invoking that lost cause to defend Marxist prejudices against equations conveys a presentiment of defeat.

If our prognosis is right and these innovations are accepted after proper exegesis in Marxist terminology, they will only lead to further trouble. As explained earlier, these theories of value and allocation are still seriously deficient. They take as given some very important variables in the economic system, such as the composition of the final bill of goods and, as one aspect of this, the division of the national output into investment goods and consumption goods. To employ a distinction that played an important role in the development of Western economic thought, Kantorovich's and Novozhilov's theories are *cost* theories of value. In terms of Alfred Marshall's famous metaphor, they still imply that since one blade of the scissors is stationary (that is, that demand is given) it is the action of the other blade (cost or supply) that cuts the paper. They represent an advance over the more primitive labor-cost theory of value that Marx employed, but still fall short of complete generality.

One criticism directed by Soviet writers against Kantorovich's objectively determined valuations is that they are not absolute. One of the factors that "objectively determines" them is the composition of output, which is taken as the starting point. One of the speakers at the conference on mathematical methods in economics pointed out that whether or not the objectively determined valuations mean anything depends on the "correctness" of the output mix postulated as a constraint.[14] He further suggests that maybe mathematical methods could fruitfully be used in illuminating what the correct output mix is. There is great mischief latent in that line of attack. This is indeed a valid criticism of both Kantorovich's and Novozhilov's theories, but their limitation of the problem of allocation to one of efficient production of a predetermined output program is founded on good reasons. To make determination of the correct bill of goods part of the problem involves asking what production is for, and leads directly to the introduction of the subjective category of utility into the analysis. Ideologically, that would be an unforgivable affront.

Novozhilov's approach contains in addition a special snare that will

[13] *The Application of Mathematics in Economic Research*, p. 478.
[14] See the remarks by A. G. Aganbegian in the report of the conference on mathematical methods in economics in *Voprosy Ekonomiki*, No. 8, 1960, pp. 110-12.

sooner or later cause trouble. His work has a disarming appeal since it seems to conform to the labor theory of value. He starts from the proposition that the problem is to maximize the effectiveness of labor, which sounds unexceptionable to a Marxist. Moreover, all the elements of value, including the inversely related costs, are expressed in terms of units of labor. It thus scrupulously preserves labor as the *numéraire* in which value is measured. But the consistency with the labor theory of value is completely illusory. It makes no sense to formulate the problem as one of minimizing the labor input into a given bill of goods (or to put the same idea another way, of maximizing leisure). The real problem is to maximize leisure and output together. In the Soviet setting, especially, minimizing labor input is a ridiculous goal. Nor can this absurdity be rationalized by claiming that minimizing the labor input is equivalent to maximizing output, since labor saved can be used to expand output. In Novozhilov's method labor is minimized under the condition of using up all the other inputs with which it can be combined. This flaw in the formulation of the nature of the problem is bound to be discovered sooner or later.

Furthermore it is not difficult to imagine institutional situations in the Soviet economy where anyone trying to apply Novozhilov's method of reasoning will have to take as the point of departure a fixed labor supply and formulate his problem as one of minimizing some other input. For instance, we might realistically pose the problem of agricultural planning as one of finding the minimum capital investment consistent with the size of the agricultural population and the assigned output goal. Or planners in the railroad branch of the economy might be assigned the goal of choosing the patterns of resource use that would minimize fuel inputs, with everything else held constant. In these situations the conformity of Novozhilov's reasoning with the labor theory of value vanishes. In any of these problems the opportunity costs would emerge in terms of the input to be minimized as *numéraire,* and one would end up with a "capital" theory of value or a "fuel" theory of value. These anomalies will never be put right until the bill of goods is entered as part of the variables to be determined, which means resort to the idealistic magnitude utility as part of the explanation.

The reconciliation of two true but contradictory theories (that is, a "fuel" theory of value and the labor theory of value) is only possible when they are recognized as special cases of a general theory under different assumptions; and in the theory of value and allocation this general theory must involve some conception of utility. Utility is the more general, abstract, common denominator into which all other explanations can be translated. The discovery of this general theory and the final collapse of the labor theory of value is by no means only a hypothetical danger. As a matter of fact, the other half of the theory of value—the theory of consumption—has already been worked out and published in the Soviet Union. This is a paper by A. A. Konius in a prestigious volume of essays published by the Academy of Sciences of the USSR in honor of the eightieth birthday of S. G. Strumilin.[15] The theory of consumption is just hanging in the air, waiting to be joined to what Novozhilov and Kantorovich have already done for the theory of production. When someone brings the two together, the rediscovery of Western value theory will be complete.

Konius poses the problem of finding the proper relationship of prices to labor input of different consumer goods for the purpose of minimizing the total labor input for a given level of what he calls vaguely "consumption." Actually the content he gives this vague term makes it identical with the "welfare" or "utility" of Western value theory. Incidentally, Konius' question is not one made up in the quiet of the professor's study but one that has long agitated those who plan the prices of consumer goods in the Soviet Union. The answer given by Western economists to this question appears in every elementary economics textbook as "prices should be proportional both to the marginal rates of substitution and the marginal rates of transformation of the goods in question." Not being accustomed to consulting this kind of source for answers to questions of socialist political economy, Konius enlisted the aid of a professor of mathematics (duly thanked in a footnote) and worked out the answer himself. Not surprisingly, he came to the same conclusion. Neither will it be a surprise to the economist that Konius could demonstrate his proposition only by specifying some assumptions about the nature of the "consumption" he was talking about. Specifically, his proof depends on the postulation of the familiar ordinal utility function or preference surface of Western economics. This assumption is there in the relatively inconspicuous form of some equations, it is true, but it is there.

Conclusion

Konius' case can serve as the thesis for our summary. The search for theoretical clarification of almost any important economic issue will ultimately require the elaboration of normative models regarding allocation of resources and conceptions of value, and these two problems ultimately merge. The rigor and power of mathematics is almost essential for describing and investigating such models, and there is thus great pressure in any science to employ mathematics. It will be diffi-

[15] *Problems of Economics, Planning and Statistics* (Moscow, Publishing House of the Academy of Sciences USSR, 1957). The article by Konius is entitled "Theoretical Problems of Prices and Consumption in the Works of S. G. Strumilin and a Way for Future Research into Them."

cult for economics to escape this pressure. As one indication, Nesmeyanov, the president of the Academy of Sciences, has admonished economists to make theirs a "real science" by using mathematics and modern computational technology.[16] But when one sits down with a mathematician, as Konius did, to demonstrate a general line of argument, the mathematician's role can only be to check whether the intuitively felt conclusion does or does not follow from the assumptions, or what assumptions might be required to prove it. As the mathematician A. N. Kolmogorov remarked in a speech at the conference on mathematical methods in economics, the advantage of having mathematicians and economists cooperate with each other is that the mathematicians force the economists to define more carefully some of their fuzzy conceptions.[17] If the conclusions are given and the task of economic science is to defend them, as Boiarskii claims in his review of Kantorovich, then it might be better to leave the conceptions fuzzy. But the really novel circumstance in the Soviet Union today is that this is no longer an adequate interpretation of the task of economic science. The planners feel so strongly the need for improvements in calculation and allocation that they must discover a more sophisticated theory of value than that willed them by Marx. It is to this end that they have delivered themselves into the hands of the mathematicians.

40

The Decline and Rise of Soviet Economic Science [*]

WASSILY LEONTIEF
Harvard University

One of the notable aspects of Soviet reality is the paradoxical coexistence of the old and the new, of the modern side by side with the old-fashioned. A visitor to Moscow cannot but be struck by the contrast between the 40-story skyscraper of the Hotel Ukraina and the prerevolutionary log cabin with intricately carved window frames nestling

---

[16] In a speech at the 21st Congress of the Communist Party quoted in *The Application of Mathematics in Economic Research*, p. 3.

[17] *Voprosy Ekonomiki*, No. 8, 1960, p. 114.

[*] Reprinted from *Foreign Affairs*, January, 1960, pp. 261-272, by permission of the publisher. (Articles in *Foreign Affairs* are copyrighted by the Council on Foreign Relations, Inc., New York.)

practically within its long shadow. Contemporary Russian literature and art present a striking example of revolutionary, socialist content poured into Victorian forms. One of the most notable paradoxes of this kind was—until recently—the contrast between the Soviet economy and Soviet economics.

The Soviet economy, directed with determined ruthless skill, has been advancing for years at such a fast and steady pace that in total—if not per capita—national income, Russia is now second only to the United States; the output of certain of its key industries, such as machine tool building, for example, has even exceeded that of ours. By contrast, Soviet economics, that is, Soviet economic science, has remained static and essentially sterile over a period of more than 30 years—a huge, impassive and immovable monument to Marx—with scores of caretakers engaged in its upkeep, fresh flowers placed in slightly different arrangements at its feet from time to time, and lines of dutiful visitors guided past in never-ending streams.

The decline of economics in Soviet Russia dates back to the late 1920s, to the time of the inauguration of the original Five Year Plan. The first decade of the Communist régime—the years of civil war and famine and then of economic rehabilitation and "primitive accumulation" assisted by the partial restoration of private enterprise—was marked by lively economic discussion. It ranged from immediate issues of economic policy to the most general problems of economic theory. This was the time when the Communist, Basarov, expounded his mathematical theory of economic growth and Professor Kondratieff, director of the Moscow Business Cycle Institute, developed the statistical analysis of long and short waves of economic growth which has exerted considerable influence on Western theory of business cycles. (A few years later both of these men vanished without a trace.)

Looking back it is not difficult to explain the decline of economic science in the first planned socialist economy. Marx was a prophet of socialism, but he was a student of capitalism; to be more exact, he was a student of the first hundred years—vital and incredibly creative, but also ruthless and destructive—of modern, mechanized large-scale industry. Marxism, as an economic theory, is a theory of rampant private enterprise, not of the centrally guided economy. Whatever references Marx made to the economy of the socialist order were brief, quite general and extremely vague. Some of his most poisonous verbal darts were reserved for Lassalle, Proudhon and other contemporary social reformers who took delight in minute descriptions of production, distribution and consumption in ideal socialist or anarchist communes. He considered these men naïve and impractical and dubbed them "Utopists."

The Soviet economists of the Stalin era were no "Utopists" in any possible sense of that word; for sound practical reasons they devoted their undivided attention to paraphrasing and interpreting Marx and Lenin. The fact that capitalism—the subject of all these labors—had been by this time abolished in Russia in a sense simplified their assigned job. Meanwhile, the Communist leaders were engaged in the unprecedented task of transforming literally at breakneck speed a technologically backward, predominantly peasant country into an industrialized military power dedicated to the pursuit of further economic growth. They were their own economists.

The fundamental proposition which explains the high rate of Soviet economic development is simple enough. Nearly 200 years ago it had already been clearly stated by Adam Smith and in more homely language by Ben Franklin. To expand one's income fast, one must channel as large a part of it as possible—and then more—into productive capital investment. This means that consumption must be restricted; while thus holding down the living standard of the masses, one must at the same time keep them working hard. Marx, in his theory of capitalist accumulation, describes exactly such a process, except that he refers to it in pejorative terms: the owners of the means of production use their monopolistic position vis-à-vis the working classes to keep wage rates down and profits up. Low wages mean a low level of consumption. High profits—the high "rate of exploitation"—mean a high rate of accumulation, since the capitalists forever strive to increase their capital so as to be able to compete better with each other and also to employ more workers to exploit. This prescription was followed by Communists in Russia steadily over a period of 30 years. However, the unmistakable success of that ruthless experiment bears testimony not so much to the economic sophistication of the Soviet rulers as to their political perspicacity and determination.

So far as the Russian technique of economic planning is concerned, one can apply to it in paraphrase what was said about a talking horse: the remarkable thing about it is not what it says, but that it speaks at all. Western economists have often tried to discover "the principle" of the Soviet technique of planning. They never succeeded, since, up to now, there has been no such thing. The "Method of Balances," to which the Soviet writers themselves invariably refer, hardly deserves its high-sounding name. It simply requires that the over-all national economic plan be constructed in such a way that the total output of each kind of goods be equal to the quantity which all its users are supposed to receive. The method does not, however, say what information and what computational procedure can be used to achieve the simultaneous balancing of many thousands of different goods and services covered by a comprehensive blueprint of a national economy.

The immense scope of the problem becomes clear if one considers the fact that each item requires for its production several other items directly, and many more—as a matter of fact, all others—indirectly. Thus whenever the planner attempts to balance the supply and demand of any one particular item, by expanding its output or by reducing its consumption, he is bound to disturb the balance of many, and ultimately of all other, goods and services. Moreover, an efficient planner must compute more than a single over-all balance. Land can be tilled with horses or with tractors; electric energy can be generated by burning coal, oil or natural gas as well as by harnessing water power. All such alternatives can be used in innumerable combinations and each combination will require a different kind of over-all economic balance. However, some of these will serve the national objectives—whatever they may be—more effectively than others.

Soviet planning procedures, in practice, do not—or at least did not up to now—differ very much from those that were used during the war by our War Production Board, by the English Supply Ministries, and by their counterpart in Germany. The larger decisions are first made by balancing the requirements for selected high-priority objectives with the available amounts of the strategic resources, that is, the most important scarce ones. Next, the details of the plan are worked out through application of standard ratios based on past experience. Final adjustments are left to informal trial-and-error procedures of the actual month-by-month and week-by-week operations.

Soviet press reports over the years abound in examples of obvious miscalculations. For instance, too much ore is mined and not enough coke is made to produce the planned amount of steel; or insufficient quantities of spare parts are turned out to keep in good repair machinery installed in new plants. More difficult to detect, because it does not show up in a glaring imbalance between the supply and the demand of some specific item, but probably not less deleterious in its effect on the over-all efficiency of the system, is the failure to make correct choices among several possible alternatives. The failure to substitute gas for coal on the supply side of the national fuel balance, or too hurried a substitution, might mean an even larger potential loss of national income than that which is brought about by the more obvious kinds of miscalculations mentioned above.

To solve all these problems in a systematic way, the planning technician must be able to compute not only one balanced plan, but many, and then he must be able to compare the efficiency of all these alternative plans in attaining whatever the specific, over-all objective of the national economic policy might be. This is an assignment easy enough to envisage, but most difficult to accomplish; it is, moreover, a highly technical task which even a very shrewd politician and powerful dictator cannot perform by himself, any more than he can, by himself, build an atomic bomb or send a rocket to the moon. He can, however, decide that the solution of this problem is worth the cost involved in solving it; he can set the experts to work on it and give them all possible support. This is what actually happened in Russia two or three years ago in respect to the important problems of economic planning discussed above. The top leadership, with Khrushchev probably taking a hand in it, apparently decided that with the rapid increase in the size and complexity of the Soviet economy, rule-of-thumb planning procedures would do no longer and must be replaced as soon as possible by more efficient, scientific methods.

The high price the Russian rulers have shown themselves willing to pay is, in this instance, not so much material as, one might say, moral: as in the case of atomic power, the scientific basis of the new techniques is being borrowed wholesale from the West—to be more specific, from the United States. This time it is "bourgeois economics" rather than physics that is about to be used to serve Soviet aims. For Communists and Marxists to concede the superiority of Western science in this particular field must be especially painful from both the ideological and the propaganda points of view; but just because of this, the significance of the move must be considered to be particularly great. To avoid any possible misunderstanding, let it be emphasized that what the Soviets are about to adopt is Western economic science, not Western economic institutions. There is good reason to believe that this can actually be done. Those Western observers who say that this cannot be done and who believe that the use of interest on capital in planning calculations presages at least a partial restoration of the system of private enterprise misunderstand, I think, the internal logic of Soviet evolution.

II

The early mid-nineteenth century successors of Adam Smith—and Marx was one of them—were concerned mainly with problems of economic growth, that is, of increasing wealth and income and of the distribution of that increasing income among labor, capital and the landowning groups. Later, the focal point of theoretical inquiry shifted to problems of economic efficiency and has remained centered on these problems ever since. It is true that the catastrophe of the Great Depression dramatically raised the question of full employment, and the recurring smaller ups and downs in business conditions continue to keep it on the map. However, looking back at the Keynesian Revolution, with its paradoxical advocacy of spending for spending's sake and the implied fear of a rapid rise in the productivity of labor, one must recognize it for what it was: a long detour rather than a basic change in the general orientation of Western economics. The question of efficiency and of rational allocation of scarce resources dominates the field of advanced scientific inquiry again. It was restored to that central position, however, with a new and different emphasis.

The traditional approach to these problems was broad, abstract and purely deductive; the new post-Keynesian, postwar inquiry is concise, specific, factual and eminently practical. The so-called "neoclassical" school, which carried on the classical theoretical tradition between the two world wars, mainly expounded and elaborated the liberal free-trade theme of the "invisible hand." It demonstrated in great detail, occasionally even making use of mathematical language, the automatic efficiency of competitive pricing. It classified and reclassified various theoretically possible situations, particularly those in which free competition breaks down or in any case does not bring about the most efficient allocation of economic resources. The "neoclassical" economists made it very clear that efficiency is a relative concept, that an allocation most efficient for the achievement of one economic end might be quite inefficient from the point of view of another. Incidentally, they have also shown that in a free competitive economy the over-all economic goal is determined by a kind of universal suffrage in which everyone has a multiple vote proportional to his dollar income.

The postwar generation of American economists takes up where the neoclassical analysts left off. Discussion of general principles is extended into the solution of specific problems, hypothetical assumptions are replaced by actual observation and purely symbolic mathematics are carried down to numerical computations. The entire national economy is viewed by the modern theorist as a gigantic, automatic computing machine, the price system being interpreted as an ingenious computing aid. To test and to extend his understanding of the operation of this machine, the economist now often identifies the specific problem it is supposed to solve, determines through detailed, direct observation the basic numerical data which are supposed to go into the solution, performs the necessary computation and then compares the final answer obtained from it with the answer to the same question arrived at in real life by operation of the impersonal forces of free competition.

To give a simple example: coal is produced in several parts of the United States, the cost of production and the maximum possible annual output varying from place to place mainly because of differing geological conditions. It moves them by either rail, water or truck to consuming areas. The actual total output can be allocated in many different ways among the producing regions and the proper amounts can be carried to the consuming regions by many means along various routes. However, some of the possible arrangements must obviously be more economical than others in terms of total combined production and transportation costs. Traditional economic theory explains why—under certain simplifying assumptions—the free competitive pricing mechanism can be expected in this case, as in many others, to bring about the establishment of the cheapest possible production and transportation pattern. The modern analyst goes further. He collects detailed information on the actual cost of production in all the different coal mining regions and on the actual rail, water and truck rates from these regions to places of consumption; and then he determines by himself—using, if necessary, a modern high speed computer—the most efficient, *i.e.* the cheapest, of all the possible alternative production and transportation patterns.

The computational procedure the economist uses might be designed in imitation of the process of trial-and-error approximation that is supposed to operate in a free-exchange economy. Or he might decide to use one of the advanced textbook methods of numerical analysis. A comparison of this answer with the observed production and the transportation pattern of coal might show that the economist has, indeed, reached a satisfactory scientific explanation of the actual process. On the other hand, he might turn up a discrepancy which will indicate the direction of necessary improvement in the theoretical formulation of the problem, the computational routine or the nature of the factual data used. Since these elements are mutually interdependent, the modification in any one of them will usually require a corresponding adjustment in the other two. On the second or third try, the result usually turns out to be more satisfactory. If nothing helps, the very assumption that costs are minimized in the economy might itself be questioned.

Such relatively simple questions as that of minimizing the combined production and transportation costs are ordinarily formulated as so-called linear programming problems and are solved through application of a computational procedure known as the Simplex method. Conceptually akin to linear programming is the so-called input-output analysis which, for example, has been effectively used in quantitative empirical analysis of the balance or the imbalance, as the case may be, between several hundreds of individual sectors of the United States economy. The application of this method requires a comprehensive statistical mapping of the structural relationship determining the flows of goods and services between all the sectors and a solution of large systems of mathematical equations based on the hundreds or thousands of figures contained in a typical input-output table. The Russians expect this method to be particularly helpful in the solution of their larger planning problems.

Under such names as "operations research," "logistics analysis" or "management science," the new techniques are now being successfully used by most large American corporations in the solution of production scheduling, inventory control, investment planning and many other of their internal problems which hitherto were met by routine application of conventional and mostly rather wasteful rules of thumb. But certain business circles in the United States have viewed with unconcealed alarm the application of these methods to the traditional problems of the economic system as a whole—the very purpose for which some of the more powerful of the new analytical devices were designed in the first place. No doubt this attitude reflects the fear that too close and too detailed an understanding of the structure of the economic machine and of its operation might encourage undesirable attempts to regulate its course.

III

The first cursory references in Russia to new developments in the West appeared some years ago in the typical polemical forays against "bourgeois economics" published from time to time in *Economic Problems* and similar Soviet journals. Gradually the polemical part of these surveys became less virulent and shorter while the factual description of the new methods became more systematic and longer. Oskar Lange, former Professor at the University of Chicago and now a prominent public figure and the leading economist in Poland, has apparently been instrumental in arousing a positive interest in linear programming and input-output economics among his high-placed Russian colleagues. The last edition of the "Textbook of Political Economy" published late in 1958 mentions a bourgeois science called Econometrics, some methods of which—it is significantly stated—might prove to be of interest to socialist economists and planners. Early in 1959 the "Studies on the Structure of the American Economy," a rather technical volume published six years ago in the United States by the author of this article and several collaborators, appeared in a Russian translation (which incidentally was edited by Professor A. A. Konus, the last surviving mathematical economist of the pre-revolutionary generation). Another straw in the wind was a popular pamphlet on problems of economic planning written by a prominent member of the research staff of the *Gosplan*—the central planning commission—and printed in several hundred thousand copies. It describes in great detail the use of the mathematical input-output method for balancing planned production and requirements. At the last two meetings of the International Statistical Institute, the official Soviet delegation made input-output analysis the subject of its principal scientific papers. Its leader used this opportunity to declare this to be a topic singularly well-suited for scientific exchange between East and West.

As soon as the baby was adopted, the question of its intellectual parentage was investigated with great diligence and it was found to be, after all, of respectable Soviet Russian ancestry. A search through old economic journals revealed that in 1925 a short article on the then newly compiled balance of the Russian national economy was published in one of these periodicals over my signature. (Actually, I wrote this paper when still a student at the University of Berlin; it was first published in Germany and then translated and published in Russia.) Another Soviet priority claim seems to be more substantial. In 1939 a young Leningrad mathematician, L. V. Kantorovich, published two papers in which he presented a general mathematical formulation of certain problems of production planning and transportation scheduling, which in fact did anticipate the conceptual framework of the linear programming theory developed a few years later by Koopmans and Dantzig in the United States. Kantorovich did not, however, devise an efficient computational solution of these problems; Dantzig did, thus opening the door to the practical, large-scale application of the linear programming approach. In any case, Kantorovich's original contribution found no response and recognition till the time when information about new developments in the West reached Moscow and the top decision was made to put them into the service of socialist planning. Professor Kantorovich is now a member of the Academy of Sciences and, according to recent newspaper reports, he even can allow himself, at its public sessions, to make disparaging remarks about "the meaningless discourse" of stalwart Marxist theorists.

Once the crucial decision was made, scientific resources were rapidly mobilized to conquer the field. The details of what actually goes on are shrouded by a veil of secrecy, but it is known that many American articles and books on the subject have been translated into Russian and circulated "privately" among the specialists assigned the task of mastering the new methods. For example, though the Russian edition of "Studies on the Structure of the American Economy" was published in 1959, the translation of that book was actually completed and widely circulated as early as 1955 or 1956.

Among the scores of young economists and mathematicians whom I had an opportunity to meet during a brief visit to Moscow and Leningrad early in 1959, many showed through questions they asked and remarks they made that they had a good acquaintance, both theoretical and practical, with input-output research. Some of these belonged to the selected group of "aspirants" (corresponding to our young post-doctoral scholars) who at the time were completing a course of intensive training in methods of modern quantitative economics under the personal direction of Academicians Kantorovich and Nemchinov. (The latter, an economist and statistician, headed until recently the Section of Social and Philosophical Sciences of the Academy of Sciences and was also a member of the Academy's all-powerful Executive Board; a few months ago he was appointed Chairman of the Academy's Commission on the Study of the Productive Resources of the U.S.S.R.) This fall, they are being transferred from Moscow and Leningrad to the new Science City in Novosibirsk, the seat of the rapidly expanding Siberian branch of the Academy of Sciences. Equipped with large-scale computational facilities, this will apparently become the new center of advanced economic research.

It was interesting to note that young men with mathematical or engineering backgrounds and some of the older practical planners and economic administrators took easily to the new discipline, while those who as students had concentrated on regular economic courses were still prone to be beset by doubts. The use—in so-called dynamic allocation theory—of a positive rate of interest on invested capital, for instance, is accepted by the former as a logical necessity, while the latter ask questions which indicate considerable resistance to such un-Marxist thought. As a result of this, the manipulative aspects of the new methodology seem at the present time more advanced in the Soviet Union than the understanding and the exploration of its deeper fundamental levels. This aspect of the problem, however, is also being taken care of: mathematics has been made an obligatory subject in the economics departments of the Universities of Moscow and Leningrad and, in both, new chairs of Econometrics were recently established—but not yet filled, apparently because of lack of suitable candidates.

The massive support which the Soviet Government has given to the development of the natural sciences is widely known. The fact that it is now prepared to discard some of the central themes of traditional Communist lore in order to gain command of the promising new intellectual tools of modern social science indicates that it expects to receive an equally high return from their use.

It will take some time before the Soviet planners will be able to apply in practice the new techniques their economists are now acquiring in theory. Not only must the vast training program, launched only a few years ago, be advanced much further, but the activities of the huge and clumsy Central Statistical Office will have to be reorganized from top to bottom. The new methods of economic analysis can make effective use of a much larger volume of much more detailed statistical and other factual information than was considered practicable heretofore. But first the information must be made available. Lenin's slogan, "Socialism is electrification plus statistics," will once again be often quoted in the Soviet press.

There can be little doubt that in the years to come the introduction of scientific planning techniques will increase the over-all productivity of the Soviet economy, just as the adoption of new methods of scientific management by our own large corporations has raised the efficiency of their internal operations. A centrally planned economy depends on the efficiency—or the inefficiency—of managerial decision to a much greater extent than does the free-market economy, which benefits from the economizing functions of competitive pricing. So, the advantage that the Russians will derive from any improvement in such decision-making procedures is bound to be particularly great. Whether the increased productivity will be used to accelerate still further the high rate of their economic growth, to step up military preparations or, as the free world should hope, to raise their standard of living, one cannot predict.

IV

In the present world-wide contest between the United States and the Soviet Union for the friendship of underdeveloped countries, the re-orientation of Soviet economics will probably have an even more immediate effect. For better or worse, these have-not countries are not content to allow their fervently desired economic growth to take care of itself. They regulate their exports and imports, they encourage new industries, their governments finance and build not only dams and roads, but also steel, chemical and other kinds of plants. In short, most undeveloped countries plan; they also ask for help. Financial support and engineering advice they get both from the Russians and from us. But so far as help on methods of economic planning is concerned, neither side has thus far been able to offer them much. Our advice is long on general wisdom, but short on teachable and learnable techniques. It is the latter, however, that they want; wisdom is not easily transmitted and furthermore no self-respecting politician has even been known to admit the lack of it. The Russians could have been expected to teach how to plan, but for reasons explained above they were able only to refer to the "method of balances," which raises an important question but does not answer it. Until now, as technical advisors on development economics, the Russians have not done any better than we have.

Having adopted modern analytical and programming techniques for large-scale domestic application, the Russians are bound to offer them for export too, and the demand is great. Since the new approach to economics originated in the United States, one would think that in this line of intellectual competition we could hold our own. But as things stand now, this is not the case.

The scientific treatment of management and business problems is expanding rapidly in the United States. But, for reasons noted before, large-scale basic research aimed at the application of these newer methods to the analysis of the structure and the operation of the economic system as a whole has slowed down in recent years. As a matter of fact, in its crucial empirical phase, this fundamental work has now come to a complete standstill because of lack of financial and organizational support. Over 20 countries—not counting the Soviet Union and its satellites—are ahead of us in this field.

41

The Revival of Theoretical Discussion Among Soviet Economists *

MAURICE DOBB
Trinity College, Cambridge, England

To convey the true shadings of a discussion is difficult if not impossible unless one is part of it. Not only will its finer nuances be missed, but also essential links, particularly policy implications, and unseen antagonists taken for granted by participants even when not openly stated. Only some rare act of intuition will enable an interpreter at a distance to grasp these nonapparent links, let alone the subtler shades. This has always been the trouble with the so-called "Soviet experts" in the West with their guessing-games and confident interpolations, whether they are part of the intelligence brigade of the cold war or "independent" and unstipended amateurs.

This might seem a very good reason for not embarking on the present article. However, awareness of one's own limitations can be a pretty effective antidote to the grosser stupidities of *soi-disant* "experts"; and knowledge of likely pitfalls may enable the cautious observer, while making some pedestrian recordings of the more obvious events, to avoid the major fallacies of "interpretation." At any rate, the reader has been warned to read what follows with proper circumspection and without inflated expectations.

One thing, at least, seems quite certain: after a fairly long period of dormancy, there has been in the last few years quite a remarkable revival (one is tempted to use the word *renaissance*) of economic discussion and theoretical activity in the Soviet Union, as well as in some other of the socialist countries, and signs of a new and more creative approach to the problems of a socialist economy.

* Reprinted from *Science and Society,* Fall, 1960, pp. 289-311, by permission of the author and the publisher.

I. The Period of Quiescence

After the animated debates of the 1920's, it seemed as though a pall had descended over economic discussion during the next two decades. At first one was inclined to consider this to be not unnatural in view of intense preoccupation with practice in the "heroic" prewar decade and the decade of the war and its aftermath—preoccupation with details of policy within a fairly narrow time-horizon and with issues that were politico-social in character so far as the general objectives of policy were concerned. One was inclined to assume that more strictly economic questions of planning were the subject of intra-departmental discussion which seldom emerged into print, but the products of which one would be able some day to discern.

There were some straws in the wind, however, that caused one to think there might be more to explain than this. On the one hand, there were recurrent complaints about the low level of economic theory, the prevalence of "narrow practicalism" and purely descriptive writings, and the failure to generalize the experience of a socialist economy—complaints that became more emphatic after the war.[1] On the other hand, when occasional *ex cathedra* pronouncements on matters of economic theory were made, the subsequent commentaries on them, alike in the U.S.S.R. and other socialist countries, were surprisingly empty of content and bore an exceptionally abstract, even scholastic, character. One may instance the question of the law of value and its continuing "influence" under socialism; about which we were told little more than that this law was used "consciously" in planning; that this did not mean that price-relations coincided with value-relations, but that in a manner unexplained they "deviated from values" in the interest of the objectives of the plan—though in such a way as to leave "total prices equal to total values." Such generalizations were apparently accepted as the sufficient essence of wisdom. At any rate, no more than this showed above the surface to form even the prolegomena to a Political Economy of Socialism. Thirty to forty years after the revolution, this was a little strange, to say the least, despite the interruptions of two major wars.

During the past quinquennium it has become fairly evident that there were several other factors in the situation to explain the grave theoretical lag in advancing towards a new Political Economy of Socialism. Firstly, there was, apparently, a prevalent assumption that anything in the way of an original departure in theoretical generalization could only come "from the top" (an obvious product of the "personality cult" of the period). This was not an atmosphere in which younger or

---

[1] Cf. p. 334 of the present writer's *Soviet Economic Development* since 1917.

lesser men were disposed to "stick their necks out" and risk a novel hypothesis—however much they might be prodded by official pronouncements deploring the "low level of theoretical work." Secondly, there seems to have been something of a "Chinese wall" between political economy (with the academic economists concerned in its teaching and cultivation) and the problems and techniques of economic planning. A hint of this separation was contained in Stalin's surprising statement to the effect that political economy is concerned exclusively with "the laws of development of men's relations of production" and that "to foist upon political economy problems of economic policy is to kill it as a science." [2] Price policy, it seems, fell within the province of planners and of economic practitioners in industrial Ministries, but not of "political economists" proper. Such a glaring divorce of theory from practice could hardly fail to breed scholasticism and dogmatism—a dogmatism probably reinforced by the fact that much of the inspiration and even the personnel of political economy at *vyshaya shkola* level tended to be from agitprop departments, the horizon of scholarship for which was too often "talmudism" (as Stalin himself dubbed it). Thirdly (and obviously connected with what we have just said), it now transpires that a dominant view was that political economy was primarily (if not exclusively) concerned with the study of the *qualitative* aspects and *differentia* of economic and social phenomena. This emphasis (resulting in a kind of economic sociology) is well exemplified in the Soviet *Political Economy Textbook* of a few years ago, and may serve to explain the scarcely-concealed dissatisfaction with it on the part of many Marxists both within and without the Soviet Union. Attention to the *quantitative* aspect of economic relations was liable to be denounced as "formalism," and "bourgeois formalism" to boot. As Academician V. Nemchinov writes in a recent issue of *Voprosy Ekonomiki* (1960, No. 6, pp. 13 f.):

Quantitative analysis of economic phenomena stands at the present time as one of the bottlenecks of Soviet economic science. The reason for this consists not only in the sharp raising of the level of demands upon Soviet economic science, but also in a definite underestimation by a section of economists of the necessity for scientific analysis of the quantitative side of economic processes in socialist economy. . . . Some economists began incorrectly to regard economic science, and particularly political economy, as a science only of qualitative economic laws, leaving out of sight the huge significance of theoretical methods of analysis of the quantitative aspect of economic laws of development of socialist society. In the recent past our economists even denied the possibility of a theoretical approach to the quantitative side of the laws [*zakonomernost*] of development of socialist society. . . . It is impossible for the political economy of socialism to limit itself merely to qualitative analysis. Economic science . . . in conditions of socialism can and must become an exact science.

[2] *Economic Problems of Socialism in the U.S.S.R.* (Moscow, 1952), p. 81.

II. The Economic Effectiveness of Investment

In the circumstances it is, indeed, quite surprising that discussion about the problem of "calculating the economic effectiveness of investment" should have occupied Soviet economists as early as it did (from the late forties) and should have had the outcome that it has. Probably some of the credit for this should go to the veteran economist Strumilin, who opened up the question in his much-quoted article on "The Time Factor in Planning Capital Investment," published in the *Izvestia* of the Academy just after the end of the war.[3] But it seems likely that a more important part of the explanation is that the question arose from the demands of practice itself, and hence had the strong backing, if not of Gosplan, of engineering-economists in the industrial *glavki*. Perhaps the fact that long-term planning came to be placed on the agenda after the war had something to do with it. At any rate, if what we have said is true, both the initiative and the continuing impetus came from outside, rather than from inside, academic political economy—came from the research staffs of Ministries and of specialized industrial institutes who had the actual handling of problems of choice between technical variants. The formulation of operational criteria, such as the recoupment-period and ratio of effectiveness, was largely the work, apparently, of transport-economists and their opposite numbers in electricity-generation and construction; and it is noteworthy that Professor T. S. Khachaturov, who deserves so much of the credit for carrying forward this discussion to a successful issue, was a transport specialist and author of a well-known textbook on transport problems. If opposition to this raising of (or way of raising) the issue came, as one supposes, from the dogmatists (who smelled a "rate-of-interest heresy" in it), then it was a clash between the *doctrinaires* and the practical men, with the latter having quite a few notable cards stacked in their favor.

The main issue in this debate can be explained in non-technical terms quite simply. Most industrial construction, whether it be a power plant or a clothing factory or an engineering works, is capable of being planned according to several so-called "technical variants." Once planned investment has been allocated between various industries (and even before this stage is reached) this presents itself as the crucial problem of investment planning (or project-making as it is usually called in Soviet literature). These technical variants will differ:

(a) in their initial cost of construction;
(b) in the results which they will subsequently yield when in operation—results which may be alternatively regarded as an increase

---

[3] *Izvestia Akademii Nauk U.S.S.R.*, Economics and Law Series, 1946, No. 3; also translated in *International Economic Papers*, No. 1.

in productivity of labor or as a decreased expenditure of labor (or prime cost) required to produce a given output.

In any given case, (b) can be expressed as a ratio to (a); and different variants or projects can be arranged in an order according to the size of this ratio in each case. It will not follow, of course, that a higher labor productivity in operation (*e. g.* when a new machine is installed and in use) will always be associated with a higher initial (investment) cost. When it is not, there is no doubt which of the alternatives to use: for practical purposes only one of them, that which yields the higher productivity, will ever come upon the planning agenda, the others being rejected from the start as inferior. But a real problem of choice will arise in the case of any pair of alternatives in which higher productivity is associated with higher investment-cost.

For example, by expending large additional sums on the construction of an expensive hydro-electric plant much cheaper electricity [4] can be produced eventually than if cheaper (and possibly smaller) coal-burning powerplants are constructed. How to decide which to construct? If one had enough steel and equipment etc. at any one time to place no ceiling on the total construction the economy could undertake (or the size of its general investment plan), there would be no problem—hydro-electric stations would win every time. But in actuality this is never so—some ceiling is necessarily imposed by the existing size and productive capacity of the capital goods industries (Marx's Department I). Hence a limit has to be placed at some point on the additional investment-cost that it is worthwhile to incur in order to achieve a given result.

The Soviet ratio of effectiveness is one way of imposing such a limit. A standard ratio is set which any project must fulfill if it is to qualify for inclusion in the plan; anything that fails to fulfill this minimum requirement being rejected. The effectiveness coefficient or ratio is usually expressed as the ratio of the difference in operating cost (or prime cost) to the difference in initial investment-cost (*e. g.* of a hydro-electric plant compared with a coal-burning one of equivalent capacity). Essentially the same ratio is sometimes expressed in a different form (the one being simply the inverse of the other) as a so-called "period of recoupment" of the original investment—the number of years within which the original investment cost will be recovered, or recouped, by the annual saving of operating cost.

In comparing investment projects there are also questions of differing periods of construction (*e. g.* a hydro-electric plant usually takes longer to construct; so will a railway line which, to reduce gradients or detours goes in for a lot of tunnelling and embankments) and different durabili-

---

[4] Provided that there is not a big seasonal variation in the flow of water, preventing full-capacity utilization from being maintained throughout the year.

ties of a plant or equipment once installed. If a more durable plant costs more to build, *how much* additional cost is worthwhile to achieve a given lengthening of life? Then, again, there is the kind of alternative where constructing the *complete* project now (whether building, power-plant or railway) is cheaper in the long run but involves the larger expenditure here and now; whereas developing it in stages, doing part now and then finishing the remaining part later, will place less strain on present resources but at the cost of a larger total expenditure over time. An effectiveness ratio can be used to decide this type of question also by providing a discount-factor by means of which future expenditures or costs are reduced to terms of present values, to enable a comparison in terms of the latter to be made and hence a choice of the alternative that comes out more advantageous or cheaper.

There was evidently a good deal of opposition in the early stages to the use of this sort of device. This opposition was first of all in principle to the use of such an "un-Marxist" notion. Had not Marx exposed the "myth of compound interest" as a metaphysical notion?, one writer asked; was this not the bourgeois notion of a specific "productivity of capital" in disguise? Investment, it was also argued, could never be decided on economic grounds alone, still less according to mechanical rules: "political" considerations which could not be quantified were always an element in planning decisions. Others claimed that such a device was too selective, and as used tended to ignore a lot of the side-effects of an investment project—what were called "supplementary investments" such as those involved in housing the additional labor force or even in re-equipping other industries so as to release the labor required for the new plant in question. (Mstislavsky tried out a complex and unusable construction in terms of the total of supplementary investments that would be needed elsewhere to replace the additional labor employed.) [5] Yet other critics concentrated on subordinate issues of interpretation: whether it was proper to use as a standard ratio one expressing the average or the marginal effectiveness in a particular industry; whether such a standard ratio should differ as between industries and sectors, or alternatively be uniform for the whole economy; whether the use of such a rule would retard technical progress.[6]

[5] This and one or two other contributions to the 1949 discussion are summarized in Charles Bettelheim's interesting work, *Studies in the Theory of Planning* (Bombay and London, 1959), pp. 155 ff.

[6] One thing that has always been puzzling about Strumilin's article mentioned above is that he seemed to be opposed to the use of such ratios, while at the same time stressing the crucial importance of the *problem* that such ratios were designated to handle. It now seems clear that his main criticism was directed against their application in a situation where prices were "arbitrary" (in the sense of diverging from "values"), and that he was looking for something more fundamental in which to express such a relation, *i.e.* in terms of labor and labor-productivity.

There was, however, another criticism that he made and which he has continued to

The debate, however, was to go in favor of the advocates of such ratios. In 1954 there was an interim summing-up of the question in the journal *Voprosy Ekonomiki,* which declared in principle in favor of the "comparability of investment expenditures and their resulting economies" and the use of such calculations in industry intra-branch investment-decisions. No agreement was reached, however, as to the proper basis for fixing a standard or minimum effectiveness-ratio. In 1956 there was issued a "temporary standard method" for calculating effectiveness of investment; and in June 1958 there was convened in Moscow an All-Union Scientific-Technical Conference on Problems of Determining the Economic Effectiveness of Capital Investment and New Techniques, with Professor T. S. Khachaturov delivering the chief report [7] (followed by Strumilin). Just previously to this, towards the end of 1957, a special Scientific Council had been instituted by the Academy of Sciences to direct and coordinate research work on this problem—a problem now promoted to being "one of the most important problems in the building of communism." Meanwhile a resolution of the Twenty-First Party Congress emphasized "the outstanding significance of the most effective direction of capital investment, providing for the least expenditure of means in cultivating productive power"; and Mr. Khrushchev was to stress the need "for calculation of the time factor," in connection with the com-

---

repeat more recently: namely, that one should not measure the results of investment merely in terms of the saving in *wages,* but should measure the resulting saving of labor in terms of the *full value* (wages *plus* surplus, or v + s in Marx's notation). Hence effectiveness-ratios, he thought, were unduly biased against the introduction of new technique. Actually there is a very simple answer to Strumilin on this point. Firstly, whether one measures the "saving of labor" at wages only or at "full value" will make no difference to the *comparative* effectiveness of alternative technical variants. Secondly, with a given size of the investment plan, no more investment could be undertaken than there were capital goods provided; hence a mere numerical change in the ratio as calculated could not affect the *real* volume or nature of investment projects (as Vaag and Zakharov, in an article we cite later, point out very aptly in relation to an analogous objection to the raising of capital-goods prices from their present low level). All that would happen if Strumilin's proposal were adopted would be that the *standard* effectiveness-ratio would have to be set equivalently higher so as to bring the aggregate cost of all the separate construction-projects into line with the total investment-plan.

[7] Khachaturov had been made a Corresponding Member of the Academy and, early in 1957, became one of the editors of *Voprosy Ekonomiki* (which for a time seemed to have been in opposition to the Khachaturov school in this matter). Among others, Kantorovich, the mathematician, Nemchinov and Novozhilov (whom we shall mention again below) took part in the discussion at this conference.

Curiously, however, Khachaturov expressed himself in favor, not of a uniform ratio, but of a ratio that differed in different sectors and industrial branches—and for reasons that do not seem convincing to the present writer, apart, perhaps, from a reference to different rates of technical progress, which may be intended to imply a reference to different rates of obsolescence and the need to adjust ratios to them. (See his article, "Problems of the Economic Effectiveness of Capital Investment" in *Voprosy Ekonomiki,* 1957, No. 2, p. 118). This compromise (if this is what it represented) is embodied in the final proposals that have emerged, although definite limits are set to the inter-branch variation.

parative advantages of hydro-electric and coal-burning power-plants. Finally, in 1960, there was issued, by joint agreement of the Economics Institute of the Academy and the Scientific Research Institute of Gosplan, a definitive "Standard Method" (*Tipovaya Metodika*), which was summarized in the Gosplan journal *Planovoye Khozyaistvo*, 1960, No. 3, (p. 56), and also published separately as *Tipovaya Metodika Opredeleniya Ekonomicheskoi Effectivnosti Kapitalnykh Vlozheni* (Moscow, 1960).

There were here enunciated standard rules for fixing effectiveness-ratios in industry, construction and transport; and (making a concession to the view that there should be some inter-branch variation in this ratio instead of uniformity) the statement advocated the setting up by each industrial branch of standard coefficients of "not less than .15 to .3," with transport and electrical power as exceptions where as low as .1 (or a recoupment-period of 10 years) was suggested.[8]

III. Prices and The Law of Value

As soon as the use of such ratios is regarded in the setting of the most efficient use of economic resources in the economy as a whole, it becomes obvious that the whole question of price-policy is inevitably raised. Any comparison of investment cost with subsequent economies in operating cost is a comparison in price terms; and the result is likely to be different according to the relative prices of the various commodities entering into the comparison. For example, suppose that one is comparing construction projects involving different constructional materials, say the use in one case of cement, in another of stone and in a third case of timber. Evidently it will make all the difference to the comparative effectiveness-ratio of these projects whether cement is dear and timber cheap, or conversely cement is the cheapest building material and compared with it stone and timber are expensive. In Poland a complaint of critics of the old pre-1956 price-policy was that the setting of an abnormally low price for coal prejudiced the comparison between coal-burning and hydro-electric power stations—and this at a time when coal was scarce and urgently needed for export. The debate on price-policy, which was open in the middle fifties was accordingly the heir to the discussion of effectiveness-ratios in investment-planning.[9]

[8] Following its publication, however, two writers in *Voprosy Ekonomiki* (L. Vaag and S. Zakharov, "On Calculating What is the Most Economical" [Ekonomichnost], 1960, No. 7, p. 103) complained that, despite this measure of agreement as to practice, there was still insufficient theoretical clarity on the reasons for it and called for further discussion of the theoretical issues involved. The article emphasizes the connection between calculating economic effectiveness and pricing according to the principle of prices of production, and is largely concerned with a carefully argued reply to theoretical objections made by critics of effectiveness-ratios, including that of Strumilin mentioned in an earlier footnote above. (Agricultural Supplement).

[9] Cf. Khachaturov's remark that deviation of prices from values may cause "untrue expression of actual effectiveness" (Planovoye Khozyaistvo, 1959, No. 8, p. 80).

The door was opened, if as yet only slightly, to a discussion of price-policy by Stalin's much-quoted declaration, in one of his last published statements, to the effect that the law of value, even if it "has no regulating function in our socialist production," "nevertheless influences production, and this fact cannot be ignored when directing production"; "consumer goods, which are needed to compensate the labor power expended in the process of production, are produced and realized in our country as commodities coming under the operation of the law of value." [10] Discussion started cautiously, and to begin with remained at an abstract level, concerning itself with such questions as whether the operation of the law of value depended upon the "existence of two forms of property" (State property and collective farm property), and hence upon commodity-relations in the exchange between industry and agriculture, or upon the "specific character of social labor under socialism" (payment of wages according to work, and the existence of a retail market where these wages were spent).

In December 1956, however, the sluice-gates were opened. A full-dress discussion was organized under the auspices of the Institute of Economics of the Academy, and attended both by economics teachers in the University and also by members of the research departments of Gosplan and of the Ministries of Finance and of Trade and of the Central Statistical Department. The note preceding the published summary of the discussion in *Voprosy Ekonomiki* said: "As is well known, in this sphere there are many unsettled questions. A number of positions taken up in our literature until now and widely adopted need more precise working out, and some of them appropriate emendation. . . . Reform of price-policy has great economic significance since directly linked with it is an improvement in the forms of economic accounting, planning of prime costs and the profitability of production, questions of calculating the effectiveness of capital investment and of introducing new techniques, etc." [11] This was followed by a further discussion six months later (with Ostrovitianov as chief *rapporteur*).

The main report at the first discussion, "On the Law of Value and Questions of Price-Formation in U.S.S.R.," was given by Kronrod who advanced the thesis that prices ought to be brought into greater conformity with values; [12] the particular corollary of this upon which emphasis was laid being the prices of means of production (Group A

[10] *Op. cit.*, p. 23.

[11] *Voprosy Ekonomiki*, 1957, No. 2, p. 71.

[12] Kronrod introduced his report with the statement that it was the peculiarities of labor under socialism that lay at the base of commodity-exchange and the law of value; since with these peculiarities of labor was linked the need for material incentives to labor, and this "necessitated the exchange of products on the principle of compensating for the expenditure of labor, i.e., economic exchange" (*Voprosy Ekonomiki*, 1957, No. 2, pp. 71-2, 79-82).

products). These were in most cases sold below values. The wholesale transfer-price at which they passed between State enterprises was based on prime cost *plus* a small profit-margin, but *without* turnover tax and hence without any proportional share in the "surplus product" of society. The alleged result was to encourage wasteful use of capital goods and insufficient incentive to economize in the use of fuel and power and raw materials and machinery. This stand-point was supported by Strumilin among others. Some speakers criticized the existing reign of what they termed "arbitrary" prices (Malyshev spoke of "subjectivism in price-formation"). These prices were arbitrary in the sense that they were fixed, not according to any general economic principle, but in order to achieve this or that particular administrative objective of the moment, the implication being that this was the sole ground of most of those "deviations of prices from values" of which so much had been heard. Academician Nemchinov called on economists to recognize their "obligation to create a theory of planned prices."

Once this general issue had been raised, numerous subsidiary issues, of varying degrees of importance, came to the fore. There was the question raised by Strumilin in an article in *Promishlennaya-Ekonomicheskaya Gazeta* [13] whether in extractive industries the wholesale selling price should not be based on cost (or value) under the least favorable natural conditions, rather than on an averaging of the different costs of various differently-situated enterprises. (This was a question which also occupied Polish economists about the same time in the form of the familiar marginal *versus* average cost principle.) More fundamental, and in many ways more interesting, was the discussion between advocates of different interpretations of the "value" principle as basis for price-reform: those who interpreted this as meaning literally that prices should be made proportional to values and those who interpreted it as meaning proportional to "prices of production" (in the sense of Marx's Volume III of *Capital*).

Manifestly, if the "surplus product" of society was to be distributed over all commodities in some uniform proportion, there were three main ways in which this could be done. Firstly, the "surplus product" could be distributed over different products and industries so that it bore a uniform proportion to the wage-bill of each industry (in Marxian terminology, with s standing for surplus and v for variable capital, this would be roughly equivalent to making s/v uniformly equal in all lines of production). Secondly, the surplus production could be so distributed as to make it uniformly proportional to the prime cost (*sebestoimost*) of production (*i.e.,* so as to make s/ (used-up c + v) uniformly equal in all industries). In practice this would mean building-up the selling-price from the prime cost by adding to the latter everywhere a proportional

[13] April 7th, 1957.

mark-up (*e. g.*, by means of a uniform rate of turnover tax). Thirdly, the surplus product could be so distributed as to make it proportional to the amount of capital (both constant and variable, fixed and circulating) normally employed in that industry. This was Marx's "prices of production" (equals cost-price *plus* a share of total surplus, made proportional, *not* to this cost-price itself, but to the total stock of C + V employed).[14]

In the 1956 debate the third interpretation was sponsored in particular by Bachurin (of the Ministry of Finance) and by Malyshev (of Gosplan); later by others including Z. V. Atlas, a well-known writer on monetary questions.[15] A link was immediately established, by implication, with the effectiveness-ratio discussion, because the main practical argument employed by this school of thought was that both criteria and incentives for the economic employment and usage of capital goods would be disturbed *unless* prices of capital goods were constructed in this way. Said Bachurin: "Distribution of net income [surplus product] proportionately to expenditure of living labor . . . will be unfavorable to branches [of industry] with a large specific weight of expenditure of stored-up labor. . . . Prices built on this principle would not stimulate technical progress, since net income would be greater where manual labor had the larger specific weight."[16] Malyshev pointed out that to base prices directly on values, as Kronrod had proposed, would cause the profitability of various branches of production to differ widely, causing it to be lower "the higher the technical level of the branch," thus discouraging technical progress. "In our conditions," he said, "the basis of price-formation must be the more developed, enriched, concrete form of value, prices of production, with a different social content from what this has under capitalism. . . . Profitability must be determined, not in relation to prime cost or to the wage-bill, but in relation to the value of all basic and turnover funds [fixed and circulating capital] of an enterprise. This gives the possibility of more fully calculating the effectiveness of capital investment."[17]

The arguments on the other side were that prices of production are a value-form belonging to capitalism which could have no place under socialism: they depended on the existence of competition with its tendency to a uniform profit-rate, and the latter had no function outside those conditions of market competition from which it arose. To impose an

14 Cf. the articles by S. Turetsky and by Bronislaw Minc in *Voprosy Ekonomiki*, 1957, No. 5, p. 62, and 1958, No. 1, p. 96.

15 "On Profitability of Socialist Enterprises" in *Voprosy Ekonomiki*, 1958, No. 7, esp. pp. 123-5. In a postscript-note to a book of last year to which we shall refer below Academician Nemchinov listed as advocates of the "prices of production" standpoint the following: I. Malyshev, L. A. Vaag, V. D. Belkin, Z. V. Atlas, V. A. Sobol, M. V. Kolganov.

16 The last sentence is from his contribution to the second discussion in May 1957, reported in *Voprosy Ekonomiki*, 1957, No. 8, p. 91.

17 *Voprosy Ekonomiki*, 1957, No. 2, p. 73, and No. 3, pp. 99-105.

equal profit-rate on industries would, indeed, conceal real expenditures of social labor and stand in contradiction to the principle of maximum economy of social labor. Some, indeed, seem to have thought that it would somehow stand in contradiction to giving priority in development to the capital goods sector of industry. Another rather curious objection was that prices of production restricted the expansion of more technically advanced industries by raising the price of things produced under conditions of high organic composition of capital (the direct contrary to Malyshev's argument that such prices would alone make these "advanced" techniques profitable).

It does not appear that any general agreement was reached on the major issues of the debate, much less so, at any rate, than in Poland where a substantial measure of agreement was arrived at and embodied in the so-called "New Economic Model" of 1957, drawn up by the State Economic Council under Professor Oskar Lange's chairmanship, and adopted in principle by the Council of Ministers. In the U.S.S.R. there was a magisterial summing-up by Ostrovitianov in *Kommunist*; but this confined itself to the more abstract issues. There was also a kind of interim summing-up by *Voprosy Ekonomiki,* giving the views of its editors, in the form of replies to a variety of correspondents, and an article by Kulikov with which the editors expressed substantial agreement.[18] But these pronouncements do not seem to have closed discussion, unlike previous occasions when *ex cathedra* pronouncements wrote *finis* to publicly expressed disagreements. (Perhaps historians looking back on these years may even point to this as the most significant change of all.) Although the existing price-system had and continues to have stout defenders (for example Maisenberg and Turetsky, both of whom spoke in a conservative sense in the 1956–7 discussion)[19] one has the impression that they may be now rather on the defensive, and that the idea that prices ought to bear a closer relation to values than they do, and "deviations" therefrom require specific justification,[20] has made quite a strong impact. So far no more than minor changes seem to have been made in administrative practice as regards pricing, though the tendency of these has been towards greater flexibility. In the case of consumer goods, some lessons have been learned from the experience of the price-reductions of the 1950's as to the need for adjusting particular

[18] *Voprosy Ekonomiki,* 1958, No. 2 and No. 8.

[19] Cf. S. Turetsky, *loc. cit.;* also his interesting book, *Ocherki Planovogo Tsenobrazovaniya,* in the first chapter of which he defends the existing system (while admitting some of its imperfections) against the price-reformers—without, however, mentioning any names. It may be noted that a forthcoming book on the subject by Malyshev has also been announced.

[20] One such justification could well be the raising of price to encourage economy in the use of some temporarily scarce commodity. Both the effectiveness and the need for such a price-change will depend, however, on the strictness or otherwise of the system of supply-allocation.

retail prices to varying demand conditions.[21] The attention of planners
and administrators has evidently been preoccupied with the sweeping
measures of regional decentralization adopted in 1957, one consequence
of which may well be a greater tendency to experimentation by particular
regional Economic Councils (Sovnarkhoze). The greater measure of
decentralization of decisions (about output-plans, about supplies, and
even about investment and about price-fixing) is likely to give increased
importance to questions of price-policy; so that the next round in the
price-discussion may, like that on effectiveness of investment, be immediately provoked by "the demands of practical life" rather than by
a priori considerations. At any rate, the advocates of price-reform, especially the price-of-productionists, continue to sustain their argument, and
with some confidence.[22]

IV. Mathematical Economics

The third main direction in which economic thought and discussion
have shown a welcome revival in the last few years is the development of
mathematical economics and an increasing interest, if a critical interest,
in developments in this direction in the West during the past two decades.
Partly, but by no means entirely, this has a simple technological explanation: the increasing employment of electronic computers in industry and planning, and an admitted neglect previously of the study of
"cybernetics," has emphasized the need for developing programming-
techniques for handling economic material in this way. At first there
was a good deal of prejudice against the introduction of any of these
methods, which were regarded as a "Trojan horse" of bourgeois concepts
imported into Soviet economic thought and practice. The term "mathematical economics" had always been used to denote the kind of general
equilibrium theory derived from Walras and Pareto, and hence in
essence a justification of competitive equilibrium in a market economy
in subjective terms. What truck could Marxism have with this kind of
thing?

For some little time, however, there has evidently been an influential

---

[21] Turetsky, *op. cit.*, pp. 411-14. In one of the last articles of the late Prof. Blyumin
(I. Blyumin and V. Shliapentok, "On the Econometric School in Bourgeois Political
Economy," in *Voprosy Ekonomiki*, 1958, No. 11, pp. 79-93, the "practical usefulness" of
the concept of demand-elasticity (both price- and income-elasticity) in the study of
market conditions was explicitly recognized; the work of Prof. H. Schultz in the United
States on demand-studies being singled out for approval (pp. 88-9). Emphasis was laid
in the article on the need to distinguish "problems of political economy" from "technico-
economic problems."

[22] Cf. the recent article by Vaag and Zakharov cited above. A new and connected discussion now taking place is on "differential rent in conditions of socialism."

group, particularly among statisticians, who saw the grave limitations and defects of so parochial a view. Russian mathematics was pre-eminent: why should the social sciences alone be barred from enrichment from this source? Some mathematicians (such as Kantorovitch of whom we shall speak in a moment) had already made some contribution to techniques of economic and social accounting, but were in danger of being ignored because of the prevailing prejudice. Apart from the technical needs of the new computing machines, what seems to have sapped previous distrust and prejudice is the demonstration by mathematical economists and statisticians that two of the principal techniques in question had their roots in Soviet reality and not in the bourgeois world as had been supposed. Firstly, it was emphasized that the input-output method, associated with the name of Wassily Leontief, was in fact derived from the "method of material balances" developed by Soviet planners in the twenties (about which Leontief had indeed written an article in *Planovoye Khozyaistvo*, the Gosplan organ, in December 1925). This has been repeatedly underlined in articles by Nemchinov and others during the past few years. Secondly, the technique known in the West as "linear programming" was, it now appears, developed by the Leningrad mathematician Kantorovitch, and published by the University of Leningrad in 1939 under the title of *Matematicheskie Metodi Organisatsii i Planirovania Proizvodstvo (Mathematical Methods of Organizing and Planning Production)*.[23] This was several years before the public appearance of the American inventors of the method.

True, it looks as though little attention was paid to Kantorovitch's discovery at the time (perhaps the fact that Leningrad was under siege within two-and-a-half years of its publication had at least something to do with this); and although the presentation of input-output data in a matrix (or chessboard as it was called) was common in planning, the algebraic refinements of matrix techniques and iterative methods do not seem to have been developed. They were even discouraged officially in the thirties, Kuibyshev when in charge of Gosplan condemning the "statistical-arithmetical deviation in planning."[24] However, in both respects it is clear that this lag is now (roughly since 1956) being overcome. One writer in 1957 tells us that "in recent times the question of elaborating the chessboard balance has been raised repeatedly, in particular at the All-Union Conference of Statistics in June 1957."[25] Linear programming techniques have been applied not only in transport but also in a number of individual industrial plants and even farms in the

[23] The method was called by him that of "decisive multipliers."
[24] Cited approvingly by G. Sorokin of Gosplan in *Planovoye Khozyaistvo*, 1956, No. 1, p. 43, in the course of a criticism of planning by "abstract models."
[25] V. Belkin in *Voprosy Ekonomiki*, 1957, No. 12, p. 147.

Leningrad region.[26] A new work by Kantorovitch was published last year by the Academy, entitled *Ekonomicheskii Raschot Nailuchshego Ispol'zovania Resursov* (*Economic Calculation of the Best Utilization of Resources*). An article by him, explaining his calculation in terms of what he calls "indirect" as well as "direct" expenditures of labor, was even published in *Voprosy Ekonomiki*, usually cautious in such matters.[27] His critic in a later number of that journal fully recognized the value of Kantorovitch's method when applied to the handling of particular scarcities (*i.e.*, scarcities of particular productive resources) in a short period situation; what he disputed was its validity in a dynamic setting (and hence as a general basis for pricing) when the task of socialist planning consisted essentially of changing and liquidating previous scarcities, for which purpose he considered that calculation in terms of actual or "direct" labor-expenditure was appropriate.[28]

Indeed, quite a number of articles on econometric topics have recently appeared in the journals.[29] In addition to the Laboratory of Computing Machines and Methods of the U.S.S.R. Academy, a special institute attached to the Siberian branch of the Academy in Novosibirsk has been set up to study economic applications of electronic computer-techniques, and has worked in close association with the regional economic council. A new department of mathematical economics is to be formed this year in the Economics Faculty at Leningrad (and similarly in Moscow at the State Economics Institute) and extra-mural lectures on linear programming and other mathematical techniques are being organized for engineers and workers in industry. At the same time the Leningrad Institute of Mathematics is working in conjunction with the Leningrad *Sovnarkhoz* which is itself setting up a computer section. In April 1960 in Moscow a scientific conference on the use of mathematical methods in economics

[26] Another interesting example was that a Working Brigade of the Cheliabinsk Polytechnical Institute together with workers of the local tractor factory used linear programming methods "with positive results" (A. Aganbegian in *Planovoye Khozyaistvo*, 1960, No. 2, p. 54 seq.).

[27] "On Calculating Productive Expenditures" in *Voprosy Ekonomiki*, 1960, No. 1. However, a note was appended to the effect that "the editors differ from a number of points of view in this article and propose to submit these to critical examination in a forthcoming number of this journal."

[28] A. Katz, *Voprosy Ekonomiki*, 1960, No. 5, pp. 117 f. In general Nemchinov seems to agree with this criticism.

[29] One of the earliest of them, in *Voprosy Ekonomiki*, 1957, No. 12, about input-output matrices was by V. E. Belkin of the new Laboratory of Computing Machines and Systems of the Academy; Blyumin's survey of Econometrics in 1958 we have already mentioned; the following year came A. Boyarsky, "On Econometrics and the Use of Mathematics in Economics Analysis" in *Planovoye Khozyaistvo*, 1959. No. 7, which was a review of the subject from Walras, through the Cobb-Douglas theorem and Leontif, to Kantorovitch and the Theory of Games; A. Aganbegian in *Planovoye Khozyaistvo*, 1960, No. 2, dealt mainly with linear programming; and in *Voprosy Ekonomiki*, the most recent articles by Kantorovich and Nemchinov have been already mentioned.

and planning was called jointly by the Economics-Philosophy-Law Section of the Academy and the Academy's Siberian branch. This heard as many as 56 papers read (in plenary session and in six specialized sections) with more than ninety persons taking part in discussion.[30] A further conference is mooted for the autumn of 1961, and also this year the setting up in the Academy of an inter-departmental scientific council for the study of mathematical methods in economics and planning. Already at the end of 1959 there had been held in Warsaw a conference of all the socialist countries on questions of elaborating the balance of the national economy, in the course of which the question of input-output tables and work being done on them received particular attention.[31] And in his recent *Voprosy Ekonomiki* article Academician Nemchinov called for the publication of a special journal devoted to mathematical economics. How far the specific input-output techniques associated with Leontief are being used by Gosplan itself is not quite clear. Probably their precise use and application are still matters of some controversy, one of the incidental difficulties apparently being that statistical information is not always available to Gosplan at present in the requisite form.

This is how Nemchinov sums up the attitude to input-output analysis etc. in his most recent article:

Rejecting bourgeois conceptions of the American economist V. Leontief, we can successfully utilize the "input-output" method of analysis, or, more strictly, the method of analysis of inter-branch productive relations, especially as this method without doubt arose under the direct and immediate influence of the first Soviet balance of the national economy built by the U.S.S.R. Central Statistical Department in 1923–4. We must not shun, still less fear the term "econometric investigation," properly understood, of course, and properly utilized in the conditions of socialist economy. It is essential to study critically investigations in the region of foreign econometrics and mathematical economics, and all that is useful and valuable in accounting and mathematical instruments, suitable for the analysis of economic relations, must be utilized in the practice of our planned economy." [32]

Indicative of these new developments was the publication last year of a collective work edited by Academician Nemchinov entitled *The Use of Mathematics in Economic Investigations*. In addition to two contributions by Kantorovitch, there is a set of elementary lectures on linear programming delivered by a Hungarian economist in Budapest, chapters on the applications of linear programming, especially to transport prob-

[30] *Planovoye Khozyaistvo*, 1960, No. 5, pp. 88-90. Nemchinov gave the main report. The conference was extensively reported in *Voprosy Ekonomiki*, 1960, No. 8, pp. 100-128.
[31] *Plan. Khoz.*, 1960, No. 5, pp. 92-6.
[32] *Voprosy Ekonomiki*, 1960, No. 6, p. 19. For adherence to the more traditional emphasis in East Germany, however, see *Wirtschaftswissenschaft*, 8 Jahygang, 7. Sonderheft; also I. Dvorkin in *Voprosy Ekon.* 1960, No. 8.

lems, and the translation of an article by Professor Oskar Lange (written originally for the Indian statistical journal *Sankhya* and embodied in his *Textbook on Econometrics*) in which he compares Leontief's input-output method with Marx's schema of expanded reproduction. Of particular interest to the present writer is a long contribution, running to nearly 200 pages, by Professor V. V. Novozhilov, one of the Leningrad group of pioneers of the linear programming approach.[33] What is specially interesting about his contribution is his linking up of the effectiveness of investment coefficient with the question of prices. In this connection he suggests a new cost-category which he calls "national economy cost," to include, in addition to prime cost (*sebestoimost*), a quantity designed to measure the effectiveness of investment in the economy as a whole. He shows that a cost-price constructed in this way will show the method of production that yields the standard ratio of effectiveness as the least-cost method—*i.e.* it will ensure that a thing produced under this method of production will show a lower cost than the same product when produced under any alternative technical method.[34] This he claims is an application of the only correct principle of calculation for a socialist economy, that of minimizing labor expenditures (through minimizing expenditures of labor *subject to a given output of capital goods,* governed by the existing size of Department I industries).

It is of interest to note in this connection that, in a postcript-note to the volume, the editor, while drawing attention to the analogy between Novozhilov's "national economic cost" and "price of production," emphasizes that it has certain qualitative differences which make it a superior version of a "transformed form of value" relevant to socialist society: in particular, that it can be treated as an accounting-price category only, and does not imply "market autonomism" as its background; moreover that it does not necessarily depend on the use of a rigidly uniform effectiveness-ratio for all sectors and branches. It is, further, interesting (and may possibly be significant in connection with future changes in the system of actual prices) that as an accounting-price for use in investment-decisions Novozhilov's proposal has been embodied

33 See his early articles of 1939 and 1946 published in translation in *International Economic Papers*, No. 6.

34 Specifically what Novozhilov suggests is that, if r stands for the standard effectiveness-ratio (as defined earlier in the present article), K for the capital-cost involved, and C for the prime cost, then what he calls "national economic cost" should be calculated in each case as rK + C. This solution can be shown to be essentially the same as that proposed by the present writer in his *Essay on Economic Growth and Planning*, Chapter VI, where it is suggested that if (in the so-called "normal" case) price is so fixed as to include a proportional share of surplus product in addition to wage-cost, that technique will be most profitable to use which maximizes growth (maximizing growth with a *given* labor force being, of course, the same as minimizing the labor needed to produce a given output).

in the recent "Standard Methods of Determining the Economic Effectiveness of Capital Investment." [35]

V. "Copying the West" or "Towards a Political Economy of Socialism?"

The reaction of most economists in the West to these developments is that they represent simply a belated importation of previously neglected notions of "bourgeois economics," and that while this can be welcomed as a rational step it is hardly an intellectual innovation to admire. This view is based, I believe, on a crucial misconception: a misconception that rests on an underestimate of the ideological element in thought. By this I mean, not simply the intrusion of ethical ideas and so-called "value judgments" into our thinking, but the fact that ideas have significance as part of a complex "picture of the real world," and this picture is inevitably influenced by the perspective in which we view the world and the presuppositions which we inherit as part of our mode of thought and belief. In the social sciences at any rate it is not at all a simple matter to separate a purely formal notion from the whole framework of thought, with its tangle of implicit definitions and assumptions, in which it has been traditionally embodied. Such a notion cannot, therefore, be as easily transferred from one context to another as the simplifiers and eclectics think: that is, it cannot be easily transferred without importing along with it a whole number of associated ideas, of a more institutional or historically relative kind, that have become inextricably entwined with it. Take, for instance, the notion of "elasticity"—a purely quantitative ratio borrowed from mathematics. What could be more purely a non-ideological, non- "superstructural" "tool"? But does it not at once imply some entity, called a "demand curve," *of which* it is a measure—an entity about whose nature there may be much controversy and whose very "existence" could be called in question? Moreover, in contemporary economic thought that entity is connected with a whole conceptual system of "indifference curves" or "behavior lines," from which it has been derived, together with a series of assumptions about individual consumers' behavior or thought-processes which these abstract notions were created to express. And what is true of an elasticity is true, *mutatis mutandis,* of the notion of an interest-rate, however much we may regard

---

[35] It is advocated for use at the enterprise-level as a special "coefficient of profitability" of investment. Whenever several variants are to be compared, the formula "C + E · K = minimum" is recommended, where E is the standard coefficient of effectiveness for the branch (*Planovoye Khozyaistvo,* 1960 No. 3, pp. 56 f.). See also Khachaturov's reference to "including in current expenses of production of a percentage of original expenditures, equal to the established coefficient of effectiveness of that branch" (*Voprosy Ekonomiki,* 1957 No. 2, p. 120).

it, abstractly, as a "pure ratio" connecting entities having different dat-
ings in time.

In other words, it is only by an astringent process of critical analysis
that one can separate out notions from their historical-ideological content
and from other institutionally-relative notions with which they are associated, and hence be in a position to discover what meaning (if any)
and relevance the former may have when transferred to a qualitatively
different social context. In the absence of such a critical examination it
may well be a sound instinct to oppose such a "transfer," by reason of
the large amount of dross that an ounce of gold may bear with it. Yet
to oppose is, at the same time, an admission of intellectual poverty—of
the immaturity of one's own critical thought.

Partly no doubt it is true to regard what has been happening recently
in the U.S.S.R. (and in some of the contiguous countries) as an emerging
from the shades of dogmatism, which cramped enquiry and discussion
for too long. But this is no more than part of it, possibly a minor aspect.
More important, and certainly more encouraging, about this new stage
in theory and discussion is the extent to which it betokens a new maturity
of Marxist thought—a maturity when it can use its tools of criticism, no
longer only negatively but also positively, so as to make constructive use,
within its own conceptual framework, of ideas and techniques that it
once feared, and at the same time foster creative thought and discussion
to the end of "generalizing the experience of socialist economy" and
building a Political Economy of Socialism.

42

The Use of Mathematical Methods in Economic Research and Planning *

V. S. NEMCHINOV
*Head, Laboratory for the Applicaton of
Mathematical Methods in Economics,
Academy of Sciences, USSR*

In today's conditions of building communism socialist society requires far higher scientific standards. The founders of Marxism-Leninism pointed out that the function of science is not merely to learn the laws of nature and society, but also to work out the ways and means of placing those laws at the service of social progress and the full development of the material and cultural standards of all members of society. This makes it necessary for the science of economics to solve in good time the problems posed by socialist construction, for our practical efforts today require improvement in the application of the known laws of development of nature and society.

Guided by the experience in socialist construction, the Communist Party and the Soviet government are perfecting the planning and management of the national economy, ensuring the successful forward movement of our society in communist construction. In connection with this progress, the standards of requirements of economic science have been further raised. Yet economics continues to lag behind the needs of actual practice.

The Soviet public today regards the economist as a social engineer whose duty it is to ensure the working out of a system of economic measures for the continuous and accelerated development of social production for the purpose of producing an abundance of material and cultural values. Today, the results of economic research must be raised to such a degree of exactness and concreteness that they will convert the laws which have been apprehended into an efficient, scientific and exact mechanism for the planned direction of the national economy.

* From *Voprosy Ekonomiki,* 1960, No. 6. Translated in and excerpts reprinted from *Problems of Economics,* November, 1960, pp. 15-25, by permission of the publisher.

Deliberate use of economic laws requires knowledge not only of the qualitative but also of the quantitative aspect of economic phenomena. Without a theoretical approach to analyzing the quantitative relationships in the socialist economy, it is impossible thoroughly and deliberately to use the economic laws of socialism, in particular to improve scientific planning for the purpose of developing the national economy and culture. Yet, along with certain problems of theoretical qualitative analysis of the ways and means of building communism, a quantitative analysis of economic phenomena has today become one of the "weak points" of Soviet economics. This is due not only to the much higher requirements set for Soviet economic science, but also to a certain underestimation by individual economists of the need for a scientific analysis of the quantitative side of the economic processes at work in the socialist national economy. . . .

In every science a quantitative analysis is inseparably bound up with the use of measures and numbers, with mathematical methods, and in economic science it is bound up, in addition, with extensive use of statistical methods, including the methods of mathematical statistics.

In economics, as is the case in all other sciences, the chief condition for the application of mathematical methods is a preliminary qualitative analysis of the nature of the economic phenomena being studied. Otherwise there arises the danger of substance disappearing and leaving nothing but equations, and secondary indexes beginning illegitimately to take the place of meaningful social and economic categories. On the other hand, the history of the development of any science shows that it becomes exact after its main criteria and basic laws are given a quantitative, mathematically formulated expression. Economic science is no exception.

The science of mathematics requires precise formulation of the initial conditions and characteristics of the phenomena studied as an essential prerequisite for consequent logical constructions. . . . It should always be remembered that mathematics has been compared to a millstone and if you place weeds under it you will never get wheat flour.

While warning against the abuse of mathematics, we must at the same time not underestimate the highly positive and salutary role played by mathematics in improving other sciences. Marx believed that a science attains perfection only when it has succeeded in making use of mathematics.[1] Testifying to this estimate by Marx are the memoirs of M. Kovalevskii[2] and mathematical notebooks left by Marx.

Proper scientific application of mathematical methods in the various sciences undoubtedly enriches them and helps improve them, but abuse

[1] See *Reminiscences About Marx and Engels,* Gospolitizdat, 1956, p. 66 (Russian edition).

[2] *Ibid.,* p. 311.

of mathematics could, of course, play the part of a "Trojan horse," making for the penetration of an alien and inimical ideology. To avoid this, the necessary measures should be taken, one of which is to raise the standard of mathematical knowledge and mathematical culture of our economists.

Some economists believe that another precaution is to fix the limits of application of mathematics in economics. Yet we should speak not of the limits of application of mathematics in economics, but only of the primacy of a preliminary qualitative analysis as the basic condition for scientific application of mathematical methods and of the need for taking into account the complexity of the conditions of the use of mathematics in the socio-economic field. Nor should it be forgotten that there are economists who still hold the incorrect view that the application of mathematical methods in economics is useless and even harmful.

In employing mathematical methods in economic research we should not, on the one hand, forget that mathematics plays a subsidiary role in the sciences in which it is applied, but on the other hand, we should not reduce the importance of mathematics to a narrow, technical feature and underestimate its great possibilities for developing the theory of the particular field of science in which it is used. . . .

The increasing attention given to analysis of the quantitative side of economic phenomena and to the development of the mathematical methods of this analysis stems from the progress of the Soviet economy, the increasingly complex tasks which we have set ourselves in the transition to the building of a communist society.

The greater attention given to theoretical and practical questions of analysis of the quantitative interconnections of the Soviet economy, far from contradicting the basic principles of the Marxist-Leninist political economy of socialism, actually follows directly from them. Yet some Western economists see in this signs of a certain deviation from Marxist-Leninist ideology. To illustrate, the January 1960 issue of the magazine *Foreign Affairs* carried an article by W. Leontief, an American economist, in which he asserted that Soviet economists are merely using the "achievements" of bourgeois political economy in their application of mathematical methods in economic research and planning. The article contains many contradictions and improbable assertions. For instance, while admitting that optimum programming methods first originated in the Soviet Union, Leontief at the same time denies the fact that the methods used in analyzing production links among branches of industry were also first worked out in the USSR in drawing up the national economic balance-sheet for 1923–1924. In denying the priority of Soviet economists and statisticians in working out the method of inter-industry production links, Leontief, in particular, puts forward the obviously improbable version that his article printed in issue No. 12 of the magazine

Planovoe Khoziaistvo for 1925 (Leontief at the time was completing his studies in the Economics Department of Leningrad University) was a translation from an article carried by a German magazine. (The article was written by him on the occasion of the publication of the balance-sheet of the national economy of the USSR for 1923–1924, which had just then appeared in the newspaper *Ekonomicheskaia Zhizn*.) He said nothing about the fact that the mathematical equations used by him in his work *The Structure of the American Economy* are essentially the equations worked out by the Leningrad economist and mathematician V. Dmitriev (the author of *Ekonomicheskie Ocherki,* 1904) and they differ from Walras' equations.

Leontief's assertion that the Soviet method of balances merely raises important economic problems but does not solve them does not correspond to the facts either. The method of balances gives an answer to the most important economic questions, establishing a connection between the structural characteristics of the national economy and its dynamic factors. This method makes it possible, among other things, to determine the degree of dependence of the coefficient of expanded reproduction on the difference between the net production of department I (production of the means of production) and the material costs of department II (production of articles of consumption). The use of these balanced economic interrelationships furnishes a thorough explanation of the high rates of economic development of the Soviet economy, which can hardly be said about Leontief's primitive formula (which he identifies with Adam Smith's economic thesis and Benjamin Franklin's "homely" formula), according to which an expansion of income requires that a constantly increasing share of it be channeled into productive capital investment at the expense of consumption. If the balanced interrelationships of the structural economic characteristics and dynamic factors are properly understood, productive capital investments not only do not require a restriction of consumption, but on the contrary they ensure a steady rise on consumption over a long period, a rise which would be impossible without the corresponding earlier productive capital investments.

Properly and scientifically used, the Soviet method of balances permits us to reveal with sufficient thoroughness and detail the entire complex structure of the economic mechanism, and on the basis of knowledge of the laws of the functioning of the economy helps to scientifically regulate the course of economic development, ensuring a high rate of economic growth.

Probably what hinders bourgeois economists from understanding the full importance of the method of balances used in Soviet planning calculations is their fear of a deeper knowledge of the mechanics of operation of economic laws, laws which open up the prospect—an "undesirable" one for bourgeois economists—for attempts to regulate the national economy, which, incidentally, Leontief admits in his article.

Thorough scientific research in quantitative interrelations is expressed in the USSR in the application not only of the method of balances but also of other methods used by our planning agencies.

How incorrect is Leontief's notion of the methodology of Soviet planning can be seen from his assertion that Soviet planning methods do not actually differ from the methods employed during World War II by the American War Production Board, the British Ministry of Supply and their counterparts in Germany. He fails to see the profound fundamental difference between Soviet planning and the methods of intervention used by military circles in the national economy. However, progressive Western economists and sociologists rightly hold that only the aggregate of social measures which systematically assure a country's economic growth and which are taken for the purpose of raising the material and cultural standards of the population may be called planning. At the Fourth International Sociological Congress held in Italy in 1959 this viewpoint was graphically expressed in the reports of Myrdal and Bettelheim. However, in economic literature abroad national economic planning is usually erroneously identified with any system of long-range synthetic economic computations and with programming technique. Such, for instance, are some of the documents covering Asian countries put out by the Economic and Social Council of the United Nations.

Carried away by his "manipulator aspect," Leontief goes even further. He not only completely denies the fundamental special characteristics of Soviet planning but even asserts that there are no principles whatever underlying the methodology and technique of planning in the USSR, since neither he nor other bourgeois economists have been able to discover any. This assertion is accompanied by another alleged paradox involving an imaginary contrast between the unparalleled successes in transforming the earlier technically backward Russia into a great industrial power and an imaginary decline in Soviet economic science. However, the rapid economic advance of a country is incompatible with a decline of economics. Our country's rapid economic expansion certainly is based on the achievements of Marxist-Leninist economic thought, achievements which were expressed in the correct and scientific principles underlying Soviet economic policy. And Leontief's statement that the communist leaders are their own economists merely testifies to the fact that in our country economic practice and theory are closely interwoven. The scientific correctness and accuracy of the fundamental principles of Marxist-Leninist economic theory are undoubtedly the major condition for our practical achievements in the economic construction of socialism.

The greater attention given to the theoretical approach and the more profound analysis of quantitative interrelations in the country's economy should make our economic and planning calculations even more accurate. Improvement and greater accuracy of economic and planning calculations, far from altering the principles of Soviet economic policy and of national economic planning, actually follow from them. They stem only from the further complexity and expansion of the Soviet economy. . . .

43

Soviet Economists Debate the Economics of Socialism: Excerpts from Recent Writings by Some of the Most Famous Participants in the Great Value—Price Controversy

a. On the Importance of the Correct Determination of Value in a Socialist Society *

S. G. STRUMILIN
Academician of the Academy of Sciences, USSR

As we know, the definition of value remains an important task under socialism. Moreover, with the abolition of the capitalist method of production this task and the accounting system serving it "becomes more important than ever," in Marx's words.[1] Socialism opens up the widest prospects for the application of value in national economic planning, primarily in regulating labor time and in the distribution of social labor between the different categories of production in proportion to their requirements. But a determination of value is needed not only here. The reduction of value may serve as a measure of the efficiency of our planned capital investments and, therefore, as an indispensable guide to their optimal planned distribution in the interests of a maximum saving of time and the highest rate of growth of labor productivity. Comparison of the relative value and local labor requirements used to produce one and the same amount of goods in the different republics and regions

---

* From *Voprosy Ekonomiki*, 1959, No. 8. Translated under the title "On the Determination of Value and its Application under Socialism," in *Problems of Economics*, January, 1960, pp. 3-9. Excerpts reprinted from the translation by permission of the publisher.
[1] K. Marx, *Capital*, Volume III, 1954, p. 865 (Russian Edition).

of the USSR will facilitate the planning and rational distribution of the productive forces in the country, while a similar comparison within the framework of the world system of socialist countries may be used in the interests of the most rational international distribution of labor, co-operation and specialization of production. Finally, the determination of the value of different goods is of the utmost importance for the rational planning of the prices of these goods and for the accounting of the corresponding accumulations, as well as for the maintenance of an adequate equivalence of exchange in domestic trade and the highest possible profitability of exports and imports.

True, up to a certain time we were content in our planning practice to do without a determination of the value of products. Prices were planned with a partial view towards accounts of the cost of production, and where they were inadequate our failings were sometimes corrected by market elements. But these failings always played only into the hands of profiteers, to the detriment of the vital interests of the social economy. Such failings are particularly dangerous when they are made in the planning of the prices of commodities used in the exchange between town and country. For a long time we did not even have any accounting of production costs of agricultural produce, and agricultural prices were planned without any proper bearings. The practice of fixing grain delivery and procurement prices up to 1953, teaches us that serious disproportions and delays in economic development are caused by blunders in planning in this field. The greater our plans for increasing investments in the different branches of the economy and the greater the mass of commodities realized on the home and foreign markets, the more accurate must be the computation of the effectiveness of these investments and the more important it is to determine the value of products.

The need to determine the full social value of the goods produced, along with an account of their production costs, i.e., the individual expenses involved in their production by each cost accounting enterprise taken separately, has become more and more pressing in recent years. The reorganization of the MTS and the change in the system of planning of collective farm production have greatly facilitated the determination of the value of food and raw material resources of the countryside, while the reorganization of industrial and construction management and the setting up of economic councils have created new opportunities for solving this problem in these spheres too. At the same time these measures confront the planning of prices with new demands. . . .

Lower prices for products of the advanced enterprises in their competitive struggle with the more backward ones is a method practiced under capitalism. Selling goods a dime cheaper than the competitor, reducing him to bankruptcy and winning the market, is the direct means of achieving an equal rate of profit under capitalist conditions. Our socialist enterprises have no need for such competition. But equal prices for equal goods under unequal labor equipment in different enterprises means an unequal rate of profit for them. Considering this soberly in the planning of investments for optimal use of all the resources of past labor, it is necessary to orient our prices to the level of the *social value* of all goods.

The advocates of prices of production believe that the principle of profitability oriented towards an equal rate of profit, as proposed by them, is not "a far-fetched principle." It would be more correct to say, however, that it is a flimsy principle of price formation or at least one whose implications have not been considered by them. . . .

b. On the Determination of the Economic Effectiveness of Capital Investments *

T. S. KHACHATUROV
Corresponding member of the Academy of Sciences, USSR

Among the most important economic problems of communist construction are those of the economic effectiveness of capital investments in the national economy. Capital investments must be used most effectively because the rates of growth of production and the period required for the solution of the USSR's chief economic task depend on this. . . .

The determination of capital investment effectiveness is closely linked with national economic planning and should become an integral part of it. . . .

In order to obtain a comprehensive solution of the capital investment effectiveness problem and to elaborate the most correct and accurate methods of determining this effectiveness, it is essential to know the value of the concrete items produced and to employ it for the calculations involved. A knowledge of the value involved provides the possibility of applying the capital investment effectiveness indices in planning and, in particular, of employing these indices when apportioning capital investments to the individual production branches.

At present such calculations are rather difficult, due to considerable

* From Planovoe Khoziaistvo, 1959, No. 8. Translated under the title "Methodological Questions of Determining the Economic Effectiveness of Capital Investments," in *Problems of Economics,* January, 1960, pp. 17-21. Excerpts reprinted from the translation by permission of the publisher.

differences in the relationships between prices and value in different industries and for different articles. Therefore, until the value of concrete items of produce is determined, prices and production costs may be used as approximations to it. It is necessary here to find out the degree of the deviation of price from value due to turnover tax, etc., and to study the problem of the possible use of conventional prices for some economic effectiveness calculations.

Research on capital investment effectiveness under socialism covers a wide range of problems. These include the study of the factors that determine the possible volume of capital investments with due consideration for the accumulations in the preceding period (the effectiveness factor depends on the volume of capital investments); the role played by capital investment effectiveness calculations in national economic planning and the distribution of capital investments among the production branches, economic areas, and enterprises; the study of the absolute effect of capital investments in terms of the increase of the physical volume of the national income; the possibility of determining the absolute effect of capital investments both as a whole and by production branches and individual enterprises; the study of the relative economic effectiveness of capital investments in the selection of the most expedient variants of capital investments; the study of the economic effectiveness of capital investments in new machinery.

A study of all these questions makes it possible to determine what economic factors influence the effectiveness level and how to establish the economic effectiveness of capital investments in planning the development of the national economy, its individual branches, economic areas, and enterprises, so as to obtain an optimal combination of all these factors. The mathematical determination of such an optimum represents a solution of an extreme problem involving the finding of the greatest possible production effect for society with the least possible input of social labor. . . .

c. On the Calculation of Production Inputs *

L. V. KANTOROVICH
Leningrad State University

Socialist society is interested in the maximum saving of social labor in order to satisfy most fully the needs of all of its members. The saving of labor requires the appropriate reckoning and estimation of the social labor input required for the production of various goods.

The magnitude of the input of social labor-time in the production of a given article is not constant but changes with every variation in the productive power of labor. The latter "is determined by various circumstances, among others by the average degree of skill of the workmen, the state of science and the degree of its practical application, the social organization of production, the scale and effectiveness of the means of production, and by natural conditions." [1] The input of social labor is a concrete magnitude, quite definite for the given point of time, given situation and conditions. This magnitude cannot, however, be found directly. In reality, practically no commodity is produced under socially average conditions. Different enterprises turning out similar commodities do not have the same technical facilities, work in different physical conditions, and so on. But the magnitude of the social-labor input is the same for each unit of the given output, regardless of how it is produced, as each individual unit of a commodity is but "an average sample of its class." [2] The task is to compute correctly, on the basis of concrete data for individual labor inputs, the magnitude of social labor inputs required for the production of a unit of the given output.

In this connection, also, the following problem arises in socialist society: how to consider the effect of selecting one or another method of producing a given commodity on the level of labor inputs in other types of output or in other sectors of production? For with modern, highly developed technology, the production of different commodities is closely interrelated. Provision of favorable conditions and allocation of definite resources for the production of one commodity to a certain extent affect the production conditions of other commodities. Therefore, a given operation or the production of a given commodity cannot be examined

* The editors of *Voprosy Ekonomiki* differ with the author on a number of propositions put forward in this article and intend to comment on them critically in an early issue of the magazine. From *Voprosy Ekonomiki*, 1960, No. 1. Translated in and excerpts reprinted from *Problems of Economics*, May, 1960, pp. 3-10, by permission of the publisher.

[1] Karl Marx, *Capital*, Moscow, 1954, Vol. 1, p. 40 (English edition).
[2] *Ibid.*, p. 39.

in isolation. To solve this complex problem we deem it natural to examine first a narrower problem, namely, to ascertain the effect of selecting a production method for a given commodity on the level of inputs in the production of other types of output within the limits of a certain production complex that puts out several different commodities. The object here is to determine "the inputs in the complex as a whole" per unit of each output, considering the interrelations of these inputs. Such inputs may be termed aggregate [3] inputs. . . .

The foregoing shows that to calculate aggregate labor inputs it is necessary in each case to consider indirect as well as direct labor inputs. Only by adding indirect labor inputs to the direct ones is it possible to convert concrete individual labor inputs into uniform standards and thus derive the aggregate labor inputs for the given output.

Consideration of indirect inputs makes it possible to decide correctly the question of using favorable natural conditions (good land in our examples). The proposed method eliminates the possibility of accidental, incomplete use of these conditions. Besides more fertile land, such conditions may be: water for irrigation, forests, fishing ground, rich oil fields, mineral deposits, etc.

Output estimates which take account of indirect inputs, particularly the inclusion of rent in regard to production under limited favorable physical conditions, facilitate the proper allocations of scarce commodities, their economy, and substitution by other commodities. Under socialism rent must certainly be considered in planning. The amount of rent must be such as to ensure the most rational use of natural resources. . . .

d. Concerning a Fallacious Concept of Economic Calculations [*]

A. I. KATS
Scientific Research Institute of Labor of the State Committee of the Council of Ministers, USSR, on Questions of Labor and Wages

Last year L. V. Kantorovich, Corresponding Member of the Academy of Sciences of the USSR, published his book *Economic Calculation of the Best Use of Resources,* and No. 1 of the journal *Voprosy Ekonomiki* for

[3] Translator's note: *kompleksnymi.*
[*] From *Voprosy Ekonomiki*, 1960, No. 5. Translated in and excerpts reprinted from *Problems of Economics,* November, 1960, pp. 42-52, by permission of the publisher.

1960 carried his article on the same subject entitled "On the Calculation of Production Inputs." As a mathematician L. V. Kantorovich deserves credit for formulating in the late '30s the main principles of a new branch of applied mathematics—linear programming—which has been increasingly used for solving complex economic problems. In his latest works, however, L. V. Kantorovich appears more as an economist than a mathematician and presents a general system of economic calculations.

It is quite obvious that even the best mathematical methods can be misapplied in a certain field of objective phenomena and lead to fallacious results. Of primary importance, therefore, is not only the degree of refinement of the mathematical means used, but also a correct interpretation of their real essence. L. V. Kantorovich's general concept, unfortunately, provides a classic example of the unjustified application of correct mathematical methods in a particular field. The use of this concept may result in major miscalculations, and this applies especially to the solution of dynamic problems of the national economy. . . .

It can be easily seen that at the bottom of all the above-listed errors is the fact that L. V. Kantorovich ignores the Marxist theory of the expenditure of labor as the substance of social costs of production. This leads, in particular, to the totally unsound nature of his suggestions in the field of price formation.

From this erroneous approach in applying higher mathematics for purposes of general economic calculations it does not follow that higher mathematics cannot be widely applied in the general economic calculations of planning. This conclusion would be absurd. On the contrary, a vast field for the application of mathematics in economics is opening up in connection with electronic computing techniques. This refers, above all, to the accurate calculation of actual costs of production, against which L. V. Kantorovich rails for no reason at all; these estimates underlying any correct economic calculation cannot be performed without applying higher mathematics and electronic computing techniques.

e. Calculation of Outlays in a Socialist Economy *

V. V. NOVOZHILOV
Leningrad State University

Economic literature today gives much attention to the problem of the planned utilization of the law of value and to methods of calculating outlays. Economists differ, however, over the nature of the shortcomings in the calculation of outlays and how they can be eliminated. Some believe that prices of output should be set at the level of its value, while outlays should be calculated according to the individual value of each product. Other economists hold that price formation and calculation of outlays should be based on the price of production formula. Still others think that the principles of price formation and calculation of outlays in a socialist economy do not fit within any price formation formulas of past systems and that a special, transformed form of value operates in a socialist economy which is specifically characteristic of it.

All of the participants in this discussion proceed from the same premise: outlays actually consist only of labor and value is determined by its outlay. Controversy arises only over the principles and methods of calculating outlays. In our opinion it is desirable to apply mathematics when solving this question. By means of mathematics and modern computing techniques we can greatly improve the methods of calculating outlays in a socialist economy.

The problem of the principles involved in the calculation of outlays under socialism can be solved only on the basis of Marx's theory of value. Consistent application of the major propositions of this theory under socialism is of decisive importance for elaborating the principles of optimum planning. . . .

Planning is complicated by the fact that as a consequence of the scarcity of the best means of production the minimums of the individual costs of products in whose manufacture these best resources can be used become *incompatible* with each other. . . .

After all, the economy derived by a given enterprise through the application of raw materials that are in short supply may be exceeded by the additional outlays at other enterprises, which could have used the rare raw materials to much greater advantage, but were deprived of this

* From *Voprosy Ekonomiki*, 1961, No. 2. Translated in and excerpts reprinted from *Problems of Economics*, December, 1961, pp. 18-28, by permission of the publisher.

opportunity. For instance, if the use of critical raw materials at one enterprise yields an economy of one million rubles, while other enterprises could have saved two million rubles by using them, it will mean depriving the national economy of a saving of one million rubles. . . .

f. On the Proper Relationship Between Mathematics and Economics in a Socialist Society *

A. BOIARSKII
Moscow State University

The problems of applying mathematical methods in economic science have been worked on intensively in our country for several years now. This work is being conducted by a special laboratory of the USSR Academy of Sciences, the Institute of Economic Research of the State Economic Council, the Institute of Complex Transport Problems of the USSR Academy of Sciences, by a number of universities, Moscow and Leningrad Universities, the Moscow State Institute of Economics, the Moscow Institute of Engineering Economics, the Siberian Branch of the USSR Academy of Sciences, the Armenian Academy of Sciences, and others. In April 1960 the USSR Academy of Sciences held a special conference at which economists and mathematicians met for joint creative discussions.[1] The problems involved in applying mathematics to economics are dealt with in monographs and economic journals.[2] This is unquestionably a progressive phenomenon.

The application of mathematics in economics essentially means that the use of mathematical methods allows for a more complete, profound and precise study of the quantitative aspect of economic phenomena, which is especially necessary in economic planning. The importance of exact quantitive relations in economics has been well understood at least

---

* The editors of *Voprosy Ekonomiki* agree with the basic criticisms of the author with respect to the works of L. V. Kantorovich and V. V. Novozhilov. From *Voprosy Ekonomiki*, 1961, No. 2. Translated under the title "On the Application of Mathematics in Economics," in *Problems of Economics*, January, 1962, pp. 12-24. Excerpts reprinted from the translation by permission of the publisher.

1 See the review of the scientific conference on the application of mathematical methods in economic investigations and planning in *Voprosy Ekonomiki*, 1960, No. 8.

2 See the journals *Voprosy Ekonomiki* and *Planovoe Khoziaistvo* for the past few years, and the pamphlet *O Primenenii Matematiki v Ekonomicheskikh Issledovaniiakh i Ob Otnoshenii k Ekonometrike*, Gosstatizdat, 1959.

since the times of William Petty. As Karl Marx pointed out, "instead of weaving together a whole series of words in comparative and superlative degrees and speculative arguments, he began to speak in terms of numbers, weights and measures. . . ." [3] The mere designation "political arithmetic" indicates that even at that time the close tie between economic science and mathematics was clearly understood. This tie was stressed by Marx time and again. . . .

Economics is particularly based on *partiinost*. This is equally true of the application of mathematics in economics. Its propositions cannot lose their *partiinost* because they come dressed in mathematical formulas, as can be demonstrated from a number of examples. . . .

The so-called "optimum planning" proposed by L. V. Kantorovich is an example of the erroneous inferences resulting from an attempt to proceed not from economic content to mathematical relationships, but the other way, from mathematics to economic content. . . .

The very character of dependence of marginal outlays in Kantorovich's system is in full accord with the usual concepts of the marginalists. His system includes the whole notorious arsenal of "laws" of marginalism: the law of declining productivity, the law of declining fertility, the law of declining effectiveness of outlays, etc. And yet it is a well-known fact that increasing production in existing enterprises results in lower outlays per unit of output, providing this increase does not go beyond the reasonable limits set by the modern level of technology. Beyond these limits an increase in output is achieved through construction of new enterprises, which, in turn, are not built after the image and likeness of the old ones, but according to the latest achievements of science and technology. As a result, outlays on them will be still lower. . . .

Some elements of Kantorovich's totally fallacious conception can be found in V. V. Novozhilov's ideas, although he uses different terminology and designations. . . . [4]

What has been said so far does not mean, of course, that in calculations one should not resort to mathematical methods, in particular to linear programming. It is just not necessary to make linear programming the basis for price policy. The great Russian mathematician P. L. Chebyshev wrote that mathematics came into being and advanced under the influence of the basic common task of human activity: to utilize to maximum advantage the available resources. Linear programming is one of the means of achieving this end. With its aid one can solve problems for

3 *K Kritike Politicheskoi Ekonomii*, Gospolitizdat, 1953, p. 41 [Russian edition; the quotation has been retranslated from the Russian—Editor].

4 See his article "Izmerenie Zatrat i Ikh Rezul'tatov v Sotsialisticheskom Khoziaistve," in the collection *Primenenie Matematiki v Ekonomicheskikh Issledovaniiakh*, Sotsekgiz, 1959; and his article "Ischislenie Zatrat v Sotsialisticheskom Khoziaistve," published in this issue of *Voprosy Ekonomiki* [the latter article was published in the December 1961 issue of *Problems of Economics*—Editor] (and excerpted above. [Editor's Note.])

determining the best plan of freightage, a number of problems concerning the distribution of assignments to enterprises, choice of the best variant for using a scarce material if the latter is needed by several production units, the choice of the best technological variants, and many other problems. All of the above constitute a fruitful field for the application of linear programming, which can yield an immense effect in the national economy. . . .

Mathematical analysis of economics cannot be detached from economic science because this analysis cannot be achieved separately from qualitative analysis. Mathematical investigations of economic phenomena should not be made at some point of "junction" of mathematics and economics, nor in a "no man's land" between them, where the principles of economics are no longer operative—especially the principle of *partiinost*—and where one may arbitrarily devise economic laws. These investigations should be carried out obligatorily as a part of economic science, within its bounds. The point of "junction" of mathematical and economical objects, to our mind, does not constitute an object for a special, third science. If quantitative analysis goes hand in hand with qualitative analysis and is based on the latter it is a part of economic science. If it is divorced from it, it is at best an analysis of the abstract quantities which form a part of mathematics. Mathematics must be incorporated into economics, not separated from it. Mathematical analysis of the economy must become the business of the economists themselves—it should not be turned over to the so-called "econometricians," or to anybody else. To this end the economists should themselves acquire the necessary mathematical knowledge. . . .

All of this is indispensable for a rapid development of the effective use of mathematics on the basis of Marxist-Leninist theory. Based on the latter, it will promote a more thorough understanding of the functioning of economic laws, exact measurement of their action, and therefore their even more effective application in economic practice, a more rational economy, and a more efficient use of the latest techniques.

g. The Law of Value in a Socialist Economy *

S. PERVUSHIN
Editor-in-Chief, Planovoe Khoziaistvo.

A vigorous discussion of the principles of price formation has been going on in our country and the other socialist countries for many years. The heightened interest of scientists and practical workers in this problem is quite understandable and justified, for basic socio-economic and organizational problems are involved in price policy. Economically substantiated prices are essential for the organization of planning, for determining the effectiveness of economic measures, for consistent implementation of the principle of material incentive and for the establishment of proper relations between town and country.

Everyone now recognizes that the practice of price formation which has developed requires considerable improvement. The existing practice of price formation results in prices failing to reflect the real changes in outlays of socially necessary labor, and therefore hampers the introduction of cost accounting and does not induce economic administrators to make effective use of fixed and working capital. Because of faulty prices the principle of material incentive cannot be consistently implemented in a number of cases. The present practice of price formation hampers the elaboration of long-range plans. Insofar as outlays of social labor are very inexactly reflected in prices it is difficult to express the rate and proportions of development of the different branches of industry in value indices, to determine the advantages of new techniques, the economic indices of particular measures of economic organization. . . .

Unfortunately a satisfactory solution has not yet been found for the problem of using the law of value and value categories in socialist economics. Some economists and philosophers have not yet overcome the metaphysical approach in their interpretation of the law of value and value categories. In view of this the law of value and value categories are either denied or their existence is recognized but the necessary inferences concerning their changed social and economic nature are not drawn. Yet the chief function of research is not to argue about whether the law of value does or does not exist, since experience has long since and convincingly shown that the law of value and value categories do exist, but

* From *Planovoe Khoziaistvo*, 1961, No. 7. Translated in and excerpts reprinted from *Problems of Economics*, December, 1961, pp. 11-18.

to study the specific forms in which the law of value appears in the different stages of building socialism. . . .

Anyone even slightly familiar with socialist practice in running the economy well knows that in a socialist society it is not the law of value which "governs" prices, but government bodies, which do so in accordance with the price policy adopted by the state, a policy worked out on the basis of analyzing the objective economic processes and the concrete tasks in building communism. In a number of cases prices are set to achieve a revolutionary shift of the economic structure of production despite objective tendencies in the movement of value. For instance, in order to achieve the most rapid industrialization of the national economy, prices served for a considerable time, and continue to serve even now, as a means of redistributing accumulations in favor of those branches which must be developed at a rapid rate, despite their losses in the initial period of development. . . .

The problem therefore is not who governs the process of planned price formation but how to make sure that the best methods of setting prices are worked out, that the objective factors which make it necessary to change prices in the different stages of building communism are taken more fully into account. . . .

44

Introducing Electronic Computers in Planning Practice *

N. KOVALEV
Chief, Computer Center,
State Economic Council of the USSR

The new draft Program of the Communist Party of the Soviet Union defines the specific ways of creating the material and technical base of communism, based on the flourishing of science and technological progress in all branches of the national economy. Our own mathematical machine-building and, first of all, our electronic computers are to play an important part in accelerating the rates of technological progress.

* From *Planovoe Khoziaistvo*, 1961, No. 8. Translated [under the title "Introducing Mathematical Methods and Computers in Planning Practice] in *Problems of Economics*, May, 1962, pp. 32-39. Excerpts reprinted from the translation by permission of the publisher.

This equipment is now widely used for technical and scientific calculations. It opens up vast, highly promising prospects for creating higher forms of automation and control of production and technological processes, and thus for the conversion of physical labor into mental labor.

The use of electronic computers has a great future in the sphere of economic management, and in improving the methods and practice of national economic planning and economic analysis. . .

Electronic Computer Technique as a Means of Automating Economic Planning Calculations

We know that the complex socio-economic dependencies and categories of the process of socialist expanded reproduction, the object of planning, appear in the plan in the form of specific quantitative magnitudes of a definite system of economic plan indices. . . . There cannot be scientifically validated planning without careful calculations, because scientific methodology is based on precise quantitative analysis and a developed mathematical apparatus. . . .

Modern computers and mathematics could place the analytical elaboration of economic plans and problems on a scientific basis. They could automate and improve economic plan calculations. The available experience in applying electronic computers in economics shows that the methods of machine mathematics are highly effective for the automation of economic plan calculations.

The Computer Center of the State Economic Council of the USSR has recently used high-speed electronic computers to perform calculations involved in a number of economic planning tasks.

A program has been worked out and adjusted for long-term demographic calculations. For this program, the "Ural-Il" electronic computer makes a detailed calculation of population increases per year and for the various stages of the long-term perspective in different categories within less than half an hour. Key machines would have taken several weeks to make the calculation, and would have required a large number of operatives.

At the request of the USSR State Planning Committee, the Computer Center worked out a program and experimentally calculated the optimum exploitation of equipment at machine-building enterprises and in certain branches of machine-building. It provided the possibility of determining the assortment and output of an enterprise or branch obtained from employing the available equipment most effectively (with a minimum of redundant equipment and equipment in short supply).

The calculation takes about an hour on the "Ural-Il" electronic computer. The attempt by Gosplan personnel to perform it manually took a great deal of time and was, as the subsequent check with the computer revealed, inaccurate.

Other types of economic plan calculations have also been made on electronic computers. . . .

The Computer Center, jointly with the Economic Research Institute of the USSR State Economic Council, has worked out and tested the possibility of effectively automating calculations connected with material and technical supply on practical data related to the distribution of rolled sheet iron. Computers are now being used to calculate the requirements and to plan the output of items distributed by the USSR State Planning Committee's Main Administration of Special Industries.

Wider use of computers will make it possible to improve fundamentally the planning of material and technical supply. . . .

Machine Mathematics and Perfecting the Methodology and Practice of Planning

Machine mathematics offers immense opportunities for improving the methodology of economic planning and for investigating the existing and newly-developing production ties between various branches and between regions.

As we know, the method of balancing is the most important method of planning the national economy. With its help we are assured of uniformity and mutual coordination of all the indices and sections of the national economic plan, in accordance with the demands of the law of planned proportionate development. It takes a great deal of effort to balance all the indices of the national economic plan by means of the ordinary instruments. What is more, the fact that sections and indices of the plan dovetail does not always mean that the plan contains the optimum variant of economic development providing the greatest economic effect with the least outlays of material and labor in the shortest time. Yet this is a most important demand, determining the level of planning and management of the national economy.

Machine mathematics will enable us to coordinate and dovetail various sections of the plan on an entirely new qualitative basis, and to produce multivariant and most economically expedient optimum elaborations of the plan according to the assigned criteria of economic effectiveness (the optimum).

When solving economic problems, the majority of which involve many measures (problems with many unknowns), it is practically impossible to sort out all the variants which meet the assigned condition and to pick the best one. Yet the mathematical apparatus now developed enables us to find the desired variant at once, provided the so-called criterion of the optimum has been formulated, that is, if one of the extreme values (minimum or maximum) of the desired function has been determined.

In a number of cases some one particular index, for example achievement of the maximum output or the achievement of the minimum cost of production, may serve as a criterion of the optimum in selecting the best variant of the production plan. When planning the volume of transport work, the minimum outlay of transport may act as this criterion. But for many economic planning problems an exhaustive answer to the question of economic desirability may only be obtained after comparing a number of economic indices. The mathematical solution of such problems boils down, in a number of cases, to establishing the minimum or maximum of several linear or non-linear functions. Effective methods have not yet been developed for solving these problems. . . .

At present the Computer Center of the USSR State Economic Council is collaborating with a number of organizations and research institutes on a plan inter-branch balance for 1962 covering a very wide range of goods (350 items and branches). In accordance with the results of this elaboration, a proposal should be presented to make inter-branch balances a part of planning practice. This will evidently make it possible to transform inter-branch balances from an object of discussion and experimentation into an effective instrument of economic planning.

This is the first time a plan inter-branch balance of production and consumption of the national economy for a wide range of goods is being drawn up in the economic planning practice of our country. Its scheme will be essentially the same as that of the reported 1959 inter-branch balance compiled by the Central Statistical Administration of the USSR. At the same time the possibility has been provided of expanding that scheme by introducing a series of fresh indices. . . .

The Computer Center is at work this year, jointly with the Council for the Study of the Productive Forces of the USSR State Economic Council and with several other agencies, on determining by means of computers the most rational long-term distribution of the various branches of industry, taking into account production costs, transportation and other factors. This work is being conducted for the cement, coal and pipe industries, and for the production of certain types of rolled goods.

An attempt is being made to arrive at comprehensive calculations of the rise in the standard of living in our country for the various stages of the long run. The coordination plan breaks the problem down into a number of work stages, involving calculation of the primary and ultimate incomes of workers, employees and collective farmers, determination of consumer demand, calculation of the personal and public consumption funds and, lastly, computation of the working people's living standard for the various stages of the general perspective. The bulk of the work is to be completed in 1962. At present some of the calculations listed in the coordination plan have already been made.

Creating a Rational System of Economic Information

Computers can be of use in other ways besides that of solving economic planning problems. This equipment contains vast possibilities in formulating standard plan indices and for building up a rational system of economic information. . . .

The volume of economic information will increase steadily as planning improves and analytical elaborations go deeper. It will not be possible to collect and process all this information without computers, or to formulate aggregate plan indices in accordance with the requirements of national economic planning.

That is why the problem of creating a rational system of collecting and developing economic information by means of modern computers is especially important among the problems involved in the introduction of mathematical methods in economics and planning. Electronic computers, connected by means of long-distance communication channels with the computer centers of the economic councils, the planning committees of the republics and the central planning bodies, should collect and process economic information automatically with the required efficiency and reliability.

A successive condensation of information and a consolidation (aggregation) of standard plan indices at the various stages of planning (enterprise—economic council—republic—central planning agencies) would be the most desirable approach to developing plan economic information. Some of the economic information and norm data may also be forwarded directly through automatic communication channels to the central planning link. . . .

The Level of Economic Work and Use of Machine Mathematics

The most important factor in determining the success with which computers are introduced into economics and planning is an improvement of economic research as a whole. Theoretical investigations must be raised to a level where they can be used in concrete calculations of practical problems; planning practice should, in a number of cases, be reorganized; the quality of primary and normative data should be improved; and, what is more important, economic elaborations of problems must be expanded and deepened.

All talk to the effect that the use of computers in planning will reduce the role played by economics must be thoroughly repudiated as mistaken and harmful. . . .

The personnel of the Computer Center have become convinced in the course of their practical work that when economic problems are solved by machine mathematics without qualified economic substantiation and appropriate preparation the level at which they are solved is substantially reduced. Before using the powerful computer apparatus for any problem, it is necessary to provide a clear economic interpretation, to establish basic economic interconnections, and to express them quantitatively. Since it is impossible to determine all the connections, it is necessary to find the means of correctly reflecting in the plans the socio-economic factors which follow from the tasks set by society for the period in question, to prepare the norms, to analyze more deeply the initial economic level.

It is evident from what has been said that an improvement in economic work and economic analysis is the starting point for the successful introduction in practice of the methods of machine mathematics. What is more, these methods will make it possible to place all economic work and planning on an entirely new qualitative basis.

Shortcomings in the Organization of Work and Some Questions About the Future

The amount of work done to introduce mathematical methods in economics and, what is more important, the effectiveness of this work still fall short of the possibilities and the role of computers in the improvement of planning. The main organizational shortcomings may be classified under three heads.

The first is the lack of cohesion in the work done. Efforts are scattered over a number of chance problems of little urgency, without any concentration on the principal problems of national economic planning. Removal of this shortcoming calls for a unification of the efforts of research bodies and planning agencies, and for thorough coordination of operations. Experience has shown that major modern scientific investigations are inconceivable without extensive and well organized coordination of the many institutions and enterprises. . . .

The other major shortcoming in the use of electronic computers in planning is the fact that some of the investigations are divorced from practical planning and do not get down to the substance of the economic problems involved. Experimental calculations are based on conventional data which assume limitations and situations inconsistent with reality. . . .

The time has now come, while continuing the exploratory research in this field, to concentrate more attention on introducing mathematical methods and computers in practical planning. Valuable experience is being accumulated by the Laboratory for the Application of Mathematical Methods in Economics of the USSR Academy of Sciences (headed by Academician V. S. Nemchinov) and the State Committee on Questions of Labor and Wages of the Council of Ministers of the USSR, which are using electronic computers effectively in some of their calculations.

The main task of the Computer Center of the State Economic Council of the USSR is to introduce machine mathematics in economics and thereby to improve the methodology and practice of national economic planning and economic analysis. This task can be solved only if the sections of the USSR State Economic Council, the USSR State Planning Committee and other planning agencies participate directly and continuously in the work carried out by the Computer Center, especially in defining and formulating the top priority tasks. The USSR State Economic Council is collaborating with a number of organizations in drawing up a long-term plan for the introduction of mathematical methods and computer machinery in practical planning.

Finally, with respect to the third group of shortcomings in this field, a large number of investigations of new economic-mathematical models and new methods of planning proceed without the participation of economists. Some mathematicians try simply to apply the mathematical apparatus developed for specific technical fields to the field of economics. In so doing they make assumptions which may be permissible in physical investigations but are completely unjustified in the socio-economic sphere.

For this reason it is necessary to establish closer cooperation between economists, mathematicians and experts in computer technique. The economists should go deeper into the methods in question so as to exploit their possibilities extensively and effectively in practical planning. They must not tolerate a nihilistic approach to questions involving the future application of machine mathematics in the sphere of economics; their criticism should be based on the principles of Marxist economic science and center on individual imperfections in the work done on these problems. They must be able to find what is rational and creative in such work.

A number of articles have recently appeared in our press by Boiarskii, Katz and others, criticizing the work of certain mathematicians (Kantorovich, Novozhilov) who devoted many years to new mathematical methods applicable in economics and have undoubtedly done a great deal in this field.

Boiarskii and Katz do right to criticize the defects and errors in the economic interpretation of certain mathematical inferences and dependencies. But they generally restrict themselves to the negative side of the matter, without trying to find and, especially, to use and apply what is of value in these investigations in practice. Some reviews deny in general the right of mathematicians to invade the sphere of economics.

They interpret it as a kind of incursion into a domain belonging solely to economists. The discussion in the press strikes one as being one-sided, chiefly involving economists. It does not seem possible that the mathematicians have no reasons for participating in it.

Extensive introduction of mathematical methods and electronic computers in the sphere of economics and national economic planning requires the training of economists who know the fundamentals of computing mathematics, and of mathematicians who have a knowledge of the fundamentals of economics, and also of specialists on electronic computers. Very few such specialists are being trained at present. In 1961 no more than 10 to 15% of the minimum number of mathematicians and computer operatives needed to ensure normal operation of the newly-produced electronic computers were graduated.

There is an obvious miscalculation in the plan for training young specialists: it contains a disproportion between the output of computer machines and the training of personnel to operate them. Broad training of medium-grade specialists (programmers), needed wherever electronic computers exist, should be organized. Programmers can be trained fairly quickly, but at present, unfortunately, they are trained in fewer numbers than the top-grade specialists.

There is no room for doubt that mathematical methods and computers will assume an appropriate place in national economic planning and will serve to improve its methodology and practice.

XI

INTERNATIONAL ECONOMIC RELATIONS BETWEEN THE SOVIET UNION AND THE OTHER SOCIALIST BLOC COUNTRIES: PROBLEMS AND BENEFITS

MARXISTS have always maintained that industrially advanced capitalist nations utilize international trade to exploit and keep in poverty the less developed and economically less advanced parts of the world. Since, in recent years, the foreign trade of the Soviet Union had increased considerably (reaching, by 1960, several times its pre-World War II level), Western economists and statisticians have engaged in extensive research to discover whether the USSR utilizes its position of supreme power within the Socialist bloc of nations to exploit its economically and politically weaker neighbors. As is to be expected, these Western scholars disagree on their findings. Horst Mendershausen, for instance, analyzed the economic relations between the Soviet Union and the smaller Communist countries for the years 1955–58 and arrived at the conclusion that the Bloc nations paid a higher average price for Soviet exports than did the nations of Western Europe and, on the average, sold their products to the Soviet Union below prices prevailing in the markets of Western Europe.[1] Franklyn D. Holzman, on the other hand, disputes Menderhausen's findings of "discrimination," presenting considerable evidence to the contrary.[2]

Without going into the Menderhausen-Holzman debate *per se*, Nicolas Spulber, in the selection of *Western Views* below, discusses some of the problems connected with the calculation of the effectiveness and profitability of trade among planned-economy countries, questions whether this trade is equally beneficial to all participants, and arrives at the

[1] "Terms of Trade between the Soviet Union and Smaller Communist Countries, 1955–57," *The Review of Economics and Statistics,* May, 1959, pp. 106-118. Also, "The Terms of Soviet-Satellite Trade: A Broadened Analysis," *The Review of Economics and Statistics,* May, 1960, pp. 152-163.

[2] "Soviet Foreign Trade Pricing and the Question of Discrimination," *The Review of Economics and Statistics,* May, 1962, pp. 134-147.

conclusion that the monopoly in foreign trade has become a powerful political and economic weapon in the arsenal of the USSR.

Representing *Soviet Views,* I. Dudinskii stresses the "complete equality, mutual benefit, and fraternal assistance" among socialist countries, claims stability of trade and price relations in the world socialist market as one of its major advantages over relations in the world capitalist market, and expresses his conviction that mutually beneficial trade relations will not only contribute to the economic growth of the socialist nations but will also strengthen the economic basis for the peaceful coexistence of the two world systems. It should be pointed out, perhaps, that Dudinskii's views on the proper determination of prices in intra-Bloc trading do not stand unchallenged among economists in socialist countries. At one extreme is the school of thought that wants to see intra-Bloc prices based on cost of production within the Bloc, at the other extreme the school of thought that maintains that the lowest price at which a commodity could be obtained anywhere is the highest any Bloc country should have to pay for it. Many economists in Eastern Europe and in the USSR take a stand somewhere between these two extremes, as does Dudinskii.[3]

WESTERN VIEWS

45

Economic Problems of Socialist Cooperation [*]

NICOLAS SPULBER
Indiana University

Economically, the Soviet bloc is not exactly a great big family sharing in some utopian way the investible resources of all. Each of the countries of this ideological, political, and military association is autonomous on the economic plane; i.e., each one's growth depends first and foremost on its own resources. Differences in factor endowments, however, difficulties in foreign trade with the West, and a general policy of developing

[3] This point is touched upon in selection 45. For somewhat greater details on this controversy, see Frederic L. Pryor, "Foreign Trade Theory in the Communist Bloc," *Soviet Studies,* July, 1962, pp. 55-57.

[*] Reprinted from Nicolas Spulber, *The Soviet Economy: Structure, Principles, Problems* (1962), pp. 245-256, by permission of W. W. Norton & Company, Inc.

mutual economic relations for a variety of political, strategic, and economic reasons render the output and foreign trade plans of each of these countries dependent in varying degrees on the output and foreign trade plans of all the others. Because the Soviet Union has advantages of size, resources, and level of industrial development and because the other countries, though less richly endowed, follow similar industrialization policies, the Soviet Union's output and foreign trade plans assume a cardinal position in relation to the output plans of certain bloc countries. In effect, the Soviet Union is the main supplier of industrial raw materials to the East European members of the bloc and the key supplier of machinery to China. The output and development of certain basic East European industries—notably steel and chemicals—are increasingly dependent on Soviet supplies. On the other hand, the massive increase in China's industrial and military potential may eventually make it less dependent on the Soviet Union. The emergence of China as the second great center of power within the Soviet bloc increasingly limits the USSR's freedom of political and economic action. In time, China may lend its support not only to a small and insignificant satellite like Albania, but also to some other more important satellite country ready and willing to assert its own demands vis-à-vis the USSR.[1]

It has often been stated that national planning is by definition hostile to international trade since it disregards the needs and requirements of other countries. In the 1940's in "The Influence of National Economic Planning on Commercial Policy," Professor Jacob Viner stated, "The less the degree of dependence of a national economy in its ordinary operations on trade with other countries, the less, *ceteris paribus,* will be the difficulties of setting up and operating a comprehensive national economic plan." "There is planning logic, therefore," Viner added, "in the marked association in recent years between the movement toward comprehensive economic planning and the movement toward autarky, most conspicuous in Soviet Russia but by no means confined to it."

Statements like Viner's imply that the planned economy bent on balancing domestic supply and demand for a number of what it considers cardinal commodities necessarily omits any test of comparative advantage; in other words, the planned economy naturally tends to become autarkic since isolation from world market prices and trade fluctuations (on which that country's trade may have little or no influence) simplifies the tasks of domestic planning. Indeed, so long as the Soviet Union felt

[1] Since the 22nd Congress of the Communist Party of the Soviet Union in October 1961, tiny Albania has been denounced in the Soviet and East European satellite press for its "criminal police system," its "provocative actions against the USSR," and its "inconsiderate claims for gratuitous help" from the other socialist countries. China has, however, openly lent its support to Albania, allegedly on doctrinal grounds only. Actually the Chinese have thus for the first time openly manifested their bid for political control in the bloc.

politically and militarily isolated, it restricted its foreign trade to a "tolerable minimum"—to borrow Viner's expression. But this changed rapidly when a number of other economies of the Soviet type came into being. The USSR expanded its foreign trade as it discovered that it could thus cushion the imbalances of its own output plans and as it established long-term foreign trade agreements ensuring that certain supplies which could help its own domestic plans would be available at fixed delivery periods and at stable prices.

It is now clear that foreign trade and comparative advantage may benefit a planned economy just as much if not more than a non-planned one. For countries like Czechoslovakia or Hungary, which are completely devoid of certain natural resources, restricting foreign trade to a "tolerable minimum" is simply suicidal. The emergence of a number of economies of the Soviet type has in fact opened up significant possibilities for interlocking their output and foreign trade plans and hence for vastly expanding mutual interchanges. And, indeed, this trade has expanded appreciably. Some of the basic output plans of certain Eastern European countries are now securely tied to the scheduled outputs of certain Soviet raw materials. If the division of labor, however, has not been broader, the explanation lies—outside power politics—in the difficulty of ascertaining, given the prevailing bloc price systems, the kind or amounts of goods to be traded and in the dogmatic approach of most bloc policy makers to the problem of industrialization. Economic calculation and dogma are the key factors behind the reluctance of these countries to adjust both their short-term output plans and their long-term investment choices to the need for expanding their interchanges.

Calculation of "Effectiveness" in Bloc Trade

The manipulation of prices within each bloc country complicates enormously the computation of the profitability of any given foreign trade operation. Let us note that Marxists do not reject the basic Ricardian approach to comparative advantage. Indeed, bloc economists stress that the objective of foreign trade is to save domestic labor; hence the smaller the socially necessary (domestic) labor embodied in exports relative to the socially necessary (domestic) labor used for producing the imported goods, the more profitable trade should be assumed to be. In practice, however, it is quite difficult to assess the economic meaning of any foreign trade operation carried on by the bloc.

Generally, the ministry of foreign trade in each bloc country computes, at various intervals, a so-called coefficient of foreign exchange, based on the country's export operations, and a so-called coefficient of domestic realization, based on its import operations. Involved in the computation of both coefficients are the domestic and foreign prices paid and obtained and the official rate of exchange. Assume that, in the case of Hungary, for instance, the established rate of exchange is $1 for 6 forints and 1 (old) ruble for 1.5 forints. Assume also that a given commodity is purchased by the exporting enterprise at 1,400 forints and sold for $200 (i.e., 1,200 forints at the official rate of exchange). The *coefficient of foreign exchange* is taken to be the ratio of the domestic price to the price obtained, computed at the official rate, i.e., $1,400 \div 1,200 = 1.16$. The coefficient is then 16 per cent above parity. If the commodity is sold for $250, the coefficient is 0.93 $(1,400 \div 1,500)$, i.e., 7 per cent below parity. The lower the coefficient, the more profitable a transaction is presumed to be. In the case of imports, if a commodity is purchased for 200 rubles and resold for 360 forints, the ruble has been "obtained" at the rate of 1.8 forints. This figure is called the *domestic rate of realization*. Since at the official rate of 1.5 forints 200 rubles equal only 300 forints, the *coefficient of domestic realization* is 1.20 $(360 \div 300 = 1.20)$, or 20 per cent above parity. If the domestic sale price is 279, the coefficient of domestic realization is 0.93, or 7 per cent below parity. This time the operation is presumed to be unprofitable.

Obviously, since all the magnitudes involved—domestic price of an exported commodity, domestic price of an imported commodity, and rate of exchange—are distorted in various ways, these calculations at best allow a comparison between two foreign trade transactions of a closely related nature, but they can hardly serve as an indicator of what is actually occurring in foreign trade as a whole. The profit rates for producers' versus consumers' goods, differentiated for other purposes altogether, may make one export operation seem more profitable than another, when actually a loss is incurred. Some bloc countries compute the differences between the foreign exchange obtained and that expended for importing the raw materials that are used in producing the given exports—a difference which may be relevant for balance of payments considerations but which no more furnishes a general criterion of "effectiveness" than the preceding computation. The difficulties appear compounded when one considers the problem of choosing whether to export a finished product, a semifinished product, or its basic raw material, and the need, for that purpose, of calculating value added at each stage of production. Furthermore, bloc trade moves in bilateral channels: thus, what must be evaluated and compared are the end results of given sets of export-import operations to be carried out with one country or another. No reliable criterion is available for ascertaining "profitability" when the domestic price differentiation does not reflect the underlying scarcities and when import-export operations must perforce be lumped together because trade is strictly confined to bilateral channels.

Further, the bloc policy makers are not satisfied with static considerations. They stress correctly that the division of labor between countries is not static; the development of each country on the basis of its own domestic plans changes the structure of its trade as well as the ratios of the socially necessary (domestic) labor for producing the goods exported and imported. But the vital initial question is how to draw up the domestic output and investment plans themselves and ensure that they are "realistic" in their assessment of the present and potential development of the respective country with regard to the goals pursued by its policy makers. In this respect, the policy makers of most of the bloc economies are dogmatically committed not only to the Soviet strategy of economic development but also to *each* of its particular emphases. There is thus an ideological block against taking into account the plans of other countries when drawing up long-term investment plans. In this case, dogma rather than the convenience of setting up an isolated domestic all-round plan appears to lend substance to Viner's statement.

Finally, the bloc economists accept the logic of comparative advantage, but only after giving it a particular twist. Followers of Marx have many misgivings about resorting to the international price pattern in intrabloc transactions since, according to Marx, a more developed country is "always" in the position of exploiting a less developed one. In Marxian terms, "an advanced country is enabled to sell its goods above their value even when it sells them cheaper than the competing countries," whereas a less developed country "may offer more materialized labor in goods than it receives and yet it may receive in return commodities cheaper than it may produce them." [2] According to the Marxian argument, the split of the gains from trade is always against the underdeveloped country because of its lagging technology. The differences in technology account for the differences in the socially necessary labor for each product within the framework of any given economy. The international market reduces the socially necessary labor of any given commodity (and hence its value and price) to its level within the most advanced country. Thus, an underdeveloped country always relinquishes more "materialized labor" (value) than it gets in exchange.[3] Differences in technology may indeed go a long way in explaining the nature of foreign trade at any given moment. But it is meaningless to assert that, because of these

[2] K. Marx, *Capital* (Untermann transl.). Chicago: Kerr & Co., 1909, Vol. III, pp. 278-279.

[3] To use a Ricardian-type illustration of comparative advantage, let country A devote 80 man-years to producing a certain quantity of wine and 90 man-years to producing a certain quantity of cloth. Let country B need to devote 100 man-years to producing the same quantity of cloth and 120 man-years to producing the wine. By exchanging country A's wine for country B's cloth, both countries would gain: in terms of the domestic cost of producing the cloth, A would save the labor of 10 man-years; B would gain in terms of the domestic cost of producing the wine the labor of 20 man-years. Here the Ricardian theory ends. For Marx, however, country A has gained from this exchange a net value of 20 man-years (100 received against 80 paid), whereas country B has incurred a net loss of 20 man-years (100 given up against 80).

differences, a ton of Soviet coal has more "value" than a ton of Polish coal or of any other goods of equivalent international price because the respective Soviet industry is more labor-intensive than the Polish one.

Since 1948, this theory of implicitly unequal exchange (more materialized labor of the underdeveloped country as against less labor of the more developed country) has been stressed by the Yugoslav Communists in order to indicate that unequal relations may also exist among socialist states. Although the Yugoslavs have been expelled from the bloc as revisionists for suggesting the possibility of socialist exploitation, the question of the utilization of the international price pattern in the socialist camp is still unsolved. In the various councils of the bloc, Soviet, Czech, and East German economists—the representatives of the more industrialized countries—have generally expressed agreement with the further utilization of the international price pattern, whereas Bulgarian and Rumanian economists have indicated serious reservations about this solution. Thus the Czech economist Vladimir Kaigl asserted that, in their present technological development, economies of the Soviet type could not evolve in their mutual trade a separate price structure completely severed from that of the world market. For this reason, he suggested that the gulf between developed and underdeveloped areas be bridged by other means than price manipulations and arbitrary deviations from world prices. On the other hand, the Rumanian economist Josef Anghel declared that the application of world prices to bloc trade had "harmful effects" and that the role of the "law of value" must be limited in intrabloc relations. He suggested that mutual trade prices be "adjusted." Until now, however, the practical consequences of this suggestion have been minimal.

As we have pointed out, world prices are used as the "base" of intrabloc trade, but the prices are kept stable during the implementation of any given foreign trade contracts, so that volume, value, structure, and delivery periods of imports and exports may be securely tied to the domestic plans. In principle, each bloc seller should charge the same price to all bloc buyers of the same commodity, but there is some evidence that sellers may charge more than the world market price in transactions with purchasers who can offer only "soft" goods in exchange. In other words, monopoly positions arise and are put to use in the imperfect intrabloc market, particularly when substantial difficulties occur in the trade of these countries with non-bloc areas (e.g., the Western embargo on "strategic" goods). Discrimination is thus practiced among the members of the Eastern trading area: it is possible, however, that in some cases a level higher than world market prices exists on *both* sides of any given bilateral trade agreement.

The impossibility of carrying out meaningful economic calculations in foreign trade because of the distortion of bloc prices and the dogmatic approaches both to the Soviet strategy of development and its emphases and to foreign trade as viewed through Marx's theory of unequal exchanges thus have seriously impeded systematic broadening of the division of labor within the bloc.

CEMA: Nature, Role, and Performance

In order to strengthen socialist cooperation, a Council of Economic Mutual Assistance (CEMA) was formed in January, 1949, by the Soviet Union and the Eastern European countries (East Germany, Poland, Czechoslovakia, Hungary, Rumania, Bulgaria, and Albania).[4] China and the Asian satellites (Outer Mongolia, North Korea, and North Vietnam) have not become members of CEMA, but China sends observers to its sessions. Since "optimal proportions" between sectors and industrial branches at the scale of the bloc, even if they could be ascertained, could not be imposed on economically autonomous countries, the Council has only advisory and consultative functions. It may make recommendations, but it lacks the executive authority to enforce them. The Council has no fixed headquarters and meets about once a year in the capital of a different member country. At its sessions, it examines the recommendations of its expert commissions—now some thirty in number and of a permanent character since 1956—each of which has its headquarters in the country best suited for its specific work. Thus, for example, the Soviet Union is host to CEMA's heavy metallurgy commission, Czechoslovakia to the machinery construction commission, East Germany to the chemical commission, Poland to the coal commission, Rumania to the oil and natural gas commission, and Bulgaria to the agricultural commission. On each commission sit the member countries' permanent representatives of the ministries and planning authorities concerned.

In the first years of CEMA's activity, the essential method of economic cooperation among the bloc countries was the establishment of long-term foreign trade agreements designed to guarantee the minimum supplies of basic materials needed for carrying out the independently drafted national output plans. Each country was attempting to reproduce in miniature the Soviet development, and at that time, coordination at the level of trade seemed to be the most appropriate method of "socialist cooperation." After a while, since the countries of the bloc began to glut their common market with a host of similar products, the problems of coordinating all the output plans and all investment plans began to receive increased attention, and CEMA was encouraged to turn its efforts to these issues. It was soon conceded that autarkic policies were harmful, that each country need not develop all the branches of heavy industry,

4 Albania was expelled from CEMA without any formalities after its official denunciation at the 22nd Congress of the Soviet Communist Party in October, 1961.

and that cooperation was necessary precisely because all these countries were genuinely interested in increasing their interchanges of highly processed products.

Thus, it was recognized that each economy of the Soviet type need not reproduce in miniature the economy of the USSR, although each one was supposed to continue to implement the same strategy of development, with its emphasis on heavy industry. But insurmountable difficulties arose in determining concretely which particular branches of industry and which products should be developed for export and by whom—i.e., how the comparative costs of different output and trade patterns should be assessed within the bloc. Moreover, because of the prevailing patterns of organization, incentives, etc.—notably the emphasis on "reaching and surpassing" some gross value of output target—each industry, sector, region, or country tends in practice to insulate itself, guarantee its own supplies, produce its own spare parts, and break its own bottlenecks. In this sense, too, Viner's contention is vindicated: insulation is related to planning, provided that one applies this contention not only to each country, but also to each region, branch, industry, or plant.

As the bloc market became glutted with identical products, however, coordination began to be worked out cautiously through technical and engineering decisions rather than by cost and price assessments. Each of CEMA's permanent commissions of experts started to examine and discuss each type of product, taking into account the production facilities offered by the various member countries. On this basis, specific technical and engineering apportionments of production among the member countries were recommended. The experts proposed, the Council recommended, and the various countries implemented, if they so decided, the specific decisions involved via their bilateral agreements. As a result of this extremely laborious procedure, certain plants in a given country were entrusted with production for the whole bloc. In some outstanding cases, certain industrial branches (e.g., the East German aviation industry) were converted to other purposes. In other cases, agreements were secured for dividing outputs of close specifications among a number of countries. In still other cases, the cooperation achieved consisted of establishing joint companies in which one country furnished the raw materials and the other the industrial facilities to exploit them. This step-by-step technical and engineering apportionment could, however, be upset or at least rendered of doubtful value if two important countries suddenly developed a very broad framework of bilateral cooperation (e.g., the Soviet-Czechoslovak agreement of January 29, 1957, in which the two countries agreed to cooperate on production of a group of key commodities). It is difficult to know in what measure such agreements actually completed or canceled out the bloc-wide apportionments already suggested by CEMA commissions. It is certain however, that future bloc-wide apportionments will have to be adjusted to agreements already reached bilaterally by the most important members of the bloc.

During the twenty years from 1960 to 1980, the East European countries will attempt to gear some of their basic investment plans to the Soviet plans of investment and output in some key industrial branches. As the main exporter of iron ore in the bloc, the Soviet Union holds sway over the expansion of steel facilities in the whole East European area. The period of investment gestation in certain industries is extremely long, and the relevant decisions, therefore, must be taken immediately. This sort of coordination, however, concerns only certain key investments and affects only part of the foreign trade of the countries concerned; a large part of this trade both within the Soviet bloc and with non-bloc countries will still be governed by short-run considerations.

The transition from coordination at the level of trade to coordination at the levels of production is thus both cautious and one-sided, among other things because of the reluctance of the very large countries—the USSR and China—to relinquish any of their own basic decisions concerning their domestic investment choices. Among the smaller but differently endowed countries, a clear differentiation is occurring in this respect. Although Czechoslovakia and East Germany, for instance, are willing and ready to engage in a very broad division of labor both between themselves and at the scale of the bloc—since they have already attained a high level of technological development—the more backward countries of the area still hope to industrialize faster by travelling a more isolated road, i.e., by following not only the Soviet strategy of development but also its emphases, thus avoiding too rapid and detailed a division of labor in the bloc.

Bloc Price Pattern and Multilateral Compensation

After the 1961 ruble reform, the Soviet Minister of Finance claimed that the new Soviet rate of exchange conformed to the actual relations of the purchasing power of currencies. He added that this exchange rate would facilitate comparisons between world prices and the average Soviet wholesale prices, since at this exchange rate, the former would be brought to the level of the latter, thus allowing a clearer valuation of the relative profitability of each export and import operation. The statement received credence in the West, but with qualifications. Professor Morris Bornstein agrees that the devaluation of the old ruble has actually brought the Soviet average price level into closer agreement with world market prices converted into rubles at the new rate. He has, however, correctly pointed out that this measure could not be viewed as sufficient in itself for solving the problems of computing the profitability of Soviet trade since it did not affect in any way the distortions prevailing in the domestic structure of Soviet prices.[5] Until now, no one has proposed the adoption of the Soviet price pattern in intrabloc transactions. Such adoption would make the foreign trade ruble convertible within the limits of the trade agreements into goods at the delivery prices prevailing in the USSR. The divergences between the Soviet price pattern and that of each bloc country is of such nature, however, that no one could ascertain who in the bloc would benefit and in what amount from any foreign trade transaction carried on at Soviet prices.

As already indicated, the prevailing system of bilateral agreements and clearing eliminates the need for the transfer of currencies as imbalances appear during, or after, the period set for carrying out a given commercial agreement. The balances are covered by the transfer of commodities, similar to the commodities included in the trade agreements and at the previously established prices. Serious difficulties seem to impede breaking away from this bilateral pattern of trade and developing a multilaterally compensatory system. Multilateral compensation would imply that each bloc country was ready to sell goods against clearing rubles, and since it might occur that some countries would build net export or import surpluses with the whole bloc (over and above their regular bilateral agreements), some limits would have to be set on the amount of clearing rubles which each country could accept. This kind of limited arrangement, somewhat similar to the one which prevailed in the defunct European Payments Union, appears to be essential in the bloc, because certain outputs and certain exportable commodities are scarce in spite of the economic imbalances created by the methodical emphasis on the so-called key planning links. A supplementary, and probably necessary, clause might be required to provide for converting some of the balances built in clearing rubles into gold. The need to ensure planned supplies and hence the preference for bilateral arrangements, the scarcity of certain key exportable goods above and beyond the plan, the need to limit the amounts of freely convertible clearing rubles and to provide for the conversion of the latter into gold up to a certain amount—all these elements, along with other factors, are likely to keep multilateral compensation within narrow margins.

Concluding Comments

The monopoly of foreign trade has proved to be an important political defensive and offensive tool for the USSR. Defensively, the monopoly has ensured maximum protection against capitalist competition and maximum assistance to the national plan because it has made imports

---

[5] Morris Bornstein, "The Reform and Revaluation of the Ruble," *The American Economic Review*, March, 1961, p. 120.

from non-bloc sources dependent on plan needs and has tailored exports to pay for the required imports. As an instrument of political attack, the monopoly has ensured the Soviet Union's freedom to shift rapidly from one market to another, to adjust purchases and sales to political considerations,[6] and to maximize the impact of its operations, especially when the international market is in distress. In fact, the more unsettled the world market, the more effective the monopoly appears as an instrument of commercial warfare. Furthermore, the more delicate the balance of power in the so-called non-committed countries, the more powerful looms the Soviet capacity to adjust its trade to its political objectives. Since 1954, systematically and in strict accordance with those objectives, the Soviet Union has expanded its trade with, and aid to, underdeveloped areas. It has concentrated its efforts on a few key spots: in the Middle East, until 1961, on Egypt; in Asia, on India and Indonesia. The USSR, Czechoslovakia, and China are now a source of military supplies for almost any group or faction ready to take arms against the West. In periods of international tension there is always talk in the West of counteracting the Soviet monopoly of foreign trade by creating a similar foreign trade monopoly on either a national or an international scale. Such a move, however, is extremely difficult to implement within the framework of free enterprise economies, and as yet no specific measures have been taken to this end.

6 The rapid adjustment of Soviet foreign trade and aid to political considerations can best be observed in the case of former bloc countries. Immediately after the political denunciation of Albania, the USSR discarded its trade agreement with that country, cancelled its credits for the period 1961–65, withdrew the Soviet technicians from Albania, and expelled the Albanian students and cadets from the Soviet Union. Khrushchev thus applied in 1961 exactly the same gamut of economic measures that Stalin did in 1948 when he expelled Yugoslavia.

46

Mutual Benefits Derived from Socialist Cooperation *

I. DUDINSKII
Head, Section on the Economy of Socialist Countries,
State Economic Council of the USSR

The constant expansion of cooperation and mutual aid among the fraternal socialist countries is a major factor in the development of the world system of socialism. . . .

Foreign trade plays an essential role in the development of economic cooperation among the socialist countries. All major forms of economic association among the socialist countries—the joint utilization of natural resources, a broader coordination of national economic plans, economic specialization and cooperation, allocation of credits—lead to the expansion of trade among these countries, to the growth of the world socialist market, i.e., an inter-state sphere of commodity and money relations among the member countries of the world socialist system. The laws of development of this market and the structural principles of the socialist countries' foreign trade stem from the nature of the socialist system and the prevalence of the social ownership of the means of production in the socialist countries.

The incentive for development of international trade in the world socialist system is not profit, but to contribute to the rapid growth of social production and to improve the working people's welfare on this basis. Reciprocal trade among the socialist countries is subordinated to the same chief objectives which determine the development of the national economy of each socialist country. Organically linked with the planned proportional development of the entire socialist economy, the foreign trade of the socialist countries helps accelerate their economic development and is an important instrument for overcoming possible disproportions or "bottle-necks" in the economies of individual coun-

---

* From *Voprosy Ekonomiki,* 1961, No. 2. Translated under the title "Some Features of the Development of the World Socialist Market," in *Problems of Economics,* September, 1961, pp. 55-62. Excerpts reprinted from the translation by permission of the publisher.

tries. The development of the world socialist market helps strengthen the economies of the socialist countries and expands their economic cooperation.

Foreign trade assists in the accomplishment of many important tasks of economic development in the socialist countries. Foreign trade is an important factor in the acceleration of the industrialization of those countries of socialism which once were economically underdeveloped. The expansion of foreign trade on the basis of international socialist division of labor enables the socialist countries to obtain deficient raw materials and fuels, increase their production and thus cut down costs.

Foreign trade is conducted by the socialist state in all socialist countries. This makes it possible to subordinate foreign trade to the requirements imposed by expanded socialist reproduction and to conduct export-import operations with the optimum combination of national and international tasks. At the same time the state monopoly of foreign trade protects the world socialist market against the unpredictable fluctuations of the world capitalist market.

Characteristic features of the socialist countries' foreign trade are complete equality, mutual benefit and fraternal assistance in economic development.

The development of the world socialist market is marked by a steady increase in volume, by planning in foreign trade and by the principle of equality in commodity exchange.

The socialist market's volume of interchange has been steadily increasing. This is caused by the fact that the economy of the Soviet Union and People's Democracies has been developing in accordance with the demands of the basic economic law of socialism. The continuous growth of production in all socialist countries ensures a constant expansion of their trade. The world socialist market does not have the marketing difficulties inherent in the world capitalist market. The socialist system solves the problem of sale for each individual country and for the world socialist system of economy as a whole. Difficulties in sale may arise only temporarily for individual items and are easily surmounted. Nor does the world socialist market ever experience crises or stagnation, characteristic of the foreign trade of the capitalist countries. . . .

Reciprocal trade accounts for the bulk of the socialist countries' foreign trade. Thus, in 1959 it accounted for 70% of the total volume of their foreign trade. The large proportion of reciprocal trade in the total foreign trade of the socialist countries reflects the development of economic cooperations among these countries. However, the figures cited indicate also that the reactionary circles of some Western countries have been deliberately interfering with the development of normal, mutually profitable, trade between the socialist and capitalist countries. This manifestation of the "cold war," and "the positions of strength policy" is in evidence even today, though it is clear that the discriminatory policy has boomeranged on its initiators and is actually damaging the economies of some capitalist countries. As for the socialist states, their national economy is rapidly developing, regardless of the state of their economic relations with the countries of the capitalist world.

The growth of the socialist countries' reciprocal trade reflects the process of continuous development and deepening of the division of labor among these countries through the coordination of economic plans, economic specialization and cooperation within the framework of the world socialist system. The Declaration of the Conference of Representatives of the Communist and Workers' Parties emphasizes the vital importance of steadily improving the international division of labor for the development of the world economic system of socialism. The deeper the division of labor, the larger is the share of output which goes into reciprocal trade.

Foreign trade, in turn, is conducive to the development of interstate specialization and cooperation in production in individual countries. Suffice it to indicate the continuously broadening range of goods entering into reciprocal trade. . . .

Another characteristic aspect of the world socialist market is the development of the trade of the countries of the socialist camp on a planned basis. The state economic plans of the Soviet Union and People's Democracies incorporate plans for foreign trade, realized under trade agreements between the socialist countries. Even prior to the coordination of the production plans of the socialist countries, the law of reciprocal trade was a law of the entire world socialist economic system. In contrast to the anarchy and unpredictable conjunctural fluctuations inherent in the foreign trade of the capitalist countries, trade in the world socialist market develops in conformity with the requirements of the planned economy of the socialist-camp countries, and serves as a major instrument in the coordination of their economic plans. As this coordination became more and more direct, the development of the socialist countries' trade took on a more planned character.

Extensive work on preparing and concluding reciprocal trade agreements covering the period up to 1965 was carried on in the Soviet Union and People's Democracies early in 1960. The Soviet Union has already concluded five-year trade agreements with Poland, Czechoslovakia, the GDR, Hungary and several other People's Democracies. The characteristic feature of the new trade agreements is that they reflect the work done on coordinating the socialist countries' economic plans. Thus, trade on the world socialist market depends on the direct coordination of the economic plans of the fraternal countries.

In order to contribute to the development of the ferrous metal industry in the European People's Democracies, the Soviet Union will increase significantly the deliveries of iron ore, coke and manganese ore to these countries. The export of oil, pig iron, rolled ferrous metals and pipes, aluminum and saw-timber, as well as different industrial equipment, from the USSR to the fraternal countries is being expanded. Thus, from 1961 to 1965 the USSR will deliver to Czechoslovakia 38 million tons of iron ore and 680,000 tons of manganese ore, 22 million tons of oil, 8.5 million tons of coal, 1,180,000 tons of apatite concentrate, and so on. The deliveries of Soviet machines and equipment to Czechoslovakia will increase significantly. The Soviet Union will deliver 15,000 tractors, 1,240 excavators, equipment for a high voltage transmission line to connect Rumania and Czechoslovakia, equipment for the textile industry, and so on. As in previous years, the USSR will supply grain and other foodstuffs to Czechoslovakia.

The European People's Democracies, for their part, will expand their exports to the USSR of machines and equipment, chemicals, consumer goods and foodstuffs. . . .

A characteristic feature of the world socialist market is the just, mutually advantageous interchange of goods between the socialist countries, adequately reflecting the relations between the values exchanged. The exchange of goods on the world socialist market is based on fair uniform prices which take account of the interests of the countries concerned and conform to the requirements of the law of value. The operation of this law, however, is limited in the trade between socialist countries. There is neither "free play" of prices, nor petty merchantilism and commercial excitement, or non-equivalent exchange characteristic of the capitalist countries' trade. Commodities moving on the world socialist market are, by their nature, free from the antagonistic contradictions of capitalist commodities; there is no competition, nor are there crises and recessions. This is not to say that no complex problems arise as the world socialist market expands. There can be temporary disproportions on this market, caused, for example, by inadequacies in coordinating the economic plans of the socialist states. But such disproportions are of a partial and temporary nature. These are the difficulties of growth, and not of decline. They are fully overcome as the socialist system of economy develops.

The operation of the law of value in the world socialist market differs from its operation within individual socialist countries. In these the national value of a commodity is basic to its price. On the world socialist market the international value of a commodity becomes a decisive factor in establishing its price. It is the difference in national levels of labor productivity that is responsible for a discrepancy between the national value of a commodity and its international value, the latter being determined by the conditions of production in a country or a group of countries supplying the bulk of the goods in question to the socialist market.

At present the prices of a given commodity on the principal world markets are taken by the socialist countries as the basis for establishing the prices in their trade. These prices are not transferred automatically, though. Prices on the capitalist market are subject to speculative fluctuations which have nothing to do with any changes in the conditions of production (creation of strategic stockpiles, war-inflationary spirals, dumping, and so on). The price fluctuations resulting from the inherent defects of the capitalist economy do not affect the trade relations among the socialist countries. There are no unpredictable price fluctuations in their reciprocal trade. Prices here are established for a long period, and they remain stable.

A major aspect of price formation on the world socialist market is the principle of uniformity of prices. A commodity may fetch different prices on the world capitalist market. On the socialist market, as a rule, one price is established for a commodity, and this price may only be differentiated to allow for transport costs and quality.

Viewing the matter in perspective, we believe that the socialist camp will gradually go over to its own price basis in its trade. . . .

The formation of the socialist market's price basis confronts the economists of the socialist countries with major problems. They must study a vast amount of factual data on the cost accounting systems adopted in the socialist countries, the labor productivity levels attained, and the principles and methods of price formation in the internal markets of the socialist countries. Systematized and generalized, these data will help in the search for ways and means to enable the socialist countries to go over to their own price basis in reciprocal trade.

The profitability of foreign trade in the narrow sense of the word can, in our view, be determined for each particular country by comparing (under some accepted method) the amount of socially necessary labor expended on the production of exports with that quantity of labor which is contained in the corresponding import production. Because of the difficulties comparisons of this kind involve, the existing indices of the profitability of foreign trade give only a rough idea of the gains or losses from foreign trade. These indices cannot, by their nature, reflect adequately all the advantages accruing from the international socialist division of labor. This by no means implies that the significance of a more accurate calculation of the profitability of foreign trade in the narrow sense of the word should be underestimated. At the same time, we can now refer to the profitability of the socialist countries' foreign trade in the broad sense of the word, i.e., the profitability determined by the entire pattern of economic gains derived from the reciprocal trade of the countries concerned. Profitability in the broad sense of the word is determined, apart from the exchange effectiveness of foreign trade (the amount of the foreign payments received for the exports as related to the national costs of the production of the commodities in question), by the socialist accumulation funds released owing to foreign trade and used for accelerating the pace of expanded reproduction, as well as by the reduction of the production costs, due to exports and imports, of nationally produced commodities, the acceleration, due to the same causes, of technological progress and the expansion of individual branches of production, new revenues in the state budget due to the sale of imports on the home market, and so on.

One of the most important and complicated problems involved in the development of the world socialist market is to find the correct means of combining the international division of labor and the profitability of foreign trade for each socialist country. In plan coordination, therefore, due allowances should be made for the price levels of specialized goods. Commodity prices should stimulate rational international specialization of production. . . .

The Soviet Union occupies the leading place in the world socialist market. It accounts for more than one-third of the trade of this market.

Trade with the Soviet Union enables the People's Democracies to receive the imports vital for the development of the key branches of their economies. Suffice it to say that the Soviet Union's share in the imports of the European People's Democracies has in recent years amounted to roughly 27% for machinery and equipment, about 75% for iron ore, 84% for pig iron, nearly 60% for non-ferrous metals, 97% for oil, roughly 59% for oil products, more than 60% for saw-timber, about 67% for cotton and to nearly 84% for cereals. Of special importance are the deliveries of integrated equipment sets from the USSR to other socialist countries for equipping major industrial enterprises. The USSR delivers first-class integrated equipment sets to the People's Democracies and renders scientific and technical assistance to these countries in the construction of more than 620 major industrial enterprises and 190 separate shops and installations.

As for the Soviet Union, its trade with the People's Democracies helps it to solve major economic problems and, in particular, contributes to a higher rate of development of a number of major industrial branches, a strengthening of its supply of raw materials and larger stocks of consumer goods. . . .

It should be noted that the composition of trade on the world socialist market is constantly changing as a result of changing export possibilities and import requirements of the countries concerned. Underlying these changes are the profound shifts in the economies of the socialist countries as a result of the creation of the material-technical base for socialism and communism.

The growing export of equipment, as a result of the development of machine-building in the respective countries and gradually intensified international specialization and cooperation in this branch, is a characteristic feature of the socialist countries' foreign trade. Concurrently, the export of foodstuffs and agricultural raw materials is substantially decreasing in a number of countries, due to the growth of internal consumption and the relative lag in the pace of agricultural development which has occurred.

The import of equipment to those People's Democracies which used to be backward economically has considerably increased as compared with the pre-war volume. Simultaneously, the industrially developed countries are increasing the import of equipment as a result of the development of international specialization and the expansion of capital investment.

The socialist countries are importing significantly more foodstuffs as compared with the pre-war volume, but in recent years there has been a tendency towards a decrease of these imports owing to the progress in agricultural production. Another trend in recent years is the growing import of manufactured consumer goods.

What changes can be expected in the structure of trade on the world socialist market? There is no doubt that trade among the socialist countries will continue to expand, chiefly due to the growing interchange of equipment, chemical products and major raw materials. It can be assumed, that agricultural progress in the fraternal countries will reduce the trade in cereals. It is equally obvious that the socialist countries will be expanding the import of consumer goods. The range of goods moving on the world socialist market is expected to broaden constantly.

The expansion and improvement of production in the socialist countries, as well as the further development of cooperation among them, will open up new channels for trade on the world socialist market. Thus, the development of the ores of the Kursk Magnetic Anomaly and the creation of new large industrial and power centers in the west of the USSR will intensify the trade between the western areas of the USSR and the European People's Democracies.

The levelling out of labor productivity in the different socialist countries will encourage the expansion and diversification of reciprocal trade. The development of the world socialist market will be stimulated if scientifically substantiated indices of the effectiveness of economic interchange of goods have been worked out and the system of reciprocal payments perfected.

The world socialist market exists alongside the world capitalist market at the present stage of historical development.

The principle of peaceful coexistence, realized by the socialist and many other countries, presupposes extensive economic ties between the countries belonging to the two different markets. These ties exist, and are developing, despite all artificial barriers. The socialist states are working for conditions facilitating the mutually advantageous exchange of goods among all countries. In their economic intercourse with the capitalist countries, the socialist states defend the principles of equality, mutual respect and mutual advantage. It is the interconnection of the two world markets that furnishes one of the principal media through which the socialist system can influence its capitalist counterpart. By establishing fair prices for their goods and avoiding participation in cartel collusions and speculations, the socialist countries contribute, within certain limits, to more correct price proportions on the world capitalist market. The trade policy conducted by the socialist countries curbs the monopolies' tendency to artificially force up prices for certain industrial goods and reduce prices for the raw materials expected by the economically underdeveloped countries.

The continuous growth of production and the improvement of the working people's living standards in the socialist countries are augmenting the export possibilities and import requirements of the Soviet Union and the People's Democracies, and are increasing the possibilities for mutually profitable trade with the capitalist countries. The economic basis for the peaceful coexistence of the two world systems becomes more reliable thereby. Prospects of more trade and other forms of economic cooperation between the socialist countries and the young national states which have recently become independent and struck out on their own are especially favorable. Both groups of countries are united by their community of interests against the ignominious system of colonialism, for broader international cooperation, and the consistent realization of the principles of peaceful coexistence.

List and Description of Periodicals *

CURRENT DIGEST OF THE SOVIET PRESS. (405 West 117th Street, New York 3, N. Y.) A weekly publication by the Joint Committee on Slavic Studies appointed by the American Council of Learned Societies and the Social Science Research Council. *The Current Digest of the Soviet Press* translates in full or in condensed form, without elaboration or comment, selected articles from the Soviet Press, arranged by subject matter. Each issue also contains a weekly index to *Pravda* and *Izvestia.*

ECONOMIC RECORD. (University of Melbourne, Parkville, N. 2, Victoria, Australia). A Quarterly published by the Economic Society of Australia and New Zealand at the University of Melbourne.

EKONOMICHESKAYA GAZETA (*Economic Gazette*). Weekly of the Central Committee of the Communist Party of the Soviet Union.

FOREIGN AFFAIRS. (58 East 68th Street, New York 21, N. Y.) An American Quarterly Review published by the Council on Foreign Relations, Inc. The editors explain that the articles published in *Foreign Affairs* "do not represent any consensus of beliefs," that *Foreign Affairs,* therefore, "does not accept responsibility for the views expressed in any articles," but that it "does accept . . . the responsibility for giving them a chance to appear there."

INDUSTRIAL AND LABOR RELATIONS REVIEW. (Cornell University, Ithaca, N. Y.) A Quarterly published by the New York School of Industrial and Labor Relations, a unit of the State University of New York, at Cornell University, Ithaca, N. Y.

INTERNATIONAL LABOUR REVIEW. (Geneva, Switzerland. Liaison Office with the United Nations, 345 East 46th Street, New York 17, N. Y.) A monthly publication of the International Labour Organization, an intergovernmental agency, of which 102 countries were members, as of June, 1962. The I.L.O. states that it is not responsible for opinions expressed in signed articles.

IZVESTIA (*News*). Daily newspaper of the Union of Workers Deputies (government) of the USSR.

* This list contains only *periodic* publications from which selections have been taken. The student who wishes to do further research is advised to check also many other journals such as the *American Economic Review, Economia Internazionale, The Journal of Political Economy, The Review of Economics and Statistics, Soviet Studies,* the *United Nations Economic Bulletin for Europe,* and *World Politics,* to name but a few, as well as books, monographs, government publications, etc.

MARXISM TODAY. (16 King Street, London, W.C. 2, England). The monthly theoretical and discussion journal of Britain's Communist Party.

MIROVIA EKONOMIKA I MEZHDUNARODNYE OTNOSHENIIA (*World Economics and International Relations*). Monthly, published by the Institute of World Economics and International Relations, USSR.

PLANOVOE KHOZIAISTVO (*Planned Economy*). Monthly, published by the State Planning Committee, USSR.

PRAVDA (*Truth*). Daily newspaper of the Central Committee of the Communist Party of the Soviet Union. Official newspaper of the CPSU.

PROBLEMS OF COMMUNISM. (1729 Pennsylvania Avenue, N.W., Washington 25, D.C.) A bi-monthly publication of the United States Information Agency. Each issue states that "Opinions expressed by contributors do not necessarily reflect the views or policies of the United States Government."

PROBLEMS OF ECONOMICS. (156 Fifth Avenue, New York 10, N. Y.) A monthly publication of the International Arts & Sciences Press which translates, without comments, articles from the leading Soviet economic journals. With some of the foremost American Soviet area specialists on its advisory Committee to suggest articles for translation, *Problems of Economics* is indispensable for the student of the Soviet Economy who does not master the Russian language.

RADIO FREE EUROPE/MUNICH, RESEARCH AND EVALUATION DEPARTMENT, BACKGROUND INFORMATION USSR. (Munich, Germany). A little known department of Radio Free Europe which publishes about three loose-leaf issues per week, containing commentaries on recent developments in the USSR, scholarly articles reprinted from Western journals, and translations of speeches and articles from the Russian. On July 1, 1962, the name of the department was changed to *Non-Target Communist Area Analysis Department*.

RUSSIAN REVIEW. (235 Baker Library, Hanover, N. H.) An American Quarterly with the declared purpose to "interpret the real aims and aspirations of the Russian people, and to advance general knowledge of Russian culture, history, and civilization." *The Russian Review* stresses that it publishes articles by authors of divergent views, and that, therefore, "the opinions expressed in any individual article . . . are not necessarily those of the editors."

SCIENCE AND SOCIETY. (30 East 20th Street, New York 3, N. Y.) An American academic Quarterly probably best described as representing the independent Marxist point of view.

SLAVIC REVIEW. (Manuscripts: 508 Thomson Hall, University of Washington, Seattle 5, Washington. Subscriptions: 337 Lincoln Hall, University of Illinois, Urbana, Ill.) An American Quarterly of Soviet and East European studies published at the University of Washington for the American Association for the Advancement of Slavic Studies. Former name: *The American Slavic and East European Review*.

SOCIAL RESEARCH. (66 West 12th Street, New York 11, N.Y.) An American Quarterly published by the Graduate Faculty of Political and Social Science of the New School for Social Research.

STUDIES ON THE SOVIET UNION. (Mannhardtstrasse 6, Munich 22, Germany). A Quarterly published by the Institute for the Study of the USSR. The Institute describes itself as "a body of emigre scholars from the Soviet Union whose aim is to furnish reliable information regarding conditions and trends in the Soviet Union today."

SURVEY. (Summit House, 1-2 Langham Place, London, W.1., England. American Distributors: Eastern News Distributors, Inc., 306 West 11th Street, New York 14, N. Y.) A Quarterly Journal of Soviet and East European studies published on behalf of the Congress for Cultural Freedom.

TRUD (*Labor*). Daily newspaper published by the Central Council of Trade Unions, USSR.

U.S. JOINT PUBLICATIONS RESEARCH SERVICE. (1636 Connecticut Avenue, N.W., Third Floor, Washington 25, D. C.) An agency of the United States Government established to service the translation and foreign language needs of the various federal government departments. The JPRS clearly states on each translation that "The contents of this material in no way represent the policies, views, or attitudes of the United States Government or of the parties to any distribution arrangements."

VESTNIK STATISTIKI (*Herald of Statistics*). Monthly publication of the Central Statistical Administration, USSR. *Vestnik Statistiki* is the leading journal of statistics in the Soviet Union.

VOPROSY EKONOMIKI (*Problems of Economics*). Monthly, published by the Institute of Economics of the Academy of Sciences, USSR. *Voprosy Ekonomiki* is the leading theoretical economic journal in the Soviet Union.

Glossary

accumulation fund—Net fixed investment plus or minus changes in inventories. In Soviet national income analysis, the accumulation fund and the consumption fund are the two basic divisions of national income by use.

Anti-Party Group—Name applied first to those "deviationists" who in 1957, tried to unseat Khrushchev. Molotov, Kaganovich, Malenkov, and Shepilov were among the best known individuals identified with the anti-party group.

artel—Cooperative work association. In agriculture, the term refers to a cooperative in which members work together and share the proceeds of their joint labor by some pre-arranged formula. Under this type of cooperative setup, the members are also entitled to devote part of their labor time to private production. Collective farms in the Soviet Union are organized as artels. See also **kolkhoz.**

bourgeoisie—According to Marx, one of the two classes which comprise capitalist society, i. e., the class that owns the means of production, hires workers who do not own any means of production, and obtains *surplus value* (rent, interest, and profits) from their labor. (See also **proletariat**).

cadre—Personnel or staff of an organization.

Candidate of Economic Science—Soviet economist holding a degree roughly similar to the American Ph.D. degree. The doctorate in the Soviet Union is actually a yet higher degree.

capital goods—See **producers' goods.**

C.C.T.U.—Central Council of Trade Unions.

CEMA—Council of Economic Mutual Assistance. Formed in 1949 for the declared purpose of enhancing socialist international cooperation, it originally included the USSR and the East European countries of the socialist bloc. Yugoslavia did not belong to CEMA and Albania was expelled in October, 1961. Mongolia joined in 1962.

centner—See quintal.

Central Statistical Administration—See TsSU.
collective farm—See kolkhoz.

comparative advantage, theory of—A theory of international trade developed by David Ricardo in which he endeavors to prove that a country could benefit from trade even if it would produce all commodities more cheaply (in terms of work measured by the use of factors of production) than other countries. Using two countries, two commodities, and labor time as his measure of cost in his example, Ricardo shows that both countries would benefit if the country that has an *absolute* advantage in both commodities would specialize in the production of the commodity in which it has the greatest *comparative* advantage, while the other country would produce the commodity in the production of which it has the least *comparative* disadvantage. To understand how it is possible to gain by buying what one can produce more cheaply oneself, think of a wheat farmer who purchases apples in the store, even though he could produce them more cheaply on his own farm. He does so because his gain from the production of wheat is greater than his savings would be were he to devote a part of his land to growing his own apples.

consumption fund—In Soviet national income analysis the share of the national income that is consumed by persons or institutions in the period in question. See also **accumulation fund.**

consumption fund, social—That part of the consumption fund that is distributed free of charge, according to needs. Free schooling or medicines dispensed free of charge would be examples of parts of the social consumption fund.

Council of Ministers—See **U.S.S.R. Council of Ministers.**

Council of Nationalities—See **U.S.S.R. Supreme Soviet.**

Council of the Union—See **U.S.S.R. Supreme Soviet.**

C.P.S.U.—Communist Party, Soviet Union.

Department I and Department II—See **Subdivision I and Subdivision II.**

econometrics—A branch of the science of economics which utilizes mathematical equations to express economic relationships in such a way that they are readily amenable to statistical testing.

factor—See **factor of production.**

factor of production—One of the following four: Land, labor, capital, entrepreneurship. In Western economic theory, these four are absolutely necessary for the production of anything under any economic system. Under capitalism all national income is divided among these four in the form of wages for labor, rent for land, interest for capital, and profits for the entrepreneur.

F.R.G.—Federal Republic of Germany (West Germany).

G.D.R.—German Democratic Republic (East Germany).

GNP—Gross national product. (For explanation, see **gross national product**.)

gosekonomsovet—State scientific-economic council; in 1960 placed in charge of long-term planning in the USSR (an activity formerly handled by the *gosplan*). Under the November, 1962 reform, *gosekonomsovet* was dissolved and *gosplan,* once again, was placed in charge of long-term planning.

Gosbank—State Bank. In the USSR, the *Gosbank* serves as central bank, as fiscal agent for the government, as important credit agency, and, in general, as one of the major parts of the economic control mechanism.

gosplan—State Planning Commission. Prior to the November, 1962 reform, *gosplan* was the major agency in the USSR charged with working out the national economic plan. Throughout Soviet history, the title of the gosplan has been changed back and forth from "Commission" to "Committee" as the powers of the gosplan were reduced, restored, and reduced again. Besides *gosplan* USSR, each union republic has its own *gosplan.* Under the November, 1962 reform, *gosplan* was placed in charge of long-term planning and its former functions were turned over to a newly created National Economic Council.

gross national product—In United States national income accounting, gross national product (GNP) equals the total value of all finished goods and direct services produced during a specified period of time, usually one year (with certain specified exceptions such as illegal goods, and with changes in inventories of goods in the process of production added or subtracted). GNP can be expressed in current prices or in prices adjusted to a given base. There is no GNP in Soviet national income analysis.

Group A and Group B—Industrial products classified respectively as producers' goods and consumers' goods.

hectare—Area equal to 10,000 square meters or 2.471 acres.

income, real—Goods and services that can be bought with money income. (If, for example, money income remains unchanged and the price level doubles, real income, by definition, drops to one half.)

input-output table—A checkerboard type cross reference table that shows what happens to the output of each producing branch of the economy, and what each consuming sector of the economy consumes. The producing branches (such as agriculture, iron and steel, electric power) may be listed vertically down the left margin, and one can then read horizontally across to see how much of the total output of each branch goes to each consuming sector. Listed horizontally across the top, then, are the various consuming sectors which consist of the same producing branches (since in the process of production, goods must necessarily be consumed) plus such additional consuming sectors as households and government. Reading vertically down a column, one can find out how much each consuming sector uses of the output of each producing branch. If, for instance, one million tons were listed in the cell formed by the "iron and steel" row (producing branch) and the "coal" column (consuming sector), this would indicate that one million tons of the total output of iron and steel go to the coal industry, i.e., that in the process of producing the nation's coal output, this tonnage of iron and steel is "consumed" by the coal industry.

Intourist—Official Soviet travel agency.

kilogram—Measure of weight equal to 2.205 pounds.

kolkhoz—Collective farm. In the Soviet Union, the state holds title to all land, but collective farm land has been granted in perpetuity to peasants who are members of the *kolkhoz*. Apart from the income derived from cooperative work, each peasant family is also granted a small plot of land for its private use. See also **artel.**

kolkhoznik—Member of a collective farm.

komsomol—Communist Youth League.

kray—Territory. Administrative subdivision.

labor time, socially necessary—Marxian term expressing the labor time necessary in any given stage of economic development to produce a commodity. According to Marx, the value of commodities under capitalism is equal to the labor time socially necessary to produce them.

Lenin, Nicholai (Vladimir Ilyich Ulyanov)—(1870-1924). Leader of the Russian revolution who led the uprising that resulted in the overthrow of Kerensky's government in October, 1917.

linear programming—A mathematical approach to solving the problem of determining which among many possible ways of doing something is the "best" solution, "best," that is, in terms of whatever is to be maximized or minimized. (It is used when the quantity to be maximized or minimized takes the form of a linear equation subject to a set of linear inequalities [relations in the form of greater than or less than, rather than equal to.] In such cases, the calculus cannot be used).

marginal—In Western economic theory, the term *marginal* plays a major role. Basically, *marginal* . . . refers to the last unit. Thus, for example, *marginal utility* is the satisfaction derived from the consumption of one additional unit; *marginal cost* is the increase in total cost resulting from the production of one additional unit; the *marginal product of labor* is the increase in total output brought about by the utilization of one more unit of labor input, etc.

marginalists—Economists who belong to the school which bases economic theory on marginal analysis. Marginalists teach, for instance, that the best output for any firm is that output at which marginal costs equal marginal revenues, since producers can increase their profits as long as additional inputs increase total costs by less than they increase total revenues. By the same token, as long as a producer can increase his output by shifting funds from one factor of production to another, he has not achieved the most economic way of producing a given output. Therefore, any given output will be produced most cheaply if the factors of production are combined in such a way that the marginal product of each is proportionate to its price. Similar theories have been developed for wage determination, maximization of utility, etc.

marginal rate of substitution—The quantity of one good (or service) which a consumer would require to compensate him for the loss of one unit of another good (or service) in order to feel neither better off nor worse off as a result of the exchange. As applied to a producer, the marginal rate of substitution refers to the quantity of one factor of production required to compensate him for the loss of one unit of another factor in order to leave his total output unchanged.

marginal rate of transformation—For any two goods or services the marginal rate of transformation is equal to the quantity of one good which could be produced by the factors of production made available by a one unit reduction in the output of the other.

M.T.S.—Machine-Tractor Station. Until 1958 the government-owned and -operated M.T.S.'s supplied the collectives with agricultural equipment and thus provided the government with a powerful control over the collectives. In 1958 a law was passed that provided for the sale of the agricultural machinery held by the machine-tractor stations to the collectives.

national income—See editor's introduction to Part III, pp. 57-58. See also **accumulation fund** and **consumption fund.**

national product—See **gross national product.**

oblast—Province. Administrative subdivision.

partiinost—Party allegiance; party spirit.

planometrics—New word, used especially in the USSR, to describe a branch of the science of economics which deals with the application of mathematics to economic planning.

plenum—Full assembly of all members (e. g., of the Central Committee of the Communist Party.)

pood—A measure of weight equal to 36,113 pounds.

Presidium of the Supreme Soviet—See **U.S.S.R. Presidium of the Supreme Soviet.**

price of production—As used by Marx, this term refers to the cost of production plus profits—and competition would make the rate of profits equal for all industries. The price of any given product may therefore be above or below its value, as Marx uses the term, but the aggregate of all prices would equal the aggregate of all values. (See also **value.**)

procurement price—In the case of agricultural products, the price paid by the government of the USSR to collectives for the legally required delivery of food and raw materials to the state. Prior to 1958, collective farms had to deliver a prescribed quota to the state at a very low price, often covering only a fraction of the cost of production. Higher purchase prices were paid for additional deliveries. This form of a "tax" on collectives, this multiple price system, was abolished on July 1, 1958.

producers' goods—(also referred to as *capital goods*). Goods used in the production of other goods, as distinguished from consumers' goods.

product mix—Assortment of goods.

proletariat—According to Marx, one of the two classes which comprise capitalist society, i.e., the class of wage earners who own no means of production other than their own labor power, who must sell this labor power to a capitalist employer in order to live, and who can sell it only if it is profitable for the capitalist to purchase it. After the "inevitable" downfall of capitalism, Marx foresaw an intermediate stage of the "dictatorship of the proletariat" on the road to the classless society of perfect communism. (See also **bourgeoisie.**)

proportionate development—Development of the various sectors of the economy (such as agriculture and industry, or consumers' and producers' goods sectors) in the "correct" proportions to one another. Although the Soviet Union stresses the importance of proportionate development, it is never clearly specified just what the "correct" proportions are, or how they are to be determined. Hence, the term lacks scientific precision. It frequently seems that the proportions planned or achieved are simply referred to as the correct and desirable proportionate development.

quintal—Translation of the Russian word *centner.* A measure of weight. As used in the USSR, it is the equivalent of 100 kilograms (220.46 pounds.)

real income—See **income, real.**

recoupment period—The period of time necessary to recoup a given investment. If it takes 100,000 hours of labor time to produce a certain machine and if by using this machine the factory can save 25,000 hours of labor time per year without a diminution of output, the recoupment period would be four years. Recently, some Soviet economists have proposed the use of the concept of the recoupment period to decide among various investment alternatives, although, for practical reasons, monetary savings rather than savings in hours of labor time are usually used to compute the recoupment period.

R.T.S.—Repair Technical Station. The R.T.S.'s were established when the machine tractor stations were abolished in 1958. Their double task was to perform major repair jobs for the collectives and to serve as supply depots for new agricultural equipment. Wherever possible, collective farms showed a preference for having all mechanical work performed in their own workshops. In 1961 the remaining work of the R.T.S.'s was taken over by a new machinery supply organization.

Ricardo, David—(1772-1823). Early English classical economist. Classical economists hold that the greatest social well-being will be achieved if each individual is left free to pursue his own economic interests. Free competition, price determination by the forces of supply and demand in a free market, and a minimum of government interference are the cornerstones of classical economic thought.

rouble—See **ruble.**

R.S.F.S.R.—Russian Soviet Federated Socialist Republic. The R.S.F.S.R. is the largest Union republic of the USSR.

ruble—Official currency of the Soviet Union. In January, 1961, under a currency reform, ten of the "old" rubles were exchanged for one of the "new" rubles. Since then the official exchange rate at which American tourists in the Soviet Union have been able to purchase rubles has been $1.11 per ruble. Formerly, however, the *tourist* exchange rate was ten old rubles for $1.00, but the "official" exchange rate was 4 rubles for $1.00.

SNK (Soviet narodnykh komissarov)—Council of People's Commissars. Previous official designation of what is now called Council of Ministers. (See **USSR Council of Ministers.**)

social consumption fund—See **consumption fund, social.**

social labor time—See **labor time, socially necessary.**

socially necessary labor time—See **labor time, socially necessary.**

sovkhoz—State farm. As distinguished from collective farms, state farms in the USSR are operated by the state. The farm workers on Soviet state farms are paid wages and are entitled to many of the benefits (such as paid vacations) that industrial workers enjoy. State farms, hence, are "agricultural factories." (For collective farm see **kolkhoz.**)

sovnarkhoz—Council of the economy, regional economic council. Since July 1, 1957, the control over most industrial enterprises in the USSR has passed from central ministries to the more than one hundred newly created *sovnarkhozy*. Under the November, 1962 reform the number of *sovnarkhozy* was greatly reduced and their respective territories enlarged accordingly.

SSSR—Russian abbreviation for USSR.

state farm—See **sovkhoz.**

Subdivision I and Subdivision II—The two sectors of the economy producing, respectively, producers' goods and consumers' goods.

Supreme Soviet—See **USSR Supreme Soviet.**

technicum—A type of secondary "technical" school in the Soviet Union open to qualified students after eight years of schooling. The curriculum is not limited to "technical" subjects in the narrow sense of the word, as students may take courses leading to such careers as teaching or nursing. Completion of the *technicum* is one of the ways in which a Soviet youth can complete secondary education and enter life as a "specialist of medium qualifications." Qualified students can continue their education at institutions of higher learning, as full-time students, or at evening classes plus summer schools or, in certain fields, by correspondence.

TsIK (Tsentral'nyi ispolnitel'nyi komitet)—Central Executive Committee.

TsSU (Tsentral'noe statisticheskoe upravlenie)—Central Statistical Administration. Formerly attached to the *Gosplan,* the TsSU has been a separate entity, attached to the USSR Council of Ministers, since 1948.

TsUNKhU (Tsentral'noe upravlenie narodnokhoziaistvennogo ucheta pri Gosplane SSSR)—Central Administration of Economic Record-Keeping Attached to the *Gosplan* of the USSR. This was the name of the Central Statistical Administration (TsSU) from 1930 to 1941.

turnover tax—Most important of all Soviet taxes, it is levied on practically all consumers' goods somewhere along the line, as they are transferred from enterprise to enterprise on their way to the final state or cooperative store. While turnover taxes vary from commodity to commodity, they average about 50 per cent of the retail prices of all consumers' goods. As a rule, no turnover tax is levied on producers' goods, but there are some exceptions such as oil, gas, and electricity.

USSR—Union of Soviet Socialist Republics.

USSR Council of Ministers—Highest executive and administrative branch in the Soviet Union. Has power to issue decrees and is subject to ratification by the Supreme Soviet. In the Soviet Union the executive branch of government is subordinated to the legislative branch.

USSR Presidium of the Supreme Soviet—Elected by the Supreme Soviet, the Presidium of the Supreme Soviet consists of 32 members and is in full power while the Supreme Soviet is not in session.

USSR Supreme Soviet—The highest legislative body in the USSR. It consists of two Houses, the *Council* (or *Soviet*) *of the Union* and the *Council* (or *Soviet*) *of Nationalities.* The former, somewhat similar to the United States House of Representatives, is elected according to population, with one deputy for every 300,000 population. The latter, somewhat similar to the United States Senate, is elected by political subdivisions, with 1 deputy from each *national area,* 5 from each *autonomous region,* 11 from each *autonomous republic,* and 25 from each *Union republic.*

value—Usually refers to *exchange value,* rather than *use value.* In this sense, the value of a commodity is equal to the commodities it will command in exchange in the market place. The monetary expression of the value of a commodity is its price. According to Marx, the value of commodities in capitalist society is equal to the labor time socially necessary to produce the commodities. However, Marx admits that commodities may be priced above or below their value as he defines it. (See also **price of production.**)

Vladimir Il'ich—See **Lenin, Nicholai.**

work day—A unit of account to determine the share paid to a farmer on a collective farm. The performance of a given task entitles the member of the collective to a given number of work day units. Each member participates in the "profits" of the collective according to the proportion of his work day units to the total work day units of all members.